Lecture Notes in Computer Science 14932

The series Lecture Notes in Computer Science (LNCS), including its subseries Lecture Notes in Artificial Intelligence (LNAI) and Lecture Notes in Bioinformatics (LNBI), has established itself as a medium for the publication of new developments in computer science and information technology research, teaching, and education.

LNCS enjoys close cooperation with the computer science R & D community, the series counts many renowned academics among its volume editors and paper authors, and collaborates with prestigious societies. Its mission is to serve this international community by providing an invaluable service, mainly focused on the publication of conference and workshop proceedings and postproceedings. LNCS commenced publication in 1973.

Motoshi Saeki · Leah Wong · João Araujo ·
Clara Ayora · Anna Bernasconi · Matteo Buffa ·
Silvana Castano · Peter Fettke · Hans-Georg Fill et al.
Editors

Advances in Conceptual Modeling

ER 2024 Workshops, AISA, CMLS, EmpER, QUAMES, JUSMOD
LLM4Modeling, Pittsburgh, PA, USA, October 28–31, 2024
Proceedings

Springer

Editors
Motoshi Saeki
Nanzan University
Nagoya, Japan

João Araujo
Universidade Nova de Lisboa
Costa da Caparica, Portugal

Anna Bernasconi
Politecnico di Milano
Milan, Italy

Silvana Castano
Università degli Studi di Milano
Milan, Italy

Hans-Georg Fill
University of Fribourg
Fribourg, Switzerland

Leah Wong
NIWC Pacific (Ret.)
San Diego, CA, USA

Clara Ayora
Universidad de Castilla-La Mancha
Albacete, Spain

Matteo Buffa
Università degli Studi di Milano
Milan, Italy

Peter Fettke
Saarland University and German Research
Center for Artificial Intelligence
Saarbrücken, Germany

Additional Workshop Editors *see next page*

ISSN 0302-9743 ISSN 1611-3349 (electronic)
Lecture Notes in Computer Science
ISBN 978-3-031-75598-9 ISBN 978-3-031-75599-6 (eBook)
https://doi.org/10.1007/978-3-031-75599-6

This Springer imprint is published by the registered company Springer Nature Switzerland AG
The registered company address is: Gewerbestrasse 11, 6330 Cham, Switzerland

Workshop Editors

Alberto García S.
Universitat Politècnica de València
Valencia, Spain

Miguel Goulão
Universidade Nova de Lisboa
Costa da Caparica, Portugal

Cristine Griffo
Eurac Research
Bolzano, Italy

Jin-Taek Jung
Hansung University
Seoul, South Korea

Julius Köpke
University of Klagenfurt
Klagenfurt am Wörthersee, Austria

Beatriz Marín
Universitat Politècnica de València
Valencia, Spain

Stefano Montanelli
Università degli Studi di Milano
Milan, Italy

Edelweis Rohrer
Universidad de la República
Montevideo, Uruguay

José F. Reyes Román
Universitat Politècnica de València
Valencia, Spain

Preface

The International Conference on Conceptual Modeling is the leading forum for presenting and discussing the state of the art and future challenges in **conceptual modeling** research and practice. Topics of interest include foundations of conceptual models; theories of concepts and ontologies; techniques for developing, integrating, and communicating conceptual models; and methods for transforming conceptual models into effective implementations.

The 43th International Conference on Conceptual Modeling (ER 2024) took place October 28–31, 2024 in Pittsburgh, Pennsylvania, USA, hosted by Carnegie Mellon University's Software Engineering Institute.

At five conference workshops, researchers presented initial and ongoing work, exchanged ideas about new, emerging, or established topics in conceptual modeling, and discussed their application in specific domains and potential new frontiers.

This volume contains proceedings of the workshops held in conjunction with ER 2024. After a Call for Workshops, workshop chairs and committees accepted and confirmed five high-quality workshop proposals.

The workshops took place on the first day of ER 2024. This volume contains articles from these accepted workshops:

- CMLS 2024 - The 5th International Workshop on Conceptual Modeling for Life Sciences
- JUSMOD24 - 3rd International Workshop on Digital JUStice, Digital Law and Conceptual MODeling
- LLM4Modeling - 2nd Workshop on Modeling in the Age of Large Language Models
- EmpER'24 + QUAMES 2024 -7th International Workshop on Empirical Methods in Conceptual Modeling (EmpER'24) and 5th International Workshop on Quality and Measurement of Model-Driven Software Development (QUAMES 2024)
- AISA 2024 - The First International Workshop on AI Services and Applications

CMLS 2024 and JUSMOD24 addressed conceptual modeling in life science and legal domains respectively. EmpER'24 + QUAMES 2024 discussed the topics of empirical research in conceptual modeling practice. Paper submissions responding to this year's theme of "Conceptual Modeling, Artificial Intelligence (AI), and Beyond" explored relationships between AI and conceptual modeling. At LLM4Modeling and AISA 2024, researchers and practitioners explored the role of AI and conceptual modeling in decision-making processes in various domains, in order to understand their potential and limitations.

Across the workshop program, workshop papers were submitted from the following 24 countries: Austria, Belgium, Brazil, Canada, Chile, Congo (DR), Czechia, Estonia, France, Germany, Italy, Latvia, Luxembourg, Netherlands, Norway, Pakistan, Portugal, South Korea, Spain, Sweden, Switzerland, the UK, the USA, and Uruguay. Each workshop had an independent Program Committee which was responsible for selecting papers. Papers were judged on contribution, novelty, clarity, relevance, and rigor.

Submissions were anonymized. The paper review process was double-blind and each paper was reviewed by at least three program committee members of a workshop. Out of 52 submissions overall, 22 papers were accepted for publication in the proceedings. In addition to the three invited paper presentations, one distinguished speaker gave a keynote talk, which enhanced the perspective and quality of the ER 2024 workshops. The workshop program offered participants a forum to discuss, deliberate, and provoke, with the primary goal of setting an agenda for future research in the featured areas.

We are deeply grateful to the ER 2024 general chair, Hasan Yasar, Chief Coordinator Peter Chen, and Program Chairs Hyoil Han, Wolfgang Maass, and Nick Multari for their support. Special thanks go to Peter Chen and Steve Liddle who provided advice on organizing workshops to meet ER conference requirements.

We thank the workshop organizers for putting together exciting programs with a keynote talk, invited papers, technical paper presentations, and rich discussions. We would like to express our gratitude to all workshop authors and reviewers for ensuring the high quality of the workshop programs. We appreciate Springer's support in producing another memorable ER workshop proceedings volume. Finally, we thank all workshop participants and the entire organizing team for contributing to a productive event. It was a pleasure to be part of the ER community.

October 2024

Motoshi Saeki
Leah Wong

Organization

Honorary Chair

Paul Nielsen	CMU SEI, USA

General Chair

Hasan Yasar	CMU SEI, USA

Chief Coordinator

Peter Chen	Carnegie Mellon University, USA (retired)

Distinguished Advisors

Kenneth M. Ford	Florida Institute for Human and Machine Cognition, USA
Jeffrey J.P. Tsai	Asia University, Taiwan

Program Co-chairs

Hyoil Han	Illinois State University, USA
Wolfgang Maass	Saarland University, Germany
Nick Multari	Pacific Northwest National Lab, USA

Forum Chairs

Sotirios Liaskos	York University, Canada
Patrick Marcel	University of Orléans, France

ER Steering Committee Liaisons

Stephen Liddle	Brigham Young University, USA
Il-Yeol Song	Drexel University, USA

Panels Chairs

Oscar Pastor	Universitat Politècnica de València, Spain
Veda Storey	Georgia State University, USA

Posters and Demos Chairs

Sergio de Cesare	University of Westminster, UK
Frederik Gailly	Ghent University, Belgium

Workshops Chairs

Motoshi Saeki	Nanzan University, Japan
Leah Wong	NIWC Pacific, USA (retired)

Tutorials Chairs

Carlos Ordonez	University of Houston, USA
Juan Carlos Trujillo Mondéjar	University of Alicante, Spain .

CEUR Proceedings Chair

Enrico Gallinucci	University of Bologna, Italy

Publicity Chairs

Anna Bernasconi	Politecnico di Milano, Italy
Claudenir M. Fonseca	University of Twente, The Netherlands

Sponsorship Chairs

Michele Falce	CMU SEI, USA
Hasan Yasar	CMU SEI, USA

Industrial Track Chairs

Sharma Chakravarthy	University of Texas at Arlington, USA
Paul B. Losiewicz	Quanterion Solutions Inc., USA

Treasurer

Stephen Liddle	Brigham Young University, USA

Logistics Chair

Michele Falce	CMU SEI, USA

ER 2024 Workshop Organizers

The First International Workshop on AI Services and Applications (AISA 2024)

Jin-Taek Jung	Hansung University, South Korea

The First International Workshop on AI-Driven Modeling and Management of Data (AIMM 2024) (integrated in AISA 2024)

Hyoil Han	Illinois State University, USA
Simon S. Woo	Sungkyunkwan University, South Korea
Il-Yeol Song	Drexel University, USA
Youjin Shin	Catholic University of Korea, South Korea

The 5th International Workshop on Conceptual Modeling for Life Sciences (CMLS 2024)

Alberto García S.	Universitat Politècnica de València, Spain
Anna Bernasconi	Politecnico di Milano, Italy
José F. Reyes Román	Universitat Politècnica de València, Spain
Edelweis Rohrer	Universidad de la República, Uruguay

7th International Workshop on Empirical Methods in Conceptual Modeling (EmpER'24) (EmpER'24 and QUAMES 2024 are merged to make EmpER'24 + QUAMES 2024)

João Araujo	Universidade Nova de Lisboa, Portugal
Dominik Bork	TU Wien, Austria
Miguel Goulão	Universidade Nova de Lisboa, Portugal
Jennifer Horkoff	Chalmers University of Technology and University of Gothenburg, Sweden
Sotirios Liaskos	York University, Canada

5th International Workshop on Quality and Measurement of Model-Driven Software Development (QUAMES 2024) (EmpER'24 and QUAMES 2024 are merged to EmpER'24 + QUAMES 2024)

Beatriz Marín	Universitat Politècnica de València, Spain
Giovanni Giachetti	Universitat Politècnica de València, Spain and Universidad Andrés Bello, Chile
Clara Ayora	Universidad de Castilla-La Mancha, Spain

3rd International Workshop on Digital JUStice, Digital Law and Conceptual MODeling (JUSMOD24)

Matteo Buffa	Università degli Studi di Milano, Italy
Silvana Castano	Università degli Studi di Milano, Italy
Cristine Griffo	Eurac Research, Italy
Stefano Montanelli	Università degli Studi di Milano, Italy

2nd Workshop on Modeling in the Age of Large Language Models (LLM4Modeling)

Hans-Georg Fill	University of Fribourg, Switzerland
Peter Fettke	Saarland University and German Research Center for Artificial Intelligence (DFKI), Germany
Julius Köpke	University of Klagenfurt, Austria

Big Data and Artificial Intelligence: Innovation-oriented Research to Improve Decision Making (Distinguished Talk)

Juan Trujillo

Lucentia Research Group - Department of Software and Computing Systems, University of Alicante, Carretera de Sant Vicent del Raspeig, s/n, 03690 Sant Vicent del Raspeig, Spain
jtrujillo@dlsi.ua.es

Abstract. Artificial Intelligence is currently being applied to a wide variety of daily processes to improve their decision-making processes. Within this discipline, Machine Learning (ML) is maybe the most popular technique that is being applied in many companies and organizations to different contexts such as predicting future scenarios, identifying user and employees' profiles, or even for diagnosing different illness and pathologies. Currently, the way to applying ML in real scenarios set different challenges from those several decades ago. In most of real-world projects, ML cannot directly be applied to a concrete data set as it is necessary to previously clean data, integrate data from different data sources, find hidden relationships, decide which data is most likely used as an input of the ML model/s and so on.

Are some of these late issues familiar to you? In Big Data projects, we have been tackling with these problems for many years. Even though Big Data research and ML research have been covering completely different research topics, in real-world projects Big Data and ML work together to improve the decision-making process. In this talk, I will focus on how the innovation-oriented re-search in Big Data topics is currently being used as relevant previous steps in ML projects. More-over, several projects will be introduced where the combination of Big Data and ML altogether were critical for their success. Lately, I will also point out how Big Data practitioners also need to have a deep knowledge on how ML models are defined, trained, and executed.

Keywords: Big Data, Data Integration, Artificial Intelligence, Innovation, Conceptual Modeling, Modeling of Machine Learning Applications

1 Short Bio

JUAN TRUJILLO (Senior Member, IEEE) received the Ph.D. degree, in 2001. He is a Full Professor within the Department of Software and Computing Systems, University of Alicante. He has been leading the Data Analytics and Big Data Research in the Department and has also been the Founder and the Director of the Lucentia Research Group, since 2008. He is the author of more than 200 conference papers, such as ER, AISTATS, IJCAI, UML, DAWAK, and CAiSE; and more than 80 JCR journals, such as DKE, DSS, ISOFT, IS, and InfSci. His main research interests include business intelligence, big data, data warehouses, artificial intelligence, machine learning, ethical and responsible artificial intelligence, data analytics, decision support systems and e-health. He is also the founder of the Lucentia Spin-off company as well as the Principal Investigator of many knowledge-transfer projects with companies.

2 Acknowledgment

The content of this talk has been partially funded by the AETHER-UA project (PID2020-112540RB-C43), a smart data holistic approach for context-aware data analytics: smarter machine learning for business modeling and analytics, funded by the Spanish Ministry of Science and Innovation; and the BALLADEER (PROMETEO/2021/088) project, a Big Data analytical platform for the diagnosis and treatment of Attention Deficit Hyperactivity Disorder (ADHD) featuring extended reality, funded by the Conselleria de Innovación, Universidades, Ciencia y Sociedad Digital (Generalitat Valenciana). A. Reina-Reina (I-PI 13/20) hold Industrial PhD Grants co-funded by the University of Alicante and the Lucentia Lab Spin-off Company.

Contents

AISA

CMLS

EmpER

QUAMES

JUSMOD

LLM4Modeling

AISA

AISA – 1st International Workshop on Artificial Intelligence Service and Application

Jin-Taek Jung

Hansung University, 116 Samseon-dong 2-ga, Samseongyo-ro 16-gil, Seongbuk-gu, Seoul, 02876, South Korea

Abstract. The 1st International Workshop on AI Service and Application marks a significant step in integrating AI into various services and applications, providing a platform for global experts, researchers, and practitioners to discuss the latest advancements, challenges, and future directions in AI. The workshop promotes collaboration and knowledge exchange, covering topics like AI's impact on conceptual modeling, decision-making, process automation, ethical considerations, and big data in knowledge services and business. From 20 high-quality submissions, eight papers were selected for presentation, offering valuable in-sights and contributing to a rich technical program. The organizers plan to continue this workshop in future conferences, anticipating growing interest in the field.

Keywords. AI Application · AI Service · Knowledge Service

Welcome to the 1st International Workshop on AI Service and Application. This workshop marks an exciting and important moment in the journey of integrating artificial intelligence (AI) into a wide array of services and applications. As AI continues to evolve and expand its reach, this workshop provides a platform for experts, researchers, and practitioners from around the globe to come together and explore the latest advancements, challenges, and future directions in this rapidly growing field.

The purpose of this workshop is to foster collaboration and knowledge exchange among participants, enabling them to share their insights, research findings, and experiences. Our program is designed to address a broad spectrum of topics, including The Impact of AI on Conceptual Modeling, AI in Decision-Making, AI and Process Automation in Knowledge Services & Business, Ethical Considerations in AI Applications in Knowledge Services & Business, AI and Big Data in Knowledge Services & Business, The Future of AI in Knowledge Services & Business and other Case Studies of Successful AI Applications in Knowledge Services & Business domain. The workshop aims to highlight both the technical innovations and the practical applications that are driving the current wave of AI integration across industries.

The first edition of the AISA workshop received 20 high-quality submissions focused on AI services and applications within the knowledge service domain. Following a thorough single-blind review process, in which each submission was evaluated by a minimum of three experts in the field, eight papers were selected for presentation. These papers offer valuable insights into the issues under investigation and collectively contribute to a compelling technical program designed to foster scholarly discussion. Anticipating increasing interest in this area in the coming years, we are motivated to continue our commitment to this workshop in conjunction with the ER 2024 conference.

AISA Organization

Workshop Adviser

Il-Yeol Song	Drexel University, USA

Workshop Chairs

Jin-Taek Jung	Hansung University, South Korea

Program Committee

Yudho Giri	Indonesia University, Indonesia
Viet-Vu Vu	CMC University, Vietnam
Kyung-Hye Park	Chungnam National University, South Korea
Hyung-Yong Lee	Hansung University, South Korea
Hyu-nchul Ahn	Kookmin University, South Korea
Kyoo-Sung Noh	Korea Association of Software Manpower, South Korea
Min-cheol Kim	Jeju National University, South Korea
Joon-Youn Kim	Software Policy & Research Institute, South Korea
Ho-Seok Yu	Software Policy & Research Institute, South Korea
Jae-Jin, Ko	Korea Electronics Technology Institute, South Korea
Burmaa Natsag	National University of Mongolia, Mongolia

Empirical Case Study of AI Service and Application for People with Disabilities (Invited Paper)

Jaehwan Lee and Jintaek Jung(✉)

Hansung University, 116 Samseon-dong 2-ga, Samseongyo-ro 16-gil, Seongbuk-gu, Seoul 02876, Republic of Korea
jh4126@naver.com, jungjt@hansung.ac.kr

Abstract. The ultimate goal of AI technology is to make human life more convenient. For people with disabilities, AI technology is not only a matter of convenience but also a crucial element in enabling social integration. This paper studies various cases where AI technology enhances the quality of life for individuals with disabilities. It analyzes the potential of AGI, the effectiveness of currently available AI services and applications, and discusses the innovative applications of AI in smart home systems and the utility of affordable AI tools. The study involves 2,200 individuals with disabilities, and the improvement in quality of life due to AI is evaluated through two-way ANOVA, considering age and income level. The analysis reveals that both age and income level significantly impact the improvement in quality of life due to AI.

Keywords: Disability · AI Service and Application · Artificial General Intelligence · Life Satisfaction

1 Introduction

The rapid development of artificial intelligence (AI) technology is transforming our daily lives in many areas. In particular, AI services and applications are playing an increasingly important role in improving the quality of life for people with disabilities. Various support tools and services utilizing AI technology are helping people with disabilities reduce the inconveniences they experience in their daily lives and enable them to live independently. Currently, AI technologies are mainly based on large-scale language models (LLMs), but recently, the transition to artificial general intelligence (AGI) has become an important topic. AGI refers to AI that is not limited to specific tasks but has the ability to perform a variety of cognitive functions like humans. While the realization of AGI is still a theoretical concept, given the positive impact of current AI advances on supporting people with disabilities, expectations are rising for the potential changes that AGI could bring. In this study, we discuss the potential of AGI to significantly improve the quality of life for people with disabilities.

This research is supported by the academic funding at Hansung University.

M. Saeki et al. (Eds.): ER 2024 Workshops, LNCS 14932, pp. 5–20, 2025.
https://doi.org/10.1007/978-3-031-75599-6_1

Increased Independence: AGI can provide more sophisticated and adaptive assistance in daily activities, which has the potential to surpass current AI solutions. These technological advances can help people with disabilities gain greater autonomy, resulting in the ability to perform a variety of tasks that were previously difficult or impossible. This will allow people with disabilities to live more independently in their daily lives [1].

Improved Communication: By providing more advanced and sophisticated communication tools, AGI can break down language and communication barriers for people with various disabilities. This can include more accurate speech-to-text technology, better sign language translation systems, and more intuitive augmentative and alternative communication (AAC) devices. These technologies can help people with disabilities communicate more seamlessly [2].

Personalized Assistance: AGI has the potential to understand and adapt to individual needs more comprehensively than current AI, enabling it to provide highly personalized support and interventions for people with different types of disabilities. This could significantly improve the quality of life for people with disabilities by providing individualized help tailored to each person's specific needs and circumstances [1].

Increased Accessibility: AGI has the potential to design and implement more inclusive environments and technologies, making the world more accessible to people with disabilities. These technological advances can significantly improve accessibility for people with disabilities, including smarter home automation systems, more intuitive assistive devices, and better-designed public spaces. This could help people with disabilities live more convenient and independent lives [2].

These potential effects are estimates based on current AI technologies, and the actual impact of AGI on the quality of life of people with disabilities will depend on how the technology is developed, implemented, and regulated. Therefore, continued research and ethical considerations are critical to ensure that AGI can benefit all members of society, including people with disabilities. Against this background, this study analyzes the impact of current AI services and applications on the quality of life of people with disabilities through empirical cases and explores the potential effects of AGI.

Therefore, this paper aims to explore the potential of AGI healthcare in promoting independent living and conduct empirical evaluations. Through this, we intend to present the applicability of AGI technology in the field of elderly healthcare and provide important implications for future research and practice.

2 Theoretical Background

2.1 Background of AI Service

Artificial intelligence (AI) services are technologies that make our lives easier and smarter.

Neural machine translation (NMT) is a technology used to translate foreign languages. The computer stops at turning a sentence into English. For example, we translate "hello" to "hello" and let the computer take over [3]. The Transformer Model is a technique that understands sentences and creates new sentences. This model recognizes the symbolic relationships of symbols to make them easier to explain. For example, the sentence "I eat apples" can be interpreted as "I eat apples" [4].

Sentiment analysis is the art of reacting to, and finding emotion in, sentences. For example, you can analyze whether a review is uplifting or downlifting. This technique is useful for analyzing customer reviews or media posts [5]. GPT models are a technique that learns from a large amount of textual data and generates new sentences based on it [6].

Some AI models are rewarded by people to get smarter. People look at the results the AI produces and rate it, and the AI gets better and better based on those results, so it gets smarter and smarter and becomes a more useful tool for us [7].

AI services make our lives easier and more possible. As AI technology improves, we get more and more benefits.

2.2 AI Service and Application

Artificial intelligence (AI) services leverage a variety of AI technologies, including machine learning, natural language processing, and computer vision, to provide automated services and personalized solutions to users. AI technologies are analyzing complex data, recognizing patterns, and creating predictive models to drive innovative service improvements in a variety of sectors.

In healthcare, AI technology is playing a huge role in improving the accuracy of diagnoses, predicting patient outcomes, and providing personalized treatment plans [8].

In the financial sector, AI applications are also helping to improve service quality and increase customer satisfaction. AI is being used to automate repetitive tasks, provide personalized financial advice, and detect fraudulent activity [9].

In public services, the adoption of AI is revolutionizing traditional service delivery. AI applications such as chatbots and automated decision-making systems contribute to increased efficiency and improved citizen satisfaction [10].

AI applications are redefining the way we interact with customer service. AI-powered platforms deliver personalized customer experiences, automate customer support through chatbots, and provide real-time problem resolution [11].

The adoption of AI in city services offers significant benefits despite a number of challenges. Public awareness, ease of use, and initial attitudes toward AI play a significant role in AI adoption [12].

There are many challenges to AI adoption, including data privacy concerns, the need for significant investment, and the need for specialized skills. Future research should focus on addressing these challenges, increasing the transparency of AI technologies, and developing ethical guidelines for the use of AI in services [13].

AI services and applications are revolutionizing the way services are delivered in many areas. By enhancing service quality, transforming business models, and improving customer experience, AI is positioning itself as a key technology of the future. However, addressing the challenges of AI adoption is essential to realizing its full potential and ensuring its ethical and effective use.

2.3 Utilizing AI Services and Applications for Life Satisfaction

Advances in AI technology are playing a major role in improving the quality of life in various fields. In particular, AI services and applications are making important contributions to solving various difficulties faced by people with disabilities in their daily lives, and it has been shown that AI technology can increase the happiness and satisfaction of users [14]. A study was conducted to predict life satisfaction using machine learning and explainable AI. The study explained how AI-based predictive models can contribute to improving an individual's quality of life [15].

A study on how customer satisfaction can be improved by applying AI technology to an organization's e-services. It suggests that people with disabilities can get a better user experience through AI services [16]. Similarly, we studied how human-AI interaction improves service quality, showing that people with disabilities can receive better support through AI services [17].

The impact of digital AI technologies on quality of life has been investigated from a global perspective. The study explored how AI technology can improve quality of life in different cultures and geographies, with important implications that can be applied to people with disabilities [18]. A systematic review of the benefits and challenges of applying AI technology in the healthcare sector. AI-based healthcare solutions can play an important role in improving healthcare and quality of life, especially for people with disabilities [19].

3 Case Studies

3.1 Improving Daily Tasks

AI can significantly improve the daily lives of people with disabilities in a variety of ways. AI-powered tools make life easier for people with disabilities through communication, automation, and accessibility. These technologies contribute to increasing independence and quality of life for people with disabilities.

Enhanced Communication: AI-powered tools, such as speech-to-text and text-to-speech technologies, can help people with speech or hearing impairments communicate more effectively with others. For example, an app like Voiceitt learns a user's pronunciation, becoming increasingly accurate over time, and converts impaired pronunciation into clear audio or text messages to facilitate communication [20].

Visual Assistance: For people with visual impairments, AI-powered image recognition technology analyzes photos of their surroundings and describes objects to provide visual information. Microsoft's Seeing AI is an example of technology that recognizes the environment through a camera and describes it out loud to help blind and visually impaired people better understand their surroundings and be more independent in their daily activities [21].

Personalized Assistance: AI can provide tailored assistance for different types of disabilities by adapting to an individual's specific needs and wants. This includes personalized learning experiences tailored to individual learning styles, adaptive interfaces that change to meet the user's needs, and personalized recommendations to help people with disabilities learn and live more effectively [22].

Home Automation: Virtual assistants with integrated artificial intelligence, such as Google Assistant or Amazon Alexa, are helping people with disabilities control appliances in their homes, set reminders, and manage daily tasks through voice commands. These technologies greatly improve the convenience of life by enabling users to accomplish household tasks without the use of their hands [22].

Task Automation: AI tools can reduce the burden on individuals with physical or cognitive disabilities by automating repetitive and simple tasks. For example, in the workplace, capabilities such as robotic process automation (RPA) allow AI to take over simple, repetitive tasks, freeing up employees with disabilities to focus on more creative and valuable work [23].

Improved Accessibility: AI can significantly improve the accessibility of digital content and services. For example, AI-powered tools can automatically caption video content or provide real-time sign language interpretation to make content more understandable and accessible to people with hearing impairments. By making information more accessible, these technologies enable people with disabilities to participate more equally in the digital world [24].

These AI-powered solutions have the potential to significantly improve the quality of life for people with disabilities. They can help people with disabilities in many aspects of their daily lives. In particular, they can help them live more independently by promoting independence, and they can also make digital content and services more accessible by increasing accessibility. Finally, they promote inclusion, increasing social integration and participation.

3.1.1 Most Innovative AI Services and Applications in Smart Home Systems

Based on current AI advancements, the most innovative AI applications in smart home systems for people with disabilities include the following.

AI-powered voice assistants, as shown in Table 1, allow people with limited mobility or visual impairments to easily control various aspects of their home environment through simple voice commands [25].

Table 1. Voice-activated assistant AI application

Product Name	Utilizing AI	Expected effect
Google Assistant	Control smart home devices through voice commands, integrate personalized services	Enhance convenience for individuals with disabilities
Amazon Alexa	Control lighting, appliances, and more through voice commands	Improved accessibility increases convenience for individuals with disabilities

Table 2 shows that AI-controlled smart lighting systems go beyond simply turning lights on and off, adapting to the time of day, user activity, and even emotional state.

This can improve the quality of life for people with various disabilities by providing them with an optimal lighting environment [26].

Table 2. Intelligent Lighting System AI Application

Product Name	Utilizing AI	Expected effect
Philips Hue	Automatically adjust lighting brightness and color based on time of day, activities, and emotional state	Improve quality of life by providing an optimal lighting environment
LIFX	Automatically adjust lighting to meet the user's needs	Provide an optimal lighting environment for individuals with disabilities

Table 3 shows that AI-powered mobility aids such as smart wheelchairs and walkers, although not technically part of the home system, can be integrated with the smart home environment to significantly improve overall accessibility and independence. This can help people with limited mobility to live more freely [27].

Table 3. AI-Powered Mobility Assistive Devices AI Application

Product Name	Utilizing AI	Expected effect
WHILL	Learn the user's movement patterns, provide obstacle avoidance and automatic navigation features	Enhance user mobility and independence
SmartCane by WeWALK	Provide real-time route guidance and obstacle information	Increase the safety and convenience of movement

AI systems like the one in Table 4 can continuously track a user's vital signs, movement patterns, and daily activities, and immediately alert caregivers or emergency services if an anomaly is detected. This provides an additional safety net for people with disabilities living independently, helping them to live with greater peace of mind [28].

As shown in Table 5, advanced AI systems have the ability to understand and execute more complex and context-dependent commands. This enables users with disabilities to perform complex tasks with simple voice instructions, increasing their autonomy in their daily lives [29].

Table 4. Health and safety monitoring AI applications

Product Name	Utilizing AI	Expected effect
Apple Watch	Monitor heart rate, activity level, and oxygen saturation, providing alerts when abnormalities are detected	Improve health management and emergency response capabilities
Google Nest Protect	Detect smoke and carbon monoxide, sending warnings to connected devices in case of abnormalities	Enhance real-time safety management and accident prevention

Table 5. Natural Language Processing for Complex Commands AI Application

Product Name	Utilizing AI	Expected effect
Siri	Understand and execute complex commands set by the user	Enhance user autonomy in daily life through the automation of complex tasks
Google Assistant	Perform routine-based complex commands and integrate various devices and tasks	Increase convenience in daily life by providing personalized, tailored services

Some smart home systems incorporate AI-powered robots that can help with cleaning, cooking, and other household chores. As shown in Table 6, these robots can greatly increase the independence of individuals with physical disabilities and reduce the burden of household chores [27].

Table 6. AI-powered robots for household chores AI Application

Product Name	Utilizing AI	Expected effect
iRobot Roomba	Automate household cleaning through voice commands or an app	Reduce the burden of household chores and enhance independence for individuals with physical disabilities
Moley Kitchen Robot	Automate the cooking process, including ingredient preparation and cooking according to recipes	Support independent living for individuals with physical disabilities by improving cooking abilities

These innovative applications show how AI is transforming smart home technology to create more accessible, supportive, and independent living environments for people with disabilities. As AI continues to advance, we can expect more sophisticated and personalized solutions to emerge, further improving the quality of life for people with disabilities in their homes.

3.1.2 Currently Available Low-Cost AI Services and Applications

Table 7 shows the currently available low-cost AI services and applications.

Table 7. Affordable AI Service Technology Currently Available

Product Name	Utilizing AI	Expected effect
Caption Mate	Provide real-time captions for phone calls in over 100 languages	Support communication for individuals with hearing impairments
Live Transcribe & Sound Notifications	Offer real-time speech recognition and personalized notifications	Enhance real-time information accessibility for individuals with hearing impairments
TD Talk	Provide real-time speech recognition and personalized notifications	Improve communication abilities
Grammarly	Correct writing errors and suggest vocabulary improvements	Enhance writing accuracy and quality
Siri	Perform various tasks through speech recognition	Increase convenience in daily life for individuals with disabilities
Be My Eyes	Connect with visual volunteers to provide visual information	Improve information accessibility for individuals with visual impairments
Seeing AI	Describe people, text, and objects through the camera	Support independent living for individuals with visual impairments
Tap Tap See	Explain objects through image recognition and convert text to speech	Enhance object recognition and information accessibility for individuals with visual impairments

These examples demonstrate that there are many low-cost or free AI-based assistive technologies available on a variety of platforms that can meet a wide range of accessibility needs.

Additionally, Table 8 below provides a list of AI services and application tools for people with disabilities from https://www.futuretools.io/, a website that provides information on AI tools and technologies.

Table 8. List of AI services and application tools to support people with disabilities

Division	Product	Platform	Main Features/ Website
Physically impaired	O1 Lite	Mobile app	Control computer with voice https://news.futuretools.io/unveiling-the-o1-lite-the-future-of-open-source-ai-devices/
	Wizardshot	Web-based	Automatically generate step-by-step tutorials https://www.futuretools.io/tools/wizardshot
Brain lesion impaired	Magicast.ai	Web-based	Text to audio conversion https://www.futuretools.io/tools/magicast-ai
	myReach	Web-based	Knowledge manage, information discovery https://www.futuretools.io/tools/myreach
Visually impaired	Audyo	AI-powered platform	Text to audio conversion https://www.futuretools.io/tools/audyo
	Recast	Mobile app	Text to audio conversion https://www.futuretools.io/tools/recast
Hearing impaired	SpeechFlow	MacOS, Windows	Audio to text conversion https://www.futuretools.io/tools/speechflow
	Vid2Txt	MacOS, Windows	Video, audio to text conversion https://www.futuretools.io/tools/vid2txt
Speech impaired	Peech App	Web-based	Text to audio conversion https://www.futuretools.io/tools/peech-app
	OpenVoice	Web-based	Voice cloning, multilingual support https://www.futuretools.io/tools/openvoice

4 Research Design

4.1 Research Hypothesis

Based on a review of existing literature, sets the following hypothesis to examine the interaction effect of age and average monthly income on the quality of life improvements due to artificial intelligence for people with disabilities.

H1: There will be a positive interaction effect of age and income level on the quality of life improvements due to artificial intelligence for people with disabilities.

4.2 Research Model

The research model is established based on theoretical discussions and prior studies regarding the improvement in quality of life due to artificial intelligence, according to the age and average monthly income of people with disabilities (Fig. 1). The research model structures the age, average monthly income, and quality of life improvements due to artificial intelligence for people with disabilities

The study analyzes whether there is an interaction effect on quality of life improvements due to artificial intelligence related to age, and whether there is an interaction effect between age and average monthly income. The concepts comprising the research model assume a positive (+) influence relationship.

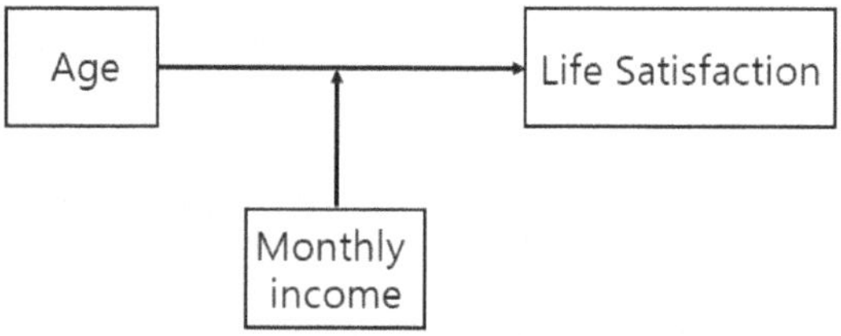

Fig. 1. Research model

4.3 Data Collection Method

This study utilizes the 2023 Digital Information Gap Survey conducted by the Korea Intelligent and Information Society Promotion Agency, which is hosted by the Ministry of Science and ICT of Korea. The data of the Digital Information Gap Survey has been measured by conducting an information gap survey by vulnerable groups on an annual basis since 2002 in accordance with the Basic Act on Intelligence and Information Society, and since 2006, the digital informatization index such as PC and mobile, the pilot calculation of the digital information gap index in 2014, and the artificial intelligence (AI) technology informatization index since 2023 have been further developed.

The 2023 Digital Divide Survey will be systematically measured and will be able to measure and utilize the interaction effect of age and average monthly income of people with disabilities on the degree of assistance in using AI.

The study sample consists of 2,200 individuals, aged 7 to 69, who are registered nationwide as of August 1, 2023, under the 'Disability Welfare Act,' based on disability types (physical impaired, brain lesion impaired, hearing impaired, visual impaired, and speech impaired).

5 Methodology

This study analyzed the interaction effect of age and average monthly income on the quality of life improvements due to artificial intelligence for people with disabilities using SPSS25 as follows.

First, frequency analysis was conducted to analyze the demographic characteristics of the subjects and descriptive statistics of the main variables were conducted. Second, a two-way analysis of variance was conducted to test the interaction effect between the main variables.

5.1 Demographic Characteristics of the Study Subjects

The gender of the people with disabilities in the study was 1,595 (72.5%) male and 605 (27.5%) female, with 218 (9.9%) under 29 years of age, 1,227 (55.8%) between 30 and 59 years of age, and 755 (34.3%) over 60 years of age. The final education level is elementary school or less 203 (9.2%), middle school 441 (20%), high school 1,139 (51.8%), and college graduate 417 (19.0%), and the type of disability is physical 1,133 (51.5%), brain lesion 481 (21. 9%), visual impairment 365 (16.6%), hearing impairment 198 (9.0%), speech impairment 23 (1.0%), and the monthly income of 802 (36.5%) less than 1.99 million won, 790 (35.9%) between 2 to 3.99 million won, and 608 (27.6%) more than 4 million won.

Table 9. General Characteristics of Participants.

Variables	Category	N	%
Gender	Male	1,595	72.5
	Female	605	27.5
Age	Under 29	218	9.9
	30 to 59	1,227	55.8
	Over 60	755	34.3
Education level	Elementary school	203	9.2
	Middle school	441	20.0
	High school	1,139	51.8
	College graduate	417	19.0
Type of disability	Physical	1,133	51.5
	Brain lesion	481	21.9
	visual	365	16.6
	hearing	198	9.0
	speech	23	1.0

(continued)

Table 9. (*continued*)

Variables	Category	N	%
Monthly income	less than 1.99 million won	802	36.5
	2 to 3.99 million won	790	35.9
	more than 4 million won	608	27.6
SUM	2,200	100/0	

5.2 Key Variable Descriptive Statistics

The results of the descriptive statistics for the main variables are as shown in Table 10. Firstly, the dependent variable, which is the quality of life expected to improve, showed a mean of 2.91 (SD = .620). The independent variable, age, had a mean of 2.24 (SD = .619), and the monthly income was reported with a mean of 1.91 (SD = .796)."

Table 10. Key variable descriptive statistics

Variable	N	Minimum	Maximum	Mean	Std. Deviation
The quality of life will be improved	2200	1	4	2.91	.620
Age	2200	1	3	2.24	.619
Monthly income	2200	1	3	1.91	.796

5.3 Two-Way ANOVA(Analysis of Variance)

To analyze the impact of artificial intelligence on the quality of life of people with disabilities, a two-way analysis of variance (Two-Way ANOVA) was conducted to verify the interaction effects of age and monthly income.

The analysis revealed that the improvement in quality of life due to artificial intelligence was statistically significant with respect to age ($F = 8.116, p = 0.00$) and monthly income ($F = 7.777$, $p = 0.00$). Additionally, the interaction effect between age and monthly income was also statistically significant ($F = 4.675, p = 0.01$) at the 0.05 significance level. Therefore, it can be concluded that there is an interaction effect between age and monthly income.

Table 11. Two-way ANOVA (Analysis of Variance)

Dependent Variable	Independent Variable	Sum of squares	Df	Mean square	F(p)	partial eta squared
The quality of life will be improved	Corrected Model	26.734[a]	8	3.342	8.952(0.00***)	.032
	Intercept	9717.228	1	9717.228	26030.549(0.00***)	.922
	Age	6.097	2	3.048	8.116(0.00***)	.007
	Monthly income	5.806	2	2.903	7.777(0.00***)	.007
	Age * income	6.980	4	1.745	4.675(0.01**)	.008
	Error	817.902	2191	.373		
	Total	19457.000	2200			
	Corrected Total	844.6336	2199			

* p<.05, ** p<.01,*** p<.001

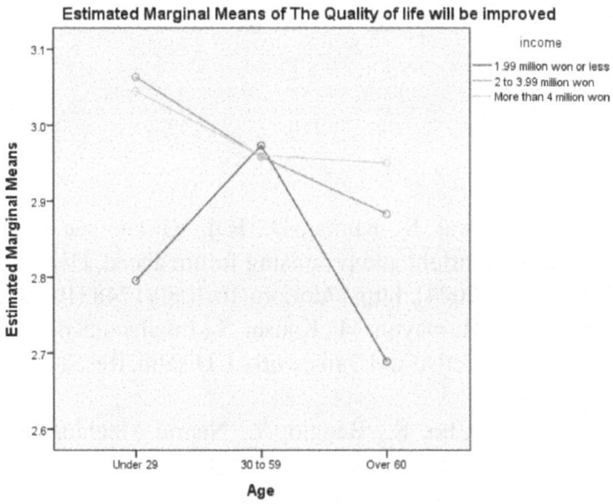

Fig. 2. Form of interaction

6 Conclusion

This This study analyzes the various ways and examples of how artificial intelligence (AI) technology can improve the quality of life for people with disabilities. AI technologies can significantly improve the independence and quality of life of people with disabilities in several areas, including communication tools, accessibility improvements, personalized assistance, and smart home systems. In particular, smart home systems such as voice-activated assistants, intelligent lighting systems, and AI-powered mobility aids can help people with disabilities live more independently and safely at home.

Research has shown that the introduction of AI technology has had a positive impact on people with disabilities in terms of reducing the inconveniences they experience in their daily lives and enabling them to live independently. For example, speech-to-text technology can help people with hearing impairments communicate, AI-powered image recognition can help people with visual impairments better understand their surroundings, and personalized learning and interfaces can help people with different types of disabilities learn and live more effectively.

The analysis of the quality of life improvements based on age and income levels with the use of AI technology showed that older and higher-income individuals tend to have a more positive perception of how AI can improve their quality of life. Particularly, the highest mean values were observed in the age group of 30–59 years and among those with a monthly income over 4,000,000 won. This analysis confirmed that the perception of AI services and applications among people with disabilities varies according to age and income. Specifically, the interaction effect between age and income suggests that the impact of AI on the quality of life of people with disabilities is complex.

Finally, various technological developments and policy support are needed to increase the accessibility and usability of AI services and applications for people with disabilities. These efforts will go a long way toward increasing the independence and quality of life of people with disabilities. We hope that AI technology will bring positive changes to the lives of people with disabilities, and we look forward to continued research and development.

References

1. Kumar, V., Barik, S., Aggarwal, S., Kumar, D., Raj, V.: The use of artificial intelligence for persons with disability: a bright and promising future ahead. Disabil. Rehabilitat. Assist. Technol. **19**(6), 2415–2417 (2024). https://doi.org/10.1080/17483107.2023.2288241
2. Almufareh, M.F., Tehsin, S., Humayun, M., Kausar, S.: Intellectual disability and technology: an artificial intelligence perspective and framework. J. Disabil. Res. **2**(4), 58-70 (2023). https://doi.org/10.57197/jdr-2023-0055
3. Bahdanau, D., Dzmitry, S., Cho, K., Bengio, Y.: Neural Machine Translation by Jointly Learning to Align and Translate. CoRR arxiv:1409.0473 (2014). https://doi.org/10.48550/arXiv.1409.0473
4. Vaswani, A., Shazeer, N.M., Parmar, N., Uszkoreit, J.: Attention is all you need. In: Neural Information Processing Systems (2017). https://www.semanticscholar.org/reader/204e3073870fae3d05bcbc2f6a8e263d9b72e776
5. Radford, A., Józefowicz, R., Sutskever, I.: Learning to generate reviews and discovering sentiment. ArXiv arxiv:1704.01444 (2017). https://www.semanticscholar.org/reader/664ec878de4b7170712baae4a7821fc2602bba25
6. Radford, A., Narasimhan, K.: Improving language understanding by generative pre-training (2018). https://gwern.net/doc/www/s3-us-west-2.amazonaws.com/d73fdc5ffa8627bce44dcda2fc012da638ffb158.pdf
7. Ouyang, L., Wu, J., Jiang, X., Almeida, D.: Training language models to follow instructions with human feedback. ArXiv arxiv:2203.02155 (2022). https://www.semanticscholar.org/reader/d766bffc357127e0dc86dd69561d5aeb520d6f4c

8. UmaMaheswaran, S.K.., et al.: Empirical analysis for improving food quality using artificial intelligence technology for enhancing healthcare sector. J. Food Qual. (2022). https://www.semanticscholar.org/reader/b0e4f2ac39af50b48e6233e685a06e46c8ee9e8a
9. Al-Araj, R., Haddad. H., Izukwe, R., Hasan, E.F., Nawaiseh, M.Y.: The effect of artificial intelligence on service quality and customer satisfaction in jordanian banking sector. WSEAS Trans. Bus. Econ. (2022). https://wseas.com/journals/bae/2022/d505107-1999.pdf
10. Henman, P.: Improving public services using artificial intelligence: possibilities, pitfalls, governance. Asia Pac. J. Public Adm. **42**(4), 209–221 (2020). https://doi.org/10.1080/23276665.2020.1816188
11. Marinchak, C.M., Forrest, E., Hoanca, B.: Artificial intelligence: redefining marketing management and the customer experience. Int. J. E-Entrepre. Innov. **8**(2), 14–24 (2018). https://doi.org/10.4018/IJEEI.2018070102
12. Yigitcanlar, T., Li, R.Y.M., Inkinen, T., Paz, A.: Public perceptions on application areas and adoption challenges of AI in urban sevices. Emerg. Sci. J. (2022).https://www.semanticscholar.org/reader/100bf2cf749656b7c0580d87fd8af6473734bd86
13. Reis, J., Amorim, M., Cohen, Y., Rodrigues, M.: Artificial intelligence in service delivery systems: a systematic literature review. In: Rocha, Á., Adeli, H., Reis, L.P., Costanzo, S., Orovic, I., Moreira, F. (eds.) Trends and Innovations in Information Systems and Technologies: Volume 1, pp. 222–233. Springer International Publishing, Cham (2020). https://doi.org/10.1007/978-3-030-45688-7_23
14. Khan, A.E., Hasan, M.J., Anjum, H., Mohammed, N., Momen, S.: Predicting life satisfaction using machine learning and explainable AI. Heliyon **10**(10), e31158 (2024). https://doi.org/10.1016/j.heliyon.2024.e31158
15. Khawan, S.F.: The use of artificial intelligence technology in the organization's e-services and the impact on customer satisfaction. SSRN Electron. J. (2023). https://doi.org/10.2139/ssrn.4595784
16. Hui, Z., Khan, A.N., Chenglong, Z., Khan, N.A.: When service quality is enhanced by human–artificial intelligence interaction: an examination of anthropomorphism, responsiveness from the perspectives of employees and customers. Int. J. Hum.–Comput. Interact. 1–16 (2023). https://doi.org/10.1080/10447318.2023.2266254
17. Kosasi, S., Lukita, C., Chakim, M.H.R., Faturahman, A., Kusumawardhani, D.A.R.: The influence of digital artificial intelligence technology on quality of life with a global perspective. Aptisi Trans. Technopreneurship (ATT) **5**(3), 240–250 (2023). https://www.semanticscholar.org/reader/28c6230dca846e4f7abfebe8168eb14ef088a5de
18. Ali, O., Abdelbaki, W., Shrestha, A., Elbasi, E., Alryalat, M.A.A., Dwivedi, Y.K.: A systematic literature review of artificial intelligence in the healthcare sector: benefits, challenges, methodologies, and functionalities. J. Innov. Knowl. **8**(1), 100333 (2023). https://doi.org/10.1016/j.jik.2023.100333
19. Antonio, E.R.P., Fadhilah, M.F., Faiq, F., Fredyan, R., Pranoto, H.:Analyzing the impact of customer service chatbots on user satisfaction. In: 2023 15th International Congress on Advanced Applied Informatics Winter (IIAI-AAIWinter), pp. 82–85 (2023).https://doi.org/10.1109/IIAI-AAI-Winter61682.2023.00023
20. White, J.J.G.: Artificial intelligence and people with disabilities: a reflection on human–ai partnerships. In: Chen, F., Zhou, J. (eds.) Humanity Driven AI: Productivity, Well-being, Sustainability and Partnership, pp. 279–310. Springer, Cham (2022). https://doi.org/10.1007/978-3-030-72188-6_14
21. Mina, P.N.R., et al.: Leveraging education through artificial intelligence virtual assistance: a case study of visually impaired learners. Int. J. Educ. Innov. Res. **2**(1), 10–22 (2023). https://doi.org/10.31949/ijeir.v2i1.3001

22. S. Venkatraman, F., A. Overmars, S., Minh Thong, T.: "Smart Home Automation - Use Cases of a Secure and Integrated Voice-Control System." Syst. 9 (2021): 77. https://doi.org/10.3390/systems9040077
23. Vieira, A.D., Leite, H., Volochtchuk, A.V.L.: The impact of voice assistant home devices on people with disabilities: a longitudinal study. Technol. Forecast. Social Change **184**, 121961 (2022). https://doi.org/10.2139/ssrn.3993227
24. Poushneh, A.: Humanizing voice assistant: the impact of voice assistant personality on consumers' attitudes and behaviors. J. Retail. Consum. Serv. **58**, 102283 (2021). https://doi.org/10.1016/j.jretconser.2020.102283
25. Lancioni, G.E., et al.: A smartphone-based program enabling people with intellectual and other disabilities to access leisure, communication, and functional activities. Univ. Access Inf. Soc. **22**(2), 581–590 (2022). https://doi.org/10.1007/s10209-021-00858-4
26. Rossetti, L., et al.: Intelligent environments and assistive technologies for assisting visually impaired people: a systematic literature review. Univ. Access Inf. Soc. (2024). https://doi.org/10.1007/s10209-024-01117-y
27. Sciarretta, E., Alimenti, L.: Smart speakers for inclusion: how can intelligent virtual assistants really assist everybody? In: Kurosu, M. (ed.) HCII 2021. LNCS, vol. 12762, pp. 77–93. Springer, Cham (2021). https://doi.org/10.1007/978-3-030-78462-1_6
28. Dutsinma, F.L.I., Pal, D., Funilkul, S., Chan, J.H.: A systematic review of voice assistant usability: an ISO 9241–11 approach. SN Comput. Sci. **3**(4) (2022). https://doi.org/10.1007/s42979-022-01172-3
29. Masina, F., et al.: VOICE actuated control systems (VACS) for accessible and assistive smart homes. a preliminary investigation on accessibility and user experience with disabled users. In: Monteriù, A., Freddi, A., Longhi, S. (eds.) Ambient Assisted Living: Italian Forum 2019, pp. 153–160. Springer, Cham (2021). https://doi.org/10.1007/978-3-030-63107-9_11

A Methodological Framework for Designing Human-Centered Artificial Intelligence Services

Thang Le Dinh[1(✉)], Tran Duc Le[1], and Jolita Ralyté[2]

[1] Business School, Université du Québec à Trois-Rivières, Trois-Rivières, Canada
thang.ledinh@uqtr.ca
[2] University of Geneva, Geneva, Switzerland
jolita.ralyte@unige.ch

Abstract. In the rapidly evolving domain of artificial intelligence (AI) technologies, integrating Human-Centered Artificial Intelligence (HCAI) within service science is increasingly pivotal for enhancing service sector performance. This paper introduces a methodological framework for HCAI service design, called HCAI-SD framework, a novel approach that incorporates HCAI principles into service science to facilitate the design of HCAI services. The framework prioritizes the harmonization of AI capabilities with human-centered design principles and HCAI guidance. While using a design science methodology, the framework effectively addresses the unique requirements of HCAI services by integrating insights from different levels of service science, including the value creation network, service system, and service levels. To demonstrate the application of the framework in a real-world scenario, a comprehensive case study is presented that aims at designing an HCAI service to enhance the systematic literature review process in the domain of AI in education. This research contributes significantly to the integration of AI capabilities within service science and provides a methodological framework for developing robust and complex HCAI services.

Keywords: Human-Centered Artificial Intelligence · Service Science · Methodological Framework · Smart Service

1 Introduction

Nowadays, artificial intelligence (AI) holds the potential to transform industries and society dramatically, yet to guarantee its effective deployment and lasting influence, both challenges and research agendas need to be tackled [1]. AI-powered services offer advantages like standardization, personalization, and relationalization, which vary based on the service task, offering, strategy, and process involved [2]. AI-powered services are reshaping the service industry by performing tasks and enabling innovation. However, they also threaten human jobs, with lower intelligence tasks replaced by higher intelligence tasks [3].

This research focuses on Human-Centered Artificial Intelligence (HCAI), an emerging discipline dedicated to developing AI applications that enhance and augment

M. Saeki et al. (Eds.): ER 2024 Workshops, LNCS 14932, pp. 21–39, 2025.
https://doi.org/10.1007/978-3-031-75599-6_2

human abilities rather than displacing them [4]. The HCAI approach emphasizes maintaining human control, ensuring that AI systems meet organizational needs, operate transparently, and uphold privacy standards.

This study aims at exploring methodologies for supporting the design and implementation of HCAI services. A new methodological framework rooted in service science for service design, called the HCAI-SD framework, is proposed to seamlessly incorporate HCAI perspectives into the development and deployment of HCAI services. More specifically, the proposed framework centers on the synergistic alignment of AI capabilities with user requirements, augmentation processes, and the principles and guidance of HCAI in AI service systems [5].

This paper is structured according to the design science research methodology [6] as follows: Sect. 2 introduces the theoretical background of the study. Section 3 presents the research design, which focuses on the objective of developing a design science-based methodological framework for designing HCAI services. Section 4 provides details on the proposed design artifacts of the HCAI-SD framework. Section 5 demonstrates the applicability and usefulness of the framework in real-world scenarios through a comprehensive case study on designing an HCAI service to enhance the systematic literature review process. Related work is discussed in Sect. 6, and conclusions and directions for future research are given in Sect. 7.

2 Background

This section briefly introduces the foundational concepts underpinning the study: Service Science and Human-Centered Artificial Intelligence.

2.1 Service Science

These days, the service sector, a key contributor to the economies of many countries, serves as an essential source of job creation and economic prosperity [7]. It frequently leads to embracing new technologies, including AI-powered tools, to boost productivity, enhance efficiency, and drive innovation. In response to its growing importance, there is a recognized need for an interdisciplinary research field called Service Science. This field focuses on service creation, design, delivery, management, and evolution. It integrates principles and methods from various disciplines, including management, computer science, economics, and social sciences, to develop a holistic understanding of services and service systems [8].

Levels of Service. Studies in Service Science should elucidate the nature of service systems, their origins, development, and the coordination between internal and external service systems [8, 9]. These studies are typically structured around three levels of service: the value creation network, the service system, and the service. A *value creation network* consists of a multitude of economic entities forming a network of service systems [10]. A *service system* is defined as "a dynamic value co-creation configuration of resources, including people, organizations, shared information, and technology, which are interconnected internally and externally to other service systems through value propositions" [11]. Finally, a *service* is described as "a change in the condition of a person or a good belonging to some business entities, resulting from the activity of another business entity, with the consent of the first person or business entity" [11]. These levels of service help dissect complex interactions and value exchanges of modern service economies.

2.2 Human-Centered Artificial Intelligence (HCAI)

The emergence of AI-powered technologies significantly impacts the global economy and offers a unique opportunity to increase customer value in the service sector [12]. As AI begins to automate routine tasks, there is a notable transformation in employment roles within the service industry. Initially, AI is replacing positions that require less cognitive effort and is progressively taking over roles that previously demanded higher analytical skills. This transition reduces the necessity for analytical skills while increasing the need for intuitive and empathetic abilities among service workers [3]. To tackle this issue, HCAI is an emerging field of study focusing on designing AI applications to enhance and support human capabilities rather than replace them. Notably, the HCAI methodology maintains human oversight, ensuring that AI systems meet organizational needs, operate transparently, and uphold privacy [4].

HCAI Principles. HCAI identifies key principles that should drive the development of AI-based services and systems [4, 5, 13–16]. The most explored and discussed principles include *Accountability*, *Explainability*, *Fairness*, and *Ethics*.

HCAI Guidance. The guidance outlines design goals and principles for HCAI in the AI life cycle, including the *Human-before-the-loop, Human-in-the-loop,* and *Human-over-the-loop* stages [17, 18].

3 Research Design

As previously mentioned, HCAI emphasizes aligning technological innovation with human-centric values. Therefore, it is vital to engage a diverse group of stakeholders in the development of HCAI services to ensure they are intuitive, accessible, and adhere to both business and societal norms [3, 4]. However, our observations suggest that there is currently a lack of focus on designing HCAI services that thoroughly embody all HCAI principles and guidance coherently.

Research Question. To address this gap, the following study proposes a framework rooted in service science for HCAI service design, named the HCAI-SD framework. The primary research question of this paper is, "*How can we build a comprehensive methodological framework for designing HCAI services to enable their adaptation in practice?*".

Research Method. To answer this research question, *design science research* (DSR) has been used as an interdisciplinary approach to create and evaluate artifacts designed to solve identified problems consistently [6]. The key components of DSR are problem space and solution space. *Problem space* refers to the environment within which a particular problem exists that needs to be addressed by designing innovative artifacts [6]. Meanwhile, *solution space* refers to the range of potential artifacts that can be developed to address the problems identified in the problem space [6].

Methodological Framework. A methodological framework offers structured, practical guidance or serves as a tool to assist the user in navigating a process through distinct stages or a sequential step-by-step approach [19]. DSR delineates primary research activities and four overarching categories of research outputs namely, *constructs*, *models*, *methods*, and *instantiations* [20].

Research Model. In alignment with the DSR process and the design of service systems [21], the study introduces a research model depicted in Fig. 1. This model outlines various steps for conducting service design (including service proposition, creation and implementation) and service operations, as well as for integrating these components into a cohesive framework. In this study, service design is considered as the whole process of studying how current human-centered design methods could be extended and adapted for service system development and delivery [22].

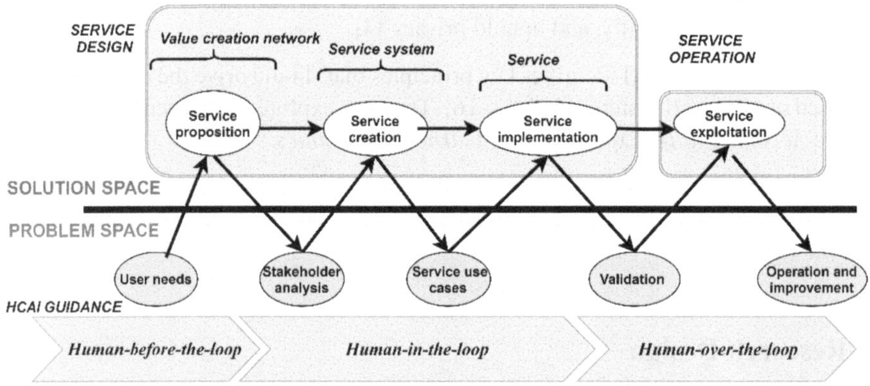

Fig. 1. Research model for the HCAI-SD framework.

As depicted in Fig. 1, *service design* entails the creation of a service concept that shapes the customer's experience and outlines the necessary physical, human, and technological resources required for service delivery. On the other hand, *service operation* encompasses all the activities and processes that facilitate customer value creation through service delivery [9].

The research model for the HCAI-SD framework is structured around different service levels. At the *value creation network* level, the focus is on service processes and leveraging the competencies of a business entity to deliver benefits and create business value for another entity [9]. The *service system* level is concerned with enhancing service systems to ensure effective management, integrating HCAI principles, and improving service system performance based on critical performance measurement dimensions [9, 23]. Finally, the *service* level examines the strategic use of AI-powered technologies tailored to specific data and model requirements to meet user needs and enhance the scalability of service systems [23].

4 HCAI-SD Framework

The DSR studies and determines the domain knowledge available to solve a problem that can take the form of a methodological framework [19, 20]. Accordingly, this section presents the basis of the HCAI-SD framework, including constructs, a model, and a method [6].

4.1 Constructs

A construct is an abstract concept specifically chosen to help understand and describe certain phenomena relevant to the field of study [24]. In other words, constructs provide a language for describing problems and solutions [24]. The HCAI-SD framework includes the following constructs at different levels of service as presented in Table 1.

Table 1. Constructs of the HCAI-SD framework.

Level	Construct	Description
Value creation network level	User needs	Refer to users' desires, goals, preferences, and expectations when they interact with a service [25]
	Value proposition	A concise description of a service that connects with customers and stakeholders to create value [26]. The value proposition may define the objectives and scope of the service [26]
Service system level	Service	A change in the condition of a person or an item belonging to a business entity, which occurs due to the activity of other business entities, with the approval of the first business entity [8, 9]
	Stakeholder	A business entity, a key player in the value creation network, encompassing roles like service providers and users [9]
	Provider	Delivers services tailored to meet users' needs [9]
	User	Engages with services, consumes them, and plays a crucial role in value creation through this consumption [9, 27]

(continued)

Table 1. (*continued*)

Level	Construct	Description
	Event	A user's request to engage with a service [28]
	Process	An action performed by a service system to the occurrence of an event triggered by a business entity that transits it from one dynamic state to another [28]
Service level	Data object	A business layer component, interconnected data to support business services to meet user needs [28]. More specifically, an object type and a set of objects of this type define a data object
	Activity	Addresses a data processing method or an AI model needed for processing a data object [23]. The Activity constructs can be specialized into three types of constructs: i) *Human-before-the-loop* outlining design goals and principles for HCAI in the initial phase; ii) *Human-in-the-loop* covering HCAI-oriented activities throughout the design, development, and deployment phases; and iii) *Human-over-the-loop* addressing HCAI-based AI governance during the later phases of deployment [17, 18]
	Measure	Deals with the performance and trustworthiness of service systems to answer how to capture and measure the result of an activity or a process [9]
	Service principle	A type of measure that can be specialized into Efficiency, Effectiveness, and Sustainability constructs (corresponding to the principles of service systems) [8, 9]: i) *Efficiency* referring to the effectiveness with which a service utilizes its resources to meet its objectives, particularly in delivering value to its users while minimizing waste, costs, and time; ii) *Effectiveness* focusing on the degree to which a service meets the needs and expectations of its users and achieves its intended outcomes; and iii) *Sustainability* concerning the capacity of a service to maintain its levels of performance and quality over the long term while responsibly managing its social, economic, and environmental impacts [29]

(*continued*)

Table 1. (*continued*)

Level	Construct	Description
	HCAI principle	A type of measure that can be specialized into Explainability, Accountability, Fairness, and Ethics constructs (corresponding to HCAI principles) [4, 5, 13–16]: i) *Accountability* ensuring that AI actions and decisions comply with the legal frame of the organization and society; ii) *Explainability* guaranteeing that AI-based decision-making processes can be explained and justified; iii) *Fairness* addressing biases and ensuring that AI benefits all segments of society; and iv) *Ethics* concerning where the morality of decisions is considered

4.2 Model

A model utilizes constructs to depict a real-world scenario encompassing the design problem and solution space. Essentially, a model describes the relationships between constructs [24]. The model of the HCAI-DC framework is depicted in Fig. 2.

As shown in Fig. 2 using the UML notation, service providers and users are stakeholders of the value creation network. A value proposition is developed according to user needs. Each value proposition has distinct objectives assessed using specific measures (or metrics). A service is created to ensure a value proposition. A service is supported by a process defined as a set of activities that can be executed in parallel or in sequence. An activity performs a data processing method or AI model on a data object. There are different types of activity, including Human-before-the-loop, Hu-man-in-the-loop, and Human-over-the-loop activities. There are two categories of measures: service principle-based and HCAI principle-based measures. An activity can be evaluated and governed by measures based on service principles (Efficiency, Effectiveness, and Sustainability) or measurements related to HCAI principles (Explainability, Accountability, Fairness, and Ethics).

4.3 Method

A method outlines specific steps that offer guidance on problem-solving, specifically detailing approaches for exploring the solution space [24]. Figure 3 presents the method of the HCAI approach, including the phases, tasks, and their key constructs. The tasks and subtasks are detailed in the following of this section.

Identify User Needs. This task involves understanding what users require from a service to meet their goals, solve their problems, or enhance their experience. It includes the following sub-tasks: i) ***Determining the AI potential*** that consists in identifying users and stakeholders needs so that the AI-powered solutions can be identified and assessed,

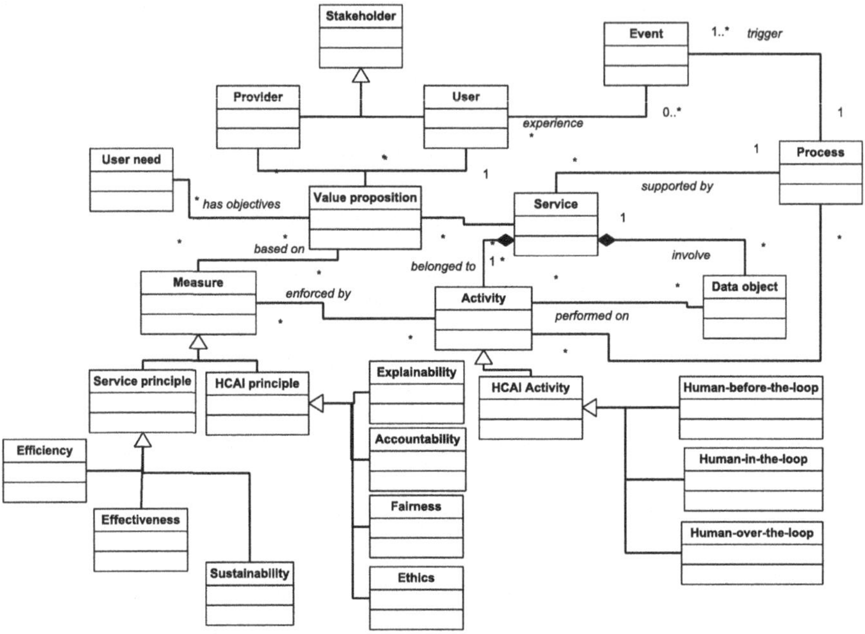

Fig. 2. Model of the HCAI-SD framework.

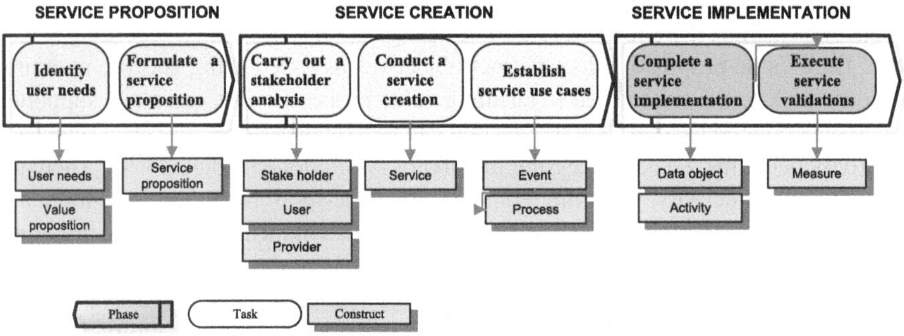

Fig. 3. Method of the HCAI-SD framework.

particularly their strengths and limits [23, 25]; ii) ***Considering the AI usage strategy*** to know whether the service will improve or automate user needs to increase efficiency and gain competitive advantages [10, 23]; and iii) ***Examining the feasibility*** which is crucial before committing significant resources to its development and deployment which involves assessing whether the project is technically viable, economically sensible, and strategically aligned with the organization's goals [23, 30].

Formulate a Service Proposition. This task consists in creating a clear statement that outlines a specific service offers to its target users. It includes: i) ***Setting the service objectives*** in terms of customers' satisfaction, operational efficiency, and overall business goals [31]; ii) ***Preparing the service description*** which specifies the service functionality and the terms at which the service is offered [32]; and iii) ***Highlighting the benefits and value creation*** which explains the service value proposition by considering the user as the determiner and creator of value, with the service provider providing potential value and facilitating value creation, which occurs when a resource is turned into a specific benefit called resourcing, performed by the service system [8, 33].

Carry Out a Stakeholder Analysis. This is a critical task aiming to help organizations identify and understand different stakeholders and their roles relevant to a service. It consists in: i) ***Identifying service stakeholders*** which can be individuals, groups, or organizations interested in or affected by the delivery, outcome, and quality of the service [8]; ii) ***Categorizing stakeholders*** in two main categories: service users and service providers. A *service user*, also called a service target, is a customer of the business entity [10]. There are two types of service providers: *primary service providers,* providing services to its service users and *secondary service providers,* providing services to its clients' users [10]; and iii) ***Assigning responsibilities*** to each stakeholder that must align with the service objectives and stakeholder's capability and area of expertise, which may provide specific AI-powered and generative AI-powered services [31].

Conduct a Service Creation. This task is crucial for organizations aiming to introduce new services that meet specific user needs. It includes: i) ***Designing the service processes*** to prepare a visual representation, also called a service blueprint, outlining all the steps, interactions, and touchpoints involved [31]; ii) ***Assuming the AI trustworthy*** *by* following the HCAI guidelines, which can be used depending on the levels of human decisions such as examining and authenticating AI decisions before implementing them, intervening and overriding AI decisions if needed, and overseeing the working and intervening if something went wrong [18]; and iii) ***Identifying key service components*** such as resources, shared information, and services provided by service providers [9, 23, 31].

Establish Service Use Cases. It is a fundamental step in service design and development that helps to clarify how a customer or user will interact with a service in real-world scenarios. It consist in: i) ***Determining service use cases*** that are detailed descriptions of how the service will be used by its intended users, including specific scenarios in which the service addresses customer needs, solves problems, or enhances the user experience [34]; ii) ***Modelling service activities*** in terms of events and associated processes, including all the steps a user and primary service provider must take from the beginning to the end of the service [23]; iii) ***Assuming the HCAI guidance*** to clarify human participation in the key phases such as *Human-before-the-loop* corresponding to the design of the HCAI service (including the planning step), *Human-in-the-loop* corresponding to the development of the HCAI service (including the data, modelling, deployment steps) and *Human-over-the-loop* corresponding to the exploitation of the HCAI service (including the oversight step) [5, 18]; and iv) ***Proposing the control points*** to evaluate the HCAI service at different levels: *control point 1* checking whether all planning requirements are met during the Human-before-the-loop phase, *control point 2* checking whether the data object collected is diverse and unbiased, *control point 3* checking whether modeling algorithms and data processing are used correctly during the Human-in-a-loop phase, and *control point 4* checking whether the testing and validation are appropriately performed during the Human-over-a-loop phase [13, 18, 27].

Complete a Service Implementation. This task involves putting a newly designed service into operation and ensuring it functions as intended for its users. It includes: i) ***Identifying data objects*** that relates to data requirements (needs for data objects and data collection methods) [23] and data collection (type and amount of data objects needed), which is based on available resources and how to interoperate with them [35]; ii) ***Developing service activities*** that consists in choosing an AI model or processing method used in activities to optimize stakeholder satisfaction in an explainable way and how the incoming data object affects the quality of model training or data processing [23]; and iii) ***Creating a service prototype*** as a practical approach to demonstrate the feasibility and scalability of a service, including data objects and activities, by implementing a specific architecture and using specific tools and services provided by service providers [36].

Execute Service Validations. It is a critical task in the development and implementation of any service that involves systematically verifying that the service meets the specified requirements and performs as expected in various scenarios. It includes: i) ***Carrying out service validation and testing*** that encompasses a range of techniques and methods to ensure that a service meets its intended requirements and operates correctly based on service performance measurements such as efficiency, effectiveness, and sustainability [9, 37]; ii) ***Correcting errors and failures*** that consists in identifying error types and sources and mitigating them by providing an action plan for how they should be addressed and fixed [23]; iii) ***Establishing feedback and user control*** that involves determining different types of feedback, how and when the feedback is used [23] and user control related to human participation in taking important decisions at different control points and the usage of different methods and tools to validate the results [13, 18, 38]; and iv) ***Maintaining explainability and trust*** *that* aims at explaining the limitations and capabilities of an HCAI service, what the service can do, and how it does it [23] and at ensuring HCAI trustworthy, which requires HCAI principles such as fairness, explainability, accountability, and ethics of AI [18].

5 Practical Applicability of the HCAI-SD Framework

In the DSR method, instantiations demonstrate that design artifacts, including constructs, models, and methods, can be integrated into a functional system [24]. To demonstrate the application of the framework in real-world scenarios, the practical applicability of the HCAI-SD framework is validated through a comprehensive case study, in which the framework is used to design an HCAI service to conduct a systematic literature review (SLR) called HCAI-SLR service.

5.1 Case Study

The case study was carried out at a research institute at the university of Quebec, Canada during the period 2023–2024. The framework for designing a HCAI-SLR service had been presented in a research seminar for about 40 participants, and then the service had been experimented in a training workshop organized for about 30 participants, including researchers and graduate students. Moreover, a software prototype had been developed and presented at different partners of the institute in Vietnam (two universities and about 100 participants). In the following, the realization of the proposed activities is presented.

Identify User Needs. The exponential growth of SLR presents significant challenges for conducting SLRs, which are essential for synthesizing knowledge and guiding future research [39]. As the volume of available data expands, the process becomes increasingly time-consuming and prone to errors [40]. While recent advancements in AI, particularly generative AI, offer to promise solutions to enhance the SLR process, it is essential to note that AI is not a complete replacement for human expertise [41].

To conduct the initial assessment of user needs for the HCAI-SLR service, the research team initiated a series of small communications and interviews with the stakeholders, which were followed by surveys. Information on various aspects, including current SLR practices and workflows, challenges in conducting SLRs, familiarity with and attitudes towards AI technologies, and desired features and functionalities for an AI-assisted SLR tool have been collected.

Formulate a Service Proposition. In the HCAI-SLR service, AI capabilities are integrated with human judgment and domain knowledge to maintain the reliability and accuracy of the service. In other words, the service can augment the capability of users to carry out SLRs efficiently and effectively while respecting the HCAI principles.

To respond to the collected user needs, the following essential service objectives have been identified: i) *Efficiency*: reduce the time and effort required for literature search, screening, and data extraction; ii) *Accuracy*: ensure the precision of data extraction and analysis to maintain the integrity of the review; iii) *Usability:* provide user-friendly interfaces and intuitive workflows; and iv) *Control*: allow users to review, validate, and override AI outputs as needed.

Thus, the key functionalities and benefits of the service are determined as i) *Initiation of Research:* utilize prompt engineering techniques [42] to suggest research titles, goals, questions, and related keywords and generate the research outline; ii) *Screening and Prioritization:* prioritize relevant titles and abstracts using keyword highlighting, exclusion keywords, and duplicate detection, reducing the manual workload; iii) *Data Extraction and Analysis:* extract and synthesize key findings information from selected papers, such as study characteristics, outcomes, and contributions, according to the research questions; iv) *Report Generation:* generate well-structured draft sections of the literature review with appropriate citations, ensuring consistency in tone and style; and v) *User Interface and Interaction:* provide an intuitive and user-friendly interface that allows researchers to easily navigate, review, and interact with the AI-generated outputs and feedback.

Carry Out Stockholder Analysis. As mentioned before, this case study is conducted within academic research setting at the Université du Québec, Canada. The *primary stakeholders* include researchers, faculty, and postgraduate students from various departments, such as the business school and the accounting department, who are engaged in

SLRs as part of their academic work. They will become *service users*. Additionally, *secondary stakeholders* include academic database providers, AI tool developers and API providers, who are responsible for developing and maintaining AI tools used in the HCAI-SLR service. Universities and research organizations that support and fund research activities also fall into the category of secondary stakeholders. They will be categorized as *service providers*.

Table 2. Roles of humans and AI in each HCAI-SLR service phase.

Phase	Role of Humans	Role of AI
Human Initiation	Set the direction of the review, define research objectives, formulate initial questions, outline scope	Assist in refining research title, research questions or suggesting relevant keywords based on initial human inputs
AI Augmentation	Oversee selection and configuration of AI tools, and ensure alignment with objectives	Manage and process large datasets, automate tasks such as data extraction, literature search, preliminary analysis, draft sections of the review, format references
AI Triangulation	Validate and cross-check AI outputs, identify discrepancies or inconsistencies, provide corrective feedback	Use multiple AI tools to cross-verify results, ensure robustness and reliability, provide synthesized data
Human Decision	Review and interpret AI-processed data, make final decision	Assist in refining the results, support human decision-making

Conduct a Service Creation. The aim of this task is to define how to implement the intelligence augmentation process and how to support the HCAI guidance:

- *HCAI intelligence augmentation process*: The design of the HCAI-SLR incorporates a comprehensive service management approach structured around the intelligence augmentation process. This process ensures a seamless integration of human expertise and AI capabilities, enhancing the efficiency and effectiveness of literature reviews while maintaining essential human oversight.
- *Multi-phase process for human-AI collaboration*: The HCAI-SLR service is structured into four key phases, each designed to facilitate specific aspects of the SLR process through collaborative efforts between humans and AI: i) *Human-before-the-loop* stage includes Human Initiation phase; ii) *Human-in-the-loop* stage includes AI Augmentation and AI Triangulation phases; and iii) *Human-over-the-loop* stage includes Human Decision phase (Table 2).

Establish Service Use Cases. To establish service use cases for the HCAI-SLR, the main scenarios are identified in which researchers will interact with the service to conduct SLRs based on the SLR process [38] including the following steps:

1. *Identification step* defines the purpose, goals, title, keywords, and research questions.
2. *Literature search step* explores various databases to locate relevant papers.
3. *Practical screening step* identifies which studies meet the review criteria for inclusion.
4. *Quality appraisal step* establishes exclusion criteria to assess the quality of studies and determine their eligibility for inclusion.
5. *Data extraction step* extracts information and content from selected research papers.
6. *Synthesis of studies step* combines the extracted facts from studies conducted in selected research papers.
7. *Review writing step* presents the results of the review in a systematic and organized manner.

Control points are proposed at different stages of the SLR process to evaluate the effectiveness and trustworthiness of the HCAI-SLR service. These control points should assess data quality, model accuracy, and service reliability, as well as data quality control points, service reliability control points, and user feedback integration.

The HCAI-SLR service requires integrating AI into the SLR process [43]. The proposed approach uses a blend of *prompt-based* and *task-oriented* AI functions, each tailored to optimize different stages of the SLR process:

- *Prompt-Based AI Functions*: These functions work like conversational AI systems like *ChatGPT*[1], *Claude*[2], and *Google Gemini*[3]. They are designed to interact through natural language prompts. Their use is primarily during the phases of the SLR, where creative synthesis and integration of information are required. Prompt-based functions can be particularly useful in the following SLR steps: *Identification, Synthesis of Studies, and Writing.*
- *Task-Oriented AI Functions*: These functions are designed to support specific tasks, including features for screening, quality assessment, and data extraction. Task-oriented functions are crucial in the initial stages of the SLR, such as data collection and preliminary analysis, where structured tasks like identifying relevant studies and extracting key data are performed. They can be particularly useful in the following SLR steps: *Searching for the Literature, Practical Screening, Quality Appraisal, and Data Extraction.*

Complete Service Implementation. To complete the service implementation for the HCAI-SLR, the study identifies the key data objects, develops service activities, and creates a service prototype that demonstrates the functionality and user experience of the HCAI-SLR service:

- ***Identifying data objects***: The primary data objects that will be used throughout the SLR process include: i) *List of papers*: the initial set of papers retrieved from the literature search, including metadata such as titles, abstracts, authors, and publication details; ii) *Selected papers*: the subset of papers that meet the eligibility criteria after

[1] https://chat.openai.com/.
[2] https://claude.ai/.
[3] https://gemini.google.com/.

the screening process, which will be included in the SLR; iii) *Units of analysis*: the specific data elements that will be extracted from the selected papers, such as study characteristics, participant demographics, intervention details, and outcome measures; iv) *Extracted data*: the actual data values extracted from the selected papers based on the defined units of analysis, which will be used for data synthesis and analysis; and v) *Synthesized results*: the aggregated and summarized findings from the extracted data, which will form the basis of the SLR conclusions and recommendations.

- ***Developing service activities***: Based on the identified data objects, service activities are developed that leverage AI and processing methods to support researchers conducting the SLR. Some examples of service activities include: i) *Data collection*: utilize academic databases (e.g., Scopus[4], WoS[5]) to source relevant papers; ii) *Title and abstract screening*: screen the list of papers based on the eligibility criteria and prioritize them for human review; iii) *Full-text assessment*: analyze the full-text of the screened papers and identify relevant sections and data elements for extraction; iv) *Data extraction*: extract the defined units of analysis from the selected papers and populate them into a structured database; and v) *Data synthesis*: synthesize the extracted data and generate summary statistics and visualizations.
- ***Creating a service prototype***: To demonstrate the feasibility and potential benefits of the HCAI-SLR service, a service prototype is created that integrates the developed service activities and AI into a user-friendly interface. The service prototype should include the following features: i) *a web-based dashboard* for researchers to input their prompts and data; ii) an *interactive search interface* that allows researchers to review and refine the automatically generated search queries and results; iii) a *screening interface* that presents the prioritized list of papers for human review and allows researchers to make inclusion/exclusion decisions; iv) an *extraction interface* that displays the automatically extracted data elements for each selected paper and allows researchers to validate and edit the extractions; v) a *synthesis interface* that presents the automatically generated summary statistics and visualizations and allows researchers to customize and interpret the results; and vi) *collaborative features* that enable multiple researchers to work on the same SLR project, share comments and feedback, and track the progress of the SLR process.

Execute Service Validations. To ensure the reliability, effectiveness, and trustworthiness of the service, it is essential to perform the following subtasks:

- *Carry out service validation and testing:* Perform thorough testing, including functional, usability, and performance tests, along with end-to-end tests to validate the entire SLR process. It ensures the service operates effectively from start to finish.
- *Correct errors and failures:* Based on testing results, identify and prioritize errors, failures, or issues. Debug software defects, optimize performance, and address usability issues to ensure the service functions effectively and meets user expectations.
- *Establish feedback and user control mechanisms:* Provide in-app feedback forms and user preference settings to gather user input. Implement clear communication channels for user assistance and feedback, allowing users to share their experiences.

[4] https://www.scopus.com/.

[5] https://www.webofscience.com/wos.

Analyze user feedback and behavior data to enhance and personalize the service, making continuous improvements based on user needs and preferences.

- *Maintain explainability and trust:* Document and communicate AI-powered tools' assumptions, limitations, and potential biases. Provide clear explanations and visualizations of AI-generated results and recommendations to help users understand and trust the outcomes. Conduct regular audits and assessments of AI functions to detect and mitigate performance drift, bias, or fairness issues. Engage with the research community and domain experts to ensure the service meets scientific rigor, ethical standards, and considers societal implications.

5.2 Findings and Lessons Learned

The case study demonstrates the effectiveness of the HCAI-SD framework in designing the HCAI-SLR service. The application of the framework in higher education, particularly within the HCAI-SLR service, has received positive feedback from a focus group of 21 participants, consisting of researchers (66.7%), graduate students (23.8%), and practitioners (9.5%). An ongoing action research project is implementing HCAI services in education and research at the research institute and business school. The majority of participants in this project confirm that utilizing AI in research can enhance their performance, including the effectiveness, efficiency, and impact of their research activities. Specifically, 38.1% of participants were very satisfied with the performance, and 33.3% were satisfied. In addition, 52.4% of participants found the framework convenient in organizing the SLR process, with 19% rating it as very convenient. Moreover, 57.1% of respondents strongly agreed that there was a clear benefit to the human-AI collaborative approach, while 38.1% agreed.

Indeed, the concept of *Artificial Intelligence in Education* (AIED) has advanced significantly in recent years, demonstrating a growing interest and adoption of AI technologies in educational settings [44]. Furthermore, the transition towards Human-Centered AI (HCAI) services in education underscores the importance of utilizing AI as a tool for human enhancement while maintaining a balance between high levels of automation and user control [45]. This evolution prioritizes user experience, ethical considerations, and societal impacts, aiming to create HCAI services in higher education that are accessible, transparent, and beneficial for academic communities.

Concerning the validation of the HCAI-SLR application based on design science research, the HCAI-SLR has been evaluated using different methods [46]. Firstly, the *case study* demonstrates the application of the HCAI-SD framework as an artifact to a real-world situation and evaluates its effect on the real-world situation. Secondly, the *prototype* and its experiments highlight the utility and suitability of the proposed framework. Fourthly, the research seminars and training workshops are indeed *an expert evaluation* that indicates the assessment of the framework by experts in different domains. Finally, the higher education experiment can be considered as a *subject-based experiment* involving different subjects related research and education to evaluate whether the practical application of the framework is realistic.

Following the framework's structured approach, key aspects of HCAI service design are systematically addressed, including user needs, service proposition, stakeholder analysis, service creation, use cases, implementation, and validation. This comprehensive method ensures that the HCAI-SLR service is user-centered, technically robust, and ethically responsible. However, the design process revealed challenges and lessons learned. A significant challenge was balancing AI automation with the need for human oversight in the SLR process. While AI can enhance efficiency in some tasks, human judgment remains crucial in data interpretation and synthesis. Ensuring the explainability and transparency of AI models and algorithms was also vital for researcher trust. Despite these challenges, the case study underscores the substantial benefits of the HCAI-SLR service. By integrating AI and human collaboration, the service reduces the time and effort required for systematic literature reviews, enhancing the quality, consistency, and reproducibility of results. It enables researchers to keep pace with the expanding scientific literature and make well-informed decisions. Furthermore, the HCAI-SLR service fosters collaboration and knowledge sharing among researchers by providing a centralized platform for conducting and disseminating SLRs.

6 Discussion

In our observation, the proposals for approaches and methods for designing HCAI services and systems are still scarce. There are still many difficulties to design Human-AI interactions. Among them the difficulty to articulate what AI can/cannot do, to foresee the potential effects of AI, to explain AI behavior, and to design shared control between AI and the users [47]. Furthermore, design and evaluation framework for HCAI service is one of the most important challenges [48]. This study is one of the first studies that focus on the methodological framework for designing HCAI services based on service science perspective.

Compared with the HCAI-based studies such as [17, 47, 48], the proposed approach, focusing on applying service science principles, effectively meets the unique requirements of HCAI services by integrating insights from various levels of service, including value creation networks, service systems, and service levels. For instance, the HCAI approach presented in [17] consists of two key elements: i) the three dimensions of user, technology, and ethics and ii) the seven primary HCAI design goals enabling the integration of specific design goals into the HCAI approach. This approach was not proposed particularly for HCAI services and, therefore, did not consider the specific requirements of the service sector.

Compared with software engineering and service science approaches such as [23, 26–28], this methodological framework provides structured and actionable guidance as a tool to help systematically navigate a process through clearly defined stages in a coherent manner. For example, the service science-based approach such as [27] proposes a knowledge-based framework for context-ware service modelling; however, the HCAI principles and guidance are not considered seriously. Another example, the RE4HCAI framework consists of three distinct layers for outlining human-centered guidelines, presenting a catalog designed to assist in eliciting requirements for building HCAI-based software and proposing a modeling language to visually represent the requirements [22]. Compared with this approach, our approach is based on DSR that concentrates on the presentation of a framework in a logical manner, integrating the artefacts, their interrelationships, and the development process of service design.

7 Conclusion

This paper introduces the HCAI-SD framework, a methodological structure that integrates Human-Centered AI principles into service science to design HCAI services. The framework harmonizes AI capabilities with human-centered design, promoting the integration of HCAI across diverse services and enhancing the synergy between human intelligence and AI. This not only improves service efficiency and effectiveness but also fosters trust and acceptance of AI innovations.

The research contributes the theoretical advancements by merging AI with service science and offers a strategic guide for organizations deploying HCAI solutions that are effective and ethically responsible. Practically, the framework facilitates the creation of AI-powered services that align with human needs and values. Specifically, the framework and its case study highlight the synergy between human intelligence and AI applications in education and research. This synergy demonstrates AI's potential to augment human capabilities and addresses critical issues of transparency and trustworthiness, essential for the continued development of human-centric AI in higher education.

Future research stemming from this study could expand and enhance the understanding and application of HCAI-SD framework in various ways. Firstly, future studies could focus on the empirical testing of the HCAI methodological framework. Implementing the framework in real-world scenarios across different industries could provide practical insights and validate its effectiveness. Secondly, future research could delve deeper into developing methods or tools that enhance clarity around the capabilities and limitations of AI systems. Finally, research could explore how HCAI services can be personalized to meet individual user needs more effectively, potentially through adaptive AI that learns from user interactions to tailor context-aware services [27].

References

1. Dwivedi, Y.K., et al.: Artificial Intelligence (AI): Multidisciplinary perspectives on emerging challenges, opportunities, and agenda for research, practice and policy. Int. J. Inf. Manag. **57**, 101994 (2021)
2. Huang, M.-H., Rust, R.T.: Engaged to a robot? the role of AI in service. J. Serv. Res. **24**, 30–41 (2021)
3. Huang, M.-H., Rust, R.T.: Artificial intelligence in service. J. Serv. Res. **21**, 155–172 (2018)
4. Shneiderman, B.: Human-centered AI. Oxford University Press (2022)
5. Smuha, N.A.: The EU approach to ethics guidelines for trustworthy artificial intelligence. Comput. Law Rev. Int. **20**, 97–106 (2019)
6. Vom Brocke, J., Hevner, A., Maedche, A.: Introduction to design science research. Design science research. Cases 1–13 (2020)
7. Kim, J., Wood, J.: Service sector development in Asia: an important instrument of growth. Asian-Pac. Econ. Literat. **34**, 12–25 (2020)
8. Maglio, P.P., Spohrer, J.: Fundamentals of service science. J. Acad. Mark. Sci. **36**, 18–20 (2008)
9. Le Dinh, T., Leonard, M.: A conceptual framework for modelling service value creation networks. In: 2009 International Conference on Network-Based Information Systems, pp. 463–468. IEEE (2009)

10. Maglio, P.P., Srinivasan, S., Kreulen, J.T., Spohrer, J.: Service systems, service scientists, SSME, and innovation. Commun. ACM **49**, 81–85 (2006)
11. Spohrer, J., Maglio, P.P., Bailey, J., Gruhl, D.: Steps toward a science of service systems. Computer **40**, 71–77 (2007)
12. Belk, R.W., Belanche, D., Flavián, C.: Key concepts in artificial intelligence and technologies 4.0 in services. Serv. Bus. **17**, 1–9 (2023)
13. ISO: ISO/IEC TR 24028: 2020 Information Technology—Artificial Intelligence—Overview of Trustworthiness in Artificial Intelligence. International Organization for Standardization Geneva (2020)
14. Arrieta, A.B., et al.: Explainable Artificial Intelligence (XAI): concepts, taxonomies, opportunities and challenges toward responsible AI. Inf. Fusion **58**, 82–115 (2020)
15. van Berkel, N., Tag, B., Goncalves, J., Hosio, S.: Human-centred artificial intelligence: a contextual morality perspective. Behav. Inf. Technol. **41**, 502–518 (2022)
16. Tahaei, M., Constantinides, M., Quercia, D., Muller, M.: A systematic literature review of human-centered, ethical, and responsible AI. arXiv preprint arXiv:2302.05284 (2023)
17. Xu, W., Gao, Z.: Enabling Human-Centered AI: A Methodological Perspective. arXiv preprint arXiv:2311.06703 (2023)
18. Kaur, D., Uslu, S., Rittichier, K.J., Durresi, A.: Trustworthy artificial intelligence: a review. ACM Comput. Surv. (CSUR) **55**, 1–38 (2022)
19. McMeekin, N., Wu, O., Germeni, E., Briggs, A.: How methodological frameworks are being developed: evidence from a scoping review. BMC Med. Res. Methodol. **20**, 1–9 (2020)
20. Bai, X., White, D.C., Sundaram, D.: Multi-methodological approaches in design science: a review, proposal and application. PACIS **159** (2013)
21. Annarelli, A., Battistella, C., Nonino, F.: Product service system: a conceptual framework from a systematic review. J. Clean. Prod. **139**, 1011–1032 (2016)
22. Sangiorgi, D., Eun, Y.: Service design as an approach to new service Development: reflections and future studies. In: ServDes. 2014 Service Future; Proceedings of the fourth Service Design and Service Innovation Conference. Linköping Electronic Conference Proceedings, pp. 194–204 (2014)
23. Ahmad, K., Abdelrazek, M., Arora, C., Baniya, A.A., Bano, M., Grundy, J.: Requirements engineering framework for human-centered artificial intelligence software systems. Appl. Soft Comput. **143**, 110455 (2023)
24. Bichler, M.: Design science in information systems research. Wirtschaftsinformatik **48**(2), 133–135 (2006). https://doi.org/10.1007/s11576-006-0028-8
25. Torres, A., Miranda, C.: Understanding service design and design thinking differences between research and practice: An empirical study. In: Nóvoa, H., Drăgoicea, M., Kühl, N. (eds.) IESS 2020. LNBIP, vol. 377, pp. 259–272. Springer, Cham (2020). https://doi.org/10.1007/978-3-030-38724-2_19
26. Radziwill, N.: Value Proposition Design. Taylor & Francis (2015)
27. Le Dinh, T., Vu, T.M.H., Dam, N.A.K., Ralyté, J.: Context-aware service modelling: a knowledge-centric framework (2023)
28. Dinh, T., Thi, T.T.P.: A conceptual framework for service modelling in a network of service systems. In: Morin, J.-H., Ralyté, J., Snene, M. (eds.) IESS 2010. LNBIP, vol. 53, pp. 192–206. Springer, Heidelberg (2010). https://doi.org/10.1007/978-3-642-14319-9_15
29. Wolfson, A., Tavor, D., Mark, S.: Sustainability as service. Sustainabil. Account. Manag. Policy J. **4**(1), 103–114 (2013)
30. Bowen, D.J., et al.: How we design feasibility studies. Am. J. Prev. Med. **36**, 452–457 (2009)
31. Stickdorn, M., Hormess, M.E., Lawrence, A., Schneider, J.: This is Service Design Doing. O'Reilly Media Inc, Newton (2018)
32. Jegadeesan, H., Balasubramaniam, S.: A Model-driven approach to service policies. J. Object Technol. **8**, 163–186 (2009)

33. Grönroos, C.: On value and value creation in service: a management perspective. J. Creat. Value **3**, 125–141 (2017)
34. Kim, Y., Doh, K.-G.: Use-case driven service modelling with XML-based tailoring for SOA. Int. J. Web Grid Serv. **9**, 35–53 (2013)
35. Le Dinh, T., Le, T.H.: Towards an approach for modeling interoperability of information systems. In: 2007 IEEE International Conference on Research, Innovation and Vision for the Future, pp. 22–28. IEEE (2007)
36. Han, S.N., Lee, G.M., Crespi, N.: Semantic context-aware service composition for building automation system. IEEE Trans. Ind. Inf. **10**, 752–761 (2013)
37. Kelly, B., Crowther, M., King, J., Masson, R., DeLapeyre, J.: Service validation and testing. In: FIW, pp. 173–184. Citeseer (1995)
38. Le Dinh, T., Le, T.D., Uwizeyemungu, S., Nguyen, C.N.: Literature review as a service: a human-centered artificial intelligence approach. In: 2024 the 8th International Conference on Innovation in Artificial Intelligence (ICIAI 2024). ACM, Tokyo (2024)
39. Linnenluecke, M.K., Marrone, M., Singh, A.K.: Conducting systematic literature reviews and bibliometric analyses. Aust. J. Manag. **45**, 175–194 (2020)
40. Siddaway, A.P., Wood, A.M., Hedges, L.V.: How to do a systematic review: a best practice guide for conducting and reporting narrative reviews, meta-analyses, and meta-syntheses. Ann. Rev. Psychol. **70**, 747–770 (2019)
41. Castillo-Segura, P., Alario-Hoyos, C., Kloos, C.D., Panadero, C.F.: Leveraging the potential of generative AI to accelerate systematic literature reviews: an example in the area of educational technology. In: 2023 World Engineering Education Forum-Global Engineering Deans Council (WEEF-GEDC), pp. 1–8. IEEE (2023)
42. Giray, L.G.: Prompt engineering with ChatGPT: a guide for academic writers. Ann. Biomed. Eng. **51**, 2629–2633 (2023)
43. Okoli, C.: A guide to conducting a standalone systematic literature review. Commun. Assoc. Inf. Syst. **37** (2015)
44. Chen, L., Chen, P., Lin, Z.: Artificial intelligence in education: a review. Ieee Access **8**, 75264–75278 (2020)
45. Zhang, K., Aslan, A.B.: AI technologies for education: recent research & future directions. Comput. Educ. Artif. Intell. **2**, 100025 (2021)
46. Peffers, K., Rothenberger, M., Tuunanen, T., Vaezi, R.: Design science research evaluation. In: Peffers, K., Rothenberger, M., Kuechler, B. (eds.) DESRIST 2012. LNCS, vol. 7286, pp. 398–410. Springer, Heidelberg (2012). https://doi.org/10.1007/978-3-642-29863-9_29
47. Yang, Q., Steinfeld, A., Rosé, C.P., Zimmerman, J.: Re-examining whether, why, and how human-AI interaction is uniquely difficult to design. In: Proceedings of the 2020 CHI Conference on Human Factors in Computing Systems (2020)
48. Ozmen Garibay, O., et al.: Six human-centered artificial intelligence grand challenges. Int. J. Hum.-Comput. Interact. **39**, 391–437 (2023)

Beyond One-Fits-All: A Case Study Approach to AI System Design Methods

Sabine Janzen[1] and Hannah Stein[1,2(✉)]

[1] German Research Center for Artificial Intelligence, Stuhlsatzenhausweg 3, 66123 Saarbruecken, Germany
{sabine.janzen,hannah.stein}@dfki.de
[2] Saarland University, Campus, 66123 Saarbruecken, Germany

Abstract. Despite the widespread application of artificial intelligence (AI) as universal solution for complex business problems, there remains a significant gap in design methods for AI systems, distinguishing them sharply from traditional software systems. This research aims to address the lack of standardized design methods tailored for AI projects, which are often impeded by unique challenges such as data sensitivity, model performance, and regulatory compliance. Through an exploratory case study of four AI projects, this paper investigates correlations between characteristics of AI projects and the design methods applied, introducing a set of If-This-Then-That (IFTTT) patterns. These patterns are intended to aid in selecting and combining design method components that align with the specific needs of AI projects. Results highlight the importance of understanding project-specific characteristics to enhance the effectiveness of design methods in AI engineering, offering practitioners actionable insights for improving quality and reliability of AI systems through tailored design approaches.

Keywords: Artificial Intelligence · Design method · Case study · AI systems · AI project characteristics · Correlation pattern

1 Introduction

Artificial Intelligence (AI) is considered as one-fits-all-solution for often sparsely specified business problems [5,16]. But, practice shows that designing solution-oriented AI systems is still an open research topic [24,25]. This is due to the ambiguous relation between AI systems and traditional software systems leading to uncertainties on how AI systems should be designed [6,10,24]. AI systems can be defined as software systems with symbolic and sub symbolic AI components [6] implementing algorithms on perception, attention, action selection, learning, memory and reasoning [31]. Their deterministic as well as probabilistic nature leads to high error rates and therefore an inability to predict final outcomes of an AI system or to reproduce the same output [24]. This aspect is

M. Saeki et al. (Eds.): ER 2024 Workshops, LNCS 14932, pp. 40–57, 2025.
https://doi.org/10.1007/978-3-031-75599-6_3

reinforced by the central role of data in AI systems, being enabler on the one hand and constraint on the other. When asking for design methods handling these challenging aspects, contrary positions are given ranging from just applying established software engineering methods [10] to missing guidelines in design of AI systems not comparable with conventional software systems [13,24]. The application of integrated and well-managed development processes for AI systems results in higher quality outcomes and decreases the risk for project failure [36,38], especially within the first phases of analysis and design (cf. Glass' law, Boehms First Law).

But, in contrast to the current AI hype, clear guidelines and design methods for AI systems development are missing both in practice and in research. Mostly, practitioners do not apply any design method for developing AI systems because available methods do not match with the specific characteristics of AI projects, e.g., availability and sensitivity of data [32]. "Companies experience challenges related to data quality, design methods and processes, performance of models as well as deployment and compliance." [6, p. 1] And in research, related work focuses on design methods for data analytics projects, i.e., developing pure sub symbolic AI systems [3,20]. But, additional and new tasks around data analytics like data collection, cleansing, management, and continuous updates are not conform with traditional software engineering processes and required resources for data management are often underestimated [13,24].

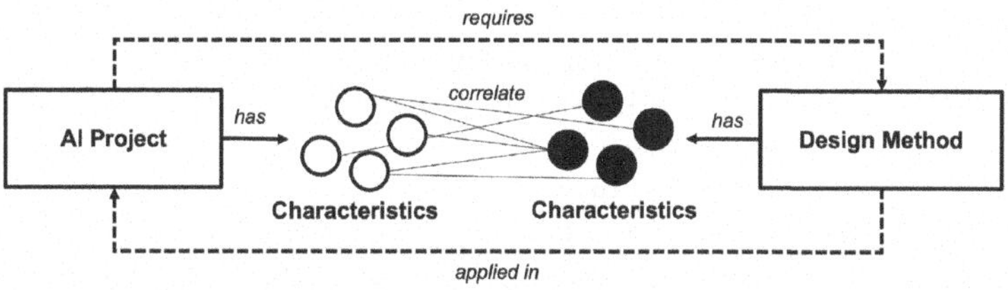

Fig. 1. Investigation of correlations between characteristics of AI projects and design methods to determine appropriate design methods for AI systems development

Objective of this research is the **investigation of appropriate design methods for AI systems development**. We assume that there is no 1:1 mapping from design method to AI project type [3]; therefore we applied an approach that additionally uses characteristics of design methods as a mediator between types of AI projects and potential design methods (cf. Fig. 1). In the assumption of correlation patterns between deducted AI project and design method characteristics, **four AI projects solving business problems in practice were analyzed** with respect to applied design methods in a case study for deriving If-This-Then-That (IFTTT) patterns. For instance, if an AI project shows characteristics a, b, then an applied design method should offer characteristic c. Contribution of this paper is a pool of fine-granular correlation patterns between AI projects showing specific characteristics and potential design methods to be applied in these types of projects (cf. Fig. 1). With focus on the analysis and design phase of AI system development, qualitative results provide guidance for the appropriate selection and aggregation of design method components as required by AI projects in practice as well as implications for the growing research field AI systems design and AI engineering.

The paper is structured as follows. Next, we present the theoretical background on the design of AI systems with respect to existing requirements and design methods as well as characteristics of AI projects. Afterwards, our research method is described. We then systematically present the four AI projects analyzed within our case study before we discuss the results of the analysis of the AI projects, the according design methods, as well as correlation patterns between AI project and design method characteristics. Last, we present a conclusion with future work.

2 Design Methods and Characteristics

A simplified design method (*DM*) model consists of analysis, design, implementation and testing phase. Several research fields like AI, Human-Computer-Interaction (HCI), Software Engineering, Requirements Engineering, Service Engineering and Product Development cover and apply diverse design methods. So far, in **AI** no specific design methods are used; instead pure technical and implementation-oriented approaches are applied that neglect system requirements or specific design knowledge [23,31]. Besides participatory design, User-centered design and Design Thinking, design methods in **HCI** also cover "wild-west" design. In **software engineering**, sequential, iterative and incremental or agile design methods are distinguished, e.g., waterfall model, spiral model, prototyping [14], rational unified process, SCRUM, XP. In **requirements engineering**, functional and non-functional requirements are derived, capturing the behaviour of intended software system [28]. Design methods therein apply diverse techniques in order to derive requirements, e.g., specifying goals and responsibilities [9] determining scenarios [37], deriving agents and roles (i*) [9] or analyzing business context and business events [28]. In **service engineering**, design methods are applied to specific service types based on reference models such as waterfall, spiral and prototyping,e.g., service blueprinting [35]. In **product development** problem-oriented approaches are used to capture requirements of design problems and to generate solutions with respect to production issues, e.g., concept screening and scoring [26]. According to literature, several characteristics can be derived for analyzing these existing design methods with respect to AI systems development. Table 1 lists these six design method characteristics with descriptions, potential values and examples.

3 AI Projects and Characteristics

Related work identifies several characteristics to define AI project types, e.g., project triggers, deployment, type of data analysis (e.g., [3,21,33]). With respect

Table 1. Characteristics of design methods DM

Characteristic	Description	Values	Example of application
Business context understanding [28]	Availability of phases, steps, guidelines for analysis of business context of system	$[low, high]$	Designing systems for optimization of industrial production processes requires *high* business context understanding.
Service focus [28,35]	Allocation of guidelines and schemas for capturing user-centered services	$[low, high]$	When designing middleware systems, strong service provision to users is beyond the scope of the project (*low*).
Evaluation and consolidation [26,33]	Provision of in-between steps for evaluation of system design artifacts and consolidation of opportunities	$[low, high]$	In development of iPhone (1st gen), design methods with *high* number of evaluation steps were used for testing and pruning preliminary design results
Role of data [21]	Capturing data role in system through guidelines (post) and application of relevant data in design process itself (pre)	$[pre, post]$	For crisis warning systems, amount, type and format of available data streams constrain early system design (*pre*) and must be captured in requirements during design process (*post*).
Situational approach [11,21]	Offer of narrative techniques, user stories in analysis and design phase for translating implicit to explicit knowledge	$[informal, semi, formal]$	Social media tools are framed by complex usage situations intuitively captured by narrative techniques in text form ($informal$) and translated to ER models ($semi - formal$).
Physical objects [19]	Methodical acquisition of relevant physical objects of intended system	$[low, high]$	When designing ambient assisted living systems, physical objects, e.g., space, devices, have to be captured during design process.

to methodical AI systems development, we adopted and extended this list of nine characteristics of AI projects P given in Table 2 accompanied by potential values. **Scope** means the application scope of an intended AI system that can be outside or within existing business units, e.g., a new planning system for the controlling unit (*inner*). **Deployment** refers to the frequency the project outcome is deployed [4]. We distinguish between single use projects with limited time and shorter development cycles and continuous use projects with longer development cycles and undefined end. For instance, the deployment of an AI system showing COVID vaccination status of employees over time represents a *single* use project, since it fulfills ad hoc information requests regarding a specific business question. **Project triggers** can be (1) data used to gain new insights, (2) solutions for well-defined problems requested by management for answering business questions, and (3) ill-defined problems lacking clear link to business questions [3]. For instance, analyzing available IoT data of production lines of diverse locations of past 48 months for deriving potential new insights represents a $data - triggered$ project (cf. Table 2). **Integration** of AI systems can be defined as greenfield, i.e., developed from scratch and standalone without constraints by already existing IT infrastructure, or brownfield, means in form of a fully integrated service. An AI system generating recommendations for optimized and health promoting shift schedules by processing production plans and past sick leaves has to be fully integrated into IT infrastructure ($brownfield$). Furthermore, the **team size** of AI projects represents a driver of project productivity. According to [29] average team size of less than nine and larger or equal to nine people is distinguished. As AI systems represent software systems with

Table 2. Characteristics of AI projects P

Characteristic	Values
Scope [8,10,16]	$[inner, outer]$
Deployment [3,4]	$[single, continuous]$
Project trigger [3,13]	$[data, problem, solution]$
Integration [6,10,16]	$[greenfield, brownfield]$
Team size [33]	$[< 9, >= 9]$
Share of AI [6,13]	$[low, medium, high]$
Interaction [2]	$[linear, non-linear]$
Data sensitivity [22]	$[low, high]$
Data availability [7,13]	$[none, insufficient, sufficient]$

AI components [6], **share of AI** in intended systems differs from low [0–24%] to medium [25–74%] to high share [75–100%] (cf. Table 2). For instance, a natural language assistant service (e.g., Apple Siri, Amazon Alexa) possesses a *high* share of AI components. Another essential characteristic of AI projects is **interaction** [2] as AI systems are developed according to interaction settings with users, services, devices etc. These can be either linear (e.g., client-server) or non-linear (e.g., broker or blackboard systems). As an example, when developing AI systems for multi-sided data platforms complex $non-linear$ interaction settings have to be captured within the project (e.g., [18]). Last, as data play a crucial role in AI projects, **data sensitivity** and **data availability** represent significant characteristics (cf. Table 2). AI project teams working with highly sensitive data must assure protection against unauthorized access during project and by the AI system itself [22], e.g., HR data processed by an AI system for specifying gaps in required team skills represent *highly* sensitive data. But without data, no AI. Availability of sufficient data is a crucial point in AI projects driving design decisions [7]. For instance, in case of $insufficient$ data, available data lacks relevant features, so additional data sources have to be explored and acquired (data crawling).

4 Research Method

This work intends to investigate design methods that are appropriate for AI projects. We assume that there is no 1:1 mapping from design method to AI project type [3]; therefore we applied an approach that additionally uses characteristics of design methods as a mediator between types of AI projects and potential design methods. This allows us to derive fine-granular correlation patterns between AI projects showing specific characteristics and potential design methods offering characteristics to be applied in the project. Specified correlation patterns enable an individual selection and re-aggregation of design method components in AI projects in practice. Within the previous section, we derived specific characteristics of design methods (cf. Table 1) and AI projects (cf. Table 2). Next, we explored potential correlations between these characteristics that seem to influence the choice of a design method in practice. For that, we applied a case study approach. To select cases, we used theoretical sampling, i.e., AI projects in practice were selected that applied a design method and could be analyzed according to the derived characteristics (cf. Table 2).

4.1 Data Collection

A total of four AI projects $P_{\mathrm{A}}, P_{\mathrm{B}}, P_{\mathrm{C}}, P_{\mathrm{D}}$ was selected to be included in the case study. These AI projects applied a design method $DM_{\mathrm{A}}, DM_{\mathrm{B}}, DM_{\mathrm{C}}, DM_{\mathrm{D}}$ and showed expressiveness with respect to specified characteristics. Data were collected by a focus group discussion with representatives of the projects selected according to their long-term involvement within the methodical development of the intended AI system. The focus group followed a semi-structured approach consisting of (1) AI project and its characterization, and (2) applied design method with characteristics assessment, for each case (cf. Table 1 and 2).

4.2 Data Analysis

The assessment of characteristics of (1) AI projects $P_{\mathrm{A}}, P_{\mathrm{B}}, P_{\mathrm{C}}, P_{\mathrm{D}}$, and (2) applied design methods DM_{A}, $DM_{\mathrm{B}}, DM_{\mathrm{C}}, DM_{\mathrm{D}}$ by a focus group was documented with respect to defined values, e.g., project trigger of AI project P_{A} was data-driven or not. Based on this, an undirected multigraph $G = (V, E)$ was specified with characteristics and their value unfolding as vertices V and a function $E : W \rightarrow \mathbb{N}_0$ with W representing a multiset of all 2-elements subsets of V showing the assessment of the focus group for AI projects $P_{\mathrm{A}}, P_{\mathrm{B}}, P_{\mathrm{C}}$, P_{D}. For extracting correlation patterns between characteristics of AI projects and design methods, the adjacency matrix $AD = [a_{\mathrm{ij}}]$ of multigraph G was specified with:

$$a_{ij} = \begin{cases} |K(i,j)|, & \text{if } i,j \in E, \\ 0 & \text{else.} \end{cases} \tag{1}$$

AD shows vertices of multigraph G connected by edges, i.e., potential correlations between characteristics of AI projects and design methods that were found in results of the focus group discussion. As G is a multigraph, multiple edges can exist between two vertices, i.e., correlations are found in multiple cases means projects. $|K(i,j)|$ indicates the number of edges connecting vertex i and j. Last, the resulting mxn adjacency matrix AD was used as input for the generation of a flow diagram (Sankey diagram) that enables the identification of striking flows and thereby potential correlation patterns.

5 Case Study

Four AI research projects $P_{\mathrm{A}}, P_{\mathrm{B}}, P_{\mathrm{C}}, P_{\mathrm{D}}$ were selected for the case study; in each project a design method was applied for developing the intended AI system in a specific domain. Each project represents one case. For each case, the problem statement of the AI project, the applied solution as well as the characteristics assessment by project representatives will be given. Aggregated results in terms of the adjacency matrix AD and the Sankey diagram are showing potential correlation patterns are discussed in the next section.

5.1 Case 1: AI Project P_A

Problem Statement: Objective of AI project P_A was the development of an AI system for optimization of potato harvesting and prevention of crop failures. Potatoes suffer from high speeds of harvesting belts, that cause damages and therefore rotting during storage that can only be recognized after harvesting. For minimizing loss, harvesting needs to be optimized in real-time.

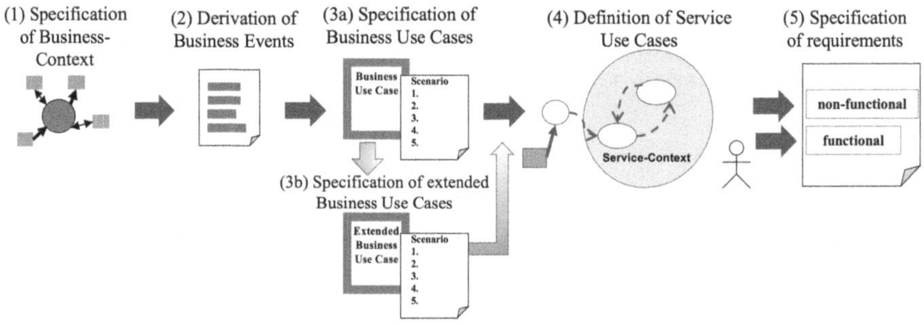

Fig. 2. Design method DM_A applied in AI project P_A

Solution: The project team developed a "pain-sensitive" nPotato - a cyber-physical potato-like system. Harvested with real potatoes, nPotato classifies impacts, predicts damages and expected loss based on an edge AI approach in real-time. As a result, farmers are able to optimize the harvesting process with respect to volume and quality on site; e.g., slow down driving speed of harvester. The project team applied a design method DM_A that stems from requirements engineering [28] (Fig. 2). DM_A specifies the business context of the intended AI system and derives relevant business events to be able to create business use cases. Those are used to integrate service use cases of the AI system before defining functional and non-functional requirements.

Assessment: P_A representatives assessed characteristics of the project as shown in Table 3. Application scope of the nPotato system was within the inner core business unit of farmers and potato harvesters. As a R&D project, P_A was a single use project with limited time and short development cycle (six months). Project trigger was the management request to find a solution for the well-defined problem of potato damage during harvesting. Integration aspects of

Table 3. Characteristics assessment of AI projects P_A, P_B, P_C, P_D (filled boxes = characteristic that applies) (cf. Table 2)

Characteristic	Value	P_A	P_B	P_C	P_D
Scope	*inner*	■		■	■
	outer		■		
Deployment	*single*	■			■
	continuous		■	■	
Project trigger	*data*		■		
	problem			■	■
	solution	■			
Integration	*greenfield*	■	■		■
	brownfield			■	
Team size	*average*	■	■		■
	large			■	
Proportion of AI	*small*				
	medium	■			
	large		■	■	■
Interaction	*linear*	■		■	■
	non − linear		■		
Data sensitivity	*low*				
	high	■	■	■	■
Data availability	*none*				■
	insufficient		■	■	
	sufficient	■			

nPotato were assessed as greenfield and brownfield as the cyber-physical system represents an edge device, that was developed in a standalone manner from scratch. But, service endpoints of nPotato were integrated into existing infrastructure of harvesters by means of an API. The medium-sized P_A team was composed by domain experts, business people, developers and data scientists. Having a medium share of AI, nPotato supports linear interaction settings with users, devices and services. Sensitivity of harvesting and crop-related data was high whereas data availability was sufficient since data required for training the prediction model were obtained in experiments by domain experts (cf. Table 3). The assessment of the design method DM_A applied in P_A is shown in Table 4. We can see, that DM_A offers guidelines for comprehensive business context understanding. Service focus of DM_A was high supporting the development of a user-centered nPotato service. The role of in-between steps for evaluating and consolidating design opportunities was low and according to representatives not needed. Role of data was explicitly captured during design process within use cases. But, DM_A did not apply a situational approach. Since P_A developed a cyber-physical system, DM_{A} shows methodical support and integration of physical objects within the design process.

Table 4. Characteristics assessment of design methods DM_{A}, DM_{B}, DM_{C}, DM_{D} applied in AI projects P (filled boxes = characteristic that applies) (cf. Table 1)

Characteristic	Business context		Service focus		Evaluation & consolidation		Data Role		Situational approach			Physical objects	
Value	*low*	*high*	*low*	*high*	*low*	*high*	*pre*	*post*	*inf.*	*sem.*	*form.*	*low*	*high*
DM_{A}		■		■	■			■					■
DM_{B}	■		■			■		■		■		■	
DM_{C}		■		■		■	■		■				■
DM_{D}		■		■		■	■		■				■

5.2 Case 2: AI Project P_{B}

Problem Statement: Goal of P_{B} was the development of an AI system for enabling semi-automatic generation and trading of sophisticated data products in food industry. Here, sensor-based data are gathered during production, but sparsely used across corporate boundaries due to data sovereignty issues. By sharing aggregated data products, food producers get comprehensive data insights serving as decision support for optimizing production lines and outcomes.

Solution: The P_{B} team developed an AI-based multi-sided data platform FAST that enables generation, annotation, searching for and trading of higher-value data products. Data sovereignty issues were solved by a technical solution in form of a decentralized edge computing setting. Core of FAST is a broker that realizes distributed generation of data products and their sovereign trading secured by automatic electronic contracts [18]. The project team applied a design method DM_{B} (cf. Fig. 3) that combines approaches of requirements engineering and HCI. DM_{B} specifies the business context and derives relevant business events in order to create business use cases. Used as input for narrative techniques, informal conceptual models were derived capturing intended usage situations of FAST. After translating those into semi-formal conceptual models that helped for identifying required information objects (e.g., raw data streams, data products), user roles and services, functional, non-functional and data-driven requirements were specified.

Assessment: The application scope of FAST was beyond the core business of food producers (cf. Table 3). P_{B} was classified as both single and continuous use project with limited time due to its R&D status but longer development cycles within the core architecture of FAST. Trigger of P_{B} were sensor-based data already gathered during food production. Developed from scratch and standalone, integration of FAST was classified as greenfield. The medium-sized team was composed of domain and legal experts, business people, developers and data

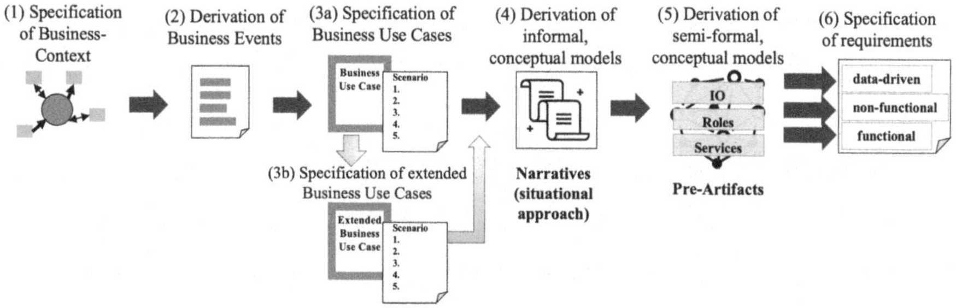

Fig. 3. Design method DM_B applied in AI project P_B

scientists. With a high share of AI, FAST supports non-linear interaction settings in networks of users, services and data products. According to high data sensitivity, data availability was insufficient in P_B. Due to the fact, that the focus of FAST was beyond the core business of food producers, we see that support of business context understanding and service focus as well as integration of physical objects of the applied DM_B was quite low (cf. Table 4). Steps for evaluating and consolidating preliminary design artifacts were essential since FAST was intended to open up completely new business models for food producers. This is also the reason for the explicit integration of a situational approach in DM_B working with formal and semi-formal conceptual models. Role of data was explicitly captured during design process within so called pre-artifacts (cf. Fig. 3).

5.3 Case 3: AI Project P_C

Problem Statement: Objective of AI project P_C was the AI-supported strengthening of manufacturers' resilience to disruptions. P_C addressed this need by the target of smart resilience services (SRS) that enable anticipation of and measure-based response to potential disruptions in manufacturing, e.g., tool wear, bottlenecks in the supply of raw materials, anomalies in processes, failures of suppliers.

Solution: The P_C team developed an AI-based service platform SmartReS that enables sharing, annotation, searching for and customized usage of SRS based on existing hyperscaler platforms. SRS support manufacturers in optimizing resilience operationalized by a resilience indexer. Core of SmartReS are SRS implementing hybrid AI architectures, i.e., merging symbolic and subsymbolic AI components, for (1) anticipating disruptions based on heterogeneous data streams, and (2) recommending pro-active measures rated by a resilience indexer. The team applied a design method DM_C that combines concepts from HCI, requirements engineering, service engineering and product development [12] (Fig. 4). DM_C specifies as-is and to-be of the intended system's application scope that are used to derive narratives of potential SRS usage situations.

Internally and externally evaluated narratives were analyzed regarding required information objects, actor roles and services before specifying requirements [12].

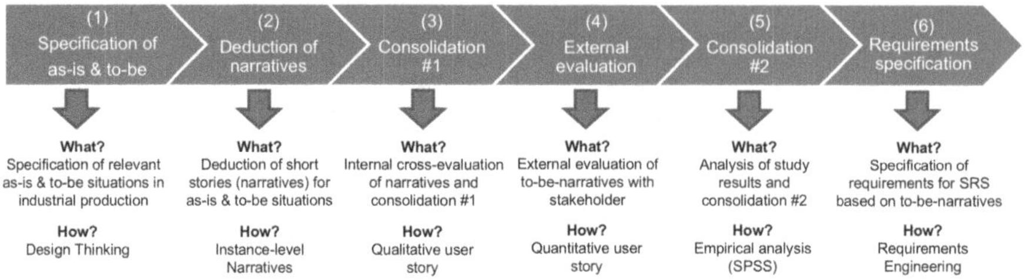

Fig. 4. Design method DM_{C} applied in AI project P_{C}

Assessment: Application scope of SmartReS was within the inner core business unit of manufacturing (cf. Table 3). P_{C} was a continuous use project with long development cycle and deployment of long-term SRS. Trigger of P_{C} was the ill-defined problem of resilience optimization in manufacturing, i.e., clear business questions had to be specified in P_{C}. The large team consisted of domain experts, business people, developers and data scientists. With a medium to high share of AI in SRS, SmartReS supports both, linear and non-linear interaction settings with users, devices and services. Due to high sensitivity of production data, data availability was insufficient or non-existent whereby workarounds had to be found in P_{C}. As SmartReS enters the core business in manufacturing, the applied DM_{C} ensured a deep business context understanding as well as the methodical integration of physical objects, i.e., industrial IoT (cf. Table 3). Service focus was high supporting the development of user-centered SRS. DM_{C} combined a situational approach with a high number of steps for internal and external evaluation and consolidation of preliminary design artifacts. This was essential according to representatives of P_{C} for capturing the ill-defined problem of resilience optimization. This hypothesis is supported by the significant role that DM_{C} gives to data, both in requirements (post) and within the SRS design itself (pre).

5.4 Case 4: AI Project $\mathbf{P}_D$

Problem Statement: Objective of AI project P_{D} was the development of an AI system for predicting the stress level of customers while shopping in-store for providing tailored mobile services in real time, e.g., advertisement or offer of product bundles in retailing.

Solution: The team of project P_{D} developed a stress-based smart retail service system (SBRS) that collects unobtrusively measured heart rate data from a smartwatch and acceleration data from a mobile phone during in-store shopping. The heart rate stream as well as acceleration data is analyzed with the help of machine learning to classify in-store customers regarding their stress levels. Based on the results, the SBRS provides individually tailored services in real-time. Similar to AI project P_C, the project team applied a design method DM_D (cf. Fig. 5) that combines approaches especially from requirements engineering, service engineering and product development. The project team first derived as-is situations and to-be situations of the envisioned system's application scope. Based on the to-be situations, narratives describing how SBRS could be used in a real shopping environment have been created. In a further step, the narratives have been externally evaluated by applying a quantitative study amongst potential in-store shoppers. Externally evaluated narratives were analyzed regarding required information objects, actor roles and services before specifying requirements.

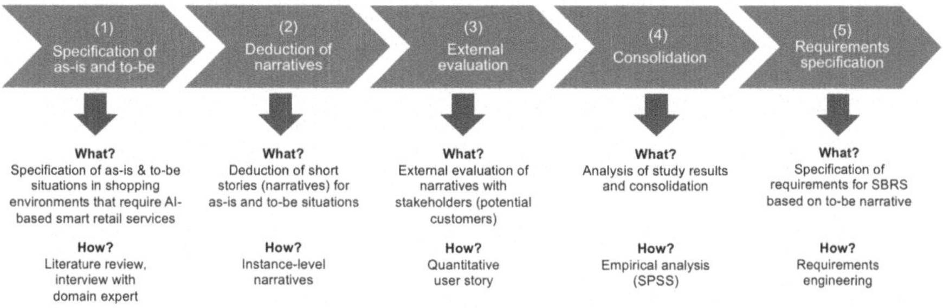

Fig. 5. Design method DM_D applied in AI project P_D

Assessment: The intended AI system SBRS was specifically designed for in-store shoppers as well as for retailers providing tailored services and thus, its application scope was assessed as to be within the inner business unit of retailers (cf. Table 3). As a R&D project, P_D was a single use project with limited time and short development cycle (12 months). Trigger of project P_D was the ill-defined problem of providing tailored services for customers during in-store shopping, i.e. clear business questions had to be specified within the project. DM_D supported the development of user-centered SBRS representing a high service focus. The average-sized team of project P_D mainly consisted of domain experts, developers and data scientists. With a large proportion of AI components, SBRS supports linear settings with users, devices and services. Due to high sensitivity of vital signs and movement data by customers necessary for classifying them regarding their stress levels, data was not available. A specific workaround had to be found for gathering data and training the machine learning model. As SBRS penetrates the core business of retailing, the applied design method DM_D ensured a deep business context understanding as well as the methodical integration of physical objects, i.e., required devices such as mobile sensors (cf. Table 4). According to representatives of the project, the applied design method offered a high number of in-between steps for evaluating and consolidating preliminary results in the design process. Furthermore, the role of data was captured in the early design process (pre) and a situational approach has been applied using narrative techniques in text form (informal).

6 Discussion

Gathered results of the characteristics assessment of AI projects $P_{\mathrm{A}}, P_{\mathrm{B}}, P_{\mathrm{C}}, P_{\mathrm{D}}$ and of the design methods DM_{A}, DM_{B}, DM_{C}, DM_{D} applied in these AI projects are shown in Table 3 and 4. They were mapped onto the multigraph $G = (V, E)$ showing the assessment of the focus group for the AI projects of the case study. The resulting $13x21$ adjacency matrix AD specifies multiple edges that exist between two vertices, i.e., correlations between project and design method characteristics that were found in multiple cases means $P_{\mathrm{A}}, P_{\mathrm{B}}, P_{\mathrm{C}}, P_{\mathrm{D}}$ (A, B, C, D in AD):

$$AD = \begin{pmatrix}
0 & [A,C,D] & 0 & [A,C,D] & [A] & [C,D] & [C,D] & A & [C,D] & 0 & 0 & 0 & [A,C,D] \\
B & 0 & B & 0 & 0 & B & 0 & B & 0 & B & 0 & B & 0 \\
0 & [A,D] & 0 & [A,D] & A & D & D & A & D & 0 & 0 & 0 & [A,D] \\
B & C & B & C & 0 & [B,C] & C & B & C & B & 0 & B & C \\
B & 0 & B & 0 & 0 & B & 0 & B & 0 & B & 0 & B & 0 \\
0 & [C,D] & 0 & [C,D] & 0 & [C,D] & [C,D] & 0 & [C,D] & 0 & 0 & 0 & [C,D] \\
0 & A & 0 & A & A & 0 & 0 & A & 0 & 0 & 0 & 0 & A \\
B & [A,D] & B & [A,D] & A & [B,D] & D & [A,B] & D & B & 0 & B & [A,D] \\
0 & C & 0 & C & 0 & C & C & 0 & C & 0 & 0 & 0 & C \\
B & [A,D] & B & [A,D] & A & [B,D] & D & [A,B] & D & B & 0 & B & [A,D] \\
0 & C & 0 & C & 0 & C & C & 0 & C & 0 & 0 & 0 & C \\
0 & 0 & 0 & 0 & 0 & 0 & 0 & 0 & 0 & 0 & 0 & 0 & 0 \\
0 & A & 0 & A & A & 0 & 0 & A & 0 & 0 & 0 & 0 & A \\
B & [C,D] & B & [C,D] & 0 & [B,C,D] & [C,D] & B & [C,D] & B & 0 & B & [C,D] \\
0 & [A,C,D] & 0 & [A,C,D] & A & [C,D] & [C,D] & A & [C,D] & 0 & 0 & 0 & [A,C,D] \\
B & 0 & B & 0 & 0 & B & 0 & B & 0 & B & 0 & B & 0 \\
0 & 0 & 0 & 0 & 0 & 0 & 0 & 0 & 0 & 0 & 0 & 0 & 0 \\
B & [A,C,D] & B & [A,C,D] & A & [B,C,D] & [C,D] & [A,B] & [C,D] & B & 0 & B & [A,C,D] \\
0 & D & 0 & D & 0 & D & D & 0 & D & 0 & 0 & 0 & D \\
B & C & B & C & 0 & [C,B] & C & B & C & B & 0 & B & C \\
0 & A & 0 & A & A & 0 & 0 & A & 0 & 0 & 0 & 0 & A
\end{pmatrix} = \begin{pmatrix}
0 & 3 & 0 & 3 & 1 & 2 & 2 & 1 & 2 & 0 & 0 & 0 & 3 \\
1 & 0 & 1 & 0 & 0 & 1 & 0 & 1 & 0 & 1 & 0 & 1 & 0 \\
0 & 2 & 0 & 2 & 1 & 1 & 1 & 1 & 1 & 0 & 0 & 0 & 2 \\
1 & 1 & 1 & 1 & 0 & 2 & 1 & 1 & 1 & 1 & 0 & 1 & 1 \\
1 & 0 & 1 & 0 & 0 & 1 & 0 & 1 & 0 & 1 & 0 & 1 & 0 \\
0 & 2 & 0 & 2 & 0 & 2 & 2 & 0 & 2 & 0 & 0 & 0 & 2 \\
0 & 1 & 0 & 1 & 1 & 0 & 0 & 1 & 0 & 0 & 0 & 0 & 1 \\
1 & 2 & 1 & 2 & 1 & 2 & 1 & 2 & 1 & 1 & 0 & 1 & 2 \\
0 & 1 & 0 & 1 & 0 & 1 & 1 & 0 & 1 & 0 & 0 & 0 & 1 \\
1 & 2 & 1 & 2 & 1 & 2 & 1 & 2 & 1 & 1 & 0 & 1 & 2 \\
0 & 1 & 0 & 1 & 0 & 1 & 1 & 0 & 1 & 0 & 0 & 0 & 1 \\
0 & 0 & 0 & 0 & 0 & 0 & 0 & 0 & 0 & 0 & 0 & 0 & 0 \\
0 & 1 & 0 & 1 & 1 & 0 & 0 & 1 & 0 & 0 & 0 & 0 & 1 \\
1 & 2 & 1 & 2 & 0 & 3 & 2 & 1 & 2 & 1 & 0 & 1 & 2 \\
0 & 3 & 0 & 3 & 1 & 2 & 2 & 1 & 2 & 0 & 0 & 0 & 3 \\
1 & 0 & 1 & 0 & 0 & 1 & 0 & 1 & 0 & 1 & 0 & 1 & 0 \\
0 & 0 & 0 & 0 & 0 & 0 & 0 & 0 & 0 & 0 & 0 & 0 & 0 \\
1 & 3 & 1 & 3 & 1 & 3 & 2 & 2 & 2 & 1 & 0 & 1 & 3 \\
0 & 1 & 0 & 1 & 0 & 1 & 1 & 0 & 1 & 0 & 0 & 0 & 1 \\
1 & 1 & 1 & 1 & 0 & 2 & 1 & 1 & 1 & 1 & 0 & 1 & 1 \\
0 & 1 & 0 & 1 & 1 & 0 & 0 & 1 & 0 & 0 & 0 & 0 & 1
\end{pmatrix} \quad (2)$$

Based on AD, a Sankey diagram was generated showing 162 flows between 31 vertices of multigraph G with $|K(i,j)| \neq 0$ (cf. Fig. 6). Flows with $|K(i,j)| > 2$ are highlighted as they represent indicators for clusters of correlations between project and design method characteristics. Based on this, a class of relevant correlation patterns was arranged according to the number of covered flows with $|K(i,j)| > 2$. This class contains four project characteristics **Scope (inner), Interaction (linear), Data sensitivity (high)** and **Proportion of AI (large)** correlating with four design method characteristics in 111 flows: **Business context (high), Service focus (high), Evaluation (high)** and **Physical objects (high)** (cf. Fig. 6). Next, we will discuss identified If-This-Then-That correlation patterns between AI projects showing specific characteristics and potential design methods appropriate for this kind of projects in detail.

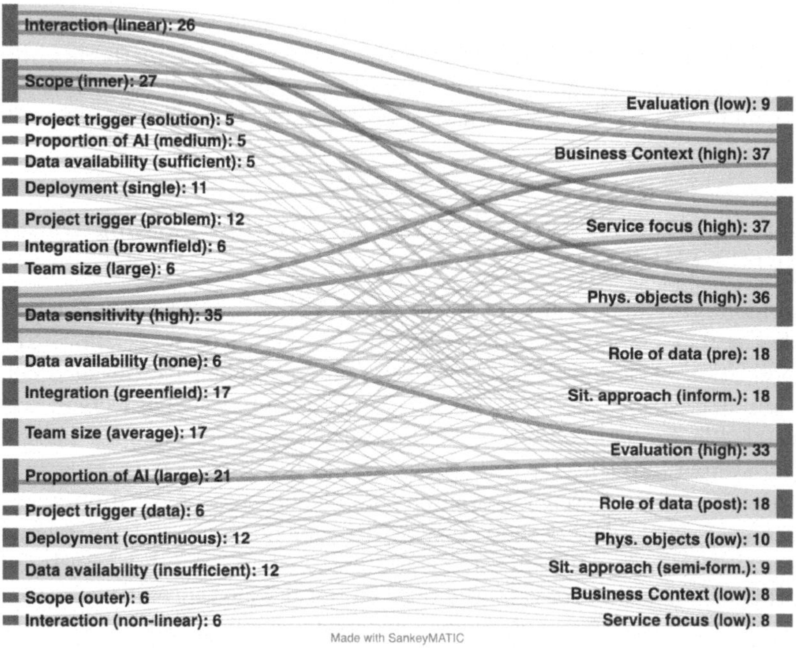

Fig. 6. Sankey diagram with 162 flows between 31 vertices of multigraph G. Indicators for clusters of correlations between project and design method characteristics are marked blue ($|K(i,j)| > 2$). (Color figure online)

6.1 IF Sensitivity of Data Is High THEN ...

When analyzing identified correlations patterns, we saw a strong correlation between AI projects facing high data sensitivity (#flows:35) and the application of design methods with high relevance of business context understanding, service focus, in-between steps for evaluating system design artifacts as well as the acquisition of system-relevant physical objects in the design process (cf. Fig. 6). The correlation between high data sensitivity in projects and methodical business context understanding is also supported by literature. For instance, in case of highly sensitive data such as medical data, input by domain experts is usually needed for data tasks that require experience-based knowledge as well as judgment [27]. Furthermore, there is a striking relationship between high data sensitivity in projects and the application of design methods with strong service focus. This can be explained by the fact that data are often to be claimed as sensitive due to their reference to persons; and this per se establishes a correlation to the design of user-centered services working on these data, e.g., in the medical field or finance [15,17]. Another relevant correlation is given between AI projects that are characterized by high data sensitivity and the methodical provision of sophisticated in-between steps for evaluation and consolidation of system artifacts as well as strong methodical acquisition of relevant physical objects of the intended system. We assume that AI projects working with sensitive data are driven by uncertainties and technical challenges. Here, design methods providing iterative build and evaluate cycles [8] as well as an integrated view of all system components - either physical or non-physical - help to pull risks forward and reduce blind spots.

6.2 IF Intended AI System's Scope Lies Within Existing Business Units THEN ...

Furthermore, results indicate a strong correlation between AI projects where the intended system's scope lies with existing business units (inner) (#flows:27) and the application of design methods focusing on comprehensive business context understanding, strong service focus and capturing of physical objects in systems design (cf. Fig. 6). This finding follows intuition, since an intended integration of an AI system into core business (inner scope) requires deep analyses of existing processes, users, systems as well as components and physical objects (e.g., IoT, sensors) during the design process with domain experts [1]. Understanding as-is situations in daily business is a prerequisite for developing AI systems that provide beneficial user-centered business services for specified target states. Means, in case of AI systems planned to penetrate existing business units, related projects benefit from the application of design methods helping in analyzing as-is situations of the business, specifying services for target states and capturing relevant processes, users, systems, and physical objects.

6.3 IF Intended Interaction Settings are Linear THEN ...

Regarding the classification of intended interaction settings with users, services, devices etc. [2], we saw that the development of AI systems with linear interaction setting (#flows:26) also benefits from methodical support in business context understanding, keeping a strong service focus as well as the consideration of physical objects. This is comparable with the aforementioned correlation pattern tackling the development of AI systems those scopes lie within existing business units. We conclude from this, that AI systems planned to penetrate existing business units are often characterized rather by more traditional linear interaction settings than non-linear settings (e.g., broker, blackboard, peer to peer). So, in case of AI systems with linear interaction settings, related projects require design methods giving guidance in analyzing as-is situations of the business, deriving user-centered services for target states and capturing physical objects in the design process, such as devices (sensors) independent from the observed domain [30].

6.4 IF Proportion of AI Components in Intended System is Large THEN ..

Last, there was a strong correlation found between projects facing a large proportion of AI components in the intended system (#flows:21) [6] and the application of design methods that provide sophisticated in-between steps for evaluation and consolidation of system design artifacts. This is due to the deterministic as well as probabilistic nature of AI components that leads to high error rates and therefore an inability to predict final outcomes of the intended system or to reproduce the same output [24]. The larger the proportion of AI components, the larger the need for risk mitigation through the use of methods with build and evaluation cycles. This enables tackling of hidden technical challenges in AI systems development caused by difficulties given in the combination of traditional software engineering with AI engineering [13,24,34].

7 Conclusion

We considered appropriate design methods for AI systems development. In contrast to the current AI hype, little attention has been given to the methodical design of symbolic and sub-symbolic AI systems leading to missing guidelines and design methods for AI projects in practice. Contribution of this paper was a pool of $If - This - Then - That(IFTTT)$ correlation patterns between AI projects showing specific characteristics and potential design methods appropriate for this kind of projects. With focus on the analysis and design phase of AI system development, qualitative results of a case study that analyzed four AI projects and their design methods were used to discuss implications of identified fine-granular correlation patterns in designing AI systems. A falsification of other potential correlations is not given by this research. Instead, results represent a starting point for further quantitative investigation of required design method characteristics for AI systems and application development.

Acknowledgement. This work was part-funded by the European Union within the project INTEGRATE in the European Regional Development Fund (ERDF), managed by the Saarland State Chancellery; and by the German Federal Ministry for Economic Affairs and Climate Action (BMWK) within the research projects SPAICER (grant number: 01MK20015A), PAIRS (grant number: 01MK21008B), EVAREST (grant number: 01MT19003B) and Smart Farming World (grant number: 01MD16007F).

References

1. Allen, M., Leung, R., McGrenere, J., Purves, B.: Involving domain experts in assistive technology research. Univ. Access Inf. Soc. **7**(3), 145–154 (2008)
2. Alter, S.: System interaction patterns. In: Proceedings of IEEE CBI 2016, vol. 1, pp. 16–25 (2016)
3. Baijens, J., Helms, R., Kusters, R.: Data analytics project methodologies: which one to choose? In: Proceedings of ICBDM 2020, pp. 41–47 (2020)
4. Baijens, J., Helms, R.W.: Developments in knowledge discovery processes and methodologies: anything new? In: Proceedings of AMCIS 2019, pp. 1–10 (2019)
5. Bécue, A., Praça, I., Gama, J.: Artificial intelligence, cyber-threats and industry 4.0: challenges and opportunities. Artif. Intell. Rev. **54**(5), 3849–3886 (2021)

6. Bosch, J., Olsson, H.H., Crnkovic, I.: Engineering AI systems: a research agenda. In: AI Paradigms for Smart Cyber-Physical Systems, pp. 1–19. IGI Global (2021)
7. Gröger, C.: There is no AI without data. Commun. ACM **64**(11), 98–108 (2021)
8. Hevner, A.R., March, S.T., Park, J., Ram, S.: Design science in information systems research. MIS Q, 75–105 (2004)
9. Horkoff, J., Yu, E.: Interactive goal model analysis for early requirements engineering. Requir. Eng. **21**(1), 29–61 (2016)
10. Horneman, A., Mellinger, A., Ozkaya, I.: Ai engineering: 11 foundational practices. Carnegie Mellon University Pittsburgh United States, Technical report (2020)
11. Janzen, S., Kowatsch, T., Maass, W.: A methodology for content-centered design of ambient environments. In: Proceedings of DESRIST 2010, pp. 210–225 (2010)
12. Janzen, S., öksüz, N., Sporkmann, J., et al.: Smart resilience services for industrial production. In: VDI-Kongress AUTOMATION 2021 (2021)
13. Kim, M., Zimmermann, T., DeLine, R., et al.: The emerging role of data scientists on software development teams. In: Proceedings of IEEE ICSE 2016, pp. 96–107 (2016)
14. Larman, C., Basili, V.R.: Iterative and incremental developments: a brief history. Computer **36**(6), 47–56 (2003)
15. Lee, C., Kim, T., Hyun, S.J.: A data acquisition architecture for healthcare services in mobile sensor networks. In: Proceedings of IEEE BigComp 2016, pp. 439–442 (2016)
16. Li, J., Li, M., Wang, X., Thatcher, J.B.: Strategic directions for AI: the role of cios and boards of directors. MIS Q **45**(3) (2021)
17. Lyko, K., Nitzschke, M., Ngonga Ngomo, A.-C.: Big data acquisition. In: Cavanillas, J.M., Curry, E., Wahlster, W. (eds.) New Horizons for a Data-Driven Economy, pp. 39–61. Springer, Cham (2016). https://doi.org/10.1007/978-3-319-21569-3_4
18. Maass, W.: Contract-based data-sharing for ai-based decision making on the web. In: Proceedings of HICSS 2022 (2022)
19. Maass, W., Janzen, S.: Towards design engineering of ubiquitous information systems. In: Proceedings of DESRIST 2012, pp. 206–219 (2012)
20. Mariscal, G., Marban, O., Fernandez, C.: A survey of data mining and knowledge discovery process models. Knowl. Eng. Rev. **25**(2), 137–166 (2010)
21. Martinez-Plumed, F., Contreras-Ochando, L., Ferri, C., et al.: Crisp-dm twenty years later: from data mining processes to data science trajectories. IEEE Trans. Knowl. Data Eng. **33**, 3048–3061 (2019)
22. McGilvray, D.: Executing Data Quality Projects: Ten Steps to Quality Data and Trusted Information (TM). Elsevier Science, Amsterdam (2021)
23. Negnevitsky, M.: Artificial Intelligence: A Guide to Intelligent Systems. Pearson, Boston (2005)
24. Ozkaya, I.: What is really different in engineering AI-enabled systems? IEEE Softw. **37**(4), 3–6 (2020)
25. Pons, L., Ozkaya, I.: Priority quality attributes for engineering ai-enabled systems. arXiv preprint arXiv:1911.02912 (2019)
26. Pugh, S., Clausing, D., Andrade, R.: Creating Innovative Products Using Total Design: The Living Legacy of Stuart Pugh. Addison-Wesley, Boston (1996)
27. Rahman, P., Nandi, A., Hebert, C.: Amplifying domain expertise in clinical data pipelines. JMIR Med. Inf. **8**, e19612 (2020)
28. Robertson, S., Robertson, J.: Mastering the Requirements Process: Getting Requirements Right. Addison-Wesley, Boston (2012)
29. Rodríguez, D., Sicilia, M., García, E., Harrison, R.: Empirical findings on team size and productivity in software development. J. Syst. Softw. **85**(3), 562–570 (2012)

30. Ross, P., Keyson, D.V.: The case of sculpting atmospheres: towards design principles for expressive tangible interaction in control of ambient systems. Pers. Ubiq. Comput. **11**(2), 69–79 (2007)
31. Russell, S., Norvig, P.: Artificial Intelligence: A Modern Approach. Pearson, Boston (2002)
32. Saltz, J., Hotz, N., Wild, D., Stirling, K.: Exploring project management methodologies used within data science teams. In: Proceedings of AMCIS 2018 (2018)
33. Saltz, J., Shamshurin, I., Connors, C.: Predicting data science sociotechnical execution challenges by categorizing data science projects. J. Assoc. Inf. Sci. Technol. **68**(12), 2720–2728 (2017)
34. Sculley, D., et al.: Hidden technical debt in machine learning systems. Adv. Neural Inf. Process. Syst. **28** (2015)
35. Shostack, G.L.: How to design a service. Eur. J. Mark. **16**(1), 49–63 (1993)
36. Stackowiak, R., Kelly, T.: Design Thinking in Software and AI Projects: Proving Ideas Through Rapid Prototyping. Springer, Heidelberg (2020). https://doi.org/10.1007/978-1-4842-6153-8
37. Sutcliffe, A.: Scenario-based requirements analysis. Requir. Eng. **3**(1), 48–65 (1998)
38. Uren, V.: Critical success factors for artificial intelligence projects. In: Proceedings of EurOMA 2020 (2020)

GRASPER: Leveraging Knowledge Graphs for Predictive Supply Chain Analytics

Sabine Janzen[1], Hannah Stein[1,2(✉)], and Sebastian Baer[1]

[1] German Research Center for Artificial Intelligence, Stuhlsatzenhausweg 3, 66123 Saarbruecken, Germany
{sabine.janzen,hannah.stein,sebastian.baer}@dfki.de
[2] Saarland University, Campus, 66123 Saarbruecken, Germany

Abstract. Supply chain disruptions in manufacturing are increasingly prevalent due to the complexity and lack of transparency beyond direct suppliers. Early-stage disruptions often remain undetected, propagate in the network and pose significant challenges to industries reliant on component-based products such as sensors, engines, and electronics. We introduce GRASPER, an AI-based approach for detecting hidden problems in supply chains through graph-theoretic analysis of component shortages. Unlike traditional top-down market analyses, GRASPER converts Bill-of-Material (BOM) data into a semantically enriched knowledge graph in JSON-LD, incorporating historical and current market data on prices, availability, and lead times. By applying and combining graph-theoretical measures, GRASPER identifies critical components, manufacturers, and suppliers that could jeopardize production. The model's effectiveness was validated using a prototype in the sensor manufacturing industry, leveraging an open dataset from social network analysis to assess its performance in pinpointing critical nodes in the knowledge graph. This approach enhances supply chain transparency and resilience, offering significant support for manufacturers in mitigating risks and making informed decisions.

Keywords: Knowledge graph · Supply chain disruptions · AI-based analytics · Component shortages · Graph-theoretical measures

1 Introduction

Supply chain disruptions are a mass phenomenon driven by the increasing trade in intermediate goods, shortage of specific components like semiconductors, greater richness of variants in manufacturing industry as well as the global increase in lead times [2,12,19,22,28,32]. When manufacturing component-based products like sensors, engines or electronics, underlying supply chains are complex and increasingly non-transparent beyond the direct suppliers (tier 1) [1,7,13]. Those supply chains represent a hierarchy of components starting with an item that consists of several components, i.e., assemblies, individual parts

M. Saeki et al. (Eds.): ER 2024 Workshops, LNCS 14932, pp. 58–70, 2025.
https://doi.org/10.1007/978-3-031-75599-6_4

(own parts, purchased parts) and raw materials, that, except of the latter, again are composed of further components (see Fig. 1) [26]. If disruptions with respect to volatile market prices, decreasing availabilities and uncontrollable lead times of components occur in early stages of the supply chain, they usually remain undetected by companies [9,27]. They propagate and reinforce through the supply chain network before popping up as critical situation if not even crisis at tier 1 level (see Fig. 1). Those hidden problems threaten production plans as well as the fulfillment of customer orders in companies [30]. To minimize risks, demand forecasts are developed on a large scale and component orders are placed early and in large quantities to fill warehouses [21]. In case missing components cannot be substituted, this leads to unplanned downtimes, loss of production, fail to fulfill customer orders and job cuts [4,30].

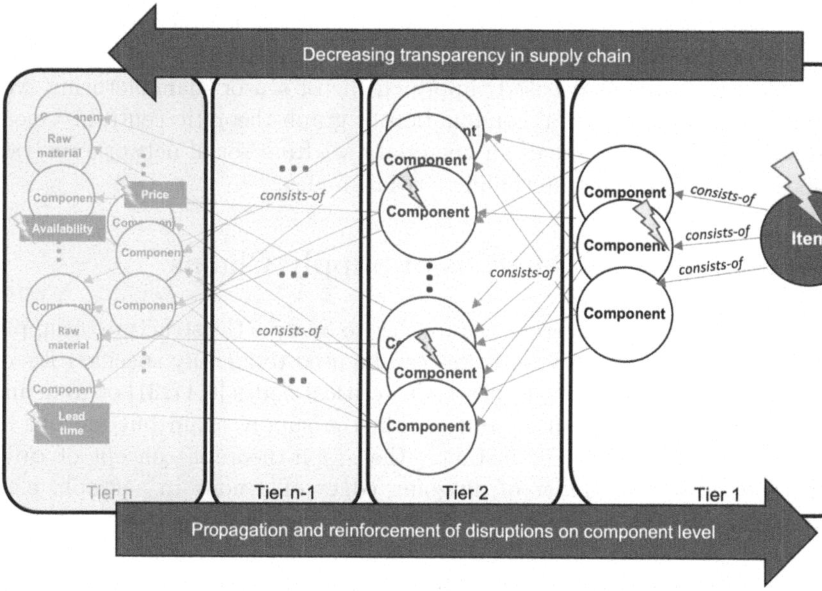

Fig. 1. Hidden problems in component-based supply chains.

In research, related work on detecting hidden problems in component-based supply chains focuses on building monitoring or tracking systems to improve supply chain visibility [11,18,20] or to virtualize supply chains in form of multi-agent systems [14,23]. In addition to that, there is related work focusing on supply chain resilience in general, referring to risk mitigation strategies [3,8] as well as disruption strategies [16,29].

Objective of our research is the detection of hidden problems in supply chains by an AI-based graph-theoretic analysis of shortage trends at component level for improving transparency of supply chains in industrial manufacturing. Focusing on the decision space of manufacturers support in the implementation of existing measures is provided, e.g., searching for missing parts at the spot market. In this work, we propose **GRASPER** - a model for graph-theoretic analysis of component criticality for detecting hidden problems in component-based supply chains. In this context, we define a critical component as a component whose shortage leads to supply chain disruptions, i.e., has a negative impact on timely and cost-effective production of the final product. In contrast to existing top-down approaches for analyzing the market situation [5], components of Bill-of-Materials (BOMs)[1] are conceptually captured by being transformed into a knowledge graph operationalized in JSON-LD.This knowledge graph is semantically enriched and fed with historical and current market data (prices, availability, lead times). The AI-based analysis with respect to the graph-theoretical concepts in-degree, out-degree, out-strength, and betweenness-centrality of nodes enables answering of various questions, e.g., "Which are critical components/manufacturers/suppliers?", "Are there changes in lead times/availabilities/prices, that could be critical for the entire product range?". The model was exemplified within a service prototype for detecting hidden problems in component-based supply chains of sensor manufacturing. We were able to evaluate a partial combination of graph-theoretic centrality measures in GRASPER by means of an open data set from social network analysis in terms of performance in determining critical nodes.

2 Graph-Theoretic Analysis of Supply Chains

There exist several graph-theoretic approaches to analyze the structure of supply chains [6,17,30,31]. Centrality measures can be used to identify specific roles of nodes in the supply chain, e.g., to determine critical nodes [6,17,31] or to define suppliers that play an important role within the supply chain but are out of scope of the company [31]. For instance, the graph-theoretic concept of **out-degree** represents the number of outgoing edges of a node in a graph, e.g., supplier-nodes with high out-degree are shared by many downstream supplier-nodes [17,31]. The concept of **in-degree** measures the number of incoming edges of a node; those nodes can be considered as integrators, which source a lot of material [17]. Nodes with high **betweenness-centrality** act as hubs having influence on the performance of downstream nodes [17,31]. The **out-strength** concept represents the sum of weights of outgoing edges of a node in a graph. It shows the involvement of a node in the supply chain with respect to the production of the final product, e.g., quantity of component needed to realize product. [10] applied centrality measures to determine critical components in a graph obtained from BOM data. They show that the risk for rescheduling of production plans is higher in case of required components with high out-strength and high out-degree [10]. GRASPER extends these contributions by

[1] A Bill of Materials (BOM) is a detailed list of all raw materials, components, and assemblies required to manufacture a product, including part numbers, descriptions, and quantities. It serves as a blueprint for the manufacturing process, ensuring all necessary parts are available and correctly assembled.

the embedding of multiple centrality measures for determination of component criticality as well as the integration of market data about prices, availabilities, and lead times on component level.

3 Model for Graph-Theoretic Analysis of Component Criticality

We present GRASPER, a model for graph-theoretic analysis of component criticality in supply chains consisting of four main modules following [10] (see Fig. 2): **Mapper, Semantifier, Criticality Controller, and Hidden Problem Detector**.

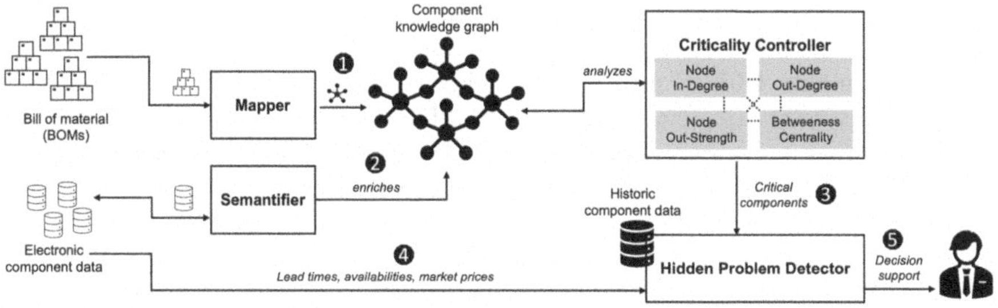

Fig. 2. Model for graph-theoretic analysis of component criticality in supply chains (GRASPER).

GRASPER operates on a knowledge graph obtained from BOMs that are mapped onto a graph structure. Furthermore, **GRASPER** uses electronic component data by Octopart[2] for continuously enriching the knowledge graph with semantic specifications of components (e.g., category) as well as with market information on manufacturers, suppliers, availabilities, prices, and lead times. The enriched knowledge graph serves as input for the model's core components, **Criticality Controller** and **Hidden Problem Detector** (see Fig. 2). The **Criticality Controller** consists of several modules charged with executing the task of determining the criticality of components of the supply chain by combining graph-theoretic concepts **in-degree, out-degree, out-strength and betweenness centrality** of nodes. Output of this module are identified critical components in the graph as well as detailed information about these components, e.g., manufacturer or seller of the component or its category. Finally passed to the **Hidden Problem Detector**, this module checks actual and historic data about these components regarding lead times, availabilities, and market prices for identifying potential hidden problems and creating an alert as decision support for end users (see Fig. 2).

[2] https://octopart.com/.

3.1 Algorithm and Example Course

For introducing the proposed approach, we will give an example course of determining critical components in supply chains starting with the mapping of BOMs onto a knowledge graph and ending with an alert for critical components as decision support for end users. The description of the process will be supported by the model view marked with step numbers (see Fig. 2). In the example, we apply GRASPER on BOMs from sensor manufacturing (# of data entries: 976) as well as electronic component data by Octopart (# of requested components: 621).

Generation of Component Knowledge Graph: The Mapper receives BOMs in form of excel files (see Fig. 2, step 1) representing the composition of the product in a tree-like structure. Furthermore, BOM data cover IDs, potential manufacturers, descriptions as well as the stage of the component within the BOM tree (see Table 1). For instance, the component with ID A0B7C is built of the components D0E3F and G0H5I. Those sub-components are again built of other components (e.g., component with ID J3K4L) (see Table 1). To source component G0H5I, components X01S and X04T are given as alternatives, i.e., those components can substitute the component G0H5I.

Table 1. Example Bill-of-Material (BOM) data (anonymized extract).

Stage	ID	Manufacturer	Short description	Stage wrt BOM	Source description
|1.26|	A0B7C	N/A	....	2. Stage	N/A
|1.26.9|	D0E3F	N/A	....	3. Stage	N/A
|1.26.9.29|	J3K4L	N/A	....	4. Stage	N/A
|1.26.11|	G0H5I	N/A	....	3. Stage	N/A
|1.26.11.4|	X01S	MANU5CF	....	4. Stage	933628580215
|1.26.11.8|	X04T	MANU8GD	....	4. Stage	TBC807-40

The Mapper module (see Fig. 2, step 1) maps the BOM data onto a graph. All components and given manufacturers are represented as nodes within the graph (see Fig. 3). In case of "is component" or "is substitute" relations between two components, the Mapper creates a corresponding edge between the resulting nodes. The resulting component knowledge graph covers 621 component and 83 manufacturer nodes as well as 380 "is substitute"-edges, 305 "is component"-edges, and 382 "produce"-edges between components and manufacturers.

Semantic Enrichment of Knowledge Graph: The Semantifier (see Fig. 2, step 2) enriches the knowledge graph by electronic component data obtained from Octopart. Thus, source or short description of components can be used as search string (see Table 1) for receiving manufacturing part numbers, names and locations of manufacturers as well as sellers, category of components, median prices, market availabilities and lead times. Additional nodes for categories and sellers as well as manufacturers if not already existing are generated and linked by corresponding edges (see Fig. 3). Data like manufacturing part numbers, median prices, market availabilities and lead times are integrated as node properties. The enriched component knowledge graph contains 621 component and 105 manufacturer nodes, 34 category nodes, 154 seller nodes as well as 305 "is component"-edges, 380 "is substitute"-edges, 494 "produce"-edges, 267 "is category"-edges and 6438 "sells"-edges.

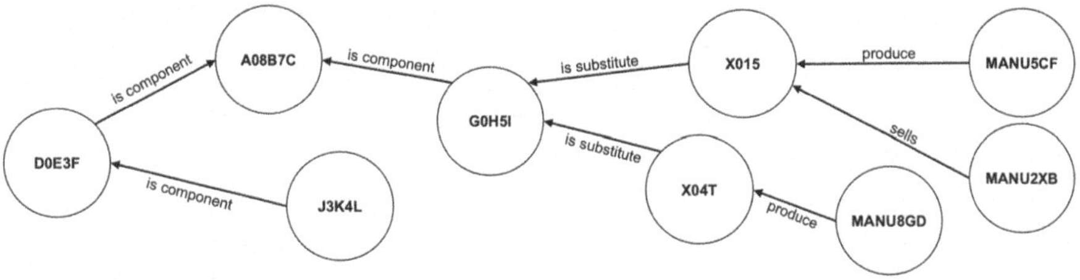

Fig. 3. Example component knowledge graph based on extract of BOM data given in Table 1 (extract).

Determination of Critical Components: The Criticality Controller (see Fig. 2, step 3) analyzes the component knowledge graph with respect to critical components. As mentioned before, shortages in critical components lead to supply chain disruptions, i.e., have a negative impact on timely and cost-effective production of the product. This is due to shortages of upstream components, decreasing availabilities, lack of substitution options or increasing market prices and lead times. This is operationalized by means of a graph-theoretic approach. With $G = (V, E)$, the component knowledge graph is a directed graph with set of nodes V, i.e., components, and set of edges E. Every node, i.e., component, has a degree, representing the number of edges of node v: $d_G(v)$. The **in-degree** $d_G^-(v)$ is the number of incoming edges of a node v. A high in-degree shows that (a) the component consists of many upstream components ($d_{GA}^-(v)$) or (b) that there are several alternative components available ($d_{GB}^-(v)$). If substitutes are available for sourcing material, this mitigates the severity of supply chain disruptions [24,29], i.e., option (a) reinforces component criticality whereas option (b) mitigates it. The **out-degree** $d_G^+(v)$ is the number of outgoing edges of a node v. A high out-degree shows that the component is part of many downstream components; this reinforces component criticality. **Out-strength** of a component node represents the sum of weights of outgoing edges, i.e., how often the component is required in downstream components: $s_G(v) = \sum w(e_v)$. The concept **betweenness-centrality** $c_G(v)$ represents the influence of a component v within the component knowledge graph. The more often a node v takes the role of an intermediary for a pair of nodes (i, j), the more central v is and the higher its betweenness-centrality. Components with high criticality $CR(v)$ have (1) high out-strength, and/or (2) high out-degree, and/or (3) high in-degree with respect to upstream components, and/or (4) low in-degree with respect to alternatives, and/or (5) high betweenness-centrality:

$$CR(v) = \frac{d_G^+(v) + s_G(v) + c_G(v)}{d_{GB}^-(v)} + d_{GA}^-(v)$$

Applied to the example knowledge graph in Fig. 3, we see high criticality of component D0E3F (see Table 2) in contrast to component G0H5I that is less critical due to its potential alternatives. The Criticality Controller determines the criticality for all 621 components. To mitigate normal volatility and background noise in supply chains, a box plot procedure is used to identify outliers of the normally distributed CR values (upper whisker). Those outliers represent critical components indicating a $CR(v)$ above 4.14. In total, the Criticality Controller identified 75 of 621 component nodes as critical with $CR(v)$ ranging from 4.15 to 6.00.

Table 2. Determination of criticality of example components in knowledge graph given in Fig. 2.

Node	Criticality $CR(v)$	Out-Degree $d_G^+(v)$	In-Degree $d_{GB}^-(v)$	In-Degree $d_{GA}^-(v)$	Out-Strength $s_G(v)$	Betweenness Centrality $c_G(v)$
A0B7C	2	0	0	2	0	0
D0E3F	4	1	0	1	1	1
J3K4L	2	1	0	0	1	0
G0H5I	1	1	2	0	1	0

Integration of Market Data: The components listed as critical are augmented with actual market data if available. The Hidden Problem Detector requests electronic component data regarding actual market availability, estimated lead time (given in days), as well as median price on a daily basis (see Fig. 2, step 4) and aggregates historical data. Collecting this data allows the model to plot the market trend for most critical components.

Decision Support for End Users: The Hidden Problem Detector generates an overview of detected critical components augmented with actual and historical data regarding availabilities, prices, and lead times (see Fig. 2, step 5). Therefore, severe shortage trends can be identified, e.g., decreasing market availability (-36%) with simultaneous increase in lead time (+40%) for critical components. In this case, the Hidden Problem Detector would trigger an alert for creating decision support for the end user, i.e., indicating the critical component with manufacturer, seller and potential substitutes as well as justifying the detected shortage trend by means of analysed market data.

4 Implementation and Evaluation

Based on the proposed GRASPER model (see Fig. 2), we implemented a service prototype for hidden problem detection in supply chains in form of a web interface.[3]

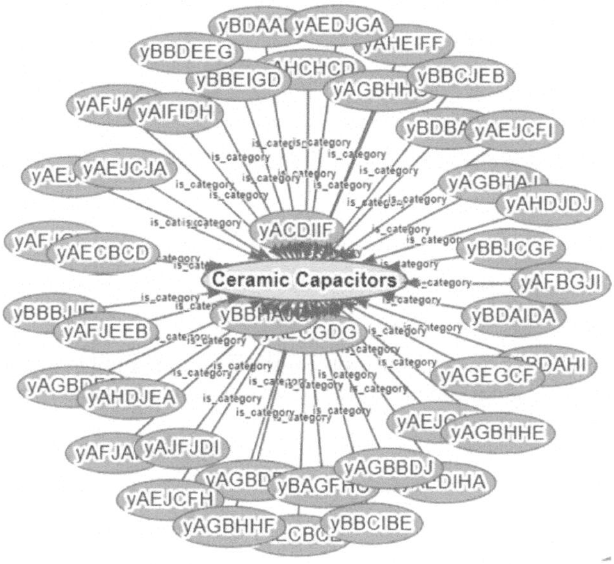

Fig. 4. Service prototype for hidden problem detection in supply chains: enriched knowledge graph based on BOM data

Figure 4 shows an insight into the service prototype. In order to be able to process BOMs in form of a knowledge graph, realizing graph-theoretic analyses, integrated external market data and displaying results to the user, a server-client architecture has been deployed by using Flask[4], Python, Neo4j[5] and the Octopart API. On client side, the interface has been implemented as a web interface (HTML, JavaScript) that accepts uploads of BOM files (xlsx). Having confirmed the selected file(s), the resulting component knowledge graph is shown as thumbnail due to its size (see Fig. 4) and the list of detected critical components is displayed to the user with additional information, e.g., criticality $CR(v)$, manufacturer, category. Furthermore, an overview of market data regarding those components is given in form of text, table, and diagram, e.g., lead time development in past 30 days (see Fig. 5). In case of detected shortage trends, relevant components are highlighted, and an alert is given. A prerequisite

[3] Link to GitHub will be provided.
[4] https://flask.palletsprojects.com/en/2.2.x/.
[5] https://neo4j.com/.

for the service is the availability of (1) BOM files following a valid schema, and (2) external electronic component data that can be requested for the components given in BOMs, e.g., via Octopart.

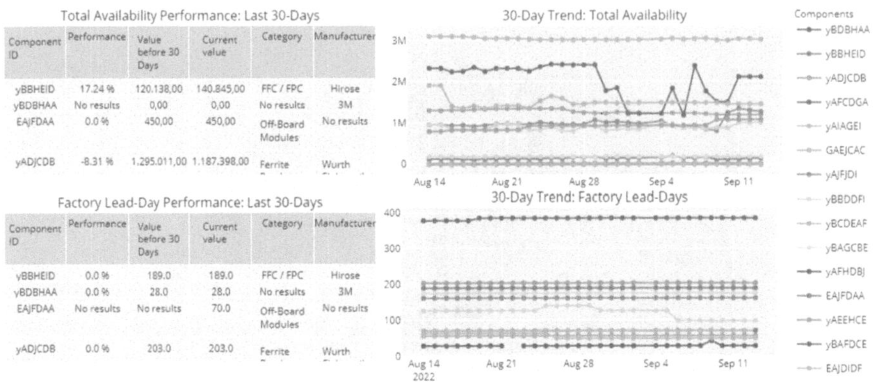

Fig. 5. Service prototype for hidden problem detection in supply chains: Overview of market data regarding determined critical components, e.g., availability and lead days of components in the last 30 days.

4.1 Setting

To evaluate our approach, we conducted a runtime study with the implemented service prototype. Goal of this study was to assess the performance in determining critical nodes in knowledge graphs. In absence of open BOM data[6], we applied the USAir97 data set and mapped it onto a directed and unweighted graph. The resulting knowledge graph contains airports as nodes (#332) and corresponding edges (#2126) representing flight connections. Similar to critical nodes in the supply chain graph, influential nodes, i.e., airports, have many direct flights from or to other airports. In case these airports were affected by strikes, staff shortages, technical problems etc.; disruptions would propagate massively within the graph. As the applied data set covers no information about substitutes and the resulting graph is unweighted due to the airport domain, the assessment of the performance in determining critical nodes by GRASPER is focused on the combination of in-degree, out-degree and betweenness-centrality, i.e.,

$$CR(v) = d_G^+(v) + c_G(v) + d_{GA}^-(v)$$

According to the SI spreading model [34] as well as the SIR spreading model [15], each 10 nodes, i.e., airports of the USAir97 data set are labeled as influential, i.e., critical.

[6] https://networkrepository.com/USAir97.php.

4.2 Results

In summary, a knowledge graph with 332 nodes and 2126 corresponding edges according to the USAir97 data set was included in the experiment. Based on the SI spreading model and SIR spreading model 20 nodes were labelled as critical; here, 4 nodes were identified as duplicates. The experiment was conducted in two runs for determining nodes labeled as critical by (1) SI, and (2) SIR spreading model. A **reduced GRASPER model** was applied in the experiment due to the airport topic indicating no substitutes as well as the unweighted nature of the resulting graph. That means, the graph-theoretic concepts in-degree for substitute edges and out-strength were skipped. 3 out of 5 concepts (60%) of the GRASPER model were applied within the performance evaluation. The service prototype was able to determine 7 out of 10 critical nodes with respect to the ground truth by SIR spreading model (see Table 3). Additionally, 60% of nodes labeled as critical by the SI spreading model were detected correctly with the reduced GRASPER model. We detected that the performance of the model in the run with SIR spreading model was quite good (correctness of 70%) whereas correctness in context of labeling by SI spreading model was lower (60%). Table 3 shows evaluation results in comparison with the models CKI [33] and CEC [25] also proposing metrics for determining influential nodes labeled by means of SI or SIR spreading model within the USAir97 data set. In contrast to GRASPER, both models were designed to detect influential, respectively critical nodes for the airport data set. Therefore, they applied full model functionality (100%, see Table 3) within the performance evaluation.

Table 3. Correctness in terms of determined critical nodes in comparison with selected models.

		SI spreading model [34]		SIR spreading model [15]	
Model	Applicability of model on data set	Determined critical nodes	Correctness	Determined ritical nodes	Correctness
CKI [33]	100%	n/a	n/a	8	80.0%
CEC [25]	100%	9	90.0%	n/a	n/a
GRASPER	60%	6	60.0%	7	70.0%

Overall, this indicates a positive evaluation of the reduced GRASPER model regarding its ability to determine critical nodes in knowledge graphs. Next steps will be to evaluate the full GRASPER model on large scale BOM data labelled with respect to critical components by domain experts. Furthermore, the final product node will be semantically enriched by data on the product's share of sales, related orders by high-ranked customers, production plans etc. to be able to simulate shortage trends in the graph and their effects on production, sales, revenue, and profit.

5 Conclusion

Manufacturers of component-based products like sensors or engines are confronted with complex supply chains characterized by an increasing nontransparence beyond tier 1. Disruptions in early stages of these supply chains usually remain undetected, propagate, and reinforce before popping up as critical situation if not even crisis at tier 1 level. Despite the risk of threatening production plans as well as the fulfillment of customer orders, handling of these hidden problems concentrates on traditional supply chain and risk management enabling reactive measures at tier 1 or 2. Focusing on the decision space of manufacturers, we introduced GRASPER, a model for graph-theoretic analysis of component criticality for detecting hidden problems in component-based supply chains. GRASPER uses a multiple graph-theoretic centrality measures for determining the criticality of components, i.e., in-degree, out-degree, out-strength, and betweenness-centrality of nodes. Bill-of-Materials (BOM) data are automatically transformed into a knowledge graph operationalized in JSON-LD, semantically enriched, and fed with historical and actual market data (e.g., prices). The model was exemplified within a service prototype for detecting hidden problems in supply chains of sensor manufacturing. We evaluated the proposed approach by means of a data set from social network analysis in terms of performance in determining critical nodes.

Acknowledgement. This work was part-funded by the German Federal Ministry for Economic Affairs and Climate Action (BMWK) within the research project PAIRS under grant number 01MK21008B.

References

1. Agrawal, T.K., Kalaiarasan, R., Olhager, J., Wiktorsson, M.: Supply chain visibility: a delphi study on managerial perspectives and priorities. Int. J. Prod. Res. **62**, 1–16 (2022)
2. Amighini, A.A.: China and India in the international fragmentation of automobile production. China Econ. Rev. **23**, 325–341 (2012)
3. Aqlan, F., Lam, S.S.: Supply chain risk modelling and mitigation. Int. J. Prod. Res. **53**, 5640–5656 (2015)
4. Attinasi, M., Balatti, M., Mancini, M., Metelli, L.: (2021). https://www.ecb.europa.eu/pub/economic-bulletin/focus/2022/html/ecb.ebbox202108_01~e8ceebe51f.en.html. Accessed 14 Nov 2022
5. Benigno, G., Di Giovanni, J., Groen, J.J., Noble, A.I.: The gscpi: a new barometer of global supply chain pressures. FRB of New York Staff Report (2022)
6. Borgatti, S.P., Li, X.: On social network analysis in a supply chain context. J. Supply Chain Manag. **45**, 5–22 (2009)
7. Caridi, M., Crippa, L., Perego, A., Sianesi, A., Tumino, A.: Do virtuality and complexity affect supply chain visibility? Int. J. Prod. Econ. **127**, 372–383 (2010)
8. Chang, W., Ellinger, A.E., Blackhurst, J.: A contextual approach to supply chain risk mitigation. Int. J. Logist. Manag. **26**, 642–656 (2015)
9. Choi, T.Y., Rogers, D., Vakil, B.: Coronavirus is a wake-up call for supply chain management. Harv. Bus. Rev. **27**, 364–398 (2020)
10. Cinelli, M., Ferraro, G., Iovanella, A., Lucci, G., Schiraldi, M.M.: A network perspective on the visualization and analysis of bill of materials. Int. J. Eng. Bus. Manag. **9**, 1847979017732638 (2017)

11. Costa, F., Do Sameiro Carvalho, M., Fernandes, J.M., Alves, A.C., Silva, P.: Improving visibility using rfid-the case of a company in the automotive sector. Procedia Manuf. **13**, 1261–1268 (2017)
12. D'Antonio, G., Mottola, S., Prencipe, G., Brusin, A.R., Sauza Bedolla, J., Chiabert, P.: Deployment of product configurators: analysis of impacts within and outside the user company. In: Ríos, J., Bernard, A., Bouras, A., Foufou, S. (eds.) PLM 2017. IAICT, vol. 517, pp. 440–449. Springer, Cham (2017). https://doi.org/10.1007/978-3-319-72905-3_39
13. Elliot, R.: Bci-supply chain resilience report (2021). https://www.thebci.org/static/e02a3e5f-82e5-4ff1-b8bc61de9657e9c8/BCI-0007h-Supply-Chain-Resilience-ReportLow-Singles.pdf. Accessed 12 Nov 2022
14. Giannakis, M., Louis, M.: A multi-agent based system with big data processing for enhanced supply chain agility. J. Enterp. Inf. Manag. **29**, 706–727 (2016)
15. Hethcote, H.W.: The mathematics of infectious diseases. SIAM Rev. **42**, 599–653 (2000)
16. Kamalahmadi, M., Parast, M.M.: An assessment of supply chain disruption mitigation strategies. Int. J. Prod. Econ. **184**, 210–230 (2017)
17. Kim, Y., Choi, T.Y., Yan, T., Dooley, K.: Structural investigation of supply networks: a social network analysis approach. J. Oper. Manag. **29**, 194–211 (2011)
18. Kärkkäinen, M., Ala-Risku, T., Främling, K.: Efficient tracking for short-term multi-company networks. Int. J. Phys. Distrib. Logist. Manag. **34**, 545–564 (2004)
19. Lechner, A., Klingebiel, K., Wagenitz, A.: Evaluation of product variant-driven complexity costs and performance impacts in the automotive logistics with variety-driven activity-based costing. In: World Congress on Engineering 2012, London, UK, pp. 1088–1096 (2012)
20. Lee, D., Park, J.: Rfid-based traceability in the supply chain. Ind. Manag. Data Syst. **108**, 713–725 (2008)
21. Lee, H.L., Padmanabhan, V., Whang, S.: The bullwhip effect in supply chains. Sloan Manag. Rev. **38**, 93–102 (1997)
22. Los, B., Timmer, M.P., De Vries, G.J.: How global are global value chains? a new approach to measure international fragmentation. J. Reg. Sci. **55**, 66–92 (2015)
23. Matsuda, M., Nishi, T., Hasegawa, M., Matsumoto, S.: Virtualization of a supply chain from the manufacturing enterprise view using e-catalogues. Procedia CIRP **81**, 932–937 (2019)
24. Pettit, T.J., Fiksel, J., Croxton, K.L.: Ensuring supply chain resilience: development of a conceptual framework. J. Bus. Logist. **31**, 1–21 (2010)
25. Qiang, R., Yang, J.: Influential spreader identification in complex networks based on network connectivity and efficiency. Wirel. Commun. Mob. Comput. **2022**, 7896380 (2022)
26. Schönsleben, P.: Logistik- Operations und Supply Chain Management. Springer, Heidelberg (2016)
27. Sheffi, Y.: Preparing for disruptions through early detection. MIT Sloan Manag. Rev. **57**, 31 (2015)
28. Shou, Y., Li, Y., Park, Y.W., Kang, M.: The impact of product complexity and variety on supply chain integration. Int. J. Phys. Distrib. Logist. Manag. **47**, 297–317 (2017)
29. Tang, C.S.: Robust strategies for mitigating supply chain disruptions. Int. J. Log. Res. Appl. **9**, 33–45 (2006)
30. Wagner, S.M., Bode, C.: An empirical examination of supply chain performance along several dimensions of risk. J. Bus. Logist. **29**, 307–325 (2008)

31. Yan, T., Choi, T.Y., Kim, Y., Yang, Y.: A theory of the nexus supplier: a critical supplier from a network perspective. J. Supply Chain Manag. **51**, 52–66 (2015)
32. Zeddies, G.: Determinants of international fragmentation of production in European union. Empirica **38**, 511–537 (2011)
33. Zhang, L., Sun, X., Wang, P., Hou, J., Sun, G.: Identifying influential nodes with a community structure measure. In: 2019 IEEE Fourth International Conference on Data Science in Cyberspace (DSC), pp. 264–269. IEEE (2019)
34. Zhou, T., Liu, J.G., Bai, W.J., Chen, G., Wang, B.H.: Behaviors of susceptible-infected epidemics on scale-free networks with identical infectivity. Phys. Rev. E **74**, 056109 (2006)

An MLOps Framework to Data-Driven Modelling of Digital Twins with an Application to Virtual Test Rigs

Denis Kruschinski[1(✉)], Dylan Tchawou Ngassam[1], Umut Durak[2], and Sven Hartmann[1]

[1] Clausthal University of Technology, Clausthal-Zellerfeld, Germany
denis.kruschinski@tu-clausthal.de
[2] DLR Institute of Flight Systems, Braunschweig, Germany

Abstract. The use of data-driven modeling for digital twins (DTs) is growing in popularity. However, many models do not make it into production. Those that do quickly become outdated. Streamlined model update is still a major challenge. There is a need to establish methods and techniques for managing data-driven digital twins throughout their entire life cycle. Machine learning operations (MLOps) recently emerged as an effective means to foster the integration of Machine Learning (ML) models and their operational workflows. In this paper, we exploit MLOps for development and operation of data-driven digital twins. To validate our approach, a case study is conducted in which an ML model of a physical test rig is trained in accordance with the MLOps principles. The work aims to demonstrate how MLOps practices can contribute to overcoming issues related to scalability, accuracy, and adaptability in the context of digital twin training.

Keywords: Machine learning operations · Digital twin · Data-driven modelling · Digital twin lifecycle

1 Introduction

The digital twin (DT) concept involves creating a virtual representation of a physical asset, system, or process, effectively duplicating it in a digital format [5]. A notable example is during the Apollo 13 mission, where multiple replicas of the spacecraft modules were used to diagnose technical issues on the ground and help guide the crew back to Earth [1]. These replicas bore certain characteristics that are typical for digital twins: they had a physical basis, connected and responsive, adapting to different scenarios and functioned as part of a network of various simulators. The DT concept is advantageous in several ways, as physical assets go through numerous life-cycle stages [10]. These include the design, manufacturing, service, and retirement phases. From this, several application scenarios for digital twins can be deduced, with possible uses such as

M. Saeki et al. (Eds.): ER 2024 Workshops, LNCS 14932, pp. 71–86, 2025.
https://doi.org/10.1007/978-3-031-75599-6_5

virtual evaluation and verification during the design phase, process evaluation and optimisation, and performance prediction during the service phase, among others.

A practical example of the digital twin application is in developing new aircraft wings. Instead of performing extensive testing with expensive test rigs such as the iron bird, digital twin concept could mitigate transit some of the testing efforts to a virtual environment, enabling easy scaling with instant deployment multiple simultaneous tests, reducing the utilisation of expensive test rigs and their associated maintenance costs, and scaling the training of employees with simulations.

There are multiple methods available to create digital twins [12]. These may consist of a CAD model that matches the aforementioned five characteristics and serves to visualise the components of an asset. Alternatively, there are physics-based models employing mathematical equations to compute specific properties of a physical asset in given operative environments. Moreover, data-driven models (e.g. a feedforward neural network (FNN) [6,7]) can be used to predict or mimic a component's behaviour based on historical data. Among them, data-driven method demonstrates its promise in recent work [3], which uses DT in developing virtual test rigs, off-line training of a virtual test rig through data-driven modelling was proposed in [3]. However, there are some challenges in the application of data-driven methods. In particular, constantly updating the model to capture the life-cycle of the physical asset has not been investigated yet, nor has a workflow for off-line rebuilding of the model.

MLOps is developed to support the development of machine learning (ML) models, such as the DT. Moreover, MLOps provides a workflow for deploying ML models.

In this paper, we aim to propose a new MLOps approach for DT to support data-driven model development, deployment, monitoring and update.

The main contributions of this paper are the following:

- A framework for data-driven modelling of DTs based on MLOps. To the best of our knowledge, it is the first data-driven modelling approach that integrates both the development and the ongoing updates and maintenance of DT models.
- A case study of a DT for a drone accelerometer aligning with principles promoted by MLOps. Our case study demonstrates the applicability of MLOps to data-driven modelling for DT of test rigs.

Organization of the Paper. This paper is organized as follows: Sect. 2 presents preliminaries and the background of our work. Section 3 presents our proposed MLOps based approach for data modelling of DTs. Section 4 presents a case study that we conducted to demonstrate the applicability of our approach to the development of DTs for virtual test rigs. Section 5 provides conclusions and suggestions for future research.

2 Background and Related Work

2.1 Background

Test rigs play a crucial role in the verification and validation of an aircraft (sub)system. These examinations are conducted on the ground, mimicking the real flight or environmental conditions that an aircraft may encounter. An aircraft can face a range of different forces accompanied by error conditions in flight, necessitating a rigorous test bench to verify system requirements.

A prominent example of such test rigs is the "Iron Bird" [2,11]. These are large-scale test rigs primarily used to test the aircraft's mechanical control systems. Critical to the validation of aircraft control and hydraulic systems, an Iron Bird encompasses all the key components of a flight control system. These include the flight control computer, actuators, fasteners, either dummy or real surfaces, and loading systems. The use of an Iron Bird at early stages of an aircraft's design enables early identification of any design flaws, thereby reducing cost and schedule risks. Moreover, these test rigs remain active throughout the aircraft's life cycle, which is about 30 years, providing valuable data analysis means.

Figure 1 depicts the interplay between virtual test rigs, data collection systems, and MLOps platforms within the context of hardware-in-the-loop (HITL) simulations. In this environment, a platform developed on MLOps principles is utilised for the purpose of training and refining ML models. These ML models have the capacity to serve as virtual test rigs, and in particular scenarios, they can replace their physical equivalents.

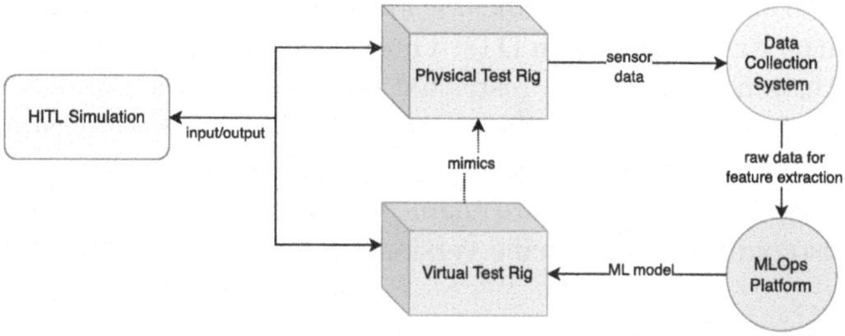

Fig. 1. A DT concept for a virtual test rig that mimics the physical counterpart using data driven modeling and MLOps principles

2.2 Related Work

In [3], a practical utilization of a virtual test rig was presented. This was realized through the modeling of a DT as a FNN using sensory data derived from a hydraulic actuator. Despite the progress made in this work, it did not delve into additional critical aspects such as supporting infrastructure for pipeline automation, online training, model refinement, and deployment. However, examining other fields reveals that these elements have been extensively researched and applied across a range of different use cases. MLOps [8], for instance, is an approach that has gained significant traction within the scientific community. It reflects a popular and effective strategy for managing the complexities of model deployment and monitoring, providing valuable insight on how these challenges might be addressed.

A recent survey paper [8] presents a generic MLOps architecture with five components. The first is MLOps *Product Initiation* which involves the early steps taken when implementing machine learning practices within an organization. This facilitates technological decision-making and lays the foundation for automated ML deployment. The second is *Feature Pipeline Engineering*, which is a defined process of creating, transforming, and selecting features that will be used to train ML models. The next component is *Experimentation*, during which data scientists perform the ML algorithm selection, re-validation of features, and hyper parameter tuning takes place. The goal of this step is to come up with the best ML model and the optimal hyper parameters. The fourth component is the *Automated ML workflow pipeline*. This step streamlines and automates the entire process of operationalizing robust ML models, transforming manual efforts into an orchestrated and efficient pipeline. Lastly, the architecture includes a component for monitoring of the Model, Data, and Infrastructure. This component incorporates feedback loops to identify potential model degradation over time. This component is crucial to keeping machine learning models reliable and aligned with evolving business needs by prompting retraining when necessary.

The reference architecture in [8] was created with a generic ML workflow in mind, where various roles are responsible for different activities and components. Our paper, in contrast, focuses on DTs. This led us to simplify the architecture by eliminating certain features. We restricted ourselves to using only services that can be locally hosted, such as offline databases. For the sake of simplicity, we discarded the role separation described in the reference architecture, including roles such as data scientist, software engineer, or DevOps engineers. For the same reason, we also omitted any specific versioning system for feature data.

3 The MLOps Framework for Modeling Digital Twins (DTs)

In this section, we present the ML framework for the data-driven modeling of DTs. The diagram shown in Fig. 2 encapsulates all vital components and processes, starting from the initial requirements analysis to the resulting model, incorporating automated model refinement as well.

Within this framework, certain pipelines necessitate human interaction, while others can be automated. The essential components of the ML workflow operate within a container orchestration platform like a Kubernetes cluster. A cluster

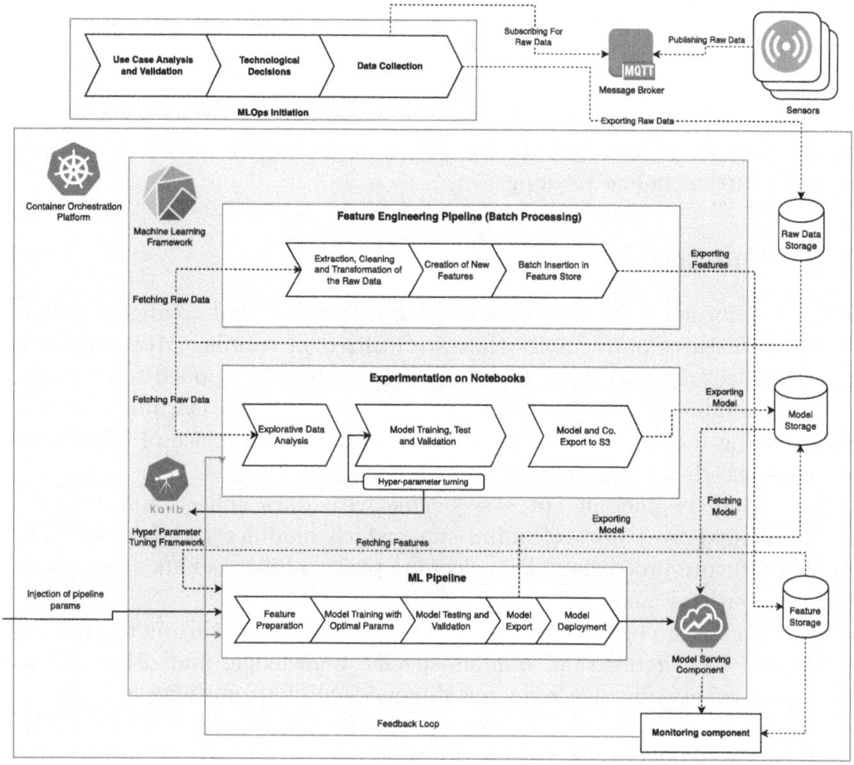

Fig. 2. An MLOps framework adapted from [8] for modeling digital twin (DT)

assists in scaling processes and ensures high availability of services due to built-in replication mechanisms.

Contrarily, there are also components within the framework that are not dependent on the orchestration platform. These include the requirements analysis and the development of components assigned for the initial and subsequent data collection from embedded sensors, all of which operate independently. In the following subsections we describe these components in more detail.

3.1 MLOps Initiation

Initial manual tasks are required, and these involve the analysis and validation of the DT use case, which includes estimating feasibility, assessing the quality of possible outcomes, and specifying the requirements of the DT and the operating environment.

After the analysis, the next step is to make technological decisions, such as determining which software products are necessary to meet the specified requirements. This could range from data storage, data protocols, sensors, machine learning frameworks, infrastructure, observability tools, and container orchestration, among others.

Following that is the collection of data from experiments, which is done by executing a data aggregator for data collection from an experiment. The gathered data can then be utilized for preliminary data analysis, feature engineering, as well as for further online training.

3.2 Feature Engineering Pipeline

The pipeline for feature engineering is a defined process that creates, transforms, and selects features or variables that are utilized in training ML models. This process involves a range of steps and operations that are applied to raw data to derive meaningful information which can serve as input for learning algorithms. By conducting feature engineering effectively, the performance of ML products can be enhanced.

The feature engineering process begins with data collection from various sources followed by a data cleaning step, which modifies the data to make it suitable for future processing. This cleaning phase addresses issues such as missing values, outliers, and inconsistencies.

New features can be created from existing raw data by utilizing mathematical transformations, aggregation, domain-specific knowledge, and other methods. This step may also involve reducing dimensionality to optimize training time and inference performance, as well as normalization, scaling, and encoding to ensure data is in a suitable range and format.

3.3 Experimentation on Notebooks

Experimentation on notebooks is a commonly performed technique by data scientists. The purpose of this exercise is to find the best model and optimize its hyper-parameters, thereby aiming to discover the most precise, generalized, and unbiased model. This process encompasses every step from connecting raw data or the feature database to exporting the ML model. Explorative data analysis (EDA) is a method that enables data professionals to gain substantial insights into data distributions, relationships, and characteristics. This plays a pivotal role in identifying potential features.

Even though a feature store may already contain model-ready data, raw data can again be re-validated during the stage of experimentation. This can allow for fine-tuning the feature engineering pipeline as needed. The experimentation also involves dividing the dataset into three subsets: training, testing, and validation. Methods used for this division could be random splits, considering chronological sequence (in the case of time series data), or based on the size of the subsets. Modelling steps follow, which include selecting the correct machine learning algorithm and tuning the hyper-parameters of the selected algorithm. In the case of deep learning models, considerations include adjusting the number of epochs, the learning rate, and the configuration of the neural network. These processes can be automated using tools like Katib [4] (a part of Kubeflow[1]).

The resulting ML model and metadata are then exported to object storage like S3-compatible storage. ML automation frameworks like Kubeflow/Katib are employed to handle experiments tracking, storing experiment data for further analysis.

3.4 ML Pipeline

The automation of the ML pipeline enables a continuous injection of information from the experiment phase directly into the automated ML pipeline. The automated process is capable of performing all the necessary ML operations in a single run, ranging from retrieving features to the final steps of model deployment.

This ML pipeline could be launched either manually or automatically, given certain triggers. There are several possible triggers for this process including, but not limited to, periodically rebuilding the ML model, an event-triggered launch due to the degradation of the model's performance, or a shift in the distribution of online data.

Finally, the end product of the ML pipeline automation is the ML model itself, which can then be utilized as a digital twin. Once deployed, the ML model is sent to a component specifically designed for model serving, which then exposes the model as a service. This service can then be readily consumed by other systems or the components operating within the DT's environment.

4 Case Study for Validation

In this section, we demonstrate the applicability of MLOps to the data-driven modeling of virtual test rigs. For that we conduct a case study of a *DT for a drone accelerometer* aligning with the principles promoted by the MLOps framework described above and displayed in Fig. 2.

In the following we will present the details of our case study with respect to the application of MLOps in data-driven modelling on four aspects: high-level system architecture, data collection, data analysis and feature engineering, and experimentation.

4.1 High-Level System Architecture

We used a test environment with the following components: *Simulated Drone*, *MQTT Broker*, *Drone Subscriber*, *Digital Twin (DT) of the drone accelerometer*, *Digital Twin (DT) Consumer*, *Data Store Systems*, *Visualization Component*, *ETL (Extract, Transform, Load) component*, and *Automated ML Pipeline* (Fig. 3).

[1] https://www.kubeflow.org/.

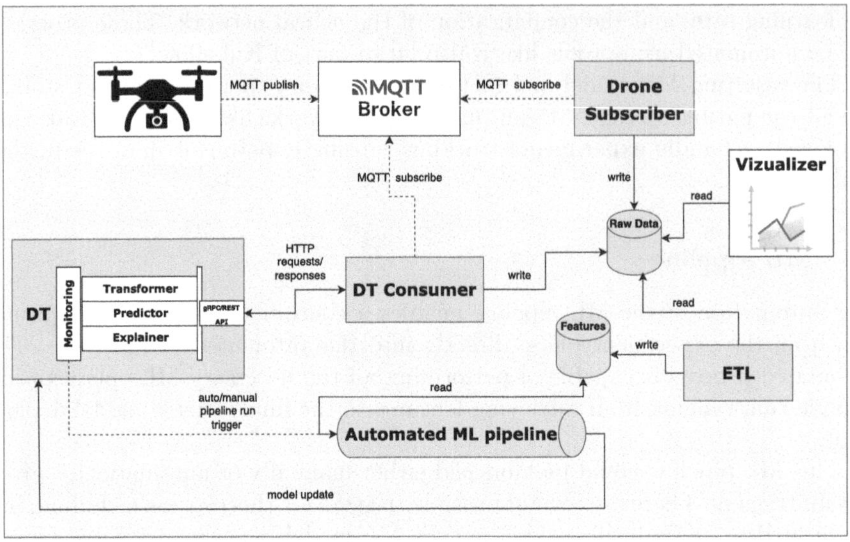

Fig. 3. High-level system architecture of our test environment

The *simulated drone* publishes its sensor data on the *publish-subscribe based messaging protocol (MQTT) broker*. Subsequently, the published data is subscribed to by two services: the *drone-subscriber* and the *DT-consumer*. The *drone subscriber* acts as the primary data collection component, storing raw data in the *data store system*. After undergoing transformation operations, the raw data is loaded into a Feature Store System, providing training-ready data or features to the *Automated ML Pipeline component*. The batch Extract-Transform-Load (ETL) component handles the transformation process. The *DT Consumer* acts as an intermediary between the DT and its physical counterpart, subscribing real-time data to the *MQTT broker* and sending HTTP requests to the *DT REST/gRPC API*. The *DT REST/gRPC API*, deployed with a transformer service, enables raw data to be pre-processed before being transmitted to its inference service.

Additionally, the DT includes model monitoring and model explainability subcomponents, ensuring ongoing performance monitoring and providing explanations for model predictions, respectively. In the event of degraded model performance, a retraining operation on actual data and a model update operation can be initiated manually or automatically. This ensures the adaptability of the DT model through its life cycle.

4.2 Simulations Conducted

Several parameters are passed to the drone at the beginning of a simulation, in particular the sensor readings' transmission rate and the predefined waypoints describing the drone's trajectory. The sequence of waypoints is depicted in Fig. 4. A total of six experiments were conducted to gather data.

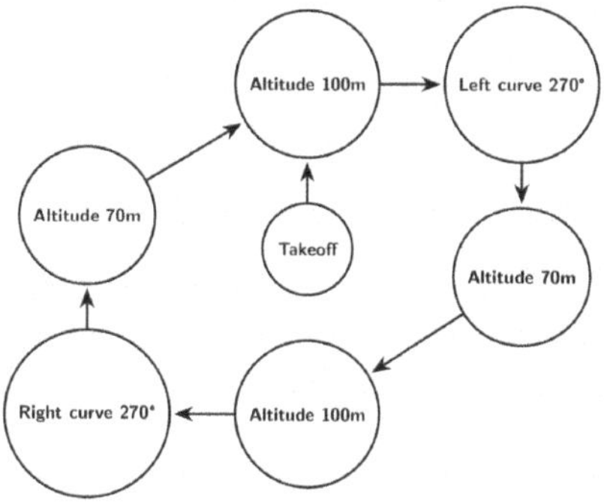

Fig. 4. State diagram describing the drone trajectory

4.3 Data Collection

For training the ML model, which will serve later as the DT of the drone accelerometer, synthetic data was generated by the software-in-the-loop (SITL) drone simulator. The generated data is subsequently published to an MQTT broker. To collect the published data efficiently, a service named *drone-subscriber* was developed. Originally, the intention was to implement the *drone-subscriber* service to leverage the shared subscription feature provided by MQTT, aiming for horizontal scalability as the rate of data generation increases. This approach would enable multiple instances of *drone-subscriber* to share the message load for a single subscription, ensuring that only one instance in the group receives a particular message for a shared topic. The *drone-subscriber* service was thus designed to function as a single instance. Even in this single-instance configuration, the service is optimized to manage data subscription to the MQTT broker and bulk insertion into TimescaleDB in separate threads. The thread responsible for MQTT subscriptions stores the data in a buffer until it reaches a defined size. The second thread then performs bulk insertions of the data objects from the queue. The drone experiments vary based on the parameters provided at the outset. To effectively track each experiment, the database was structured as shown in Fig. 5. One table houses experiment-related data, while the other table stores sensor data published throughout each experiment, referencing the experiment table to establish a clear association between the data and the corresponding experiment. The stored sensor data includes readings of the IMU sensor, GPS sensor, Attitude sensor, and the flight maneuver sent to the drone. The data are stored in JSON format.

The information about the experiments that are conducted is stored in the experiment table. The table below provides more information about the JSON data structure.

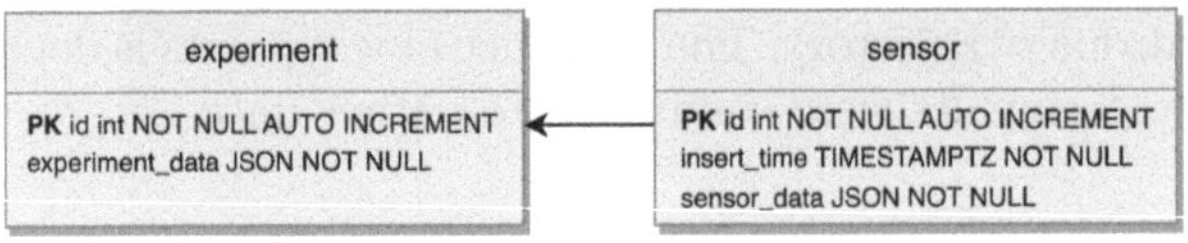

Fig. 5. Structure of the database for storing raw data

4.4 Data Analysis and Feature Engineering

Data analysis and feature engineering are two closely related stages in MLOps that play a crucial role in extracting meaningful insights and creating accurate predictive models from raw data. While data analysis focuses on understanding the characteristics and patterns of data, feature engineering transforms raw data into more meaningful and actionable features that can be effectively utilized by ML algorithms. The data analysis usually serves as the foundation of feature engineering. Based on the acceleration in the x, y, and z directions given by the IMU sensor, the gravity force can be calculated as $\sqrt{xacc^2 + yacc^2 + zacc^2}$.

In our case study, we use three techniques to analyze the data and extract the features that can have an impact on the G-force. These techniques include correlation analysis, visualization, and domain knowledge.

Starting with correlation analysis, the main objective was to identify the relationship between variables to reduce the training data's dimensionality.

The correlation matrix in Fig. 6 provides insights into how the various aspects of the drone's sensor data are related. The analysis reveals significant correlations between key variables in the dataset. Altitude and relative altitude exhibit a perfect positive linear relationship, emphasizing their inherent coherence, as relative altitude is typically derived from the reference point. Yaw speed is strongly correlated with the z-component of angular acceleration `zgyro, roll` and y-axis acceleration **yacc**, highlighting the close association between changes in yaw speed and gyroscopic and acceleration readings. Pitch speed shows notable correlations with gravity force and z-axis acceleration `zacc`, indicating a substantial link between pitch speed variations and gravitational effects. Additionally, the high correlation between the x-component of velocity `vx` and magnetic field strength `xmag` implies a connection between linear velocity in the x-direction and the magnetic field.

We analysed the relationships between the various variables and made some initial observations. When looking at the sensor readings the temperature values seem to increase linearly throughout the flight maneuver. In contrast, other sensor readings show fluctuating and recurring patterns, characteristics that can be captured by neural networks. The evaluation of factors influencing the measurement of gravitational force reveals several key variables. Acceleration in the z-axis (`zacc`) is fundamental, given gravity itself is a form of acceleration, but `zacc` is not part of explanatory variables in the model as the model will serve as the digital twin (DT) of the acceleration sensor. The speed of pitch changes (`pitchspeed`) is another influential factor, especially for drones, which undergo rotational movements. Gyroscopic measurements (`ygyro`), capturing

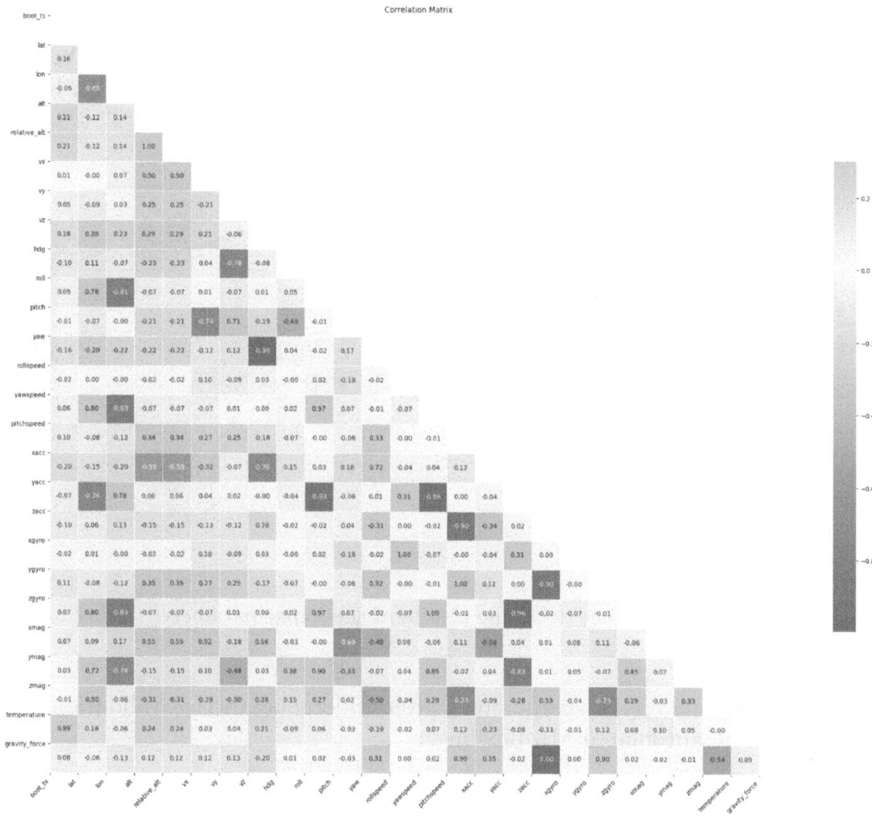

Fig. 6. Correlation Matrix

angular velocity, also play a role, particularly in drone systems with rotational dynamics. Additionally, variables like velocity (`vx`, `vy`, `vz`) can impact gravitational force due to inertia during velocity changes. Magnetic field strength (`xmag`, `ymag`, `zmag`) may indirectly influence gravitational force in systems where magnetic fields interact with charged particles. Object orientation (`roll`, `pitch`, `yaw`) is crucial, affecting both the direction and magnitude of perceived gravity. Furthermore, altitude (`alt`, `relative_alt`) changes directly impact the actual gravitational force.

4.5 Experimentation Phase

The goal of this phase is to train, fine-tune, and evaluate a model for gravitational force prediction tasks based on sensor readings. This involves selecting an appropriate learning algorithm, selecting the model architecture, and optimizing parameters to achieve the highest performance. Following the training, the model is assessed using relevant metrics, and iterations are made to fine-tune its configuration for improved accuracy.

We employed Katib, an integral part of Kubeflow, for hyper-parameter tuning. For details on using Kubeflow and Katib, the reader is referred to the official's documentation [9]. The results of the hyper-parameter tuning with Katib are shown in Fig. 7.

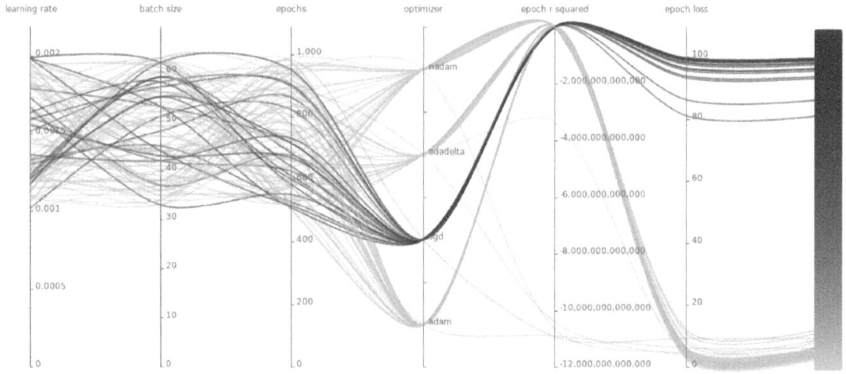

Fig. 7. Katib summary with the results of the hyper-parameter tuning

The optimal set of hyper-parameters, after undergoing further validation, can be passed to the automated ML pipeline.

4.6 Load Testing

To assess the scalability of the DT model serving infrastructure, we conduct a load test on the DT model inference service. This load testing aims to determine the DT's capability to handle real-world conditions through the simulation of concurrent increased inference requests. The key parameters considered include the simulation duration and the request rate (i.e., the number of requests per second). For example, Fig. 8 depicts the latencies of the requests experienced in our experiments when the duration is set to 30 s and request rate is set to 100 per second.

4.7 Automation of the ML Pipeline

The major advantage of an automated ML pipeline is to reduce the manual effort required in various stages of the ML life-cycle, making the process more efficient, reliable, reproducible, and adaptable to changing data and business needs. Kubeflow Pipeline (KFP) was used for automating the ML pipeline in this case study which consists of four crucial steps, depicted in Fig. 9: data preparation, model training and validation, model export, and model deployment.

All ML operations, encompassing data preparation, model training and validation, model export, and model deployment, were encapsulated as lightweight

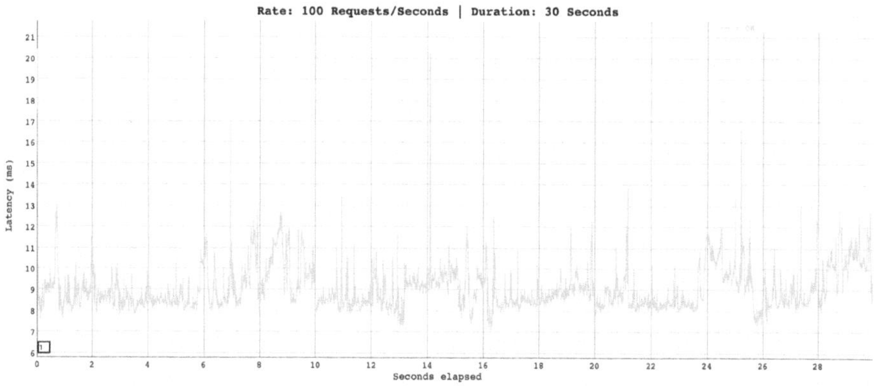

Fig. 8. Results of the load testing of the inference service

Python components. Each component adheres to a standardized structure featuring inputs, well-defined logic within its body, and the potentially generated outputs, commonly referred to as artifacts. Notably, KFP proficiently manages the storage of artifacts in the MinIO[2] object storage. This allows the artifacts produced by a preceding component to seamlessly serve as inputs for the subsequent component in the pipeline, fostering a cohesive and streamlined execution of the entire ML workflow. Notably, the artifact of a component is not the direct representation of the Python object itself; rather, it is a reference to the object stored within the file system or the object storage. The pipeline can dynamically receive a set of parameters encompassing model training and testing, object storage, Postgres connection details, transformer, and predictor configurations. This dynamic approach to passing arguments to the pipeline before each run offers a significant advantage. Coupled with the monitoring component, this strategy empowers the DT model to effectively tackle challenges associated with the dynamic behavior inherent in its physical counterpart. By allowing flexibility in the adjustment of key parameters, the DT can adapt to varying conditions, ensuring a more robust and responsive modeling of the dynamic system it represents.

4.8 Discussion

As seen from the above observations, the adapted MLOps has been successfully applied to data-driven modelling of DTs throughout the life cyle, demonstrating its applicability to not only support data modeling development, deployment but also updating and maintenance. We have also demonstrated the scalability of the DT.

From its initiation phase, MLOps emphasizes a thorough understanding of the business problem, derivation of the ML problem, and making informed design

[2] https://min.io/.

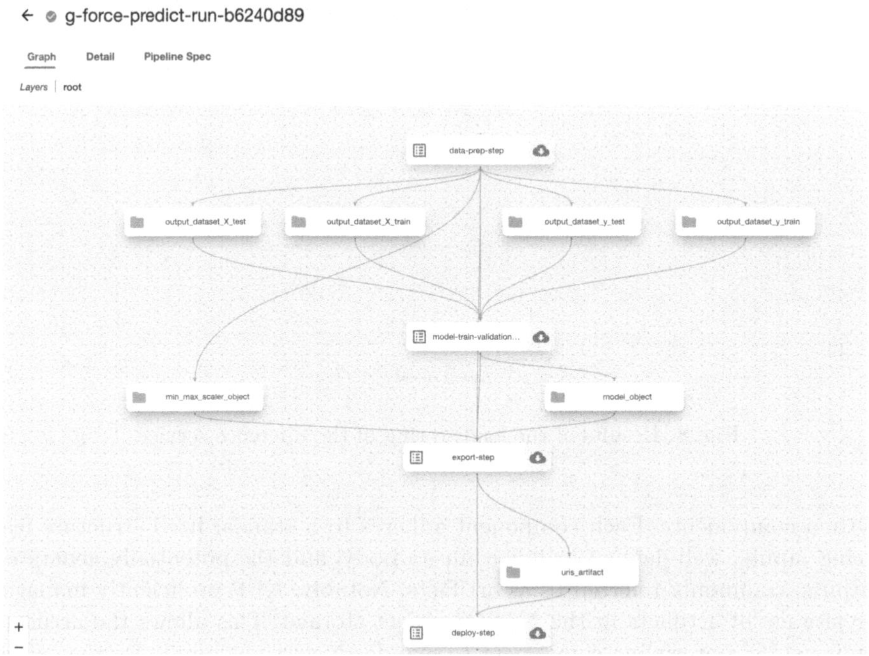

Fig. 9. Direct acyclic graph of the Kubeflow pipeline implemented for this case study

design and technological decisions. These initial steps in MLOps additionally include the critical steps of collecting, exploring, and understanding the data that will be used as the foundational layer for modeling. As the field of MLOps evolves rapidly, choosing the appropriate MLOps platform and tools becomes instrumental in proactively tackling upcoming infrastructural challenges associated with the dynamic nature of data and model requirements.

As a prominent open-source MLOps platform, Kubeflow serves as a cohesive ecosystem that integrates tools for designing, running, automating, and monitoring ML operations at scale, as illustrated by this case study. Additionally, leveraging Kubeflow played an important role in tackling intricacies related to scalability and observability of the DT model or model inference service. The utilization of Katib, one of the most important components of Kubeflow, facilitated the discovery of optimal hyper-parameters for the DT model, thereby enhancing its accuracy.

The MLOps framework presented in Fig. 2 provides a good basis for how data-driven DTs can be conceptualized, experienced, and then productionalized. It is noticeable that this framework additionally promotes collaboration between experts of diverse fields, such as data scientists, and data engineers.

5 Conclusions and Future Work

In this paper, we proposed a new framework based on MLOps to guide the development and operation of data-driven DT. After an exploration of relevant literature to find out common challenges and requirements for digital twinning and state-of-the-art architectural considerations of MLOps, we conducted a case study of a DT for a drone accelerometer aligning with principles promoted by MLOps. Leveraging Kubeflow as the MLOps platform, the study case showcased how MLOps workflow increases the effectiveness and efficiency of the data-driven digital twinning process and how the application of MLOps principles and practices help mitigate the challenges related to scalability, fidelity, and adaptability of the DT model.

Looking ahead, this study emphasizes the significance of a standardized framework, particularly MLOps, in guiding the creation and management of data-driven DTs during their entire life cycle. The recommendations derived from this study encourage practitioners and organizations to consider MLOps as an essential component in the dynamic landscape of digital twinning. The rapid evolution of platforms and tools in the MLOps landscape offers promising opportunities for the future, facilitating a more informed and efficient selection of solutions suitable for specific challenges, thus contributing to continuous improvement and innovation in the field of digital twinning.

Acknowledgement. This research was funded by the German Federal Ministry for Economic Affairs and Climate Action (BMWK) under project number 20A2103E (MuStHaF).

References

1. Apollo 13: The first digital twin (2020). https://blogs.sw.siemens.com/simcenter/apollo-13-the-first-digital-twin/
2. Aydemir, H., Zengin, U., Durak, U., Hartmann, S.: Designing a virtual iron bird as a digital twin. In: AIAA Scitech Forum, pp. 0239.1–11 (2021). https://doi.org/10.2514/6.2021-0239
3. Aydemir, H., Zengin, U., Kruschinski, D., Hartmann, S., Durak, U.: Developing a virtual actuator as a digital twin. In: AIAA Aviation Forum, pp. 3629.1–11 (2022). https://doi.org/10.2514/6.2022-3629
4. George, J., Saha, A.: End-to-end machine learning using kubeflow. In: Joint International Conference on Data Science & Management of Data (ACM IKDD CODS and COMAD), pp. 336–338 (2022)
5. Grieves, M., Vickers, J.: Digital twin: mitigating unpredictable, undesirable emergent behavior in complex systems. In: Kahlen, F.-J., Flumerfelt, S., Alves, A. (eds.) Transdisciplinary Perspectives on Complex Systems, pp. 85–113. Springer, Cham (2017). https://doi.org/10.1007/978-3-319-38756-7_4
6. He, R., Dong, C., Chen, G., Sun, S., Shen, X.: Data-driven digital twin technology for optimized control in process systems. ISA Trans. **95**, 221–234 (2019)
7. Izacard, G., Mohan, S., Fernandez-Granda, C.: Data-driven estimation of sinusoid frequencies. In: Conference on Neural Information Processing Systems (NeurIPS) (2019)

8. Kreuzberger, D., Kühl, N., Hirschl, S.: Machine learning operations (mlops): overview, definition, and architecture. IEEE Access **11**, 31866–31879 (2023). https://doi.org/10.1109/ACCESS.2023.3262138
9. Kubeflow: The machine learning toolkit for kubernetes. https://www.kubeflow.org/
10. Liu, M., Fang, S., Dong, H., Xu, C.: Review of digital twin about concepts, technologies, and industrial applications. J. Manuf. Syst. **58**, 346–361 (2021)
11. SAE-Aerospace: Description of systems integration test rigs (iron birds) for aerospace application (AIR 5992) (2023). https://www.sae.org/standards/content/air5992/
12. Thelen, A., et al.: A comprehensive review of digital twin—part 1: modeling and twinning enabling technologies. Struct. Multidisc. Optim. **65**, 354ff (2022)

Empirical Study on the Use of Artificial General Intelligence Healthcare in the Elderly (Invited Paper)

Seungho Seo and Jintaek Jung(✉)

Hansung University, 116 Samseon-dong 2-ga, Samseongyo-ro 16-gil, Seongbuk-gu, Seoul 02876, South Korea
shseo@vtex.co.kr, jungjt@hansung.ac.kr

Abstract. This paper explores the potential use of artificial intelligence (AI) and AI-based healthcare systems for the elderly and empirically analyzes the impact of these technologies on the daily life satisfaction of elderly individuals. Recent advancements in Artificial General Intelligence (AGI) have opened up innovative possibilities in the healthcare sector, particularly in systems that monitor and support the health conditions of elderly individuals, providing personalized health management and daily life assistance. This study utilized data from the '2023 Digital Divide Survey' collected by the National Information Society Agency of Korea, analyzing the impact of the degree of AI usage assistance on the daily life satisfaction of 2,300 elderly individuals aged 55 and older. The results showed that the degree of AI usage assistance had a significant positive impact on daily life satisfaction, while education level and monthly household income also had positive effects. Conversely, age had a negative impact. This study suggests that AGI technology can play a crucial role in enhancing the quality of life for the elderly, emphasizing the need for policy support to facilitate this.

Keywords: Artificial General Intelligence · Elderly Healthcare · Digital Divide

1 Introduction

Over the past decade, the rapid advancement of artificial intelligence (AI) has led to significant breakthroughs in various fields such as healthcare, finance, and natural language processing. Particularly, Artificial General Intelligence (AGI), which possesses cognitive abilities similar to humans and can adapt to various tasks and situations, has emerged as an innovative concept. Unlike narrow AI, which is optimized for specific tasks, AGI mimics the broad and adaptive intelligence of humans. Although the concept of AGI is not new, recent developments in machine learning and neural networks have brought this vision closer to reality. Bahdanau, Cho, and Bengio (2014) proposed a new approach that jointly learns to align and translate by creating a translation system, demonstrating the potential for AI systems to perform complex language processing tasks [1]. Oord et al. (2016) introduced Wavenet, a model capable of generating raw audio, showcasing AI's

This research is supported by the academic funding at Hansung University.

M. Saeki et al. (Eds.): ER 2024 Workshops, LNCS 14932, pp. 87–98, 2025.
https://doi.org/10.1007/978-3-031-75599-6_6

ability to produce highly realistic audio [2]. The research by Radford, Jozefowicz, and Sutskever (2017) made progress in training AI to understand and generate text similar to human language [3]. Following this, Radford et al. (2018) conducted research on improving language comprehension through generative pre-training, significantly enhancing AI systems' ability to understand and generate coherent text [4]. Recently, Ouyang et al. (2022) demonstrated a crucial step towards developing AGI systems that can adapt to new tasks with minimal supervision by training language models with human feedback [5].

AGI healthcare for the elderly involves using AGI to monitor the health conditions of seniors, support diagnosis, and provide personalized health care and daily living assistance. The goal is to enhance the health management and welfare of the elderly [6, 7]. The transition to an aging society is becoming a significant social issue worldwide, emphasizing the need for improved health care and welfare for seniors. AGI has opened up various possibilities in elderly health management [6]. However, there are several challenges in the practical application of AGI in healthcare. Seniors may face cognitive, physical, and psychological barriers in adopting new technologies, necessitating research to overcome these barriers. Additionally, thorough examination of the safety and ethical issues related to AGI systems is required.

Therefore, this paper aims to explore the potential of AGI healthcare in promoting independent living and empirically evaluate its application. Through this, we hope to present the applicability of AGI technology in the field of elderly healthcare and provide important implications for future research and practice.

2 Literature Review

2.1 AGI-Based Independent Living Services for the Elderly

Supporting independent living for the elderly in an aging society is a critical issue. AI technology can play a significant role in maintaining the independence of the elderly and improving their quality of life. Various studies have suggested ways in which AI and robotic technology can promote independent living for the elderly. In the study by Padhan et al. (2023), the ways in which AI and robots enhance the independence and quality of life of the elderly were explored. It concluded that AI and robotic technologies significantly support daily living activities, ensure safety, and reduce social isolation for the elderly [8]. O'Connor's (2022) study indicated that AI technology could contribute to improving elderly care practices and found that AI is useful in monitoring the health status of the elderly and providing personalized care services [9]. Bizjak et al. (2018) explored the potential of intelligent assistive systems for the elderly and confirmed that these systems are effective in aiding daily living and enhancing autonomy [10]. Iqbal (2023) reviewed various AI tools that are useful in supporting the health care and independent living of the elderly [11]. Koç's (2023) study showed that AI plays a crucial role in maintaining independent living by real-time monitoring of the health status of the elderly and providing necessary support[12].

AI-based smart homes support the independence of the elderly in the following ways:

- **Automation of Daily Tasks**: Smart lighting systems, smart thermostats, and other devices automate routine tasks [13, 14].

- **Health Monitoring and Safety**: Wearable devices and fall detection sensors monitor health indicators and provide alerts in case of incidents [13, 16, 17].
- **Personalized Support**: AI-based personal assistants help with daily tasks, medication reminders, appointment scheduling, and more [15–17].
- **Cognitive Support**: AI applications offer memory enhancement and cognitive stimulation [16, 18].
- **Enhanced Mobility**: Mobility solutions like self-driving cars provide safe and accessible transportation options [13, 16].
- **Social Engagement**: Online platforms and virtual events promote social participation [13, 17].
- **Customized Living Environment**: Smart home systems adjust lighting and other settings according to individual preferences [15, 17].

In summary, AI-based smart homes significantly enhance the independence of the elderly, supporting autonomous and comfortable living and ultimately improving their overall quality of life.

2.2 AGI-Based Independent Living Services for the Elderly

In an aging society, the importance of smart home technology is increasing to ensure the health and safety of the elderly and to support independent living. Particularly, advancements in artificial intelligence technology are bringing significant changes to smart home systems. AGI (Artificial General Intelligence)-based smart home technology plays a crucial role in enhancing the quality of life for the elderly and maintaining independent living.

Rong et al. (2022) explored the design of AI-based healthcare products for elderly families, confirming that these products can enhance the convenience and safety of the elderly. This demonstrates the potential for effectively supporting elderly health management and safety in smart home environments [19]. O'Connor (2022) discussed how AI technology can improve elderly care practices, emphasizing that AI can support independent living by monitoring the health status of the elderly in real-time and providing personalized healthcare services [9]. Dilip et al. (2022) investigated how AI-based smart companion robots can be utilized in elderly healthcare and rescue systems, showing that smart robots can continuously monitor the health conditions of the elderly and respond quickly in emergency situations [20].

AGI-based smart homes can assist the daily lives of the elderly in various ways. The smart home services that can enhance the daily life of the elderly are as follows (Table 1).

By integrating these AI-based technologies, smart homes can significantly improve the ability of the elderly to perform daily activities independently, enhance safety, and maintain a higher quality of life while aging in place.

2.3 Smart Home Application Services for Promoting Independent Living for the Elderly

One of the most popular smart home application services for the elderly is the AI-based personal assistant. AI-based personal assistants offer several key benefits, as shown in Table 2, enhancing the independence, safety, and quality of life for the elderly.

Table 1. Smart Home Services to Enhance the Daily Life of the Elderly.

Smart Home Service	Description
Automation of Daily Tasks	Controlling lights, temperature, and appliances through voice commands or preset schedules. Adjusting lighting and temperature settings according to personal preferences and routines [17, 18]
Medication Management	Reminders to take medication at appropriate times. Notifying caregivers if medication is missed [17, 18]
Health and Safety Monitoring	Wearable devices and sensors track vital signs and detect abnormalities, providing real-time alerts to caregivers or medical professionals. Fall detection sensors identify accidents and automatically request assistance. Smart cameras with facial recognition enhance home security [17, 18]
Cognitive Support	AI applications provide memory prompts and reminders for daily activities. Virtual assistants schedule appointments and manage tasks [19]
Enhanced Mobility	AI-based mobility aids, such as smart walking assistants, help maintain balance and prevent falls. Autonomous vehicles equipped with AI provide safe transportation options for the elderly [13, 18]
Social Engagement	AI-based platforms connect the elderly with peers who share similar interests, recommending activities and strengthening social connections [17]
Personalized Living Environment	Smart home systems offer comfortable and customized living spaces tailored to the daily routines and preferences of the elderly [17, 18]

The most popular AI-based personal assistants for the elderly include:

- Whisper: An automatic speech recognition system that can convert audio to text [23].
- DBRX Instruct: An AI model that follows instructions [24].
- ChatDoctor: An interactive AI system focused on medical topics [25].

A comparison of these three AI-based personal assistant services is shown in Table 3.

The analysis concluded that Whisper is the most suitable AI-based personal assistant service for the elderly for the following reasons:

- **Speech Recognition Feature**: Whisper's ability to convert speech to text is very useful in situations where using a keyboard is challenging.
- **Various Functions**: Whisper offers multiple functions, including an AI chatbot, writing prompts, and image generation, supporting information retrieval, schedule management, and simple writing tasks.
- **Personalized Recommendations**: Whisper learns from the user's previous behaviors and preferences to provide customized services.

Table 2. Benefits of AI-based Personal Assistants

AI Personal Assistant Service	Description
Enhanced	AI assistants support daily tasks, reminders, access to information and entertainment, helping the elderly maintain autonomy [22]
Independence	They monitor the home environment, detect emergencies, and alert caregivers or emergency services, ensuring the safety of the elderly [22]
Improved Safety	AI assistants provide timely medication reminders, helping to adhere to prescribed therapies and prevent missed doses or errors [22]
Cognitive Support	AI assistants offer reminders for daily activities, appointments, and medication schedules, providing valuable cognitive support for those with memory difficulties [21]
Streamlined Communication	Voice-activated assistance makes it easier for the elderly to make phone calls, send messages, and engage in video chats, strengthening social connections [22]
Health Monitoring	Integrated with wearable devices, they track vital signs and detect anomalies, offering early warnings of potential health issues [21]
Personalized Care	They learn individual preferences and provide personalized recommendations for health care, nutrition, and lifestyle choices [21]
Ease of Use	Voice control interfaces make it easier for the elderly to interact with technology, overcoming potential barriers associated with touchscreens or complex controls [22]
Peace of Mind for Caregivers	AI assistants provide continuous support and monitoring, reducing caregiver burden and offering peace of mind [21]

- **Voice Output Function**: Whisper includes a text-to-speech feature, making information easily accessible for those with visual limitations.
- **Usage Patterns**: Whisper's conversational security technology makes it easy for the general public to use.

Due to these features, Whisper was evaluated as the most suitable service to support the independence of the elderly and reduce barriers to using digital devices.

3 Research Design

3.1 Research Hypothesis

Based on the review of existing literature, this study aims to examine the impact of the degree of AI usage assistance on the daily life satisfaction of the elderly by setting the following hypothesis.

Table 3. Comparison of AI-based Personal Assistant Services

Service Name	Main Features	Specialization	Input Type	Output Type	Use Cases
Whisper	Speech recognition and transcription	Audio processing	Voice	Text	Voice commands, communication log creation
DBRX Instruct	Instruction-following AI model	Performing various AI inferences	Text	Text	Performing various tasks
ChatDoctor	Multi-domain specialized interactive AI	Medical information and consultation	Text	Text	Medical consultation, information provision

H1: The degree of AI usage assistance for the elderly will affect their daily life satisfaction.

3.2 Research Model

To analyze the impact of the degree of AI usage assistance on the daily life satisfaction of the elderly, this study established a research model as shown in Fig. 1. Daily life satisfaction was set as the dependent variable, while the degree of AI usage assistance was set as the independent variable. The control variables were gender, age, educational background, and monthly household income.

Fig. 1. Research model

3.3 Data Collection Method

To verify the research model, this study utilized data from the '2023 Digital Divide Survey' collected by the National Information Society Agency of Korea[26]. The survey targeted citizens aged 7 and older nationwide, and additional data were collected for vulnerable groups such as the elderly, disabled, low-income individuals, farmers and fishermen, North Korean defectors, and marriage immigrants. The Digital Divide Survey is an annual time-series survey used as basic data to review the performance of policies aimed at bridging the digital divide in Korea and to derive improvement plans for enhancing the effectiveness of future related policies. The sample was extracted through stratified proportional sampling by metropolitan municipalities, and data were collected through one-on-one structured interviews. For this study, 2,300 elderly individuals aged 55 and older from the 2023 Digital Divide Survey targeting the general public were selected.

4 Empirical Study

4.1 Characteristics of the Sample

Before analyzing the reliability and validity of this study, a frequency analysis was conducted to examine the demographic characteristics of the survey respondents. The results are shown in Table 4. Among the respondents, there were 1,073 males and 1,027 females. In terms of education level, 352 had an elementary or middle school education or less, 537 were middle school graduates, 1,104 were high school graduates, and 308 were college graduates. Regarding monthly household income, the largest group consisted of those with an income of less than 3 million KRW, with 1,082 respondents falling into this category.

Table 4. Demographic and Sociological Characteristics of Research Subjects.

Division	Item	Frequency	Ratio (%)
Gender	Male	1,073	46.7
	Female	1,227	53.3
Age	the elderly in their 50s	525	22.8
	the elderly in their 60s	972	42.3
	the elderly in their 70s	803	34.9
Educational background	Undergraduates of elementary school	352	15.3
	Middle school graduation	537	23.3
	High school graduation	1,104	48.0
	College graduate or higher	308	13.4
Monthly household income	less than 2.99 million won	1082	47.0
	3 million won to 5.99 million won	972	42.3
	more than 6 million won	248	10.7
SUM	2,300	100/0	

4.2 Key Variables Descriptive Statistics

The descriptive statistics for the key variables are shown in Table 5. The dependent variable, daily life satisfaction, had a mean of 21.18 (SD = 3.56). The degree of AI usage assistance, which affects daily life satisfaction, had a mean of 24.83 (SD = 6.85).

Table 5. Key variable descriptive statistics

Variable	N	Minimum	Maximum	Mean	Std. Deviation
Daily life satisfaction	2300	8	32	21.18	3.56
The degree of help in using AI	2300	10	40	24.83	6.85
Gender	2300	1	4	2.17	.83
Age	2300	1	2	1.54	.49
Educational background	2300	1	4	2.56	.92
Monthly household income	2300	1	1	1.63	.66

4.3 Validity and Reliability Analysis

Table 6 shows the correlation coefficients between key variables related to the degree of AI usage assistance and daily life satisfaction of the elderly. The variables include daily life satisfaction, degree of AI usage assistance, gender, age, educational background, and monthly household income.

Table 6. Key variable descriptive statistics

Variable	Daily life satisfaction	The degree of help in using AI	Gender	Age	Educational background	Monthly household income
Daily life satisfaction	1					
The degree of help in using AI	.254**	1				
Gender	−.067**	−.068**	1			
Age	−.262**	−.273**	.066**	1		
Educational background	.326**	.317**	−.176**	−.573**	1	
Monthly household income	.305**	.246**	−.037	−.467**	.514**	1

* p<.05, ** p<01,*** p<.001

Daily life satisfaction showed a positive correlation with the degree of AI usage assistance (.254**), educational background (.326**), and monthly household income (.305**).

It showed a negative correlation with age (−.262**).

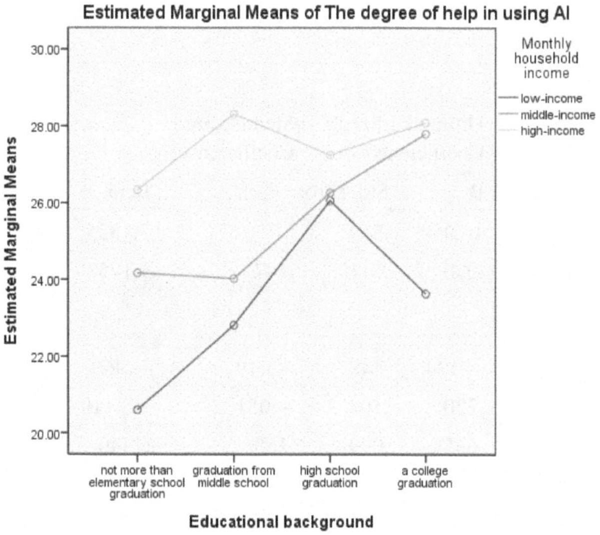

Fig. 2. Analysis of variance for the degree of AI usage assistance, educational background, and monthly household income

Figure 2 visually shows how the degree of AI usage assistance is distributed according to various levels of educational background and monthly household income. It can be concluded that the higher the educational background and monthly household income, the more assistance is received from AI usage. This indicates that while AI technology is effective in improving the daily lives of the elderly, these benefits may be unevenly distributed based on education and income levels. Therefore, it suggests the need for policies and education to increase accessibility so that all elderly individuals can equally benefit from AI technology.

5 Empirical Results

5.1 The Impact of the Degree of AI Usage Assistance on Daily Life Satisfaction of the Elderly

Table 7 presents the results of a regression analysis with daily life satisfaction set as the dependent variable, and the degree of AI usage assistance, gender, age, educational background, and monthly household income set as independent variables.

- These results indicate that the degree of AI usage assistance has a significantly positive impact on daily life satisfaction. The more AI is utilized, the higher the daily life satisfaction (Beta = .147, t = 7.175, p = .000).
- Age has a significantly negative impact on daily life satisfaction. The older the individual, the lower the daily life satisfaction tends to be (Beta = –-.051, t = –-2.119, p = .034).

Table 7. Demographic and Sociological Characteristics of Research Subjects.

Coefficients								
Model		Unstandardized Coefficients		Standardized Coefficients		t	P	F
		B	Std. Error		Beta			
Daily life satisfaction	(Constant)	16,950	.559		30.325	.000	83.848	.153
	The degree of help in using AI	.076	.011	.147	7.175	.000		
	Gender	−.134	.140	−.019	−.960	.337		
	Age	.220	.104	−.051	−2.119	.034		
	Educational background	.635	.099	.165	6.440	.000		
	Monthly household income	.851	.124	.159	6.875	.000		

p*<.05, **p<01,***p<.001.

- Educational background has a significantly positive impact on daily life satisfaction. The higher the educational background, the higher the daily life satisfaction tends to be (Beta = .165, t = 6.440, p = .000).
- Monthly household income has a significantly positive impact on daily life satisfaction. The higher the income, the higher the daily life satisfaction tends to be (Beta = .159, t = 6.875, p = .000).

In conclusion, the degree of AI usage assistance plays an important role in enhancing the daily life satisfaction of the elderly. While age has a negative impact, educational background and monthly household income have positive impacts. These analysis results suggest that AI technology can be a crucial tool for improving the daily life satisfaction of the elderly, especially for those with higher education and income levels.

6 Conclusion

6.1 Summary of Research Findings

This study investigated the impact of the degree of AI usage assistance on the daily life satisfaction of the elderly. The study analyzed a total of 2,300 elderly individuals, examining their gender, age, educational background, and monthly household income. The main findings are as follows:

- Daily life satisfaction showed a positive correlation with the degree of AI usage assistance. The more AI was utilized, the higher the daily life satisfaction of the elderly tended to be.

- Educational background and monthly household income also positively affected daily life satisfaction, whereas age had a negative impact.
- The results indicated that the higher the educational background and monthly household income, the more assistance was received from AI usage. This suggests that the benefits of AI technology may be unevenly distributed based on education and income levels.

6.2 Policy Implications

The results of this study suggest the following policy implications:

- Policies are needed to increase accessibility so that all elderly individuals can equally benefit from AI technology. For example, support measures such as reducing the cost of smart home technology and providing subsidies are necessary.
- Educational programs should be provided to help the elderly easily understand and utilize AI technology. Customized education for the elderly with lower educational levels is particularly needed.
- A comprehensive support system considering the age, education, and income levels of the elderly should be established to ensure that all elderly individuals can equally benefit from AI technology.
- The safety and ethical issues of AI technology should be thoroughly reviewed to create an environment where the elderly can use AI with trust.

This study suggests that AI technology can play a crucial role in enhancing the daily life satisfaction of the elderly, emphasizing the need for policy support to facilitate this.

References

1. Bahdanau, D., Cho, K., Bengio, Y.: Neural machine translation by jointly learning to align and translate. arXiv preprint arXiv:1409.0473 (2014)
2. van den Oord, A.: Wavenet: a generative model for raw audio. arXiv preprint arXiv:1609.03499 (2016)
3. Radford, A., Jozefowicz, R., Sutskever, I.: Learning to generate reviews and discovering sentiment. arXiv preprint arXiv:1704.01444 (2017)
4. Radford, A., Narasimhan, K.: Improving language understanding by generative pre-training (2018)
5. Ouyang, L.: Training language models to follow instructions with human feedback. Adv. Neural. Inf. Process. Syst. **35**, 27730–27744 (2022)
6. Paiva, J.O.: Mobile applications for elderly healthcare: a systematic mapping. PLoS ONE **15**(7), e0236091 (2020)
7. Tun, S.Y.Y., Madanian, S., Mirza, F.: Internet of things (IoT) applications for elderly care: a reflective review. Aging Clin. Exp. Res. **33**(4), 855–867 (2021). https://doi.org/10.1007/s40520-020-01545-9
8. Padhan, S.: Artificial Intelligence (AI) and robotics in elderly healthcare: enabling independence and quality of life. Cureus **15** (2023)
9. O'Connor, S.: Artificial intelligence for older adult health: opportunities for advancing gerontological nursing practice. J. Gerontol. Nurs. **48**(12), 3–5 (2022)
10. Bizjak, J., Gradišek, A., Gams, M.: Intelligent assistant for elderly. In: International Joint Conference on Artificial Intelligence (2018)

11. Iqbal, S., Iqbal, S.: Artificial Intelligence tools and applications for elderly healthcare - review. In: Proceedings of the 2023 9th International Conference on Computing and Artificial Intelligence (2023)
12. Koç, M.: Artificial intelligence in geriatrics. Turk. J. Geriat. **26**, 352–360 (2023)
13. Powell, M.: Artificial Intelligence Helps Meet the Changing Needs of the Aging Population. Provider Magazine, Articles (2023)
14. Huggingface: MagicAnimate. https://huggingface.co/spaces/zcxu-eric/magicanimate. Accessed 20 July 2024
15. Aging with Dignity: How AI Can Support Independence and Autonomy
16. How AI Technology Can Improve the Lives of the Elderly. https://www.seniorhelpers.ca/resources/blogs/how-ai-technology-can-improve-the-lives-of-the-elderly/. Accessed 20 July 2024
17. Ethical AI: Enriching The Lives Of Seniors Through Independent Living. https://www.forbes.com/sites/forbestechcouncil/2023/09/25/ethical-ai-enriching-the-lives-of-seniors-through-independent-living/. Accessed 20 July 2024
18. Sahota, N.: AI: A Beacon Of Hope In Elder Care. Forbe (2023). https://www.forbes.com/sites/neilsahota/2024/04/23/ai-a-beacon-of-hope-in-elder-care/. Accessed 20 July 2024
19. Rong, J.: Research on material design of medical products for elderly families based on artificial intelligence. Appl. Bionics Biomech. **2022** (2022)
20. Dilip, G.: Artificial intelligence-based smart comrade robot for elders healthcare with strait rescue system. J. Healthc. Eng. **2022** (2022)
21. AI Assistant for the Elderly: Empowering Independence and Enhancing Quality of Life. Scholarly (2023). https://scholarly.so/blog/ai-assistant-for-the-elderly-empowering-independence-and-enhancing-quality-of-life. Accessed 20 July 2024
22. Bradley-Cobb, H.: Benefits of AI-powered voice assistant for aging adults. https://randolph.ces.ncsu.edu/2024/03/ai-voice-assistant-aging-adults/. Accessed 20 July 2024
23. Huggingface: Whisper. https://huggingface.co/spaces?sort=trending&search=Whisper. Accessed 20 July 2024
24. Huggingface: DBRX Instruct. https://huggingface.co/spaces?sort=trending&search=DBRX+Instruct. Accessed 20 July 2024
25. Huggingface: ChatDoctor. https://huggingface.co/spaces?sort=trending&search=ChatDoctor. Accessed 20 July 2024
26. National Information Society Agency, 2023 The Report on the Digital Divide. National Information Society Agency (2024). https://www.nia.or.kr/site/nia_kor/ex/bbs/View.do?cbIdx=81623&bcIdx=26517&parentSeq=26517

Effects of Perceived Ease of Use and Perceived Usefulness of Technology Acceptance Model on Intention to Continue Using Generative AI: Focusing on the Mediating Effect of Satisfaction and Moderating Effect of Innovation Resistance

Sarang Jeong, Sihoo Kim, and Seunghee Lee(✉)

Kumoh National Institute of Technology, 61, Daehak-ro, Gumi-si, Gyeongsangbuk-do, South Korea
{sarang,marketing}@kumoh.ac.kr, kimshlife@naver.com

Abstract. This study analyzed whether perceived ease of use and perceived usefulness influence the intention to continue using generative AI based on the Technology Acceptance Model (TAM). Furthermore, this study analyzed whether user satisfaction has a mediating effect between perceived ease and usefulness and continuance use intention and whether innovation resistance has a moderating effect between perceived ease and usefulness and continuance use intention and between satisfaction and continuance use intention. Using a survey of 281 generative AI users, we found that perceived usefulness has a positive effect on intention to continue using AI. Furthermore, user satisfaction mediated this relationship, and innovation resistance had a negative moderating effect. These results suggest strategic measures to promote the acceptance of AI technologies, and future research should further analyze the factors of technical proficiency and innovation resistance.

Keywords: Generative AI · Technology Acceptance Model · User Satisfaction · Innovation Resistance · Intention to Continue Using

1 Introduction

In recent years, the development of artificial intelligence (AI) technology has been rapidly progressing, and generative AI is leading a revolutionary change in various industries. Generative AI has the ability to generate data in various forms, such as text, images, and voice, and is being utilized in various applications such as content creation, customer service, and data analysis. These advances in AI technology are creating new opportunities for individuals and organizations alike, but they also pose a variety of challenges to user acceptance of the technology. The Technology Acceptance Model (TAM) is a widely used theoretical tool to explain the process of user adoption of new technologies. The TAM suggests that users' intention

M. Saeki et al. (Eds.): ER 2024 Workshops, LNCS 14932, pp. 99–106, 2025.
https://doi.org/10.1007/978-3-031-75599-6_7

to adopt a technology is primarily determined by its perceived ease of use and usefulness. However, in the case of advanced technologies such as generative AI, mere perceived ease of use and usefulness are not sufficient explanations for user acceptance intention. The purpose of this study was to examine the intention to continue using generative AI by adding the mediating effect of user satisfaction and the moderating effect of innovation resistance to the perceived ease of use and usefulness based on the Technology Acceptance Model (TAM). In other words, we analyzed the effect of perceived ease of use and usefulness on the intention to continue using generative AI, explored the mediating effect of user satisfaction, and analyzed how innovation resistance moderates this relationship. By doing so, we aim to explore strategic measures to promote the continuous use of generative AI and provide practical implications for technology development and user education.

2 Literature Review

2.1 Generative AI

Generative AI is a technology that generates similar or new outputs based on pre-trained data, and the outputs include text, images, video, audio, and code [1]. Generative AI differs from existing technologies in that it actively generates responses in response to user needs [2]. It has great potential because it can be used across a wide range of industries, including language, images, and speech [3]. It is only with the advent of ChatGPT that the technology has grown in influence to the point where it is generative rather than discriminative in categorizing and understanding text [4]. ChatGPT can be used for a variety of purposes, including entertainment, educational tools, technical support, and counseling, but the technology is not yet perfect and can sometimes produce unexpected results or fail to fully understand certain contexts [3].

2.2 Perceived Usefulness

According to the Technology Acceptance Model (TAM), the perceived usefulness of generative AI is that it enhances the learning experience by generating new outputs in response to learners' input prompts [5]. Furthermore, learners find it very useful for experimentation, practice, and problem-based learning because it allows them to solve more complex problems [6]. In addition, it is a very useful educational tool because it has many benefits for education and research, such as improving equity of access to information, facilitating personalized learning, improving critical thinking skills, and developing AI literacy [7].

2.3 Perceived Ease of Use

Perceived ease of use and perceived usefulness are important antecedents of the technology acceptance model (TAM) and have a significant impact on customers' behavioral intention to use the new technology [8].

2.4 Continuous Use Intention

Continuance intention is defined as a user's intention to continue to use a particular system after the first time they try it, or the intention to continue to use the service as a form of loyalty to the service provider [9]. Continuance usage intention is defined as a deep commitment to repurchase or reuse a product or service in the future, which results in a willingness to reuse the product or service in an attempt to switch [10]. In the Information Systems Success Model (IS Success Model), it was argued that user satisfaction has a significant impact on the success of using a system and the intention to continue using it [11]. The Technology Acceptance Model (TAM) explained that user satisfaction plays an important role in technology acceptance and intention to continue using.

2.5 User Satisfaction

When users perceive a technology as useful and easy to use, they are more likely to be satisfied, which leads to their intention to continue using it [12]. They argued that the response diversity and contextual understanding of ChatGPT, a generative AI, have a significant impact on user satisfaction and proposed an algorithmic approach to improve these factors [13]. ChatGPT user satisfaction is influenced by the system's usability, response accuracy, and response time [10].

2.6 Moderating Effect of Innovation Resistance

Innovation resistance can be defined as 'the behavior of consumers to maintain the previous status quo against the changes imposed by innovation in the process of accepting a new product, and the decision of consumers to continue to stick with the existing product or not to accept the innovative product in response to the change' [14]. Innovation Resistance Theory was proposed to criticize the fact that much of the existing research on innovation has focused on diffusion and adoption [15].

3 Research Methodology

Based on the Technology Acceptance Model (TAM), this study systematically analyzed the main factors affecting the intention to continue using generative AI through the mediating effect of user satisfaction and the moderating effect of innovation resistance.

3.1 Research Model

(See Fig. 1).

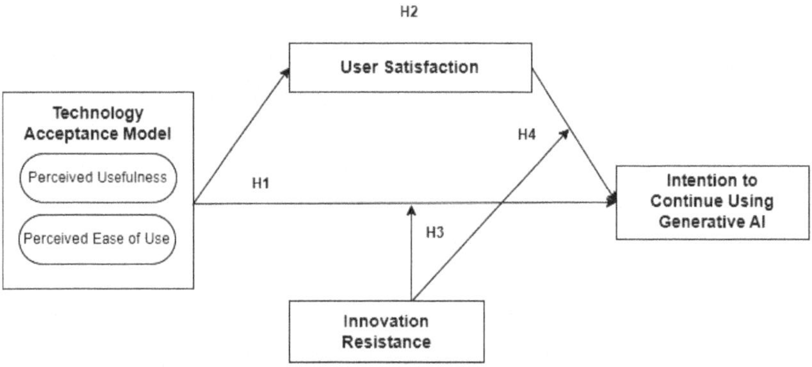

Fig. 1. Research model

3.2 Research Hypothesis

H1: Perceived ease of use (technology acceptance model) will have a positive effect on intention to continue using generative AI.

H1-1: Perceived ease of use will have a positive effect on intention to continue using generative AI.

H1-2: Perceived usefulness will have a positive effect on intention to continue using generative AI.

H2: User satisfaction will mediate the relationship between technology acceptance model and intention to continue using generative AI.

H2-1: User satisfaction will mediate the relationship between perceived ease of use and intention to continue using generative AI.

H2-2: User satisfaction will mediate the relationship between perceived usefulness and intention to continue using generative AI.

H3: Innovation resistance will moderate the relationship between technology acceptance model and intention to continue using generative AI.

H3-1: Innovation resistance will moderate the relationship between perceived ease of use and intention to continue using generative AI.

H3-2: Innovation resistance will moderate the relationship between perceived usefulness and intention to continue using generative AI.

H4: Innovation resistance will moderate the relationship between user satisfaction and intention to continue using generative AI.

3.3 Data Collection and Analysis Method

This study collected data through a questionnaire survey and analyzed the relationship between variables using multiple regression analysis, mediation effect regression analysis, and moderation effect regression analysis. The study population is limited to users who have experience with generative AI technology, and the sample was organized by considering their demographic characteristics. The questionnaire and items are composed of items that measure the perceived ease and usefulness of technology acceptance model, user satisfaction, innovation resistance, and intention to continue using generative AI. To test the validity of the variable measures used in this study, the KMO (kaiser meyer olkin) test was performed in the confirmatory factor analysis using SPSS V29, and all of them were above 0.6, and the Cronbach-α value was above 0.883 in the reliability test, which ensured internal consistency among the measurement items. The goodness of fit of the research model is also good because the modified R^2 = .531, F value is 106.523, P value is less than 0.05, and Durbin-watson's statistic is more than 2, so the research model is suitable.

4 Results

4.1 Testing Hypothesis 1: The Effect of Perceived Ease of Use and Usability on Intention to Continue Using Generative AI

Hypothesis 1-1: Ease of use will have a positive effect on the intention to continue using generative AI. The regression analysis showed that the independent variables explained 44.2% of the dependent variable with R^2 = .442. The effect of Perceived Ease of Use on Intention to Continue Using Generative AI is not statistically significant ($\beta = 0.015$, $t = 0.785$, $p > 0.05$). This result suggests that users' perception that using a generative AI tool does not require much effort does not increase their intention to continue using it. Therefore, Hypothesis 1-1 is rejected.

Hypothesis 1-2: Perceived usefulness will have a positive effect on the intention to continue using generative AI. On the other hand, Perceived Usefulness was found to have a positive effect on Continuance Intention ($\beta = 0.655$, $t = 14.848$, $p < 0.001$). This indicates that the more users perceive the technology to be beneficial, the more they intend to continue using it. Therefore, hypotheses 1-2 are accepted.

4.2 Testing Hypothesis 2: The Mediating Effect of User Satisfaction

Hypothesis 2-1: Satisfaction will mediate the relationship between perceived ease of use and intention to continue using generative AI. The regression analysis showed a significant mediating effect of satisfaction on the relationship between perceived ease of use and intention to continue using generative AI ($\beta = 0.405$, $t = 7.400$, $p < 0.001$). This suggests that the perceived ease of use of a technology can increase users' satisfaction and influence their intention to continue using it. Therefore, Hy-pothesis 2-1 is accepted.

Hypothesis 2-2: Satisfaction will mediate the relationship between perceived usefulness and intention to continue using generative AI. Satisfaction had a significant mediating effect on the relationship between perceived usefulness and intention to continue using generative AI ($\beta = 0.482$, $t = 7.340$, $p < 0.001$). It can be seen that usability increases user satisfaction, which in turn leads to continuance intention. Therefore, Hypothesis 2-2 is accepted.

4.3 Testing Hypothesis 3: Moderating Effect of Innovation Resistance

Hypothesis 3-1: Innovation resistance will moderate the relationship between perceived ease of use and intention to continue using generative AI. We analyzed whether innovation resistance moderates the relationship between perceived ease of use and intention to continue using generative AI, and found that innovation resistance negatively moderates this relationship ($\beta = -0.451$, $t = -9.329$, $p < 0.001$). In other words, users with higher innovation resistance are less likely to continue using the technology even if they perceive the technology to be easy to use. Therefore, Hypothesis 3-1 is accepted.

Hypothesis 3-2: Innovation resistance will moderate the relationship between perceived usefulness and intention to continue using generative AI. Similarly, innovation resistance had a negative moderating effect on the relationship between perceived usefulness and intention to continue using generative AI ($\beta = -0.314$, $t = -7.707$, $p < 0.001$). This suggests that even if a technology is perceived as useful, users with high innovation resistance are less likely to continue using it. Therefore, Hypothesis 3-2 is also accepted.

4.4 Testing Hypothesis 4: Moderating Effect of Innovation Resistance on Satisfaction and Intention to Continue Using Generative AI

The regression analysis shows that innovation resistance moderates the relationship between satisfaction and intention to continue using generative AI. Higher innovation resistance has a negative moderating effect on the intention to continue using generative AI ($\beta = -.321$, $t = -7.096$, $p < 0.001$). Therefore, Hypothesis 4 is accepted.

4.5 Summary and Interpretation of the Findings

The results of this study show that perceived usefulness of the technology acceptance model has a positive effect on continuance use intention, user satisfaction has a mediating effect on the relationship between perceived ease of use and perceived usefulness of the technology acceptance model and continuance use intention, and innovation resistance has a negative moderating effect on the relationship between perceived ease of use and perceived usefulness of the technology acceptance model and continuance use intention. These findings emphasize that strategies to reduce users' resistance to innovation are necessary for successful adoption of AI technologies.

5 Conclusion

This study analyzed the influence of technology acceptance model (TAM) on the intention to continue using generative AI. The results show that perceived ease of use has no significant effect on the intention to continue using generative AI, while perceived usefulness has a significant effect. User satisfaction mediated this relationship, and perceived ease of use and perceived usefulness were adopted in the intention to continue using generative AI. The moderating effect of innovation resistance on user satisfaction and intention to continue using generative AI was negative, and the moderating effect of perceived ease of use and perceived usefulness on intention to continue using generative AI was negative. Practical implications: To increase user satisfaction, generative AI technology developers and companies should optimize user experience, provide personalized services, and establish feedback loops to increase user satisfaction. In addition, user education and awareness-raising activities are necessary to reduce innovation resistance, which can promote technology acceptance. Future research should further investigate perceived risk, suitability, complexity, and attitudes as influential factors on specific innovation resistance and analyze the moderating effect of training on generative AI. These implications will be important contributions to the acceptance and diffusion of generative AI technologies. On the other hand, this study is limited by the fact that the sample is biased toward one country and lacks a global perspective.

References

1. Glesias, A., Gálvez, A., Suárez, P.: The role of artificial intelligence and machine learning for the fight against COVID-19. In: Hammouch, Z., Lahby, M., Baleanu, D. (eds.) Mathematical Modeling and Intelligent Control for Combating Pandemics. Springer Optimization and Its Applications, LNCS, vol. 203, pp. 111–128. Springer, Cham (2023). https://doi.org/10.1007/978-3-031-33183-1_7
2. Jihoon, Y., Sanghyuk, Y.: Beyond ChatGPT to the Generative AI Era: Media and Content Generative AI Service Cases and Competitiveness. Korea Broadcasting and Telecommunications Agency (2023). https://www.kca.kr/Media_Issue_Trend/vol55/pdf/Media_Issue_Trend(vol55)_22.pdf
3. Lee, S.-A., Jung, T.-H.: Analysis and forecast of venture capital investment on generative AI startups: focusing on the U.S. and South Korea. Ventur. Startup Res. **18**(4), 21–35 (2023). https://doi.org/10.16972/apjbve.18.4.202308.21
4. Chang, S.: ChatGPT has changed the future of writing education – focusing on the response of riting education in the era of artificial intelligence. Writ. Res. **56**, 7–34 (2023). https://doi.org/10.31565/korrow.2023.56.001
5. Chan, C.K.Y., Hu, W.: Students' voices on generative AI: perceptions, benefits, and challenges in higher education. Int. J. Educ. Technol. High. Educ. **20**(1), 43 (2023). https://doi.org/10.1186/s41239-023-00411-8
6. Rahman, M.M., Watanobe, Y.: ChatGPT for education and research: opportunities, threats, and strategies. Appl. Sci. **13**(9), 578–593 (2023). https://doi.org/10.3390/app13095783
7. Ivanov, S., Soliman, M.: Game of algorithms: ChatGPT implications for the future of tourism education and research. J. Tour. Futures **9**(2), 214–221 (2023). https://doi.org/10.1108/JTF-02-2023-0038
8. Davis, F.D., Bagozzi, R.P., Warshaw, P.R.: Technology acceptance model. J. Manag. Sci. **35**(8), 982–1003 (1989). https://doi.org/10.1007/978-3-030-45274-2

9. Bhattacherjee, A.: Understanding information systems continuance: an expectation-confirmation model. MIS Q. 351–370 (2001). https://doi.org/10.2307/3250921
10. Oliver, R.L.: A cognitive model of the antecedents and consequences of satisfaction decisions. J. Mark. Res. **17**(4), 460–469 (1980). https://doi.org/10.1177/002224378001700405
11. DeLone, W.H., McLean, E.R.: Information systems success: the quest for the dependent variable. Inf. Syst. Res. **3**(1), 60–95 (1992). https://doi.org/10.1287/isre.3.1.60
12. Venkatesh, V., Morris, M.G., Davis, G.B., Davis, F.D.: User acceptance of information technology: toward a unified view. MIS Q. **27**(3), 425–478 (2003). https://doi.org/10.2307/30036540
13. Fornell, C., Johnson, M.D., Anderson, E.W., Cha, J., Bryant, B.E.: The American customer satisfaction index: nature, purpose, and findings. J. Mark. **60**(4), 7–18 (1996). https://doi.org/10.1177/002224299606000403
14. Seung, H.L.: "(A) Study on the Innovation Resistance of Consumers in Adoption Process of New Product" Sungkyunkwan University, Doctoral dissertation (1993). http://imgsvr.riss4u.net/contents3/td_contents9/01986/725//01986725.pdf
15. Ram, S.: A model of innovation resistance. Adv. Consum. Res. **14**(1), 208–212 (1987)

Conceptual Modeling for Public AI Systems

Seonghwan Ju[1](✉), Seoltae Ko[1], and Andrew Lim[2]

[1] Seoul Digital Foundation, Seoul, South Korea
{shju,kost}@sdf.seoul.kr
[2] Quebec Government Office, London, USA
andrew.lim@mri.gouv.qc.ca

Abstract. The Korean government has declared a transition from e-government to AI-based intelligent government through policy master plans, such as the 2nd E-Government Basic Plan (2021–2025) and the National AI Everyday Life Action Plan (2023). This is largely due to the rapid spread of generative AI, represented by ChatGPT, in everyday life, as a significant number of citizens expect AI transformation of public services. However, due to the early stage of the diffusion of generative AI technology, there are not many studies on how to implement AI systems in the public sector, and there is an urgent need to clarify the related concepts, considering that not only technical aspects, but also institutional aspects and social impact aspects should be considered together. Therefore, this study proposes a conceptual modelling of public AI systems considering the Korean context. For this purpose, we used the "conceptual framework development" method of Varpio et al. (2020) to organise the attributes of 82 related literatures and concepts derived from the PRISMA guidelines, and conceptually derived a public AI system by connecting the relationships of each attribute. We distinguished four stages in the development of AI systems in the public sector - AI adoption, AI implementation, AI transformation, and AI evaluation - and defined the concept of a public AI system by linking the components of each stage, defining the attributes, and connecting the relationships between the factors. This can be used as a practical guide for the public sector, including the government, and will contribute to promoting the adoption of AI systems.

Keywords: public AI system · intelligent government · generative AI · conceptual modeling

1 Introduction

The informatization of government and public institutions, represented by the e-government that began in the 1980s, has seen Korea establish and operate a world-class e-government since the 2000s. Recently, various attempts to introduce AI technology across all areas of society have been ongoing due to innovations in generative AI technology, and the Korean government is also planning to introduce generative AI technology into public systems and services. This effort aims to advance from the existing e-government to an AI-based intelligent government, driven by the public's high expectations for AI-adopted public services [1].

M. Saeki et al. (Eds.): ER 2024 Workshops, LNCS 14932, pp. 107–123, 2025.
https://doi.org/10.1007/978-3-031-75599-6_8

However, there are several obstacles, such as costs, security, and technological capabilities, and as generative AI technology is in its early stages, there is no clear definition of what AI systems and services will look like in the public sector or their impacts. Furthermore, as discussions on the social and ethical impacts of AI continue globally, a conceptual modeling of AI systems that considers both technical and social aspects is needed. Also, with the spread of AI adoption by governments and public institutions, there must be standard operating procedures and criteria that align with social norms, as AI systems, due to their learning ability, can act autonomously and even modify their behavior independently, making such procedures and criteria even more crucial [39].

Therefore, this study aims to define the concept of public AI systems based on domestic and international research. Through systematic literature review, key components will be derived, and a conceptual framework defining public AI systems will be developed by setting attributes for these components and establishing their relationships.

2 Literature Review

2.1 Concept and Types of Public AI Systems

Public AI systems refer to AI systems developed and utilized by government and public institutions. Although the core technology is mainly developed in the private sector, system development and utilization based on this technology are actively progressing in various forms in the public sector, with several researchers discussing this.

According to Gartner (2021), AI technology in the global public sector is utilized in the order of chatbots and conversational agents (26%), machine learning-based data mining (16%), and biometric recognition (14%). In Korea, public services (51.2%), research and analysis (20.3%), and internal management (15.3%) are the primary applications [62].

Several scholars have theoretically categorized the types of public AI systems. Bataller & Harris (2016) classified public AI system types into automation and augmentation, explaining that automation is used to enhance efficiency by having AI perform repetitive tasks, while augmentation supports decision-making and improves work effectiveness by enhancing workers' skills, knowledge, and experience [5]. Demolino et al. (2018) suggested that public AI systems could be developed for enhancing interaction, intelligent automation, and decision-making improvement, with applications in case management, customer service, human capital management, fraud and risk management, and inspection and maintenance [22]. Pencheva et al. (2020) argued that AI could be applied in government and public institutions for policy research and evaluation, agenda setting and policy making, and policy implementation across the entire cycle from strategy to operations [77]. Han (2021) used the example of e-Estonia to argue that AI systems are developed for public service to citizens, support tools for public officials, maintenance of national public records, operation of physical infrastructure, compliance with and utilization of laws, and public policy development [29].

2.2 Development of Public AI Systems

The procedures and methods for developing AI are generally similar, but government and public institutions differ from the private sector in terms of technological capability, organizational purpose, governance, security level, and social and ethical responsibilities, necessitating a different concept for AI development. Several researchers have studied and presented concepts for developing public AI systems.

Mehr (2017) proposed six strategies for effective AI development, considering the slower adoption speed and capability compared to the private sector: starting as part of a public program, collecting citizen opinions, developing AI based on existing resources, preparing data and privacy protection, establishing strategies to mitigate ethical risks, and avoiding blind reliance on AI in decision-making processes [55]. Yang et al. (2020) proposed an AI model for science and technology administration, consisting of four stages: problem exploration, AI applicability review, AI model development through public research institutions, and field application and monitoring of the initial AI model [107]. The OECD (2022) presented five concepts explaining public AI systems, considering both technical and social aspects: human and earth, economic context, data and input, AI model, and tasks and output. Additionally, they argued that data and input, AI model, and tasks and output must go through an experimental stage (AI in the lab) before full-scale service deployment [73]. Straub et al. (2023) proposed three concepts explaining public AI systems using the term AI-GOV: operational fitness (whether the AI system achieved its intended goals in terms of efficiency, effectiveness, safety, reliability, etc.), epistemic alignment (whether the AI system's data is appropriate in terms of transparency, explainability, reproducibility, etc.), and normative divergence (whether the AI system's outcomes comply with acceptable behavioral norms) [89]. Madan (2023) proposed the AI Innovation Stage Model based on the diffusion of innovations (DOI) theory, consisting of three stages: AI adoption, AI implementation, and AI diffusion. The AI adoption stage involves recognizing the need for AI and planning solutions influenced by technology, organization, and environmental factors. The AI implementation stage involves starting and progressing through the technology development project to testing. The AI diffusion stage refers to the period until AI becomes a routine function after several pilot projects, where both technological completeness and social acceptance must be considered [52].

2.3 AI Risks

Public services have a significant impact on the general public, making AI risks more sensitive. Several researchers and research institutions have presented risks and preventive measures associated with AI.

The NIA (2023) highlighted new risks to manage due to the emergence of generative AI, such as sensitive data sharing, data misuse, privacy protection, data security, reduced public interest, increased costs due to monopoly, and utilization restrictions [65]. The NIS (2023), overseeing Korea's national information, issued security guidelines for the development and use of generative AI, identifying major security threats like misinformation, AI model abuse, similar model service pretext, and data leakage [67]. Madan (2023) presented five conflicting values that can arise during the AI implementation process, termed AI tensions: automation vs. augmentation, collective rights vs. individual autonomy, data accessibility vs. security and privacy, prediction accuracy vs. citizens' rights. Although each concept differs, they highlight factors to consider when tempted to develop AI that conflicts with public values [52]. The NIST (2023) proposed seven AI risks and an AI risk management framework, including validity and reliability, safety, fairness and bias management, security and resilience, transparency and accountability, explainability and interpretability, and privacy. The risk management framework consists of governance for risk management, a map for identifying risks, risk measurement, and risk management tools [69].

2.4 Analysis of Previous Research

(Table 1).

Table 1. Summary of Previous Studies Related to Public AI Systems

	Researcher	Concepts
concepts and type	Bataller&Harris (2016)	automation, augmentation
	Demolino, D. et al. (2018)	case management, customer service, human capital management, fraud and risk management, inspection and maintenance
	Han (2021)	public service, public support tools, maintenance of national public records, operation of infrastructure, compliance with and utilization of laws, development of public policies
Development	Yang et al. (2020)	problem exploration, AI application suitability review, AI model development, monitoring result-based advancement
	OECD (2022)	human and earth, economic context, data and input, AI model, task and output
	Straub et al. (2023)	operational fitness, epistemic alignment, normative divergence
	Madan (2023)	AI adoption, AI implementation, AI diffusion, Public Administration Transformation
Risk	NIA (2023)	sensitive data sharing, data misuse, personal information protection, data security, reduced public interest, increased costs due to monopoly, restrictions on utilization
	NIS (2023)	incorrect information, AI model abuse, similar model service pretext, data leakage

The key implications of previous research on public AI systems can be summarized as follows:

1. AI in government and public institutions can be categorized by purpose, which can be used as reasons and purposes for AI adoption by future institutions.

2. Both technical and non-technical factors should be considered to promote AI adoption acceptance during development.
3. Public AI system development, like the private sector, follows linear procedural steps.
4. Ethical and social risks exist, and preventive measures are essential.

These analysis results formed the theoretical background for developing the conceptual framework.

3 Research Methodology

3.1 Research Model

This study aims to conceptually organize a framework for developing public AI systems based on Varpio et al. (2020)'s 'Conceptual Framework Development Model' [100]. The conceptual framework development process involves a bottom-up approach starting from data related to a specific phenomenon, through which researchers search for overall patterns and provide a conceptual explanation of the phenomenon [49]. The study proceeds in the order of data collection, theoretical exploration, theoretical framework formation, and conceptual framework development.

3.2 Research Procedure and Methods

1. Data Collection: Data collection was carried out using the systematic literature review method PRISMA (Preferred Reporting Items for Systematic Reviews and Meta-Analyses) to ensure the validity of literature selection. PRISMA provides practical guidelines for systematic literature collection and selection [57]. The systematic literature review process involves identification, screening, eligibility, and inclusion. According to these steps, previous research related to public AI systems was selected for theoretical exploration.
2. Theoretical Exploration: For the analysis of collected literature, the AI Innovation Stage Model by Madan (2023) was used as the basic analytical framework, which was modified using various previous research results. This framework was used to derive components related to public AI systems.
3. Theoretical Framework Formation: The elements analyzed through the AI Innovation Stage Model during theoretical exploration were presented in the form of a framework. Attributes to be included in each stage were classified, with similar attributes integrated, and ambiguous attributes excluded.
4. Conceptual Framework Development: This step involved refining the theoretical framework, reorganizing each component, and connecting the attributes and relationships of each component to present a conceptual framework for public AI systems.

3.3 Model Data Collection and Theoretical Exploration

The data collection phase involved a systematic literature review using PRISMA, progressing through identification, screening, eligibility, and inclusion.

In the identification phase, the target databases and search terms were set. Domestic papers were searched on RISS, and international papers on Scopus, with search terms limited to 'artificial intelligence implementation.' Additional terms such as 'public' and 'government' were included to focus on the public sector. This yielded 117,472 papers, of which 110,320 were excluded.

The screening phase involved checking the search period, research fields, document types, publication status, and levels. The search period was from January 2015 to May 2024, focusing on social sciences and targeting final published journal papers. Both fully open and partially open papers were included, targeting SCI, SCIE, SSCI, and KCI-listed papers. As a result, 5,629 papers were excluded from 7,152, selecting 1,523 papers.

In the eligibility phase, evaluation criteria matching the research purpose were set, and full-text reviews were conducted. The criteria were: (i) studies related to the public sector, (ii) excluding papers on AI background, concepts, and necessity, (iii) excluding papers analyzing AI trends, (iv) excluding papers with overlapping or similar variables, (v) excluding papers with overlapping or similar research methods. This resulted in excluding 1,440 out of 1,523 papers. The inclusion phase finalized 82 papers as the basic sample for theoretical exploration to analyze the components of the public AI system development framework.

The theoretical exploration phase analyzed 82 selected papers based on an activity system model. Contexts were analyzed by dividing into planning, implementation, transformation, infra, and risk, deriving basic components for the framework and constructing a public AI development framework.

The theoretical framework formation phase integrated the derived components into an empirically validated theoretical framework. The process involved refining the analysis results through redundancy removal, categorization, and proceduralization. Redundancy removal involved eliminating duplicate words, integrating synonyms, and removing contextually irrelevant words. Categorization identified shared attributes among words to cluster them, maintaining the activity system model's domains.

4 Conceptual Model for Public AI System Development Framework

To comprehensively approach public AI systems, it is necessary to understand not only the technical but also the social and ethical aspects. Therefore, this study proposes the PITIR (Planning, Implementation, Transformation, Infra, Risk) model, a conceptual model for public AI systems, redesigned based on various previous studies and data, using AI Innovation Stage Model [52] as the basic analytical framework. Infra and Risk are dimensions that affect the entire public AI system development process, while Planning, Implementation, and Transformation are dimensions related to the development process (Fig. 1).

4.1 Planning

The first dimension, Planning, refers to pre-planning for AI system development.

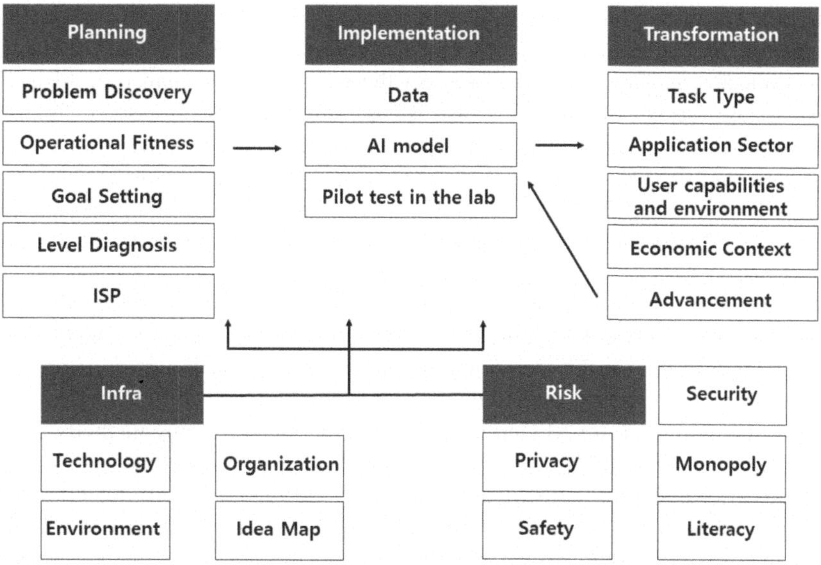

Fig. 1. PITIR (Planning, Implementation, Transformation, Infra, Risk) Model.

Initially, it is necessary to explore the problems to be solved. This process should involve collecting opinions from stakeholders, such as traffic experts and citizens, for system development for traffic services.

Next, operational suitability evaluation is needed to determine if AI systems are an appropriate means to solve the identified problems. This requires understanding the advantages of AI and assessing if these advantages align with the development organization's goals, such as cost reduction and productivity improvement, effectiveness in service and decision-making enhancement, accuracy and speed improvement, safety, reliability, and innovation in new business model planning.

Subsequently, the target system should be designed according to the nature of the problems and solutions. This involves detailing problems and solutions, designing the information system/data/technology/security architecture based on the detailed content, and estimating related costs.

Additionally, assessing the technical and organizational readiness levels to determine if the designed AI system can be effectively operated is essential. Technical readiness can be judged by existing data and infrastructure, while organizational readiness is judged by expert personnel, organizational structure, and institutional factors.

The Korean government and public institutions encourage strategic system planning that includes these factors and procedures, and submitting an ISP (Information Strategy Planning) report is mandatory to receive system construction budget approval.

4.2 Implementation

The second dimension, Implementation, refers to the construction of an AI system.

The first factor for building an AI system is training data. Training data is the material for creating AI models, and like a black box, the results of AI can be determined by what data is collected and trained, and can affect the technical performance of AI models and socio-ethical expectations. The properties of training data are described with this in mind. The data collection method is an important attribute because it defines the format of the data, and the identification of the data source makes it possible to explain the output of the AI model. Data format and scale can infer the type and performance of AI models, and data quality can determine the accuracy and reliability of AI model performance.

The second factor is the AI model. AI models are algorithms derived from data training, and can be said to be the engine of an AI system. The following are the properties of AI model descriptions that determine the nature of AI models. Information on the source model, which is a pre-trained model; the nature of the AI model, such as natural language processing, vision AI, and machine learning; deep learning methods, such as reinforcement learning, RNN, and CNN; AI model construction methods, such as indirect construction and direct construction; and finally, information on the final developed AI model, such as scale and accuracy. In particular, the AI model construction method, which can be classified into indirect construction and direct construction, is a factor that reflects Korea's unique institutional characteristics stemming from data security issues. Indirect construction is a method of creating a new model by learning the retained data after connecting an external foundation model with an API, while direct construction is a method of creating a new model by learning the retained data after downloading open source models to an internal server.

The third factor is experimentation and pilot testing. Experiments and pilot tests are essential to ensure the reliability of AI systems. In particular, it is important to increase the accuracy and completeness of AI systems through experiments and pilot tests because, unlike existing ICT, the outcome of AI systems is uncertain.

4.3 Transformation

The third dimension, Transformation, refers to driving changes in public administration as a result of AI system construction.

The first factor is understanding the types of tasks that will be possible through AI systems. In the planning phase, several types of benefits from AI adoption were explained, such as efficiency, safety, effectiveness, and innovation. Task types refer to more specific outcomes. For example, promoting a type of task like RPA work automation system introduction to enhance work efficiency.

The second factor is the AI application field suitable for public purposes. Regardless of the excellent performance of developed AI systems, it must be appropriately applied to the public sector to have significance and sustainable operation, making the public purpose of the application field important.

The third factor is the user's AI capability and surrounding environment. The user's AI capability level needs to be high, and AI systems need to be conveniently constructed for easy operation to increase usage rates. Additionally, the user's surrounding environment is important as AI system outcomes need to positively impact the surrounding environment for comfortable use.

The fourth factor is economic factors. The industry domain the developed AI system belongs to and its related businesses can affect development costs, impacting the sustainability of AI systems.

Finally, AI system operation and enhancement capabilities are crucial. Due to the characteristics of AI systems, continuous performance improvement and error correction are needed even after the initial system development, requiring preparation and additional learning of related data. Thus, it is very important for the AI system operation organization to possess the relevant capabilities.

4.4 Infra

The fourth dimension, Infra, affects the entire process of public AI system development, and the higher the level of infrastructural readiness, the easier it is to build and operate AI systems. Infra is not just hardware or technology-related infrastructure, but also non-technical factors such as organisational culture and institutions that are related to the acceptance of AI adoption.

The theory underlying the derivation of these factors is the technology-organisation-environment (TOE) framework, which has been used to study technology adoption in various environments (Tornatzky and Fleischer, 1990).

Technology is a factor for the development and operation of AI systems, such as cloud computing, database infrastructure, networks, and data governance.

Organisation can be described in terms of three components: human capabilities, governance, and organisational culture, and these three components are interconnected, i.e., if human capabilities are insufficient, governance can compensate for them, or if human capabilities and governance work properly, they need to be supported by a good organisational culture. In the case of Korea, the human capacity of the government and public institutions is low compared to the private sector, so the government is trying to offset this weakness by strengthening collaboration with the private sector or changing governance.

Environment acts as an external trigger for public administration to respond to certain stimuli. The political environment, policy directives, regulations or laws, and AI guidelines are vertical pressures, while intergovernmental competition, media scrutiny, citizen demands, and industry pressures are horizontal pressures.

Finally, idea maps can serve as guidelines for governments and public organisations that are new to AI adoption. The idea map is a demand-supply matching guide that lists the types of systems that can be developed according to the purpose of solving the problem and matches the detailed technology to develop the system. For example, there is a demand to develop a chatbot for responding to complaints, and RNNs are matched with the technology required to develop this system.

4.5 Risk

The fifth dimension, Risk, includes social and ethical risks arising from the development and utilization of public AI systems and countermeasures to prevent them. With the rapid spread of generative AI, the scope and impact of risks have significantly increased, leading to comprehensive discussions.

Unauthorized misuse of personal information is a representative risk, as using personal data randomly to enhance AI performance infringes on individual rights.

The safety of training data is also a crucial risk, where infringing on others' copyrights during data collection or using biased data in AI model training negatively impacts data safety.

Data security is a serious risk, as confidential or sensitive data leaked through communication networks during the AI model training process can severely impact internal operations, which can result from intentional acts like hacking or unintentional acts like data leaks when using external AI models through clouds, necessitating related preventive guidelines.

The monopolistic dominance of big tech in AI models poses a non-technical and social risk. Developing AI foundation models requires substantial resources and costs, making it highly likely to be monopolized by a few large tech companies, potentially leading to increased costs, decreased public interest due to lack of updates, and monopolization of social safety nets by profit-driven companies.

Finally, the technical and ethical capabilities of AI users also pose a risk. Users should not misuse AI tools for malicious purposes, such as spreading fake news or infringing on others' rights, and must have the ability to identify bias or discrimination risks in AI service outcomes. Institutional measures to overcome these risks in the development and operation process of public AI systems are necessary.

5 Conclusion

As explained above, despite the increasing need for AI adoption in government and public institutions due to the rapid spread of generative AI, there is limited practical guidance from research on adoption, development, and operation. In this context, this study is significant as it lays the foundation for practical guide development through conceptual modeling.

The PITIR (Planning, Implementation, Transformation, Infra, Risk) model proposed in this study organizes factors to consider in each dimension when government and public institutions develop and operate AI systems. Regarding the development process, the Planning dimension includes problem identification, suitability review, target system setting, technical and organizational readiness diagnosis, and ISP implementation. The Implementation dimension includes training data, AI models, experiments, and pilot tests. The Transformation dimension includes types of tasks, applicable fields for public purposes, user capabilities and surrounding environment, economic context, and operation and enhancement capabilities. The Infra dimension, affecting the entire process, includes technology, organization, environment, and idea mapping. The Risk dimension includes personal information protection, data safety, data security, big tech monopoly, and AI user capabilities. The PITIR model can be used throughout the public AI system development process, considering technical, social, and ethical factors from planning to operation and enhancement, making it a comprehensive model.

However, this study is an initial model based on theoretical exploration of previous studies, and further empirical research in actual AI system development and operation processes is needed to refine and supplement each dimension.

References

1. 4th Industrial Revolution Commitee.: A public awareness survey on the use of AI to "pupularize AI". 4th Industrial Revolution Commitee, Seoul (2021)
2. Atabekov, A.: Artificial intelligence in contemporary societies: legal status and definition, implementation in public sector across various countries. Soc. Sci. **12**(3) (2023). https://doi.org/10.3390/socsci12030178
3. Balashov O.V., Bukachev D.S., Gnezdova J.V.: The use of artificial intelligence in automation of planning and operational management of organizational and technical systems in the covid-19 pandemic. Post-COVID Economic Revival, Volume II: Sectors, Institutions, and Policy, 2, 187-201 (2022). https://doi.org/10.1007/978-3-030-83566-8_12
4. Bannister, F., Connolly, R.: Administration by algorithm: a risk management framework. Inf. Polity **25**(4), 471–490 (2020). https://doi.org/10.3233/IP-200249
5. Bataller, C., Harris, J.: Turing Artificial Intelligence into Business Value, Today. Accenture, Arlington (2016)
6. Bednarchuk, M., Tyukov, A., Janovsky, T., Sokolov, A., Shcherbakov, M.: Energy service contract as a key factor of innovative development of budgetary organizations. In: 2017 8th International Conference on Information, Intelligence, Systems and Applications, IISA 2017, 2018-January, pp. 1–6 (2017). https://doi.org/10.1109/IISA.2017.8316383
7. Bhowmick, A., Seetharaman, A.: Influence of digital infrastructure, data integration & ethical dimension on artificial intelligence in product development. In: 2024 10th International Conference on Mechatronics and Robotics Engineering, ICMRE 2024, nan, pp. 201–208 (2024). https://doi.org/10.1109/ICMRE60776.2024.10532203
8. Bogatinov, D., Nacev, A.: Artificial intelligence gainst terrorist use of cyberspace - a brief review. Countering Terrorist Activities in Cyberspace, nan, pp. 95–105 (2018). https://doi.org/10.3233/978-1-61499-847-1-95
9. Bonsu, K.O., Song, J.: Turbulence on the global economy influenced by artificial intelligence and foreign policy inefficiencies. J. Liberty Int. Aff. **6**(2), 113–122 (2020)
10. Broomfield, H., Reutter, L.: Towards a data-driven public administration: an empirical analysis of nascent phase implementation. Scand. J. Public Admin. **25**(2), 73–97 (2021)
11. Chadwick, S.: Rise of the (planning) machines? J. Plan. Environ. Law **2020**(8), 841–848 (2020)
12. Chae, G.-Y., An, S.-H., Lee, C.-Y.: Demand forecasting for liquified natural gas bunkering by country and region using meta-analysis and artificial intelligence. Sustainability (Switzerland) **13**(16) (2021). https://doi.org/10.3390/su13169058
13. Charles, V., Rana, N.P., Carter, L.: Artificial intelligence for data-driven decision-making and governance in public affairs. Gov. Inf. Q. **39**(4) (2022). https://doi.org/10.1016/j.giq.2022.101742
14. Chatterjee, S., Khorana, S., Kizgin, H.: Harnessing the potential of artificial intelligence to foster citizens' satisfaction: an empirical study on India. Gov. Inf. Q. **39**(4) (2022). https://doi.org/10.1016/j.giq.2021.101621
15. Chen, T., Gascó-Hernandez, M., Esteve, M.: The adoption and implementation of artificial intelligence Chatbots in public organizations: evidence from U.S. state governments. Am. Rev. Public Adm. **54**(3), 255–270 (2024). https://doi.org/10.1177/02750740231200522
16. Chohan, S.R., Akhter, Z.H.: Electronic government services value creation from artificial intelligence: ai-based e-government services for Pakistan. Electron. Gov. **17**(3), 374–390 (2021). https://doi.org/10.1504/EG.2021.116003
17. Chong, Y.-W., Villanueva-Libunao, K., Chee, S.-Y., Alvarez, M.J., Yau, K.-L.A., Keoh, S.L.: Artificial intelligence policies to enhance urban mobility in Southeast Asia. Front. Sustain. Cities **4** (2022). https://doi.org/10.3389/frsc.2022.824391

18. Constantin, I., Patachia, C., Patrascu, C., Avadanei, A., Nitescu, L.: Threat classification in current communication infrastructures. In: Proceedings of the 11th International Conference on Electronics, Computers and Artificial Intelligence, ECAI 2019, nan (2019). https://doi.org/10.1109/ECAI46879.2019.9042079
19. Cortez, E.K., Maslej, N.: Adjudication of artificial intelligence and automated decision-making cases in Europe and the USA. Eur. J. Risk Regul. **14**(3), 457–475 (2023). https://doi.org/10.1017/err.2023.61
20. Cui, D., Wu, F.: The influence of media use on public perceptions of artificial intelligence in china: evidence from an online survey. Inf. Dev. **37**(1), 45–57 (2021). https://doi.org/10.1177/0266666919893411
21. Dai, P., Chen, Y., Feng, Y.: Big data analysis of applying artificial intelligence to criminal justice and their prevention. In: Proceedings of the International Conference on Computation, Big-Data and Engineering 2022, ICCBE 2022, nan, pp. 58–63 (2022). https://doi.org/10.1109/ICCBE56101.2022.9888156
22. Demchenko, M.V., Gulieva, M.E., Larina, T.V., Simaeva, E.P.: Digital transformation of legal education: problems, risks and prospects. Eur. J. Contemp. Educ. **10**(2), 297–307 (2021). https://doi.org/10.13187/ejced.2021.2.297
23. Demolino, D., Gebre, B., Whitehouse, M.: Essential Insights: Artificial Intelligence Unleashed. Accenture, Arlington (2018)
24. Du, H., et al.: City infrastructure ontologies. Comput. Environ. Urban Syst. **104** (2023). https://doi.org/10.1016/j.compenvurbsys.2023.101991
25. Duke, S.A.: Deny, dismiss and downplay: developers' attitudes towards risk and their role in risk creation in the field of healthcare-ai. Ethics Inf. Technol. **24**(1) (2022)
26. Engin, Z., et al.: Data-driven urban management: mapping the landscape. J. Urban Manag. **9**(2), 140–150 (2020). https://doi.org/10.1016/j.jum.2019.12.001
27. Faiz, A., Shah, B.H., Faiz, A.: Climate resilient slope stabilization for transport infrastructures. In: Transport Infrastructure and Systems - Proceedings of the AIIT International Congress on Transport Infrastructure and Systems, TIS 2017, nan, pp. 55–62 (2017)
28. Ghose, A.: An integrated spatial decision support system (SDSS) for rural development department of orissa. Int. Arch. Photogramm. Remote Sens. Spat. Inf. Sci. - ISPRS Arch. **35**, 1278–1282 (2004)
29. Güney, C., Ala, T.: The insights of publications in the field of artificial intelligence (AI)-based risk management in public sector: a bibliometric overview. EDPACS **69**(1), 41–68 (2024). https://doi.org/10.1080/07366981.2024.2312002
30. Han.: The governemnt appearance and orientation in the era of artficial intelligence transformation: artificial intelligence government. J. Korean Assoc. Reg. Inf. Soc. **24**(4), 137–158 (2021)
31. Haqbeen, J., Sahab, S., Ito, T., Rizzi, P.: Using decision support system to enable crowd identify neighborhood issues and its solutions for policy makers: an online experiment at Kabul municipal level. Sustainability (Switzerland) **13**(10) (2021). https://doi.org/10.3390/su13105453
32. Hemphill, T.A., Kelley, K.J.: Artificial intelligence and the fifth phase of political risk management: an application to regulatory expropriation. Thunderbird Int. Bus. Rev. **63**(5), 585–595 (2021). https://doi.org/10.1002/tie.22222
33. James, A., Whelan, A.: 'ethical' artificial intelligence in the welfare state: discourse and discrepancy in Australian social services. Crit. Soc. Policy **42**(1), 22–42 (2022). https://doi.org/10.1177/0261018320985463
34. Jordan, S.R.: Designing artificial intelligence review boards: creating risk metrics for review of AI. In: International Symposium on Technology and Society, Proceedings, 2019-November 2019. https://doi.org/10.1109/ISTAS48451.2019.8937942

35. Kasych, A., Cherniavska, O., Ruban, D., Glukhova, V., Golub, V., Nefedova, T.: Artificial intelligence as a tool of local self-government and democracy development during the formation of industry 5.0 and society 5.0. In: Proceedings of the 5th International Conference on Modern Electrical and Energy System, MEES 2023, nan (2023). https://doi.org/10.1109/MEES61502.2023.10402417
36. Kell, N.: How can CISOs use AI in their business? Comput. Fraud Secur. **2019**(9), 14–16 (2019). https://doi.org/10.1016/S1361-3723(19)30097-1
37. Kempeneer, S., Heylen, F.: Virtual state, where are you? A literature review, framework and agenda for failed digital transformation. Big Data Soc. **10**(1) (2023). https://doi.org/10.1177/20539517231160528
38. Khisamova, Z.I., Begishev, I.R., Sidorenko, E.L.: Artificial intelligence and problems of ensuring cyber security. Int. J. Cyber Criminol. **13**(2), 564–577 (2019)
39. Klingberg, S.: Countering terrorism: digital policing of open source intelligence and social updates media using artificial intelligence. In: Artificial Intelligence and National Security, nan, 101–111 (2022). https://doi.org/10.1007/978-3-031-06709-9_6
40. Kobis, N., Starke, C., Rahwan, I.: The promise and perils of using artificial intelligence to fight corruption. Nat. Mach. Intell. **4**, 418–424 (2022)
41. Kuberkar, S., Singh, S., Singhal, T.K.: Adoption intention of artificial intelligence enabled smart city services from citizens' perspective. Int. J. Hum. Cap. Urban Manag. **9**(1), 29–46 (2024). https://doi.org/10.22034/IJHCUM.2024.01.03
42. Kulal, A., Rahiman, H.U., Suvarna, H., Abhishek, N., Dinesh, S.: Enhancing public service delivery efficiency: exploring the impact of AI. J. Open Innov. Technol. Mark. Complex. **10**(3) (2024). https://doi.org/10.1016/j.joitmc.2024.100329
43. Latupeirissa, J.J.P., Dewi, N.L.Y., Prayana, I.K.R., Srikandi, M.B., Ramadiansyah, S.A., Pramana, I.B.G.A.Y.: Transforming public service delivery: a comprehensive review of digitization initiatives. Sustainability (Switzerland) **16**(7) (2024). https://doi.org/10.3390/su16072818
44. Lăzăroiu, G., Harrison, A.: Internet of things sensing infrastructures and data-driven planning technologies in smart sustainable city governance and management. Geopolit. Hist. Int. Relat. **13**(2), 23–36 (2021)
45. Lee, H.S., Kuang, K.S., Liew, P.X., Har, W.M.: Do applications of artificial intelligence (AI) contribute to the mitigation of hazardous environments? An analysis based on various pillars of AI. In: 2024 10th International Conference on Mechatronics and Robotics Engineering, ICMRE 2024, nan, pp. 287–292 (2024). https://doi.org/10.1109/ICMRE60776.2024.10532166
46. Leonard, P., Tyers, R.: Engineering the revolution? Imagining the role of new digital technologies in infrastructure work futures. N. Technol. Work. Employ. **38**(2), 291–310 (2023). https://doi.org/10.1111/ntwe.12226
47. Lewis, A., Stachowicz-Stanusch, A., Elshareif, E.: Is the UAE ready for the fourth industrial revolution in the age artificial intelligence? Development of artificial intelligence in the United Arab Emirates. In: Proceedings of International Conference on Research in Education and Science, vol. 9, no. 1, pp. 162–171 (2023)
48. Li, C., Yang, L.: Responsible AI: the revolution in governance technology in China. In: Proceedings - 2021 2nd International Conference on Artificial Intelligence and Education, ICAIE 2021, nan, pp. 76–80 (2021). https://doi.org/10.1109/ICAIE53562.2021.00023
49. Li, D., Azman, N.H.N.: The impact of artificial intelligence (AI) on the low-carbon economy: a prospective study on the long-term rental housing market in Guangxi, China. Chin. J. Urban Environ. Stud. **10**(4) (2022). https://doi.org/10.1142/S2345748122500245
50. Lim.: Development of Conceptual Framework for Application of Learning Analysis in Virtual World Metaverse Learning Environment. Chungbuk National University, Cheongju (2023)

51. Lyu, K., Hao, M.: Definition and history of smart cities: the development of cities and application of artificial intelligence technology in smart cities. AI-Based Services for Smart Cities and Urban Infrastructure, nan, pp. 1–22 (2020). https://doi.org/10.4018/978-1-7998-5024-3.ch001
52. Madan, R.: Artificial intelligence diffusion in public administration. In: AIES 2022 - Proceedings of the 2022 AAAI/ACM Conference on AI, Ethics, and Society, nan (2022). https://doi.org/10.1145/3514094.353952
53. Madan, R.: Artificial Intelligence adoption in Canadian public administration: a mixed-methods study. PhD thesis, University of Reading, Reading (2023). https://doi.org/10.48683/1926.00114444
54. Marasinghe, R., Yigitcanlar, T., Mayere, S., Washington, T., Limb, M.: Computer vision applications for urban planning: a systematic review of opportunities and constraints. Sustain. Cities Soc. **100** (2024). https://doi.org/10.1016/j.scs.2023.105047
55. McKenzie, M., Gulson, K.N.: The incommensurability of digital and climate change priorities in schooling: an infrastructural analysis and implications for education governance. Res. Educ. **117**(1), 58–72 (2023). https://doi.org/10.1177/00345237231208658
56. Mehr, H.: Artificial Intelligence for Citizen Services and Government. Havard Kennedy School, Ash Center for Democratic Governance and Innovation, Cambridge (2016)
57. Mellouli, S., Janssen, M., Ojo, A.: Introduction to the issue on artificial intelligence in the public sector: risks and benefits of AI for governments. Digit. Gov. Res. Pract. **5**(1) (2024). https://doi.org/10.1145/363655
58. Moher, D., Liberati, A., Tetzlaff, J., Altman, D.: Perferred reporting items for systematic reviews and meta-analyses: the PRISMA statement. PLOS Med. **6**(7) (2009). https://doi.org/10.1371/journal.pmed.1000097
59. Morkhat, P.M., Ponkin, I.V., Markhgeym, M.V., Botnev, V.K., Turganbayev, A.O.: Artificial intelligence versus public administration: limitations of application. Humanit. Soc. Sci. Rev. **7**(3), 516–520 (2019)
60. Murdoch, B.: Privacy and artificial intelligence: challenges for protecting health information in a new era. BMC Med. Ethics **22**(1) (2021). https://doi.org/10.1186/s12910-021-00687-3
61. Muthumanikandan, V., Bhuvaneswari, A., Easwaran, B., Perumal, T.S.R.: Cyber-physical system solutions for smart cities. Cyber-Physical System Solutions for Smart Cities, nan, pp. 1–182 (2023)
62. Nalbandian, L.: An eye for an 'i:' a critical assessment of artificial intelligence tools in migration and asylum management. Comparat. Migr. Stud. **10**(1) (2022). https://doi.org/10.1186/s40878-022-00305-0
63. Ahn, N., Lee, J.: Analysis and Implications on the Use of the Artificial Intelligence by the Public Sector in the Domestic and Foreign Countries. Software Policy & Research Institute, Seongnam (2021)
64. Ndumbe, S.I., Velikov, P.: Government strategies on cybersecurity and how artificial intelligence can impact cybersecurity in healthcare with special reference to the UK. In: Jahankhani, H., Bowen, G., Sharif, M.S., Hussien, O. (eds.) Cybersecurity and Artificial Intelligence. Advanced Sciences and Technologies for Security Applications, pp. 217–236, LNCS. Springer, Cham (2024). https://doi.org/10.1007/978-3-031-52272-7_9
65. Newman, J., Mintrom, M., O'Neill, D.: Digital technologies, artificial intelligence, and bureaucratic transformation. Futures **136** (2022). https://doi.org/10.1016/j.futures.2021.102886
66. NIA.: Directions for utilizing super-large AI private platforms in the public sector. National Information Society Agency, Daegu (2023)
67. Nindler, R.: The united nation's capability to manage existential risks with a focus on artificial intelligence. Int. Community Law Rev. **21**(1), 5–34 (2019). https://doi.org/10.1163/18719732-12341388

68. NIS.: Security guidelines for using generative AI such as ChatGPT. National Intelligence Service, Republic of Korea (2023)
69. Nishimura, S., Ikaruga, S., Tsuboi, S., Kobayashi, T., Song, J.: Using the expert system theory in the development of support methods for a compact city plan. Design and Decision Support Systems in Architecture and Urban Planning - 13th International Conference on Design and Decision Support Systems in Architecture and Urban Planning, DDSS 2016, nan (2016)
70. NIST.: AI Risk Management Framework. Second Draft. National Institute of Standards and Technology, Gaithersburg (2022)
71. Novokmet, A., Tomičić, Z., Vinković, Z.: Pretrial risk assessment instruments in the us criminal justice system - what lessons can be learned for the European union. Int. J. Law Inf. Technol. **30**(1), 1–22 (2022). https://doi.org/10.1093/ijlit/eaac006
72. Noymanee, J., Iewwongcharoen, B., Theeramunkong, T.: Artificial intelligence maturity model for government administration and service. In: International Conference on Digital Government Technology and Innovation, DGTi-Con 2022 - Proceedings, nan, pp. 66–70 (2022). https://doi.org/10.1109/DGTi-CON53875.2022.9849184
73. Ntanda, A., Carolissen, R., Adegbaju, F.: Restorative social justice through digital transformation in South African metropolitan cities. In: 2023 IEEE European Technology and Engineering Management Summit, E-TEMS 2023 - Conference Proceedings, nan, pp. 111–116 (2023). https://doi.org/10.1109/E-TEMS57541.2023.10424566
74. OECD: OECD Framework for the Classification of AI systems. OECD publishing, Paris (2022)
75. Okuda, A., Ofa, S.V.: Artificial intelligence and broadband development through the Asia-pacific information superhighway. J. Infrast. Policy Dev. **2**(2), 319–342 (2018). https://doi.org/10.24294/jipd.v2i2.1047
76. Orlandić, M., Đukić, T., Mladenović, M.: Upcoming digital transformation and artificial intelligence trends in the public sector. Administratie si Management Public, **2024**(42), 45–59 (2024). https://doi.org/10.24818/amp/2024.42-03
77. Pasupuleti, R., Vadapalli, R., Mader, C.: Cyber security issues and challenges related to generative ai and chatgpt. In: Proceedings - 2023 10th International Conference on Social Networks Analysis, Management and Security, SNAMS 2023, nan, (2023). https://doi.org/10.1109/SNAMS60348.2023.10375472
78. Pencheva, I., Esteve, M., Mikhaylov, S.J.: Big Data and AI – a transformational shift for government: so, what next for research? Public Policy Adm. **35**(1), 24–44 (2020). https://doi.org/10.1177/0952076718780537
79. Plantinga, P.: Digital discretion and public administration in Africa: implications for the use of artificial intelligence. Inf. Dev. **40**(2), 332–352 (2024). https://doi.org/10.1177/02666669221117526
80. Popova, A.V., Balashkina, I.V., Nikitin, P.V., Prokopovich, G.A.: Ontology of artificial intelligence: on the question of the dehumanization of social regulators. Stud. Syst. Decis. Control **314**, 81–88 (2021). https://doi.org/10.1007/978-3-030-56433-9_10
81. Porwol, L., Garcia, P.A., Dumas, C.: Transforming e-participation: VR-dialogue – building and evaluating an ai-supported framework for next-gen VR-enabled e-participation research. Transform. Gov. People Process Policy **17**(2), 233–250 (2023). https://doi.org/10.1108/TG-12-2021-0205
82. Qiao-Franco, G., Zhu, R.: China's artificial intelligence ethics: policy development in an emergent community of practice. J. Contemp. China **33**(146), 189–205 (2024). https://doi.org/10.1080/10670564.2022.2153016
83. Salmon, P.M., et al.: When tomorrow comes: a prospective risk assessment of a future artificial general intelligence-based uncrewed combat aerial vehicle system. Appl. Ergon. **117** (2024). https://doi.org/10.1016/j.apergo.2024.104245

84. Sanchez, T.W.: Planning on the verge of AI, or AI on the verge of planning. Urban Sci. **7**(3) (2023). https://doi.org/10.3390/urbansci7030070
85. Schiff, D.S., Schiff, K.J., Pierson, P.: Assessing public value failure in government adoption of artificial intelligence. Public Adm. **100**(3), 653–673 (2022). https://doi.org/10.1111/padm.12742
86. Sharma, M., Luthra, S., Joshi, S., Kumar, A.: Implementing challenges of artificial intelligence: evidence from public manufacturing sector of an emerging economy. Gov. Inf. Q. **39**(4) (2022). https://doi.org/10.1016/j.giq.2021.101624
87. Son, T.H., Weedon, Z., Yigitcanlar, T., Sanchez, T., Corchado, J.M., Mehmood, R.: Algorithmic urban planning for smart and sustainable development: systematic review of the literature. Sustain. Cities Soc. **94** (2023). https://doi.org/10.1016/j.scs.2023.104562
88. Spalević, Ž., Kaljević, J., Vučetić, S., Milić, P.: Enhancing legally-based e-government services in education through artificial intelligence. Int. J. Cogn. Res. Sci. Eng. Educ. **11**(3), 511–518 (2023). https://doi.org/10.23947/2334-8496-2023-11-3-511-518
89. Štefanišinová, N., Muthová, N.J., Štrangfeldová, J., Šulajová, K.: Implementation and application of artificial intelligence in selected public services; [implementacija i primjena umjetne inteligencije u odabranim javnim službama]. Croat. Comp. Public Admin. **21**(4), 601–622 (2021). https://doi.org/10.31297/hkju.21.4.2
90. Straub, V.J., Morgan, D., Bright, J., Margetts, H.: Artificial intelligence in government: concepts, standards, and a unified framework. Gov. Inf. Q. **40**(4), 1–34(2023). https://doi.org/10.1016/j.giq.2023.101881
91. Suneja, N., Shah, J.P., Shah, Z.H., Holia, M.S.: A neural network approach to design reality oriented cost estimate model for infrastructure projects. Reliab. Theory Appl. **16**, 254–263 (2021)
92. Swanson, T., Zelner, J., Guikema, S.: Covid-19 has illuminated the need for clearer AI-based risk management strategies. J. Risk Res. **25**(10), 1223–1238 (2022). https://doi.org/10.1080/13669877.2022.2077411
93. Swinney, C.J.: The challenges of artificial intelligence: Britain's bright future. Air Space Power Rev. **24**(2), 118–139 (2022)
94. Tariq M.U.: The role of emerging technologies in shaping the global digital government landscape. Emerging Developments and Technologies in Digital Government, nan, pp. 160–180 (2024). https://doi.org/10.4018/979-8-3693-2363-2.ch009
95. Thoene U., Alonso R.G., Benavides D.E.D.: Ethical frameworks and regulatory governance: an exploratory analysis of the colombian strategy for artificial intelligence. Revista de Direito, Estado e Telecomunicacoes **16**(1), 146–171 (2024). https://doi.org/10.26512/lstr.v16i1.48974
96. Titu, M.A., Stanciu, A.: Human and aritificial intelligence: the partnership that imparts hope. In: Proceedings of the 11th International Conference on Electronics, Computers and Artificial Intelligence, ECAI 2019, nan (2019). https://doi.org/10.1109/ECAI46879.2019.9041998
97. Tsabedze, V.: Managing records in the age of artificial intelligence: how prepared are archives and records management professionals in eswatini? Internet Ref. Serv. Q. **28**(1), 77–95 (2024). https://doi.org/10.1080/10875301.2023.2284898
98. Tsuboi, S., Ikaruga, S., Kobayashi, T., Nishimura, S.: The effectiveness of the compact city plan of local government after abolishing the area division system. Design and Decision Support Systems in Architecture and Urban Planning - 13th International Conference on Design and Decision Support Systems in Architecture and Urban Planning, DDSS 2016, nan (2016)
99. Tuptuk, N., Hazell, P., Watson, J., Hailes, S.: A systematic review of the state of cybersecurity in water systems. Water (Switzerland) **13**(1) (2021). https://doi.org/10.3390/w13010081

100. van der Vlist, F., Helmond, A., Ferrari, F.: Big AI: cloud infrastructure dependence and the industrialisation of artificial intelligence. Big Data Soc. **11**(1) (2024). https://doi.org/10.1177/20539517241232630
101. Varpio, L., Paradis, E., Uijtdehaage, S., Young, M.: The distinctions between theory, theoretical framework, and conceptual framework. Acad. Med. **95**(7), 989–994 (2020). https://doi.org/10.1097/ACM.0000000000003075
102. Wasserman, D., Flaxman, M.: Artificial intelligence and planning practice. Plan. Advi. Serv. Memo, nan (111) (2022)
103. Whittle, T., Gregova, E., Podhorska, I., Rowland, Z.: Smart manufacturing technologies: data-driven algorithms in production planning, sustainable value creation, and operational performance improvement. Econ. Manag. Financ. Mark. **14**(2), 52–57 (2019)
104. Williamson, B.: Policy networks, performance metrics and platform markets: charting the expanding data infrastructure of higher education. Br. J. Edu. Technol. **50**(6), 2794–2809 (2019). https://doi.org/10.1111/bjet.12849
105. Wirtz, B.W., Müller, W.M.: An integrated artificial intelligence framework for public management. Public Manag. Rev. **21**(7), 1076–1100 (2019). https://doi.org/10.1080/14719037.2018.1549268
106. Wolniak, R., Stecuła, K.: Artificial intelligence in smart cities—applications, barriers, and future directions: a review. Smart Cities **7**(3), 1346–1389 (2024). https://doi.org/10.3390/smartcities7030057
107. Wu, J.: Quality evaluation model of artificial intelligence general education online course based on AI algorithm. In: Proceedings - 2022 International Conference on Education, Network and Information Technology, ICENIT 2022, nan, pp. 129–133 (2022). https://doi.org/10.1109/ICENIT57306.2022.00035
108. Park, Y., Um, M.: A study on the Application of Artificial Intelligence for the Administrative Innovation of Science and Technology. Science and Technology Policy Institute, Sejong (2020)
109. Yee, D.-H., You, Y.-Y.: The impact of awareness of new artificial intelligence technologies on policy governance on risk. Res. World Econ. **11**(2), 152–158 (2020). https://doi.org/10.5430/rwe.v11n2p152
110. Yfantis, V., Ntalianis, K., Ntalianis, F.: Exploring the implementation of artificial intelligence in the public sector: welcome to the clerkless public offices. Applications in education. Adv. Eng. Educ. **17**, 76–79 (2020). https://doi.org/10.37394/232010.2020.17.9
111. Yigitcanlar T., et al.: Artificial intelligence and the local government: a five-decade scientometric analysis on the evolution, state-of-the-art, and emerging trends. Cities **152** (2024). https://doi.org/10.1016/j.cities.2024.105151
112. Zhang, W., Zuo, N., He, W., Li, S., Yu, L.: Factors influencing the use of artificial intelligence in government: evidence from china. Technol. Soc. **66** (2021). https://doi.org/10.1016/j.techsoc.2021.101675
113. Zhu, Q.: A financial risk network assessment model based on artificial intelligence and machine learning. In: IEEE International Conference on Knowledge Engineering and Communication Systems, ICKES 2022, nan (2022). https://doi.org/10.1109/ICKECS56523.2022.10060821

Self-explanatory Retrieval-Augmented Generation for SDG Evidence Identification

Darío Garigliotti(✉)

University of Bergen, Bergen, Norway
dario.garigliotti@uib.no

Abstract. With the establishment of the Sustainable Development Goals (SDG) framework, practitioners in environmental impact assessment have an increasing requirement to detect relevant information centered on this frame of reference. The task of automatically identifying evidence that supports the project actually addressing a particular SDG target becomes crucial for enabling assessment digitalization across long, heterogeneous documents. In this work, we tackle SDG evidence identification via the well-suited Retrieval-augmented Generation (RAG) approach powered by Large Language Models (LLM). The identified evidence may also support further related tasks in conceptual modeling where reports or parts of their content are to be assigned to entries in a structured resource such as a domain-specific ontology. Beyond the measurement of performance of a series of method configurations on this task, we also assess RAG abilities for making this kind of decisions when the LLM is requested to explain its own mechanisms alongside the answer it generates. Our evaluation resources are made publicly available.

Keywords: Sustainable Development Goals · Retrieval-augmented Generation · Large Language Models · Explainable AI

1 Introduction

The requirement for addressing Sustainable Development Goals (SDG)[1] has become more prominent across many spheres of human activity. SDGs, established by United Nations to serve as a common ground for high-level policy arcs, have indeed become a frame of reference in a multiplicity of development regulations at all scales and in almost every domain (Del Campo et al., 2020). Distinguishedly, professionals in areas of environmental assessment, ranging from expert assessors to authorities, as well as key personnel on the side of project developers, are regularly faced with the need to process documentation pertaining SDGs. These kind of documents, *environmental (impact) assessment* (EIA) reports, are typically long, and are presented in heterogeneous formats, through

[1] https://sdgs.un.org/goals.

M. Saeki et al. (Eds.): ER 2024 Workshops, LNCS 14932, pp. 124–132, 2025.
https://doi.org/10.1007/978-3-031-75599-6_9

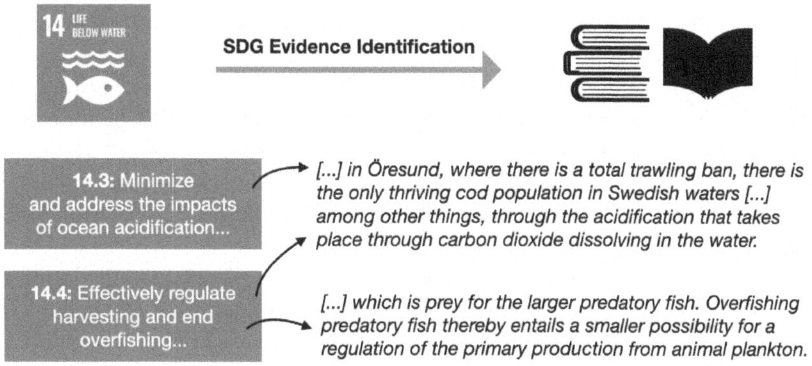

Fig. 1. Overview of the SDG Evidence Identification task.

which these experts endure the difficult task of finding the relevant information that is needed, in particular, that which addresses a given SDG of interest. Plus, the information need of environmental assessors for detecting textual passages addressing an SDG, and mostly SDG targets as focused, actionable SDG subgoals, often clashes subtly with incentives in the documents' narrative for aggrandazing the ways by which the SDG target is being addressed by the developer behind the report (Del Campo et al., 2020). There is clearly an increasing need for information systems that enable larger digital access to this kind of analysis by all actors involved. We argue that a crucial component of such a system deals with detecting relevant passages in a EIA report addressing a given SDG target. This information extraction problem is the one that we address in our paper. An overview of this task is depicted in Fig. 1.

A series of recent advancements in key components of their training (architecture, regime, data acquisition and usage) has made significant improvements in language modeling technology with the establishment of Large Language Models (LLMs) as the dominant technology in several information processing tasks (Touvron and et al., 2023; Radford et al., 2019). These models, trained over very large corpora of scrapped content and prominent datasets with powerful transformers-based neural networks and human feedback, provide themselves vast knowledge implicitly stored in their billions of parameters (Elazar and et al., 2024). Yet, for knowledge domains, problems and content sources with limited or altogether null presence in the underlying data of an LLM, the incorporation of explicit, relevant knowledge often results decisive to achieve desired performances. Retrieval-augmented Generation (RAG) (Lewis and et al., 2020) is a general umbrella of methods that integrate external knowledge to complement the capabilities of an LLM. This approach suits very well with our problem, where we intend to predict a decision making answer regarding whether a candidate passage truly addresses an SDG target.

Our work subscribes within the emerging research between areas such as Natural Language Processing (NLP), Knowledge Representation (KR) or Information Extraction (IE) overlapping in the applicability of their techniques on the relevant phenomena within climate change. Whether to respond questionnaires (Spokoyny et al., 2023) or to detect climate claims in text (Stammbach and et al., 2023), more studies address environmental scenarios of information access. Fundamental research is also focused on building dedicated language models (Webersinke et al., 2022; Thulke and et al., 2024), as well as chat systems (Vaghefi and et al., 2023) and EIA-centric ontologies (Nielsen and et al., 2023; Garigliotti and et al., 2023).

Alongside the convenience of using LLMs in multiple tasks and domains, a common drawback is the presence of hallucinations that very often hurt their performance, and altogether diminish the trustworthiness in decisions supported by these models (Liu et al., 2023; Asai et al., 2022). Hence, in this work, we study mechanisms within Explainable AI (XAI) (Cambria et al., 2023) to elicit, from an LLM, not only the prediction for the correct assessment of a target being addressed by a passage, but also the ability of the same model to explain the rationales behind its generated answer. The potential explanations, together with the evidence naturally provided by the identification task, would increase the factors of trust in the users of these environmental assessment systems (Menick and et al., 2022).

The resources developed in this work are made publicly available at https://bit.ly/AIMM_at_ER_2024-SDG_EI_XAI-Materials.

The rest of the paper defines in detail the problem that we address, describes the approach and the data and metrics we use for its evaluation, and analyzes the experimental results guided by our research questions.

2 Methodology

2.1 Problem

Given an SDG target, and one or more passages from environmental impact assessment (EIA) reports, *SDG Target Evidence Identification* (or *SDG-EI* for short) is the task of deciding which of the passages, if any, is a relevant evidence supporting that the content of the target is addressed (Garigliotti, 2024). We assume an instantiation of this problem where a method, specifically an Large Language Model (LLM), is required to generate an answer –to a question asking for deciding which among the candidate passage(s) is relevant– such that the answer contains the correct passages, each referred to by a unique string identifier also included in the prompt used to generate with the LLM. Figure 1 presents an overview of our problem and illustrates it with examples of evidence identification for SDG targets.

2.2 Retrieval-Augmented Generation

We approach the SDG-EI problem by instantiating the Retrieval-Augmented Generation (RAG) framework in a series of methods. A main characteristic of

RAG is its ability to complement the parametric or implicit information in an LLM with external, domain-specific knowledge provided in the prompt issued to the generator LLM (Lewis and et al., 2020; Gao et al., 2023). As its name indicates, RAG consists in three main stages. The first one, *retrieval*, obtains a ranked list of documents for a query from a given document index. In our scenario, a collection of EIA reports is indexed and retrieved from by issuing the content of an SDG target as the query. In the second stage, a standard prompt –designed to ask an LLM to answer about relevant EIA passages for a given target– is *augmented* with the retrieved passages so that the generator is provided with these as context for the question. Otherwise, the SDG-EI task in it would be left to face the entirety of the space of implicit knowledge in the LLM where most likely the desired output for the passages of interest would not be found. The final phase involves inputting this augmented prompt into an LLM from which to *generate* an answer containing the desired output, in this case, the mention of the passages relevant to the SDG target, if any.

A template of the prompts developed in this work is shown in Table 1. The settings for the parameters studied here are described in Sect. 3.2.

2.3 Explainable SDG-EI

In order to operationalize the elicitation to a model for inspecting its own rationales used to produce the generated output, we directly request to the LLM to complement its answer about passage relevance to a target with an explanation. Specifically, we also add to the prompt, during augmentation, (i) an additional instruction, mentioning the intention to ask for this self-inspection, and (ii) a complementary question asking for explaining on the generated answer.

In the template presented in Table 1, the placeholders [XAI instr.] and [XAI Q.] are replaced by the actual explainability-oriented instruction and question, according to experimentation with relevant parameters described in Sect. 3.2.

3 Experimental Setup

3.1 Dataset

We make use of a collection based on environmental reports made publicly available by the Ministry of Climate of the Republic of Estonia.[2] These reports correspond to projects developed in the country and other European countries nearby, hence determining a particular environment with the geography, the human activities and regulations that exists in these locations. The collection comprises 16,474 passages obtained from 33 reports. It also collects the relevance of passages –obtained with a baseline lexical retrieval method– for a selection of 30 SDG targets, out of the 157 targets within the SDG framework. These targets are relevant to the environmental assessment carried out in said environment of

[2] https://kliimaministeerium.ee/piiriulene-moju-hindamine#piiriulese-moju-hind.

Fig. 2. The 30 SDG targets in the dataset.

provenance for the reports, and so more likely to be addressed in them. Figure 2 lists all the 30 selected SDG targets.

The dataset is included in our resources made publicly available.[3]

3.2 RAG Configurations

In this work, each SDG-EI method is an instance of the RAG framework, where a particular assignment of values is set to our RAG parameters of interest, in what we refer to as a (parameter) configuration.

For the **retrieval** phase, we use the SDG target as query to retrieve the top 3 passages (i.e. 3 the cut-off) from the indexed collection of passages, via both traditional lexical retrieval (lexical, for short) and learned dense retrieval (dense, for short) (Gao et al., 2023). The well-established Pyserini library[4] is here used to perform retrieval.

In the second stage, **augmentation**, we experiment with the way that the retrieved passages are integrated. Within a common format where each passage is provided preceded by its unique identifier from the collection, a straightforward augmentation lists the passages in the same order as in the retrieval output. Since the presence of implicit artefacts was detected where the model tries to memorize the top positions of the relevant passages in the retrieval order, we also experiment with an alternative *ordering* where passages appear in the prompt in a random order. In this same stage we also experiment on few-shot learning, specifically, with the *number of examples* provided in the prompt to help

[3] https://bit.ly/AIMM_at_ER_2024-SDG_EI_XAI-Materials.
[4] https://github.com/castorini/pyserini.

Table 1. Template to build the basic prompt during augmentation. The templates for the XAI-aware prompts are almost identical except for the enabled explainability components **[XAI instr.]** and **[XAI Q.]** omitted in the basic prompt.

Prompt template
You are an assistant for tasks in environmental impact assessment (EIA). A few excerpts from the textual content of EIA reports are provided by the user as contexts. Please ANSWER the QUESTION about the possible relevance of these contexts for the given Sustainable Development Goal (SDG) target. Please answer to the best of your ability. If you don't know the answer, just say that you don't know. Keep the answer concise. When you refer to a context in your answer, always cite the corresponding context ID (which must be among the given CONTEXTS) between square brackets (e.g. [a1b2x34d]), as it's done in each example. Examples are given below, each example between the '<example>' and '</example>' tags. After that, you are given the actual SDG target with contexts so that you answer about it. **[XAI instr.]**

Prompt template (ctd.)
⟨example⟩ ... ⟨/example⟩ ... QUESTION: Which one(s), if any, of the provided context(s) is a relevant evidence where the SDG target is addressed? **[XAI Q.]** CONTEXTS: Context ID: ... Context: ... ... ANSWER:

narrow down the generation space of the LLM –the possible values are 1 and 2, i.e. one-shot and two-shot. A third parameter of interest is the actual *explanation question* that elicits the rationales from the LLM. We distinguish the basic prompt, i.e. without explanation elicitation, from the alternative ones that we refer to as XAI-aware prompts. A direct XAI question, *X-direct*, asks "Why do you think that this is the answer to the question?" right after the question for passage relevance to the SDG target. A counterfactual strategy, *X-counter*, instead, inquires for alternative prompting scenarios challenging the augmented LLM input itself: "What would you have answered to the same question if the order of the passages in the prompt was different?" Each of these XAI-aware prompts correspond to the template in Table 1 where the respective question mentioned above is put in the [XAI Q.] placeholder. With the same template, in a XAI-aware prompt the placeholder [XAI Instr.] at the end of the prompt header is replaced by the additional instruction "You are also asked about why you are giving this answer to the question. Please respond to it right after."

Generation is finally performed by inputting the prompt into the GPT-3.5 (gpt-3.5-turbo-0125) LLM (Radford et al., 2019).

3.3 Evaluation Metrics

We evaluate the SDG-EI performance of each of the proposed RAG methods by the means of standard set metrics of precision, recall and F-score with respect to the predicted and relevant passages for an SDG target. Given a method, we report the average performance across all its SDG targets.

4 Experimental Results

Table 2 presents the results for all our experimental configurations. Each block in the table corresponds to one of the prompting strategies: basic, X-direct, and X-counterfactual, resp. The corresponding files with the full results for every RAG stage are made available in the public directory with our resources.[5]

Table 2. Experimental results for all the configurations in the SDG Evidence Identification task. A metric group indicates the setting for the parameter about number of few-shot examples in the prompt (one or two). In all these experiments, the retrieval cut-off is top 3 results and the generator LLM is GPT-3.5. In each block of this table, the best performance on a metric is shown in **bold**.

Retrieval method	Passage order	One-shot			Two-shot		
		Prec.	Rec.	F-Sco.	Prec.	Rec.	F-Sco.
Prompt: Basic (no XAI elements)							
Lexical	By ranking	0.7222	**0.6611**	**0.6656**	0.7667	**0.6778**	0.6944
	Random	**0.7444**	0.6	0.6411	**0.7944**	0.6722	**0.6956**
Dense	By ranking	0.6556	0.6389	0.62	0.6556	0.5667	0.5878
	Random	0.6833	0.5833	0.5989	0.7	0.6056	0.6322
Prompt: X-direct							
Lexical	By ranking	**0.7889**	**0.8167**	**0.7689**	**0.7889**	**0.6611**	**0.6833**
	Random	0.7333	0.6	0.6111	0.7867	0.6389	0.6617
Dense	By ranking	0.6889	0.6111	0.5989	0.7667	0.5778	0.6156
	Random	0.6889	0.65	0.6456	0.7111	0.5389	0.58
Prompt: X-counter							
Lexical	By ranking	**0.8**	**0.4444**	**0.5489**	0.7667	0.3889	0.4956
	Random	0.7333	0.3444	0.46	**0.8333**	**0.4389**	**0.5511**
Dense	By ranking	0.7333	0.3722	0.4711	0.7	0.3722	0.46
	Random	0.7	0.3944	0.48	0.7667	0.4333	0.5222

We analyze these experimental results by answering our research questions.

RQ1: *How do methods perform in terms of retrieval-stage and few-shot parameters?* In all the settings and for every metric, lexical retrieval clearly results to perform better. Qualitatively, these cases are often favoured by few words that are very relevant for correctly matching query –target– and passage during retrieval. These are words that, while distinctive for a target and/or passage, become less distinctive when combined with the semantics of other words by dense retrieval. Examples of these key words found in our data are "transport" (for target 11.2), "acidification" (for target 14.3), "overfishing" (strong signal for SDG target 14.4), and "alien" (for target 15.8 about invasive species).

[5] https://bit.ly/AIMM_at_ER_2024-SDG_EI_XAI-Materials.

RQ2: *What is the impact of the order of the passages in the prompt?* We observe strong indications for our hypothesis about the existence of artefacts in the LLM that make it favour the top passages. The methods where the passages are provided for augmentation in the same order as in the retrieval ranking outperform the counterparts with random order of passages in the prompt, i.e. the respective method with order by ranking gets affected when its passages do not keep the best on top. In the particular cases of X-counter prompt with two examples we observe the inverted pattern, and we suspect it has to do with an LLM confused by the counterfactual request.

RQ3: *Does self-explanatory generation help improve the performance on SDG-EI?* In both precision and recall metrics, and hence in their harmonic mean F-score too, SDG-EI is mostly benefited by X-direct as a simple explainable generation mechanism that we request in the prompt. X-counter, too, shows improvements for the best performing configurations in terms of precision. However, measuring by recall, X-counter clearly hurts the performance with large drops by the increased absence of correct passages in proportion in the answer. It seems then to confirm the confusion phenomena when inquired by counterfactual about passage ordering.

5 Conclusions and Future Work

In this paper, we study the usage of Retrieval-augmented Generation methods powered by an established commercial LLM for SDG evidence identification. We assess the fundamental ability of the LLM to generate the expected output when provided with explicit, external knowledge in a well-engineered prompt. Plus, we evaluate it in comparison with simple strategies to enable explainable generations by eliciting self-explanatory answers.

This evidence not only aims to confirm the prediction of a model about the content of a report addressing the SDG target in question, but also may serve to support related conceptual modeling tasks. Prominently, we envision addressing the mapping of a report –or particular parts of its content– into the structured counterparts in an ontology of environment-centered items such as activities, impacts and targets. The study of problems on linking mentions of these environmental elements to the uniquely identified entries in a structured knowledge resource is a main line of future work.

References

Asai, A., Gardner, M., Hajishirzi, H.: Evidentiality-guided generation for knowledge-intensive NLP tasks. In: Proceedings of NAACL-HLT, pp. 2226–2243. ACL (2022)

Cambria, E., Malandri, L., Mercorio, F., Mezzanzanica, M., Nobani, N.: A survey on XAI and natural language explanations. Inf. Process. Manag. **60**(1), 103111 (2023). ISSN 0306-4573

Del Campo, A.G., Gazzola, P., Onyango, V.: The mutualism of strategic environmental assessment and sustainable development goals. Environ. Impact Assess. Rev. **82**, 1–9 (2020). ISSN 0195-9255

Elazar, Y.A.B., et al.: What's in my big data? ArXiv, abs/2310.20707, 2024
Gao, T., Yen, H., Yu, J., Chen, D.: Enabling large language models to generate text with citations. In: Proceedings of the 2023 Conference on Empirical Methods in Natural Language Processing, pp. 6465–6488. Association for Computational Linguistics (2023)
Garigliotti, D.: SDG target detection in environmental reports using retrieval-augmented generation with LLMs. In: Proceedings of the 1st ClimateNLP Workshop, pp. 241–250. ACL (2024)
Garigliotti, D., et al.: Do bridges dream of water pollutants? Towards DreamsKG, a knowledge graph to make digital access for sustainable environmental assessment come true. In: Proceedings of the ACM Web Conference (2023)
Lewis, P., et al.: Retrieval-augmented generation for knowledge-intensive NLP tasks. Adv. Neural Inf. Process. Syst. **33**, 9459–9474. Curran Associates, Inc. (2020)
Liu, N., Zhang, T., Liang, P.: Evaluating verifiability in generative search engines. In: Findings of the Association for Computational Linguistics: EMNLP 2023, pp. 7001–7025. ACL (2023)
Menick, J., Trebacz, M., et al.: Teaching language models to support answers with verified quotes. ArXiv, abs/2203.11147, 2022
Nielsen, F.Å., Lyhne, I., et al.: Environmental impact assessment reports in wikidata and a wikibase. In: ESWC Workshops (2023)
Radford, A., Wu, J., Child, R., Luan, D., Amodei, D., Sutskever, I.: Language models are unsupervised multitask learners, 2019
Spokoyny, D., Laud, T., Corringham, T., Berg-Kirkpatrick, T.: Towards answering climate questionnaires from unstructured climate reports, 2023
Stammbach, D., Webersinke, N., et al.: Environmental claim detection. In: Proceedings of the ACL (Volume 2: Short Papers), pp. 1051–1066. ACL (2023)
Thulke, D., et al.: ClimateGPT: towards AI synthesizing interdisciplinary research on climate change. ArXiv, abs/2401.09646, 2024
Touvron, H., et al.: Llama 2: open foundation and fine-tuned chat models. ArXiv, abs/2307.09288, 2023
Vaghefi, S.A., Stammbach, D., et al.: ChatClimate: grounding conversational AI in climate science. Commun. Earth Environ. **4** (2023). CRIS-Team Scopus Importer:2023-12-29
Webersinke, N., Kraus, M., Bingler, J.A., Leippold, M.: ClimateBert: a pretrained language model for climate-related text. In: Proceedings of AAAI 2022 Fall Symposium (2022)

CMLS

CMLS – 5th International Workshop on Conceptual Modeling for Life Sciences

Alberto García S.[1], Anna Bernasconi[2], José Fabián Reyes Román[1], and Edelweis Rohrer[3]

[1] Universitat Politècnica de València, Spain
[2] Politecnico di Milano, Italy
[3] Universidad de la República, Uruguay

Recent advances in understanding human conditions and diseases have opened new opportunities for prevention, diagnosis, and treatment. The exponential growth of information in this field impacts the design and development of data management pipelines, highlighting the need for novel approaches to processing healthcare data and knowledge.

The 5th International Workshop on Conceptual Modeling in Life Sciences (CMLS) was held in 2024 as part of the ER 2024 conference. This workshop continues to bring together researchers in Information Systems (IS), Conceptual Modeling (CM), Data Management (DM), and Artificial Intelligence (AI) who are working on healthcare and life science challenges. The combined efforts of the IS, CM, DM, and AI research communities are critical to the precise ontological characterization of components in complex biological systems, as well as the modeling of operational processes and decision-support methods for disease diagnosis and prevention. These disciplines must work together to develop practical solutions for high-quality, efficient healthcare.

The submissions covered a wide range of topics, such as conceptual modeling for genetic risk assessment, modeling biological processes, ontologies for mental health disorders, AI applications in vaccine development and prediction, and data integration in healthcare. These contributions demonstrate various modeling techniques and AI approaches to address critical challenges in life sciences and healthcare. CMLS aims to foster discussions on the conceptual modeling community's role in supporting life sciences research and applications. We hope the ideas presented will inspire further research and collaborations in these critical areas.

Acknowledgments. The organizers express their gratitude to the authors, members of the program committee, organizers of ER 2024, and the invited speaker for their valuable contributions to the success of CMLS 2024. CMLS 2024 was organized within the framework of the projects PID2021-123824OB-I00 – Spanish State Research Agency and CIPROM/2021/023 – Generalitat Valenciana. Anna Bernasconi is supported by Ministero dell'Università e della Ricerca (PRIN PNRR 2022 "SENSIBLE" project, n. P2022CNN2J), funded by the European Union, Next Generation EU, within PNRR M4.C2.1.1.

CMLS Organization

Workshop Chairs

Alberto García S.	Universitat Politécnica de Valéncia, Spain
Anna Bernasconi	Politecnico di Milano, Italy
José F. Reyes Román	Universitat Politécnica de Valéncia, Spain
Edelweis Rohrer	Universidad de la República, Uruguay

Program Committee

Bernardo Breve	Università degli Studi di Salerno, Italy
Raffaele Calogero	University of Turin, Italy
Stefano Ceri	Politecnico di Milano, Italy
Stefano Cirillo	Università degli Studi di Salerno, Italy
Nelly Condori	Universidad Santiago de Compostela, Spain
Tommaso Dolci	Politecnico di Milano, Italy
Giovanni Giachetti	Universitat Politécnica de Valéncia, Spain
Giancarlo Guizzardi	University of Twente, The Netherlands
Sergio Lifschitz	Pontifical Catholic University of Rio de Janeiro, Brazil
Giovanni Meroni	Technical University of Denmark, Denmark
Paolo Missier	Newcastle University, UK
José Palazzo	Federal University of Rio Grande do Sul, Brazil
Ignacio Panach	University of Valencia, Spain
Oscar Pastor	Universitat Politécnica de Valéncia, Spain
Barbara Pernici	Politecnico di Milano, Italy
Tiago Prince Sales	University of Twente, The Netherlands
Monjoy Saha	National Cancer Institute, USA
Veda Storey	Georgia State University, USA
Lisa Trigiante	University of Modena and Reggio Emilia, Italy
Juan Carlos Trujillo	University of Alicante, Spain

On the Expressiveness of Petri Nets for Modeling Biological Processes: The Case for mRNA Translation and Protein Synthesis

Luis Henrique Costa Neto[1(✉)], S. Lifschitz[1], F. Baião[2], M. Catanho[3], A. B. de Miranda[3], and E. H. Haeusler[1]

[1] Informatics Dept., Pontifical Catholic Univ. of Rio de Janeiro (PUC-Rio), Rio de Janeiro, Brazil
{lneto,sergio,hermann}@inf.puc-rio.br

[2] Industrial Eng. Dept., Pontifical Catholic Univ. of Rio de Janeiro (PUC-Rio), Rio de Janeiro, Brazil
fbaiao@puc-rio.br

[3] Laboratório de Genética Molecular de Microrganismos, Instituto Oswaldo Cruz, Fundação Oswaldo Cruz, Rio de Janeiro, Brazil
{mcatanho,amiranda}@fiocruz.br

Abstract. The translation process in Molecular Biology has been extensively studied, and several modeling frameworks have been used, including Petri Networks. We propose an approach that models mRNA translation at the codon level for the elongation phase, improving the expressiveness, extending from single transitions to representing each elongation step. We use the proposed model to run simulations comparing the effects of the relative availability between mRNA and amino acid.

Keywords: protein synthesis · mRNA translation · Petri Networks

1 Introduction

The Central Dogma of Molecular Biology describes the flow of genetic information within a biological system: DNA is replicated, transcribed into RNA, and then translated into proteins. Genetic information is abstracted using an alphabet of four nucleotides (A, G, T, and C) deciphered from sets of three nucleotides

L. H. Costa Neto, S. Lifschitz, F. Baião, and E. H. Haeusler are partially funded by CAPES (Brazilian Ministry of Education Funding Agency) institutional grant.
S. Lifschitz is partially funded by the National Council for Scientific and Technological Development (CNPq), grant 306525/2021-6.
F Baião is partially funded by Rio de Janeiro State Funding Agency (FAPERJ) grants 200.514/2023 and 211.308/2019) and CNPq grants 312059/2022-1 and 422810/2021-5.
E.H. Haeusler is partially funded by FAPERJ grant APQ1 E-26/210.258/2019 249292) and CNPq grant 309287/2023-5.

M. Saeki et al. (Eds.): ER 2024 Workshops, LNCS 14932, pp. 137–147, 2025.
https://doi.org/10.1007/978-3-031-75599-6_10

(codons). Out of the 64 existing codons, 61 encode one of the 20 canonical amino acids, while the remaining three direct translation initiation and termination.

Modeling the transmission of genetic information is crucial for understanding life's functions, evolution, and advancing scientific knowledge. It provides fundamental knowledge about the storage, replication, and utilization of genetic information within cells, revealing the complexity of life and the roles of DNA, RNA, proteins, and the cellular machinery.

In this article, we agree with [5] that modeling the bio-molecular dynamics at the most basic and computational level provides a universal and intentional, in computational terms, model feature. The intentionality comes from the principle stated in [5] that each molecule or molecular complex is primarily associated with its activity and only lately to an alleged biological function, providing a more observational than interpretational meaning to each process performed by the biomolecule. Thus, we analyze the process of mRNA translation as a computational process and conclude that the observational perspectives that can be taken can contribute to observing different activities in the processes. The semantics is expressed in Petri Nets. We remind the reader about this formalization and show how some decisions made during the formalization imply different activities, according to both quantitative and qualitative perspectives.

As described in [4], the translation process is generally divided into three stages: initiation, elongation, and termination. The initiation stage involves the binding of the ribosomal unit to the mRNA. The elongation stage is when the polypeptide chain is built by reading codon after codon and binding the amino acids together to form the chain. Finally, the termination stage begins when a stop codon is recognized, and the necessary reactions release the ribosomal unit and the completed polypeptide chain. Several papers have modeled the translation process in a codon-by-codon manner; we also take this approach instead of a one-shot process.

We use the tooling of Petri Networks to show the possible outcomes that might occur using the more detailed approach, which is not possible in the one-shot version. Although the usual model for translation is the ODE/Reaction Kinetics as in [1,3,6], Petri Networks have also been used to model this process as in [2] and [13]. In [14], the authors compare the main modeling strategies for mRNA translation. It is worth mentioning that experimentally verifying the results of the many formalisms for modelling protein synthesis may be achieved with the help of CFPS[1] as mentioned in [10].

The Petri Network framework demonstrates the differences between the one-shot vs codon-by-codon model. In doing so, we both arrive at a conclusion first drawn by [1] that the longer the codon chain, the less likely the process is to conclude, as well as a novel conclusion regarding the effects of abundant mRNA within the cell.

The main idea is to highlight that the one-shot model leaves out the non-linearity of the process. Given the simultaneity of several reactions occurring within the cell, including several parallel elongation reactions, the process can

[1] Cell-free Protein Synthesis.

consume too much of an amino acid in the initial steps of elongation, which leads to some amino acids composing only partial polypeptides and, therefore, not making their way to finished proteins. This conclusion is similar to the one achieved by [6]; we invert the analysis and investigate the effects of what happens to protein output as we increase the amount of mRNA given a fixed amount of aminoacids.

2 Background

We begin by recalling the definition of Petri Networks; for a comprehensive review, see [9].

Definition 1. *We define a Petri Net as a tuple* (P, T, I, O, M), *where*

- P *is a finite set of places:* $P = \{P_1, P_2, ..., P_n\}$
- T *is a finite set of transitions:* $T = \{T_1, T_2, ..., T_m\}$
- I *is a function assigning weights to input arcs:* $I : P \times T \to \mathbb{N}$
- O *is a function assigning weights to output arcs:* $O : T \times P \to \mathbb{N}$
- M_i *is the marking of the places at epoch* i[2]*:* $M_i : P \to \mathbb{N}, i \geqslant 0$.

The initial marking can be identified with a tuple in $\mathbb{N}^n$ with $n = |P|$.

Given a transition $t \in T$ and a marking M, we say that t is a valid transition for M iff $\forall p M(p) \geqslant I(t, p)$. After a valid transition t is fired, the network goes from the current marking M to M' respecting the input and output functions, which means:

$$\forall p \; M'(p) = M(p) - I(t, p) + O(t, p)$$

If we view the input and output functions as $n \times m$ matrices[3], we can define the transition matrix $A = O - I \in \mathbb{N}^m \times \mathbb{N}^n$, and the marking M as a vector, it is correct to affirm that:

$$M' = A(t)M$$

We assume that only one transition is fired at a time. Hence, it is possible to consider a sequence of transition firings: $[T_1, T_2, T_3, T_2, T_1, T_1, T_3, ...]$.

In summary, we can only fire a transition if the preceding places have enough tokens to match the input for that transition, and given a fired transition, tokens are consumed or produced according to the amounts defined by the input and output arcs, respectively.

3 Translation Modeling

We revisit why it is relevant to model mRNA translation in detail rather than take the entire process as a single reaction. Focusing solely on elongation and

---

[2] $M_0(p) = k$ is equivalent to saying we have k tokens in place p at epoch 0.

[3] n is the number of places and m the number of transitions.

analyzing the relationship between the process and amino acid availability is sufficient. As such, we do not consider otherwise relevant processes and molecules, such as tRNAs, tRNA aminoacylation, ribosomes, termination factors, etc. We also do not take into account the post-processing steps.

For this simplified version, we consider that the amino acid sequence (e.g., $a_1a_2a_2a_3$) is sufficient to build the network in each model so that we can compare the models for the same amino acid sequence.

3.1 Simple One-Shot Model

In this model, we treat the translation process as a single network transition.[4]

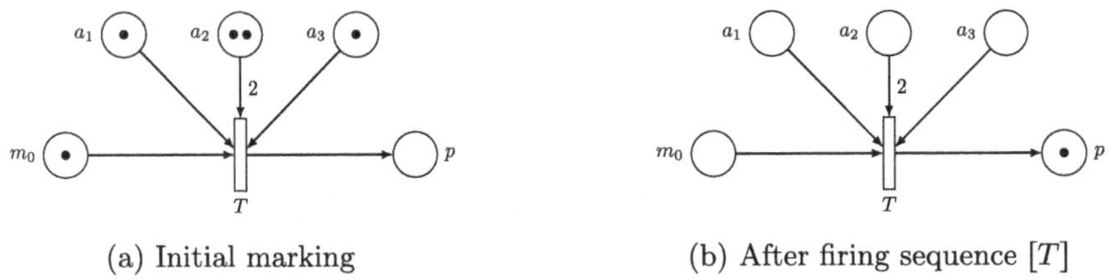

Fig. 1. Example of conventional model for sequence $a_1a_2a_2a_3$

As we see in Fig. 1, the network has only one transition and, by definition, can only fire if the marking for place M is not empty and the aminoacids places have the necessary amount of tokens. Therefore, the only achievable markings are:

- No transition is fired, and we end up with no changes in any initial markings (and therefore no proteins).
- The transition is fired once, and we have one protein as output.
- If there are more amino acids than shown in Fig. 1, then the transition might be fired multiple times, and the process finishes with as many proteins as the number of times the transition was fired.

3.2 Simple Codon-by-Codon Model

This model breaks down the translation process in many steps, with the mRNA molecule being in different states as the elongation subprocess unfolds. The main difference is that we do not consume all necessary amino acids in a single transition and do not get a protein until the last amino acid is attached.

In Fig. 2, it is possible to see that the codon-by-codon network gives rise to more probable states due to the increased number of places and transitions. To level the ground and have a reasonable comparison of models, we will compare only the areas that are common among the models, that is, the amino acids A_i, mRNA (M), and synthesized protein (P). To compare the two networks, we are interested in the submarking reachability of the networks.

[4] As a convention, we do not label edges with weight = 1.

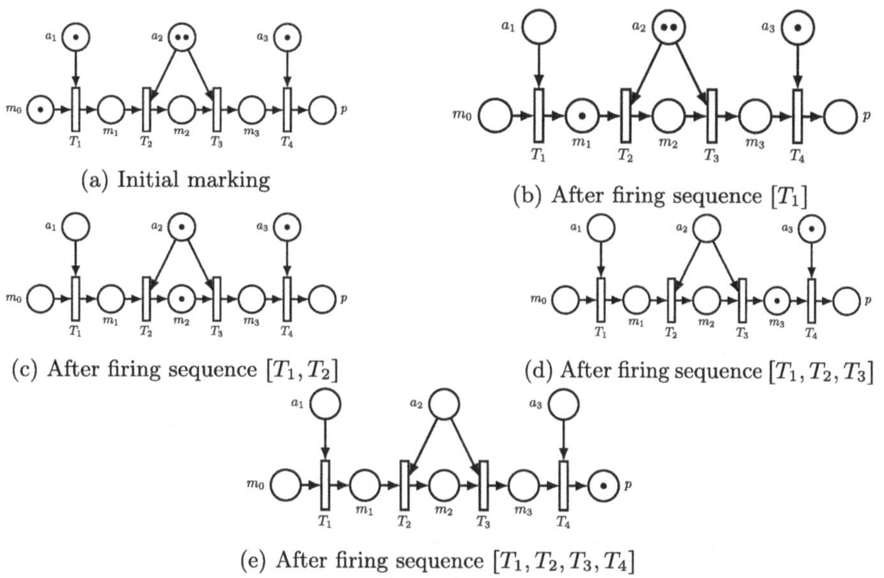

Fig. 2. Codon-by-Codon model for sequence $a_1a_2a_2a_3$

4 Qualitative Comparison

In the literature of Petri Networks, one way to qualitatively compare two networks is to look at the reachable markings from an initial marking M_0 in [9]. This property is referred to as a behavioral property of the network, that is, a property that depends on the initial marking, distinguishing it from structural properties that do not depend on the initial marking.

Definition 2. *For a Petri Network with initial marking M, a marking M' is said to be reachable if a firing sequence $[T_{i_1}, T_{i_2}, T_{i_3}, ..., T_{i_k}]$ exists such that the application of the sequence results in the network marking being M'.*

Definition 3. *For a Petri Network with initial marking M, the reachability graph of the network is a tree, with the root node representing the initial marking*[5] *and the branches representing possible firing sequences.*

To better visualize the effects of the detailed model, we will take a network even simpler than the ones for aminoacid sequence $a_1a_2a_2a_3$ and consider the simplest case possible of a single amino acid and a codon chain of size 2, as can be seen in Fig. 3 and Fig. 4.

[5] We represent the nodes of the tree with the tuple defining the marking $(M(p_1), M(p_2), ..., M(p_n))$.

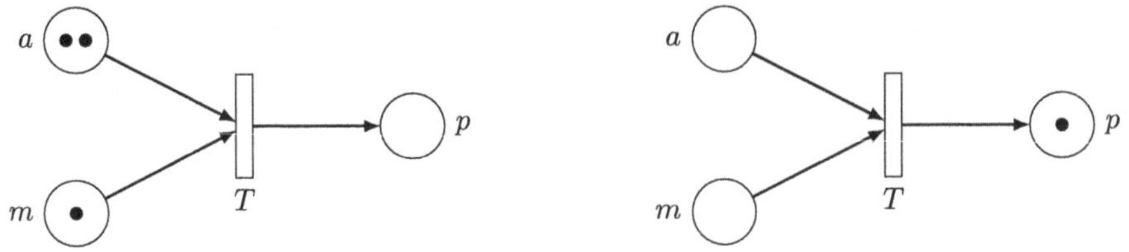

(a) Initial marking (b) After firing sequence $[T]$

Fig. 3. One-shot model for sequence a_1a_1

(a) Initial marking (b) After firing sequence $[T_1]$

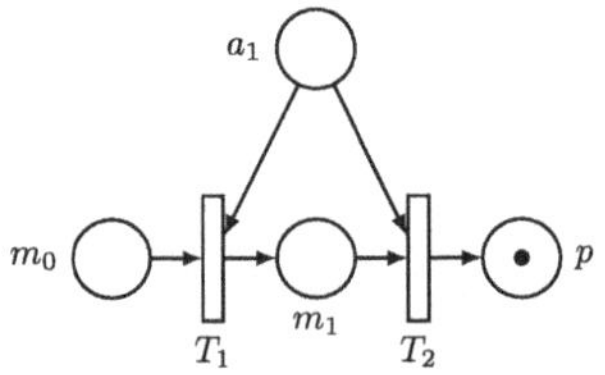

(c) After firing sequence $[T_1, T_2]$

Fig. 4. Codon-by-codon model for sequence a_1a_1

4.1 Comparing Reachable Markings

To compare both structures, we consider an initial marking in which we have:

- m mRNA molecules;
- a of a_1 amino acids;
- 0 proteins;
- 0 mRNA in intermediary states (detailed model only).

Given this initial condition, we see that the reachability graph for the networks defined in figures Fig. 3 and Fig. 4 is as shown in Fig. 5.

Not only do we have a richer possible dynamic, but we also have essentially different possible achievable states. In the single transition model, if we have sufficient mRNA molecules of amino acids, we end up with as many proteins as possible. In the codon-by-codon model, the amino acids may be mostly consumed for the transition t_1, thus achieving a lower level of protein output in the process.

The range of possible outcomes is, of course, dependent on the relative abundance of the input molecules. In an abundance of amino acids ($a \gg m$), at some

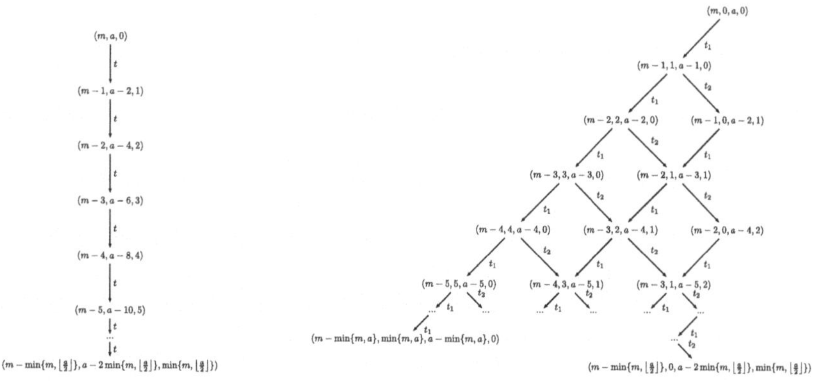

(a) Reachability graph for the single transition model

(b) Reachability graph for the codon-by-codon model

Fig. 5. Comparison of reachability graphs for both models

point, m_0 will be exhausted, and it is only possible to fire t_2 after this, and then we achieve an outcome similar to the single transition model. If, on the other hand, we have a relative abundance of mRNA molecules, it is possible that only transition t_1 fires, and even though the process consumed all amino acids, it ends up with no protein.

Comparing figures Fig. 5a and Fig. 5b, it is easy to see that while the single transition model can only achieve a final state with $\min\{m, \lfloor \frac{a}{2} \rfloor\}$ proteins, the codon-by-codon model can achieve the whole range going from $\min \max 0, a - m, m$ to $\min\{m, \lfloor \frac{a}{2} \rfloor\}$, recovering the result of the single transition model only in the case of absolute amino acid abundance. This means that the one-shot model will achieve the maximum possible protein output, whereas the codon-by-codon model has a range of potential outcomes.

Hence, given the concurrency of processes occurring within the cell, and the possible existence of several mRNA molecules locally competing for the same resources, it is possible (and likely, as we will see) that the first steps will consume amino acids and the elongation process will get stuck before it can be finished.

Since the mRNA molecule is a long chain commonly comprising hundreds or thousands of codons, it requires a varied of amino acids to produce a polipeptide. Given the locality of reactions withing the cell, the measure of the local abundance of all 20 canonical amino acids would be necessary to achieve the expected results with the one-shot model. In the next section, we explore whether or not these results are theoretically probable.

5 Probabilistic Dynamics

We have previously revisited the qualitative differences in a more detailed translation modeling vis-a-vis the simpler model of a single transition. However, the fact that the reachable markings are different might not be so incoherent with reality if the probability of a process of greedy consumption of amino acids for the intermediary transitions is low.

To investigate the relevance of the difference in a probabilistic fashion, we need to consider the probability that a specific firing sequence will happen, given an initial marking. To do this, we must assume certain behaviors and assign these probabilities. As only the codon level model allows for a non-deterministic behaviour[6], from here on, we will use it exclusively.

Arguably, the simplest possible probabilistic model for the transitions is assigning each valid transition with the same probability. With this assumption, we use the method of Monte Carlo Simulation[7] to analyze the probability distribution of firing sequences given an initial marking.

5.1 Effects of Chain Length in Protein Output

In [1], there is mention of the effects of chain size in protein synthesis output, but the conclusion is that chain sizes have little impact on the synthesis rate. Additionally, in [8], the authors investigate the effects of ribosome abortion[8] and propose a mathematical model for it. One of the conclusions is that ribosome abortion may be needed to retrieve ribosomal units stuck on mRNA without moving forward in the elongation process. Still, why ribosomes might get stuck or how likely it is is not discussed. Without the PNet model, we ran a simulation that may shed some light on this phenomenon.

More specifically, we analyze how protein output varies when we change chain length and the relative amounts of amino acids vs mRNA. For simplicity, we assume chains composed of a single codon. Also, we measure abundance vs scarcity of amino acids/mRNA as follows:

- We fix the number of amino acid tokens as $chainsize \times 100$, so we have enough amino acids to produce 100 proteins;
- We initiate the mRNA with varying quantities, starting from 100 and moving up 10 at a time;
- Therefore we start with a relative mRNA abundance of 1.0 and increase it by 0.1 for each experiment

We ran the experiment for varying chain sizes (going from 10 to 100 in 10 codon increments); for each chain size and relative abundance, we simulate the Petri Network for as many steps as there are aminoacids[9] and check the tokens in the protein place at the end. The heatmap with the results for this experiment can be seen in Fig. 6.

---

[6] In the one-shot model, at all times, we have only one possible transition, and it fires until it consumes all its inputs, and then the process stops.

[7] The simulation code can be found in https://github.com/lhcnetop/mrna_petrinet.

[8] Ribossome being disconnected from the mRNA.

[9] As in the codon-by-codon model, for each transition exactly one amino acid is consumed, this ensures the network reached its final state and no transition can be fired after that.

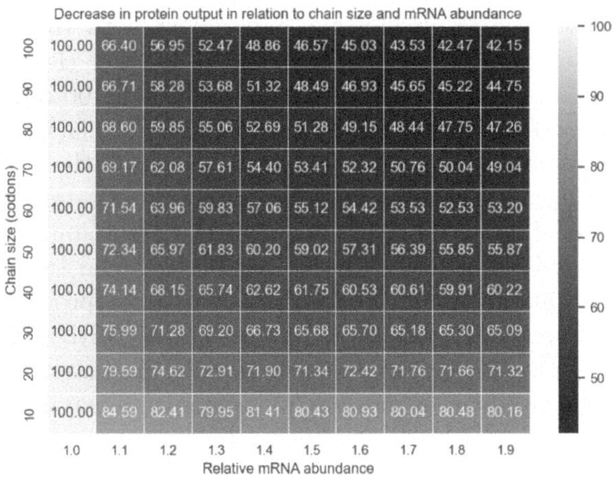

Fig. 6. Simulation experiment results relating chain length with protein output

The heatmap shows that, as the chain size increases, the protein output becomes more sensitive to the relative abundance of mRNA. The intuition behind this is that the larger the chain size, the greater the translation capacity to be stuck in intermediary states that consume more amino acids. The next step is to simulate this for a realistic sequence. We chose the translation of preprotoinsulin as it is widely documented and a comparably small polypeptide.

5.2 Simulation for Preprotoinsulin

As we take a scenario with fixed chain size, the remaining variable to be analyzed is the relative abundance of mRNA vs amino acids. As the natural protein needs several different amino acids, we started the model with precisely the amino acids required to translate 100 proteins.

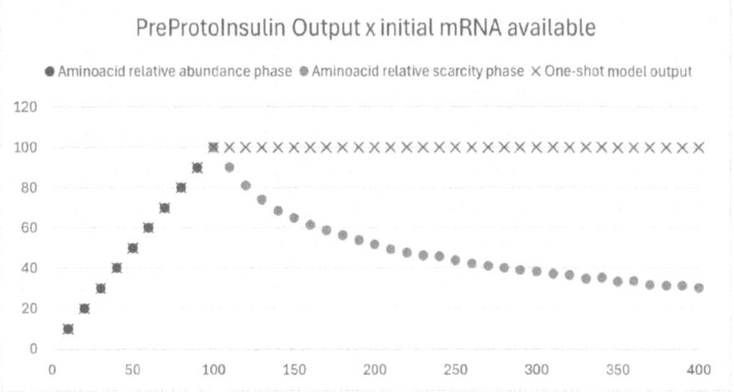

Fig. 7. Results of the simulation experiment for preprotoinsulin

In Fig. 7, we see the results for the experiment with the codon-by-codon model in two phases: a phase with amino acid abundance (less than 100 input mRNAs) and a phase of amino acid scarcity (more than 100 input mRNAs). In this simulation, it becomes clear that the one-shot model's lack of variability can manifest itself in potentially relevant practical scenarios rather than being just a theoretical advantage. It is also possible to see that the greater expressiveness of the codon level model is only appropriate in scenarios of amino acid starvation for these models. This is in line with the results obtained by [6], in the sense that starvation will induce more errors in the translation process.

In particular, the model indicates that increasing mRNA above a certain threshold could harm protein synthesis given a certain amount of amino acids. Considering the recent advances in mRNA vaccines, this may be an exciting line of investigation.

6 Conclusions

In this work, we proposed a Petri Net model for mRNA translation and explored its advantages relative to a one-shot model. Given the tractability of Petri Networks, it was simple to build a simulation model for different mRNA chains and examine it to understand better the effects of chain length and aminoacid scarcity/mRNA abundance in the process. In particular, we know that an advantage of this model relative to others is that it can shed light on why some processes tend to happen in specific scenarios.

For example, in [6], the authors investigate the effects of amino acid starvation on translation errors. They build a model to connect the starvation with the errors, but they do not explore why those errors might occur. In contrast, our model shows that these errors might occur due to the process becoming stuck in specific steps due to a lack of amino acid substrate to continue. This is in line with [7] and [11] findings regarding the correlation of abundance of tRNAs and their respective codon occurence in genes, as well as relevance to gene expression, our proposed model may help in analyzing what would happen if that was not the case and quantify the potential impact on overall protein synthesis.

Furthermore, looking at [8], the authors introduce a model to deal with ribosome abortions; one of the mentioned reasons for ribosome abortion is a pause of the ribosome at a particular site in the mRNA chain. Our model suggests that these pauses might occur because of a lack of aminoacid availability[10] in that region. With recent techniques such as ribossome profiling, it might become possible to better estimate the parameters of the model to draw new insights on the mRNA translation process as mentioned in [12].

With these conclusions, we add to the rich literature on using the Petri Nets formalism and its many derivations to better model and understand fundamental biochemical processes. The flexible nature of this formalism helps to extend any current models to add elements, functions, and activities while retaining

[10] More precisely, the scarcity of the required tRNA.

comparability to simpler models. Also, the computational aspect of Petri Nets renders itself to simulate diverse behaviors.

References

1. Bergmann, J., Lodish, H.: A kinetic model of protein synthesis. Application to hemoglobin synthesis and translational control. J. Biol. Chem. **254**(23), 11927–11937 (1979)
2. Brackley, C.A., Broomhead, D.S., Romano, M.C., Thiel, M.: A max-plus model of ribosome dynamics during mRNA translation. J. Theor. Biol. **303**, 128–140 (2012)
3. Gilchrist, M.A., Wagner, A.: A model of protein translation including codon bias, nonsense errors, and ribosome recycling. J. Theor. Biol. **239**(4), 417–434 (2006)
4. GM, C.: The Cell: A Molecular Approach. Sunderland (MA): Sinauer Associates (2000). https://www.ncbi.nlm.nih.gov/books/NBK9849/. Accessed 14 Feb 2024
5. Haeusler, E.H., et al.: Intentional semantics for molecular biology. In: Reis, M.S., de Melo-Minardi, R.C. (eds.) Advances in Bioinformatics and Computational Biology. BSB 2023. LNCS, vol. 13954, pp. 94–105. Springer, Cham (2023). https://doi.org/10.1007/978-3-031-42715-2_9
6. Harley, C., Pollard, J., Stanners, C., Goldstein, S.: Model for messenger RNA translation during amino acid starvation applied to the calculation of protein synthetic error rates. J. Biol. Chem. **256**(21), 10786–10794 (1981)
7. Ikemura, T.: Correlation between the abundance of yeast transfer rnas and the occurrence of the respective codons in protein genes: Differences in synonymous codon choice patterns of yeast and escherichia coli with reference to the abundance of isoaccepting transfer rnas. J. Mol. Biol. **158**(4), 573–597 (1982). https://doi.org/10.1016/0022-2836(82)90250-9, https://www.sciencedirect.com/science/article/pii/0022283682902509
8. Jain, A., Gupta, A.K.: Modeling mRNA translation with ribosome abortions. IEEE/ACM Trans. Comput. Biol. Bioinf. **20**(2), 1600–1605 (2023)
9. Murata, T.: Petri nets: properties, analysis and applications. Proc. IEEE **77**(4), 541–580 (1989)
10. Müller, J., Siemann-Herzberg, M., Takors, R.: Modeling cell-free protein synthesis systems-approaches and applications. Front. Bioeng. Biotechnol. **8** (2020). https://doi.org/10.3389/fbioe.2020.584178, https://www.frontiersin.org/journals/bioengineering-and-biotechnology/articles/10.3389/fbioe.2020.584178
11. Shields, D.C., Sharp, P.M.: Synonymous codon usage in bacillus subtilis reflects both translational selection and mutational biases. Nucleic Acids Res. **15**(19), 8023–8040 (1987). https://doi.org/10.1093/nar/15.19.8023, https://www.ncbi.nlm.nih.gov/pmc/articles/PMC306324/
12. Yadav, V., Ullah Irshad, I., Kumar, H., Sharma, A.K.: Quantitative modeling of protein synthesis using ribosome profiling data. Front. Mol. Biosci. **8** (2021). https://doi.org/10.3389/fmolb.2021.688700, https://www.frontiersin.org/journals/molecular-biosciences/articles/10.3389/fmolb.2021.688700
13. Yang, J., Pu, H., Lian, J., Gu, J., Fan, M.: Modeling and analysis of protein synthesis and DNA mutation using colored petri nets. IEEE Access **6**, 22386–22400 (2018). https://doi.org/10.1109/ACCESS.2018.2825782
14. Zhao, Y.B., Krishnan, J.: mRNA translation and protein synthesis: an analysis of different modelling methodologies and a new PBN based approach. BMC Syst. Biol. **8**(1), 25 (2014)

Enhancing Vaxign-DL for Vaccine Candidate Prediction with Added ESM-Generated Features

Yichao Chen[1,2], Yuhan Zhang[1], and Yongqun He[1](✉)

[1] University of Michigan, Ann Arbor, MI 48109, USA
yongqunh@med.umich.edu
[2] Penn State University, State College, PA 16803, USA
ypc5501@psu.edu

Abstract. Many vaccine design programs have been developed, including our own machine learning approaches Vaxign-ML and Vaxign-DL. Using deep learning techniques, Vaxign-DL predicts bacterial protective antigens by calculating 509 biological and biomedical features from protein sequences. In this study, we first used the protein folding ESM program to calculate a set of 1,280 features from individual protein sequences, and then utilized the new set of features separately or in combination with the traditional set of 509 features to predict protective antigens. Our results showed that the usage of ESM-derived features alone was able to accurately predict vaccine antigens with a performance similar to the orginal Vaxign-DL prediction method, and the usage of the combined ESM-derived and orginal Vaxign-DL features significantly improved the prediction performance according to a set of seven scores including specificity, sensitivity, and AUROC. To further evaluate the updated methods, we conducted a Leave-One-Pathogen-Out Validation (LOPOV) study, and found that the usage of ESM-derived features significantly improved the prediction of vaccine antigens from 10 bacterial pathogens. This research is the first reported study demonstrating the added value of protein folding features for vaccine antigen prediction.

Keywords: Vaccine Antigen · Reverse Vaccinology · Protein Folding · Evolutionary Scale Modeling (ESM) · Deep Learning · Vaxign-ML · Vaxign-DL

1 Introduction

Vaccine design is a hot research topic, esp. after the COVID-19 pandemic. Reverse vaccinology (RV) is a method for predicting vaccine candidates by analyzing genomics and proteomics sequences [1]. There are two types of RV prediction strategies currently available. One is the filtering type, which predicts protective vaccine antigens using specific filtering criteria such as subcellular localization, adhesin probability, and the number of transmembrane helices. For example, depending on a pre-designed filtering strategy, if a protein is found

M. Saeki et al. (Eds.): ER 2024 Workshops, LNCS 14932, pp. 148–158, 2025.
https://doi.org/10.1007/978-3-031-75599-6_11

to have any transmembrane helices, a vaccine antigen prediction program such as Vaxign may filter out the protein [2]. The limitation of this type of method is that the evaluation criteria may not be complete and the filtering method may be too restrictive, which may lead to low sensitivity. The other strategy is machine learning based. Specifically, the second strategy is able to learn from the same set of training data and make effective predictions using specific machine learning methods such as logistic regression, support vector machine, random forest, extreme gradient boosting, and neural networks [3,4].

Our laboratory has developed many vaccine candidate prediction tools including Vaxign [2], Vaxign-ML [4], and Vaxign-DL [3]. For example, Vaxign is the first web-based reverse vaccinology method [2] Vaxign-ML [4] which is trained using a four-layer neural network to improve the prediction results. Vaxign uses the filtering method [2] Vaxign-ML uses the extreme gradient boosting method, and Vaxign-DL uses a neural network deep learning method. Vaxign is the first web-based RV method that achieved high specificity but relatively low sensitivity [2]. Vaxign-ML shows high specificity and sensitivity [4]. Vaxign-DL shows a performance similar to Vaxign-ML in terms of specificity and sensitivity [3]. How to further improve deep learning-base vaccine antigen prediction has become a challenge.

There are many protein folding programs, including two popular deep learning-based prediction methods AlphaFold [5] and ESM (Evolutionary Scale Modeling) [6]. As an self-supervised neural language model, the AlphaFold method takes multiple sequence alignments of evolutionarily related proteins as inputs, while the ESM method requires only single input sequences. The ESM transformer protein language model scales a deep contextual language model with unsupervised learning to protein sequences with evolutionary diversity. Compared to AlphaFold, ESM runs much faster.

In this study, we hypothesized that the utilization of the intermediate features generated by a protein folding program such as the ESM program would significantly enhance our vaccine antigne prediction performance. The ESM-1b function in ESM generated 1,280 features, and our previous Vaxig-DL and Vaxign-ML used 509 features. To evaluate our hypothesis, we calculated and used these two sets of features separately or in combination to evaluate how the usage of the ESM-generated features would enhance our vaccine antigen prediction performance. Our evaluation confirmed the value of the additional ESM-generated features in vaccine antigen prediction. In addition, we utilized our methods to predict vaccine antigens from a set of ten pathogens using a Leave-One-Pathogen-Out Validation (LOPOV) test, and further verified the value of our improved Vaxign-DL method.

2 Methods

2.1 Collection of Positive and Negative Protein Sequences

The training and testing data used were the same dataset used in [3] and [4]. Specifically, the dataset includes positive and negative samples. The positive samples refer to those proteins that can induce protective immune responses against virulent pathogen infections. These proteins have been verified from laboratory animal testing as valuable candidates for vaccine development. These positive sample proteins were originally downloaded from the Protegen protective antigen database [7]. Additionally, since the 584 bacterial protective antigens (BPAgs) from 50 Gram-positive and Gram-negative pathogens downloaded from the Protegen database may have potential biases, homologous proteins with sequence similarity exceeding 30% have been removed in [4]. Consequently, the final positive sample data contains 397 BPAgs. To obtain negative sample data, [4] used pathogen proteins with BPAgs sequence similarity less than 30% and removed homologous proteins. These methods for obtaining positive and negative samples are consistent with those described in [8].

2.2 ESM Generation of New Features Based on Protein Sequences

To ensure the model stability, we used the "ESM-1b" model, a pre-trained model with 33 layers and 650M parameters, and "$UR50/S-2018-03$" as the training set. It can eventually generate 1,280 embedding dimension features.

Because data differs between Gram positive/negative bacterial strains, the datasets of protein sequences were classified as GNN (Gram-negative protection-negative), GNP (Gram-negative protection-positive), GPN (Gram-positive protection-negative), and GPP (Gram-positive protection-positive). For example, GPP proteins are Gram-positive protection-Positive proteins that come from Gram-positive bacteria and are experimentally verified vaccine antigens. Protection-negative are negative control proteins that are likely not protective vaccine antigens. Each protein sequence data is used separately through "ESM-1b" to generate each group of results. Then, by merging the results produced by GNP and GPP, we can get the merged positive samples. Similarly, we can also get a combined protection-negative data by merging GNN and GPN feature results. Eventually We got two datasets, protection Positive and Negative. Finally, by combining the results generated by ESM-1b with our original Vaxign-ML and Vaxign-DL data [3,4], we got two sets of combined datasets with 1,789 features each.

Note that the ESM-1b model can only use up to 1,024 amino acids for the ESM protein folding prediction process. For those large size proteins, the additional amino acids beyond the 1,024 amino acids cannot be used for ESM calculation. Our study found only a small number of proteins in our datasets have the size over 1,024 amino acids. To deal with this situation, two methods were applied. The first method was to skip those proteins that have the protein sequence length exceeding 1,024 amino acids. The final data obtained is 372 positive samples and 3,969 negative sample, both have 1,789 features. Therefore, our second method was to use only the first 1,024 amino acids if a protein has over 1,024 amino acids. The results of the two methods were also compared and analyzed.

2.3 Leave-One-Pathogen-Out Validation

To test vaccine candidates against novel pathogens, we retained the [3] Leave-One-Pathogen-Out Validation (LOPOV) dataset from the Vaxign-ML and Vaxign-DL studied, and calculated and added 1,280 features generated by ESM to the original datasets. This approach involved a set of ten pathogens, including four Gram-positive pathogens (*Mycobacterium tuberculosis*, *Staphylococcus aureus*, *Streptococcus pneumoniae*, and *Streptococcus pyogenes*) and six Gram-negative pathogens (*Helicobacter pylori*, *Neisseria meningitidis*, *Brucella* spp., *Escherichia coli*, *Yersinia pestis*, and *Hemophilus influenzae*). For each LOPOV analysis, the positive and negative protein samples from one specific pathogen were left out, and the samples from the remaining nine pathogens were used for model training. The trained model with the nine pathogen samples was then used to predict vaccine antigens from the left-out pathogen.

2.4 Deep Learning Pipeline

The overall pipeline is shown in Fig. 1. Through the ESM protein folding program, we got 1,280 features generated by the ESM pre-trained model. Different from the biological or chemical features from the traditional Vaxign-ML method, these ESM features are named "Feature 1", "Feature 2", etc., so it is difficult to identify the specific meaning of these ESM features. By combine these new ESM features with 509 features from the original Vaxign-DL/Vaxign-ML studies, we obtained the total of 1,789 features for each protein.

The original data samples include 397 positive protein samples and 3,970 negative protein samples. After we removed those protein sequences that have over 1,024 amino acids, our data samples used for ESM processing are only

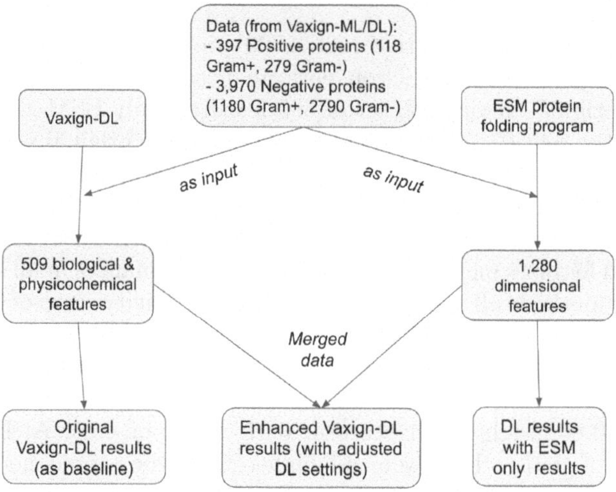

Fig. 1. Overall Pipeline

372 positive samples. To maintain the original 1:10 data ratio, we randomly deleted many negative samples, resulting in the number of 3,720 negative protein samples. Due to the change of the sample sizes, we fine-tuned the weights of the data in our deep learning process.

Our deep learning method used Multi-layer Perceptrons (MLP) model, the same classic deep learning model as used in Vaxign-DL [3]. The MLP model uses the sequential layering of nonlinear processing units and the back-propagation optimization method [9]. In addition to the same three-layer hidden MLP model as used in Vaxign-DL, we also tested a five-layer hidden MLP model in our study. The two middle hidden layers have 256 units and 128 units respectively. Each fully connected layer used LeakyReLU [10] activation function with a slight slope of 0.005 to maintain activity. After LeakyReLU, batch normalization was applied to improve optimization and stability. In addition, in order to increase Robustness and prevent Overfitting, each fully connected layer also had dropout layers with a dropout rate of 0.1. The final output layer used softmax activation function to ensure that the result is the probability of each category.

2.5 Performance Evaluation

For the evaluation model, in order to be able to clearly compare the results, the original evaluation criteria were applied. Specifically, our result evaluation calculated seven scores: value accuracy, sensitivity, specificity, weighted F1 score, Matthews correlation coefficient (MCC), Area under the Receiver Operating Characteristic (AUROC), and Area under Precision-Recall Curve (AUPRC).

3 Results

3.1 Performance Analysis ESM Enhance Vaxign-DL Model

Using the 372 protection-positive and 3,720 protection-negative samples, we tested and compared the prediction performances with three different sets of features: the original Vexing-DL set of 509 features, only ESM-generated 1,280 features, and the set of 1,789 features by combining the original set and the new ESM features (Table 1). By calculating the seven evaluation scores as defined in the Methods, we found that overall original Vaxign-DL method (baseline) and the ESM only method achieved similar prediction performances and the method with combined features method achieved higher performances in all scores expect that the three methods all achieve the same high specificity score of $0.99 + 0.004$.

Out of the seven scores calculated, all except sensitivity and MCC were over 0.9 with all the three methods, suggesting the high performances for all the methods. The combined method achieved achieved a value accuracy of 0.97, sensitivity of 0.83, wighted F1 score of 0.97, MCC of 0.85, AUPRC of 0.92, and AUROC of 0.97, which were all higher than the scored generated from the original and ESM only methods. For example, the original, ESM only, and combined method achieved an AUROC score of 0.94, 0.94, and 0.97, respectively;

and they achieved a sensitivity score of 0.74, 0.75, and 0.83, respectively. Given the specificity scores similar among the three methods, the higher sensitivity score from the combined method might be an important factor to its higher AUROC score.

Overall, additional features from the ESM protein folding program helped the Vaxign-DL model achieve better performance of protective vaccine antigen prediction.

Table 1. Performance metrics for different models

	Val Accuracy	Sensitivity	Specificity	Weighted F1	MCC	AUPRC	AUROC
Original	0.96 ± 0.008	0.74 ± 0.071	0.99 ± 0.004	0.96 ± 0.008	0.78 ± 0.046	0.84 ± 0.049	0.94
ESM Only	0.96 ± 0.005	0.75 ± 0.063	0.98 ± 0.004	0.96 ± 0.007	0.77 ± 0.043	0.85 ± 0.036	0.94
Combined	**0.97 ± 0.004**	**0.83 ± 0.045**	0.99 ± 0.004	**0.97 ± 0.004**	**0.85 ± 0.021**	**0.92 ± 0.013**	**0.97**

3.2 Hyperparameter Optimization Study

In the Vexign-DL model, four hidden layers were originally used [3]. In order to further improve the prediction results of Vaxign-DL combined with ESM, we

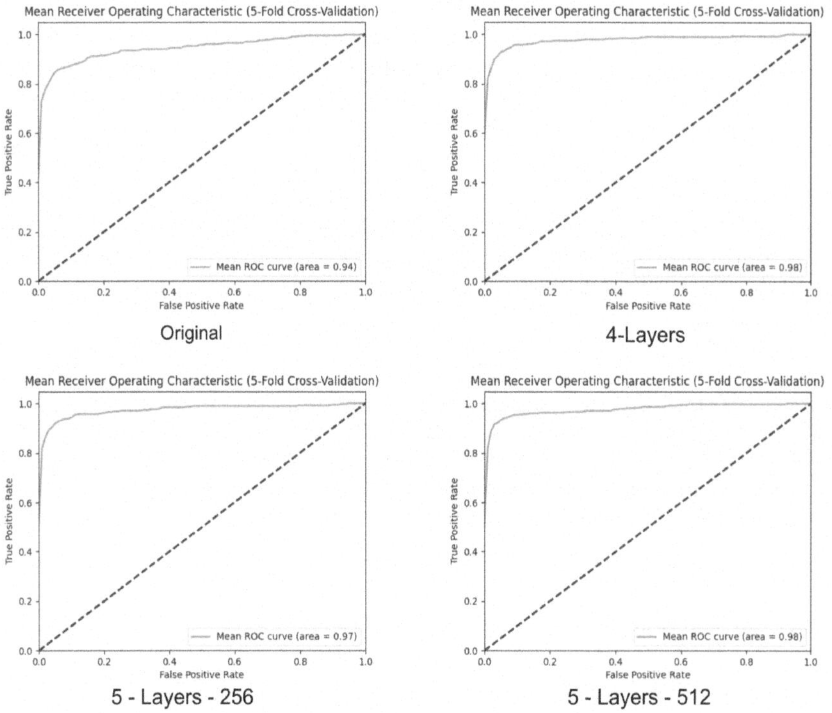

Fig. 2. Mean ROC result

further explored whether more Neural Network layers could improve the prediction results of the model. To this end, we added a fully connected layer to the original model, 256, 128, 64. After testing the five-layer fully connected layer, it was found that more layers did not significantly improve the performance (Fig. 2). For this reason, we changed the dimensions of the fully connected layer to 512, 256, 128. The results were consistent and there was no significant change between these two settings. The four-layer model indeed achieved the best sensitivity (0.83 ± 0.045) (Table 2). In the end, the original four-layer fully connected layer model was retained as our optimal setting in the later studies.

Table 2. Performance metrics for different number of Layers

Combined Skip	Val Accuracy	Sensitivity	Specificity	Weighted F1	MCC	AUPRC	AUROC
4 Layerss	**0.97 ± 0.004**	**0.83 ± 0.045**	0.99 ± 0.004	**0.97 ± 0.004**	**0.85 ± 0.021**	**0.92 ± 0.013**	**0.97**
5 Laysers 256	0.97 ± 0.006	0.81 ± 0.031	0.98 ± 0.005	0.97 ± 0.005	0.83 ± 0.035	0.91 ± 0.027	0.97
5 Layers 512	0.97 ± 0.004	0.80 ± 0.021	0.99 ± 0.004	0.97 ± 0.004	0.83 ± 0.025	0.91 ± 0.033	0.97

Comparison of Two ESM Methods for Processing Long Sequence Proteins

Out of the 397 positive vaccine antigens in our dataset, 25 (6%) have the size over 1,024 amino acids. Since ESM can generate features for proteins up to 1,024 amino acids, we designed and tested two different methods to include these large size proteins. The "Skip" way was that when the amino acid length of a protein is over 1,024, the protein would be skipped for further usage in prediction. The "Cut" method was that when the amino acid length is over 1,024, only the first 1,024 amino acids were used as input. Table 3 shows the results of the two different methods. The "Skip" method achieved better results in all aspects. It is possible that the "Cut" could not get the accurate prediction of all the features for the large-size protein sequence using ESM-1b, which might have led to a bias in the prediction.

Table 3. Performance metrics for different ESM Processing

ESM-1b	Val Accuracy	Sensitivity	Specificity	Weighted F1	MCC	AUPRC	AUROC
Skip	**0.97 ± 0.004**	**0.83 ± 0.045**	**0.99 ± 0.004**	**0.97 ± 0.004**	**0.85 ± 0.021**	**0.92 ± 0.013**	**0.97**
Cut	0.96 ± 0.005	0.75 ± 0.063	0.98 ± 0.004	0.96 ± 0.007	0.77 ± 0.043	0.85 ± 0.036	0.94

Leave-One-Pathogen-Out Validation

To further evaluate different deep learning methods tested in this study, we applied the Leave-one-pathogen-out Validation (LOPOV) approach, which tested how a deep learning method learned from using only 9 bacterial pathogens'

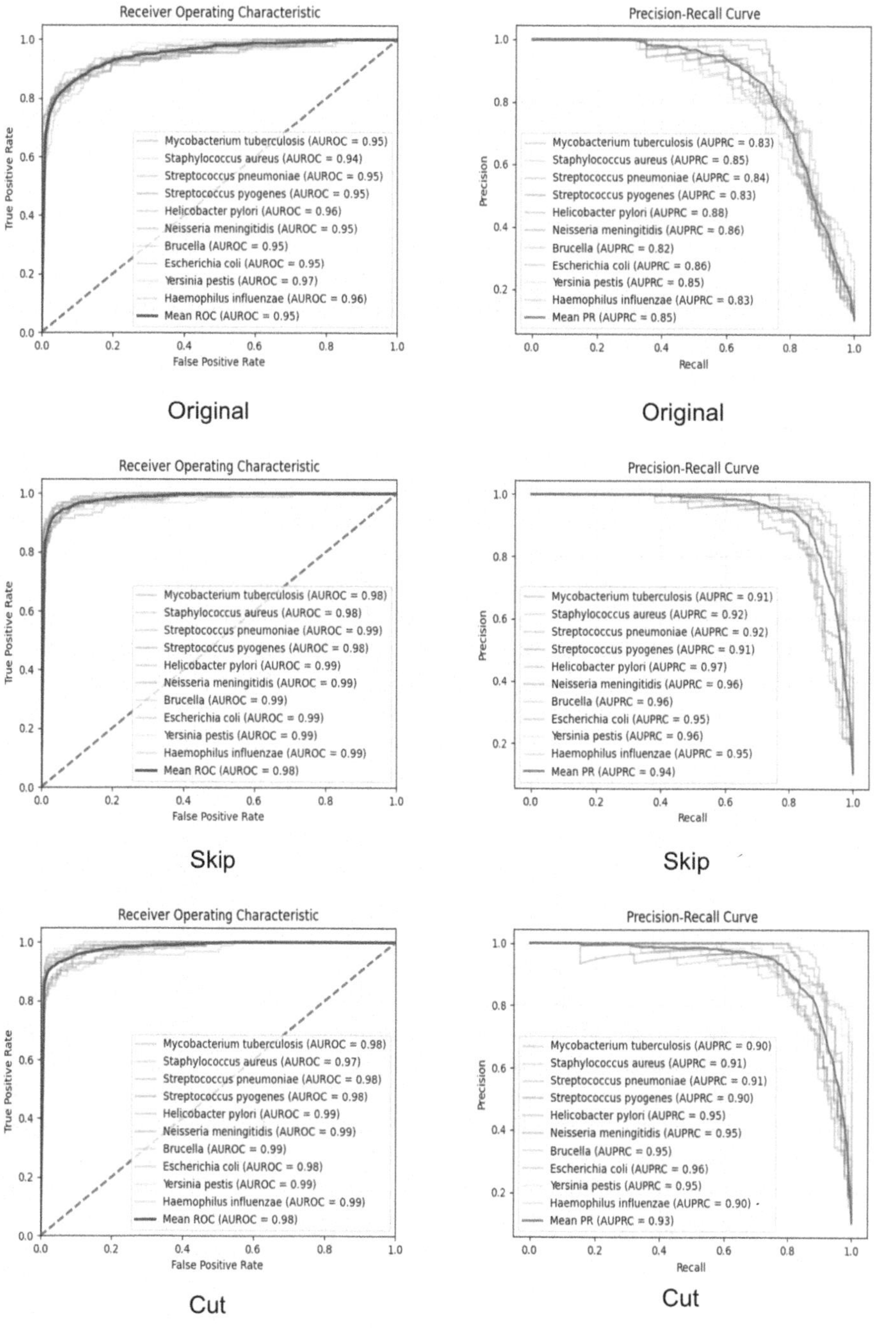

Fig. 3. LOPOV evaluations using different deep learning methods

data could be used to predict vaccine candidates from another new bacterial pathogen. This was the method originally used in Vaxign-ML [4]. The scores, the Area under the Receiver Operating Characteristic (ROC) score and the Area under the Precision-Recall curve (ROC) score were calculated (Fig. 3). Our results showed that the "Skip" and "Cut" methods that used the ESM-derived features in combination with the original Vaxign-DL features both performed better than the original Vaxign-DL method. The Cut method achieved an average AUC of 0.98 and AUPRC of 0.94, and Skip method achieved an average AUC of 0.98 and AUPRC of 0.93, both were better than the Original method results of AUC of 0.95 and AUPRC of 0.85. These confirmed the improved performance using the ESM pre-training model.

4 Discussion

To our best knowledge, our work represents the first deep learning-based vaccine antigen prediction program that uses the intermediate features out of a protein folding program (i.e., ESM). Our results showed that such a protein folding based method enhanced the vaccine prediction performance. The improved performance of the enhanced Vaxign-DL model for vaccine antigen prediction using features generated from a protein folding prediction program has significant implications and applications for accelerating vaccine development processes.

In this study, the ESM program was used due to its advantages in speed and accuracy, making it a preferred choice for vaccine antigen prediction. While AlphaFold could have been an alternative, we did not use it primarily because of its slower runtime compared to ESM. Nonetheless, considering the other benefits of AlphaFold, we plan to test it in future research. Additionally, we will assess the statistical significance of performance improvements across different methods.

While the abstract nature of the 1,280 ESM-derived features enhances predictive power, these features are unlikely to be directly associated with specific biological meanings, which poses a concern in a field where understanding model predictions is equally important. In future work, we will further explore how to balance predictive performance with interpretability by identifying biological relevance of features and introducing additional methods of interpretability analysis. We also plan to explore more advanced "ESM2" models, such as the "ESM2-t48-15B-UR50D" model [11], which features 15 billion parameters, a 48-layer Transformer architecture, and multi-task learning [12]. We may also evaluate other methods than current multilayer perceptron (MLP) method, such as Long Short-Term Memory (LSTM) [13], to further strengthen the model.

A limitation of the ESM program is its calculation of proteins with a maximum of 1,024 AAs. Since bacterial proteins average 320 AAs [14], only 25 out of 397 (6%) positive vaccine antigens in our study exceed this length, indicating that the number of affected proteins is small. In addition to the "Skip" and "Cut" methods used, we plan to explore more sophisticated techniques, such as sliding window and subsequence selection, which may better handle long sequences by extracting multiple overlapping fragments or selecting important subsequences for embedding. Furthermore, we intend to analyze the characteristics of these long proteins to determine if they share common features, represent specific antigenic classes, or exhibit distinct distributions across bacteria.

Acknowledgments. This research is funded by a NIH-NIAID grant U24AI171008. We also acknowledge the usage of the training data originally generated in the published Vaxign-ML study.

Disclosure of Interests. The authors have no competing interests to declare that are relevant to the content of this article.

References

1. Huffman, A., et al.: COVID-19 vaccine design using reverse and structural vaccinology, ontology-based literature mining and machine learning. Brief. Bioinform. **23**(4), bbac190 (2022). https://doi.org/10.1093/bib/bbac190
2. He, Y., et al.: Vaxign: the first web-based vaccine design program for reverse vaccinology and applications for vaccine development. J. Biomed. Biotechnol. **2010**, 297505 (2010). https://doi.org/10.1155/2010/297505
3. Zhang, Y., Huffman, A., Johnson, J., He, Y.: Vaxign-DL: A Deep Learning-based Method for Vaccine Design and its Evaluation. bioRxiv (2023). https://doi.org/10.1101/2023.11.29.569096v1
4. Ong, E., Wang, H., Wong, M.U., Seetharaman, M., Valdez, N., He, Y.: Vaxign-ML: supervised machine learning reverse vaccinology model for improved prediction of bacterial protective antigens. Bioinformatics **36**(10), 3185–3191 (2020). https://doi.org/10.1093/bioinformatics/btaa119
5. Jumper, J., Evans, R., Pritzel, A., et al.: Highly accurate protein structure prediction with AlphaFold. Nature **596**, 583-589 (2021). https://doi.org/10.1038/s41586-021-03819-2
6. Yan, R., Zhang, Y., Li, Y., Xia, L., Guo, Y., Zhou, Q.: Molecular architecture and conformational dynamics of SARS-CoV-2 spike protein in complex with ACE2 receptor. Proc. Natl. Acad. Sci. **117**(21), 2020–2025 (2020). https://doi.org/10.1073/pnas.2016239118
7. Yang, B., Sayers, S., Xiang, Z., He, Y.: Protegen: a web-based protective antigen database and analysis system. Nucleic Acids Res. **39**(Database issue), D1073–D1078 (2011). https://doi.org/10.1093/nar/gkq944 PMID: 20959289; PMCID: PMC3013795
8. Bowman, B.N., et al.: Improving reverse vaccinology with a machine learning approach. Vaccine **29**(45), 8156–8164 (2011). https://doi.org/10.1016/j.vaccine.2011.07.142
9. Hornik, K., Stinchcombe, M., White, H.: Multilayer feedforward networks are universal approximators. Neural Netw. **2**(5), 359–366 (1989)
10. Maas, A.L., Hannun, A.Y., Ng, A.Y.: Rectifier nonlinearities improve neural network acoustic models. In: Proceedings of the 30th International Conference on Machine Learning (ICML), vol. 30, no. 1 (2013)
11. Lin, Z., et al.: Evolutionary-scale prediction of atomic level protein structure with a language model. Originally published in bioRxiv. https://doi.org/10.1101/2022.07.20.500902. Now published in Science. https://doi.org/10.1126/science.ade2574

12. Rives, A., Meier, J., Sercu, T., Fergus, R., et al.: Biological structure and function emerge from scaling unsupervised learning to 250 million protein sequences. bioRxiv (2021). https://doi.org/10.1101/2020.11.20.391069
13. Hochreiter, S., Schmidhuber, J.: Long short-term memory. Neural Comput. **9**(8), 1735–1780 (1997)
14. Tiessen, A., Pérez-Rodríguez, P., Delaye-Arredondo, L.J.: Mathematical modeling and comparison of protein size distribution in different plant, animal, fungal and microbial species reveals a negative correlation between protein size and protein number, thus providing insight into the evolution of proteomes. BMC. Res. Notes **5**, 85 (2012). https://doi.org/10.1186/1756-0500-5-85, PMID: 22296664; PMCID: PMC3296660

Conceptual Modeling for Polygenic Risk Score Research: Improving Domain Understanding and Clinical Utility

Diana Martínez-Minguet(✉) and Óscar Pastor

PROS Group, Valencian Research Institute of Artificial Intelligence (VRAIN), Universitat Politècnica de València, Camí de Vera, s/n, 46022 València, Spain
dmarmin@vrain.upv.es, opastor@dsic.upv.es

Abstract. The Polygenic Risk Score (PRS) research domain holds great promise for significant contributions to precision medicine by providing insights into genetic predispositions for common diseases. However, the field faces challenges in terminology standardization and precise conceptualization, which hinder domain comprehension and consequently the effective data management and application in clinical practice. With the aim of providing clarification in domain-specific terms and relationships, in this paper we apply conceptual modeling techniques to the PRS research domain. We develop two conceptual models, one for the definition of a PRS Model and another for defining the PRS Models in context, in order to clarify terminology and disambiguate concepts typically used in studies. Finally, we instantiate a study as a use case which illustrates how the proposed solution clarifies the domain. Our approach enhances domain comprehension and promotes standardization. In addition, it serves for the benchmarking of PRS Models, helping clinicians to better select PRS Models for practical application in clinical settings.

Keywords: Polygenic Risk Score · Conceptual Modeling · Healthcare · Precision Medicine

1 Introduction

Common diseases such as diabetes and cancer are of great interest in medical research because they significantly impact healthcare systems. If they could be characterized by just a relevant gene their genetic diagnosis would be much easier, but reality is much more complex. These diseases are usually polygenic, meaning that many small genetic variants contribute to the overall risk of developing the disease [12]. Understanding and managing such a polygenic dimension has become a crucial aspect. The representation of this complex genetic liability can be obtained by computing a Polygenic Risk Score (PRS) [8], which is a measure of the genetic predisposition of an individual to having a certain disease. PRSs, when combined with other risk factors, can have the power to assist

M. Saeki et al. (Eds.): ER 2024 Workshops, LNCS 14932, pp. 159–168, 2025.
https://doi.org/10.1007/978-3-031-75599-6_12

clinical decision-making and treatment choices, aiding in the development of precision medicine, and contribute to risk stratification of the population [7,14].

Understanding and computing PRSs requires knowledge of the PRS research field, which can be particularly challenging to navigate specially for researchers who are external to the domain, such as clinicians and epidemiologists aiming to perform PRS analyses for patients or populations [4]. In fact, there are some scientific papers with the aim of providing clarification and making the domain more approachable [3,4,9,11]. However, this novel research field is characterized by a lack of standardization in terminology and inconsistencies in conceptualizations [3,13]. As a result, knowledge on the relevant elements that take part in the PRS research context and their relations are difficult to establish and domain comprehension is hampered, which eventually prevents the potential application of PRS research in other research areas.

Given this problematic, conceptual modeling (CM) can play a role in resolving the stated barriers. CM has proven to be an effective solution to improve comprehension and standardization of other areas also related to the biological domain [1,5]. In addition, the elements represented in a conceptual model delimit the framework of a certain domain addressed to the specific stakeholders. In this work, we apply CM techniques to characterize the PRS research domain using the Unified Modeling Language (UML) Class Diagram [2]. So far, we are not aware of any other work that has applied CM for the stated purpose. The expected benefits of applying CM techniques for the PRS research domain are: (i) to provide clarification of the domain and (ii) to delimit the framework of the PRS research domain addressed to clinicians and epidemiologists. Only by clarifying the domain and delimiting the framework, a valuable data management process intended to generate valid knowledge will be feasible. As an added value of the contribution of this paper, the results can serve as a common framework for the benchmarking of PRS models, particularly useful for researchers aiming to select a suitable PRS Model for performing a PRS analysis.

The remaining of the paper is organized as follows: in Sect. 2 we expose the inconsistencies arising in the domain that have motivated our work. Section 3 describes the proposed solution applying CM techniques, and an example study is instantiated as a use case. The contributions obtained from the proposed solution are discussed in Sect. 4. Finally, Sect. 5 draws the main conclusions and foresees future work.

2 Background

In this section we present the barriers to comprehension arising in the PRS research domain that have motivated our work.

As a first statement regarding nomenclature, PRSs appear in the literature under other names, such as Polygenic Scores (PGS) or Genetic Risk Scores (GRS). Depending on the study consulted, these terms can be synonyms or have subtle differences [8]. For instance, it is common to find that a PGS is a measure of predisposition to any trait, such as height, while the PRS is associated to a disease. In this study we are in the context of common diseases, hence we will refer to PRSs.

We start by discussing how the term PRS refers in practice to three different concepts. A **PRS** is a value –a score– associated to an individual, that gives a measure of the predisposition to have a certain disease [8]. This score is the result of the aggregation of the gene variants that contribute to disease risk in varying degrees, i.e., each variant has its weight (or effect size). Therefore, a PRS is computed by simply performing a weighted sum of the variants found in the individual. The particular set of variants and effect sizes –the scoring set– that need to be considered for computing the PRS is provided by a PRS model. A **PRS model** applies a statistical method to a set of variants and provides them with effect sizes, producing as a result the scoring set [11]. For a PRS to be correctly interpreted it is required information on the PRS model used and result representation details, information provided in the **PRS analysis** [4]. A major confusion in the PRS research domain comes from the fact that these three concepts: (i) a PRS –the score associated to an individual–, (ii) a PRS model –the tool for obtaining the PRS– and (iii) a PRS analysis –the process of applying a PRS model to an individual–, although being completely different are usually all referred to as PRS.

Given this widespread malpractice, expressions such as "PRS performance" or "apply a PRS" appear frequently, while in the same study a PRS has been defined as a value associated to an individual, as can be seen in [6,10]. These inconsistencies in conceptualization make sense for an expert having a clear understanding the domain. However, they cause much confusion to a non-expert given that the same term is describing different concepts which, in addition, are strongly interrelated between them. Our position is that only with a sound, shared understanding of the domain, a correct and valuable data management process is possible, and this is where conceptual modeling –as a precise strategy to face the conceptualization of a given domain– becomes a key artifact.

Another example of heterogeneity in terminology is regarded to the definition of datasets involved in PRS Model development and evaluation. PRS research studies agree that there are three possible dataset roles. Two roles are involved in PRS Model development, one that provides the baseline data and another for refinement; the third role is for PRS Model evaluation. In addition, each dataset exists in one of two types: summary statistics (SS) or individual-level data (IL). However, the role name of a dataset and the type varies depending on the study consulted. In Table 1 we can see how four studies use different terminology for each role and different possible types. Again, accurate conceptualization of these concepts is necessary for enhancing domain comprehension.

Clarification efforts are present in the field, such as the aforementioned studies as well as guideline recommendations [13]. However, there is still a lack of standardization in PRS research studies, and its formal conceptualization has not been addressed, which can hamper the effective data management and knowledge extraction. With the aim of contributing to clarification efforts, in the next

Table 1. Comparison of terminology used by four different studies on dataset roles used in PRS Model development and evaluation. In brackets it is specified the dataset type, individual-level (IL) or GWAS summary statistics (SS), for each dataset role.

Article	Development (role 1)	Development (role 2)	Evaluation (role 3)
Ma et al. [8]	Training - Discovery (SS/IL)	Validation (-)	Test - Target (SS/IL)
Babb de Villiers et al. [11]	Base - Input - Discovery (SS/IL)	Test - Training (IL)	Validation (IL)
Osterman et al. [9]	Base - Training (SS)	Validation (-)	Target - Test (IL)
Choi et al. [3]	Base (SS)	Target - Training (IL)	Test - Validation (IL)

section we apply CM techniques for the precise conceptualization of the PRS research domain.

3 The Conceptual Models

Here we present our solution to the stated barriers by applying CM techniques. Our stakeholders are clinicians and epidemiologists who aim to perform PRS analyses, for which they have to compare, verify information completeness and eventually apply a PRS Model. We first provide a simple conceptual model to depict the essential elements that define a PRS Model. Secondly, we conceptualize the PRS Models in context, where they are developed, evaluated and applied, thus with the PRS Model as the cornerstone of the conceptual model.

We leverage PRS research studies and guideline recommendations to delimit the framework and select appropriate terminology. In addition, following the standardization and centralization efforts that are ubiquitous in the genomic field, we consider identifiers for ontologies or database repositories whenever possible.

3.1 A PRS Model

In the literature, the definition of what a PRS Model is can be vague. A PRS Model is often identified as simply the statistical method or algorithm applied, while the data used for developing a PRS Model clearly defines the final outcome. The essential elements that constitute a PRS Model are depicted in Fig. 1.

We define a PRS Model as a set of variants that acquire an effect size when a method is applied. The variants involved are known as single nucleotide polymorphisms (SNPs) which are the smallest possible change in a gene, i.e., the gene has one of its units altered compared to the reference genome, known as the assembly (analogous to a cardinal system). Thus a VARIANT is defined by an identifier (*snp_id*) and its location within a gene, given by the *chromosome*, the *position* within the chromosome and the *assembly*. The possible options that the variant can have are known as alleles. The specific change is specified by the allele information, which consists of the allele appearing in the assembly –reference allele–, the possible alleles available –alternative alleles–, and the concrete allele that confers risk to the disease of study –risk allele– (*ref_allele*, *alt_allele* and *risk_allele*, respectively). When the method is applied, some variants may be discarded and the remaining ones will be assigned an effect size, represented by the WEIGHTED VARIANT class and the *effect_size* attribute. The set of weighted variants conforms the SCORING SET, a class defined by the total number of variants finally considered in the outcome (the derived attribute *n_snp*) and the *assembly* attribute, which is the same for all variants in a PRS Model. The METHOD is defined by a *name*, which identifies a statistical method such as penalized regression, a *description* of the method and the *software* used, if available. The *LD_technique* attribute refers to how linkage desequilibrium (LD) is addressed. LD refers to the non-random association between near variants. LD has an influence in the final risk prediction to the disease since a low-risk variant strongly correlated with a high-risk variant might appear also as high risk. This is a relevant issue that has to be reported when taken into account within the method. Finally, the method is composed of parameters whose value can be chosen or optimized (PARAMETER class, with the *name* and *value*).

With this conceptual model for a single PRS Model we emphasize that each PRS Model is defined by the set of variants, the method applied and the resulting scoring set, which is evidenced by the relations of cardinality.

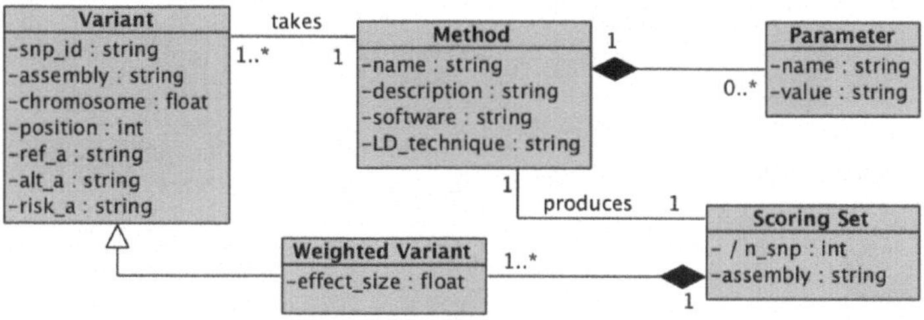

Fig. 1. Conceptual model of a PRS Model.

3.2 A PRS Model in Context

With this conceptual model (Fig. 2) we aim to delimit the framework of the PRS research domain addressed to clinicians and epidemiologists. We take the PRS Model as the cornerstone, which has been characterized in the previous subsection.

A PRS MODEL can be identified by a *name* and two identifiers, the article in which it is reported (*pub_id*, for instance the PubMed ID) and ideally an identifier in the PGS Catalog database (*PGSC_id*) which is the most widely known repository of PRS Models. As previously explained, a PRS Model provides the means for computing the predisposition of an individual to having a certain disease. However, a more specific purpose such as risk of death due to a disease can also be defined. For the appropriate application and interpretation of the results provided by a PRS Model, the *intended_ use* and *predicted_ outcome* need to be specified.

A PRS Model is associated to a disease (or a group of diseases), more technically a PHENOTYPE, which is the observable or measurable trait of a disease, identified by the *name* and the *EFO_ id*, an identifier in the widely used Experimental Factor Ontology (EFO). Also, many PRS Models can be developed for the same phenotype. A PRS Model is composed of a SCORING SET, as depicted in the first conceptual model, with *n_ snp* and *assembly* attributes. It is also depicted in this conceptual model to make explicit that it is the element required for performing the PRS analysis. We remind that the PRS ANALYSIS applies a PRS Model (specifically the scoring set) to a patient, and computes the individual's PRS. The variants and effect sizes necessary for the PRS analysis can be obtained by considering the conceptual model previously presented. The interpretation of the PRS is made according to the *description* of the PRS analysis. The PATIENT has an identifier (*patient_ id*) and an *ancestry*. When a PRS analysis is performed for a patient, the patient's *PRS* measure is obtained. With this description we clearly establish the interrelation of the three key concepts described in Sect. 2: the PRS, the PRS Model and the PRS analysis.

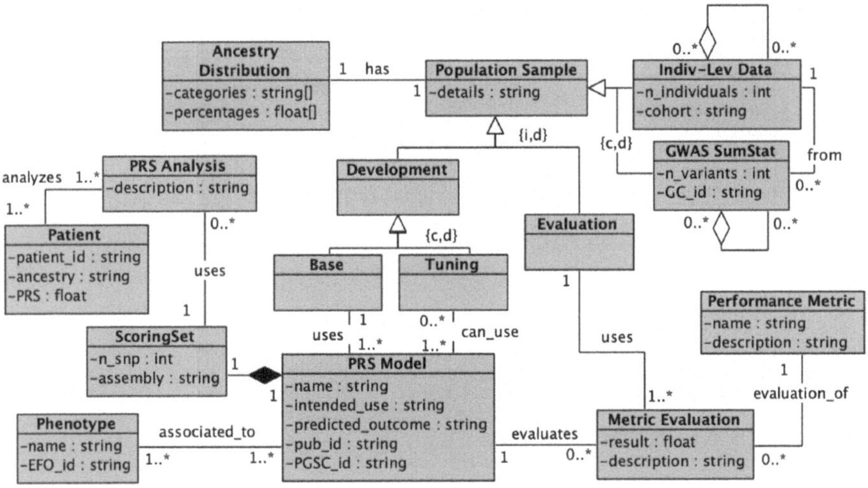

Fig. 2. Conceptual model of PRS Models in context.

Regarding the datasets involved in the development and evaluation of a PRS Model, all these datasets are population samples (POPULATION SAMPLE class), for which relevant *details* such as how the dataset has been generated or age and sex details of the population can be specified, if applicable. A population sample is obtained from a group of individuals, hence it is associated with an ANCESTRY DISTRIBUTION, defined by the *categories* and their *percentages*. As explained in Sect. 2, each dataset (population sample) can exist in one of two types: a GWAS summary statistics or individual-level data, GWAS SumSat and Indiv-Lev Data, respectively. A GWAS summary statistics sample is ideally catalogued in the GWAS Catalog database (*GC_id*), and it has a set of variants (*n_variants*) which have been obtained from the analysis performed in an individual-level data sample, with a total number of individuals (*n_individuals*). A dataset can be obtained from the aggregation of other datasets of the same type, which is represented by the white diamonds in the dataset type classes. The other specialisation of the population sample relates to the dataset roles. Independent datasets are used for Development or Evaluation of a PRS Model. For the development of a PRS Model, at least one dataset providing the initial set of variants is required, the Base. Optional datasets can be used for optimizing parameters or for method selection, the Tuning datasets. The terminology used to refer to the dataset roles (Development –Base and Tuning– and Evaluation) has been chosen according to guideline recommendations and to the scientific studies revised. We decided on terminology that is unlikely to fit in another role, hence we have avoid the use of Training, Test, Target or Validation terms that appear in Table 1.

Finally, a PRS Model is evaluated by a Performance metric, defined with a *name* and the *description* of what is being evaluated, for instance discriminatory ability or association between phenotype and outcome. For a Metric evaluation the metric evaluated and an evaluation sample is required, giving the metric *result* that is associated to the PRS Model.

Relevant features to be considered in PRS Model selection are the phenotype of interest, the ancestry for which the PRS Model has been defined, or the metric evaluations, also influenced by the the ancestry of the evaluation sample, among others. With this conceptual model, we can navigate all the relevant features and understand their impact in PRS model suitability for a PRS analysis.

3.3 Instantiation of a Use Case

Here we take the study presented in [15] as a use case and instantiate it in both conceptual models. In this study the authors develop a PRS Model as part of an effective survival prediction tool for reducing colorectal cancer mortality.

The conceptual model of the PRS Model can be seen in Fig. 3. Of the 300 variants taken by the PRS Model, 287 conform the scoring set. We have represented variant rs703931 as an example, whose information is provided according to the GRCh37 assembly and for which an effect size of 0.160 has been associated. The method used is a Random Survival Forest, which is a random forests method for the analysis of right-censored survival data. The LD has been addressed by using a LD reference panel, and variants with a squared correlation of $r^2 < 1$ were kept.

The conceptual model of the framework is presented in Fig. 4. The PRS Model is reported in a study that can be found in the PubMed database, and it also reported in the PGS Catalog repository. It is intended for use in prognosis of the risk of death in patients with colorectal cancer. The phenotype studied is colorectal cancer, which can be associated to an EFO identifier. The datasets used

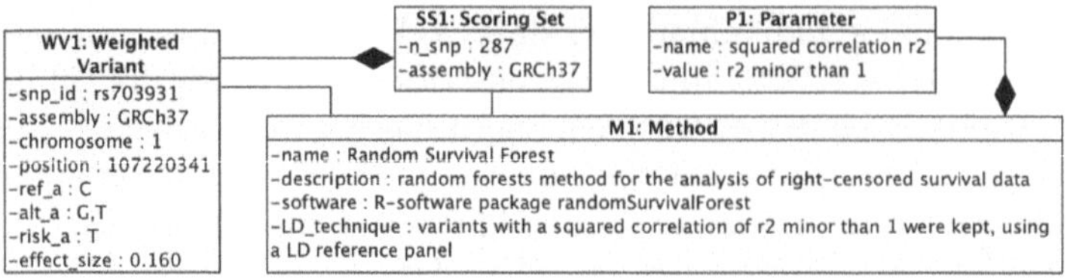

Fig. 3. Instance of a PRS Model developed in [15].

initially are five individual-level data population samples. They perform a GWAS meta-analysis in two of them (NJCRC and UK Biobank cohorts) and obtain the Base sample, which is a GWAS summary statistics. The Tuning dataset is the TCGA cohort, used for choosing the optimal method among 8 different methods for the PRS Model. The two last datasets (PLCO and ZJCRC cohorts) are used for evaluation of the final PRS Model. For each evaluation sample, two performance metrics are evaluated. For simplicity, we instantiate one of them, the Area Under the Curve (AUC). AUC performance metric represents the discriminatory ability of the PRS Model for 5-year overall colorectal cancer survival prediction. Two evaluations are obtained, one for each evaluation sample. The scoring set consists of 278 variants and their information is provided according to the GRCh37 assembly. There is no PRS analysis performed in this study, as the PRS Analysis and Patient classes are absent.

Relevant comments regarding terminology used in this study are: they refer to the PRS Model as a Polygenic Prognosis Score (PPS), or 'score'; they refer to the dataset roles as 'derivation', 'validation' and 'testing', which can potentially be misunderstood by other roles, specially for the 'validation' and 'testing' terms.

4 Discussion

In this study we have exposed the barriers in domain comprehension arising in the PRS research domain due to the lack of standardization in terminology and inconsistencies in conceptualization. As a solution we have applied CM techniques as a precise strategy to face the conceptualization of the domain of study. In the following paragraphs we analyze the benefits and potential improvements of our proposed solution:

The two Conceptual Models allow for the differentiation of the inner elements of a PRS Model (CM1) and the external ones, related to the general framework (CM2). CM1 clarifies in a simple representation which are the essential elements that conform a PRS Model. It could be further disambiguated for the purpose of defining the development of a PRS Model, for instance further specialisation of the method for higher level of detail, but this is out of the scope of applying PRS models into a clinical setting. With CM2 we have clarified the inconsistencies in conceptualization and the heterogeneity of terminology presented in Sect. 2. The interrelation between a PRS, a PRS Model and a PRS analysis is well defined. Regarding dataset characterization, accurate nomenclature has been selected to

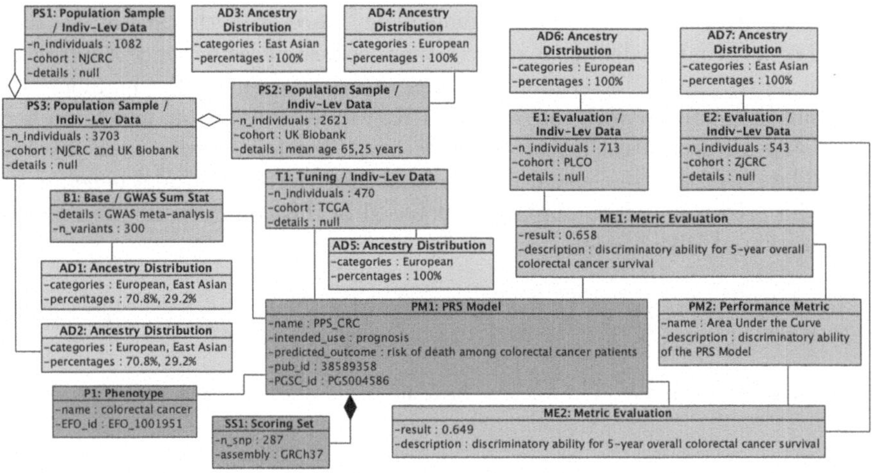

Fig. 4. Instance of the PRS Model developed in [15] in context. It is depicted the PRS Model, associated phenotype and scoring set (green), the datasets (blue) and their ancestries (orange), and the description and evaluations of the performance metric (purple).

designate the three different roles, and both dataset types are allowed in every case, as is the most general situation. With these clarifications we contribute to a shared understanding of the domain, since we have made explicit the underlying content explained in [3,8,9,11] under a common schema. In addition, how a PRS Model is applied is clarified since CM1 and CM2 are connected by the scoring set, which is the element of the PRS Model required when computing the PRS of a patient.

The instantiation of the use case has shown a practical application of the two conceptual models. We can clearly see that a PRS Model has been developed and evaluated but not applied in a PRS analysis. The datasets taking part in PRS Model development and evaluation are easily traced to their original sources and their roles are clearly depicted. The terminology used in the study has been successfully mapped to the conceptual model. Note that if another PRS model were to be compared with the one presented, it would be possible to perform a direct comparative evaluation by representing both PRS models using this common framework. This significantly faces the heterogeneity in PRS Model reporting claimed by domain experts [13]. This is a major contribution since it enables efficient PRS Model selection, a crucial step that clinicians and epidemiologists face when performing a PRS analysis.

5 Conclusions and Future Work

The PRS research domain is a promising field that will bring major advancements in precision medicine for common diseases. Its translation to clinical practice is hampered due to domain comprehension, which can have a negative impact in the correct and valuable data management process. In this study, we have applied conceptual modeling to address the inconsistencies in conceptualization and the heterogeneity in terminology present in the domain. We highlight the contribution of a framework that enables PRS Model comparison, which is a necessary step for accurate PRS Model selection. Therefore, future work involves the validation of the conceptual models to be used for PRS Model benchmarking, and a proposal of data management based in this conceptualization for the prioritization of PRS Models.

Acknowledgments. This work was supported by the Generalitat Valenciana through the CoMoDiD project (CIPROM/2021/023).

Disclosure of Interests. The authors have no competing interests to declare.

References

1. Bernasconi, A., García S., A., Ceri, S., Pastor, O.: A comprehensive approach for the conceptual modeling of genomic data. In: Ralyte, J., Chakravarthy, S., Mohania, M., Jeusfeld, M.A., Karlapalem, K. (eds.) Conceptual Modeling. ER 2022. LNCS, vol. 13607, pp. 194–208. Springer, Cham (2022). https://doi.org/10.1007/978-3-031-17995-2_14
2. Booch, G., et al.: The unified modeling language. Unix Rev. **14**(13), 5 (1996)
3. Choi, S.W.S., et al.: Tutorial: a guide to performing polygenic risk score analyses. Nat. Protoc. **15** (2020)
4. Collister, J., et al.: Calculating polygenic risk scores (PRS) in UK biobank: a practical guide for epidemiologists. Front. Genet. **13** (2022)
5. García, A., et al.: A conceptual model-based approach to improve the representation and management of omics data in precision medicine. IEEE Access **PP**, 1 (2021)
6. Kachuri, L., et al.: Principles and methods for transferring polygenic risk scores across global populations. Nat. Rev. Genet. **25** (2023)
7. Lewis, C., Vassos, E.: Polygenic risk scores: from research tools to clinical instruments. Genome Med. **12** (2020)
8. Ma, Y., et al.: Genetic prediction of complex traits with polygenic scores: a statistical review. Trends Genet. **37** (2021)
9. Osterman, M., et al.: Polygenic risk scores. Curr. Protoc. **1** (2021)
10. Roberts, E., et al.: Polygenic risk scores and breast cancer risk prediction. Breast **67** (2023)
11. Babb de Villiers, C., et al.: Understanding polygenic models, their development and the potential application of polygenic scores in healthcare. J. Med. Genet. **57** (2020)
12. Visscher, P., et al.: Discovery and implications of polygenicity of common diseases. Science **373**, 1468–1473 (2021)
13. Wand, H., et al.: Improving reporting standards for polygenic scores in risk prediction studies. Nature **591**, 211–219 (2021)
14. Wray, N., et al.: From basic science to clinical application of polygenic risk scores: a primer. JAMA Psychiatry **78** (2020)
15. Xin, J., et al.: Integration of pathologic characteristics, genetic risk and lifestyle exposure for colorectal cancer survival assessment. Nat. Commun. **15** (2024)

Integrative Ontology of Bipolar Disorder (OBD): Advancing Bipolar Disorder Research Through an Interoperable Ontological Framework

Yujia Tian[1,3], Yongqun He[1,2], Rachel Richesson[1,3], and Melvin Mclnnis[1,4](✉)

[1] University of Michigan Medical School, Ann Arbor, MI 48109, USA
yujiat@umich.edu, mmcinnis@med.umich.edu
[2] Department of Computational Medicine and Bioinformatics, University of Michigan, Ann Arbor, MI 48109, USA
[3] Department of Learning Health Sciences, University of Michigan, Ann Arbor, MI 48109, USA
[4] Department of Psychiatry, University of Michigan, Ann Arbor, MI 48109, USA

Abstract. Bipolar disorder (BD) is a serious psychiatric condition of unknown etiology but thought to result from a combination of dysfunction of brain biology, on a background of genetic, social, and personal contributing factors. The complex etiology and often diverse clinical manifestations of bipolar disorder pose challenges in establishing a clinical diagnosis. To integrate the large amounts of heterogeneous illness susceptibility knowledge, data, and metadata from multiple sources, we propose the development of an interoperable and integrative ontology of bipolar disorder (OBD) as a systematic framework to combine and represent knowledge from diverse sources. The advantage of OBD is the capacity to reuse, integrate, align, link, and structure terms from multiple ontologies under the upper-level Basic Formal Ontology. In use cases, we demonstrate how an OBD can be applied to map out the genetic predispositions and clinical symptoms of BD, aimed towards facilitating improved accuracy in diagnoses and personalized treatment plans. The OBD supports data FAIRness (e.g., findability, accessibility, interoperability, and reusability)and encourages collaborative and multidisciplinary studies of BD using diverse domains and ontologies.

Keywords: Bipolar disorder · Ontology · Data Integration · FAIR · Ontology of bipolar disorder

1 Introduction

Bipolar disorder (BD) is a serious psychiatric illness characterized by pathological swings of mood that alternate between mania and depression. During manic episodes, individuals experience extremes of increased energy and mood

M. Saeki et al. (Eds.): ER 2024 Workshops, LNCS 14932, pp. 169–179, 2025.
https://doi.org/10.1007/978-3-031-75599-6_13

with a diminished need for sleep. There are often profound personal, social, and vocational consequences secondary to reckless and impulsive behaviors driven by mania. The duration of a manic episode varies (days to weeks) with multiple concomitant symptoms (hallucinations and delusions) and conditions (substance use). Conversely, depressive episodes are marked by low energy and mood, pessimism, anhedonia, and reduced speech and activity; depressions are typically the more common manifestation and enduring phase of BD, lasting weeks to months and frequently becoming chronic [1]. A comprehensive and integrated ontological framework for BD is lacking; there are few samples that have large amounts of deep clinical and biological data, despite the emerging large-scale collaboratives in the Psychiatric Genetics Consortium [2]. From a clinical standpoint, small, non-representative clinical samples with cross-sectional designs are the norm, and in order to gain deeper insights into BD (or any human condition), it will be necessary to integrate multiple sources of information in a manner outlined here below.

A current problem, in BD and other medical research, is how to integrate data from multiple sources and fields. A large amount of heterogeneous data is constantly generated in this era of rapid technological development, but this data is not well organized, integrated, and utilized. The diversity of data formats, inconsistency in data quality, and semantic differences between different research fields have led to many challenges in data integration. If these challenges can be successfully overcome, we can have a more comprehensive understanding of the complexity of the disease and quickly translate research results into clinical practice.

This new vision recognizes that knowledge in any given domain needs to be organized and securely managed to facilitate global contributions, collaborations, and analysis. For BD, the clinical focus must include detailed phenotypic descriptions with the goal of studying the relation of clinical features to basic science by collecting data through large-scale longitudinal cohorts and enhancing data interoperability and transferability of multiple datasets through a common data model approach [3]. This paradigm shift requires systems that can interact with each other and operate across different platforms. Currently, a wide variety and range of knowledge data and metadata is emerging about BD. However, these data are not in a variety of data-systems and emerging ontologies that are in variable states of maturity and are not well-organized. The resulting challenge is a major lack of data interoperability and transferability that seriously hampers progress in research, hindering global data sharing and collaborative research in understanding and treating BD.

Advancements in ontologic approaches provide opportunities for addressing these challenges. Ontology offers a structured taxonomy that designates combinations of universals, defined classes, and specifies relationships between them. It is a detailed and multidimensional map of knowledge domains. Ontology categorizes entities (through taxonomy), defines the types of entities present (universals and defined classes), and offers explanatory links between entities. There are a multitude of ontology systems; the Open Biological and Biomedical Ontologies

(OBO) Foundry includes 265 unique ontologic systems [4]. Many, such as the Human Phenotype Ontology (HPO), are clinically focused and provide a standardized vocabulary of observed phenotypic abnormalities encountered in human disease [5]. Others, such as OMIM, are more disease focused and link specific disorders with the genetic basis [6].

In the current study, we initiated the development of an integrated Ontology of Bipolar Disorder (OBD), one that is anchored in extant ontologic systems but aims to develop an interoperable ontology framework to integrate the ever-expanding and diverse amounts of knowledge data and metadata from various sources relevant to BD. This framework will generate a dynamic infrastructure to support and advance research into BD, it is designed to efficiently accommodate emerging data and information from a wide range of academic (clinical and basic science) disciplines in order to facilitate a deeper understanding and promote global collaboration in this field.

2 Methods

2.1 Data Collection and Annotation

In this study, we categorized our data from various sources related to BD, including phenotypes, diseases, genes, cells, and biomarkers. For phenotypes, data were sourced from the Heinz C. Prechter Longitudinal Study of Bipolar Disorder (Prechter Study) [7], an ongoing (2005-present) open cohort study of over 1500 adults with BD and healthy controls. We utilized the Prechter data online dictionaries (https://medicine.umich.edu/dept/prechter-program/bipolar-research/data-repositories) which include 86 questionnaire forms. We simply extracted BD-related phenotypes by reviewing all the forms. For disease and gene associations, we first searched the HPO website for "Bipolar affective disorder" (HP:0007302). We then downloaded the "disease associations" and "gene associations" from HPO. Subsequently, we used OLS ontology search [8] to manually match the terms in gene ontology and disease ontology. For biomarker associations, we conducted a search on PubMed, reviewing numerous articles to identify those discussing biomarkers and bipolar disorder. We manually abstracted the biomarkers associated with bipolar disorder from these articles. The National Cancer Institute Thesaurus (NCIT) represents such knowledge as concepts and roles (relationships) related to bipolar disorder [9], which were also incorporated into our study. By integrating these diverse data sources, we aim to create a comprehensive interoperable ontology framework that supports advanced research and a deeper understanding of bipolar disorder.

2.2 Development of OBD

The list of terms was mapped to the ontology hierarchy and classified using the BFO-based classification method. Specifically, the Ontofox tool [10] was employed to extract terms associated with bipolar disorder. The terms from the Ontofox output were then displayed using the Protege-OWL editor [11]. For ontology modeling: HPO was used to define the phenotypes related to BD; Human Disease ontology (DOID) [12] was used to define the diseases associated with BD; Cell Ontology (CL) [13] was used to define the cells related to BD; Ontology of genes and genomes (OGG) [14] was used to define the genes associated with BD; NCIT provided various terminologies related to BD. These ontologies are chosen from among all reference ontologies in the OBO Foundry ontology library (https://obofoundry.org/). OBO Foundry supports the development of interoperable ontologies, which supports data FAIRness (e.g., findability, accessibility, interoperability, and reusability) [15]. Furthermore, related terms were imported into the newly created OBD which was used to model the relationships between bipolar disorder and the confirmed associated terms. Here, we did not generate any new terms but reused and reorganized existing terms from existing ontologies.

2.3 Ontology Framework Development

The development of the OBD follows the ontology development principles initiated and promoted by OBO Foundry. Bipolar disorder domain experts and ontologists collaborated to reach a consensus on the aims, methods, and content of the OBD. This development process employs a combination of top-down and bottom-up methodologies [16], ensuring a comprehensive and well-structured ontology. Using top-down approaches, high-level concepts and structures were defined first, providing a broad framework for the ontology. Concurrently, bottom-up methodologies were employed to incorporate specific terms and relationships based on detailed data and expert input.

3 Results

3.1 Data Collection and Annotation

According to Table 1, after searching the Prechter data, we identified 44 related phenotypes. We chose to search the Prechter data first rather than directly using HPO because HPO often lacks comprehensive coverage of phenotypes related to mental health. Recently, significant efforts have been dedicated to improving and expanding the vocabulary of the HPO. A simple search for bipolar disorder in HPO does not yield all relevant phenotypes found in the disorders. Additionally, HPO itself does not include the related risk-factor phenotypes that are often related to BD, such as "childhood trauma" and "antisocial personality", which have been reported by the Prechter longitudinal group. From the HPO search, we found 33 diseases and 43 genes related to BD. For biomarkers, we reviewed several articles on BD and identified 33 related biomarkers. Subsequently, we searched for cell types associated with these biomarkers, resulting in 20 cell types. Additionally, 31 terminologies from NCIT were found to be related to BD. All these terms were then manually imported into an Excel spreadsheet for further analysis and integration into the OBD.

Table 1. Selected reused ontologies in OBD

Ontologies	Content	No. of terms imported
HPO	Phenotypes	44
OGG	Genes	43
DOID	Diseases	33
CL	Cell types	20
NCIT	Terminology	31

3.2 Development of OBD

Figure 1 illustrates the hierarchical structure and selected key ontology terms of the ontology used to represent knowledge about BD. This ontology adopts the Basic Formal Ontology (BFO) [17] as its upper-level ontology, which includes the 'continuant' and 'occurrent' branches. The continuant branch represents entities that endure through time. Within the continuant branch, we have: Material Entity (BFO), which includes Cell (CL) representing different cell types, Gene (OGG) representing genetic elements, and Terminology (NCIT) representing various terminological entries; Quality (BFO) representing characteristics or attributes of material entities; and Realizable Entity (BFO), which includes Disposition (BFO) representing the potential to develop certain conditions or behaviors, Phenotype (HP) representing observable traits or characteristics, Disease (DOID) representing diseases or pathological conditions, and Function (BFO) representing specific roles or activities of entities. The recurrent branch represents entities that occur in time. Within the current branch, we have: Process (BFO) representing processes or events that unfold over time; Temporal Region (BFO) representing periods or intervals of time; and Planned Process (OBI) [18] representing processes that are planned or intended, such as clinical interventions.

3.3 Framework Development of OBD

Figure 2 illustrates the OBD design pattern that links different types of entities within the framework of BD. Many of the entity types in Fig. 2 represent branches of hierarchical terms defined by specific ontologies. For example, numerous genes are defined in the OGG and "Neurons" defined in CL. While the BD top-level design (Fig. 1) shows the hierarchical relationships among different terms, Fig. 2 depicts the relationships of terms across different hierarchical branches of the OBD. Specifically, it includes roles such as "BP I" and "BP II" linked to "human" and highlights how mutations in genes like CHRNA7 have dispositions that lead to BD. Additionally, it shows the connection from "genes" to "cells" and subsequently to "Neurons", integrating "phenotypes" for manic and depression. Therefore, Fig. 1 and Fig. 2 provide a comprehensive framework for the OBD design, ensuring data interoperability and data reusability.

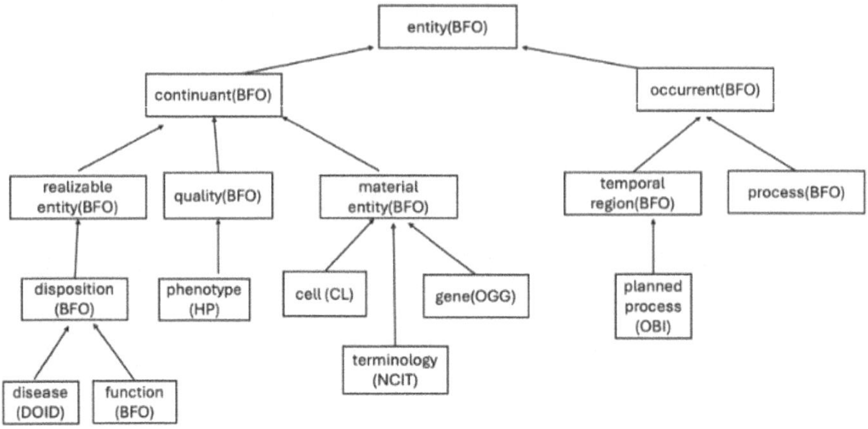

Fig. 1. Upper-level schema of OBD.

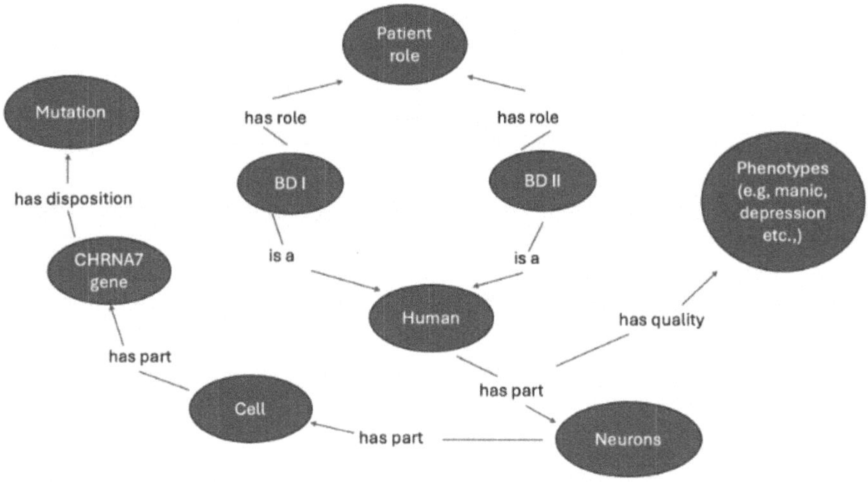

Fig. 2. Ontology overall design for interlinking different types of entities related to BD

3.4 Use Case Study 1: Integration of BD Related Knowledge from Different Sources

In order to demonstrate how OBD works, we constructed a model to facilitate better understanding as illustrated in the provided Fig. 3. This ontology model adopts multiple ontological frameworks, including the Basic Formal Ontology (BFO), Disease Ontology (DOID), Gene Ontology (OGG), Cell Ontology (CL), Human Phenotype Ontology (HPO), and the National Cancer Institute Thesaurus (NCIT). At the top level, we have "Things" which bifurcate into two main branches: "Genetic Disease" and "Disease Disorder or Findings". The "Genetic Disease" branch further specifies "Chromosome Disease", which includes "Chromosome Deletion" and the specific location "Chromosome 15q 13.3". In this context, the gene "CHRNA7" located on chromosome 15q 13.3 and expressed in glial cells is highlighted as being related to bipolar disorder. The "Disease Disorder or Findings" branch encompasses "Disease or Disorder", which includes "Psychiatric Disease" and further branches into "Mood Disorder". This category includes "Bipolar Disorder" and "Depression". "Bipolar Disorder" is subdivided into "Bipolar I Disorder", "Bipolar II Disorder", and associated conditions such as "Manic Bipolar Affective Disorder" and "Bipolar Depression". "Depression" is also connected to "Bipolar Depression", indicating that individuals with bipolar disorder may share conditions with those diagnosed with depression. Additionally, the "Phenotypic Abnormality" branch addresses "Abnormality of Mental Function", which includes "Abnormal Emotion" and is further divided into "Mania" and other emotional abnormalities. This work shows how OBD can be applied to map out the genetic predispositions and clinical symptoms of BD, facilitating more accurate diagnoses and personalized treatment plans.

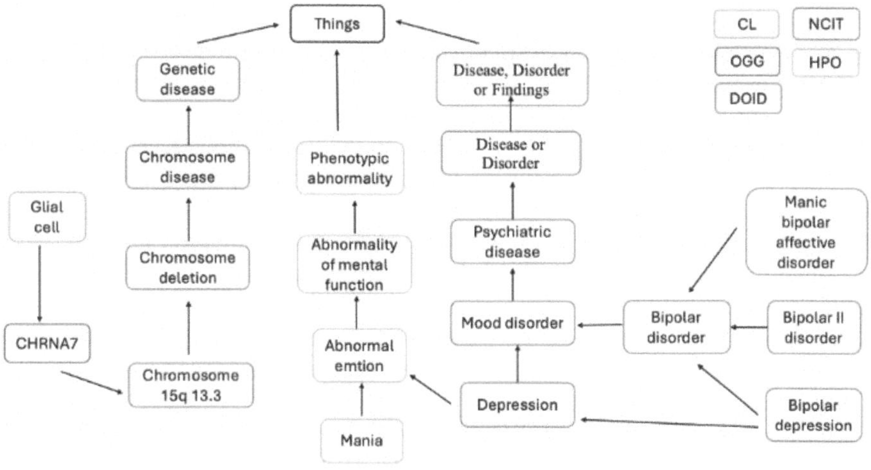

Fig. 3. Demonstrating how BD knowledge from different domains can be integrated

3.5 Use Case Study 2: Computational Logical Reasoning for OBD

Synthesize knowledge to develop new insights about BD and possible treatments by inputting genetic and phenotypic data of patients to leverage OBD for diagnosis and treatment planning. According to Fig. 4, Bipolar depression falls under both bipolar disorder and depression, indicating that individuals with bipolar disorder may share conditions with those who have depression. Interestingly, bipolar depression is also classified under non-neoplastic endocrine pancreas disorder, which is a subtype of endocrine pancreas disorder. Furthermore, non-neoplastic endocrine pancreas disorder is categorized under digestive system disorder according to NCIT.

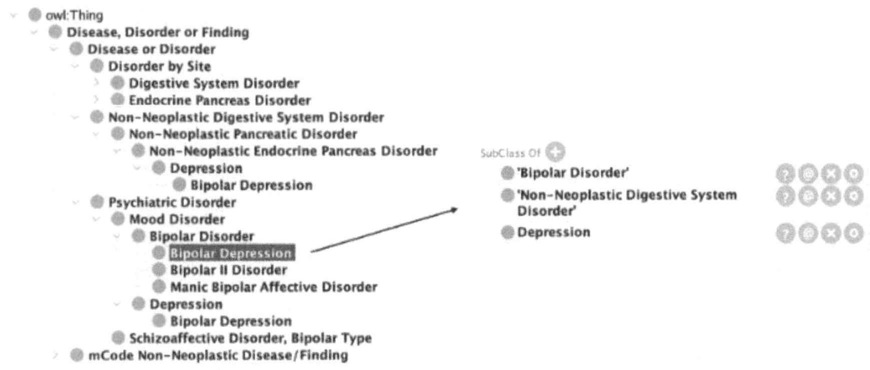

Fig. 4. An example of a logical relationship about OBD

4 Discussion

The diverse and complex clinical manifestations of mental illnesses like BD pose challenges in medical diagnosis [3]. Despite improvements in traditional psychiatric diagnostic systems such as the Diagnostic and Statistical Manual of Mental Disorders (DSM) [19] and The International Classification of Diseases (ICD) [20], they still struggle with accurately diagnosing heterogeneity and comorbidity. In contrast to traditional classifications, The Hierarchical Taxonomy of Psychopathology (HiTOP) [21] proposes an alternative classification method, offering a more continuous perspective of the disease spectrum. Research domain criteria (RDoC) [22] focuses on clinical research of brain functions. However, these infrastructures face various challenges. To address these issues, Ontology offers new possibilities for the standardization and comprehensive description of mental illnesses.

In this study, we propose a new approach, the integrated Ontology of Bipolar Disorder (OBD). In this approach, OBD leveraged existing ontologies and thereby ensured compliance with OBO foundry and BFO principles. We did not establish any new terms; all terms were reused and organized from existing ontologies. We extracted terms related to genes, phenotypes, terminologies, cells, and diseases associated with BD from five existing ontologies. These terms were then aggregated using Ontobee, Ontofox, and Protege following the BFO standards. Subsequently, we presented two relevant use cases demonstrating that BD is a heterogeneous common condition, different people showing different clinical manifestations and different disease progression. By leveraging ontology knowledge, we aim to integrate information from various data sources and metadata. This approach, using an OBD, can facilitate the integration of knowledge from multiple sources and clinical domains and enable new knowledge to be generated, perhaps leading to novel discoveries of new relationships that can inform new diagnostics or innovation.

In particular, this work could support the integration of data from electronic health records, which have promise to support discovery and research about patients in "real world settings." To date, much of the valuable information in Electronic Health Records (EHRs) [23] is locked in systems, challenging to use because of the extreme heterogeneity in EHR data across sites. Methods for accessing and using EHR data for research are badly needed and would benefit researchers in informatics and psychiatry as well as other clinical disciplines. One approach to standardizing and aggregating EHR data across sites is to use a Common Data Model (CDM) [24], such as the OMOP, to standardize and translate heterogeneous data into a common structure, thereby facilitating interoperability.

In the future study, we aim to incorporate concepts from the OMOP common data model to translate different datasets into a common structure. Our focus will be on data from EHR and the Prechter Longitudinal Study of Bipolar Disorder (Prechter Study). We will also explore additional available ontologies related to BD and create new relevant terms that address any misinformation, ensuring a more comprehensive knowledge representation of BD in our ontology framework. We plan to validate and refine the ontology to address the use cases and researcher needs. This version was developed with a small number of domain experts and simple preliminary use cases, and will likely improve with future input of BD researchers. Regardless, the current OBD includes relevant parts of existing ontologies and overcomes the limitations of current classifications widely employed in clinical care. Finally, an ontological framework lays the foundation for a paradigm shift by providing a comprehensive and multidimensional approach to BD research. By combining resources from different sites, we aim to enhance our understanding and management of bipolar disorder, unravel its complexity, and enable multiple disciplines to achieve more efficient explanations, ultimately contributing to better mental health management and outcomes.

Acknowledgments. Yujia Tan was supported in this work by the University of Michigan's Department of Learning Health Sciences (LHS) and the Program in Biomedical Sciences (PIBS) graduate training programs. Dr. Yongqun "Oliver" He is a biomedical ontologist who led the development of the Ontobee tool and OGG, and contributed to the development of the HPO and CL ontologies. Dr. Rachel Richesson is an expert in EHR and data standardization who leads the EHR Core for the NIH Health Systems Research Collaboratory, and Dr. Melvin McInnis is a domain expert in bipolar disorder who leads the Heinz C. Prechter Bipolar Research Program.

Disclosure of Interests. MGM has received research support from Janssen Pharmaceuticals and has consulted with Janssen and Otsuka Pharmaceuticals. Funding sources: This work was supported in part by the Prechter Bipolar Research Program, Prechter Family Charitable Fund, Richard Tam Foundation, and the NIH through UM1TR004404.

References

1. Jain, A., Mitra, P.: Bipolar Disorder. StatPearls, StatPearls Publishing (2024)
2. Corvin, A., Sullivan, P.F.: What next in schizophrenia genetics for the psychiatric genomics consortium? Schizophr. Bull. **42**(3), 538–541 (2016)
3. McInnis, M.G., et al.: Strategies and foundations for scientific discovery in longitudinal studies of bipolar disorder. Bipolar Disord. **24**(5), 499–508 (2022)
4. Jackson, R., et al.: OBO foundry in 2021: operationalizing open data principles to evaluate ontologies. Database (2021)
5. Gargano, M.A., et al.: The human phenotype ontology in 2024: phenotypes around the world. Nucleic Acids Res. **52**(D1), D1333–D1346 (2024)
6. Amberger, J.S., Hamosh, A.: Searching online mendelian inheritance in man (OMIM): a knowledgebase of human genes and genetic phenotypes. Curr. Protocols Bioinform. **58**, 1.2.1–1.2.12 (2017)
7. Yocum, A.K., et al.: Cohort profile update: the Heinz C. Prechter longitudinal study of bipolar disorder. Int. J. Epidemiol. **52**(6), e324–e331 (2023)
8. Barsnes, H., et al.: OLS dialog: an open-source front end to the ontology lookup service. BMC Bioinform. **11**(1), 34 (2010)
9. Cohen, B., et al.: Automated comparative auditing of NCIT genomic roles using NCBI. J. Biomed. Inform. **41**(6), 904–913 (2008)
10. Xiang, Z., et al.: OntoFox: web-based support for ontology reuse. BMC. Res. Notes **3**(1), 175 (2010)
11. Rubin, D.L., et al.: Protégé-OWL: creating ontology-driven reasoning applications with the web ontology language. In: AMIA Annual Symposium Proceedings, vol. 2005, p. 1179 (2005)
12. Schriml, L.M., et al.: The human disease ontology 2022 update. Nucleic Acids Res. **50**(D1), D1255–D1261 (2022)
13. Diehl, A.D., et al.: The cell ontology 2016: enhanced content, modularization, and ontology interoperability. J. Biomed. Semant. **7**(1), 44 (2016)
14. Liu, M., et al.: ICEO, a biological ontology for representing and analyzing bacterial integrative and conjugative elements. Sci. Data **9**(1), 11 (2022)
15. Wilkinson, M., Dumontier, M., Aalbersberg, I., et al.: The FAIR guiding principles for scientific data management and stewardship. In: Scientific Data, vol. 3, p. 160018 (2016)
16. Odeh, M., et al.: iOntoBioethics: a framework for the agile development of bioethics ontologies in pandemics applied to COVID-19. Front. Med. **8**, 619978 (2021)
17. Vogt, L., et al.: Accommodating ontologies to biological reality-top-level categories of cumulative-constitutively organized material entities. PLoS ONE **7**(1), e30004 (2012)
18. Bandrowski, A., et al.: The ontology for biomedical investigations. PLoS ONE **11**(4), e0154556 (2016)
19. Uher, R., et al.: Major depressive disorder in DSM-5: implications for clinical practice and research of changes from DSM-IV. Depression Anxiety **31**(6), 459–471 (2014)
20. Harrison, J.E., et al.: ICD-11: an international classification of diseases for the twenty-first century. BMC Med. Inform. Decis. Making **21**(6), 206 (2021)
21. Kotov, R., et al.: The hierarchical taxonomy of psychopathology (HiTOP): a dimensional alternative to traditional nosologies. J. Abnorm. Psychol. **126**(4), 454–477 (2017)

22. Insel, T., et al.: Research domain criteria (RDoC): toward a new classification framework for research on mental disorders. Am. J. Psychiatry **167**(7), 748–751 (2010)
23. Evans, R.S.: Electronic health records: then, now, and in the future. Yearb. Med. Inform. Suppl. **1**, S48–S61 (2016)
24. Choi, W., et al.: Expansion of EHR-based common data model (CDM). In: Studies in Health Technology and Informatics, vol. 264, pp. 1443–1444 (2019)

EmpER

7th International Workshop on Empirical Methods in Conceptual Modeling (EmpER 2024)

João Araujo[1], Dominik Bork[2], Miguel Goulão[3], Jennifer Horkoff[3], and Sotirios Liaskos[4]

[1] Department of Informatics, Universidade Nova de Lisboa, Lisbon, Portugal
p191@fct.unl.pt
[2] Business Informatics Group, TU Wien, Vienna, Austria
dominik.bork@tuwien.ac.at
[3] Chalmers University of Technology and University of Gothenburg, Sweden
mgoul@fct.unl.pt, jenho@chalmers.se
[4] School of Information Technology, York University, Toronto, Canada
liaskos@yorku.ca

The development and sharing of conceptual models have long been understood to support important human activities such as communication, design, reasoning, decision-making and documentation. A great variety of languages, frameworks, tools, and techniques are continuously being proposed for helping effective development and use of practical conceptual models. The key motivation behind the EmpER workshop series is the understanding that success of all these contributions depends on whether their merits can be demonstrated in practice, i.e., whether they indeed help practicing model producers and model users in achieving their goals. At the same time, production and use of conceptual models gives raise to psychological, social, organizational and other contextual phenomena that deserve to be studied if we are to understand how conceptual modeling is applied in practice. Furthermore, the act of building conceptual models is ideally informed by empirical evidence that is nowadays abundant in the form of digital data. This overabundance of data, combined with the advent of advanced data analysis and artificial intelligence (AI) techniques, introduces major opportunities and challenges for an empirically-informed conceptual modeling.

The 7th International Workshop on Empirical Methods in Conceptual Modeling (EmpER 2024) is aimed at bringing together researchers with an interest in the empirical investigation of conceptual modeling practices, as well as with the study of all forms of data-driven, evidence-based conceptual modeling. The 2024 installment of the workshop invited three kinds of papers: *full study papers* describing a completed study, *work-in-progress papers* describing a planned study or study in progress, as well as *position, vision and lessons learned papers* about the use of empirical methods for conceptual modeling. As usual the workshop particularly welcomed negative results as well as proposed empirical studies that are in their design stage so that authors can benefit from early feedback and adjust their designs prior to a real data collection. We, further, invited technical contributions, case studies, or position and vision papers on data-driven, evidence-based conceptual modeling, to reflect the expanded scope that the workshop has acquired the past few years.

The workshop received a total of nine (9) submissions. Each submission was reviewed by at least three members of a committee of twenty-two (22) subject matter experts in a double-blind fashion. Based on the outcome, four (4) submissions out of the nine were accepted for presentation at the workshop. The topics included an experiment on the effect of the addition of process step execution orders within goal models of robotic production systems to model comprehensibility, an empirical study to examine if two different large language models (LLMs) can correctly answer conceptual modeling examination questions immediately or after being given instructional material, an experiment evaluating a proposed framework for characterizing the contributions of conceptual modeling research, and a study on the use of generative AI to provide a look (visual) and sound (audio) perspective of UML diagrams.

We would like to express our gratitude the Program Committee members for their hard work in reviewing papers, the authors for submitting their works, and the ER 2024 workshop co-chairs, Leah Wong and Motoshi Saeki, as well as the ER 2024 organizing committee for their support and patience.

EmpER Organization

Organization and Steering Committee

João Araujo	Universidade Nova de Lisboa, Portugal
Dominik Bork	TU Wien, Austria
Miguel Goulão	Universidade Nova de Lisboa, Portugal
Jennifer Horkoff	Chalmers University of Technology and University of Gothenburg, Sweden
Sotirios Liaskos	York University, Canada

Program Chairs

João Araujo	Universidade Nova de Lisboa, Portugal
Miguel Goulão	Universidade Nova de Lisboa, Portugal
Jennifer Horkoff	Chalmers University of Technology and University of Gothenburg, Sweden
Sotirios Liaskos	York University, Canada

Program Committee

Camilo Almendra	Universidade Federal do Ceará, Brazil
David Aveiro	University of Madeira, Portugal
Robert Buchmann	Babeş-Bolyai University, Romania
Marian Daun	Technical University of Applied Sciences Würzburg-Schweinfurt, Germany
Edna Dias Canedo	University of Brasília, Brazil
Robson Fidalgo	Universidade Federal de Pernambuco, Brazil
Antonio Garmendia	Universidad Autónoma de Madrid, Spain
Vincenzo Gervasi	University of Pisa, Italy
José Antonio Hernández Lopez	Linköping University, Sweden
Andrea Herrmann	University of Heidelberg, Germany
John Krogstie	Norwegian University of Science and Technology, Norway
Tong Li	Beijing University of Technology, China
Lin Liu	Tsinghua University, China
Raimundas Matulevičius	University of Tartu, Estonia
Claudia Negri-Ribalta	University of Luxembourg, Luxemburg
Oscar Pastor	Universidad Politécnica de Valencia, Spain
Tiago Prince Sales	University of Twente, The Netherlands

Henderik Proper	TU Wien, Austria
Jan Recker	University of Hamburg, Germany
Ben Roelens	Open Universiteit, The Netherlands
Jéssyka Vilela	Universidade Federal de Pernambuco, Brazil
Manuel Wimmer	JKU Linz, Austria

How Does UML Look and Sound? Using AI to Interpret UML Diagrams Through Multimodal Evidence

Aleksandar Gavric(✉), Dominik Bork, and Henderik A. Proper

Business Informatics, TU Wien, Vienna, Austria
{aleksandar.gavric,dominik.bork,henderik.proper}@tuwien.ac.at

Abstract. Despite the availability of abundant digital data, there is a research gap in effectively utilizing this empirical evidence to inform the process of constructing or learning conceptual models. This gap highlights the need to address empirically-informed conceptual modeling practice. This paper underscores the potential of Artificial Intelligence (AI) for improving evidence-based conceptual modeling practice, specifically with Unified Modeling Language (UML) diagrams. We use generative AI to provide a look (visual) and sound (audio) perspective of UML diagrams. Our solution, named **mod**Sense, can link diagram elements to existing image and audio data or generate new image and audio content to improve understanding through real-world examples. Furthermore, our solution incorporates human preferences and feedback to dynamically adjust the generated or retrieved content to the user's comprehension level, providing a tailored human-model interaction experience. Through increased engagement and real-world connections in UML diagrams, we aim to make models more aligned with business logic, resulting in better conceptual models and, subsequently, more effective computer programs. We report on the initial results of **mod**Sense and the **mod**Sense**4**All empirical study that focuses on assessing the educational impact of these multimodal resources in the domain of programming assistant software for surgery applications.

Keywords: UML · Empirical Evidence · Generative AI · Multimodal Data · Conceptual Modeling

1 Introduction

"If you cannot explain a program to yourself, the chance of the computer getting it right is pretty small." – Bob Frankston

Understanding and clearly communicating the structure and behavior of a system is fundamental in software development, enabling practitioners to specify, visualize, construct, and document the artifacts of software systems. The Unified

M. Saeki et al. (Eds.): ER 2024 Workshops, LNCS 14932, pp. 187–197, 2025.
https://doi.org/10.1007/978-3-031-75599-6_14

Modeling Language (UML) provides a standardized way to visualize and document these systems, but how does UML translate beyond static diagrams? This paper explores innovative approaches to interpreting UML diagrams through generated images and audio, offering a multi-sensory experience to enhance comprehension and communication among model readers/creators and stakeholders. Although UML is fundamental in technical education and professional practice, its complexity can be daunting, particularly for newcomers [3]. This complexity necessitates innovative educational tools that enhance comprehension and facilitate a more intuitive learning process. This research contributes to the evidence-based conceptual modeling practice through pedagogical methods in software engineering education and aligns with AI advancements. We take the application of AI a step further—aiming to foster the reading and creation of UML diagrams by providing real-world examples of diagram concepts and structures. This raises our research question (**RQ**): *How can generative AI enhance the comprehension and creation of UML diagrams by providing contextual real-world examples?*

To respond to those research questions, we utilize generative AI to offer both visual and auditory perspectives on UML diagrams. Our approach can associate diagram components with specifications to generate new content and, therefore, facilitate understanding through practical, real-world examples. Moreover, our approach adapts to individual user preferences and feedback, dynamically modifying the generated or retrieved content to match the user's level of comprehension, thus providing a personalized human-model interaction experience. By increasing engagement and making real-world connections within UML diagrams, we aim to ensure that models are more closely aligned with business logic and related to the domain represented by the models. This leads to evidence-based rather than confidence- or assumption-based conceptual models and, ultimately, more effective computer programs. Our solution is particularly beneficial for simulating domains where evidence data collection is hindered by constraints such as limited time, spatial opportunities, or prohibitive costs. Our approach aims to represent and manage these constraints within our simulations. Furthermore, our approach is invaluable in domains where the content is complex and challenging for beginners, such as surgical procedures.

In the remainder of this paper, Sect. 2 provides related work. Section 3 describes our solution, termed ***modSense***, which is an umbrella term for the method and the tool used for interpreting UML diagrams with multimodal AI [7]. We report on our current evaluation results and the on-going empirical study in Sect. 4 and conclude in Sect. 5.

2 Related Work

Understanding conceptual models of business domains is a key skill for practitioners tasked with systems analysis and design [12].

2.1 Generative AI and UML

Our work is positioned in the intersection of Generative AI, such as Generative Adversarial Networks [8], that offered a generative approach to visualizing empirical knowledge and interpreting UML diagrams, such as [16]. When it comes to composing UML diagrams, natural language models have been developed to transform textual requirements into structured UML class diagrams, enhancing the comprehension and visualization of software design [1]. Conversational AI further enhances the learning experience by providing interactive and adaptive feedback to learners. Intelligent tutoring systems like *COLLECT-UML* have demonstrated the effectiveness of using constraint-based feedback to teach object-oriented analysis and design using UML. Automated tools for evaluating and correcting UML diagrams also play a fundamental role in the learning process. For example, tools that automatically classify and correct UML diagrams based on images have been developed, allowing learners to receive instant feedback on their diagrams. These tools utilize machine learning models to detect and correct errors, making the learning process more efficient and effective [10].

2.2 Education in the Context of UML

When it comes to the education of UML context, the potential of generative AI in computing education was explored by Zastudil et al. (2023) [17], who conducted interviews with students and instructors to gauge their experiences and preferences. Their findings suggest a growing acceptance of AI tools in classrooms, albeit with concerns regarding their optimal use. Farrelly et al. (2023) [5] expanded on these implications, discussing the impact of AI on higher education and the challenges of maintaining academic integrity.

These studies collectively demonstrate the potential of AI in education while also highlighting the ethical and practical challenges that must be addressed to ensure its effective and responsible use. Our empirical study is in compliance with the mentioned guidelines and takes the application of AI a step further while also taking a step toward a more specific application to foster UML diagram reading and creation by providing real-world examples of diagram concepts and structures. When it comes to organizing the empirical study, research in this field predominantly uses experiments with specific user proxy cohorts to examine factors that explain how well different types of conceptual models can be comprehended by model viewers [12]. A recent article by Abrahão et al. (2024) [2] provides significant insights into this area, highlighting key findings and methodologies that shape current practices. By synthesizing data from various sources, the authors present a nuanced view of how evidence-based approaches can drive innovation and efficiency in software development processes [2].

3 *The modSense* Method

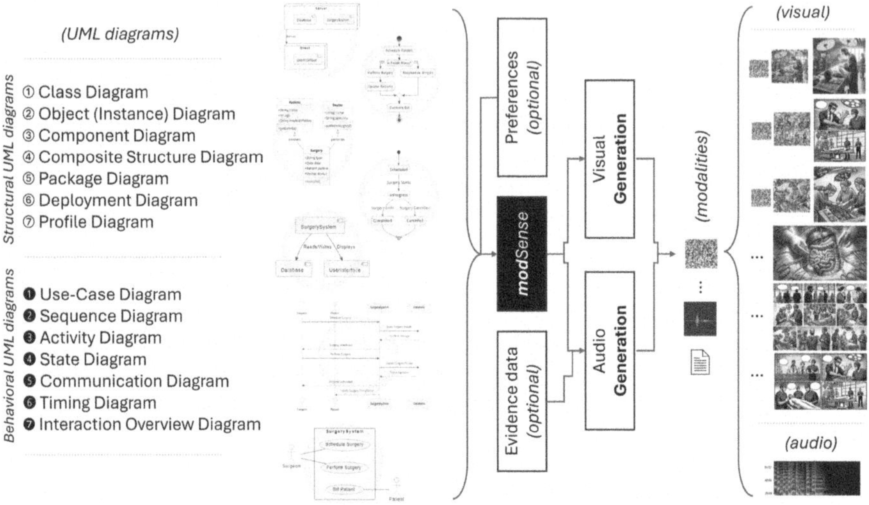

Fig. 1. *modSense* platform overview.

In conceptual modeling education, the comprehension of UML diagrams stands as a fundamental skill [9]. Recognizing the diverse learning styles and preferences of students, a learning-centric approach becomes imperative for effective pedagogy. In this paper, we present the ***mod***Sense platform that is designed to transform the interpretation of UML diagrams by placing learning at the forefront of its design philosophy. At its core, ***mod***Sense embodies a commitment to enhancing the educational experience through innovative AI-driven technologies, catering to the individual needs and preferences of learners. By prioritizing learning outcomes and adopting a multifaceted approach that integrates image and audio generation, and multimodal data retrieval, ***mod***Sense redefines the landscape of UML diagram interpretation, offering a dynamic and engaging learning environment for students in the field of conceptual modeling. Through the integration of advanced generative AI technologies, ***mod***Sense provides a multifaceted approach (see Fig. 1) to enhance the understanding of UML diagrams, catering to diverse learning styles and preferences. ***mod***Sense employs state-of-the-art Generative AI techniques to dynamically generate visual representations and audio descriptions of UML diagrams. This multimodal approach aims to enrich the learning experience by providing learners with multiple sensory inputs. Visual representations offer a clear representation of the diagram's structures, while audio descriptions provide additional context and explanation, catering to auditory learners and those with visual impairments. By presenting information in multiple modalities, ***mod***Sense accommodates different learning preferences and enhances overall comprehension and accessibility [11,15].

3.1 Understanding UML

UML diagrams [6] are a set of graphical representations that help in visualizing, specifying, constructing, and documenting the artifacts of a software system. UML diagrams are broadly categorized into structural and behavioral diagrams. Structural diagrams focus on the static aspects of the system, portraying the physical and conceptual elements and their relationships. Common structural diagrams include class diagrams, object diagrams, component diagrams, composite structure diagrams, deployment diagrams, and package diagrams. These diagrams help in detailing the system's architecture, such as classes and their relationships, system components, and the arrangement of software deployments. Our solution can interpret UML Structural diagrams as illustrated in Fig. 2.

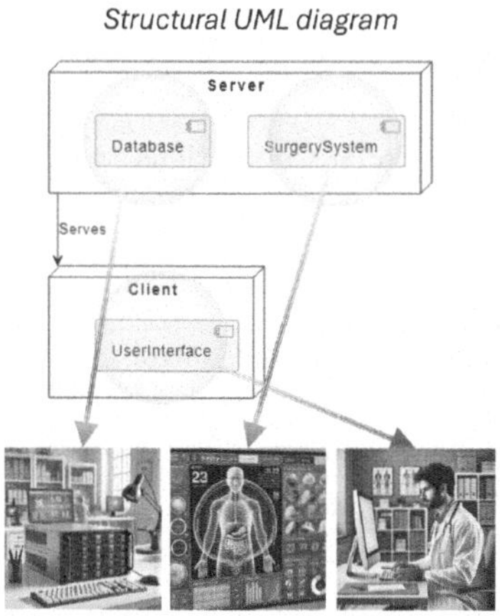

Fig. 2. Structural UML diagram mapped to generated content.

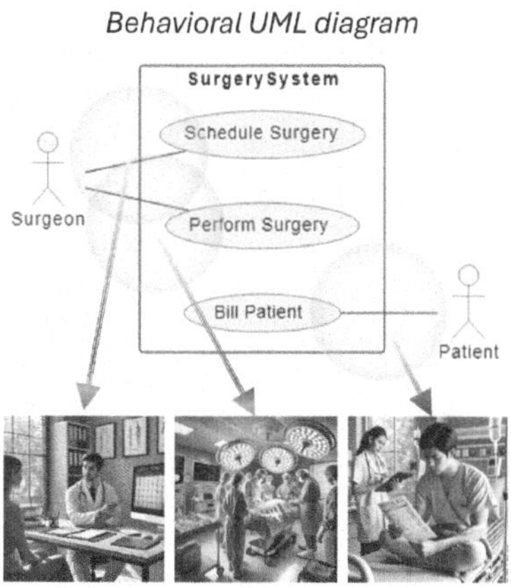

Fig. 3. Behavioral UML diagram mapped to generated content.

Behavioral diagrams, in contrast, represent the dynamic aspects, detailing how the system behaves over time and in response to events. This category includes use case diagrams, sequence diagrams, activity diagrams, state machine diagrams, communication diagrams, interaction overview diagrams, and timing diagrams. These diagrams map out the processes, workflows, and operational sequences within a software system, providing insights into the flow of data and control among different system components. Our solution can interpret UML Behavioral diagrams as illustrated in Fig. 3.

Both types of diagrams are constructed from a variety of elements that provide the building blocks for modeling software systems. We have selected 59 such elements across all 14 types of UML diagrams following the UML specification [14] (see Table 1). The elements include but are not limited to, classes, interfaces, components, use cases, actors, and various types of interaction units such as messages and transitions.

Table 1. UML Key Elements for Generating ***modSense*** interpretations

No.	UML Diagram	Key Elements for Generating *modSense* interpretations
1	Class	Classes, Interfaces, Associations, Generalizations, Dependencies
2	Object	Objects, Links, Fields
3	Use Case	Actors, Use Cases, Relationships, System Boundary
4	Sequence	Objects, Lifelines, Messages, Activation Bars, Time Constraints
5	Collaboration	Objects, Links, Messages, Sequence Numbers
6	Activity	Activities, Transitions, Swimlanes, Forks, Joins, Start/End
7	State Machine	States, Transitions, Events, Actions, Initial and Final States
8	Component	Components, Interfaces, Ports, Connections
9	Deployment	Nodes, Artifacts, Links
10	Timing	Objects, Time Rulers, State or Value Lifelines, Events
11	Interaction	Interaction Frames, Activity Nodes, Control Flows, Decisions
12	Communication	Objects, Messages, Links, Sequence Numbers
13	Composite Struct.	Parts, Connectors, Ports, Collaborations
14	Package	Packages, Dependencies, Mergings, Access

3.2 Visual Generative Capabilities

To connect theoretical knowledge and practical application in the field of conceptual modeling education, this paper introduces a novel (to the best of our knowledge) application of Generative AI to enhance the learning and understanding of UML diagrams. By taking the advanced capabilities of discrete Variational Autoencoders (dVAE), autoregressive transformers, and diffusion models [13], we employ a system capable of generating dynamic visual and auditory content that contextualizes UML diagrams.

The conditioned sample generation starts with the encoding of a textual description y, which specifies the desired image attributes. This text is converted into a sequence of Byte Pair Encoding (BPE) tokens and then embedded into the model. The autoregressive transformer models the generation process where each image token x_i is sequentially predicted based on the previously generated tokens $x_{<i}$ and the input text y.

The conditional probability of generating an image given a text description is given by:

$$p(x \mid y) = \prod_{i=1}^{N} p(x_i \mid x_{<i}, y),$$

where N is the total number of image tokens to be generated. This formulation illustrates the sequential nature of generating image tokens, where the probability of each token x_i depends on its preceding tokens $x_{<i}$ and the text y.

3.3 Auditory Generative Capabilities

For generating audio, we incorporate the solution by [13] into our platform's pipeline. This is achieved through conditioned audio generation using MUSICGEN [4]. MUSICGEN is based on autoregressive modeling, where the sequence of tokens U from the quantized representation Q is modeled such that each token U_t at time t is predicted based on all previous tokens, $p_t(U_t|U_{t-1}, \ldots, U_0) = P(U_t|U_{t-1}, \ldots, U_0)$. Here, U_0 is often a special token indicating the start of the sequence, and p_t is the autoregressive probability model at time t.

Then, the Inexact Autoregressive Decomposition approach is used for the simultaneous prediction of multiple codebooks to reduce complexity and increase efficiency. If the sequence V represents tokens with K codebooks at time t, then the probability of observing $V_{t,k}$, the token from the k-th codebook at time t, given all previous tokens is $p_{t,k}(V_{t,k}|V_{t-1}, \ldots, V_0) = P(V_{t,k}|V_{t-1}, \ldots, V_0)$ where $V_{t,k}$ is the token at time t from codebook k, and $p_{t,k}$ is the autoregressive model specific to codebook k.

3.4 Focus Masks

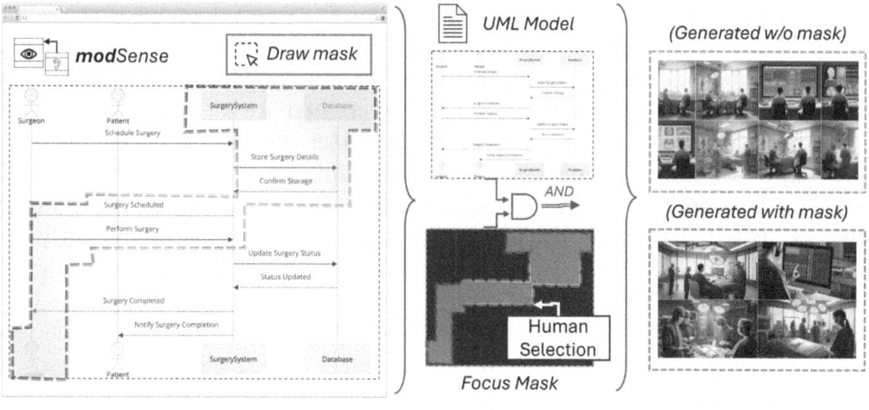

Fig. 4. Focus mask concept for human-guided selective model interpretation.

To make the generation of the content even more customized, we implemented a concept of Focus Masks (see Fig. 4). Implementing a focus mask in the context of UML diagram generation offers a highly personalized and interactive approach to learning and understanding complex systems. A focus mask is essentially a user-defined selection within a UML diagram that highlights specific parts or elements of the diagram for deeper exploration. This functionality enhances the educational experience by allowing users to concentrate on particular components of a system, simplifying the learning process by isolating complex interactions or structures. Users can apply a focus mask to any part of a UML diagram—be it a cluster of classes in a class diagram, specific interactions in a sequence diagram, or particular states in a state machine diagram.

Upon defining a focus mask, the system then generates the specific part of the UML diagram highlighted by the mask. This generation process utilizes generative AI technologies that can dynamically create or adjust the visual representation of the selected diagram portion based on user inputs and predefined modeling rules. For example, if a user selects a series of interactions in a sequence diagram, the AI generates an enhanced view of these interactions, possibly expanding on details like message sequencing, timing, and participant lifelines. This tailored generation helps users see only the relevant parts of a diagram in greater detail, making it easier to understand specific functionalities or relationships without the distraction of unrelated diagram components.

4 Empirical Study in Conceptual Modeling: Multimodal UML Education

Our current evaluation of **mod**Sense involved generating interpretations for various test domains and comparing the results. We selected test domains with intensive manual work, specifically pottery making, organic farming, and bookbinding. So far, we report positive results on diagrams where the temporal dimension is more visible. The generated visual content for these test domains is presented in Figs. 5, 6, and 7, respectively, while the generated audio content is available on our GitHub repository[1]. Through manual observation, we confirmed that the visual generations with basic UML models we created are satisfactory. However, we believe that the reasons for not achieving better results in covering all UML types and better audio generation are (1) the simplicity of the UML models chosen for the test, and (2) the lack of engagement from modelers who did not invest sufficient thought and time to customize their requirements. Consequently, we are addressing these issues with an ongoing study that tracks UML creation and learning in a control group.

The on-going empirical study, **mod**Sense**4**All, aims to investigate the efficacy of using Generative AI to synthesize images for educational purposes in the context of UML conceptual modeling. Specifically, the study focuses on the educational impact of multimodal learning resources generated by AI across 14

[1] https://github.com/aleksandargavric/modsense.

different types of UML diagrams. Participants are recruited from undergraduate and graduate computer science courses, tasked to program a surgery-assistant system, with a balanced mix of those who have prior exposure to UML and those who do not. Participants are randomly divided into two groups: a control group that receives traditional UML instruction and an experimental group that utilizes AI-generated multimodal resources. These resources include AI-synthesized images illustrating key concepts and elements of each UML diagram type, aimed at enhancing comprehension through visual learning.

The primary domain for **mod**Sense**4**All evaluation are surgery applications, given its complex and highly technical nature. The study is conducted over a period of one university semester. The first phase involves a pre-test to assess the baseline understanding of UML concepts among participants. This is followed by a four-week instructional phase where each group receives their respective learning materials. The final phase includes a post-test identical to the pre-test to measure any changes in comprehension. Throughout the study, participants' interactions with the learning materials are documented using learning management system (LMS) analytics, capturing metrics such as time spent on each resource and frequency of access. Additionally, participants complete weekly surveys to provide qualitative feedback on their learning experiences. The assessment of the study involves a comparative analysis of pre- and post-test results between the control and experimental groups, supplemented by qualitative insights from the surveys. This mixed-methods approach aims to provide a comprehensive understanding of the potential benefits and challenges of integrating AI-generated visual aids in UML education.

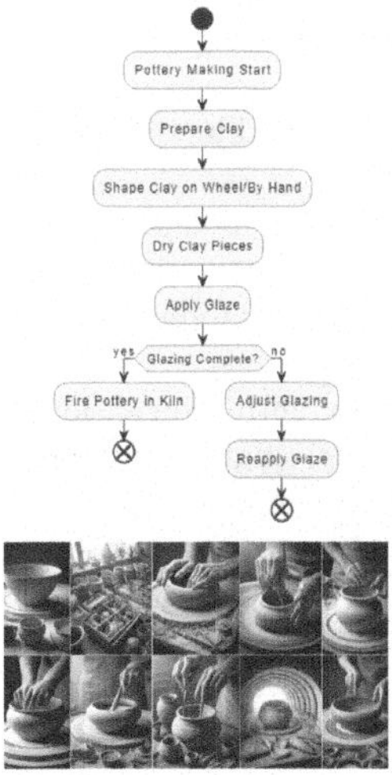

Fig. 5. Example case study in the domain of pottery making.

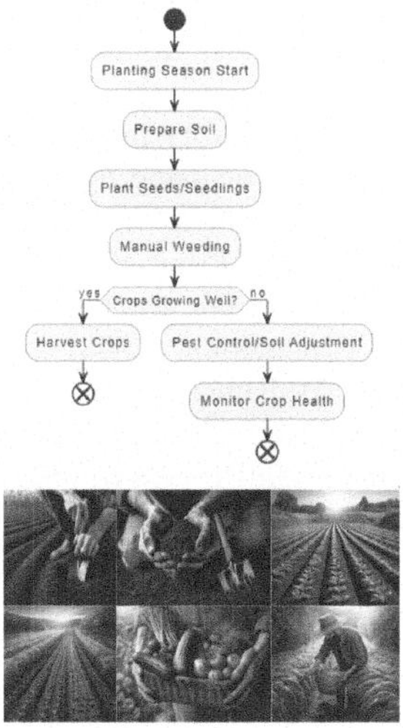

Fig. 6. Example case study in the domain of organic farming.

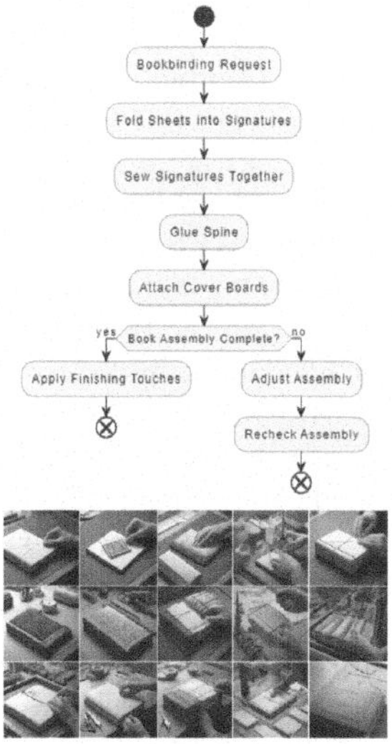

Fig. 7. Example case study in the domain of bookbinding.

5 Conclusion

This paper explored the application of AI technologies—specifically generative and conversational AI—in enhancing the teaching and understanding of Unified Modeling Language (UML) diagrams across domains. By integrating these AI capabilities, we have demonstrated a significant advancement in the educational use of UML diagrams, making them more interactive, accessible, and tailored to individual learning needs. The focus mask feature and the dynamic generation of content based on user preferences provide a customized learning experience, allowing users to focus on specific areas of a diagram relevant to their interests or challenges. Looking forward, the potential of this AI-driven approach extends beyond the initial domains tested, promising broader applications in various educational and professional training settings. By incorporating user feedback and refining AI interactions, the tool can evolve to meet educational demands and adapt to new learning environments.

References

1. Abdelnabi, E.A., Maatuk, A.M., Hagal, M.: Generating UML class diagram from natural language requirements: a survey of approaches and techniques. In: IEEE 1st International Maghreb Meeting of the Conference on Sciences and Techniques of Automatic Control and Computer Engineering MI-STA, pp. 288–293 (2021)
2. Abrahão, S., et al.: Research highlights in evidence-based software engineering. IEEE Softw. **41**, 133–136 (2024). https://doi.org/10.1109/MS.2023.3321418
3. Baghaei, N., Mitrovic, A., Irwin, W.: Supporting collaborative learning and problem-solving in a constraint-based CSCL environment for UML class diagrams. Int. J. Comput.-Support. Collab. Learn. **2**, 159–190 (2007). https://doi.org/10.1007/s11412-007-9018-0
4. Copet, J., et al.: Simple and controllable music generation. In: Thirty-seventh Conference on Neural Information Processing Systems (2023)
5. Farrelly, T., Baker, N.: Generative artificial intelligence: implications and considerations for higher education practice. Educ. Sci. (2023)
6. Fowler, M.: UML Distilled: A Brief Guide to the Standard Object Modeling Language, 3 edn. Addison-Wesley Professional (2003)
7. Gavric, A., Bork, D., Proper, H.: Multimodal process mining. In: 26th International Conference on Business Informatics. IEEE (2024). https://model-engineering.info/publications/papers/CBI-MultiModalProcessMining.pdf. In press
8. Goodfellow, I.J., et al.: Generative adversarial networks (2014). https://arxiv.org/abs/1406.2661
9. Hitz, M., Kappel, G.: UML@ work: von der Analyse zur Realisierung (2002)
10. Lokonon, M.S., Houndji, V.R.: Automatic UML defects detection based on image of diagram. In: DeLTA, pp. 193–198 (2022)
11. Lukyanenko, R., Bork, D., Storey, V.C., Parsons, J., Pastor, O.: Inclusive conceptual modeling: diversity, equity, involvement, and belonging in conceptual modeling (short paper). In: 2023 Companion Proceedings of the 42nd International Conference on Conceptual Modeling: ER Forum. CEUR Workshop Proceedings, vol. 3618 (2023)

12. Mendling, J., Recker, J., Reijers, H., Leopold, H.: An empirical review of the connection between model viewer characteristics and the comprehension of conceptual process models. Inf. Syst. Front. 1–25 (2019). https://doi.org/10.1007/S10796-017-9823-6
13. Ramesh, A., et al.: Zero-shot text-to-image generation (2021)
14. Rumbaugh, J., Jacobson, I., Booch, G.: Unified Modeling Language Reference Manual, 2nd edn. Pearson Higher Education (2004)
15. Sarioglu, A., Metin, H., Bork, D.: How inclusive is conceptual modeling? A systematic review of literature and tools for disability-aware conceptual modeling. In: Almeida, J.P.A., Borbinha, J., Guizzardi, G., Link, S., Zdravkovic, J. (eds.) ER 2023. LNCS, vol. 14320, pp. 65–83. Springer, Cham (2023). https://doi.org/10.1007/978-3-031-47262-6_4
16. Whittle, J., Jayaraman, P., Elkhodary, A., Moreira, A., Araújo, J.: MATA: a unified approach for composing UML aspect models based on graph transformation. In: Katz, S., Ossher, H., France, R., Jézéquel, J.-M. (eds.) Transactions on Aspect-Oriented Software Development VI. LNCS, vol. 5560, pp. 191–237. Springer, Heidelberg (2009). https://doi.org/10.1007/978-3-642-03764-1_6
17. Zastudil, C., Rogalska, M., Kapp, C., Vaughn, J.L., Macneil, S.: Generative AI in computing education: Perspectives of students and instructors. ArXiv abs/2308.04309 (2023)

Can Large Language Models Learn Conceptual Modeling by Looking at Slide Decks and Pass Graduate Examinations? An Empirical Study

Noé Y. Flandre[1,2] and Philippe J. Giabbanelli[1(✉)]

[1] Virginia Modeling, Analysis, and Simulation Center (VMASC), Old Dominion University, Norfolk, VA, USA
pgiabban@odu.edu
[2] IMT Mines Alès, Alès, France
noe.flandre@etu.mines-ales.fr

Abstract. Large Language Models (LLMs) have been used in numerous studies to pass written examinations, with mixed performances. Prior studies have relied on the text capability of LLMs and close ended questions (e.g., multiple choices), often examining performances without comparison to real-world test-takers. Recent studies have emphasized the need to test multiple LLMs and situate performances with respect to students' scores. In addition, recent LLMs can handle both text and images. In our empirical study, we leverage this technical improvement to examine whether LLMs can learn from the same material (i.e., readings and slide decks) that was given to students in a graduate class on conceptual modeling. Our experiments on GPT-4o and Claude 3.5 Sonnet demonstrate that both LLMs improve performances by learning from the material across five tests (covering different aspects of conceptual modeling) and across levels of mastery (e.g., understand, create). Both LLMs achieved passing grades. GPT-4o was often aligned with, or above, a median student. Our results pave the way for future studies in which LLMs may take a course in conceptual modeling, by decomposing video recordings of lectures into images.

Keywords: Computer Vision · Conceptual Modeling · Exam Performance · Graduate Course · Large Language Model

1 Introduction

An abundance of studies has recently documented the performances of Large Language Models (LLMs) in taking written examinations. Their focus was often on medical examinations, as assessed via multiple choice questions and other forms of automatically graded questions (e.g., fill-in-the-blank, matching). Reviews based on GPT 3 and GPT 3.5 reported mixed findings, as the LLM occasionally underperformed significantly compared to a hypothetical average

M. Saeki et al. (Eds.): ER 2024 Workshops, LNCS 14932, pp. 198–208, 2025.
https://doi.org/10.1007/978-3-031-75599-6_15

student [5,11], or sometimes exhibited results that were enthusiastically portrayed as signs of 'intelligence' in the popular press. Parts of the difficulty in contextualizing performances stems from the lack of a comparator group, as early works rarely compared the scores of LLMs with students taking the same tests (e.g., only one of 12 studies reviewed in [11]). A study involving an expert panel examined the discrepancy between answers proposed by an LLM vis-Ãă-vis the expected answers (i.e., 'answer key'), and they found that test questions were at times poorly constructed from vague or ambiguous statements [8]. Recent works thus stress the importance of performing empirical studies in which multiple LLMs are used to propose test answers, then compared with students' scores [8]. In this paper, we performed the first empirical study that examines the ability of different LLMs to pass examinations in conceptual modeling, in comparison with students who took the same tests. The notion of conceptual modeling is used in a broad sense, thus we *not* focus on UML or specific modeling grammars; rather, we cover the ability of students to abstract a situation into a model (i.e., form relevant and interdependent concepts) and reason about this abstraction.

Scholars have pointed out that important claims for LLMs such as "achieving human-level performance" or being "among the top 10% of test-takers" were not always assessed on a fair basis with respect to their human counterparts. For example, the bar examination for the legal profession is *closed-book* for humans, whereas LLMs can tap into their vast knowledge model inferred from massive digital collections [7]. Interestingly, there is also a challenge the other way around: students are taught *specific course material* that culminates in related examinations, whereas the ability of an LLM (who has not taken the course) relies solely on its pre-existing knowledge model and its extent to which it can make inferences. For a fair comparison, our study *(i)* allows students to bring relevant course material to their examinations and *(ii)* provides the same material to the LLM. This set-up allows us to examine a fundamental question: could an LLM learn conceptual modeling like a student by 'taking' the same course?

As stated by Newton and Xiromeriti, the technical innovations afforded by LLMs allow us to conduct "studies whose research questions were not plausible just a few months ago" [10]. While LLMs excel at retrieving information from textual corpus (e.g., course readings), students also receive instruction in higher education courses through non-textual means. For example, instructors can write on a board and lead class discussions (known as 'chalk and talk'), or they can use digital tools such as slide decks which can mix text and images. Newer LLMs such as GPT-4 have vision capability so they can deal with multimodal data consisting of images (e.g., slides, visual component of test questions) along with text (e.g., test questions, course readings). Recent studies have assessed the ability of GPT-4 in taking exams that include visual components, for example by interpreting technical diagrams and data trends [12]. In multiple instances, GPT-4 had a performance similar to humans [10] and thanks to its vision component, it scored among the top 10% of test-takers [8]. To the best of our knowledge, our empirical study in the context of conceptual modeling is the first that examines whether vision capability allows LLMs to improve their performances by learning the course material. Our inquiry complements prior research in which LLMs were enhanced with *textual* facts fetched from databases (i.e., RAG-augmented LLMs), leading to performance gains on examinations from 81% (without RAG) to 85% (with RAG), thus outperforming an average student [9].

While prior research on LLMs and examinations was often performed on automatically graded examinations (e.g., multiple choice questions) [5,11], conceptual modeling involves complex tasks such as creating and analyzing a model's validity. Although our scope is different, we echo Bork's recommendations that a conceptual modeling course should be "taught and tested comprehensively" [1]. Consequently, our tests rely primarily on open-ended questions. For example, test-takers are given a scenario and asked to propose a set of relevant states for their model (e.g., modeling disease progression), they must generate sample situations that exhibit specific characteristics (e.g., illustrate bias), or they need to articulate viable alternatives (e.g., validate a model in the absence of quantitative data). We posit that an LLM should demonstrate its skills in conceptual modeling through such 'Ill-Structured Problems' (ISPs), which are defined by admitting multiple solutions and requiring a careful analysis of the problem. While studies have compared students' and experts' solutions to ISPs [4], there is a paucity of works devoted to the assessment of LLMs for ISPs [2].

Our empirical study on conceptual modeling makes three contributions:

- We examine whether LLMs can learn conceptual modeling both articles (as text) and slide decks (via vision capability) from slide decks by exhibiting a similar performance on examinations with respect to students.
- We emphasize the ability to solve ill-structured problems, as is appropriate in a graduate-level introduction to conceptual modeling and as a reflection of the complexity of tasks involved in this domain.
- We evaluate using two LLMs (GPT-4o and Claude-3-sonnet released Feb 9th 2024) over five tests, corresponding to different themes in modeling.

The remainder of this paper is structured as follows. In Sect. 2, we summarize the course structure, learning outcomes, and thematic modules (each culminating in one quiz). In Sect. 3, we present the design of our empirical study. Our results are provided in Sect. 4 and contextualized in Sect. 5. To support transparency and further contribute to the literature on LLMs in conceptual modeling, we have released our dataset containing test questions, answers (for both LLMs and anonymized students) and associated grades on a third-party anonymized repository at https://doi.org/10.5281/zenodo.12734347.

2 Organization and Aims of the Modeling Course

Conceptual modeling is a multidisciplinary topic as it covers domains such as operations research, statistics, or computer science. The typical division of a university into departments required that we emphasized the domain pertaining to the department, thus the course was taught from the perspective of computer science. Consequently, we designed a course on conceptual modeling *for simulation*. In this context, the activities covered by a course include "(i) determining modelling objectives, (ii) specification of model scope and detail, (iii) choice of output measures, and (iv) determining experimental factors" [14]. While (i) and (ii) are also covered when conceptual modelling is taught in other disciplines such as business or software engineering [13], (iii) and (iv) are more specific about the transition from a conceptual model to performing simulation experiments. We share the views of van der Zee that learning objectives in our context boil down to improving *knowledge* about relevant methods and techniques, and gaining *skills* to execute modeling activities given the available resources [14]. According to Bork [1], these objectives can be further divided into four themes: factual (e.g., parts and purpose of conceptual models), conceptual, procedural (i.e., taking steps to create valid models), and metacognitive (e.g., who is the audience of the model, what will they do, which resources must be secured to make the model). The design of our course touches on all four of these themes.

Modeling courses use a variety of modeling languages and environments, as evidenced by international comparisons of course designs [3]. Our course used `NetLogo` and proceeded in 5 modules, each culminating in one quiz. Each module was delivered using power point presentations, which is a "prototypical way of teaching" with digital technologies in higher education [6].

In terms of assessment strategies, we follow the recommendations that a conceptual modeling course at the masters level should include opportunities to practice [14], thus we include a mandatory project conducted in small teams – a practice also followed at institutions such as Lancaster University [14] or KU Leuven at the graduate level [13]. The group project and paired assignments evaluate metacognitive knowledge, which is beyond the scope of this manuscript. We focus on the evaluation of factual and procedural knowledge through quizzes. The class had five quizzes and questions at different levels of mastery in each quiz (Table 1), which is in line with other conceptual modeling courses that featured six quizzes [13]. A reliance on Multiple Choice Questions could be appropriate in programs whose outcomes focus on the levels of understanding, analyzing, and evaluating. However, courses in conceptual modeling also require *creating* models, thus evaluation modalities include open ended questions [13].

The course was taught at Miami University in Fall 2023. Graduate students must obtain a grade of B or above (i.e., 70%) to receive credits, thus 70% is a 'passing grade'. Using a scale of 1 (worst) to 4 (best), students evaluated the extent to which examinations were deemed fair or whether the course material matched the expected learning outcomes (Table 2). These scores are compared to a department's average and used for annual personnel evaluations, thus the difficulty of a course is adjusted to align with institutional expectations. Consequently, each quiz was designed after evaluating students on the prior quiz to adjust the difficulty of questions based on prior performances.

Table 1. Each course module was assessed by one quiz, containing a varying number of questions that covered different levels of mastery.

Quiz number and theme	Understand	Analyze	Evaluate	Create	Total (n)
1: Modeling goals, compartmental models, CA	2	2	1	1	6
2: Disease models, validity	4	1	1	1	7
3: Agent-Based Models	2	0	1	3	6
4: Language models	2	2	0	0	4
5: Design of Experiments	1	3	0	1	5
%	39.29	28.57	10.71	21.43	

Table 2. Mean scores for several questions included in standardized teaching evaluations. All students responded to the anonymized survey (respondent rate 100%).

Question	Course	Department
In this course I learned to analyze complex problems or think about complex issues	4.00	3.38
My appreciation for this topic has increased as a result of this course	3.88	3.
The professor effectively explained, modeled, and/or critiqued theories, concepts and applications	4.00	3.13
The professor effectively communicated and applied expectations, course objectives and methods of evaluation	3.75	3.21
Overall teaching effectiveness	3.50	3.09

3 Design of the Empirical Study

Figure 1 summarizes our empirical approach. Each of the five course modules culminated in a quiz. Students took the five quizzes based on the teaching material for the module, consisting of a slide deck and occasionally a reading (PDF). We tested the ability of *two LLMs* to answer the same questions, based on *whether they were given the teaching material* or not. The absence of a textbook supports our empirical design, as it isolates the effect of the teaching material onto learning in an LLM. Slide decks were turned into images by saving them into JPEG files; some slides were combined given the LLM's limitations (e.g., Claude accepts 20 images). Python scripts written in Jupyter Notebooks automate all other parts of the process. For replicability, library versions and their purpose are listed in Table 3. While studies on LLMs in conceptual modeling include an element of prompt engineering, note that *each quiz question is already a prompt.* There is thus no influence of 'prompt style' as we ask the same questions to LLMs and students. We tested a total of 28 questions corresponding to different themes in modeling and at different levels of mastery (Table 1). For example, a question on *creating* compartmental models gave students a case description and asked them to identify relevant concepts (emphasis added):

> Tuberculosis (commonly known as 'TB') is one of the most common infections in the world, affecting about 2 billion people. TB is transmitted from person to person through the air. An important feature of TB infection is the latent period. Most newly infected individuals progress to a latent stage in which TB remains dormant and does not replicate. People in this stage are non-infectious. Many people with latent TB will never progress to active disease, but if they do, they are symptomatic and infectious. Half of infectious people die from the disease and the other half recovers spontaneously. TB does not confer complete immunity after recovery. Individuals who recover from active TB are not only susceptible to re-infection, but they can also relapse into active disease. *List the states that we will need to represent the disease.*

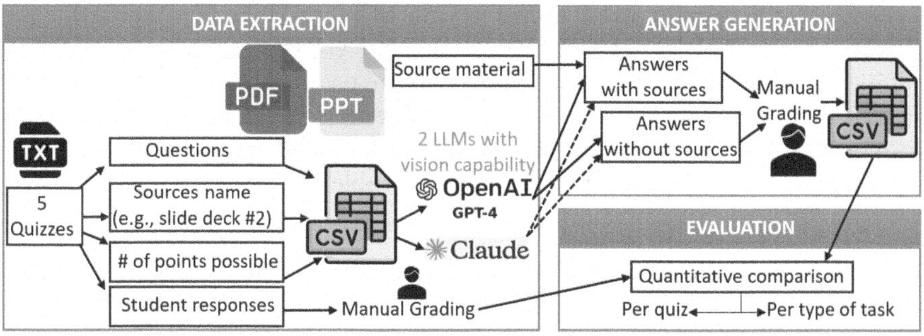

Fig. 1. Design for our empirical study on LLMs and conceptual modeling.

Students also had to propose models at different levels of complexity:

> A very abstract view of an agent posits that its "working memory" is influenced by cognition and results in actions. But it doesn't really tell us how memory works. As a modeler, propose two ways to operationalize the memory: a simple way, and a more complex way. Please be clear about the nature of data, its storage and use.

Several of the questions are highly-context dependent, as the answer would be derived from the learning experience engendered by the course. For example, a prevailing framework may only be defined with respect to a learning resource: "Propose an extension of the framework *from your reading.* Tell us what it extends and why that would be useful." In a similar manner, questions may contain acronyms that students would be expected to know in order to interpret the problem (e.g., CA for Cellular Automaton, LHD for Latin Hypercube Design).

4 Results

The LLMs and students were graded by the same instructor. Experimental results (Fig. 2) show that either LLM can produce answers whose quality falls within the distribution of the students, on any of the modeling themes studied and for any level of mastery. Without training, the answers of LLMs may receive a low score (albeit 'plausible' among students) as they occasionally misunderstand the context. With training, answers from LLMs always improved. This improvement is particularly noticeable when focusing on the percentage of answers that received full marks: without training, Claude 3.5 and GPT-4o get full marks on 28.57% and 39.28% of questions respectively, whereas training yields full marks on 57.14% (up by ↑28.57%) and 82.14% (up by ↑42.86%) of questions. For context, students get full marks on 62.03% of questions. These results highlight the important impact of an LLM, as there is a noticeable gap between Claude 3.5 Sonnet (Fig. 2; square) and GPT-4o (Fig. 2; circle). With training, Claude 3.5 Sonnet barely obtained a passing grade (with training), whereas GPT-4o often surpassed a median student. Performances from the LLMs were consistent across modeling themes (Fig. 2; left) and across levels of mastery (Fig. 2; right), as confirmed by one-ANOVA (Table 4).

Table 3. Specific libraries used in our work in addition to built-in Python functions.

Library	Version	Purpose
re	2.2.1	Parse the questions/points/sources via regular expressions
csv	1.0	Load and save our data as comma-separated values (CSV)
openai	0.28.0	Prompting GPT
fitz	1.24.7	Extracting text from readings (provided as PDF files)
anthropic	0.29.0	Prompting Claude
pandas	1.5.3	Combining input CSV files with prompts, support visualizations

Examining the LLM's answers reveals that training with resources also affects the answers' *length.* Responses without training averaged 2368.67 ± 1040.39 characters, which was reduced to 1716.53 ± 1122.12 characters after training. Overall, the distribution of answers' length shifts towards shorter responses (Fig. 3). However, shorter answers are *not always better*, as the relation between answer length and quality is mediated by the LLM (Fig. 3; inset).

Table 4. One-way ANOVA for the impact of the LLM and sources onto results across levels of mastery. p-values > 0.05 show no statistically significant difference.

LLM	Sources	Sum of squares	df	F	Pr(>F)
GPT-4o	No	7.594	3.0	1.690	0.195
	Yes	3.778	3.0	1.547	0.227
Claude 3.5 Sonnet	No	6.697	3.0	2.014	0.138
	Yes	3.925	3.0	1.350	0.281

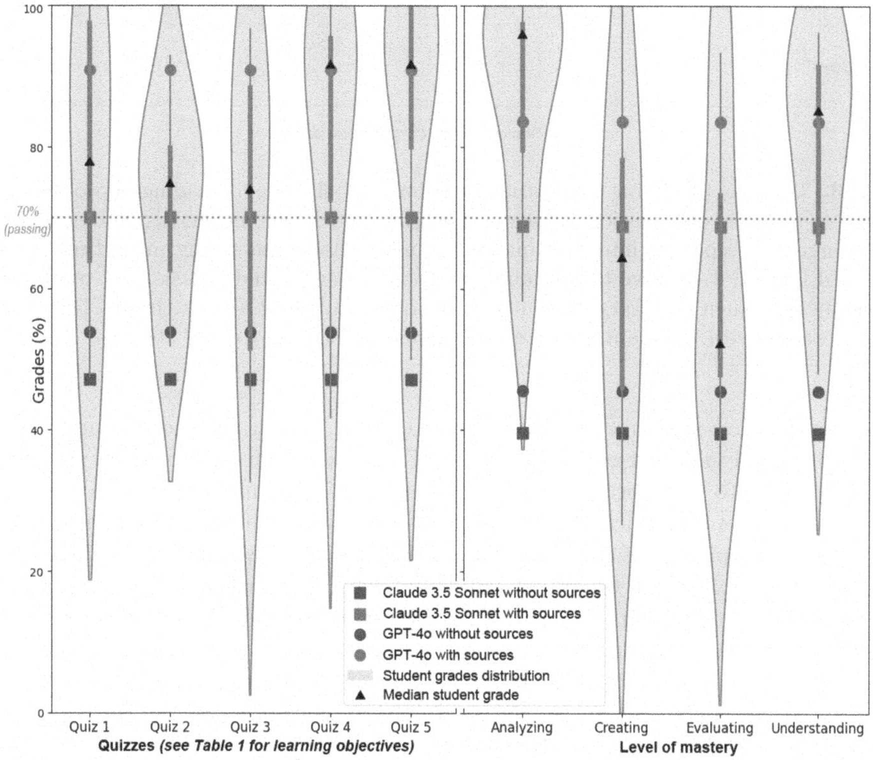

Fig. 2. Distribution of student grades per quiz and level of mastery, and our four combinations of LLMs (GPT-4o, Claude 3.5 Sonnet) with/without access to resources.

5 Discussion and Conclusion

Prior research reported mixed findings on the use of LLMs to pass examinations, which were often from the medical domain and predominantly assessed on multiple choice questions. In contrast, the LLMs' ability to learn modeling received less attention. In addition, modeling often requires the development of

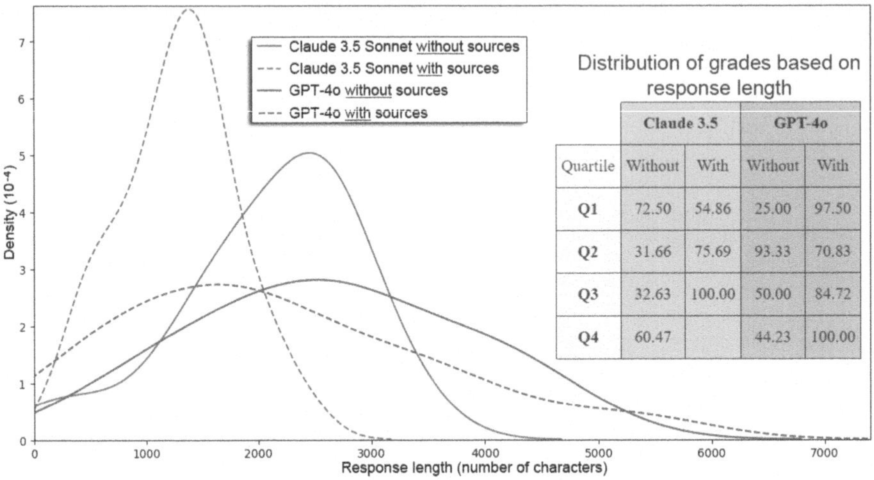

Fig. 3. Training LLMs on conceptual modeling via slides and readings (two PDFs) tends to shift the distribution of answers' lengths, which become shorter. Categorizing the length of responses into four quartiles (inset) shows the strong mediating effect of the LLM: GPT-4o gave high-quality very short answers and occasionally produced long answers when necessary. In contrast, the quality of short answers from Claude 3.5 deteriorated, with the main improvements found in medium to long answers.

process-oriented skills on ill-structured problems, which are more comprehensively assessed via open-ended questions. These skills can be taught by showing students how to transform cases into models (e.g., schematic abstractions) and how to interpret dynamics (e.g., as plots or spatial phenomena), which emphasize the *visual* component of conceptual modeling. While LLMs are notably efficient to deal with text, their vision capacity was previously limited. The integration of vision into mainstream LLMs has enabled us to examine whether they could learn conceptual modeling from the same material that was given to students. Our empirical study on a graduate class suggests that LLMs indeed learn from slides, but the effect is strongly mediated by the choice of LLM. GPT-4o demonstrated an excellent learning ability, as it comfortably exceeded passing grades on all modeling themes and at all levels of mastery. GPT-4o was often on par with, or above, a median student. While Claude 3.5 Sonnet also improved performances by learning, it barely achieved a passing score. We saw that learning affected both the quality of answers (which improved) and their length. Intuitively, without learning, the LLM provides a very comprehensive but general answer. The answer is specific once the LLM understands the particular context.

There are four limitations to this study. First, while our empirical study involved two well-known LLMs, other emerging LLMs offer both language and vision (e.g., Phi-3V). Additional models would not change our observation that results (e.g., quality, length of answers) are mediated by the choice of LLM. However, emerging models could have higher performances than observed at the present time. Second, we defined conceptual modeling broadly and the topic can be taught in different ways, for example to emphasize simulation (as we did) or focused on business processes. Our study was based on a graduate course in a computer science department, thus findings may differ if the training material and associated question stressed a different facet of conceptual modeling. Third, institutional standards for a passing grade may differ, thus the notion that "a LLM can pass an exam" is context-dependent. In our case, 70% is the threshold for a passing grade so we consider that Claude 3.5 is 'borderline', but the message would change if the standard was lowered to 50%. Fourth, it is possible that the ability of LLMs to learn text from the slides may be more important than images, which would need to be examined through ablation experiments.

We acknowledge that the teaching experiences in a course cannot be reduced to slides. Discussions and interactive examples are also typical activities in a class. Since LLMs can learn from images, it would be of particular interest in future work to provide image snapshots from recorded lectures. This would broaden the training of LLMs to more closely resemble a student who takes a class. As classes are recorded (e.g., online learning, hybrid learning), the possibility of asking a LLM to 'take a course' is now becoming a reality.

Disclosure of Interests. The authors have no competing interests to declare that are relevant to the content of this article.

References

1. Bork, D.: A framework for teaching conceptual modeling and metamodeling based on bloom's revised taxonomy of educational objectives. In: Proceedings of the 52nd Hawaii International Conference. System Sciences, pp. 7701–7710 (2019)
2. Ding, Z., Srinivasan, A., MacNeil, S., Chan, J.: Fluid transformers and creative analogies: exploring large language models' capacity for augmenting cross-domain analogical creativity. In: Proceedings of the 15th Conference on Creativity and Cognition, pp. 489–505 (2023)
3. Giabbanelli, P.J., Mago, V.K.: Teaching computational modeling in the data science era. Procedia Comput. Sci. **80**, 1968–1977 (2016)
4. Gupta, V.K., Giabbanelli, P.J., Tawfik, A.A.: An online environment to compare students' and expert solutions to ill-structured problems. In: Zaphiris, P., Ioannou, A. (eds.) LCT 2018. LNCS, vol. 10925, pp. 286–307. Springer, Cham (2018). https://doi.org/10.1007/978-3-319-91152-6_23
5. Levin, G., Horesh, N., Brezinov, Y., Meyer, R.: Performance of ChatGPT in medical examinations: a systematic review and a meta-analysis. BJOG: Int. J. Obstetr. Gynaecol. **131**(3), 378–380 (2024)
6. Lohr, A., et al.: On powerpointers, clickerers, and digital pros: Investigating the initiation of digital learning activities by teachers in higher education. Comput. Hum. Behav. **119**, 106715 (2021)
7. Martínez, E.: Re-evaluating GPT-4's bar exam performance. Artif. Intell. Law 1–24 (2024)
8. Mendonça, N.C.: Evaluating ChatGPT-4 vision on Brazil's national undergraduate computer science exam. ACM Trans. Comput. Educ. (2024)

9. Miladi, F., Psyché, V., Lemire, D.: Comparative performance of GPT-4, RAG-augmented GPT-4, and students in MOOCs. In: Basiouni, A., Frasson, C. (eds.) BBGI 2024. CCIS, vol. 2162, pp. 81–92. Springer, Cham (2024). https://doi.org/10.1007/978-3-031-65996-6_7
10. Newton, P., Xiromeriti, M.: ChatGPT performance on multiple choice question examinations in higher education. A pragmatic scoping review. Assess. Eval. High. Educ. 1–18 (2023)
11. Sumbal, A., Sumbal, R., Amir, A.: Can ChatGPT-3.5 pass a medical exam? A systematic review of ChatGPT's performance in academic testing. J. Med. Educ. Curricular Dev. **11**, 23821205241238641 (2024)
12. Susnjak, T., McIntosh, T.R.: ChatGPT: the end of online exam integrity? Educ. Sci. **14**(6), 656 (2024)
13. Vemuri, P., Poelmans, S., Serral Asensio, E., Snoeck, M.: Teaching conceptual modeling leveraging formative assessments and adaptive release paths. In: Proceedings of the 42th International Conference on Conceptual Modeling (ER2023) (2023)
14. Zee, V.D., et al.: Panel discussion: education on conceptual modeling for simulation-challenging the art. In: Johansson, B., et al. (eds.) Proceedings of the 2010 Winter Simulation Conference, pp. 290–304. IEEE (2010)

Evaluating a Framework of Conceptual Modelling Research

Jose Ignacio Panach[1(✉)], Óscar Pastor[2], Stephen W. Liddle[3], Veda C. Storey[4], Heinrich C. Mayr[5], and Bernhard Thalheim[6]

[1] Escola Tècnica Superior d'Enginyeria, Universitat de València, Valencia, Spain
joigpana@uv.es

[2] VRAIN, Universitat Politècnica de València, Valencia, Spain
opastor@dsic.upv.es

[3] Brigham Young University, Provo, UT, USA
liddle@byu.edu

[4] Georgia State University, Atlanta, GA, USA
vstorey@gsu.edu

[5] Alpen-Adria-Universität Klagenfurt, Klagenfurt, Austria
Heinrich.Mayr@aau.at

[6] Christian-Albrechts-Universität Kiel, Kiel, Germany
bernhard.thalheim@email.uni-kiel.de

Abstract. Conceptual modelling aims to abstractly represent aspects of the perceivable world for a wide range of application areas so that the relevant part of an application can be represented and appropriate data included in a useful information system. Such abstraction efforts can be challenging and the resulting research papers have a wide variety of reported results. This makes it difficult to correctly identify and categorize the contribution of a specific research paper. Prior research has proposed a framework for characterizing the contributions of conceptual modelling research. In this paper, we assess the effectiveness of the framework's use to understand whether and how it could be applied to the large field of conceptual modeling. An experiment was conducted with 24 junior researchers as subjects. The evaluation of the experiment consisted of analysing the level of agreement among the subjects in the classification of a research paper's characteristics and analysing the correctness when classifying a paper. The data analysis showed a medium level of agreement and a good level of correctness. The outcome implies that framework helps identify the type of contribution made by a research paper, even when subjects are non-experts in conceptual modelling.

Keywords: conceptual modelling · empirical software engineering · evaluating research contributions · Characterizing Conceptual Modeling Research

1 Introduction

Conceptual Modelling (CM) focuses on understanding, conceptualizing and representing 'reality' in different domains of interest, with a special emphasis on information systems design and development [1]. Consequently, the field of conceptual modelling research

M. Saeki et al. (Eds.): ER 2024 Workshops, LNCS 14932, pp. 209–218, 2025.
https://doi.org/10.1007/978-3-031-75599-6_16

has become broad, diverse, and not always easy to understand. Prior research has studied the process of learning conceptual models (e.g., Bera et al. [2]). Delcambre et al. [3, 4] introduced a framework for understanding CM research and for characterizing CM research contributions, called Characterizing Conceptual Modeling Research (CMMR), which is the basis of experiments reported in this paper.

The CCMR framework is intended to be capable of capturing the main characteristics of CM research reported in a research publication. The diversity of conceptual modelling is accommodated while maintaining the core notions that are frequently associated with CM; for example, abstraction of the real world for which an application needs to be developed and communication mechanisms. One significant aspect is how the framework materializes the goal of providing authors with a standardized way to describe their work while highlighting their main contribution. This would allow researchers to position their work and enable others to assess the value of their CM contribution. The framework aims to be suitable for any user, even for non-experts in CM.

The main contribution of this paper is the analysis of the effectiveness of using a specific framework to characterize the contribution of a conceptual modelling research publication. The evaluation is conducted in terms of agreement in answering questions of the framework, and correctness when answering questions. The sample is composed of 24 master's students who have limited knowledge of CM but have some experience with research activities. The results show a medium value for the agreement (half of the questions yield a high agreement level), and a high level of correctness.

Section 2 describes related research efforts to classify research on conceptual modelling. Section 3 describes the CCMR framework. Section 4 describes our experiment, and Sect. 5 presents the results. Section 6 concludes the paper.

2 Related Works

Several frameworks have been developed to help classify and understand research articles. Some papers focus on the evaluation of the article review process, such as the work of Bianchi et al. [5] which analyses Royal Society journals from 2006 to 2017, measuring manuscript changes during the peer review from their initial submissions. Their evaluation is based on metrics for the number of reviewers, the evaluation of reviewers, and their citations after publication. A similar work was conducted by Bolek et al. [6], which aims to analyse reviewers' attitudes towards different sections of a manuscript during its review. They examined the consistency of a reviewer's evaluation throughout the review of the different parts of the paper, whether it corresponds to the recommendations of the editors, and whether the paper needs a new revision. Leung et al. [7] studies top-quality reviewers' perceptions of peer reviews and synthesizes their approaches to build a guide that helps reviewers. The results do not identify a single, structured approach to reading and reviewing manuscripts. Brown et al. [8] proposed a framework for the peer review process. This framework aims to be useful for both academics and anyone with enough knowledge to understand the proposal.

There are other works in literature that have proposed frameworks and guidelines for reading papers but not in a systematic manner. Snyder [9], defines a guideline to conduct literature reviews. The guidelines consider different types of reviews, as well as some recommendations to know how to both conduct and evaluate a literature review paper. Storey et al. [10] proposed a framework to capture the main beneficiary of a research study (who), the main type of research contribution produced (what), and the research strategies used in the study (how). Franzago et al. [11] defined a classification framework considering as input the result of a mapping study to analyse collaborative model-driven engineering. The framework is composed of a set of concepts, references among concepts and attributes representing the set of data items extracted from each primary study. Vost et al. [12] was proposed to simplify and design case studies for comparing testing tools and make the results more reliable. That framework aims to facilitate the replication of case studies, helping in the aggregation of secondary studies.

These works provide an interesting background to classify and evaluate papers, but they are generic and do not focus specifically on CM. They are not suitable for a context beyond research. Moreover, none of the review guidelines and frameworks described here have empirical validation. Rather, they have been used to classify or aggregate papers, but lack an exhaustive analysis of their positive and negative aspects. As a step towards solving the gaps identified in the related works, this paper proposes the evaluation of a framework to classify papers that deal with conceptual modelling. The framework is composed of questions the reader must answer while (or after) reading the paper. The questions help to classify the paper and identify the contribution. They are defined so that even non-experts in conceptual modelling can apply the framework.

3 A Framework to Classify Conceptual Modelling Research Papers

This section summarizes the Characterizing Conceptual Modeling Research (CCMR) framework presented in Delcambre et al. [4]. The framework is composed of multiple questions that aim to characterize the conceptual modelling context of the work and the type of contribution associated with it. Table 1 shows the questions that compose the framework. The first part of the CCMR framework is intended to characterize the context (questions from Q1 to Q4). Concerning the possible types of contribution, three significant and distinct types of research contributions are proposed: 1) those centered on a model, language, metamodel, representation, or notation for CM (thus exploring "what" is being represented); 2) those centered on a method, process, tool, or algorithm for a CM-related purpose (thus examining "how" representations can be used); and 3) those that contribute CM vision, philosophy, principles, or a review (thereby encompassing a variety of CM aspects in a high-level way). For convenience, we refer to these types as "model", "method", or "vision" as a shorthand.

Once the subject chooses the contribution type (model, method, or vision), the questions are specific to that type. Questions specific to the model are from Q5 to Q6, questions specific to the method are from Q7 to Q9, and the question specific to vision is Q10. Q11 appears in all three contribution types, letting users introduce an additional free-text description. We are aware that some of the questions in Table 1 could be seen as ambiguous and open to multiple interpretations. Our experiment aimed to analyze how this ambiguity manifested in the specific practical setting we selected.

Table 1. Questions of the CCMR framework

1. Characterize the conceptual modelling context of this work	
Q1	List the representation used/treated as a conceptual model in this work
Q2	Which groups of users are likely to create, modify, read or otherwise use this representation
Q3	What is captured in this representation
Q4	What is the level of abstraction for this representation
2. Contribution type: a model, language, metamodel, notation	
Q5	List the model, conceptual modelling language, notation, or metamodel
Q6	What is the nature of the significant contribution?
Q11	Briefly describe the contribution
3. Contribution type: method/process, tool, algorithm	
Q7	List the method, process, tool or algorithm
Q8	What is its purpose?
Q9	What is the nature of the significant contribution?
Q11	Briefly describe the contribution
4. Contribution type: CM vision, philosophy, principles, or review of the CM	
Q10	What type of high-level contribution is made?
Q11	Briefly describe the contribution

4 Experimental Design

The analysis is done for each question, identified from Q1 to Q11 as shown in Table 1. The experiment was conducted at the Universitat Politècnica de València (Spain) in the Master of Engineering and Software System Technology program with 24 subjects. Participation in the experiment was mandatory since it was an evaluable task as part of the course, among other activities. The pedagogical value for students was that they would learn how to interpret and classify CM papers. Even though the CCMR framework can be helpful for CM experts, it is not expected that all CCMR users will have significant experience. We recruited inexperienced researchers to study whether CM characteristics included in the framework are understandable by subjects with minimal CM background. Even though subjects have a minimum level of experience reading research papers, most of them have not dealt with conceptual models previously.

4.1 Research Questions, Response Variables, and Metrics

We focus on studying the framework from the point of view of helping in the analysis of a selected paper. **RQ1:** *Does the framework help to achieve an agreement among several reviewers of the paper evaluation?* The response variable to answer this research question is "agreement". IEEE [13] defines agreement as "mutual acknowledgement of terms and conditions under which a working relationship is conducted." By "agreement" we refer to whether the criteria and classification established by each subject are the same as the criteria and classification of the other subjects for the same article. It is important to understand what criteria were used to classify the questions. We measure the agreement level using Blau's Index [14], which quantifies the probability that two subjects randomly recruited from a population are in different categories of a variable. Its minimum value, zero, would indicate that all members agree on the same category, so there would be no variety. The maximum number, 1, means that subjects selected all the possibilities in the same proportion. Based on the Blau Index, we consider values less than or equal to 0.4 as a high agreement. To classify the possible results into quantifiable metrics, before conducting the experiment we designed an experimenter's solution, where we divided the possible answers to each question of the framework into several categories. The proposed solution was obtained as a major agreement reached by the authors, senior researchers in the CM domain.

RQ2: *Does the framework help in the correctness of the paper evaluation?* The response variable to answer this research question is "correctness". IEEE [13] defines correctness as "the degree to which software, documentation, or other items meet user needs and expectations, whether specified or not." By "correctness" we mean whether the options marked in the framework by subjects agree with what experimenters have considered as possible correct answers for the evaluated paper. Gold standard answers were created by major agreement of the experimenter's team, who are experts in CM. Possible values for correctness are 1 or 0. Value 1 means that the subject's answer agrees with the experimenters' solution. Value 0 means the contrary. Note that the experimenters' solution may involve several possible correct answers since there are some subjective aspects that, depending on how a paper is interpreted, may lead to multiple correct answers.

4.2 Procedure

Our design consists of reading three papers and applying the framework. We selected three papers to represent the three proposed contribution types (model, method, vision). Fonseca et al. [15], coded as Paper A, represents the "model" contribution type; Bour et al. [16], coded as Paper B, represents the "method" contribution type; and Harer et al. [17], coded as Paper C, represents the "vision" contribution type. All three papers were published recently in the International Conference on Conceptual Modeling (ER). The choice of this conference is justified by the fact that its topics match well the central topic of the framework: conceptual modelling.

Our experiment focuses on studying which aspects of the framework can be enhanced, rather than investigating differences between using our framework and not using it. To avoid bias from the order in which the papers are read, we divided subjects into three groups (G1, G2 and G3) and had them read papers in three balanced rounds of different papers. These are the steps of the experimental procedure:

- **Step 1: Demographic questionnaire**. Subjects fill out a demographic questionnaire.
- **Step 2: Framework introduction**. In a class session, one experimenter describes the framework to be used, and how to work with it.

- **Step 3: Training with the framework.** Subjects use the framework to analyse a paper. All subjects use the same paper for training, guided by the experimenter. The protocol and the instruments used in this training exercise are the same as those used in the experimental tasks. Subjects read the paper and fill out the questionnaire. These data are not analysed, as they are outside of the experiment.
- **Step 4: Applying the framework to the first paper**. The first paper to be analysed depends on the group where each subject has been classified. Subjects first read the paper and then applied the framework, reporting their analysis using a questionnaire.
- **Step 5: Applying the framework to the second paper**. This is a repetition of Step 4 but with another paper.
- **Step 6: Applying the framework to the third paper**. This is a repetition of Step 4 but with another paper (the third one).
- **Step 7: Filling satisfaction questionnaire**. At the end of using the framework, subjects fill out the satisfaction questionnaire.

5 Results

The results and replication package are available in Zenodo [18]. First, we analyse the agreement for the specific questions for each contribution type, only considering the subjects that made the correct identification of the type.

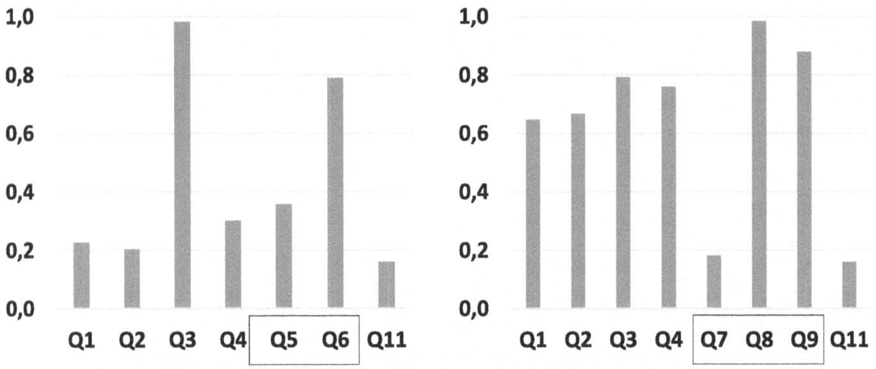

Fig. 1. a) Results for agreement of Paper A. b) Results of Paper B

Figure 1.a quantifies agreement for Paper A [15], a paper of type "model." Results show that the level of agreement is quite good for most common questions except for Q3. Note that specific questions for a paper of type "model" are highlighted in a rectangle (Q5 and Q6). We can conclude that the identification of the nature of the contribution (Q6) seems to affect agreement analysis. Figure 1.b quantifies agreement for Paper B [16], a method paper. Q1 yields poor agreement. This means that the determination of the conceptual models used in the paper is fuzzy. Q2 yields a low level of agreement. This leads to thinking that the target audience needs to be clarified. Q11 (brief contribution description) yields good agreement. Q8 and Q9, which are questions specific to this type of paper, yield a low agreement. This means that the purpose and the nature of the contribution are not clearly identified. Q7, which is also specific to the "method" contribution type, yields a high agreement which means that subjects agree on the method identification.

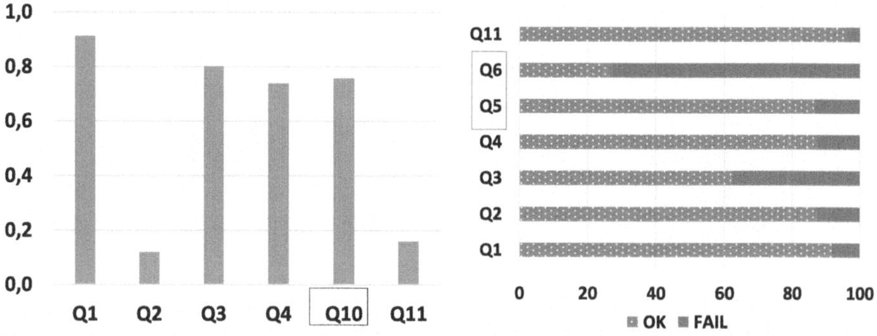

Fig. 2. a) Results for agreement of Paper C. b) Results for correctness of Paper A

Figure 2.a shows the results for agreement of Paper C [17]. The only strong agreement appears in Q2, representing the groups interested in the conceptual model. This result for Q2 is shared in Paper A and Paper C. Q1 fluctuates between both replications, and Q3 shows a low agreement, similar to the other papers. Q11, which represents the contribution of the article, has a very strong agreement. Q10, which is the only specific question for this type of paper, does not yield a large agreement, which means that there is confusion in delimiting the main contribution of the paper.

Even if it is not easy to generalize the results because there are some discrepancies among papers, we can answer to RQ1 that the agreement level of the questions depends on the analysed question. Some questions have good agreement (Q1, Q2, Q5, Q7, Q11), at least in some cases, while other questions almost always have poor agreement (Q3, Q4, Q6, Q8, Q9, Q10). It seems to be clear that conclusions cannot be generalized for all questions that compose the framework. We want to emphasize that our purpose is to get concrete insights about the framework's use to identify points of improvement, and this goal is achieved with the information collected and reported in the paper.

To analyse the **correctness** of each type of paper independently, questions specific to each type of paper are analysed only if the subject correctly identifies the type of paper. Figure 2.b shows the results of correctness for Paper A [15]. Q1 and Q2 yield the best values, which means that the models used in the paper and the target users are identified with almost no error. The lowest correctness arises in Q6, which means that the nature of the contribution is fuzzy. Q3 also shows a low value, which means that subjects of such replication did not properly identify what is captured in the representation, while Q4 had a good value, indicating that what is the level of abstraction was well-identified. Q5 and Q11 show high correctness, which means that subjects correctly identified the type of contribution and its summary.

Figure 3a shows the correctness results for Paper B [16]. Q1, Q4, Q7 and Q11 yield the best value. This means that the subjects in this paper identified the conceptual representations, the abstraction level, the method, and the contribution properly. The

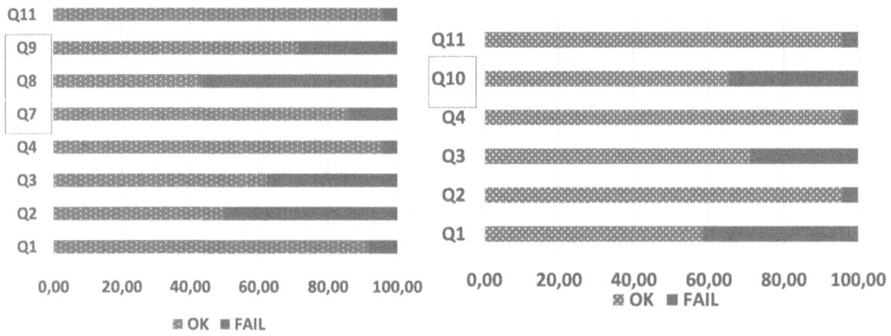

Fig. 3. a) Results for the correctness of Paper B. b) Results for the correctness of Paper C

lowest correctness values arise in Q2, Q8, and Q9. This means that subjects did not identify the paper's target group of users, the purpose, and the nature of the significant contribution. Q3, although showing a low value of correctness, yields that many of the subjects appropriately identified what is captured in the representation (values are close to 60% of correctness). Figure 3b shows the graphics for the correctness of Paper C [17]. It shows a good correctness level (more than 80% of correctness) for Q2 and Q4. This means that the target groups of the conceptual models and the level of abstraction are identified with a low error. The lowest correctness appears in Q1. There is a wide variety of answers when subjects have to specify the conceptual models used in the paper. Other questions (Q3, Q10, Q11) yield values between 60% and 80% of correctness, which means that there are a few errors when subjects identify what is captured in the conceptual model representation, what the contribution type is, and when the model or notation is listed. Thus, the answer to RQ2 is that, even though most of the questions that compose the framework are answered correctly (Q1, Q4, Q5, Q7, Q10, Q11) in most of the papers, there are some questions with many errors among the subjects (Q2, Q3, Q6, Q8, Q9).

To conclude this section, we discuss potential threats to the validity of our study. Following the conventional approach, we categorize these threats into four types: construct, internal, external, and conclusion validity threats. First, by selecting three specific papers—one for each type of possible contribution—it is possible that this choice introduced some bias. However, these papers were carefully chosen by the authors as adequate representatives of each contribution type, with a high level of agreement among them. Regarding internal validity, it could be affected by the criteria used to classify the selected papers. The team of authors, all of whom are experts in CM, reached a strong consensus on what should be considered the correct classification, and this consensus was used as the baseline, thereby mitigating the threat to internal validity. For conclusion validity, the evaluation of agreement could be influenced by the dispersion and subjectivity associated with some of the responses. To address this threat, we defined and employed a specific measurement criterion (based on the Blau Index, where values less than or equal to 0.4 indicate high agreement). In terms of correctness, another threat to conclusion validity could stem from subjectivity, as the experimenters' solutions might involve several possible correct answers. We mitigated this by collectively discussing the various answers to reach a unanimous decision. Finally, conclusion validity can also be impacted by the specific characteristics of the study population. While the feedback obtained helped us answer the two research questions (RQs), the reliability and generalizability of the results are limited due to the composition and size of the sample, which may introduce bias.

6 Conclusion

This paper presents the validation of a framework for characterizing conceptual modeling research that is intended to help understand and classify research papers related to conceptual modeling. The three main types of research contributions proopsed by the CCMR framework guide the work. An experiment was conducted with subjects with a low level of experience in research and conceptual modelling and, thus, were non-experts. The results reveal that, even though subjects are not experts in the conceptual modelling field, they obtained good agreement, and a very high value for correctness. The results have specific implications. First, the CCMR framework works in a similar way for the three possible types of contribution of the paper. Second, the correct application of the framework requires a modest amount of training. A brief introduction of 30 min to the framework is enough to apply it correctly. Third, some questions of the framework may lead to different correct answers. Finally, the results helped to identify the most subjective questions. Future research will involve replicating the experiment with different papers and additional subjects to further assess the generalizability of the results independently. We will also refine the CCMR framework by facing subjectivity in the answers that have generated low agreement and/or low correctness.

Acknowledgments. This work has been developed with the financial support of the Generalitat Valenciana under the project TENTACLE (GVRTE/2023/4592166) and the Spanish Ministry of Science and Innovation SREC (PID2021-123824OB-I00).

References

1. Embley, D.W., Liddle, S., Pastor, Ó.: Conceptual-model programming: a manifesto. In: Embley, D., Thalheim, B. (eds) Handbook of Conceptual Modeling, pp. 3–16. Springer, Heidelberg (2011). https://doi.org/10.1007/978-3-642-15865-0_1
2. Bera, P., Poels, G.: How quickly do we learn conceptual models? Eur. J. Inf. Syst. **28**, 663–680 (2019)
3. Delcambre, L.M.L., Liddle, S.W., Pastor, O., Storey, V.C.: Characterizing conceptual modeling research. In: Panetto, H., Debruyne, C., Hepp, M., Lewis, D., Ardagna, C., Meersman, R. (eds) OTM 2019. LNCS, vol. 11877, pp. 40–57. Springer, Cham (2019)
4. Delcambre, L.M.L., Liddle, S.W., Pastor, O., Storey, V.C.: Articulating conceptual modeling research contributions. In: Reinhartz-Berger, I., Sadiq, S. (eds.) ER 2021. LNCS, vol. 13012, pp. 45–60. Springer, Cham (2021). https://doi.org/10.1007/978-3-030-88358-4_5
5. Bianchi, F., García-Costa, D., Grimaldo, F., Squazzoni, F.: Measuring the effect of reviewers on manuscript change: a study on a sample of submissions to royal society journals (2006–2017). J. Informet. **16**, 101316 (2022)

6. Bolek, M., Bolek, C., Shopovski, J., Marolov, D.: The consistency of peer-reviewers: assessment of separate parts of the manuscripts vs final recommendations. Account. Res. 1–23 (2022)
7. Leung, D., Law, R., Kucukusta, D., Guillet, B.D.: How to review journal manuscripts: a lesson learnt from the world's excellent reviewers. Tour. Manage. Perspect. **10**, 46–56 (2014)
8. Brown, L.M., David, E.A., Karamlou, T., Nason, K.S.: Reviewing scientific manuscripts: a comprehensive guide for peer reviewers. Ann. Thorac. Surg. **103**, 1365–1370 (2017)
9. Snyder, H.: Literature review as a research methodology: an overview and guidelines. J. Bus. Res. **104**, 333–339 (2019)
10. Storey, M.-A., Ernst, N.A., Williams, C., Kalliamvakou, E.: The who, what, how of software engineering research: a socio-technical framework. Empir. Softw. Eng. **25**, 4097–4129 (2020)
11. Franzago, M., Ruscio, D.D., Malavolta, I., Muccini, H.: Collaborative model-driven software engineering: a classification framework and a research map. IEEE Trans. Software Eng. **44**, 1146–1175 (2018)
12. Vos, T.E.J., Marín, B., Escalona, M.J., Marchetto, A.: A methodological framework for evaluating software testing techniques and tools. In: 2012 12th International Conference on Quality Software, pp. 230–239 (2012)
13. IEEE: IEEE standard computer dictionary. A compilation of IEEE standard computer glossaries. Institute of Electrical and Electronics Engineers. New York, EE.UU (1991)
14. Blau, P.M.: Inequality and Heterogeneity: A Primitive Theory of Social Structure, vol. 7. Free Press, New York (1977)
15. Fonseca Garcia, L., Carbonera, J.L., Rodrigues, F.H., Roca Antunes, C., Abel, M.: What rocks are made of: towards an ontological pattern for material constitution in the geological domain. In: Laender, A., Pernici, B., Lim, EP., de Oliveira, J. (eds) ER 2019. LNCS, vol. 11788, pp. 275–286. Springer, Cham (2019). https://doi.org/10.1007/978-3-030-33223-5_23
16. Bour, R., Soule-Dupuy, C., Vallès-Parlangeau, N.: DEMOS: a participatory design approach for democratic empowerment of IS users. In: Laender, A.H.F., Pernici, B., Lim, E.-P., de Oliveira, J.P.M. (eds.) ER 2021. LNCS, vol. 11788, pp. 387–394. Springer, Cham (2019). https://doi.org/10.1007/978-3-030-33223-5_32
17. Härer, F., Fill, H.-G.: Past trends and future prospects in conceptual modeling - a bibliometric analysis. In: Dobbie, G., Frank, U., Kappel, G., Liddle, S.W., Mayr, H.C. (eds.) ER 2021. LNCS, vol. 12400, pp. 34–47. Springer, Cham (2020). https://doi.org/10.1007/978-3-030-62522-1_3
18. Panach, J.I., Pastor, O., Liddle, S.W., Storey, V.C., Mayr, H.C., Thalheim, B.: Dataset of the article evaluating a framework of conceptual modelling research (2024)

Extending Goal Models with Execution Orders: An Investigation of the Impact on Comprehensibility

Jeshwitha Jesus Raja[1], Akhila Vissom Raju[1], Jennifer Brings[2], and Marian Daun[1(✉)]

[1] Center for Robotics, Technical University of Applied Sciences Würzburg-Schweinfurt, Schweinfurt, Germany
marian.daun@thws.de
[2] Bingen Technical University of Applied Sciences, Bingen, Germany
j.brings@th-bingen.de

Abstract. Goal models are used in early development phases to specify the system under development and conduct early feasibility analyses. Therefore, goal models show an abstract representation of the system not detailing the system behavior, which is typically specified in later stages. In the development of robotic production systems, the execution order of different tasks is important and must be considered when deciding upon feasibility of approaches and weighing different solution alternatives. The order of production steps can be easily integrated into goal models, as this can be behavior specified on a very high and abstract level. However, integrating more and more complexity into a goal model bears the risk of reducing its comprehensibility. In this paper, we report a controlled experiment investigating the effect the introduction of process step execution orders within goal models of robotic production systems has on the models' comprehensibility. Results show that the introduction of execution orders can even increase comprehensibility.

Keywords: Robotic Production System · Goal Modeling · Execution Order · Controlled Experiment

1 Introduction

Goal modeling is an established approach in requirements engineering that supports systematic analysis in early development stages [27]. Common goal modeling approaches include KAOS [7,28], iStar [2,6,29], and the Goal-oriented Requirement Language (GRL) [19]. Goal modeling has been valued for supporting early analyses of complex technical systems. For instance, goal modeling has successfully been used for Dynamically Adaptive Systems [14], Industry Automation systems [21], Cyber-Physical Systems [3], ATM systems [5] and so on. In this paper, we investigate the use of GRL goal models in the context of collaborative robotic production systems.

M. Saeki et al. (Eds.): ER 2024 Workshops, LNCS 14932, pp. 219–228, 2025.
https://doi.org/10.1007/978-3-031-75599-6_17

Typically, GRL goal models used in the early phases of development do not detail system behavior, as this is reserved for later stages. However, in the context of robotic production systems, understanding the execution order of tasks is not only crucial for discussing security and usability issues, but also for assessing feasibility and comparing different solutions. For instance, when assembling a computer, the components that need to be mounted must be secured first before any wiring is done. If a robot connects the wires before mounting the parts, it could lead to disastrous results or make the assembly impossible. Therefore, integrating execution orders into goal models can enhance their relevance, but it also introduces additional complexity that may affect the comprehensibility of the goal model. One challenge with goal models is achieving a shared understanding of the model, particularly as the complexity increases with model extensions [23]. Therefore, alongside the introduction of new syntaxes, it is also important to ensure that comprehensibility is maintained or improved and that the model's efficacy is enhanced in its specific domain, such as industry automation.

This paper contributes an investigation of the impact of extending goal models with new syntaxes on their comprehensibility and efficacy in the context of robotic production systems. Through a controlled experiment, we aim to assess how these extensions affect the ability to accurately interpret and utilize the models for decision-making and system analysis. Our goal is to determine whether these extensions improve or hinder the overall effectiveness and comprehensibility of goal models in the domain of industry automation.

The paper is outlined as follows: Sect. 2 discusses the related work. Section 3 describes the experiment and its design, and Sect. 4 presents the results. Finally, Sect. 5 concludes the paper.

2 Related Work

Goal-oriented requirements engineering (GORE) is a method used to uncover, analyze, and describe stakeholder goals, which then lead to software and system requirements. Analysis through GRL can help assess the satisfaction of goals and facilitate the evaluation of high-level design alternatives. It can also aid in deciding on high-level requirements and the design of the system based on the required structure, behavior, and function [1]. The syntax of GRL is based on the syntax of the i* or iStar language [29]. iStar is a general-purpose, goal-based modeling language used in both industrial and academic projects. One advantage of iStar is its extensibility, allowing new constructs to be incorporated to meet the specific needs of different application areas [15].

Goal models are regarded as critical instruments for analyzing stakeholder needs and problems. It can be done in different ways depending on the nature of the problem and the purpose of the analysis. A specific goal modeling language construct, the contribution of goal satisfaction of one goal to another, plays a central role in supporting decision problem exploration within goal models [18]. To model many modern systems, various iStar profiles have been proposed that take the particularities of collaborative cyber-physical systems and their developers' needs into account [11]. They also take into account the interactions (dependencies) among the individual systems and networks (actors).

Goal model extensions are proposed on a regular basis to accommodate specific needs encountered in various domains [17]. Particularly, for process oriented domains – as industry automation which is dependent on the production process – the sequence in which tasks are carried out is of importance. Therefore, goal models have been extended with action sequences (e.g., [26]), positive and negative preferences (e.g., [24]), or execution orders (e.g., [22]). These inter-actor dependencies present an additional source of complexity, which is measurable [16]. However, these inter-actor dependencies and other complexity measures have not been related to the comprehensibility of the goal model. The comprehensibility (or understandability) of a given notation is inherently subjective, so a more objective way to evaluate it is through performance-based measures [25]. Hence, how well a participant performs a given task can help determine their understanding of it [10]. Therefore, in this paper, we investigate the influence the extension with execution order dependencies have on comprehensibility and efficacy of goal models through a controlled experiment.

Previously, a model-based approach to systematically define and analyze robotic systems and their digital twins in the early stages of development was introduced [20,22]. The goal model extension included the introduction of monitoring systems as actors, monitoring resources and dependencies as resources and dependencies of GRL goal modeling, and order of execution. These are important for defining the monitoring data needed by the digital twin to observe the current production tasks. Adding to the previous work, in this paper, we test the comprehensibility and efficacy of this approach through an experiment involving participants with knowledge in the domain of industry automation. We use an experimental design that has been previously used and published (e.g., [8–10]) for analyzing and comparing comprehensibility of modeling approaches, ensuring consistency with established methodologies. By doing so, we aimed to enhance the reliability and comparability of our findings with existing literature.

3 Study Setup

3.1 Research Goal

The primary goal of this experiment is to investigate the comprehensibility of having an execution order in GRL goal modeling. We want to test how comprehensible this approach is to engineers, considering their knowledge in the field of industry automation.

3.2 Research Questions

In this paper, we focus on two research questions:

- *RQ1: Does the introduction of execution orders within goal models influence the comprehensibility of the goal model?*
- *RQ2: Does the introduction of execution orders within goal models affect the overall efficacy in assessing GRL goal models?*

3.3 Variables

Independent Variable. The independent variable is the type of goal model shown, thus it has two levels:

- *Standard Goal Model (SGM)*: GRL goal model without modeling extension for execution order.
- *Extended Goal Model (EGM)*: GRL goal model using modeling extension for execution order.

Dependent Variables

- *Comprehensibility* refers to the participants' ability to understand and correctly determine the execution order based on their performance in the survey. For comprehensibility, the participants are given performance tasks, where they answer questions about the model. Comprehensibility is measured as percentage of correct answers.
- *Efficacy* relates to how effective participants find the model for use in the development of robotic systems in the industry automation domain. Efficacy is measured as self-rated value on a 10-point semantic differential scale.

We further investigated several covariates like *Age*, *Gender*, *Individual cognitive abilities* and *Pre-existing knowledge about goal models* as potential confounding variables that could influence the experiment's outcomes. However, we did not find any influence of these factors, and thus do not report results related to this.

3.4 Hypotheses

Based on the research questions and the variables, the following hypotheses are defined for the study.

For **RQ1**, the hypotheses are:

- **H1-0:** There is no significant difference in the comprehensibility of standard goal models and extended goal models.
- **H1-a:** The comprehensibility of extended goal models is higher compared to standard goal models.
- **H1-b:** The comprehensibility of standard goal models is higher compared to extended goal models.

For **RQ2**, the hypotheses are:

- **H2-0:** The introduced execution order does not affect the overall efficacy in assessing GRL goal models.
- **H2-a:** The introduced execution order positively affects the overall efficacy in assessing GRL goal models.
- **H2-b:** The introduced execution order negatively affects the overall efficacy in assessing GRL goal models.

3.5 Participants

The experiment was conducted among engineering students enrolled in the Bachelor's Engineering (B.Eng) programs in 'Robotics' and 'Mechatronics'. There were 57 participants in total, with 10 from the Robotics program and the remainder from Mechatronics. This group included participants aged between 20 and 38, comprising at least 43 males and 10 females. The students had previous knowledge of conceptual modeling from earlier semesters. However, despite their familiarity with conceptual modeling, goal modeling was a relatively new topic introduced only in the sixth semester, specifically under the course 'Requirements Engineering'.

3.6 Experiment Material

A questionnaire[1] with two sections was created and given to participants to fill out. The questionnaire started with a basic introduction to goal models, including the syntax and important terms of GRL goal modeling. The first section contained a goal model with two actors, their goals, tasks, and the standard dependencies between the given tasks. This example was followed by questions regarding the provided goal model. In the second section, the standard goal model was extended with the order of execution. This section also contained the same kind of questions as the previous section. Both sections had 10 questions each, totaling 20 questions, excluding the personal data section. To minimize crossover effects, the examples in both sections were different and randomized across participants. Although the base idea between the examples was the same, the goals and tasks were different.

The GRL goal models used in the experiment were for an assembly line that welds car parts onto their chassis. This assembly line is fully automated and consists of four sets of collaborative robots: 'Pneumatic Gripper Cobot', 'Spot Arc Welding Cobot', 'Laser Welding Cobot', and 'Plasma Welding Cobot'. Among these, we specifically utilized the 'Laser Welding Cobot' and the 'Plasma Welding Cobot'. For SGM, we modeled this situation using the standard constructs of GRL. Figure 1 presents the EGM, with the cobots and their monitoring systems depicted, along with the order of execution. The blue arrows represent the order in which the actors (cobots in our case) work, while the green arrows indicate the sequence of tasks within an actor. The red arrows denote the monitoring dependencies between the cobot and its monitoring system.

To minimize crossover and learning effects, the SGM and the EGM featured different actors. Half the participants received an SGM with the actors 'Pneumatic Gripper Cobot' and 'Spot Arc Welding Cobot', and an EGM with the actors 'Laser Welding Cobot' and 'Plasma Welding Cobot'. The other half received an SGM with the actors 'Laser Welding Cobot' and 'Plasma Welding Cobot', and an extended model with the actors 'Pneumatic Gripper Cobot'

[1] The complete questionnaire along the data set can be found in the supplement available at https://dx.doi.org/10.6084/m9.figshare.26828266.

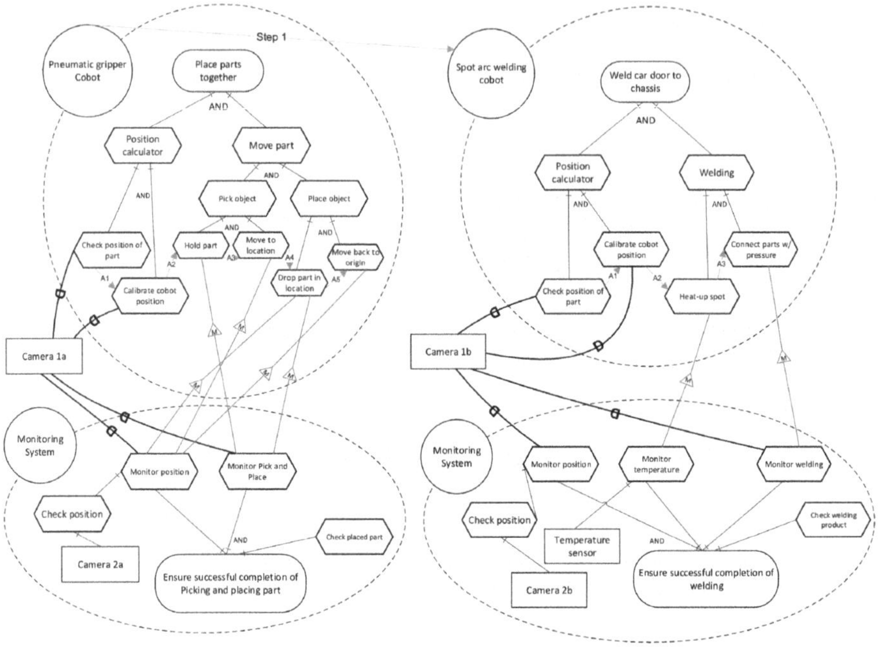

Fig. 1. Extended goal model of two cobots and their monitoring systems

and Spot Arc Welding Cobot'. The two types of questionnaires were randomly distributed amongst participants.

3.7 Procedure

The controlled experiment was conducted in a classroom, where the participants were given the questionnaire with no time restriction. Most participants completed the experiment in approximately 20 min. To maintain the integrity of the experiment, participants were not allowed to discuss the questionnaire during the session. Additionally, there was no communication between the researchers and the participants during the experiment. The participants were only informed about the topic of the experiment on the spot to ensure the authenticity of their responses.

3.8 Data Analysis

We calculated descriptive statistics for the comprehensibility and efficacy, including the mean, standard deviation, and range, to summarize the central tendency and variability of the data.

To evaluate the hypothesis for comprehensibility, we conducted a paired-samples t-test. A paired samples t-test compares the means of two related groups to determine if there is a statistically significant difference between them [12].

This test is used as we use a within subject design and the independent variable has two levels (SGM and EGM).

We used a one-sample t-test to analyze the data for efficacy. A one-sample t-test compares the mean of a single sample to a known or hypothesized population mean to determine if there is a statistically significant difference between them. As we are using a 10-point semantic scale, it tests whether the sample mean significantly differs from a hypothesized midpoint or expected value on that scale. According to the central limit theorem, parametric tests are applicable even in the case of deviations from the normal distribution in case of a large sample size [12].

4 Results

4.1 Descriptive Statistics

Descriptive statistics are given by Table 1. A certain number of participants did not complete all questions, resulting in a varied total number of responses for each section. For efficacy, participants rated EGM better than SGM (4.393 compared to 4.936 on a 10-point semantic differential scale, where 1 means best and 10 worst). The percentage of correctly answered questions was calculated for each participant based on their responses. For comprehensibility, the average percentage of correct solutions for participants was 50.0% (SD = .1875) with the SGM, compared to 70.18% (SD = .2495) with EGM.

Table 1. Descriptive Statistics

	N	Range	Min	Max	Mean	Std. Err.	Std. Dev.	Variance
Efficacy SGM	55	8.000	1.000	9.000	4.936	0,295	2.186	4.778
Efficacy EGM	56	7.000	1.000	8.000	4.393	0,275	2.060	4.243
Comprehensibility SGM	57	.875	.125	1	.500	.0248	.188	3.516
Comprehensibility EGM	57	1	.000	1	.702	.030	.249	6.224
Valid N (listwise)	54							

4.2 Result per Research Question

Research Question 1. T-test results for the percentage of correct solutions show that this difference is statistically significant, $t(56) = -5.452, p < .001$. This shows that participants performed significantly better interpreting the core concepts of the goal model with execution orders than those without execution orders. Therefore, we reject the null hypothesis H1-0 and accept the alternative hypothesis H1-a, which posits that the goal model is better understood with execution orders.

Research Question 2. We analyzed the ratings given by the participants on the efficacy of the given models (where 1 indicates the model is very efficient and 10 indicates it is less efficient). The average rating for SGM was 4.94 and 4.39 for EGM. T-test results show that this difference is not statistically significant, $t(53) = 1.584, p > .05$. Thus, we cannot reject the null hypothesis H2-0, indicating that the introduction of execution orders does not significantly affect the overall efficacy in assessing GRL goal models subjectively for the participants.

The results of the study indicate that the understandability of the goal models is significantly higher when execution orders are included, with correct answers improving by 20.18% percentage. A majority of participants expressed a preference for using these extensions in the future, highlighting their acceptance.

4.3 Threats to Validity

Internal Validity: Internal validity refers to what extent researchers can conclude that changes in the dependent variable are caused by manipulations to the independent variable [4]. Despite the differences between the SGM and the EGM, the underlying concepts remain consistent. Since the experiment was conducted within subjects, there is a possibility of a learning effect when participants move on to the second section. To minimize biases, we randomly assigned participants to different conditions.

External Validity: External validity refers to the extent to which inferences drawn from a given study's sample can be applied to a broader population or other target populations [13]. The experiment involved 57 engineering students. While this sample may be representative of students in engineering programs, it may not be generalizable to professionals in industry or to students from diverse cultural or educational backgrounds. Additionally, the controlled environment (a classroom in our case) may not reflect the complexities and distractions of real-world scenarios.

Construct Validity: Construct Validity refers to the extent to which an experiment accurately measures the theoretical constructs it is intended to assess. The instruments used to measure comprehensibility and efficacy (i.e., questionnaires and performance tasks) were validated through pilot testing, to ensure they capture the intended constructs.

Conclusion Validity: Conclusion validity refers to the extent to which the results and conclusions of the experiment are reasonable with regard to the collected data. This is crucial for determining whether the findings of the study can be trusted and if they accurately reflect the reality being investigated. In this study, we had a large sample size, and t-test reached level of significance for RQ 1.

5 Conclusion and Future Work

In this paper, we evaluated the comprehensibility of goal models extended with execution orders of tasks. These extensions are crucial to describe process dependent goal, as the tasks follow a specific order. This is, for instance, the case in production processes. To do so, we conducted a controlled experiment to investigate comprehensibility and efficacy for robotic production systems. In conclusion, the integration of goal models with execution orders resulted in a significantly increased comprehensibility of the goal model. The experiment demonstrated that goal models, when combined with execution orders, are intuitive and beneficial, as indicated by participants' willingness to use them in future applications.

A single experiment is not reliable enough to make broad conclusions; therefore, more experiments are needed in the future. Future work will also involve testing the integration of goal models with execution orders in real-world settings. This will help validate the approach in practical scenarios and provide insights into any adjustments needed to optimize its effectiveness and usability in various domains.

References

1. Amyot, D., Ghanavati, S., Horkoff, J., Mussbacher, G., Peyton, L., Yu, E.: Evaluating goal models within the goal-oriented requirement language. Int. J. Intell. Syst. **25**(8), 841–877 (2010)
2. Amyot, D., Horkoff, J., Gross, D., Mussbacher, G.: A lightweight GRL profile for i* modeling. In: Heuser, C.A., Pernul, G. (eds.) ER 2009. LNCS, vol. 5833, pp. 254–264. Springer, Heidelberg (2009). https://doi.org/10.1007/978-3-642-04947-7_31
3. Brings, J., Daun, M., Weyer, T., Pohl, K.: Goal-based configuration analysis for networks of collaborative cyber-physical systems. In: 35th Annual ACM Symposium on Applied Computing, pp. 1387–1396 (2020)
4. Cahit, K.: Internal validity: a must in research designs. Educ. Res. Rev. **10**(2), 111–118 (2015)
5. Dalpiaz, F., Borgida, A., Horkoff, J., Mylopoulos, J.: Runtime goal models: keynote. In: IEEE 7th International Conference on Research Challenges in Information Science (RCIS), pp. 1–11. IEEE (2013)
6. Dalpiaz, F., Franch, X., Horkoff, J.: iStar 2.0 language guide. arXiv preprint arXiv:1605.07767 (2016)
7. Dardenne, A., Van Lamsweerde, A., Fickas, S.: Goal-directed requirements acquisition. Sci. Comput. Program. **20**(1–2), 3–50 (1993)
8. Daun, M., Brings, J.: Investigating factors influencing students' assessment of conceptual models. In: 27th International Conference on Evaluation and Assessment in Software Engineering, pp. 470–474 (2023)
9. Daun, M., Brings, J., Krajinski, L., Weyer, T.: On the benefits of using dedicated models in validation processes for behavioral specifications. In: IEEE/ACM International Conference on Software and System Processes, pp. 44–53. IEEE (2019)
10. Daun, M., Brings, J., Obe, P.A., Stenkova, V.: Reliability of self-rated experience and confidence as predictors for students' performance in software engineering. Empir. Softw. Eng. **26**(4), 80 (2021)

11. Daun, M., Stenkova, V., Krajinski, L., Brings, J., Bandyszak, T., Weyer, T.: Goal modeling for collaborative groups of cyber-physical systems with GRL. In: 34th ACM/SIGAPP Symposium on Applied Computing, pp. 1600–1609 (2019)
12. Field, A.: Discovering Statistics Using IBM SPSS Statistics. Sage Publications limited (2024)
13. Findley, M.G., Kikuta, K., Denly, M.: External validity. Annu. Rev. Polit. Sci. **24**(1), 365–393 (2021)
14. Goldsby, H.J., Sawyer, P., Bencomo, N., Cheng, B.H., Hughes, D.: Goal-based modeling of dynamically adaptive system requirements. In: IEEE International Conference on the Engineering of Computer Based Systems, pp. 36–45. IEEE (2008)
15. Gonçalves, E., Castro, J., Araújo, J., Heineck, T.: A systematic literature review of iStar extensions. J. Syst. Softw. **137**, 1–33 (2018)
16. Hassine, J., Tukur, M.: Measurement and classification of inter-actor dependencies in goal models. Softw. Syst. Model. **21**(6), 2267–2310 (2022)
17. Horkoff, J., et al.: Goal-oriented requirements engineering: an extended systematic mapping study. Requirements Eng. **24**, 133–160 (2019)
18. Horkoff, J., Yu, E.: Interactive goal model analysis for early requirements engineering. Requirements Eng. **21**, 29–61 (2016)
19. ITU Int. Telecommunication Union: Recommendation ITU-T z.151: User Requirements Notation (URN). Technical report (2018)
20. Jesus Raja, J., Manjunath, M., Daun, M.: Towards a goal-oriented approach for engineering digital twins of robotic systems. In: ENASE, pp. 466–473 (2024)
21. Jesus Raja, J., Manjunath, M., Kranz, P., Schirmer, F., Daun, M.: Using goal modeling for defining digital twins in industry automation. In: ER (Companion) (2023)
22. Jesus Raja, J., Manjunath, M., Daun, M.: Model-based specification of robotic digital twins. In: 28th IEEE International Conference on Emerging Technologies and Factory Automation. IEEE (2024)
23. Jureta, I., Faulkner, S.: Clarifying goal models. ER (Tutor. Posters Panels Industr.Contributions) **83**, 139–144 (2007)
24. Liaskos, S., McIlraith, S.A., Sohrabi, S., Mylopoulos, J.: Integrating preferences into goal models for requirements engineering. In: 2010 18th IEEE International Requirements Engineering Conference, pp. 135–144. IEEE (2010)
25. Morales, J.M., Navarro, E., Sánchez, P., Alonso, D.: A family of experiments to evaluate the understandability of TRiStar and i* for modeling teleo-reactive systems. J. Syst. Softw. **114**, 82–100 (2016)
26. Trafton, J.G., Altmann, E.M., Ratwani, R.M.: A memory for goals model of sequence errors. Cogn. Syst. Res. **12**(2), 134–143 (2011)
27. Van Lamsweerde, A.: Goal-oriented requirements engineering: a guided tour. In: Fifth IEEE International Symposium on Requirements Engineering, pp. 249–262. IEEE (2001)
28. Van Lamsweerde, A.: Requirements Engineering: From System Goals to UML Models to Software, vol. 10. Wiley, Chichester (2009)
29. Yu, E.S.: Towards modelling and reasoning support for early-phase requirements engineering. In: ISRE 1997: 3rd IEEE International Symposium on Requirements Engineering, pp. 226–235. IEEE (1997)

QUAMES

5th International Workshop on Quality and Measurement of Model-Driven Software Development (QUAMES 2024)

Beatriz Marín[1], Giovanni Giachetti[1,2], and Clara Ayora[3]

[1] Universitat Politècnica de València, Spain
bmarin@dsic.upv.es, giovanni.giachetti@unab.cl
[2] Universidad Andrés Bello, Chile
[3] Universidad Castilla – La Mancha, Spain
clara.ayora@uclm.es

We welcome you to the fifth edition of the International Workshop on Quality and Measurement of Software Model-Driven Development (QUAMES), co-located with the 43nd International Conference on Conceptual Modeling (ER 2024) in Pittsburgh.

The success of software development projects depends on the productivity of human resources and the efficiency of development processes to deliver high-quality products. Model-driven development (MDD) is a widely adopted paradigm that automates software generation by means of model transformations and reuse of development knowledge. Nowadays, MDD is also known as zero-code or no-code paradigm. The MDD advantages have motivated the emergence of several modeling proposals and MDD tools related to different application domains and stages of the development lifecycle.

In MDD contexts, it is essential to assess the quality of conceptual models, as it has a direct impact on the quality of the final software systems. Also, project management needs to be adapted to take into account that programming effort is replaced by modelling effort at an earlier stage. To address these challenges, QUAMES aims to attract research on methods, procedures, techniques, and tools for measuring and evaluating the quality of conceptual models that can be used in MDD environments. Its primary goal is to enable the development of high-quality software systems by promoting quality assurance in the modeling process.

In this edition of QUAMES, one submission titled *Towards leveraging gamified code-testing for effective model validation* was accepted for publication. This paper presents a gamified tool to test conceptual models used in MDD environments. We want to express our gratitude to all the authors for their valuable contributions, the dedicated program committee members for their reviews and discussion for QUAMES 2024, and the supportive organizers of ER 2024.

Acknowledgments. This workshop is partially supported by European Commission under the ENACTEST project (ERASMUS+ No 101055874, 2022-2025); the Music360 project (HORIZON-RIA No 101094872); the REBECCA project (HORIZON-KDT ref. 101097224; MCIN/AEI ref. PCI2022-135043-2; NextGen. EU/PRTR); and AETERNAL project (MCIN/AEI ref. PID2023-149753OB-C21; ERDF).

QUAMES Organization

Workshop Chairs

Beatriz Marín	Universitat Politècnica de Valencia, Spain
Giovanni Giachetti	Universitat Politècnica de Valencia, Spain, and Universidad Andrés Bello, Chile
Clara Ayora	Universidad de Castilla-La Mancha, Spain

Program Committee

Oscar Pastor	Universidad Politécnica de Valencia, Spain
Yves Wautelet	KU Leuven, Belgium
Jose Luis de la Vara	Universidad de Castilla-La Mancha, Spain
Tanja Vos	Universidad Politécnica de Valencia, Spain
Rene Noel	Universidad de Valparaíso, Chile and Universidad Politécnica de Valencia, Spain
Stefan Biffl	Vienna University of Technology, Austria
Ignacio Panach	Universidad de Valencia, Spain
Jolita Ralyté	University of Geneva, Switzerland
Maya Daneva	University of Twente, The Netherlands
Dietmar Winkler	Vienna University of Technology, Austria
Porfirio Tramontana	University of Naples Federico II, Italy
Ignacio García	University of Castilla-La Mancha, Spain
Ana Paiva	University of Porto, Portugal
Mehrdad Saadatmand	RISE Research Institutes of Sweden, Sweden
Shaukat Ali	Simula Research Laboratory, Norway
Isabel Brito	Instituto Politécnico de Beja, Portugal
Juan Cuadrado-Gallego	University of Alcalá, Spain
Anna Rita Fasolino	University of Naples Federico II, Italy

Towards Leveraging Gamified Code-Testing for Effective Model Validation

Felix Cammaerts(✉) and Monique Snoeck

KU Leuven, 3000 Leuven, Belgium
{felix.cammaerts,monique.snoeck}@kuleuven.be

Abstract. Software testing educators often struggle to educate the next generation of software engineers. However, in recent years, gamification approaches have been applied specifically to software testing education and have been found to increase student engagement with the subject. Similarly, recent years have seen an increase in the use of Model-Driven Engineering (MDE). While this has enabled non-technical students to develop fully functional programs through model-to-code transformations, these non-technical students often perform limited testing on their developed models. Therefore, we have proposed a new solution, based on an existing proposal for gamifying code-testing, by reusing the already existing knowledge from gamified code-testing and applying it to model-testing to create a gamified model-testing approach. In this paper we discuss an initial evaluation of our new solution in terms of user friendliness. We delve deeper into the pitfalls that had to be considered for the specific tool translation, as well as some other issues that need to be considered when translating any gamified code-testing approach into a similar model-testing approach. These findings are then translated into recommendations for the future translation of gamified code-testing approaches into gamified model-testing approaches.

Keywords: Model-testing · Gamification · ModelDefenders

1 Introduction

Software testing is an important part of the software development lifecycle. Through validation and verification it is possible to gain confidence in the correctness of the system under test. In fact, it has been found that developers spend between 35–50% of their time debugging and validating software [6].

Unfortunately, software testing is a difficult subject to teach in higher education. On the one hand, software testing is poorly integrated with current software engineering degrees. A recent study found that only 39% of universities in Europe

M. Saeki et al. (Eds.): ER 2024 Workshops, LNCS 14932, pp. 233–248, 2025.
https://doi.org/10.1007/978-3-031-75599-6_18

offer a course fully dedicated to software testing [32]. On the other hand, it was reported that students enrolled in software testing courses would like their software testing course to be enhanced with more practical experience [13]. A study with software testing experts in the field [17] revealed that the uncertainty of a tester's job position, lack of attractiveness and poor career development for testers negatively influence the practice of software testing.

Gamification has been proposed as a way to reduce the lack of enthusiasm felt by students during testing and to provide them with a more engaging environment [2,27]. Gamification is defined as a process in which motivational affordances can induce game-like experiences and further behavioural outcomes [22]. Specifically in software testing, several gamification approaches have already been introduced and evaluated, as mentioned by [18]. Examples include CodinGame [8], CodeHunt [4], CodeDefenders [28] and Bug Hunt [16].

In recent years, the use of MDE has increased. MDE is a development approach in which software is automatically generated from a model representing the requirements of the system using a transformation engine. The benefits of MDE include rapid development and the ability to develop a model rather than writing code from the requirements, which has enabled more non-technical people to develop software systems. In fact, one study reported that MDE adoption yields productivity gains of 800% [25]. Furthermore, the market for low-code/no-code platforms has been reported to have a compound annual growth rate of over 44% [1], making it increasingly important to train students to test applications created using a no-code approach.

However, while designing a model rather than writing code directly may seem to protect the user from common programming errors, the validation and verification of such models still plays a key role. There is no guarantee that the model reflects the requirements, even if the translation engine works perfectly.

Just as software testing is a difficult subject to teach, model-testing is also a difficult subject to teach. Just like in software development, in model development students are not engaged to perform testing. One study had found that about 40% of student models contained deadlock situations [10]. In addition, students were found to make many types of errors in their models [5,30], such as missing associations, missing object types in class diagrams, determining the correct cardinalities for a class diagram association, and deciding between an entity type or a relationship type. More testing could reduce the number of errors identified by students when designing models: a study by Sedrakyan et al. [31] has shown that simulating models by generating an application and testing it does reduce modelling errors, but that "naive" testing of the generated application is still deficient. So there is room to improve model quality by teaching students how to better test their models, as evidenced by the higher coverage students achieve when given feedback on their testing efforts [12,14].

To avoid squandering the research on using gamification to teach software testing, we use an already existing and well-validated gamified code-testing approach. This will avoid reinventing the wheel for the growing field of MDE and engage students in model-testing.

Specifically, we have chosen CodeDefenders [28] for this. CodeDefenders is a player-against-player competitive game, where two students compete against each other to test a class under test based on mutation testing. After a literal one-to-one translation of CodeDefenders into an equivalent game for model-testing called ModelDefenders [11], we apply an iterative (re)design approach. With this iterative design approach, we aim to evaluate and improve the user-friendliness of ModelDefenders resulting from the direct translation from code-testing to model-testing. After this initial evaluation of ModelDefenders, it is our aim to further evaluate the tool in terms of desired learning outcomes concerning modelling, such as model coverage, understanding and quality in our future work. However, in this paper we mainly focus on providing recommendations to translating gamified code-testing approaches into similar gamified model-testing approaches. These recommendations are useful for further engagement in model-testing via already established gamified code-testing approaches.

Our research questions are therefore:

- RQ1. How can a gamified code-testing approach be translated into a model-testing approach with similar game mechanics?
- RQ2. What pitfalls and issues should be considered when applying such a translation to any gamified code-testing approach?

In what follows, we provide related work concerning other gamified modelling approaches and the game mechanics of CodeDefenders in Sect. 2. Section 3 explains the method we used to translate CodeDefenders into ModelDefenders and how further evaluation was performed. Section 4 presents the results of this evaluation, which are then discussed in Sect. 5 and translated into recommendations for gamification approaches. Section 6 concludes the paper.

2 Related Work

2.1 Gamified Modelling

UMLegend [9] is a game where students receive feedback on their class diagram for a list of exercises. The feedback provided falls into three categories: syntax errors (UML class diagram specific), semantic errors (exercise specific) and pragmatic quality warnings (e.g. unnecessary associations between classes). UMLegend consists of levels, avatars and feedback as gamification elements.

Papygame [7] is a gamified approach to help Master students in Computer Science to learn the specific modelling aspects of Papyrus for UML. In the Papygame tool, students can solve exercises of different levels, and passing a level unlocks the next exercise. Each exercise is associated with a specific game type, either 'Hangman', where each wrong answer causes the next part of the man to be drawn, or 'On Your Own', where students complete exercises without help.

Jurgelaitis et al. [24] have integrated gamification into a higher education modelling course. This consists of providing students with levels of increasing difficulty to master the syntax and semantics of modelling languages. The integration has been found to have a positive impact on grades and motivation.

LearnER [15] is a gamified editor for developing ER diagrams. LearnER provides students with automatic feedback on their ER models. Feedback is further enhanced with gamification approaches by a leaderboard where students who have requested the least amount of feedback from the tool receive higher scores. The addition of gamification to the tool was found to be beneficial in increasing the number of exercises completed by students.

BIPMIN [21] is a gamified BPMN tool that gives students feedback on the syntactic quality of their BPMN model. Students were found to appreciate the tool and rate its usability as high.

Unfortunately, we have not been able to identify any gamified tool that aims to teach students to test their models more properly. The tools that have been discussed tend to focus on syntactic quality. Although syntactic correctness is a prerequisite for testing code, just having syntactically correct code does not guarantee correct programme behaviour. The same can be said for models. Like code, models should be tested to see if they produce the correct output given the prior state of the system and the given inputs. Therefore, in our research we translate CodeDefenders into ModelDefenders, which, to the best of our knowledge, is the first attempt to introduce a gamified model-testing tool.

2.2 CodeDefenders

CodeDefenders is a player-versus-player game in which two players compete against each other [28]. The players are assigned as either attackers or defenders. Both are given the same class to test. The attacker's task is to define a mutant of the class under test, while the defender's task is to write a test case for the class under test. The test case is then executed on the mutant. If the test case fails, the mutant is said to be dead, in line with mutation testing. If the test case passes, the mutant is said to be alive. If the mutant dies, the defender gets a point, while if the mutant stays alive, the attacker gets a point. This incentivises the defender to test the class under test as thoroughly as possible, while motivating the attacker to come up with good mutants that are difficult to write test cases against. CodeDefenders has already been rigorously evaluated with students [3,29], for course integration [20] and the subsequent positive learning effects on students in that course [19]. We have opted to use CodeDefenders in this research, as we believe it to be the only player-against-player non-cooperative game for code-testing and thus has more complex mechanics. The experiment conducted in this research would thus allow us to also make recommendations towards translating other gamified code-testing approaches.

2.3 ModelDefenders

ModelDefenders [11] works in a similar way as CodeDefenders. However, instead of doing testing on a class under test, testing is done on a Model Under Test (MUT). This MUT can be based on any type of modelling language such as class diagrams or statecharts. On this MUT mutants can be defined by means of small syntactic deviations to the models, for example changing the multiplicity of an association in a class diagram. Test cases for a MUT can be defined as a sequence of actions (e.g. creating or removing objects of an object type) and an expected outcome (pass/fail). The models under test can be any kind of model, ranging from structural and behavioural models, and any kind of level ranging from organization and process level up to code level.

3 Method

The design of ModelDefenders based on CodeDefenders was done using the design science approach as adapted by Hevner et al. [23] to an information systems research framework. We chose this framework because our goal was to develop a gamified model-testing tool based on the existing literature on code-testing tools, in order to provide the modelling community with a practical solution to engage practitioners and students in testing their models. As discussed by Hevner et al. [23], design science research consists of three cycles of activities called the relevance cycle, the rigour cycle and the design cycle. The relevance cycle consists of the initial part of the research in which requirements are elicited and possible solutions within the environment are identified. The rigor cycle consists of the selection and application of relevant methods, theories and frameworks in the construction of the new solution. The design cycle, which is the core of design science research, consists of generating different alternative solutions and evaluating them against the requirements. An overview of the design process is given in Fig. 1. The orange boxes also provide an overview of the feedback received during each iteration, which is more elaborately discussed in the results. The applied changes to the next iteration of the game are given in the discussion.

The usage of this design science approach allows us to find answers to the research questions. For RQ1, each of the subsequent prototypes developed using the design cycle yield a gamified model-testing approach (ModelDefenders) which is based on a code-testing approach with similar game mechanics (CodeDefenders). For RQ2, the evaluations that were conducted to accompany the design cycle allow to diminish any issues that arose from this translation, thus these evaluations can be used to identify any pitfalls and issues when applying a translation of a gamified code-testing to a gamified model-testing approach.

The experimental design consists of recruiting participants to evaluate each version of the game in terms of user-friendliness. Taking into account the feedback from the evaluations, the game is improved for the next iteration of the design cycle. In these evaluations, the self-reported user-friendliness of ModelDefenders by the participants is used as quality metric and thus forms the dependent variable. To measure the user-friendliness, participants answer several Likert-scale questions concerning a.o. the ease of use and learnability of the game. During each design cycle, a new prototype of ModelDefenders is introduced, which is then again evaluated. These different versions of the game thus form the independent variable.

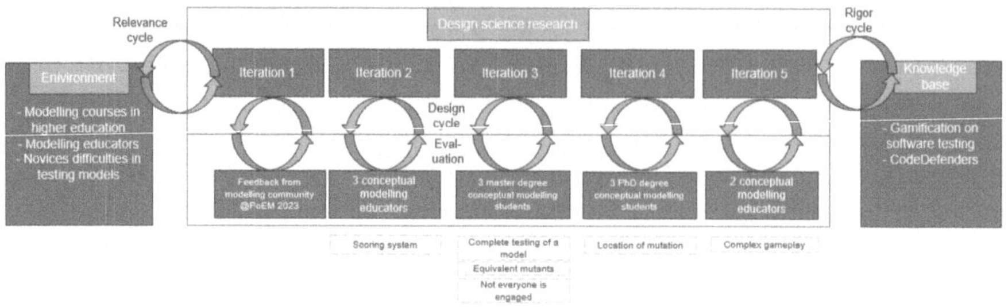

Fig. 1. Design science approach applied during this research and the yielded feedback for each iteration (orange boxes). (Color figure online)

For the design cycle we went through five iterations of ModelDefenders. Iterations 2–5 consist of an updated version of the game based on feedback from the previous iteration. The first version (resulting from iteration 1) was presented to the modelling community at the PoEM 2023 conference. The feedback received from the audience constituted the first evaluation. As this first version consists of a literal one-to-one translation of the CodeDefenders game, we refer to the full paper [11]. From the next iterations, ModelDefenders was evaluated by students and teachers in conceptual modelling. After each iteration the identified issues were fixed and the new version was used for the next iteration. This was done until no more important issues with the gameplay were reported by the participants, thus reaching a saturation effect.

In each subsequent iteration, participants played the current version of ModelDefenders. Several different models under test were used during gameplay, which acted as different difficulty levels of the game. These were given to the participants in increasing order of complexity. After completing the level of one model, the next model was used. As this was a competitive game, participants played against each other. When there were 3 participants, as was the case for iterations 2, 3 and 4, two of the participants played together as a team. This also made facilitated them to say out their thought process, which the researcher could use to identify any further issues. At the end of the game, each participant was given the opportunity to give verbal feedback on any aspect of the game.

4 Results

A total of 11 participants were recruited for the evaluation part of iterations 2–5 of the ModelDefenders design research cycle. In the second design cycle, the game was played by 3 conceptual modelling educators, after the game had been adapted to the feedback from the first evaluation. The feedback from this second iteration was used to update the game, and in the third round an evaluation was conducted with 3 Masters students in conceptual modelling. This was followed in round 4 by an evaluation with 3 PhD conceptual modelling students and finally in round 5 by an evaluation with 2 new conceptual modelling educators. After each of these evaluations, the identified issues were resolved and the game was updated accordingly before the next evaluation was conducted.

4.1 Demographics and Pre-questionnaire

Eight of the 11 participants completed the pre-questionnaire, 4 of whom identified as male and 4 as female. The average age of the participants was 28.5 years. Seven of the eight participants had at least some knowledge of modelling, while only 2 participants had some or more knowledge of mutation testing. On the basis of the four questions about technical competence, all participants felt confident about their ability to learn how to use a new software application.

4.2 Feedback During Gameplay

From the evaluations carried out during the design cycle of ModelDefenders, several gameplay issues have been identified and resolved, as discussed below.

Complete Testing of a Model. The way the test cases were designed in the initial version of ModelDefenders did not allow a model to be fully tested with a single gameplay turn. This is due to the fact that there are multiple execution traces for an artefact. More specifically, because states of a statechart may have several next states, states are not always accessible from each other, and it is therefore not possible to traverse all states of a statechart with just one test case consisting of one token. For example, consider the statechart in Fig. 2a and the test case in Table 1. The test case fully tests one of the paths of the statechart by checking for each state that none of the forbidden events can be executed, and then executing an event that can be executed to go to the next state. However, this test case has not fully tested the statechart as it has never visited the *approved* state. This is because the *approved* and *disapproved* states are not accessible from each other. It is therefore not possible to write a test case that passes through both states.

In code-testing, a similar problem arises because different paths are possible in a control flow graph. However, these different paths can be visited by changing the input to a function call, as this could change the parts of the code that are visited. This means that allowing multiple assert statements in a single test case would allow all paths of the control flow graph to be visited. The difference is that in code-testing, a single input value can evaluate an entire function, whereas in model-testing, after providing an input event, only the state of the model is updated and not the entire model has been traversed.

Stating the Location of the Mutation on the MUT. When a mutant is submitted, the location of the mutation on the MUT is indicated. This is done by placing a marker on the MUT. This information can be used to write a test case to defend against that mutant, as it indicates whether an association/transition is added, removed or renamed. In CodeDefenders, this marker can simply be

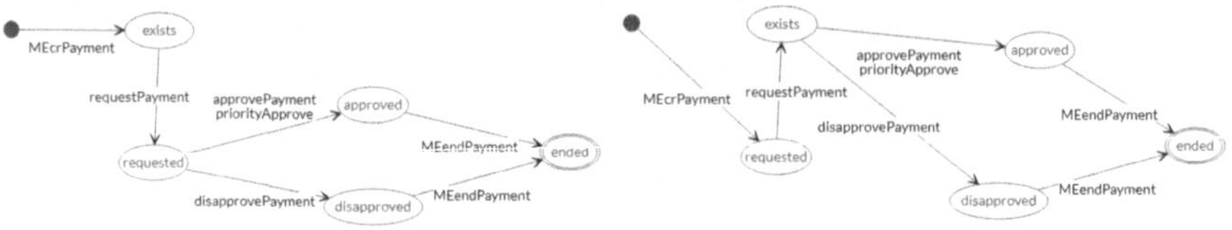

(a) Statechart as MUT (b) Equivalent mutant

Fig. 2. Example statechart as MUT and an equivalent mutant.

Table 1. Example of one test case for the model given in Fig. 2a.

Step	Event	Outcome	Step	Event	Outcome	Step	Event	Outcome
1	requestPayment	fail	9	priorityApprove	fail	17	endPayment	fail
2	approvePayment	fail	10	disapprovePayment	fail	18	disapprovePayment	pass
3	priorityApprove	fail	11	endPayment	fail	19	crPayment	fail
4	disapprovePayment	fail	12	requestPayment	pass	20	approvePayment	fail
5	endPayment	fail	13	crPayment	fail	21	priorityApprove	fail
6	crPayment	pass	14	approvePayment	fail	22	requestPayment	fail
7	crPayment	fail	15	priorityApprove	fail	23	disapprovePayment	fail
8	approvePayment	fail	16	requestPayment	fail	24	endPayment	pass

placed next to the lines of code that have been changed in the class under test. In ModelDefenders, however, since models are tested instead of code, it is less trivial to place a marker in a sensible location. There are several types of model mutation, namely relabelling, omitting and adding modelling constructs. When a modelling construct is relabelled or omitted, such as changing the multiplicity of an association or removing the association altogether, the marker can simply be placed on the modelling construct. However, when modelling constructs are added, such as adding a new association between two object types or a new transition between two states, there is no readily available modelling construct on the MUT to mark. In this case, the marker should be placed at the start and end positions for the new modelling construct. Concretely, this means that when adding an association in a class diagram, the object types that are related by that relationship will be marked. For a statechart, the source and target states of an added transition are selected.

Scoring. In the original game, points were calculated each time a new valid mutant or test case was submitted. For each mutant killed by the new test case, the defender would receive one point, while for each test case survived by a new mutant, the attacker would receive one point. However, it turned out that this gave the attacker an unfair advantage, as it is easier to create new mutants that survive all test cases than it is to create new test cases that kill all mutants [26]. This also meant that mistakes made early in the game, such as creating a test case that is too simple, would result in the opponent getting extra points for that mistake in all subsequent rounds.

This problem arises again from the fact that an input event to a model only changes the state of the model, rather than fully traversing it. This means that a test case potentially does not fully traverse a model, and test cases are potentially very short, such as traversing only the first few states of a statechart. As a result, any mutations to subsequent states without any changes to those initial states would always score a point for the attacker.

Not Everyone is Engaged. There are two approaches players can take to playing their turn. A player can decide to play the game more ad hoc, making a mutation or test case more quickly, just to see what happens, to understand the gameplay better. Conversely, a player may decide to take a more methodical approach and make a test case or mutation in their first turn to the best of their ability. In general, defenders seemed to take more time to define a test case than an attacker to define a mutation. This means that the attacker often has to wait for the defender to finish writing their test case.

Equivalent Mutants An interesting equivalent mutant was designed by an attacker during gameplay. Given the MUT in Fig. 2a, the mutant in Fig. 2b is equivalent to this MUT, even though it is semantically different in the sense that the states have wrong names. For example, when testing the statechart in Fig. 2a, after creating a payment we would expect the payment to be in the state exists, but in the equivalent mutant in Fig. 2b the payment would be in the state requested. This means that it is impossible to define a valid test case for the MUT that would kill the mutant. For every step of a sequence of events that would be successful on the MUT, that step would also be successful on the mutant. Similarly, any step in a sequence of events that would fail on the MUT would also fail on the mutant. There is therefore no way of distinguishing between the MUT and the mutant in the current way of defining test cases. An example of such a test case is shown in Table 1.

Complex Gameplay. Even though the participants were provided with elaborate gameboard-like instructions, some of them still struggled to understand how to start playing the game. Participants often found it challenging to define their first test case, as they had never written explicit test cases for a model before, and similarly to define mutants, as it was their first encounter with mutation testing and the concept of a mutant. Others also had difficulty understanding when a mutant was valid and why it was killed by a particular test case.

4.3 Post-questionnaire

For the post-questionnaire, one participant's responses were omitted because he did not answer the control questions. For the other 7 participants, the post-questionnaire shows that they rate the ease of use, learnability, perceived satisfaction, perceived effectiveness, overall usefulness, system support, game experience and learning experience as positive. Meanwhile, participants rated the difficulty in terms of complexity as low. An overview of the mean, minimum and maximum ratings per construct is given in Table 2.

Table 2. Ratings per construct of the post-questionnaire. (1 = strongly disagree, 5 = strongly agree)

Construct	Avg.	Min.	Max.	Construct	Avg.	Min.	Max.
Ease of use	3.19	1	4	Overall usefulness perception	3.97	2	5
Learnability	3.42	2	4	System support	3.81	2	5
Perceived satisfaction	4.31	3	5	Game experience	4.05	1	5
Perceived difficulties	2	1	5	Learning experience	4.05	1	5
Perceived effectiveness	3.82	1	5				

5 Discussion

Based on our findings, we make some recommendations for the future development of gamified model-testing approaches from gamified code-testing approaches. We divide our recommendations according to their area of applicability: recommendations for mutation-based approaches, recommendations for gamification approaches, and recommendations for general model-testing.

5.1 General Model Testing

Number of Test Cases to Fully Test a Model. For behavioural models such as statecharts and process models, the number of test cases in a test suite for a model should be equal to the number of distinct paths from the initial to the final states of the model. To have a test suite that would fully test all scenarios, several test cases would have to be part of the test suite. In the example statechart shown in the results (Fig. 2a), one test case would go through the approved state, while a second test case would go through the disapproved state. To fully test this model, the tester should therefore write two test cases. This is also the number of paths from the initial state to the final state. This also applies to BPMN, where an exclusive gateway means that a token can only go through one of the subsequent paths, and additional tokens are needed to test all paths [33].

Granularity of Test Cases and Ill-Defined Oracle. The granularity with which test cases, and by extension the oracle, are defined should be at the right level. During gameplay we saw that there are mutants equivalent to the MUT. Such a mutant has the same morphological structure as the MUT, but has a different semantic meaning, making it incorrect with respect to the requirements. For example, the MUT in Fig. 2a has the same morphological structure as the equivalent mutant in 2b because it has the same initial, intermediate and final states, which are also connected in the same way. To test a model more accurately, it is therefore necessary to define the oracle of a test case in more detail than just a pass/fail, but rather by explicitly stating the expected state for the model. This can be done at each step of a test case. However, this comes at the additional cost of first having to know what state is expected at each step. This is not always trivial, as for some requirements there is no explicit oracle. For example, the requirements for the model in Fig. 2a state that a payment must be requested before it can be approved or rejected. This does not provide an explicit oracle as to what state the payment should be in once it has been requested.

5.2 Mutation-Based Approaches

Marking Mutations on the MUT. Marking where a mutation has occurred in the MUT is less trivial than in code-based approaches. In code-based approaches, it is possible to simply place a marker next to each line of code that has changed in the mutant. In model-testing, this can also be done when a modelling construct is relabelled or omitted, by highlighting the modelling construct on the MUT that has been relabelled or omitted. However, when adding a construct, it is not possible to highlight the modelling construct on the MUT as it has been added to the model. Instead, the marking should be done as shown in Fig. 3. In Fig. 3 two MUTs are given, on the left a statechart, on the right a class diagram. For the statechart, a mutation is made by adding a transition between the approved and disapproved states, as indicated in green. For the class diagram, a new association is placed between the merchant and credit card object types, also indicated in green. The markers that would be given based on these changes are shown in red. For the statechart, this would consist of marking both the source and target states of the newly added transition, in this case the approved and disapproved states. For the class diagram, this would consist of marking both the object types that are linked by the association, in this case the merchant and credit card object types. These markings can be of interest for model mutation testing in general, where such markings can inform the modeller of the changes in a MUT of which the mutations have survived all test cases.

Eliminating Equivalent Mutants. To avoid the problem of equivalent mutants, a well-known problem in mutation testing, the granularity at which test cases are defined can be changed, as discussed in the recommendations for general model-testing. For a statechart, a test case could be defined that includes explicitly naming the state that the model is expected to be in after an event. This would mean that equivalent mutants could no longer be defined, since during the execution of the test case, at each step, the outcome on the mutant will also be checked for being in the correct state. More generally, it can be said that allowing test cases to be defined in a more detailed way, for example by explicitly adding which (error) state a model would be in after an event, can help to avoid the problem of equivalent mutants when using model mutation testing.

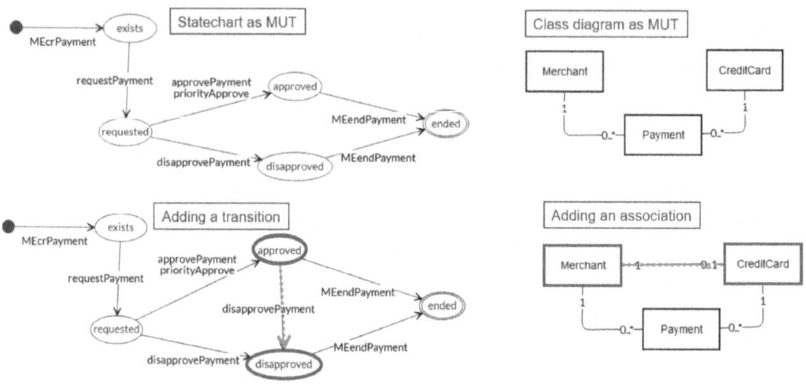

Fig. 3. Example mutations on a statechart and class diagram in which modelling constructs have been added (green) and their markings (red). (Color figure online)

5.3 Gamification Approaches

Keeping Everyone Engaged. Unfortunately, the attacker often had to wait for the defender to write a test case. This problem could be alleviated by allowing players to be both attacker and defender at the same time. Specifically, this means that at the start of a turn, both players can define a mutant. They can then submit these mutants. Both players can then receive a message on the MUT showing where the mutations have occurred, so that they can both play as defenders. While the players are playing as defenders, they can use the MUT with the mutations they have received to try and kill the opponent's mutant. This means that the roles of attacker and defender no longer exist explicitly, but are replaced by an attacker and defender phase of a turn in which both players have the same role. After the attacker and defender phases, there is a mediator phase in which the test cases are run against the mutants and points are awarded to the players. Playing the game in this way would also remove any further unfairness in the scoring due to being initially assigned as either attacker or defender, as both players would get an equal number of opportunities to play as both defender and attacker. This would also help players to become more familiar with the gameplay, as by the time they define their first test case, they will all have defined a mutant, i.e. they will already understand the constraints under which such mutants can be defined. This also gives players an equal chance to play both defender and attacker for each of the MUTs. An updated sequence diagram of this new system is shown in Fig. 4, where the subsequent stages of a turn are named as the attacker, defender and mediator phases.

Scoring. Based on the feedback regarding the distribution of points in the game, a new scoring system was proposed. In this new scoring system, both the attacker and the defender submit their test cases and mutants at the same time. Instead of comparing the new test cases with all previous mutants, only the

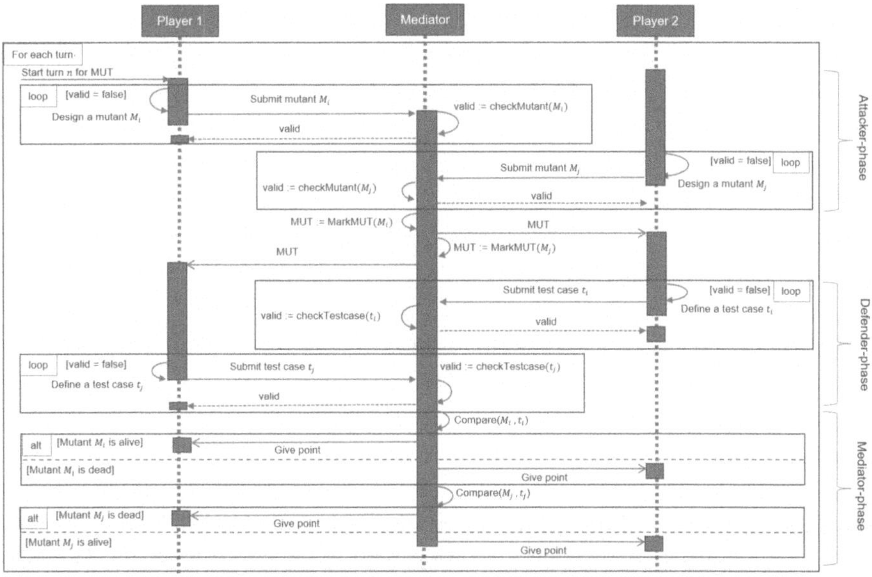

Fig. 4. Updated sequence diagram of a gameplay turn of ModelDefenders.

new mutants are compared with the new test cases. This means that neither the defender nor the attacker can gain more than 1 point per round. An example of the new scoring system is shown in Fig. 5. As no additional information is given to the attacker or defender (i.e. they do not know which mutant or test case the other player will make), they are encouraged to make mutants and test cases to the best of their ability. The unfairness of this scoring system is partly due to the fact that participants are doing model-testing for the first time and are still struggling to define good test cases for models in a formal way. Other gamification approaches can take this into account, and also ensure that mistakes are not penalised multiple times, allowing users to become familiar with model-testing without becoming demotivated.

5.4 Limitations

In terms of internal validity, given the limited number of participants, it is possible that some important usability issues were not identified during gameplay. However, as we saw that the amount of feedback generally decreased with each iteration of the game due to the changed game design in each iteration, which leads us to believe that most usability issues were still identified. In terms of the external validity of the research, only a limited sample of people participated in the research. Due to the voluntary nature of participation, there may also be a survivorship bias. Another potential issue is that no testing experts had been recruited among the participants, and that only two of the participants had prior knowledge on mutation testing. In our future work, we aim to recruit more participants who would form a more representative sample.

Turn	Phase	Player 1	Player 2	Old scoring system	New scoring system
1	Attacker phase	Designs mutant M_1	Designs mutant M_2		
	Defender phase	Defines test case t_1	Defines test case t_2		
	Mediator phase	M_1 survives t_2 M_2 is killed by t_1		1 point for player 1	1 point for player 1
2	Attacker phase	Designs mutant M_3	Designs mutant M_4		
	Defender phase	Defines test case t_3	Defines test case t_4		
	Mediator phase	M_1 survives t_4 M_2 is killed by t_3 M_3 survives t_4 M_4 survives t_3		2 points for player 1 1 point for player 2	1 point for player 1 1 point for player 2

Underlined actions are no longer done in new scoring system

Fig. 5. Two example game turns and the scores obtained by the players in the old and new scoring system.

6 Conclusion

In this paper we have discussed an initial evaluation of ModelDefenders, a gamified player-against-player model mutation testing approach based on CodeDefenders. We had used a design science research approach to develop ModelDefenders and to resolve any major issues with the gameplay. From the lessons learnt in this translation from gamified code-testing to gamified model-testing, we had made several recommendations to enable future gamified code-testing approaches to be translated into similar gamified model-testing approaches.

In terms of further work, now that we have minimised the usability issues of the game, we intend to further evaluate ModelDefenders. This will consist of having a larger group of students use the game and measuring the potential gains in terms of model-testing, model understanding and modelling skills.

References

1. Global low-code development platform market: Rising demand for innovative applications and software automation to enable market exhibit strong growth (2018). https://www.businesswire.com/news/home/20180116006370/en/27.2-Billion-Global-Low-Code-Development-Platform-Market-2017-2022
2. Alsawaier, R.S.: The effect of gamification on motivation and engagement. Int. J. Inf. Learn. Technol. **35**(1), 56–79 (2018)
3. Benjamin Clegg, J.M.R., Fraser, G.: Teaching software testing concepts using a mutation testing game. In: 2017 Proceedings of the International Conference on Software Engineering : Software Engineering and Education Track (ICSE-SEET), ICSE-SEET 2017, pp. 33–36. IEEE Press (2017)
4. Bishop, J., Horspool, R.N., Xie, T., Tillmann, N., De Halleux, J.: Code hunt: experience with coding contests at scale. In: 2015 IEEE/ACM 37th IEEE International Conference on Software Engineering, vol. 2, pp. 398–407. IEEE (2015)
5. Bogdanova, D., Snoeck, M.: Learning from errors: error-based exercises in domain modelling pedagogy. In: Buchmann, R.A., Karagiannis, D., Kirikova, M. (eds.) PoEM 2018. LNBIP, vol. 335, pp. 321–334. Springer, Cham (2018). https://doi.org/10.1007/978-3-030-02302-7_20

6. Britton, T., Jeng, L., Carver, G., Cheak, P., Katzenellenbogen, T.: Reversible debugging software. Judge Business School, University of Cambridge, Cambridge, UK, Technical report, vol. 229 (2013)
7. Bucchiarone, A., et al.: Gamifying model-based engineering: the PapyGame tool. Sci. Comput. Program. 102974 (2023)
8. Butt, P.: Students' perceptions of game-based learning using CodinGame. In: International Conference on Information Communication Technologies in Education, pp. 151–158 (2016)
9. Cagnazzo, C., Garaccione, G., Coppola, R., Ardito, L., Torchiano, M.: UMLegend: a gamified learning tool for conceptual modeling with UML class diagrams. In: Proceedings of the 2nd International Workshop on Gamification in Software Development, Verification, and Validation, pp. 2–5 (2023)
10. Cammaerts, F., Snoeck, M.: Assessing the value of incomplete deadlock verification in model-driven engineering. In: Companion Proceedings of the 42nd International Conference on Conceptual Modeling: ER Forum, 7th SCME, Project Exhibitions, Posters and Demos, and Doctoral Consortium Co-located with ER 2023 (2023)
11. Cammaerts, F., Snoeck, M.: ModelDefenders: a novel gamified mutation testing game for model-driven engineering. In: Companion Proceedings of the 16th IFIP WG 8.1 Working Conference on the Practice of Enterprise Modeling and the 13th Enterprise Design and Engineering Working Conference: BES, DTE, FACETE, Tools & Demos, Forum, EDEN Doctoral Consortium co-located with PoEM 2023 (2023)
12. Cammaerts, F., Snoeck, M.: Assessing the testing skills transfer of model-based testing on testing skill acquisition. Softw. Syst. Model. **1619–1374**, 1–19 (2024)
13. Cammaerts, F., Tramontana, P., Paiva, A.C.R., Flores, N., Pastor Ricós, F., Snoeck, M.: Exploring students' opinion on software testing courses. In: Proceedings of the 28th International Conference on Evaluation and Assessment in Software Engineering, EASE 2024, pp. 570-579. Association for Computing Machinery, New York (2024). https://doi.org/10.1145/3661167.3661276
14. Cammaerts, F., Verbruggen, C., Snoeck, M.: Investigating the effectiveness of model-based testing on testing skill acquisition. In: Barn, B.S., Sandkuhl, K. (eds.) PoEM 2022. LNBIP, vol. 456, pp. 3–17. Springer, Cham (2022). https://doi.org/10.1007/978-3-031-21488-2_1
15. Dæhli, O., Kristoffersen, B., Lauvås Jr., P., Sandnes, T.: Exploring feedback and gamification in a data modeling learning tool. Electron. J. e-Learn. **19**(6), 559–574 (2021)
16. Elbaum, S., Person, S., Dokulil, J., Jorde, M.: Bug hunt: making early software testing lessons engaging and affordable. In: 29th International Conference on Software Engineering (ICSE 2007), pp. 688–697. IEEE (2007)
17. Fernández-Sanz, L., Villalba, M.T., Hilera, J.R., Lacuesta, R.: Factors with negative influence on software testing practice in Spain: a survey. In: O'Connor, R.V., Baddoo, N., Cuadrago Gallego, J., Rejas Muslera, R., Smolander, K., Messnarz, R. (eds.) EuroSPI 2009. CCIS, vol. 42, pp. 1–12. Springer, Heidelberg (2009). https://doi.org/10.1007/978-3-642-04133-4_1
18. Fraser, G.: Gamification of software testing. In: 2017 IEEE/ACM 12th International Workshop on Automation of Software Testing (AST), pp. 2–7 (2017). https://doi.org/10.1109/AST.2017.20
19. Fraser, G., Gambi, A., Kreis, M., Rojas, J.M.: Gamifying a software testing course with code defenders. In: Proceedings of the ACM Technical Symposium on Computer Science Education (SIGCSE), SIGCSE 2019. ACM (2019)

20. Fraser, G., Gambi, A., Rojas, J.M.: A preliminary report on gamifying a software testing course with the code defenders testing game. In: Proceedings of the European Conference of Software Engineering Education (ECSEE) 2018, ECSEE 2018, pp. 50–54. ACM (2018)
21. Garaccione, G., Coppola, R., Ardito, L.: Gamifying business process modeling education: a longitudinal study. In: Proceedings of the 28th International Conference on Evaluation and Assessment in Software Engineering, pp. 580–589 (2024)
22. Hamari, J., Koivisto, J., Sarsa, H.: Does Gamification work? – A literature review of empirical studies on gamification. In: 2014 47th Hawaii International Conference on System Sciences, pp. 3025–3034 (2014). https://doi.org/10.1109/HICSS.2014.377
23. Hevner, A.R., March, S.T., Park, J., Ram, S.: Design science in information systems research. MIS Q. 75–105 (2004)
24. Jurgelaitis, M., Čeponienė, L., Čeponis, J., Drungilas, V.: Implementing gamification in a university-level UML modeling course: a case study. Comput. Appl. Eng. Educ. **27**(2), 332–343 (2019)
25. Mohagheghi, P., Dehlen, V.: Where is the proof? - A review of experiences from applying MDE in industry. In: Schieferdecker, I., Hartman, A. (eds.) ECMDA-FA 2008. LNCS, vol. 5095, pp. 432–443. Springer, Heidelberg (2008). https://doi.org/10.1007/978-3-540-69100-6_31
26. Paiva, A.C., Restivo, A., Almeida, S.: Test case generation based on mutations over user execution traces. Softw. Qual. J. **28**(3), 1173–1186 (2020)
27. da Rocha Seixas, L., Gomes, A.S., de Melo Filho, I.J.: Effectiveness of gamification in the engagement of students. Comput. Hum. Behav. **58**, 48–63 (2016)
28. Rojas, J.M., Fraser, G.: Code defenders: a mutation testing game. In: 2016 IEEE Ninth International Conference on Software Testing, Verification and Validation Workshops (ICSTW), pp. 162–167. IEEE (2016)
29. Rojas, J.M., Fraser, G.: Teaching software testing with a mutation testing game. In: Psychology of Programming Interest Group 2016 (PPIG) (2016)
30. Rosenthal, K., Strecker, S., Snoeck, M.: Modeling difficulties in creating conceptual data models: multimodal studies on individual modeling processes. Softw. Syst. Model. **22**(3), 1005–1030 (2023)
31. Sedrakyan, G., De Weerdt, J., Snoeck, M.: Process-mining enabled feedback: "tell me what i did wrong" vs. "tell me how to do it right". Comput. Hum. Behav. **57**, 352–376 (2016). https://doi.org/10.1016/j.chb.2015.12.040, https://www.sciencedirect.com/science/article/pii/S0747563215303113
32. Tramontana, P., et al.: State of the practice in software testing teaching in four European countries. In: 17th IEEE ICST (2024)
33. Vom Brocke, J., Rosemann, M.: Handbook on Business Process Management 1: Introduction, Methods, and Information Systems. Springer, Heidelberg (2014). https://doi.org/10.1007/978-3-642-45100-3

JUSMOD

Preface

Matteo Buffa[1], Silvana Castano[1], Cristine Griffo[2], and Stefano Montanelli[1]

[1] Department of Computer Science, Università degli Studi di Milano, Italy
{matteo.buffa, silvana.castano}@unimi.it,
cristine.griffo@eurac.edu
[2] Eurac Research, Bozen-Bolzano, Italy
stefano.montanelli@unimi.it

It is becoming increasingly acknowledged that law plays a pivotal role in nearly every aspect of our lives, both public and private. A vast array of legal documents is continuously generated by various institutional bodies, including Parliaments and Courts, which serve as a significant source of information and knowledge for judges, lawyers, and other professionals involved in legal decision-making. To effectively manage the growing volume, complexity, and articulation of legal documents, there is a growing commitment to digital transformation processes in the legal domain.

Conceptual modeling plays a crucial role in this scenario, to formalize features and nature of terminology used in legal documents and to promote the development and the adoption of legal ontologies, shared vocabularies, and open linked data about legislation, case law, and other relevant legal information. Furthermore, advanced functionalities for legal data and process modeling and management are advocated, embracing modern technologies like the Semantic Web, NLP, and AI, to enable semantic text search and exploration, legal knowledge extraction and formalization, legal decision-making, and legal analytics.

JUSMOD 2024, the 3rd International Workshop on Digital JUStice, digital law, and conceptual MODeling, constitutes a meeting venue for a variety of researchers involved in digital justice and digital law crossing different disciplines besides computer science, like law, legal informatics, management, economics, and social sciences. Also, it is an excellent opportunity to share, discuss, and identify new approaches and solutions for modeling, analysis, formalization, and interpretation of legal data and related processes.

In this JUSMOD edition, organized within the scope of project SERICS (PE00000014) under the NRRP MUR program funded by the EU - NGEU, the program includes three long papers and one invited paper, selected by the Program Committee following a peer-review process. The first paper addresses the topic of compliance within the context of legal and regulatory requirements. The second paper considers the possibility of reusing the UFO-L core ontology for modeling organizational rule enforcement in a healthcare context. The third paper introduces the euFAIRnews tool developed to investigate the compatibility of news sources and articles with the FAIR principles, as well as their relationship with news quality, disinformation, and digital justice. Finally, the fourth paper deals with the safety assurance of autonomous ships, with a specific focus on compliance with the International Regulations for Preventing Collisions at Sea (COLREG).

JUSMOD Organization

Workshop Chairs

Matteo Buffa	Università degli Studi di Milano, Italy
Silvana Castano	Università degli Studi di Milano, Italy
Cristine Griffo	Eurac Research, Italy
Stefano Montanelli	Università degli Studi di Milano, Italy

Program Committee

Tommaso Agnoloni	IGSG, CNR, Italy
Jean-Rémi Bourguet	University of Vila Velha, Brazil
Daniel Braun	University of Twente, The Netherlands
Juliana Justo Castello	Linhares Higher Education College-FACELI, Brazil
Samuela Marchiori	Delft University of Technology, The Netherlands
Maria das G. Teixeira	Federal University of Espírito Santo, Brazil
Davide Riva	Università degli Studi di Milano, Italy
Jaromir Savelka	Carnegie Mellon University, USA

Resignifying Compliance Between Ontologies and Epistemologies of Law (Invited Paper)

Matteo Buffa(✉)

University of Milan, Via Celoria 18, 20133 Milan, Italy
matteo.buffa@unimi.it

Abstract. This contribution is devoted to the topic of compliance in the legal-regulatory context, focusing on the need for new epistemologies of compliance that look at different, and interoperable, contexts. It is an attempt to understand and explain human and non-human cognitive processes at the basis of evaluations of a knowledge (and knowing) compliant capacity with the tension to reconstruct the different phases of the intelligibility of dispositions (and target documents that derive from them). The data analyzed so far allow us to imagine new (and plural) epistemic foundations capable of understanding and explaining this complexity. In particular, it seems to be possible to support a transition (linguistic, modeling, but also operational) from ontologies to epistemologies, all the more so when we are called upon to evaluate the issue of compliance.

Keywords: Compliance · Ontologies · Epistemologies · Philosophy of Law · GDPR

1 Compliance: Survey on an Interdisciplinary Regulatory Concept

The term "compliance" immediately evokes the closest meaning of conformity with a given standard. However, the assumptions (as well as the consequences) are to be considered very differently due to the level of identification of such standards,[1] as well as by the relative agent, which could be related to both the legal-regulatory context as well as the social, corporate and commercial one. It is, in any case, a "burden" linked

[1] With respect to the latter perspective, AGID, the Agency for Digital Italy which reports to the Presidency of the Council of Ministers, recalls that "There are international standards that refer to business continuity. Of particular relevance is the UNI CEI ISO/IEC 27001:2014 standard "Information technology - Security techniques - Information security management systems - Requirements" which, while dealing with IT security, identifies business continuity as an essential element".

M. Saeki et al. (Eds.): ER 2024 Workshops, LNCS 14932, pp. 253–266, 2025.
https://doi.org/10.1007/978-3-031-75599-6_19

to a dimension of responsibility in a broad sense, with different incidences in global market economies,[2] in sociology, psychology and education (sciences) dealing with human behavior, in medical sciences.

In the legal-regulatory context, on closer inspection, compliance is an ancient and central concept in legal systems that provide for a hierarchy of sources (I am thinking of most "civil law" systems) as well as, possibly, of Courts and rulings bound to the rule of "stare decisis" which presuppose hierarchical relationships in judicial interpretation (as per "common law"). As is well known, civil law and common law models have seen some overlaps, in particular in the face of the growing internationalization of legal systems as well as, on closer inspection, the effectiveness of the measures adopted, which increasingly extend from the national context to the supranational (European, federal) international context (from the latter point of view, the cases that the writer considers most representative are those related to the General Data Regulation Act of the Union European regulation, no. 679/2016 of 27 April 2016 promulgated with effective entry into force in 2018, thereafter only GDPR, and the legislation on Network Information Security (NIS) recently re-proposed again at European level with Directive 2555/2022 relating, in fact, to the security of critical infrastructures, which provides for new compliance obligations in terms of cybersecurity.

If we look at the Italian legal system, we know, moreover, that due to the principles of "primauté" and effectiveness of European Union law and, to a certain extent, also of primary and conventional international law, it is in accordance with Article 117 of the Italian Constitution (amended by Constitutional Law No. 3/2001) that the need to comply with, among other things, the "*(…) the constraints deriving from the Community and international legal order*". These constraints, moreover, become an interposed parameter of the constitutionality of national legislation, thus assuming a preeminent role to that

[2] "Compliance is rapidly growing across the world as regulatory requirements become more com plex and international. The compliance function is now growing faster than many other roles but, in many cases, remains operational and mechanical; relative to its level of responsibility and potential impact, compliance is low status and poorly integrated into mainstream business activities. It is often considered an expensive add-on, marginalized, seen as a barrier to successful business, bedeviled by simplistic approaches. This has to change. Compliance must show itself to be high-value and strategic". (Jackman D., 2015). On the same topic "66% of the EU IT professional say that the GDPR is a financial burden since needs up-dating and new technologies.88 With respect to the implementation of the GDPR by states, a question arises as whether is it easy to be executed? And in case the national data protection law provided detail rules for a specific issue, but the GDPR did not provide specific rules, so whether it will hampers its execution? It seems that the most crucial issue with respect to the GDPR is the proper implementation. Hence, in this situation the Board plays a significant role in an effortless implementation. The difficulties with implementation and expenses may involve all companies, governments and individuals. However, it is the nature of every new phenomena and it is inevitable to precede these steps to cope with new technologies. The different interpretations of the Regulation like the age of consent for a child are another obstacle toward a fully harmonized law. Furthermore, the GDPR new innovations like right to be forgotten or data breach notification will affect mostly the big multinational companies (Agarwal S. et al:2018) Finally, inaccuracy of the analysis of legal documents must be minimal because in the eyes of the law, there is no such thing as "near-compliance". For example, by missing an exception or a condition, one could bestow or deny an important right or obligation to the wrong party (Zeni N. et al: 2015).

of ordinary law and, therefore, constitutes a de facto constraint on the legitimacy of the activity of the national parliament, which is the only body, with some exceptional provision, entitled of legislative function.

It is possible to consider that, at least to a certain extent, in the context of legal informatics, a possible counterweight at European level lies in the so-called principle of technological neutrality. By this expression we refer to the freedom of people and organizations to choose the technology that best suits their needs. Products, services or regulatory frameworks that consider the principle of technological neutrality shall not impose or discriminate against the use of a particular type of technology. An essential reference to this principle can be found in another, and more dated, act of the European Union of 2014, in particular EU Regulation no. 283.[3]

Another significant difference, looking at the GDPR, lies in the concept closer to the term accountability,[4] "ability", and reliability that are linked to a specific subjectivity and a precise profile (again, relevant both in the legal-regulatory context and in the commercial and corporate one). Pursuant to Articles 5(2) and 25 of GDPR, we know that: "The controller shall be responsible for, and be *able* to demonstrate, compliance", in terms of *accountability*. It is therefore a principle that underlies the ability, the capacity, of the subject to prove itself reliable to an indeterminate audience also due to the recognitions prepared for this purpose. In fact, as per article 25 of the following period, provisions relating to certifiability are foreseen, i.e. a reasonable degree of certainty that has to do with "reliability" of sort: "An approved certification mechanism may be used as an element to demonstrate compliance" (see paragraphs 1 and 2 of article 25).

On the same issue, is again GDPR that provides, in subsequent provisions, for example according to Article 42, that "The Member States, the supervisory authorities, the Board and the Commission shall encourage, in particular at Union level, the establishment of data protection certification mechanisms and of data protection seals and marks, for the purpose of demonstrating compliance with this Regulation of processing operations by controllers and processors. The specific needs of micro, small and medium-sized enterprises shall be considered". In fact, even the aforementioned legislation on the protection of Network Information and Security (NIS II) as well as on important infrastructures, explicitly provides for specific obligations in this field that: "Entities

[3] See https://eur-lex.europa.eu/IT/legal-content/summary/supporting-telecommunications-networks-and-digital-service-infrastructures-across-europe.html.

[4] "The phrase 'Accountability Principle' has been used under Recital 85 and Article 5(2), but the GDPR did not define it nor allocated special provision for this issue. However, the reference of Article 5(2) as accountability, to paragraph 1 of this provision on principles with regard to the processing of personal data is the main reference of Accountability Principle envisaged by the Regulation. In a simple language, this new principle means compliance with all processing principles provided under Article 5 with special emphasis in addition to fulfilling all other required principles. Compliance with all required principles of the GDPR based on the accountability principles can be inferred from Recital 85 while addressing the data breach requirements. Under accountability, the data controller must develop a comprehensive document including the detail information on what they do and how and generally on personal data they have. This is provided under the GDPR as a new requirement. This document will use for cases like data breach notification". (Alibeigi A. et al 2019).

falling within the scope of this Directive for the purpose of compliance with cybersecurity risk-management measures and reporting obligations should be classified into two categories, essential entities and important entities, reflecting the extent to which they are critical as regards their sector or the type of service they provide, as well as their size. In that regard, due account should be taken of any relevant sectoral risk assessments or guidance by the competent authorities, where applicable. The supervisory and enforcement regimes for those two categories of entities should be differentiated to ensure a fair balance between risk-based requirements and obligations on the one hand, and the administrative burden stemming from the supervision of compliance on the other".

When we refer to data protection and governance in the context of the European Union, we can suppose it is therefore possible to distinguish between (Law) enforcement, in which the notion of compliance becomes to some extent referable to the authorities identified by the Member States as data protection authorities (DPAs), and accountability, in which the obligation of compliance falls, moreover also in the face of sanctions of a certain magnitude,[5] on public and private entities deemed essential or, although not essential, important, according to the most recent name adopted by the European legislator.

On the other hand, the repercussions of compliance can also be "individual" to some extent, as well as to their contacts with entities and bodies dealing with their personal data. If we look again at the notion of "enforcement", in particular starting from the new procedural regulation of the European Union which concerns cases between borders: "For individuals, the new rules will clarify what they need to submit when making a complaint and ensure that they are appropriately involved in the process. For businesses, the new rules will clarify their due process rights when a DPA investigates a potential breach of the GDPR. The rules will therefore bring swifter resolution of cases, meaning quicker remedies for individuals and more legal certainty for businesses".[6]

In this direction the new rules will smoothen cooperation and enhance efficiency of enforcement for data protection authorities that will be in charge for harmonizing procedural rules in cross-border cases. "The new regulation provides detailed rules to support the smooth functioning of the cooperation and consistency mechanism established by the GDPR, harmonizing rules in the following areas:

- Rights of complainants: the proposal harmonizes the requirements for a cross-border complaint to be admissible, removing current obstacles underlined by DPAs and following different criteria. It establishes common rights for complainants to be heard in cases where their complaints are fully or partially rejected. In those cases where a complaint is investigated, the proposal specifies rules for them to be properly involved.
- Rights of parties under investigation (controllers and processors): the proposal provides the parties under investigation with the right to be heard at key stages in the

[5] Recently, precisely on 3rd April 2024, Greek Data Protection Authority (DPA) issued a fine of 175.000 to the local Ministry of Asylum and Migration. Such fine imposition relates to the border management systems *Kentauros* and *Hyperion* managed by the Ministry to reception facilities and borders control and management, also considering the collection of biometric data on migrants and asylum seekers.

[6] For further details on the cross-border cases as well as concrete procedural rules to be enforced please see https://ec.europa.eu/commission/presscorner/detail/en/ip_23_3609.

procedure, including during dispute resolution by the European Data Protection Board (EDPB), and clarifies the content of the administrative file and the parties' rights of access to the file.

- Streamlining cooperation and dispute resolution: under the proposal, DPAs will be able to provide their views early on in investigations and make use of all the tools of cooperation provided by the GDPR, such as joint investigations and mutual assistance. These provisions will enhance DPAs' influence over cross-border cases, facilitate early consensus-building in the investigation, and reduce later disagreements. The proposal specifies detailed rules to facilitate the swift completion of the GDPR's dispute resolution mechanism and provides common deadlines for cross-border cooperation and dispute resolution".

Another important element is the one concerning whether - and to what extent - compliance can correspond to a subjective right, considering that the most part of EU Law in this field it's a "non [human] rights based" approach:

"One of the purposes of any institution is to routinize compliance with a given set of rules, making it more likely that the rules will be followed regardless of changing circumstances or turnover in leadership. *(Cardenas S. 2020).* The perspective under consideration, as such, cannot be exempt from certain limitations: "Though imperfect, social science approaches can help clarify answers to real world empirical questions (...) Drawing on diverse methodologies and theories, social scientists often rely on structured com parisons (small or large in number), and they attempt to rule out alternative explanations systematically. The goal is to reach relatively reliable (i.e., replicable) conclusions while offering more compelling accounts of a phenomenon. Skepticism of such approaches abounds, including claims that social complexity is not amenable to scientific inquiry or generalization, presumptions of objectivity are false, causality is impossible to establish, theory is often divorced from practice, and findings can fail to provide pragmatic solutions to concrete problems. Some social science research of course falls into these traps, but much of it is also sufficiently nuanced and self-conscious of its inherent limitations to accommodate criticism. The bottom line is that social science approaches can be deployed productively alongside legal and policy analysis, even for the study of human rights where ethics, social contestation, and humanism figure prominently".

2 From Ontologies to Epistemologies to Re-signify Compliance

The discourse (logos) on being (onto – òntos) as is well known, refers to a field (or rather, plurally, to fields) that have long been investigated and inhabited by different and, at times, conflicting philosophical approaches, including, not least, the Philosophy of Law. Such latter discipline (as well as the corresponding scientific disciplinary sector and, more recently, the equivalent scientific disciplinary group according to the recent reform of the Italian academic system by the legislator and which was implemented by ministerial decree of May 2024) then met the notion of (formal) ontology in the intersection with the fields and methods of scientific investigation of computer science and computer science. I have just referred to the theme of formal ontology in order to limit the present contribution to that ontological meaning that Edmund Husserl proposes in the union of logical-formal and mathematical gazes that allows us to identify here to isolate the birth of a hermeneutical philosophy, born close to the analytic one and then destined to depart from it.[7] The level of thought and, in part, of the imaginary is a "third place", distinct from the material and sensible as well as from the psychological. Gottlob Frege seems to be leaning towards the idea that thought can be studied, analyzed, and understood through the analysis of language. Edmund Husserl, on the other hand, proposes, in contrast to the linguistic turn, the need for a return to things or, better said, to entities. That is, the philosopher is keen to maintain that the so-called theory of multiplicity not only describes, but rather prescribes, the study of being not as being, but rather the study of entities as beings, that is, of the properties common to all the multiple forms of entity. The set of these studies, however, despite the different directions taken (i.e. analytical on the one hand and hermeneutic on the other) will lay the foundations for the neopositivist currents of thought. In any case, in our hermeneutical sense and analysis, knowledge would be destined to deal with "regional" ontologies, that is, limited, circumscribed, by a field of knowledge, of entities that intercept a competence and a speculative interest. Husserl will also distinguish between formal ontologies that are dedicated to objects divided into categories and formal logics that, on the other hand, look at different meanings. Being is, thanks to the turning point that leads – this time – to transcendence, reduced to consciousness. Above all, the general impression is that of a "family lexicon" *à la Ginzburg*,[8] for the Philosophy of Law compared to legal informatics and to what I would call the semantic turn of analytic philosophy as well as of the logical-mathematical sciences. In fact, the term ontology, as early as the last of the twentieth century,[9] looking at the so-called Semantic Web. "In this sense, the ontological aspects of a theory depend on the type of variables that can be quantified and on the semantics of the language used. The shift in meaning is particularly relevant for the significance of ontology in computer science, since it is assumed that ontology is not made up of the assertions that a theory makes about what exists and what does not exist, but about the type of meanings that the language used is able to represent. The ontological discourse is therefore no longer a discourse on being, but rather a discourse on our representation of being and on the possibilities of our language" (Castano, Ferrara, Montanelli. Course in Ontologies and Semantic Web, 2005:2). One could partly disagree with these considerations only when they look at the existence or otherwise of the entities under consideration as relevant to ontology, but one agrees on the conclusion that it is fundamental to look not only at a discourse on being but at "our" representation that we are able to give in relation to it which, necessarily, it crosses language. It is clear, then, that this accent reminds us that the claim here then becomes in some way relative to the formation of a shared identity, of a "we" that, as such, founds - and expresses itself through - a certain language.

[7] M. Barberis, *Breve storia della filosofia del diritto*, Il Mulino, Bologna, 2004, pp. 62–63.

[8] N. Ginzburg, *Lessico famigliare*, Einaudi, Turin, 1963.

[9] Semantic Web, conceptualized by Tim Berners-Lee, emerged in the late 1990s as an extension of the World Wide Web, which itself was proposed in 1989. The foundational languages for the Semantic Web, such as RDF and OWL, were developed in the early 2000s. While the term "ontology" gained prominence in AI and knowledge representation during the 1980s, the concept of the Semantic Web was introduced later, building upon these earlier discussions.

"From this conception derives the idea of formal ontology, to be read as a formal theory of modes of being. The construction of the theory coincides with the definition of the semantics of a logical language that defines the entities we are talking about and the relationships between these entities, with the aim of expressing, through this language, all the theories whose validity is accepted, or, more properly, of defining the conditions of validity of a certain theory". It is interesting, although it is precisely that particular attention to the ways of being and the *meanings* that these entities have, also thanks to the technological and algorithmic evolution that will follow the time coeval with this contribution, that it is possible to support the need for a transition (linguistic, modeling, but also operational) from ontologies to epistemologies, all the more so when we are called upon to evaluate the issue of compliance. From the possible representation of being, we pass to that of the knowledge of its meanings and of the relations that exist between them. The issue of compliance with a binding and directly applicable European regulatory standard on data protection seems adequate to support the need for such a "meta semantic" evolution.

In fact, for each provision that we consider essential to the provisions of the GDPR, we assess whether it has been transposed, in what form and we say that – from the point of view of semantics – it is compliant. We can do this, also thanks to the semantic web and, in some way, with the "lenses" of the Deming cycle, such as the ability to plan, do, check, act, when regarding a given set of entities, we can, starting from a hierarchy, establish domain relationships capable, all in all, of shaping the world (TLD).

In the formal ontological computer approach, the object, identified with a language of knowledge representation, also becomes - in some way - the ultimate mission of the instrument in question, that is, the ability to represent a "target universe". It can be potentially universal (top level domain) or limited (i.e., the legal context) in this sense Husserl's definitions of "regional" ontologies seem adequate. On closer inspection, however, it is not only the characteristics of the entities that are of interest to this semantic modelling, which has been made more complex thanks to artificial intelligence, but also its meanings and the relationships that these significations assume in relation to concepts, sub-concepts, semantic (but also factual) relationships between concepts (e.g. between the concept of normative provision and the concept of crime). If the existence of both hierarchical and non-hierarchical relationships is known and has been formalized for some time, it is the choice, i.e. the presence of a certain degree of agreement, consensus (accordance) to establish whether a given content, with respect to its properties, is to some extent related to the standard. The larger the reference set, the more the validation by the knowledge involved by this context will lead to its breadth, variability, qualitative and quantitative.

Well, artificial intelligence models involve the use of a "trained" algorithm, capable - among other things - of interpreting - that is, of recognizing and assigning meaning (preferably plural) to certain entities. How the algorithm is able to read and interpret reality is in some way a topic related to the so-called explainability that will not be the subject of in-depth analysis here.

However, for the purposes of this contribution, we can distinguish a descriptive knowledge, which is based on a standard defined a priori and which, therefore, can be called ontology, from an interpretative knowledge, capable of constructing, learning, interpreting the world according to standards that it is capable of constructing ex post, which we will therefore call epistemology.

"*Episteme*", guide, already as the bow of the ship in Greek culture[10] to the conquest of knowledge and reality, is what remains, what diverges from truth ("*aletheia*") in its only apparent significance which, as Aristotelian thought would have it, cannot be otherwise than how it is manife_sta(tion) and, therefore, how it is possible to know it.

"This 'staying' in an absolute way is expressed by Greek philosophy with the word *epistéme*, where the theme '*steme*' (from the Indo-European root 'sta') indicates precisely the 'staying' of what is and that imposes itself 'on' ('epi') any force that wants to deny it, shake it, knock it down. What cannot be otherwise is the incontrovertible, it is how things are (...) The principle of non-contradiction, which dominates the entire history of the West, states (...) that it is necessary for entities to be entities, 'when they are', but that it is not necessary for entities to be; which means that it is necessary that beings have been nothing, before they have been, and return to being nothing, after having been. That is, the principle of non-contradiction is, at the same time, the affirmation that the entities that manifest themselves become, that is, come out of nothingness and return to it; and in turn becoming, as it is understood in the thought of the West, is at the same time the affirmation of the principle of non-contradiction, that is, of the principle according to which it is impossible that, when beings are, they are nothing, but that it is necessary that in a different time, beings have been and return to being nothing".[11]

[10] On this etymological heterotopia perhaps lies the inveterate use of the term resilience in the field of cyber security as well as, by now, as an expression of common sense after the most recent crises of the human.

[11] E. Severino, *Discussions around the sense of truth*, Edizioni ETS, Pisa 2009, pp. 11–22.

The "discourse" on the episteme, on its historical and cognitive variability, will be made famous, through the thought of Ferrier, Kuhn, Popper, also by Foucault's reflections capable of uniting the horizon of thought with that of the language of different historical eras for the interpretation of the same as well as of the present, applied to different *entities.*[12] For all the reasons better considered above, the first theoretical and then terminological passage seems coherent and appropriate even when applied to artificial intelligence, that is, applied to machines capable of using skills usually conducted to human animals (and partly also non-humans) such as learning, evaluation, reasoning.

In the first generations of artificial intelligence, a knowledge base was created in which to formalize "rules" capable of managing all cases and for which, given a certain "problem" for the solution of the same, adequate rules were provided for the resolution of the specific case. In generative AI which, as such, is based on so-called deep learning techniques, everything changes. That is, applications are born that, looking at "natural" language, are able to learn directly by analyzing real cases (the reference to clinical-legal methodology is not irrelevant here also in the field of artificial intelligence) become somehow capable of learning by doing, of learning by doing, capable of being applied to new problems with respect to those in question and, therefore, capable of re-recognizing and interpreting the datum of reality. In this case, there is no plan to standardize all the rules, but rather "to learn how to make them" (Carnelutti would have said)[13] looking at the opportunity of real and experiential cases as a necessary result of conscious and conscious legal learning. That is, it is required to extract knowledge dynamically (i.e. by interpreting) with numerical representations and, therefore, capable of reproducing the most appropriate classification mechanism to respond. This result would be explainable through contrasting paradigms between deductive approaches, such as those grounded in symbolic AI and ontological models, rely on predefined rules and expert knowledge and inductive approaches, particularly those seen in subsymbolic AI, focusing on learning patterns and representations directly from raw data.[14]

In short, regardless of the text and classification, with a new demand for analysis, these techniques are able to reproduce meaning without an ex-ante formalization and, therefore, also of unsupervised learning, i.e. without the need for examples and cases already solved for the successful purpose of learning as was the case in the first generations, not independent of human intervention.

[12] M. Foucault, *Storia della follia nell'età classica*, Biblioteca Universale Rizzoli, Milan, 2006.

[13] F. Carnelutti, *Clinica del diritto*, Rivista di diritto processuale civile, 1935.

[14] Such brief mention highlights symbolic AI era but leaves the broader transition toward inductive, sub symbolic methods underexplored due to the space granted.

3 Compliance and ICT Challenges: From Ontologies to Epistemologies Models

The issue of compliance, however, is not without challenges in legal informatics. Such dimensions hold together not only the renewed and expanded dimension of the effectiveness of European legislation far way beyond the borders of the European Union (both in the case of the GDPR and with respect to NIS II)[15] but also the changes that society imposes on the Law and that, conversely, the law imposes on society.[16]

In any case, the data analyzed so far allow us to imagine new epistemologies of compliance that look at different "ontologies" in Philosophy of Law.

Specifically, we can distinguish regulatory compliance[17] from other forms of compliance which, in any case, do not deviate from those methods that look at the distancing from risks, thanks to certifications of reliability "on paper". This makes it possible to distinguish:

a) Hard (law) Regulatory compliance on policies and processes (and their regulatory meaning and influence) on effective adopted practices and internal documents.

[15] See M. Buffa, *The NIS II Directive.* Cybersecurity in Europa: tra innovazione, formazione e diritto vivente, Democrazia e Diritti sociali, I/2023, p.5, where it is recalled how this circumstance brings with it, according to some authors, some possible problematic drifts.

[16] "Due to the shift towards information and knowledge-driven economies, the use of software intensive information systems is increasing. When it comes to legislations such as the GDPR, companies need to ensure that the data processing and sharing carried out by such systems complies with relevant legal obligations. Ensuring compliance is important, otherwise non-compliance can lead to large penalties and reputation damage. As such, companies often rely on compliance assessment tools that can be used to help them to assess if their existing business processes and systems comply with relevant legal obligations. From a requirements perspective, it is important that compliance tool vendors are able to demonstrate the exhaustiveness of their tool in terms of legal obligations, as wrong conclusions could potentially be drawn from incomplete assessments. Ensuring traceability i.e. providing references to the legislation text is considered to be important for such tools. References, for instance, allow companies to consult the legislations in case of confusion or if they need to verify an assessment. Also, it is important that such tools are kept up-to-date and are capable of taking into account updated legal interpretation of the relevant regulations. For instance, the GDPR mentions appropriate measures for security (Article 32.1) where the measure of appropriateness can change over time". (Agarwal S.:2018).

[17] "For one type of risk there is a lack of adequate ICT support: regulatory compliance. Companies such as banks and insurance companies are required by Law to ensure compliance with a plethora of regulations. The risks of failure to comply with regulations are increasing in volume and complexity. The financial crisis, there is increasing awareness in the compliance world that information systems can play a larger role in improving regulatory compliance. Regulatory compliance is extremely complex, and there are not many legal experts in the field. Medium-sized institutions may employ compliance officers to monitor activities, but they are not really expert in the law. They trawl through various sources to find legislative changes and influential cases. For particularly difficult areas, they seek the guidance of expensive lawyers expert in this field. But the information is sought on an ad-hoc basis, is not stored and managed effectively, and not linked to terminology and relevant legislation for a true understanding of the law. (*Boella G. et al: 2019).*

b) Soft (law) compliance that seems to be more focused on lessical, semantic dimension of conformities that must be considered different from a mere textual comparison.

Regulatory compliance seems to be more complex to analyze and fulfil (also in terms of Deming's cycle perspective in terms of PDCA: Plan, do, check, act) designing a syllogistic model, able to be captured also thanks to those language modeling techniques that, when encountered with AI technologies, can make us understand and capture meanings beyond textual phrases and paraphrases. In this light, in fact, of particular interest seems to be the ability to look beyond the concepts and their plural meanings (and mechanisms underlying) of computer ontologies (and of signification) to look at new epistemological foundations capable of "understanding" and "explaining" this complexity.

The difference is philosophically (as much as it is informatic)[18] relevant. If the models of ontology proposed so far have been limited, at least in part, to a semantic perspective linked to "being" (compliant), looking at new (and plural) epistemologies in this context is an attempt to understand and explain human and non-human cognitive processes at the basis of evaluations of a knowledge (and knowing) compliant capacity with the tension to reconstruct the different phases of the intelligibility of dispositions (and target documents that derive from them).

[18] Such ontologies seems to be overall based on standards, while epistemologies will be based, as we will see, on algorithmic interpretations from AI: "The management of large repositories of norms, the semantic access to these norms, and the legal reasoning based on them are key challenges in Computational Law, the branch of Legal Informatics concerned with the computational analysis of norms occurring in legislation and related documents (jurisprudence, recommendations from authoritative sources, doctrine, etc.), which are originally available in natural language only (…) In the years 2010–2016, research in Computational Law had primarily focused on the application of Natural Language Processing (NLP) methods to legal texts, particularly to design legal document management systems to assist legal professionals in retrieving the information they are interested in (…) This is often done by transforming the source legal documents into XML standards and tagging the relevant information. Subsequent phases are devoted to archiving and querying the XML files (…) An ontology called PrOnto (Privacy Ontology) has been developed following a thorough ontology development methodology called MeLON (Palmirani et al., 2018d; Palmirani et al., 2018c; Palmirani et al., 2018b). The ontology has been then encoded in OWL2-DL. The latest version of PrOnto is described in (Palmirani et al., 2018a). PrOnto is built according to a modular structure. The ontology is designed in such a way that it models the essential European data protection rules contained in the GDPR, but these rules can be easily extended by attaching additional ontologies (for example, for domain-specific provisions, or for Member State legislation). PrOnto concepts are also tagged within the Akoma Ntoso representation mentioned in the previous point and with the predicates used in the DAPRECO knowledge base, as shown below, via LegalRuleML tags". (Robaldo et al.: 2020). It would be relevant to discuss the use of RDF/XML, or even more advanced knowledge representation frameworks. These technologies are better suited for enabling interoperability, richer querying capabilities, and more meaningful data integration in digital law and justice systems but granted space does not allow for such deepening.

4 On the Artificial Intelligence Act and NIS II Model: A Risk-Based Approach

As is well known, the issue of compliance has also recently been at the center of reflections within the institutions of the European Union on AI. The AI Act was adopted in 2024 aiming, first, to create a single market for AI thanks to the possibility of the free movement, establishment and recognition of AI systems that *comply* with EU rules. Increasing trust in AI, according to the EU institutions, will be possible only by ensuring that AI systems are liable, accountable, transparent and respecting ethical principles and fundamental rights. In this light, it is possible to anticipate how the risk-based approach is able to combine itself with a rights-based approach. Preventing and mitigating risks of AI is another main objective to be achieved by prohibiting or restricting the use of AI systems that present an unacceptable risk to the safety, health, dignity or autonomy of persons, or that could bring to a violation of democratic values. The EU is therefore interested in supporting innovation and excellence in AI systems and technologies by providing incentives, funding and guidance for the development and deployment of safe and ethical AI systems, and by promoting cooperation and coordination between Member States, institutions and stakeholders. Such recently approved Artificial Intelligence Act suggests therefore a new approach proposing an Anticipated Voluntary Compliance that could be able to retrace differences between a preventive model (voluntary, internal, reward-based) and a subsequent one (control, external/audit, sanction-fine-based). Such new regulation considers "That information is especially important with regard to general-purpose AI models that are planned to be released as open-source, given that, after open-source model release, necessary measures to ensure compliance with the obligations under this Regulation may be more difficult to implement (…) Providers should be able to rely on codes of practice to demonstrate compliance with the obligations. By means of implementing acts, the Commission may decide to approve a code of practice and give it a general validity within the Union, or, alternatively, to provide common rules for the implementation of the relevant obligations. Even if the system takes a risk-based approach and, therefore, the need for anticipating compliance proportional to minimal, limited, high, unacceptable risks, some considerations (such as the 168) reminds us that "compliance with this Regulation should be enforceable by means of the imposition of penalties and other enforcement measures. Member States should take all necessary measures to ensure that the provisions of this Regulation are implemented, including by laying down effective, proportionate and dissuasive penalties for their infringement, including in respect of the ne bis in idem principle".

Not very differently with NIS II directive, the regulation looks, in a preventive way, at the critical infrastructure system as interconnected and relevant in this light providing, by its article 8, in the section dedicated to Requirements for high-risk AI systems, that: "High-risk AI systems shall comply with the requirements laid down in this Section, taking into account their intended purposes as well as the generally acknowledged state of the art on AI and AI-related technologies" basing responsibility on providers: "providers shall be responsible for ensuring that their product is fully compliant with all applicable requirements required under applicable Union harmonization legislation. In ensuring the compliance of high-risk AI systems referred to in paragraph 1 with the requirements set out in this Section, and in order to ensure consistency, avoid duplications and minimize additional burdens, providers shall have a choice of integrating, as appropriate, the necessary testing and reporting processes, information and documentation they provide with regard to their product into documentation and procedures that already exist and are required under the Union harmonization legislation listed in Section A of Annex I". Most any (relevant) organization seeking compliance should perform a kind of preventive gap analysis to determine what existing governance structures, policies, processes, risk categories, metrics, etc., will need to be augmented so they can achieve compliance and answer regulators' questions efficiently, accurately, and to their approval. That could seem to be the easy part. The most uneasy one stays in the ability in (that doesn't sound just enforcement, but in the ability of) operationalizing and/or implementing the different steps to close the distances.

5 Conclusions and Implications

In such distances, it seems unavoidable that there is an unsurpassable need – consistent with national cybersecurity strategies – not to neglect a security assessment aimed at understanding what the most relevant risk factors and critical issues are. It can be a different assessment: in general, on a single area, or even on a process, which serves to understand the risk factors and identify the interventions that need to be implemented, taking into account active, passive, technological, human, but also organizational defenses, from which a plan of actions, roles, who and, finally, monitoring over time, with maintenance, variance analysis, stress test, follow-up. A cyclical process, where the continuous verifying seems to be necessary to ensure the capacity of demonstrating to be compliant, always consistent with the Deming cycle. Such models suggest the need for new epistemologies of compliance even more urgent to be adopted in different, and interoperable, contexts.

Acknowledgements. This work was supported in part by project SERICS (PE00000014) under the NRRP MUR program funded by the EU - NGEU. Views and opinions expressed are however those of the author only and do not necessarily reflect those of the European Union or the Italian MUR. Neither the European Union nor the Italian MUR can be held responsible for them.

References

Agarwal, S., Steyksal, S., Antunovic, F., Kirrane, S.: Legislative Compliance Assessment: Framework. Vienna University of Economics and Business, Austria, Model and GDPR Instantiation (2018)

Alibeigi, A., Munir, A.B., Karim, M.E., Asemic, A.: Towards standard information privacy, innovations of the new general data protection regulation. Lib. Philos. Pract. pp. 1–19 (2019). Retrieved from https://www.proquest.com/scholarly-journals/towards-standard-information-privacy-innovations/docview/2299763883/se-2

Barberis, M.: Breve storia della filosofia del diritto. Il Mulino, Bologna (2004)

Becher, S.I., Benoliel, U.: Law in books and law in action: the readability of privacy policies and the GDPR. In: Mathis, K., Tor, A. (eds.) Consumer Law and Economics. Economic Analysis of Law in European Legal Scholarship, vol. 9, pp. 179–204. Springer, Cham (2021). https://doi.org/10.1007/978-3-030-49028-7_9

Boella, G., Di Caro, L., Leone, V.: Semi-automatic knowledge population in a legal document management system, Artificial Intelligence and Law (2019)

Boella, G., Di Caro L., Humphreys L., Robaldo L, Torre, L.: Nlp challenges for eunomos, a tool to build and manage legal knowledge. In: Language resources and evaluation (LREC), pp 3672–3678 (2012)

Cardenas, S., National human rights institutions and state compliance. In: Assessing National Human Rights Institutions, pp. 29–51 (2020). https://doi.org/10.1017/CBO9781139019408.004

Carnelutti, F.: Clinica del diritto, Rivista di diritto processuale civile (1935)

Castano, S., Ferrara, A., Montanelli, S.: Course in ontologies and semantic web (2005)

Chayes, A.: The New Sovereignty: Compliance with International Regulatory Agreements (2008)

Foucault, M.: Storia della follia nell'età classica. Biblioteca Universale Rizzoli, Milano (2006)

Ginzburg, N.: Lessico famigliare. Einaudi, Turin (1963)

Jackman, D.: The Compliance Revolution: How Compliance Needs to Change to Survive. Wiley, Singapore (2015)

Palmirani, M.: Governatori, Modelling Legal Knowledge for GDPR Compliance Checking, IoS Press (2018)

Ross, S.: On legalities and linguistic: plain language legislation. Buffalo Law Review (1981)

Rustad, M., Koenig, T., Towards a global data privacy standard, Florida Law Review (2018)

Severino, E.: Discussions around the sense of truth, Edizioni ETS, Pisa, pp.11–22 (2009)

Zeni, N., Kiyavitskaya, N., Mich, L., Cordy. J. R., Mylopoulos, J.: supporting the extraction of rights and obligations for regulatory compliance. **20**(1), 1–22 (2015). https://doi.org/10.1007/s00766-013-0181-8 (2015)

Modelling Legal Enforcement with UFO-L: A Case from Swedish Healthcare

Jöran Lindeberg[1(✉)], Paul Johannesson[1], Erik Perjons[1], Martin Henkel[1], and Katarina Fast Lappalainen[2]

[1] Department of Computer and Systems Sciences, Stockholm University, Stockholm, Sweden
joran@dsv.su.se

[2] Department of Law, Stockholm University, Stockholm, Sweden

Abstract. Organisations are increasingly governed by complex and multilayered systems of rules and regulations. In heavily regulated sectors such as healthcare, compliance with these rules poses significant challenges. Not only can rule compliance conflict with organisational goals, but varying interpretations by enforcement actors can also lead to conflicting or unpredictable outcomes. Decisions by regulatory authorities and courts, equipped with fines and other sanctioning powers, create new institutional realities for organisations. One way to examine and understand these complex systems of rules and actors is through the use of ontologies. This paper aims to investigate how the UFO ontology, and, specifically, the legal core ontology UFO-L, can be used, or extended, for creating patterns for modelling of organisational rule enforcement. To facilitate this investigation, a legal case regarding Swedish healthcare was selected to identify requirements for an ontology for legal enforcement. These requirements were then compared with the representation capabilities of UFO-L. The investigation revealed strengths and weaknesses of UFO-L and provided suggestions for its modification.

Keywords: Enterprise modelling · Compliance · Rule enforcement · UFO-L · Ontology · Healthcare · Legal Design

1 Introduction

Organisations are increasingly controlled by vast and multilayered systems of rules and regulations. In particular in heavily regulated sectors, such as healthcare, complying with all rules is challenging. Not only do organisations have to balance compliance against other rules, such as profits or creating value for citizens, but they sometimes will also find that different rules will push them in opposite directions. What is permitted or not in a particular situation has to be determined by institutional actors at different levels.

Within an organisation, these levels can include, for example, an employee, their manager, and a compliance officer. This hierarchical chain then continues outside of the organisation. Typically, a public authority will be in charge

M. Saeki et al. (Eds.): ER 2024 Workshops, LNCS 14932, pp. 267–283, 2025.
https://doi.org/10.1007/978-3-031-75599-6_20

of enforcing compliance with the existing legislation. Organisations that do not accept this authority's decisions may have the possibility of appealing to a court, perhaps also to a second instance court. In cases of organisational collaborations, there can also exist an intermediate step between the internal rule and the external rules, composed of contracts and agreements.

Organisations, including their internal and external rules, are socio-technical systems that can be understood through the lens of *complex adaptive systems* (CAS) theory [6,20]. This is particularly strong in healthcare management [9,18, 19,22]. A CAS is composed of two fundamental elements: agents and constraints. Agents interact with each other according to the constraints, but the results of these interactions are far from certain. Agents will also receive feedback loops that allow them to evaluate the results of their actions and adapt accordingly by setting new constraints for themselves and others. As can be seen, organisations and regulations are part of a dynamic and indeterministic system in constant development at different levels. CAS theory recognises that the amount of control that can be exercised from above is limited, and even more so in organisational collaborations with loose constraints between actors.

Rules are key parts of social systems, but they are passive objects and can only achieve effects when they are mediated by actors [7]. Therefore, the enforcement of rules by institutional actors needs to be clearly understood both by the actors required to follow the rules and by those making the rules. Creating such a common understanding can be achieved through enterprise modelling. Although much research has been done on how enterprise modelling can facilitate compliance [16] and the use of ontologies in legal proceedings [21], less attention has been paid to modelling the legal enforcement apparatus that detects and corrects noncompliance.

In order to avoid having to reinvent the wheel, reusable meta-models, such as ontologies, have been developed for a multitude of domains. However, to the best of our knowledge, there is no ontology or reusable pattern for rule enforcement. One well-founded legal core ontology that has been used in a number of domains is UFO-L. This core ontology extends the Unified Foundational Ontology (UFO) to the legal domain. However, its capabilities to represent rule enforcement have not yet been investigated. Thus, our research aim in this paper is to clarify how UFO-L can be used to model organisational rule enforcement. Concretely, we propose a number of modelling patterns that can be useful for designers of information systems with aspects of legal enforcement.

Laws and regulation can be seen as externally imposed organisational rules and are often tightly intertwined with internal rules. Legislation is also usually well structured and publicly available. Such patterns can contribute to sensemaking for both lawmakers and regulated entities. Organisations need to understand their environment. In addition, at least large and formally advanced organisations will have their own procedures for monitoring, interpretation, and conflict resolution, resembling those of the legal enforcement system.

The remainder of this paper is as follows. Section 2 first presents a case of legal enforcement that is analysed and abstracted. Section 3 then reviews a number of legal modelling patterns based on UFO, which are used for designing our legal enforcement patterns. Section 4 presents our main contribution in the form of two complementary patterns of legal enforcement by regulatory authorities and courts. Section 5 discusses possible adaptations of UFO-L and presents additional preliminary patterns as illustrations. Section 6 concludes.

2 Methodology

2.1 Case Selection

The methodology involved testing UFO-L against a real-world case of rule enforcement. The case was selected according to the following criteria. First, the case should be sufficiently complex to provide a challenge for UFO-L. Previous research suggested that the domain of health data, characterised by heavy regulation, intricate care chains, and value conflicts between the right to health and the right to personal integrity, provides an interesting setting [14]. Second, the case should already have undergone a number of interventions by the legal enforcers. Third, for pragmatic reasons, the case should also be well documented. The chosen case was identified in a lawsuit between a private emergency hospital in Sweden, Capio S:t Görans sjukhus (hereafter referred to as the "Hospital") and the Swedish Authority for Privacy Protection (Integritetsskyddsmyndigheten, IMY)[1] IMY has been designated as the supervisory authority with respect to the General Data Protection Regulation, GDPR, and the Data Protection Act (2018: 218), DPA, as well as the Patient Data Act (2008:355) and other data protection laws in Sweden.

2.2 Data Collection and Data Analysis

The dominant source for information about the case is the judgment by the Stockholm Administrative Court of Appeal, which includes the judgment by the County Administrative Court as well as the decision by IMY[2]. When needed, complementary information was searched, including, for example, references in legal articles and case law, and the IMY website. The analysis searched for semantic triples that explain the interaction: how the actors interacted, what was the legal basis for the interaction, and what were the legal implications of the interaction. A *semantic triple* is a subject-predicate-object statement, e.g. "Judgment X-*cites*-Legislation Y", or "IMY-*appeals*-Judgment X". The extracted triples were represented as an informal model[3]

[1] For information in English, see https://www.imy.se/en/news/deficiencies-in-how-healthcare-providers-control-staff-access-to-patient-journal-data/.

[2] Kammarrätten i Stockholm, judgment 16 May 2022, case n° 4548-21; Förvaltningsrätten i Stockholm, judgment 26 May 2021, case n° 25868-20; Datainspektionen, decision 2 December 2020, ref. n° DI-2019-3846.

[3] The informal model is available as a Kumu.io map at https://kumu.io/joran/legal-enforcement-informal-model-jusmod2024.

2.3 Case Description

The case is summarised in the following timeline.

1. In March-April 2019 IMY conducted audits of eight health care providers, of which one was the Hospital regarding its electronic health record (EHR) systems. The legal base for the audit is Art. 58 in GDPR and Chap. 6, Sect. 1 of the DPA.
2. IMY concluded that the Hospital failed to undertake technical and organisational measures according to Art. 32 GDPR due to the lack of documentation in regard to the needs and risks analysis it is obligated to provide according to the regulations of the National Board of Health and Welfare to guide its assessments of the personnel's need to access information in the health records and the risks that this entails. IMY decided on a fine of 30 million SEK (equivalent to 2,6 million EUR). The legal basis for the sanctioning capabilities is Art. 58.2 in GDPR.
3. The Hospital appealed to the County Administrative Court (Förvaltningsrätten), the court of first instance. The court partly rejected the appeal but reduced the fine to a third.
4. Both IMY and the Hospital appealed to the Administrative Court of Appeal. The appeal court rejected the decision of IMY. It held that there was no basis in the GDPR to fine the hospital and that IMY had not proven that the hospital had not carried out its duties according to the rules and regulations applicable to the case.
5. IMY requested a leave to appeal to the Supreme Administrative Court (Högsta Förvaltningsdomstolen), the court of third instance. However, leave was not granted.

2.4 Abstracted Case Description

The IMY case was abstracted to the following general description: The case involves a public authority (in this case, IMY) using its legal mandate to audit the compliance of an organisation (in this case, the hospital) with specific regulations. Based on its findings and legal argumentation, the public authority makes an administrative decision which includes imposing sanctions if noncompliance is found. This decision is documented and creates new legal implications for the organisation, such as requirements to implement changes or payment of administrative fines. The organisation affected by the decision has the right to appeal in court. The court then reviews the case, potentially modifying or overturning the authority's decision. The final judgment can uphold, alter, or nullify the initial administrative decision by the public authority, depending on the court's interpretation of the law and the evidence provided.

2.5 Delimitations

To reduce the complexity of the model, a number of delimitations were established.

- The existing legislation was taken as given.
- The legal reasoning behind the decisions was not represented. We already know that UFO-L can do this. However, it was represented that certain legal provisions were invoked.
- We were not modelling the internal organisational events that had legal implications, such as how the Hospital managed its information systems, only the legal events that followed, such as investigation and interpretation.
- As for legal rights and duties that came into play during the process, the only ones represented were those that were made explicit from the final judgment AND involved the inspected organisation.
- People are not represented, only organisations.
- Differences in jurisdictions are not represented.

Then, we translated the informal model into a UFO-L compliant model. If needed, we would extend UFO with necessary elements. The modelling language used was OntoUML [1], a UML extension based on UFO [2]. In OntoUML, both classes and associations has stereotypes that correspond to UFO. The tool used was the OntoUML Visual Paradigm Plugin [3].

3 Fundamental Legal Modelling Patterns

We reviewed recent studies of legal modelling patterns that could provide a basis for the design of our rule enforcement patterns and found the following specific ontologies within the broader UFO framework:

- UFO-B, which is part of the foundational level of UFO, and represent events [5].
- UFO-L, a legal core ontology. It was originally created by Griffo as a doctoral thesis [10] grounded in theory by the legal scholars Wesley Newcomb Hohfeld and Robert Alexy. According to Hohfeld, all legal relations can be broken down into corresponding rights-duties, powers-liabilities, etc. [15]. In contrast, Alexy puts more emphasis on interpreting and balancing colliding principles (see, for example, [4]). UFO-L has been used to model, e.g., judicial decision making [11], and how legal powers can be manifested in legal events that create new rights and duties [12].
- A core ontology on decision making, which we will refer to as UFO-D [13].

In the following, we will present and depict the identified patterns. The presentation includes rudimentary information about UFO; for a more detailed understanding, we refer to the sources mentioned above.

Figure 1 represents that an actor with a Legal Role takes part in a Legal Event. Griffo et al. state that "legal events (e.g. signing of contracts, breaking laws, paying taxes, etc.) can create, change, or extinguish legal relations" [12, p. 5]. For practical modelling purposes, this means that a Legal Event creates, modifies, or terminates a Legal Relator between two parties. A party can be represented as an Actor or Role. It follows that the creation of general rules, such as lawmaking, also must be a Legal Event. A Legal Relator can be, for example, that a parent decides over a child, that a school must provide quality education for a child, or that the school must send reports to the ministry of education. Figure 1 also shows that a Legal Relator can be fulfilled, through manifestation, by other Legal Events.

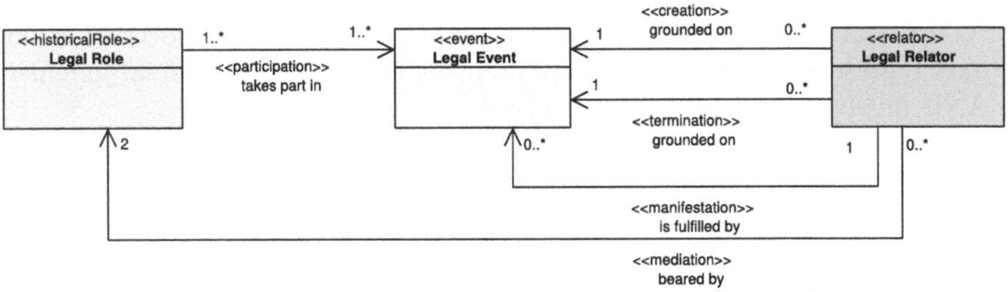

Fig. 1. The Legal Actor-Event-Relator pattern, derived from UFO-L [12, Figure 2] and UFO-B [5, Figure 4]. Note that the OntoUML plugin for Visual Paradigm that was used lacks an association stereotype for <modification>, which is why only the <creation> and <termination> stereotypes are used in the diagrams.

Figure 2 expands the workings of the Legal Relator. As mentioned, the Legal Relator is a so-called truthmaker of a relation between a Right Holder and a Duty Bearer. The Right and Duty that are parts of the Legal Relator provide details for each party. Note that Rights and Duties are Modes, which are characteristics of one party, and can also be externally dependent of the other party. Also note that the Right-Duty pair is only one out of several UFO-L patterns of corresponding relations. Another example is Power-Subjection, which is used for expressing that one party can unilaterally create Duties for the other.

Figure 3 shows that a normative legal description, such as a law, a court decision document, or a contract, is prescribed by at least one Agentive Legal Institution, i.e. a formally established organisation. It also shows that the Legal Norms that are expressed in a Legal Normative Description are separate from their description. As can be understood from the multiplicity, some norms do not need a legal document to exist, such as customary law. The figure also shows that from the UFO-L legal hierarchy it can be deduced that Legal Role, Legal Event, and Legal Relator are all subclasses of Legal Thing, which can be defined by a Legal Normative Description [11, Figure 3]. Finally, the figure shows that a Legal Normative Description must somehow be created, namely through a Legal Event. In other words, Legal Events create Legal Relators both directly (Event-*create*-Relator) and indirectly (Event-*create*-Legal Normative Description-*defines*-Legal Relator).

Figure 4 provides a basic representation of the legislative life cycle. As mentioned, lawmaking is outside the scope of this article, but this pattern is still included since we will adapt it to the life cycle of appealable legal decision documents. The figure shows how a Lawmaker makes a Legislative Enactment,

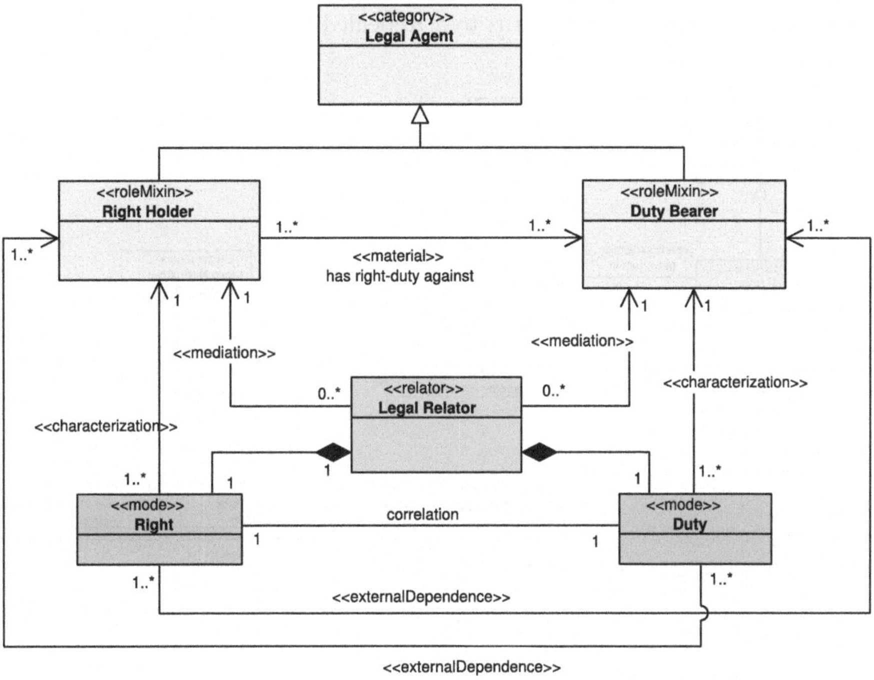

Fig. 2. The Legal Relator-Modes pattern, slightly adapted from UFO-L [11, Figure 4].

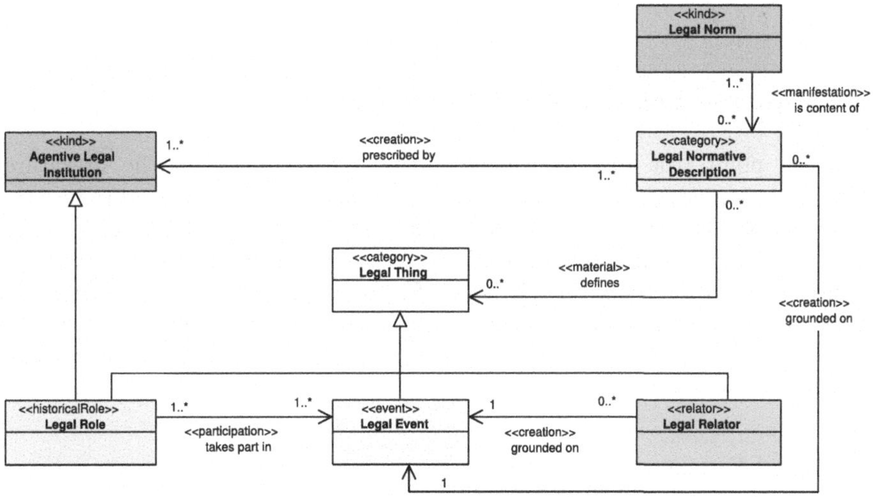

Fig. 3. The Legal Normative Description-Legal Norm-Legal Thing pattern, derived from UFO-L [11, Figure 3].

creating a new Piece of Legislation. The legislation is later repealed by the same Lawmaker, which changes its status to a Repealed Piece of Legislation.

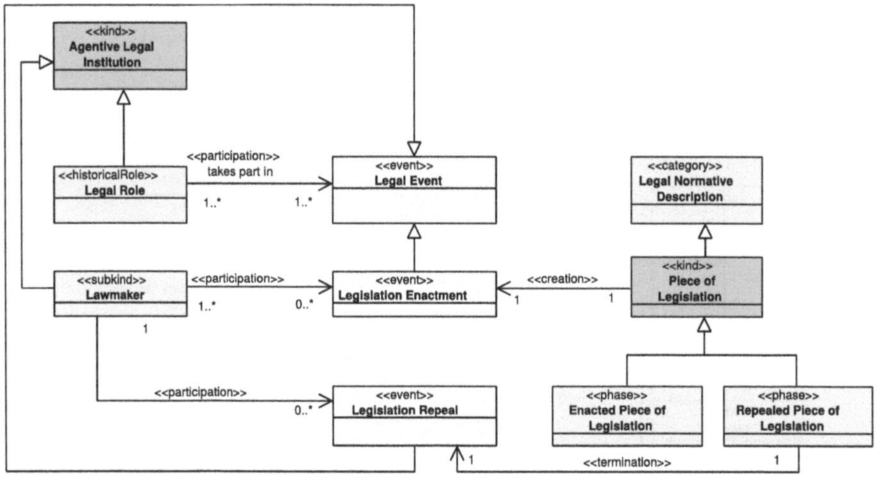

Fig. 4. The Legislation Enactment-Repeal pattern, derived from UFO-B, [5, Figure 2, Fig. 4].

The pattern from UFO-D confirms that a decision (e.g. a Legislative Enactment), is a type of Event that is done by an actor (e.g. a Lawmaker), and has a consequence (e.g. a Piece of Legislation). These relations have already been covered in Fig. 4.

4 Proposed Legal Enforcement Patterns

Until this point, the discussed patterns have been found in the literature, although presented with some adaptations, mainly to save space and reduce the complexity of the diagrams. In the following, they will be used to design two new patterns, needed to represent the legal enforcement case summarised in Sect. 2.4. The first pattern, presented in Fig. 5 and Fig. 6, covers the legal enforcement by a supervisory authority. The second pattern, presented in Figs. 7, Fig. 8, and Fig. 9, shows what happens if the supervised organisation appeals the decision of the supervisory authority.

4.1 Legal Enforcement Pattern

This pattern is divided into two overlapping diagrams. The first shows the legal situation that allows the legal enforcement, and the second depicts how the legal enforcement unfolds.

As can be seen in Fig. 5, the enactment of a law has created Legal Relators which gives a designated Supervisory Authority, for example an Independent Supervisory Authority as defined by GDPR, the right to conduct audits and also the power to impose administrative sanctions against a Supervised Organisation, including warning, reprimand, order (including restrictions and prohibitions), and an administrative fine.

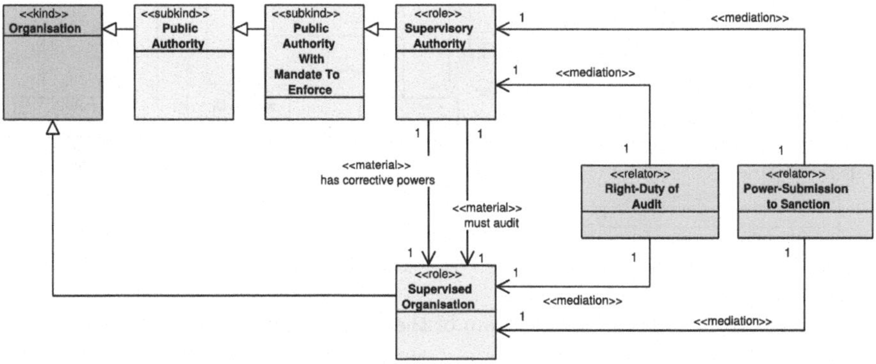

Fig. 5. The Legal Basis diagram of the Legal Enforcement Pattern.

Figure 6 expands on Fig. 5, adding the events that are manifestations of the Legal Relators. The two classes Audit and Sanction Decision are both subclasses of Legal Case Decision, which in turn is a subclass of Legal Decision. (The Audit could have been broken down into several events, from the decision to audit, to the actual audit, but to simplify, it is treated as one single event.) An Audit is eventually followed by a decision by the Supervisory Authority, which may include use of a sanctioning capability. When the deadline for appeal has passed and the decision thus come into force, Legal Order Relators From Appealable Decision will be created or terminated.

However, if the decision is appealed, another complementing pattern is needed, which is presented in the next Section.

4.2 The Appeals Cycle Pattern

The Appeals Cycle Pattern represents what unfolds if an organisation that has been subject to sanctions by a supervising authority appeals.

Actors and Roles. We will start by unfolding the actors and roles shown in Fig. 7. In the domain of rule enforcement by Supervisory Authorities, the actors are organisations, either Public Authorities or Private Companies. A relevant Public Authority is either a Court or Authority With Mandate To Enforce. A Public Authority has a Legal Level, from a common authority to third (and final) instance in the court system. Any organisation can find itself as a Case Party in a legal case, and more specifically also as an Appealing Party.

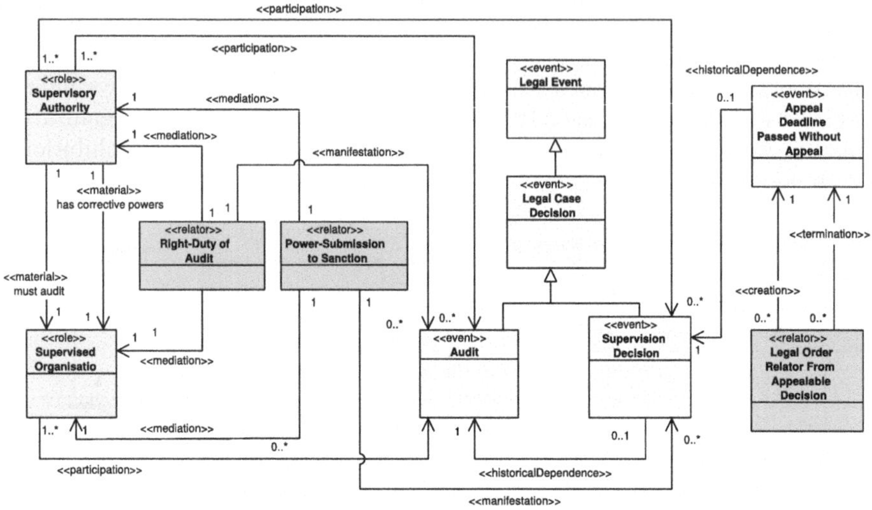

Fig. 6. The Decisions Diagram of the Legal Enforcement Pattern.

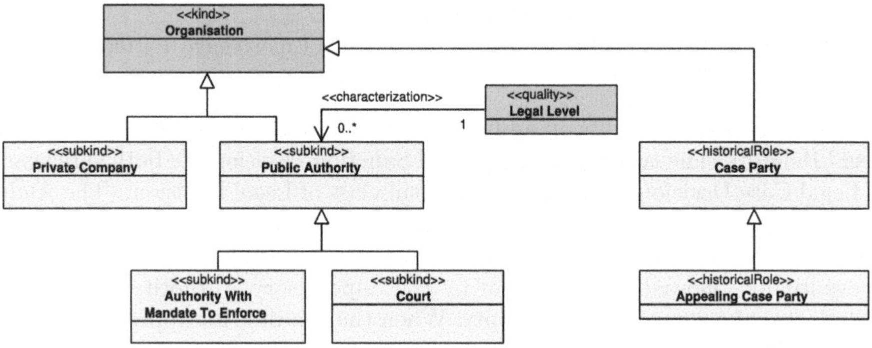

Fig. 7. The Actors and Roles diagram of the Appeals Cycle pattern.

Decisions and Legal Relators. As shown in Fig. 8, a Public Authority makes a Legal Case Decision in an individual case, which is also a manifestation of an Applicable Law Legal Relator. (The facts of the case, not shown here, are another input.) The *replaces* association expresses that an appealable decision can eventually be overruled or otherwise affected by another decision of a higher court. The most common types of legal decision would probably be to Confirm, Reject, or Modify a decision, but its also possible to Vacate (nullify/void a case due to an erroneous decision by a lower instance), or Dismiss it.

As expressed by the Object Constraint Language (OCL) restriction code next to the Legal Decision class, replacement can only be done through decisions by a higher court. An Appealable Legal Case Decision will eventually be either associated with an Appeal Made, or Appeal Deadline Passed Without Appeal

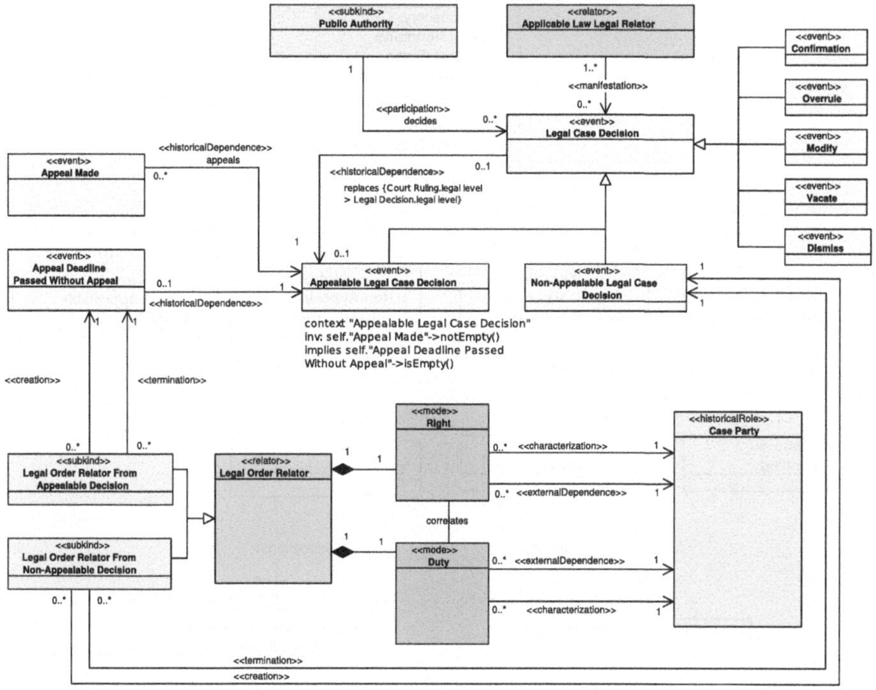

Fig. 8. The Decisions and Legal Relators Diagram of the Appeals Cycle Pattern.

will occur, as expressed by the other OCL restriction code in the centre of the figure. The latter alternative will, just as a Non-Appealable Legal Case Decision, lead to the respective subclass of Legal Order Relator entered into force.

Each Legal Relator can be broken down to a corresponding Right and Duty, which are Legal Modes. If a court has ruled, for example, that the Hospital would have to pay an administrative fine to the Swedish state, this would entail four relations. Two of those involve the right of the state to enforce and collect the fine. This right is inherent to the state, but it is also externally dependent on the actor that has the duty to pay, which in this case is the Hospital. The other two associations, in a corresponding manner, involve the duty of the Hospital to pay.

Documents and Appeals. A Legal Case Decision is formulated in a Legal Order Document, either appealable or not, as shown in Fig. 9. An Appealable Legal Order Document will first be Pending, and will then either be part of an appeal or not.

An Appeal is made by a Case Party and will also involve the Court that receives the appeal. This event ends the circle, and the new court will make a new decision.

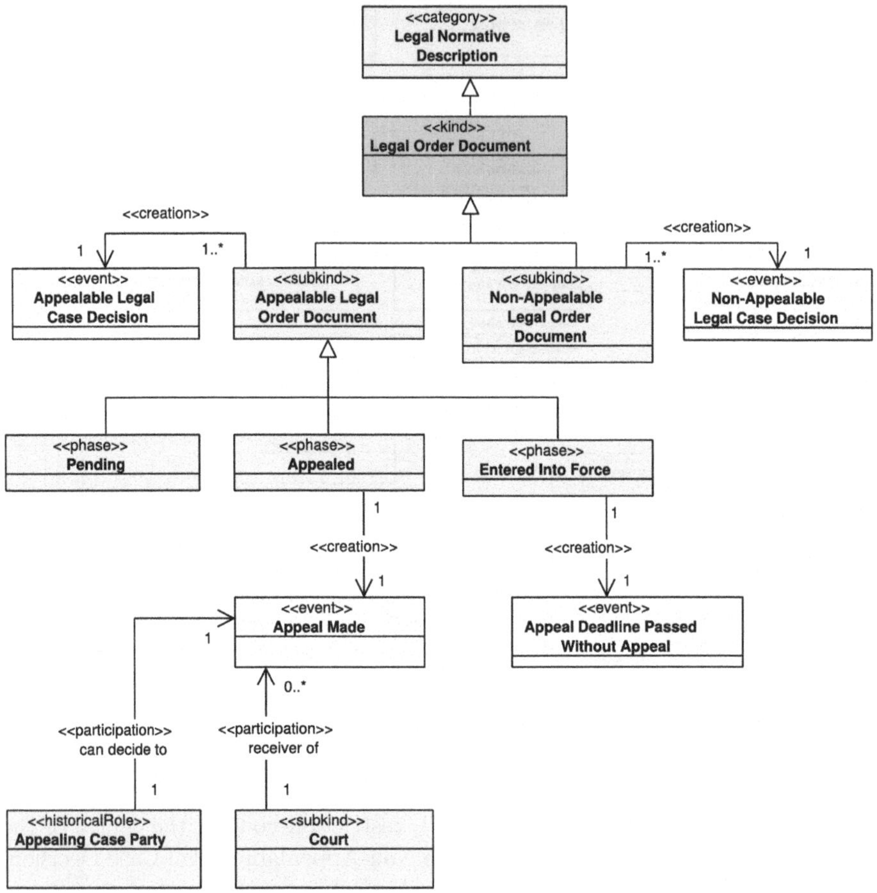

Fig. 9. The Documents and Appeals Diagram of the Appeals Cycle Pattern.

5 Discussion About Alternative Patterns

In the previous section, we proposed two new patterns for representing legal enforcement by supervisory authorities. Based on this experience, in this section, we will discuss perceived challenges with UFO-L, and explore opportunities for modifications. In so doing, we will also propose additional alternative patterns that extend the ones in this paper.

5.1 Legal Norm, Legal Relator, and Legal Decision

The relation between Legal Norm and Legal Relator requires further investigation. We consider these two constructs to be closely related; however, we do not find a relation in the UFO-L models that we have studied. As modelled by UFO-L, Legal Events create Legal Relators, which are manifested as new Legal

Events, and so forth [12]. We believe that this makes sense as long as Legal Normative Descriptions and Legal Norms [10] are not included, but when they are, it seems reasonable that at least one of these constructs could affect future legal decisions. After all, when legal experts argue their decisions, they often refer to texts and norms.

As shown in Fig. 3 presented in Sect. 3, a Legal Relator, like any Legal Thing, can be defined by a Legal Normative Description [11]. Moreover, a Legal Norm can, but does not have to, be expressed by a Legal Normative Description. A common example of Legal Norms without association to a Legal Normative Text is customary law. The question then becomes: How can UFO-L represent the association between a customary Legal Norm and a Legal Relator? It appears that it cannot, which we consider a limitation. On the other hand, in many domains, it can probably be expected that all Legal Norms are expressed in Legal Normative Descriptions. Also for pragmatic reasons it could often be best to simply associate Legal Relators to Legal Normative Descriptions, and not represent the separation between text and norm, which could probably sometimes be impractical.

A Legal Relator always defines a legal relation between parties. In contrast, a Legal Norm, in our understanding, is not limited to expressing bilateral relationships. In our understanding, Hohfeld [15] would argue that all legal realities can be expressed as relationships between two parties. However, Alexy [4] would likely consider this an over-simplification, and argue for more focus on the distinction between rules and principles, and in particular how to balance principles in case of conflicts. Certainly, there are also legal scholars who would have other views. From a pragmatic modelling point of view, expressing all norms as relators would probably not be very efficient or comprehensible. Even if we accept Hohfelds claim that all legal realities *can be* expressed as relationships between two parties, this does not mean that they *should be.*

Considering the above, we do not think it is possible to make a logically solid association between legal norms and legal relators. However, what could be represented is that a legal norm influences a legal decision. A possible pattern is shown in Fig. 10. Here, we have also included the facts of the case. The facts of the case could probably also be modelled as Legal Relators by representing the legal relations that the evidence leads to. However, that approach would not clearly distinguish between the facts and its interpreted legal implications. The advantage of the proposed pattern is its clear separation between the facts and the norms with which it is analysed. In summary, this pattern offers a new possibility for modelling decisions that constitute a vital part of legal enforcement.

5.2 Extending Legal Events

The Legal Events construct in UFO-L can be used for many different things that have legal implications. First, according to Burns and Flam [7], social actors can interact with rules in three ways: creating, interpreting, and implementing. In UFO-L, a Legal Event can be a formally defined institutional action, such as a legislator enacting new laws, or a court decision, as well as any natural act that

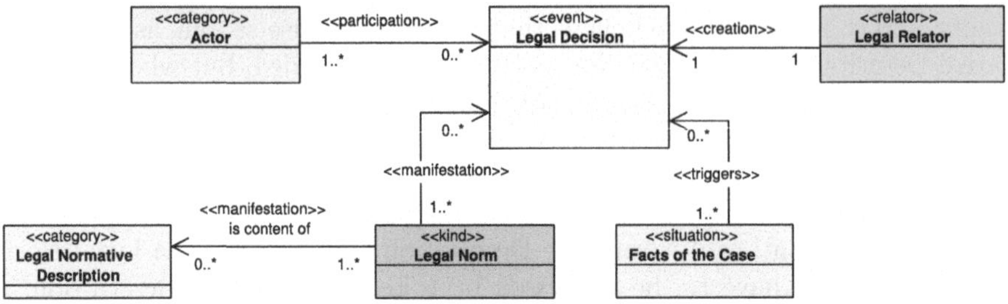

Fig. 10. Alternative Pattern 1: Facts and Legal Norms in Legal Decisions.

has legal implications, such as breaking the law [12, p. 5]. In other words, Legal Event can represent all three interaction types. Second, Legal Events can in our understanding be a) legislative acts, which can create legal relators affecting millions of people, b) court orders, that is often only between two particular parties but can also affect whole categories of actors, and c) events that are not institutional but have legal implications, such as following or breaking a law. Third, the implementation of the law can be done by both action and inaction [17]. Figure 11 shows how these dimensions could be modelled.

5.3 Who Accepts a Legal Relator?

According to UFO-L, a Legal Relator is created by a Legal Event. An example is when someone clicks "I agree" on a user agreement on the Web [12]. From that moment on, most if not all legal experts would agree that there are a number of legal relators between the two parties: the user and the company. But there would likely be some legal relator that the company believes exists, that the client or a privacy watchdog would claim does not exist. Other stakeholders could have different views. Perhaps the dispute would be settled by a court, whose decision may eventually be overruled by another court. In other words: 1) not all legal relators are recognised by all actors, 2) some actors have a legal mandate to establish the legal truth, and 3) even these truths are only preliminary until no further appeals can be made.

In our patterns in Sect. 4, we delimited the model to only show legal relators from final court judgments. However, it could be useful to also represent the different views that are constructed through the legal process, or even the conflicting legal analysis by actors without a particular mandate. In Fig. 12, we show how conflicting opinions can be modelled. We find inspiration from another part of UFO-L, which states that a Legal Normative Description must be recognised by at least two agents [10]. We propose representing that an actor can accept or contest a Legal Relator (neutral actors would have no association). If an actor is the first to accept a legal relator, this event would also include establishing it. If a legal relator is no longer accepted by anyone, it is effectively nullified.

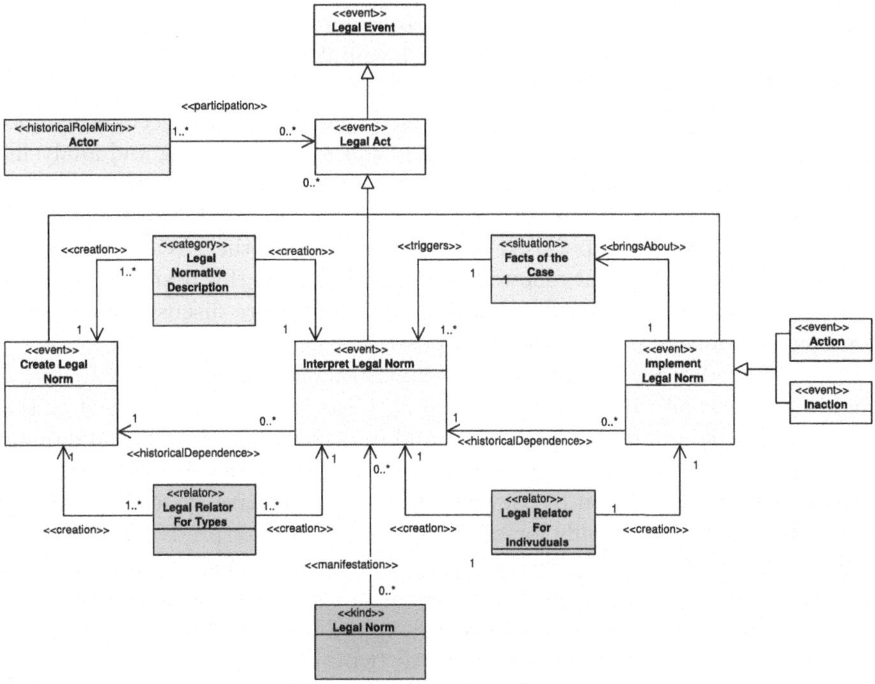

Fig. 11. Alternative Pattern 2: Extending Legal Events.

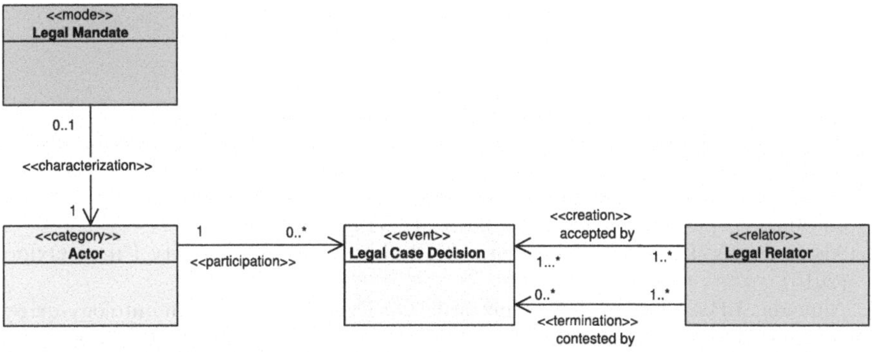

Fig. 12. Alternative Pattern 3: Legal Case Decision Accepting Legal Relator.

6 Conclusion

In this paper, UFO-L, a well-founded legal core ontology, was used to model the legal enforcement by supervisory authorities. The domain description was created through the analysis of a legal case from Swedish healthcare, in which an authority acting as independent supervisory authority, as defined by GDPR, supervised the management of a private hospital employees' access rights to electronic health records. The authority decided on a substantial administrative fine for the hospital, but the case was appealed, and eventually a second-instance court rejected the decision. The modelling began with identifying and analysing existing patterns from UFO-L and other relevant UFO contributions.

Two new patterns were designed: one for the legal process between the supervisory authority and the supervised organisation, and another, as a continuation, of the appeals processes that followed in courts. Based on this design experience, some possibilities for further development of UFO-L were discussed and corresponding preliminary patterns were proposed.

As mentioned in Sect. 1, the legal system is also interesting to study to understand organisational rules in general. The patterns for legal enforcement in this paper can also be useful for representing and understanding the internal dynamics of an organisation, or a collaboration of organisations. As also explained in Sect. 1, organisations can be viewed as complex adaptive systems (CAS). In these systems, one cannot fully foresee how rules will be interpreted and enforced, constantly recreating institutional realities. This complex and dynamic environment will be more manageable if represented in information systems. One possible future research direction could be to explore how organisational rules and their enforcement can be included in digital twins of organisations [8]. Another direction could be to design systems aimed at providing feedback for rule makers, including law makers, on how the consequences of their decisions unfold throughout an organisational system.

References

1. OntoUML specification. https://ontouml.readthedocs.io/
2. Unified Foundational Ontology (UFO) specification. https://dev.nemo.inf.ufes.br/seon/UFO.html
3. OntoUML visual paradigm plugin, May 2024. https://github.com/OntoUML/ontouml-vp-plugin, original-date: 2019-11-25T14:21:32Z
4. Alexy, R.: A Theory of Constitutional Rights. Oxford University Press, Oxford (2010)
5. Almeida, J.P.A., Falbo, R.A., Guizzardi, G.: Events as entities in ontology-driven conceptual modeling. In: Laender, A.H.F., Pernici, B., Lim, E.-P., de Oliveira, J.P.M. (eds.) ER 2019. LNCS, vol. 11788, pp. 469–483. Springer, Cham (2019). https://doi.org/10.1007/978-3-030-33223-5_39
6. Anderson, P.: Perspective: complexity theory and organization science. Organ. Sci. **10**(3), 216–232 (1999). https://doi.org/10.1287/orsc.10.3.216
7. Burns, T.R., Flam, H.: The Shaping of Social Organization. Swedish Collegium for Advanced Study in the Social Sciences. SAGE Publications, London, England, May 1987
8. Caporuscio, M., Edrisi, F., Hallberg, M., Johannesson, A., Kopf, C., Perez-Palacin, D.: Architectural concerns for digital twin of the organization. In: Jansen, A., Malavolta, I., Muccini, H., Ozkaya, I., Zimmermann, O. (eds.) ECSA 2020. LNCS, vol. 12292, pp. 265–280. Springer, Cham (2020). https://doi.org/10.1007/978-3-030-58923-3_18

9. Ellis, B.: 29. An overview of complexity theory: understanding primary care as a complex adaptive system. In: Sturmberg, J., Martin, C. (eds.) Handbook of Systems and Complexity in Health. Springer, New York (2013). http://dx.doi.org/10.1007/978-1-4614-4998-0
10. Griffo, C.: UFO-L: a core ontology of legal aspects built on legal relations perspective. Ph.D. thesis, Technological Center, Computer Science Department, Federal University of Espírito Santo State (2018)
11. Griffo, C., Almeida, J.P.A., Guizzardi, G.: Legal theories and judicial decision-making: an ontological analysis. In: Proceedings of the 11th International Conference (FOIS 2020). Frontiers in Artificial Intelligence and Applications, vol. 330, pp. 63–76 (2020), publication Title: Frontiers in Artificial Intelligence and Applications
12. Griffo, C., Almeida, J.P.A., Lima, J.A.O., Prince Sales, T., Guizzardi, G.: Legal powers, subjections, disabilities, and immunities: ontological analysis and modeling patterns. Data Knowl. Eng. **148**, 102219 (2023). https://doi.org/10.1016/j.datak.2023.102219, https://www.sciencedirect.com/science/article/pii/S0169023X23000794
13. Guizzardi, R., Carneiro, B.G., Porello, D., Guizzardi, G.: A core ontology on decision making. In: Proceedings of the XIII Seminar on Ontology Research in Brazil and IV Doctoral and Masters Consortium on Ontologies (ONTOBRAS 2020), vol. 2728, pp. 9–21. CEUR-WS (2020)
14. Henkel, M., Perjons, E., Lappalainen, K.F., Fors, U., Sjöberg, C.M.: Digitalization of health and social care collaboration: identification of problems and solutions. In: Joint Proceedings of RCIS 2024 Workshops and Research Projects Track. CEUR Workshop Proceedings, Guimarães, Portugal (2024). https://ceur-ws.org/Vol-3674/RP-paper8.pdf
15. Hohfeld, W.N.: Fundamental legal conceptions as applied in judicial reasoning. Yale Law J. **26**(8), 710–770 (1917), publisher: JSTOR
16. Kim, H., Fox, M., Sengupta, A.: how to build enterprise data models to achieve compliance to standards or regulatory requirements (and share data). J. Assoc. Inf. Syst. **8**(2) (2007). https://doi.org/10.17705/1jais.00115, https://aisel.aisnet.org/jais/vol8/iss2/5
17. Mário de Oliveira Rodrigues, C., Bezerra, C., Freitas, F., Oliveira, I.: Handling crimes of omission by reconciling a criminal core ontology with UFO. Appl. Ontol. **15**(1), 7–39 (2020). https://doi.org/10.3233/AO-200223, https://content.iospress.com/articles/applied-ontology/ao200223, publisher: IOS Press
18. Plsek, P.E., Greenhalgh, T.: Complexity science: the challenge of complexity in health care. BMJ: Br. Med. J. **323**(7313), 625–628 (2001). https://doi.org/10.1136/bmj.323.7313.625
19. Rouse, W.B.: Health care as a complex adaptive system: implications for design and management. Bridge-Washington-Natl. Acad. Eng. **38**(1), 17 (2008)
20. Turner, J.R., Baker, R.M.: Complexity theory: an overview with potential applications for the social sciences. Systems **7**(1), 4 (2019). https://doi.org/10.3390/systems7010004
21. Vafaie, M., Bruns, O., Pilz, N., Waitelonis, J., Sack, H.: CourtDocs ontology: towards a data model for representation of historical court proceedings. In: Proceedings of the 12th Knowledge Capture Conference 2023, K-CAP 2023, pp. 175–179. Association for Computing Machinery, New York, NY, USA, December 2023. https://doi.org/10.1145/3587259.3627562, https://dl.acm.org/doi/10.1145/3587259.3627562
22. Zimmerman, B.: How complexity science is transforming healthcare. In: The SAGE handbook of complexity and management, pp. 617–635. SAGE Publications Ltd (2011). https://doi.org/10.4135/9781446201084

The eu-FAIRnews: A Preliminary Exploration of Bridging Disinformation and Digital Justice Through FAIR Data Practices in Online News Sources

Antonella Calò(✉), Davide Damiano Colella, Marco Longo, Priamo Tarantino, Antonella Longo, and Marco Zappatore

Department of Engineering for Innovation, University of Salento, 73100 Lecce, Italy
{antonella.calo,antonella.longo,
marcosalvatore.zappatore}@unisalento.it, {davidedamiano.colella,
marco.longo,priamo.tarantino}@studenti.unisalento.it

Abstract. Freedom of speech is a crucial right. While the digital realm has allowed for greater expansion of free expression, it has also facilitated anonymous sharing of content. The veracity of news is increasingly threatened by the difficulty of tracking data, sources, and those responsible for data inconsistencies, which contribute to disinformation. Anonymity has become a potential threat, enabling the spread of disinformation without consequences and challenging regulations. The "untraceability" of data modifications, data inconsistencies, and anonymity of authors lead us to consider whether the FAIR (Findable, Accessible, Interoperable, Reusable) principles could be applied to news sources to determine if they can help counter disinformation, while still respecting the right to freedom of speech and enhancing the right to clear information for all and the journalists' right to professional integrity. The difficulties in regulating disinformation while respecting freedom of speech, combined with the increasing presence of anomalies in data from news sources and the lack of Italian corpora for training detection/prediction models, led us to develop the eu-FAIRnews. Initially conceived as a scraping tool to collect news and data from various sources, eu-FAIRnews is now being implemented to explore the compatibility of news sources and articles with the FAIR principles and their relation to news quality, disinformation, and digital justice. The eu-FAIRnews tool reflects real-world challenges in defending against this type of hybrid threat. Finally, the tool guides users through the visualization of data, results, and preliminary scores, enhancing transparency, accountability, and media awareness.

Keywords: FAIR Data · Disinformation · Hybrid Threat Defense · Digital Media Awareness · Digital Justice · Data Traceability · Censorship

1 Introduction and Theoretical Background

With the digital age, the dissemination of content online has become easier, allowing people to express themselves with more freedom. However, this ease has also introduced a new threat: the proliferation of disinformation. As Wardle notes [1], distinguishing truth

M. Saeki et al. (Eds.): ER 2024 Workshops, LNCS 14932, pp. 284–301, 2025.
https://doi.org/10.1007/978-3-031-75599-6_21

from falsehood in today's digital landscape has become increasingly difficult. The massive spread of the Internet and social media has led to an overload of information, where misinformation, fake news, and disinformation are prominent examples of social harm [2]. This challenge is not confined to ordinary users; fact-checking initiatives struggle to keep pace with this information overload, exacerbated by a lack of comprehensive datasets in all languages and inconsistent data availability [3].

One significant issue is the predominance of English-language corpora used to train detection and prediction models. As a result, experts often rely on translated content for multilingual solutions, which poses a problem because disinformation in each language uses specific linguistic and communication strategies tailored to its target audience that machine translation (MT) alone cannot provide without any work of creating translation or *transcreation* [4]. Further complications arise from linguistic inconsistencies, which hinder efforts to regulate disinformation. These inconsistencies affect both international regulation harmonization, where the same terms can have different interpretations [5], and the understanding of digital neologisms or abstract terminologies like "Deepfake," "echo chambers," and "DeepNudes," which lack precise definitions, thus hindering comprehension and regulatory interoperability [6]. To address these challenges, several ontologies related to online behaviors are being developed [6–9]. Buffa in [10] highlights the intersection of cybersecurity with legal and computer science fields, especially as new terms like "e-Health" and "cyberwarfare" emerge. These behaviors often facilitate cyber-crimes that transcend national jurisdictions, becoming supranational, yet regulatory responses remain fragmented. The regulation of disinformation and related phenomena, such as revenge porn (which can intersect with disinformation, as in the case of "DeepNudes"), is further complicated by data unavailability and inconsistencies. These issues are particularly evident in open-source datasets related to conflicts and terrorist attacks, which are often based on news sources [11, 12]. Such inconsistencies can result from the rapid dissemination of information and the challenges in updating data accurately [13], or from deliberate manipulation intended to harm society, such as in the context of terrorist attacks [11, 14]. Disinformation is now seen as a threat to democracy and is increasingly recognized as a hybrid threat that could play a role in cyber warfare [15, 16]. Consequently, it is important to note that disinformation is being considered in cybersecurity regulations and reports [17]. Despite growing analysis of these phenomena, data inconsistency and unavailability persist, complicating the identification and prosecution of those responsible. Anonymity, while a core principle of online free expression, also allows those spreading misinformation to evade accountability. Regulating these phenomena is further challenged by the need to balance the rule of law with respect for freedom of speech, leading to the use of non-binding soft law instruments and resulting in a weakening of protections [10]. Some scholars [18] suggest this has led to a new surveillance paradigm, where concepts like the *Panopticon* and *Synopticon* are applied to online behavior [10, 18]. In this paradigm, social media's use of soft law instruments could enable a *Synopticon*-like environment, where everyone can observe everyone else. The issues of data untraceability, anonymity, and inconsistent data in news sources underscore the need for better organization and interoperability of digital objects. This context brings the FAIR principles—Findability, Accessibility, Interoperability, and Reusability [19]—into focus as crucial guidelines for enhancing data reusability, which could be pivotal in combating disinformation. These principles advocate for 'machine actionable' data, ensuring that digital objects provide sufficient detail for machines to autonomously identify, assess, and utilize them. This includes maintaining detailed provenance records, essential for accurately citing and trusting data [19–21]. In the context of disinformation, applying the FAIR principles can help trace data origins, verify accuracy, and ensure digital objects are interoperable and reusable. By promoting a standardized framework, such as the FAIR Digital Object Framework (FDOF), digital content can be better organized, facilitating the detection and countering of false information [20]. This systematic approach enhances the traceability and reliability of data, strengthening the infrastructure for managing and mitigating disinformation.

1.1 Research Goals and Research Questions

In this context, we developed eu-FAIRnews, a tool for scraping Italian news sources to create datasets. Initially developed due to the lack of Italian language corpora for training detection and prediction models, this tool aims to compile an initial dataset of Italian news classified as real or fake. In a subsequent phase, we expanded the tool's scope to include FAIR practices, exploring the relationship between disinformation and FAIR data to enhance digital justice. This decision was informed by findings from our previous work [22, 23]. Our studies highlight the anomalies and inconsistencies in data from conflict and terrorism datasets based on news sources (e.g., ACLED[1], GTD[2]), which struggle to keep data updated and verified, sometimes leading to deliberate misinformation [22]. The studies also emphasize the regulatory challenges posed by disinformation, particularly concerning freedom of speech and linguistic data[3], while underscoring the need for media literacy to enhance user resilience [23]. The Research Questions we want to address are:

- Can FAIRness be reached in data extracted from news outlets and news websites?
- Is there a possible relation between FAIRness and fair and ethical news?
- Can FAIRness enhance transparency, accountability in information sources, and the users' media awareness?

Although at an early stage, we aim to address these issues from three perspectives: 1) **technical,** by improving data updating processes, which prevents data duplication, and by automating data collection and categorization for model training and monitoring systems; 2) **regulatory,** by exploring how FAIR data practices can enhance disinformation regulations while respecting freedom of speech and supporting journalistic integrity; 3) **educational,** by enhancing media literacy through clear labeling and visualizations to help users better understand and navigate news sources. The tool explores the connection between FAIRness and the trustworthiness of news sources evaluated by the international fact-checking organization Newsguard[4]. By comparing our findings with Newsguard's

[1] https://acleddata.com/data-export-tool/.

[2] https://www.start.umd.edu/gtd/.

[3] The interpretations of Disinformation/Misinformation are the same considered in our previous works and used in the Ontology presented in them [23].

[4] https://www.newsguardtech.com.

trustworthiness scores, we aim to investigate the potential correlation between FAIR data principles and news quality. While preliminary, our approach offers significant promising insights for future improvements and contributions to combating disinformation. In this paper, the eu-FAIRnews tool, which supported us in exploring these issues, will be presented. The paper is organized as follows: as the theoretical state of the art has been presented in the introduction, the second section will focus on the related work related to practical similar approaches. Section 3 will detail the Methodology followed. The adopted Data Model will be proposed in Sect. 4. Section 5 will describe the Case study, while results will be presented in Sect. 6 and discussed in Sect. 7. Finally, conclusions and future works will be drawn.

2 Related Work

As highlighted earlier, the rapid spread of disinformation in the digital age presents significant challenges, ranging from data integrity and trustworthiness to issues affecting users' trust and even societal security [16, 24]. One primary issue in digital journalism is data duplication and the difficulty of updating one piece of information across multiple platforms [25]. Moreover, ensuring the quality of Big Data, a critical factor in many fields remains a challenge due to data anomalies and inconsistencies. According to [26], the importance of trusted data is fundamental, emphasizing the increasing role of metrology and standardization to verify the precision and trustworthiness of all types of metadata, as demonstrated by the Korean Standard Reference Data (SRD) [26] case. However, despite these efforts, 'veracity'—the accuracy and reliability of data—remains threatened by biases, noise, and abnormality, exacerbated by data 'volume' and 'velocity' [26]. Even though this approach focuses on medical data, our research centers on information data, particularly within the context of disinformation campaigns, such as the COVID-19 infodemic. During this period, as noted by Ceri [27], the global community had to navigate a deluge of information regarding the SARS-CoV-2 virus and COVID-19. The CORD-19 initiative [27] used Natural Language Processing (NLP) and topic modeling methods to analyze trending topics, extract claims, and verify metadata presence and veracity, demonstrating the importance of data traceability and provenance in academic writing. The FAIR principles, initially developed to improve the infrastructure supporting the reuse of scholarly data [19], are increasingly applied across various industries. Despite their growing adoption, digital journalism still struggles with issues like anonymity, data duplication, and lack of unique identifiers for journalists, which contribute to phenomena such as foreign information manipulation and interference (FIMI). For instance, Doppelgänger websites—clones of trusted sites used to spread disinformation—exploit subtle differences in URLs that are hard to detect (Olaf Steenfadt and Konrad Bleyer-Simon, Eu-DisinfoLab[5] and this is why they propose Unique Media Identifiers (UMIs) to combat such Doppelgänger websites. The use of Unique Identifiers (that we do not only propose for websites but as explained later in the articles for authors too) and the necessity to find, access, exchange, and reuse data led us to hypothesize that the FAIR practices could represent a possible solution to regulating and

[5] https://www.disinfo.eu/outreach/our-webinars/why-do-we-need-unique-media-identifiers/.

monitoring disinformation while respecting freedom of speech and enhancing the digital justice related to this topic. To our knowledge, no other analysis of FAIR compatibility of (Italian) news sources, and no scraping tools that use FAIRness to enhance data quality and interoperability, and to assess the relation between information FAIRness and news quality and trustworthiness has been created. The following, represent some practical examples of approaches with similar goals related to data/information quality, which may be inspirational for our future research, but differ from our current work.

Among the studies that present solutions to the main problems of digital media related to validity, reliability, bias, and information pollution, the main technology used is blockchain. In [28] a proposed Blockchain scheme prioritizes user anonymity over transparency, potentially enabling misuse. While privacy is emphasized, the dangers of non-transparent practices like anonymity [28] are highlighted, underscoring the risks of false narratives and industry abuse. Crucial data like Data Provenance is overlooked in their platform-focused approach. Their scheme, based on Open Data and Blockchain, prioritizes platform users over authors, neglecting crucial data like Data Provenance. Data Provenance involves various metadata beyond author identity, including block metadata and timestamps, crucial for news integrity. Websites' identities, vulnerable to cloning, pose threats of disinformation dissemination as we have seen with Doppelgänger websites and their URL. In [29], a blockchain technology defines different access roles between journalists and readers. Here, certified journalists must vote on articles. This model intends to work as an agora where people brainstorm ideas and journalists take responsibility for the platform. Other approaches focus more on the use of Blockchain for the security of data storage [30] or scraping methods [31]. The former model [30] which will be considered for future works, differs from ours both in the technology used, in the main goals, and in the use of FAIR principles. The latter one [31], could also be inspirational, but it focuses only on images, social media, comparison methods, and the lack of relation with FAIR methods. These models will be considered for future developments, however, blockchain does not provide some relation properties. It cannot maintain relationships between the news and keep track of data changes preventing data duplication, which is something that has been achieved by other data-oriented solutions [25]. Generally, while these models trained on English datasets offer valuable insights, they often fail to consider the specific challenges posed by the Italian language and the European regulatory framework. These models typically do not incorporate FAIR principles, missing the opportunity to use FAIR practices as a foundation for a regulatory framework that enhances automation, preserves freedom of speech, and upholds rights to clear information and professional integrity. Our primary goal is to create a preliminary Italian news dataset to train algorithms and explore whether FAIRification [32] of news sources can impact disinformation management, defense, and users' media literacy.

3 Methodology

This paper will introduce an improvement of a tool which was originally developed solely for scraping Italian news from news websites, aimed at building g a dataset containing Italian news. During the design and development of the original tool, we noticed that because anonymity and data anomalies (in dates, numbers, etc., ...) represent some of the main issues related to the simplicity of making and disseminating fake news/disinformation, we hypothesized that applying the FAIR principles [19] to disinformation management could be related, both from the technical and regulatory aspects and from the societal and educational one. The initial version of the Tool was developed using the Software Development Life Cycle (SDLC) approach [33], which includes Planning and Requirements Analysis, where users' needs and system requirements are identified; the Architecture Design phase, followed by the Software Development. Finally, the Testing phase, where the system's functionality is verified and improved. Because we realized there may be a connection between FAIRness and trustworthiness, it can be said that the SDLC approach has been and still will be followed by an Agile Software Engineering approach[6] for ongoing improvements and maintenance. The tool uses Data Engineering methods for data analyses and preparation and Exploratory Data Visualization (EDV) methodologies to create two dashboards: an initial one for previewing scraped news sources and a final one for visualizing trustworthiness scores. These methodologies enhance transparency and the users' awareness while allowing them to address the research questions.

4 Data Model

The data model proposed (Fig. 1) primarily considers two factors:

1. Adherence to FAIR Principles [19]:
   a. F3: **Metadata clearly and explicitly includes the identifier of the data they describe.** This ensures that the metadata are directly linked to the corresponding data, facilitating accurate data referencing and retrieval.
   b. A2: **Metadata should be accessible even when the data are no longer available.** This ensures that critical information about the data remains available for future use, citation, and reference, maintaining the value and utility of the metadata independently of the primary data.
   c. I1: **Metadata utilizes a formal, accessible, shared, and broadly applicable language for knowledge representation, promoting interoperability.** In our case, we use the schema.org[7] ontology, specifically the NewsArticle schema, to ensure that our metadata is consistent and can be easily integrated with other datasets using the same ontology.
2. Challenges in News Website Structures:
   a. Inconsistencies: News websites often have significant inconsistencies in their data structures. These variations make it challenging to standardize the data extraction process, as each site may use different HTML tags, structures, and conventions.
   b. Lack of Machine-Readable Formats: Many news websites do not adequately support machine-readable formats such as JSON-LD. This lack of standardization limits the quality and quantity of data that can be automatically extracted, necessitating the use of custom scraping scripts for each site.

[6] https://agilemanifesto.org/iso/en/manifesto.html.

[7] https://schema.org/NewsArticle.

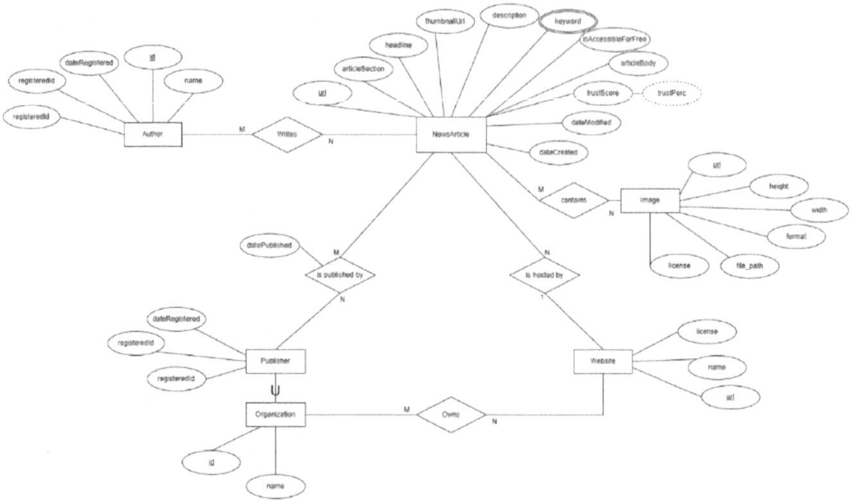

Fig. 1. Simplified ER of a certified NewsArticle

4.1 Ontology and Data Model Construction

To address these challenges and ensure adherence to the FAIR principles, we based our data model on the established considering the NewsArticle schema from schema.org. (1.c) This ontology provided a robust framework for ensuring that our data model is both scalable and interoperable. The schema.org ontology is widely recognized and used, which enhances the interoperability of our data with other systems and datasets that also adhere to this standard. Given the nature of the data and the ontology-based attribute selection, we determined that a document-oriented NoSQL database would be the most suitable. The flexibility of NoSQL databases allows for the efficient handling of semi-structured and unstructured data, which is common in web-scraped content. Utilizing JSON-LD (JavaScript Object Notation for Linked Data) documents allowed us to closely follow the ontological structure and semantic richness of the attributes defined by schema.org. JSON-LD is particularly advantageous because it embeds linked data in JSON, making it both human-readable and machine-processable, thus enhancing the data's interoperability.

4.2 Current Limitations and Future Directions

Due to the limitations of current news websites, our model is a simplified version of the full schema.org ontology. Despite this, our model provides a robust foundation that, when implemented, might have an impact. Moving forward, we plan to:

1. Expand the range of attributes and entities as more sites adopt machine-readable formats.
2. Improve data extraction techniques to handle variability in site structures.
3. Enhance database performance and scalability through optimized schema design and indexing strategies, as well as implementing sharding and replication.

4.3 Rationale for Using ER, MongoDB, and Ontology Simultaneously

1. Entity-Relationship (ER) Model: Serves as a conceptual blueprint for designing our database schema, providing clarity and structure. It helps in identifying entities, attributes, and relationships, aiding in normalization and reducing redundancy.
2. MongoDB (NoSQL Database): Chosen for its ability to handle semi-structured and unstructured data, scalability, flexibility, and compatibility with JSON-LD. It is optimized for high read/write throughput, accommodating changes in data structures without requiring a schema redesign.
3. Ontology (Schema.org and NewsArticle Schema): Ensures metadata consistency and interoperability, adhering to FAIR principles. The ontology provides a formal, shared language for knowledge representation, enhancing semantic richness.

4.4 Role of ER Model in Transition Phases

Currently, many news websites do not support machine-readable formats, leading to a simpler data model. The ER model helps clarify and define relationships, ensuring robustness even with limited attributes.

The ER model supports smooth transitions through various system evolution phases:

1. Initial Phase: Limited attributes and simplified relationships, with authors as simple attributes.
2. Intermediate Phase: Introduction of an authors' register, enhancing visibility and relationship mapping.
3. Final Phase: Comprehensive ontology integration, using schema.org in its full scope to enhance data richness and interoperability.

The ER model also provides a structured framework for the gradual incorporation of more complex relationships and entities. This ensures that our data model can evolve in a controlled and efficient manner, achieving full integration with comprehensive ontologies and supporting the principles of FAIR data management.

5 Case Study

The EU-FAIRnews is a user-friendly tool that allows scraping data from news sources, checks if data can be made FAIR, and compares the FAIRness feasibility with the Newsguard's trustworthiness scores. Users can visualize data in both the preliminary and final phases in two separate dashboards. The first gives the user an idea of the scraped content (number of articles, category, trending keywords), while the second final one clarifies to the users which source/article could be more/less trusted according to our method. Finally, the tool allows us the download datasets in.csv,.xlsx, and J-SON formats. To answer our research questions and validate our work, the tool was tested on 10 different Italian News Outlets and websites. Before describing the design and the development of the software, it is fundamental to understand the requirements needed, the technological enablers, and the Data Sources.

5.1 Requirements

To reach the prefixed goals of this study, we analyzed and defined some requirements which can be divided into **Functional Requirements** and **Non-Functional Requirements.**

Functional Requirements. The Following are the Six Functional Requirements defined:

1. **Data extraction:** The system allows users to extract information from selected national news sources.
2. **Intuitive user interface:** The system provides a clear and easy-to-use user interface to initiate data extraction.
3. **Guided crawler:** The system implements a guided crawler to efficiently gather the desired information.
4. **Data storage:** The extracted information is stored in a document database in a consistent and accessible manner.
5. **Data conversion:** The system converts raw data following FAIR principles.
6. **Source Reliability Study and Preliminary News Assessment:** The system assesses the reliability of sources and assigns an initial reliability score to news stories. However, it is important to note that this initial score will be subject to further analysis.

Non-Functional Requirements: The main system characteristics are **performance** (The system can handle large amounts of data efficiently); **reliability** (the system ensures high reliability in data extraction and storage); **scalability** (the system is designed so that it can grow and adapt to future increases in load); and **usability** (the user interface is intuitive and user-friendly to enable a pleasant experience for users).

5.2 Technological Enablers

The tool leverages a robust JavaScript ecosystem for efficient data acquisition, management, and user interaction. Puppeteer[8], a Node.js package, automates website interactions to extract news content accurately, which is stored in a MongoDB database. The code is designed to automate the process of extracting data from specific Web pages, enabling the collection of useful information for various applications such as data analysis, news monitoring, or indexing. MongoDB's flexible structure handles the heterogeneous nature of news data, ensuring rapid processing and scalability. Vue.js, a progressive JavaScript framework, is used to develop a user-friendly dashboard for exploring the data. The system offers export options in both CSV and JSON-LD formats, enhancing data accessibility and interoperability. This focus on open formats promotes transparency and the sharing of valuable news content.

5.3 Data Sources

Initially, the tool was designed to scrape news websites to check if data could be made FAIR, this highlighted the possible relation between untraceability, disinformation, and

[8] https://pptr.dev/.

findability and *accessibility*. To analyze this possibility, we decided to select a sample of trusted and non-trusted Italian News provided by Newsguard. Newsguard is a fact-checking organization, where analysts, powered by multiple AI tools, work to counter disinformation and track false narratives spreading online. It provides a browser extension, which applies a label next to links on search engines showing their trustfulness score. The levels of scores are *Maximum Caution* (0–39); *Caution* (40–59); *Credible with Exceptions* (60–74); *Generally Credible* (75–99); and *High Credibility* (100). Nine are the criteria to analyze trustworthiness in an apolitical, pass/fail way according to them.[9] We decided to select 5 trusted and 5 non-trusted news websites among which allowed scraping. Their Newsguard score will be then used, as a comparison parameter with the scoring we will then provide based on FAIR principles. In this article, we decided to pseudonymize the websites to keep this information private because further research and tests will be done. Pseudonyms that we gave to the analyzed websites are "Trusted1(2, 3, 4, 5)" and "non-Trusted1(2, 3, 4, 5)" and their Newsguard scores (100 = maximum of trustworthiness) are respectively, for the "Trusted": 75/100; 82.5/100; 87.5/100; 87.5/100; 87.5/100; for the "non-Trusted": 49.5/100; 49.5/100; 25/100; "non-Trusted4" was not labeled by Newsguard; 7.5/100. In paragraph 7, we will compare these scores to the ones we gave. After retrieving the source identifier and relevant settings, the system starts a Puppeteer instance with a browser in headless mode. The browser visits the main URL and waits for the HTML structure to load completely. Then, using JavaScript, the system searches the Document Object Model (DOM) to locate and extract relevant HTML elements from the web page. Among the elements extracted are the title, thumbnail, image and news URLs, article body, publication date, author, category, license, and keywords related to each article on the page. It should be kept in mind that not all sites considered contain all this information. The presence or absence of such data will be considered in assessing the reliability of the news and the site itself. In addition, it would have been easier to extract data directly from the JSON-LD on the news page, but this option is not always available on the various sites examined and, more importantly, does not follow a uniform pattern.

5.4 Detailed Technical Implementation

The `SettingModel` class defines the data schema for storing source-specific settings in the database, used to navigate target web pages and locate elements of interest. The schema, specified through `settingSchema`, defines data fields and their types. In this way, the system adapts to the specific structure of each data source. These settings guide the system in navigating target web pages and locating relevant elements of interest. Once settings are obtained, the system starts a headless browser, visits the main URL, loads the page, and extracts data. The `scrapeData` method orchestrates the crawling operation using selectors to retrieve information from web pages, each will have its own HTML structure and will therefore require specific selectors. For instance, the art_url selector locates article URLs e.g. in the case of National Newspaper, the selector `a.Card_card_linkgVEN4` searches for an anchor <a> element that simultaneously has the indicated class. The choice of the selector is made after observing that all

[9] https://www.newsguardtech.com/ratings/rating-process-criteria/.

<a class= "Card_cardlink_gVEN4"> elements in the DOM of the National Newspaper homepage contain the URL of the specific article as an href attribute and the title of the article as textual content (art_title). Extracted data are processed and formatted according to the data model and metadata specifications. If an article is already in the database, it is updated instead of duplicated, with the modification date tracking the last update.

5.5 Proposed Tool Architecture

The system uses a client-server architecture: the client is the user interface, and the server handles data extraction, processing, and management. Components include a database for storing data, a scraper for information extraction, and a Data Conversion Module for converting raw data into FAIR data.

Client-Side. This represents the user interface, typically built using a framework like Vue.Js. It provides an intuitive experience for users to interact with the tool's functionalities.

Dashboards. The preliminary Dashboard provides a visual overview of collected data with graphs displaying metrics like the number of analyzed news items and top keyword distribution. This helps users quickly understand trends and identify areas for further exploration. After data analysis and conversion to FAIR data, the final Dashboard, found in the "Sources Rank" section, presents news sources' trustworthiness scores, categorized as *Good, Average, or Poor.* The overall score averages individual article scores based on criteria such as category, title, URL, preview, author, keywords, source site license type, date, and compliance with JSON-LD metadata. Users can click on scored sources to view detailed article metadata and the articles' reliability scores. In 5.6 the scoring system will be illustrated in detail.

Setting View. This is an optional section that we decided to implement so that more advanced users could custom selectors or set crawling/scraping parameters.

Scraping View. The scraping can be handled automatically in the background or potentially integrated with the dashboard to provide progress updates. This view allows users to have a visual idea of the scraped articles. Users can decide to scrape from one source or all the sources at once.

Export View. Finally, users can also decide to export data in different formats.

Server-Side. This manages the core functionalities of the system, which include **data acquisition**, Using Puppeteer; **data processing** by formatting and structuring extracted data; **data storage**: MongoDB stores extracted and processed data, ensuring scalability; and **data conversion** where a module transforms raw extracted data into open data formats like CSV (comma-separated values) and JSON-LD (JavaScript Object Notation for Linked Data). This promotes data sharing, interoperability, and accessibility, adhering to FAIR principles (Findable, Accessible, Interoperable, and Reusable).

Scraping Mechanism. To better understand the Tool Architecture, an overview of the scraping mechanism is necessary. The Scraping Mechanism includes the **Selector Definition**, where the server uses predefined or custom selectors (via a "Setting View") for efficiently extracting data from websites with varying structures, targeting specific HTML elements like titles, articles, or metadata; and **Crawling Management** characterized by **scheduling**, where crawling is initiated by user actions or on a predefined schedule; **multithreading,** where the server scrapes multiple sources simultaneously, improving efficiency; and **duplicate detection,** where extracted data undergoes duplication to store unique news items.

5.6 The Preliminary FAIRnews Scoring System

The final dashboard categorizes news sources and articles into *Good, Average*, and *Poor*. This paper focuses on the preliminary phase of testing our tool, which aims to analyze the correlation between Newsguard's trustworthiness scores and adherence to FAIR principles. The scoring system evaluates key parameters from schema.org, including Genre, Headline, URL, Abstract, Author, Keywords Accessibility, License, Publisher, Date Published, and JSON-LD. We selected these parameters according to the results obtained in our previous works, as mentioned in the introduction, where the analysis showed that most unavailability/inconsistency is related to time/space dimensions and authors (because of anonymity). This early-stage scoring system is essential for understanding how metadata presence correlates with news trustworthiness, yet the lack of widespread use of JSON-LD in news sources significantly complicated our data collection process, making the assessment more labor-intensive and potentially less accurate. JSON-LD provides structured data that would allow for more streamlined data extraction and integration, supporting better interoperability and reuse, key aspects of the FAIR principles. The scoring method assigns points to each metadata attribute based on its presence and importance. For example, the Genre (G) attribute whose weight is 0.50 points (w_{Genre}), aids in categorization. The Headline (H) and the URL (U), essential for access, each receive a weight of 0.25 (w_{Head}, w_{URL}). An Abstract (Ab), offering a concise content summary, hweights0.75 (w_{Abs}). The Author (A) attribute, crucial for credibility, has a heavy weight of 1.25 (w_{Auth}). Keywords Accessibility (KW), which weighs 1.00(w_{KW}), enhances discoverability, drives website visits, and shapes echo chambers by influencing article visibility. The License attribute (L), indicating the terms under which the content can be used or shared, contributes 0.25 ($w_{license}$); Creative Commons licenses are particularly valued for promoting transparency and openness. The Publisher's name (P), essential for credibility and traceability, adds a weight of 0.25 (w_{Pub}). The Date Published (D) weights 0.50 (w_{Date}). The JSON-LD attribute, which varies in points based on readiness and quality, is crucial for data interoperability, with higher scores indicating better adherence to metadata standards[10]. The total trust score (TS), a sum of these points is then expressed as a percentage. Scores above 80% classify the article as *Good*, scores between 60% and 79.99% as *Average*, and scores below 60% as *Poor*. Our testing revealed a significant deficiency in many news websites: the absence of a proper license. Most sites either do not specify a license or rely solely on copyright notices, with only a few adopting Creative Commons licenses. This lack of licensing transparency complicates content reuse and undermines openness and accountability,

[10] $TS = w_{Genre}G + w_{Title}T + w_{URL}U + w_{Head}H + w_{Abs}Ab + +w_{Auth}A + w_{KW}KW + w_{Web}W + w_{Date}D + w_{Pub}P + +w_{license}L + w_{json\_ld}J$

which are critical in combating misinformation. Future developments will refine these parameters and expand the dataset to include a broader range of sources and metadata types, enhancing the tool's robustness and applicability. The weights assigned to each attribute were determined through heuristic evaluation, considering the relative importance of each attribute in the context of news credibility and the likelihood of their presence in credible versus non-credible sources. These initial weights are subject to refinement based on further empirical validation and feedback from domain experts. It is important to note that the news score does not aim to establish the truthfulness or falsehood of the news but to provide a probabilistic estimate; this is because a news article may have many missing data points but still be true, and vice versa, as it will be discussed in the results and discussion sections.

6 Results and Initial Insights

To conduct the tests, the crawling process was started with one site at a time for news extraction. The slowest website was "non-Trusted5," with 39 news stories extracted in 139.25 s, likely due to a low-performance server. The results show the number of news items extracted from each website during a single session and the time taken. The system also supports multithreading, allowing news scraping from all selected sources at once by launching 10 processes in parallel. Overall, 410 news items were extracted from 10 websites in 616.13 s. Node.js launched 6 processes, queuing the others, which were executed in order as processes completed. However, simultaneous HTTP requests caused long ping times, with some exceeding Puppeteer's 30-s timeout. This issue was mitigated by extending the timeout limit, ensuring proper operation. Factors causing timeouts included connection issues, limited hardware resources (virtualized server), and high website latency. When the extraction was completed, the accuracy of saving the information in the database was checked. Next, the data were transformed into various formats, including PDF, CSV, and JSON-LD. The preliminary interactive dashboard shows the number of news articles extracted from each source, the main categories, and a histogram of frequently used keywords both generally and per source. This provides a clear idea of trending topics and potential main topics of current fake news, helping identify trends and user interests. Once data are extracted and visualized, the tool automatically checks the presence of the metadata that we want to convert into FAIR. Depending on the data availability and presence, we provided a weight for the different metadata, representing the importance of its presence and extraction feasibility. The considered metadata are: Genre, Headline, URL, Abstract, Author, Keywords accessibility, License, Publisher, Date Published, and JSON-LD.

Figure 2 shows the presence of the License in most cases, we must highlight that this test accepted all types of items that could be considered as Licenses (such as the copyright logo). This was because a proper license was mostly absent as it can be seen in the results of our test to check if the license was present or not in a JSON-LD container on 51 news websites. This way, most sites would have been classified as non-trusted. That explains why we had to calculate the score related to the license differently. In total, 410 news articles were extracted from 10 websites. Figure 3 shows the eu-FAIRnews results compared to the Newsguard score:

Source	News Source	Genres	Headline	URL	Abstract	Author	Keywords	License	Publisher	DatePublishec	JSON-LD
Trusted1	✓	✓	✓	✓	✓	✓	✓	✓	✓	✓	1.0
Trusted2	✓	✓	✓	✓	X	✓	X	✓	✓	✓	0.8
Trusted3	✓	✓	✓	✓	✓	✓	✓	✓	✓	✓	0.9
Trusted4	✓	✓	✓	✓	✓	✓	✓	✓	✓	✓	0.9
Trusted5	✓	✓	✓	✓	✓	✓	✓	✓	✓	✓	0.7
Non-Trusted1	✓	✓	✓	✓	✓	✓	✓	✓	✓	✓	0.5
Non-Trusted2	X	✓	✓	X	X	X	X	✓	✓	✓	0.0
Non-Trusted3	X	✓	✓	X	X	X	X	X	✓	✓	0.0
Non-Trusted4	✓	✓	✓	X	✓	✓	✓	✓	✓	✓	0.5
Non-Trusted5	✓	✓	✓	✓	✓	✓	✓	✓	✓	✓	0.8

Fig. 2. Metadata richness in tested websites

Source	News Count	Time (s)	NewsGuard Score	eu-FAIRnews Result
Trusted1	59	70.71	75.0	74.93
Trusted2	93	93.63	82.5	69.36
Trusted3	55	42.12	87.5	80.22
Trusted4	39	29.89	87.5	83.52
Trusted5	27	33.38	87.5	83.3
Non-Trusted1	24	28.19	49.5	93.33
Non-Trusted2	40	77.56	49.5	37.5
Non-Trusted3	13	62.71	25.0	37.5
Non-Trusted4	21	38.69	nan	77.89
Non-Trusted5	39	139.25	7.5	88.93

Fig. 3. The eu-FAIRnews results compared with the Newsguard scores.

The eu-FAIRnews scores are averages of all articles' scores per source. For example, although Trusted4 has a *Good* score (83.30%), some articles have low trustworthiness scores, such as 41.67, which is rated as *Poor*. Also, all news articles in non-Trusted5 present a score of 41.67%[11] because each article provides the same metadata. Similarly, all other non-Trusted websites exhibit consistent scores for their articles. Datasets related to extracted/converted FAIR data can be downloaded, facilitating real-time updates on a powerful server without data duplication.

7 Discussion

The tests conducted on selected news sources provided various insights into the eu-FAIRnews tool's potential, highlighting areas for technical improvement and policy support. Achieving FAIRness in data extracted from news websites is challenging but feasible. Our system efficiently extracted and converted data into various formats, a crucial step toward FAIR principles. However, the inconsistent use of JSON-LD across news sources hindered data extraction, complicating the scoring process. This was less of an issue for Italian Public Administration websites, which improved their open and FAIR data quality as showed in [34], by following the EU's Data Quality Guidelines (DQGs) [35]. If news websites adopted similar guidelines, these challenges could be mitigated. Thus, our analysis mainly focused on the second metric of the first principle of FAIRness—(meta)data richness—evaluating metadata and data completeness.

The second research aim explored the relationship between FAIRness and ethical news sources. Analysis revealed a significant link between FAIRness and news quality. Trusted sources generally had higher scores, reflecting better metadata completeness. However, some Non-trusted sources could appear credible due to their metadata. For

[11] This is the score of each single article, not the source's one, which is 88.93% obtained by averaging al the single articles' scores.

instance, non-Trusted1 consistently uses the same author, uncommon in legitimate journalism, while non-Trusted4 provides author names and photos, which may be fabricated. A quick search revealed that authors from non-Trusted sources were not recognized as professional journalists, raising concerns about the authenticity of these sources. Our scoring system, reflects reality, highlighting the challenges of distinguishing factual content from unverified claims in the digital era. The ease of anonymous publishing exacerbates this issue, blurring the lines between news and opinion. Thus, it is crucial to protect freedom of expression while clearly distinguishing between verified information and personal opinions. The tool scores both sources and individual articles, revealing discrepancies in trust levels. For example, Trusted2, often lacking author information, might be rated as *Average* rather than *Good*, contrasting with NewsGuard's assessment. This discrepancy highlights the importance of detailed metadata, such as proper licensing, which many sites lack. Moreover, non-trusted sources often achieve high scores simply by presenting complete but unverified data, posing a threat to public and professional trust. To address these challenges, we propose developing guidelines and regulatory standards for news metadata quality and establishing a verification system for online authors and publishers. This initiative, integrated into the eu-FAIRnews tool, will include a continuously updated database of Trusted and non-Trusted sources. Collaboration with fact-checking organizations will be crucial for implementing these standards. Furthermore, addressing "Doppelgänger" websites, which mimic legitimate sources to spread false information, involves using Unique Media Identifiers (UMIs) for early detection of fake clones. We also propose creating an authors' registry with unified identifiers and content history, similar to academic records, to safeguard information integrity and prevent cloning risks. Utilizing specific licenses, data formats, and (Unified authors'/sources') IDs can protect freedom of speech while ensuring transparent and trustworthy information dissemination. Additionally, our tool, with further implementations, could help detect Italian disinformation by developing AI models trained on accurate Italian datasets. NLP analysis, alongside claim and trend analysis, could refine these models, using keywords to predict emerging fake news topics prediction. The user-friendly dashboard aims to enhance media literacy by guiding users through a visual understanding of trustworthiness parameters. Moreover, the planned integration of labels into online content will promote transparency, accountability, and media literacy, thus empowering users to cope with disinformation.

8 Conclusions and Future Works

In this paper we presented the eu-FAIRnews tool, to explore the possible impact that FAIR practices could have on disinformation regulation from three perspectives (technical, regulatory, and educational). Accordingly, we have defined three research questions, answered as in the following:

- **Can FAIRness be achieved in data extracted from news websites?** Yes, although challenging due to inconsistent usage of structured data formats like JSON-LD across sources, our approach demonstrates that FAIRness can be attained in news data. However, improvements in data structures and adherence to standard metadata practices are necessary for full FAIR compliance.

- **Is there a correlation between FAIRness and fair, ethical news?** Potentially, as applying FAIRness principles to news data can mitigate anonymous content dissemination, enhancing transparency and accountability. The completeness, accuracy, and veracity of metadata also support ethical journalism practices.
- **Can FAIRness promote transparency, accountability, and media awareness?** Indeed, with support from news data guidelines and an authors' registry, FAIRness can significantly enhance transparency, accountability, and media awareness. By ensuring news data's findability, accessibility, interoperability, and reusability, stakeholders and readers can trace information origins, verify authenticity, and identify misinformation patterns, ultimately safeguarding trusted professionals and sources.

Future work will focus on enhancing our tool/ scoring system by testing different source types and widening metadata analysis. Additionally, we aim to propose News Data guidelines and regulations concerning data standards like JSON-LD and licensing. Transitioning to a fully compliant data model with the NewsArticle ontology will ensure integrity, interoperability, and backward compatibility. We also plan to implement a tracking system for authors and their content, along with a trustworthiness database for news sources. Finally, performing NLP analysis on Italian content will refine our predictive and detection models, enhancing their effectiveness in the Italian language.

Acknowledgments. This work has been partially supported by the Spoke 9 "Digital Society & SMart Cities" of ICSC - Centro Nazionale di Ricerca in High Performance-Computing, Big Data and Quantum Computing, funded by the European Union - NextGenerationEU (PNRR-HPC, CUP:C83C22000560007).

Disclosure of Interests. The authors have no competing interests to declare that are relevant to the content of this article.

References

1. Goldberg, D.: Responding To "Fake News": is there an alternative to law and regulation? Southwest Law Review. **47**, 417–447 (2018)
2. Huang, J.J., et al.: Anonymous and Unlinkable identity scheme in open data environment. In: Proceedings - 2023 18th Asia Joint Conference on Information Security, AsiaJCIS 2023, pp. 73–80. Institute of Electrical and Electronics Engineers Inc. (2023). https://doi.org/10.1109/AsiaJCIS60284.2023.00022
3. Ünal, R., Çiçeklioğlu, A.Ş.: The function and importance of fact-checking organizations in the era of fake news: Teyit.org, an example from turkey. Medijske Studije. **10**, 140–160 (2019). https://doi.org/10.20901/ms.10.19.8
4. Katan, D.: Transcreation. Presented at the September 16 (2021). https://doi.org/10.1075/hts.5.tra19
5. Xu, F., Sheng, V.S., Wang, M.: A unified perspective for disinformation detection and truth discovery in social sensing: a survey. ACM Comput Surv. **55** (2021). https://doi.org/10.1145/3477138
6. Falduti, M., Griffo, C.: Modeling Cybercrime with UFO: an ontological analysis of non-consensual pornography cases. In: 41st International Conference on Conceptual Modeling (ER 2022 Proceedings)) (2022). https://doi.org/10.1007/978-3-031-17995-2_27

7. Castano, S., Falduti, M., Ferrara, A., Montanelli, S.: The LATO knowledge model for automated knowledge extraction and enrichment from court decisions corpora. Inf. Syst. **106** (2022). https://doi.org/10.1016/j.is.2021.101842
8. Castano, S., Falduti, M., Ferrara, A., Montanelli, S.: Law data science and ethics: the CRIKE approach. In: Proceedings of the 1st International Workshop on Processing Information Ethically co-located with 31st International Conference on Advanced Information Systems Engineering, pp. 1–9 (2019)
9. Castano, S., Falduti, M., Ferrara, A., Montanelli, S.: The CRIKE data-science process for legal knowledge extraction discussion paper. In: Italian Symposium on Advanced Database Systems, June 16th to 19th (2019)
10. Calzolari Zamorani, N., et al.: open journal of humanities electronic scientific journal in open access
11. McCann, W.S.: Who said we were terrorists? Issues with terrorism data and inclusion criteria. Stud. Conf. Terrorism. **46**, 964–984 (2023). https://doi.org/10.1080/1057610X.2020.1816676
12. Krieg, S.J., Smith, C.W., Chatterjee, R., Chawla, N. V.: Predicting terrorist attacks in the united states using localized news data (2022). https://doi.org/10.1371/journal.pone.0270681
13. Glass, K., Colbaugh, R., Pacific northwest national laboratory (U.S.), IEEE ITSS., Institute of electrical and electronics engineers: ISI 2013. In: 2013 IEEE International Conference on Intelligence and Security Informatics : Big Data, Emergent Threats, and Decision-Making in Security Informatics, Seattle, WA : conference venue, Grand Hyatt Seattle, 4–7 June 2013
14. Innes, M., Dobreva, D., Innes, H.: Disinformation and digital influencing after terrorism: spoofing, truthing and social proofing. Contemp Soc Sci. **16**, 241–255 (2021). https://doi.org/10.1080/21582041.2019.1569714
15. Gagliardi De Freitas, N.: Cyberterrorism as hybrid threat: a comparison between the iranian and estonian case. http://hdl.handle.net/10362/156155
16. Executive summary a comprehensive resilience ecosystem hybrid threats. https://doi.org/10.2760/382543
17. Lella, I.: Enisa threat landscape (2023). https://doi.org/10.2824/782573
18. Maestri, E.: Lex informatica. Diritto, persona e potere nell'età del cyberspazio. Annali Online della Didattica e della Formazione Docente. **9**, 302–305 (2015)
19. Wilkinson, M.D., et al.: Comment: the FAIR guiding principles for scientific data management and stewardship. Sci. Data. **3** (2016). https://doi.org/10.1038/sdata.2016.18
20. Bonino Da Silva Santos, L.O., Sales, T.P., Fonseca, C.M., Guizzardi, G.: Towards a conceptual model for the FAIR digital object framework. In: Frontiers in Artificial Intelligence and Applications, pp. 227–241. IOS Press BV (2023). https://doi.org/10.3233/FAIA231131
21. Krans, N.A., Ammar, A., Nymark, P., Willighagen, E.L., Bakker, M.I., Quik, J.T.K.: FAIR assessment tools: evaluating use and performance. NanoImpact. **27** (2022). https://doi.org/10.1016/j.impact.2022.100402
22. Calò, A., Zappatore, M., Lia, M., Longo, A.: Visual Data Engineering for Conflict and Terrorism Prediction. Sorrento, Italy (2023). https://doi.org/10.1109/BigData59044.2023.10386226
23. Calò, A., Longo, A., Zappatore, M.: Comparative analysis of disinformation regulation: a preliminary analysis. In: Advances in Conceptual Modeling. ER2023, pp. 162–171 (2023). https://doi.org/10.1007/978-3-031-47112-4_15
24. Paul, A.J., Iżewicz, P., Flatow, G., Bachmann, S.-D., Gunneriusson, H., Bowen, A.S.: The journal on terrorism and security analysis JTSA following the pivot: does NATO have a role in southeast Asia? A Case Study in Security Affairs: Israel and Sub-Saharan Africa Terrorism and Cyber Attacks as Hybrid Threats: Defining a Comprehensive Approach Threats to Global Peace and Security Introduction and Overview (2014)

25. Takan, S., Ergün, D., Katipoğlu, G.: Fair-news: digital journalism model to prevent information pollution and manipulation. Comput. Mater. Continua. **75**, 6059–6082 (2023). https://doi.org/10.32604/cmc.2023.039505
26. Lee, D.: Big data quality assurance through data traceability: a case study of the national standard reference data program of Korea. IEEE Access. **7**, 36294–36299 (2019). https://doi.org/10.1109/ACCESS.2019.2904286
27. Invernici, F., Bernasconi, A., Ceri, S.: Exploring the evolution of research topics during the COVID-19 pandemic (2023). https://doi.org/10.1016/j.eswa.2024.124028
28. Xiong, W.: IEEE Computer Society, International Association for Computer & Information Science, Pattern Recognition and Machine Intelligence Association., Institute of Electrical and Electronics Engineers. In: 17th IEEE/ACIS International Conference on Computer and Information Science (ICIS 2018), proceedings, Singapore, June 6–8, 2018
29. Kim, B., Yoon, Y.: Journalism model based on blockchain with sharing space. Symmetry (Basel). **11** (2019). https://doi.org/10.3390/sym11010019
30. Wang, X., Xie, H., Ji, S., Liu, L., Huang, D.: Blockchain-based fake news traceability and verification mechanism. Heliyon. **9** (2023). https://doi.org/10.1016/j.heliyon.2023.e17084
31. Vishwakarma, D.K., Varshney, D., Yadav, A.: Detection and veracity analysis of fake news via scrapping and authenticating the web search. Cogn. Syst. Res. **58**, 217–229 (2019). https://doi.org/10.1016/j.cogsys.2019.07.004
32. Jacobsen, A., et al.: A generic workflow for the data fairification process. Data Intell. **2**, 56–65 (2020). https://doi.org/10.1162/dint_a_00028
33. Shafiq, S., Mashkoor, A., Mayr-Dorn, C., Egyed, A.: A literature review of using machine learning in software development life cycle stages (2021). https://doi.org/10.1109/ACCESS.2021.3119746
34. Lia, M., Damiano Colella, D., Longo, A., Zappatore, M.: euFAIR: a digital tool for assessing the FAIR principles. In: Advances in Conceptual Modeling. ER223. pp. 49–58 (2023). https://doi.org/10.1007/978-3-031-47112-4_5
35. Data.europa.eu Data Quality Guidelines - August 2021. (2021). https://doi.org/10.2830/879764

Safety Assurances in Autonomous Vessels

Sreekant Sreedharan[1](✉), Muthu Ramachandran[3], Erik Røsæg[2], and Børge Rokseth[1]

[1] Department of Engineering Cybernetics, Norwegian University of Science and Technology, Trondheim, Norway
{sreekant.sreedharan,borge.rokseth}@ntnu.no
[2] Faculty of Law, University of Oslo, Oslo, Norway
erik.rosag@jus.uio.no
[3] Forti5 Technologies Limited, London, UK
muthu.ramachandran@forti5.tech

Abstract. Autonomous ships represent a transformative advancement in maritime transportation, promising significant shifts in cargo and passenger transport from road to sea, reduction in operational costs, minimized risks for crew, and lower environmental impacts. As a critical emerging infrastructure, their safety is a subject of ongoing debate. This paper explores the safety assurance of autonomous ships with a particular focus on compliance with the International Regulations for Preventing Collisions at Sea (COLREG). Central to this study is the development of a sophisticated virtual testing environment, supported by a digital twins that replicates key aspects of environment and autonomous vessels, including sensors and actuators. This virtual environment simulates complex navigational scenarios to rigorously test and validate the autonomous navigation systems against COLREG standards under varied maritime conditions. The solution integrates a dynamic test management system that not only orchestrates simulations but also automatically generates and assesses test scenarios to identify potential deficiencies in vessel performance.

Keywords: safety assurance · systems modeling · computer simulation · digital twins · COLREG · maritime regulations

1 Introduction

As advanced robotic machinery becomes increasingly integrated into our physical environment, scientists, operators, and regulators face the significant challenge of ensuring these systems operate safely and adhere to established standards. With over two million AI-controlled robots operating worldwide today, having multiplied three-fold over the past two decades alone, robotics is now expanding well beyond its industrial roots into transportation where unmanned aerial vehicles (UAV), autonomous cars and trucks, autonomous surface vessels (ASVs) and remotely operated vessels (ROVs, usually referring to underwater vessels) are proliferating across the planet. However, these robotic transport systems that are employed to pursue complex goals with limited direct supervision raise

M. Saeki et al. (Eds.): ER 2024 Workshops, LNCS 14932, pp. 302–320, 2025.
https://doi.org/10.1007/978-3-031-75599-6_22

credible safety concerns. Assuring the safety of this emerging breed of robotic maritime transportation is the general focus of our research.

1.1 Problem Statement

Verifying maritime transportation safety is a complex problem mandating a multi-disciplinary approach - spanning: maritime regulations, fluid dynamics, rigid-body dynamics, robotic control, environmental modeling, traffic modeling, behavioural science, systems testing, software engineering and a several others - to precisely model vessel dynamics, traffic behavior, weather dynamics and human behavior, before regulatory schematics can be effectively applied by authorities can assure an Autonomous Vessels (AVs) is adequately safe for operation. Accordingly, verifying the behavior of an AV pitches it against a myriad of safety and collision avoidance protocols that involves navigating a labyrinth of technological, regulatory, environmental, human, testing, and ethical challenges. Each category presents unique unaddressed hurdles to ensuring the safety and reliability of autonomous maritime operations, as outlined below.

Technological Complexity: Autonomous vessels rely on a multitude of sensors (radar, LiDAR, cameras, GPS, etc.) for situational awareness. Verifying the accuracy and reliability of these sensors under various environmental conditions (e.g., fog, heavy rain, high waves) is challenging. Sensor fusion integrating data from multiple sensors, adds another layer of complexity. Moreover, collision avoidance algorithms, often based on AI and machine learning, are complex and dynamic, requiring algorithms processing vast amounts of data in real-time to make rapid decisions. Verifying that these algorithms can handle all possible scenarios, including rare and unexpected events, is daunting.

Environmental Variability: Vessels operate in a highly dynamic marine environment that is inherently unpredictable and constantly changing. Factors such as tides, currents, and weather conditions can significantly impact the performance of collision avoidance systems. Verifying protocols under all possible environmental conditions is challenging. Compounding the problem is human activity. Maritime traffic can vary significantly in density and patterns, as busy ports and shipping lanes present different challenges compared to open sea.

Human Factors: AVs may need to interact with human-operated vessels. Predicting and verifying the responses of human operators to the actions of an AV is complex. Ensuring autonomous systems safely handles unpredictability in human is immensely challenging. Moreover, AVs must make ethical decisions in critical situations, such as choosing the lesser of two evils in an unavoidable collision scenario. Verifying that the decision-making process aligns with superior seamanship and ethical standards is complex.

Regulatory and Legal Challenges: Today, there is no universally accepted standard for the development and verification of AV systems. Different jurisdictions adopting varying requirements, makes consensus on a unified verification protocol difficult. Consequently, determining diligence and negligence in case of a collision involving AVs raises new liability and accountability questions. Verifying whether collision avoidance protocols were correctly followed or whether a failure was due to a technical glitch, a software bug, or external factors is challenging. Moreover, given AVs must also operate across international waters and through various territorial waters, each governed by different jurisdictions with varying regulatory frameworks for AVs, ensuring compliance across jurisdiction is complex and can lead to operational challenges and potential legal conflicts. Furthermore, maritime law and regulations are continually evolving to keep pace with technological advancements and because flag states (the country where a vessel is registered) may employ different standards and requirements for vessel operation and safety, an AV registered in one country may need to comply with different or additional standards when entering the waters of another country, adding a new dimension to compliance assurance.

The innumerable challenges presented by jurisdictions and flag states, the lack of harmonized regulations, varied compliance standards, inter-jurisdictional operational complexities, legal and liability issues, individually present unique and distinct hard problems for compliance assurance but together the various categories for challenges make safety assurance of AVs a near Herculean undertaking. In this research however, we limit the definition of compliance to a discrete numeric measure quantifying systemic safety within a regulatory regime.

Although several studies focused on test case generation, such as in automotive [7,17,31], aviation [16], and other industries exist, there are relatively few studies focused on either testing processes - theoretical model evaluation or formal verification - in the maritime industry, as reported in by recent authors [27,35,38,40]. Existing maritime solutions focus on idealized situations on the high sea, whereas most safety incidents occur in harbour zones and inland waterways where traffic and congestion introduces ambiguity to a vessel master's decision thus limiting the application of such solutions. The lack of safety assurances solutions modelling such complex scenarios is a crippling impediment to the broad-based adoption of AVs in transportation today. This technology gap is the central focus of our research. Additionally, assessing compliance and/or circumstances for justifiable adjudication of vessel behavior with respect to international maritime traffic regulation, is the thematic emphasis on of the research.

This paper reports the outcome of our research and is organized as follows: In Sect. 2, we present a survey of the current advances in AV safety. In Sect. 3, we describe the guiding philosophy, goals and approach adopted in our research. Section 4 discuss how a platform and a domain language can be woven into an application to implement our theory. Finally, in Sect. 5 we describe an illustrative case study demonstrating how we apply our solution in practice to ensure regulatory compliance and safety in maritime operations employing the COLREGs.

2 Related Works

We begin our exploration in this section by focusing on advances within the field of assurance systems for vessel safety verification and related subjects. We proceed by first making the following assertion that serves as guidance to our approach: *If AVs and human operated vessels must operate together in a shared environment, both ought to be held to the same evaluation practices and standards.* By extension, as humans are trained and tested by evaluators with extensive real-world experiences, AVs must also benefit from commensurate experiences in training and evaluation as well. These percepts guide our research in which we seek to develop software platforms that closely emulate how humans are evaluated so as to assure close compliance with our human experience.

Contemporary practice of safety verification in industrial applications conventionally employs simulations to reduce cost and avoid the risk of loss of life and property. A comprehensive recent survey of validation algorithms [3] recognizes that system properties are consistently misrepresented or hard to model, irrespective of design approach; leading to the author's conclusion that safety verification of complex operating environments must necessarily be conducted on the whole system, not just components. Whereas formal verification systems based on mathematical models alone can certainly identify defects, they scale poorly because of their requirement for *completeness*. Basic black-box testing is a partial panacea to the problem, eliminating the dependency of the verification system on the model of the verified system [30], but are also limited by requirements of completeness. This prompted us to exploration the properties of *adequate safety* and its fulfilment, in light of the futility of achieving *completeness*.

Vessels sail the seas traversing coastal waters where assurances of safety is guaranteed by local regulatory protocols. Therefore, in the context of a regulated environment, verification, compliance and assurance, are closely related terms that apply to both machine and human operation. Bearing in mind our particular focus on autonomous surface vessel safety, our survey explored recent developments in collision avoidance algorithms [1]. Although a family of regulations are emerging to regulate AVs, of particular research interest is the development of techniques to comply with international standard of the COLREGs [8,9,14]. Consistent across this research area we see focus narrowly limited to path planning algorithms [2,19] and collision avoidance [2,15,39] or areas pertinent to operation on the open sea. What is often overlooked is an important insight that a 'trajectory of disturbances eventually cause the system to fail' [3], emphasizing the importance of observing the vessels not just within the bounds of a few scenarios, but on its behavior during an entire journey under diverse circumstances. More recently, considerable attention has been given to evaluation platforms with a renewed focus on platform design [27], scenario generation [28] and application of risk modeling paradigms [29,36]. However, our assessment reinforces our calculus that whereas a rich palette of paradigms and algorithms already exist, an integrated platform paradigm to blend and compose them into gradually complex scenarios is missing.

As an important side note, it is also worth mentioning an emerging trend in legal scholarship exploring the intersection of AI and law exploring the codification of legal language [26] as well as the ethical and legal impact of machines in the workplace [20] that focus on evaluating societal preparedness for the emergence of AI.

In seeking to develop environments that closely emulate 'human-like' experiences, we also explored recent advances in computational neuroscience for alternative design approaches. Discussed extensively in this paper and a distinguishing feature of our approach is the application of fundamental theories in cognitive science to software design. Inspiring our approach is a core tenet of Marvin Minsky's philosophy that "minds are what brains do" [24]. The idea manifests in our approach with the development of the concept of *faculties* described later in the paper, building on Minsky's seminal work on knowledge representation four decades ago [23]. Our design also incorporates ideas from Rumelhart's conception of distributed cognitive architecture [33], while recent studies in cognitive architecture and neuroscience provides affirmation to our general approach [10–12]. Considered also are 'textbook architectures' for agency within *faculties* where we adopt intelligent agentic designs advanced by Russell [34] and Wooldridge [42] in their definitive academic treatment.

3 Research Methodology

Summarizing our observation from the previous sections - verifying collision avoidance protocol effectiveness across all scenarios is impractical due to the computational explosion of scenarios that require verification across several dimensions. Moreover, with the law evolving, keeping up with compliance requirements requires a verification system that can also evolves with both law and technology. Therefore, exhaustive testing to ensure maximal coverage of the most critical scenarios without compromising safety is the defining challenge we seek to address, and the advancement of the state of the art on this issue is the goal of our research. Succinctly, the scope of this research is falls into three areas:

1. Development of a comprehensive verification platform to cover the combinatorial explosion of scenarios required to adequately assure AV safety.
2. Development of a computer language to effectively communicate regulatory guidelines to verification software used in testing safety of AVs.
3. Demonstration of the platform and language as it is applied to verify autonomous navigation software against a class of regulatory protocol.

3.1 Design Approach

Delving deeper into the three research objectives, our research breaks down into the following body of work:

- **Platform**: We adheres to conventional practice by designing a verification platform built around a simulation environment. Here, we advance the recent research on the TestIT [27] and OSP [4] platforms respectively, by developing a novel platform to scale the scope of testing with the introduction of a containerized software and high-performance cluster computing to the mix.

- **Language**: In order to resolve the problem of contextual ambiguity and vagueness in COLREG we introduced two novelties: a) development of *Legata* a language to describe abstract legal concepts, b) development of a *Rule automata* runtime to interpret legal clauses within the dynamic context of a simulation.
- **Application**: Weaving the language into the simulation as a final step required building out the environmental components to imbue realism in the simulation, developing the library of *Legata* COLREG transcriptions and tools required to permutate through a myriad of scenarios, to be run on a massive cluster computing infrastructure. The concept diagram in Fig. 1 profiles how regulatory prose (e.g.:COLREG) is systematically decomposed into terms and clauses, that is then composed into logical propositions ingested into the verification platform to evaluate maritime scenarios.

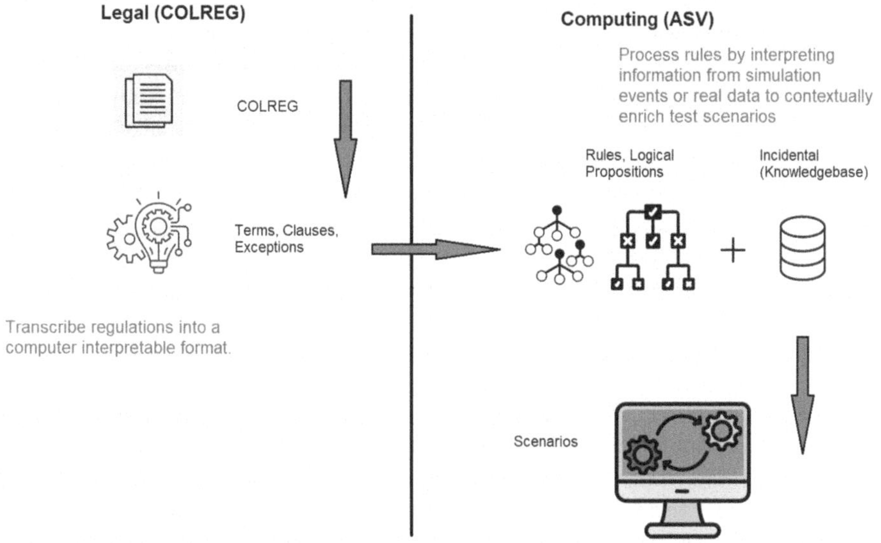

Fig. 1. A conceptual workflow explaining how terms and clauses are extracted from legal clause and encoded into a decision tree of logical propositions for use in a simulation scenario.

In aspiring for a comprehensive solution for maritime safety validation, we conceived a generic platform that makes it easier to blend the best testing techniques for autonomous systems in both mature industries - automobile and aviation - and emerging practices in the nascent autonomous maritime industry [6,25,32,37]. Although our early design concepts started out as adaptations of established maritime simulation models by Woerner [41] and Minne [22], the novelty of our research is the amalgamation of an implicitly multi-disciplinary approach with advances in language, platform and application into an integrated solution allowing simultaneous evaluation of a massive number of scenarios to assure compliance in the most ambiguous regulatory circumstances. The following section explains how this is achieved.

4 Implementation

4.1 Language

Unlike conventional computer languages, *Legata*, our language for COLREG transcription, eschews explicit definitions terms and definitions in its vocabulary. Instead, it favours a language and grammar of abstract concepts as evidenced by the COLREG transcription example shown in Fig. 2. What this means is that *Legata* describes meta concepts that can only be computed when a circumstances is presented to it. This is achieved by compiling *Legata* files into a decision tree that is processed by a runtime interpreter within the simulation. Illustrated in Fig. 3 is the model of such a *rule automata*. The automata interacts with the simulation environment to evaluate scenarios by converting abstract concepts to concrete facts pertinent to a specific instant in simulation. Thus the automata running *Legata* serves as a mediator between the simulation and the legal clause imparting situational objectivity to commonly abstract terms by resolving it at runtime. This novel approach combining a simulation with a runtime-interpreted domain language also allows *Legata* to describe complex scenarios, using an evolving linguistic vocabulary with an unlimited capacity for expression. The system abstracts concepts by introducing a concept called a *resolver* - interfaces provided to the language via the *rule automata* that allows it to peer into the simulation world of the AV software for inspection while it is being tested. *Resolvers* thus act as probes for the *automata* to enforce regulations by testing the assumptions made in a *Legata* clauses. It thus assures that the vessel is compliant with regulations at all times or flags it as non-compliant otherwise. Functionally, *Resolvers* are software modules loaded and passed to the simulation runtime at system startup; each *resolver* extends the vocabulary - namespaces and terms - that is available to describe simulation circumstances. *Resolvers* help interpret and compute simulation properties allowing us to eliminate contextual ambiguity based on circumstance.

It is important to point out here that applications of *Legata* files are not necessarily exclusive to COLREG regulations. *Legata* is a general-purpose language for codifying any kind of maritime regulations. For example a collection of *Legata* files may be used to describe traffic protocols specific to a costal state - the Oslo or Singapore harbour. Such explicit specialized rules may even apply narrowly to traffic separation schemes exclusively to a specific locale within a jurisdiction, territory or region. This important feature allows *Legata* to model a wide range of permutations of circumstantial international regulations, territorial provisions and maritime situations, to evaluate vessel behaviour during testing. That translates to tighter oversight on regulatory compliance.

Another point to note is that *Legata* terms are simply implemented as functions within a dynamically loaded software package. Within the implementation

```
# COLREG.Rule10:

define: {
    OS: OwnShip
    TS: TargetShip
    TSS: OwnShip.TrafficSeparationScheme
}


# Traffic Separation Schemes
# (a) This Rule Applies to traffic separation schemes adopted by the Organization and does not relieve
# any vessel of her obligation under any other rule.
condition: {                                                              <=  Circumstances for
    : [OS, Map.Sea@TrafficSeparationScheme].Distance in Area.Near.ProximityRange      Rule application

    # Trigger rule 10 overriding other conditions. Useful for rules in cross-reference.
    : OS.Restriction in ['COLREG.Rule10.*']
}

# (b) A vessel using a traffic separation scheme shall:
# (i) proceed in the appropriate traffic lane in the general direction of traffic flow for that
# lane;
clause['COLREG.Rule10.b.i']:{
    : {                                                                   Clauses describing conditions
        condition: { :TSS is not empty }                              <=  to activate a clause and
        assure: {                                                         assurances to verify
            :OS.Position in TSS.Area                                      compliance with protocol.
            :OS.Heading in TSS.SafeHeading
            :OS.Velocity <= TSS.SafeVelocity
            :(OS,TS).Distance >= TSS.SafeDistance
            }
    }
}
```

Fig. 2. Legata transcription of a clause in Rule-10 of the COLREG.

of these software functions - whereas the attribute (e.g.: a vessel speed) of a simulant is directly observed from its activity in the simulation, more complex terms (e.g.: safe speed in a traffic lane) may have to be computed based on the situational aspects or characteristics (e.g.: traffic density, vessel weight, class or type). This is an important feature because it allows the software package resolving the term to use a wide range of sophisticated techniques - an AI model, an ML algorithm, fuzzy logic or a database lookup - to compute the value of a term. Coincidentally, this use of external software packages to describe complex terms is also how *Legata* allows an endless evolving vocabulary to enrich the descriptive scope of the language.

4.2 Platform

For our platform design, we conceived a 'testable metaverse' for 'digital twins of autonomous vehicles'. It is a general-purpose assessment system to support contextual, realistic, large-scale simulations for testing. It is designed to run containerized environments of each simulation scenario, within a simulation capsule or '*simulule*' - distributed on server nodes running on a high-performance computing (HPC) cluster. An autonomous software to be tested is typically introduces as a software twins into the environment for assurance. Each *simulule* then runs as a fully isolated simulation instance that runs a single permutation of the assurance state space. During the run, the *simulule* observes and scores

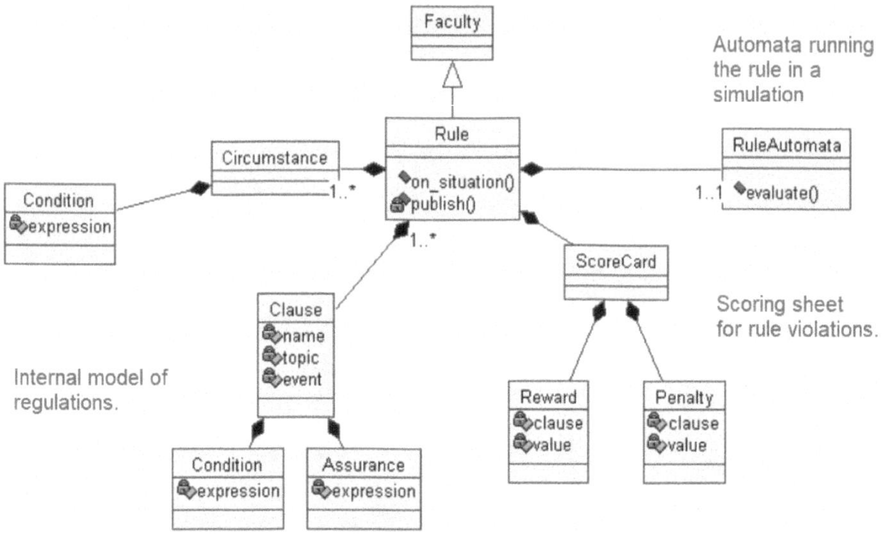

Fig. 3. Regulatory rules are composed internally as a collection of clauses and evaluated by a rule automata that scores score a circumstance to assess risks and rewards.

the actions of the tested software against a particular simulation scenario. The score results are then stored in a distinct database and once all permuted scenarios have been scored, the score collection is extracted, collated and exported into a common data warehouse for analysis using a host of verification algorithms. Finally, a summarized dashboard with performance reports is generated to simplify visualization and analysis of the strengths and weaknesses of the verified autonomous software. We concluded that the capabilities detailed above required by the simulation can be neatly achieved by building it as a comprehensive, embedded operating system running as tasks in an HPC cluster. Such an operating system was developed as the Co-Simulation Operating System (COS) - a containerized operating system purpose-built for large-scale distributed simulations of immersive, realistic, physical environments. COS, as platform delivering the features has the following features:

Scalable High-Performance Simulation Environment: The platform has a capacity to support a massive number - 10^5 to 10^7 - of individual scenarios running it parallel. It also allows us to describe the permuted scenario behavior parametrically through configuration files. The scenarios running as containerized simulation capsules (called *simulules*) appreciably simplifies software development while ensuring data isolation in a parallelized runtime environment. *simulules* are completely autonomous containers runtime environments that can model virtually all possible situations and scenarios, emulate the physical environment as closely as possible, while allowing the measurement and capture features of the environment mathematically. It is also domain agnostic (e.g.: maritime, road, rail, aerial) to facilitate multi-domain convergence in future incarnations and it has plug-in capability for new behavior as '*faculties*' to enable limitless expansion of assurance scope and capabilities.

Microkernel Design: The *simulule* are by design a complete embedded operating system with full support of a microkernel including: scheduling and time management, process management, inter-process communication, device management, file system, storage and data management services, configuration management and network services. This is desirable in two ways - Firstly, because as a hostable microkernel the *simulule* can easily run on a desktop during the simulation design stage, however modifying the *simulule* configuration should also enable it to run and scale up massively on a high-performance cluster without requiring any modification. Secondly, as a comprehensive containerized operating system, the *simulule* emulate these devices closely (GPS, LIDAR, Radar, Gyroscope, MRU etc.) allowing the import a catalog of simulated ship models as digital twins from existing solutions (e.g.: OSP [4]).

Development Tools: Supporting the platform is a suite of auxiliary tools for inspecting the runtime environment, visualizing the simulation during development, composing complex simulation from simple configurations, generating and deploying scenarios on a cluster for verification. Development tools for extensive logging and debugging tools to troubleshoot the environment are also part of the package.

A detailed evaluation of the architecture and capabilities of COS is beyond the scope of this paper. However, it is worthwhile to note here that COS is a purpose-built operating system designed exclusively to run massively large-scale simulations. As such, COS's distinguishing feature is that its kernel primarily schedules simulation processes called services, running indefinitely for the duration of the simulation. These services collaborate with each other to generate complex simulation behavior will become more evident in the following sections. A *faculty* is simply a highly specialized variant of a service.

4.3 Application

The platform and the language form the foundation on which we begin to compose the domain application for compliance assurance. To do that we build the components that emulate the world in which our autonomous software operates.

Modeling the Physical World: In keeping with our design goals, the COS world is purposefully unfettered by an imposed paradigm or model of the simulation world. Instead COS presents a clean empty canvas on which a designer can institute her own paradigms and models; consequently, COS is agnostic to domain or application and is designed to be boundlessly extensible. As an example, A built-in world building toolkit provides a foundational core on which to adapt a maritime application. The COS world is composed of four elements: world objects - that represents physical inanimate objects in the simulation, simulation objects (also referred to as simulants) that possess agency within the simulation, builders that compose the simulation world from data files, and faculties that control the behavior of the simulation. In the following case study

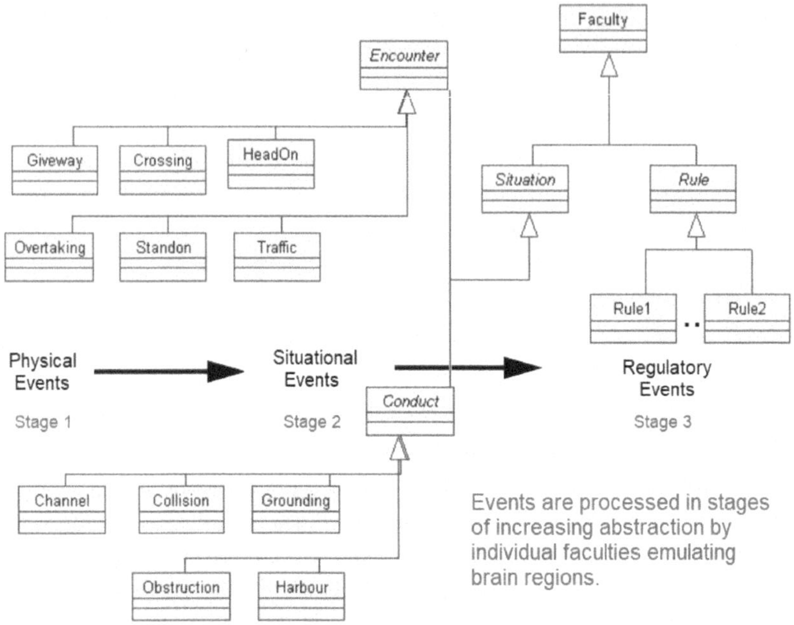

Fig. 4. Information processed in stages by faculties of increasing levels of abstraction to interpret complex concepts in a regulation (COLREG).

(Sect. 4 of this paper), we will demonstrate how we extend the core capabilities for the maritime domain.

Composing Simulation Behavioral: In the *"Society of Mind"*, Marvin Minsky [24] theorizes that the mind is a collection of semi-independent agents or processes, collectively contributing to cognition. This concept can be linked to various brain regions, which function as distinct yet interconnected modules. Recognizing these brain regions as specialized agents working in concert, we can see how Minsky's theory maps directly to modular and distributed brain function. We adopt this concept into a distinguishing feature of the COS simulation platform, calling it *faculties*. Drawing on the principles of brain anatomy, *faculties* draw on the principles of emergent complex behavior from composite interactions between regions of the brain, whereby capabilities of brain regions emanate from simple neuronal cell structures woven together into a complex super-structures [12] [13]. Illustrated in Fig. 3 a model for regulations and Fig. 4 demonstrates how we leverage simple *faculties* to compose complex ones to impart intelligence to simulations in COS. By composing *faculties* sequentially along an interaction graph - physical events (e.g. vessel movement) are interpreted as situational events (e.g. *overtaking*) and further down, situational events are interpreted as regulatory events by rules (e.g.: a violation of overtaking protocols specified in COLREG rule 13). The design mimics how regions of the human brain interact to convert raw sensory input into abstract concepts of higher intelligence through abstraction. This approach embraces Minsky's theory that - *'The power of intelligence stems from our vast diversity, not from any single, perfect principle'* [24], We find that as postulated by Minsky, such a model of abstraction makes possible extremely complex environmental behavior within our simulation, yet constructing individual *faculty* stays painless. In our system, *faculties* interact with each other asynchronously over a messaging service buttressed by a process scheduling mechanism that allows them to operate independently in parallel. Constantly observing the environment, these *faculties* evaluate and score events while interacting with a subsystem called the *data manager* that collates statistics and persists data into a local file-based database. The locally cached data is eventually aggregated into a centralized data warehouse in the upstream data pipeline of the simulation environment. Illustrated in Fig. 5 is the conceptual flow of information in the described system.

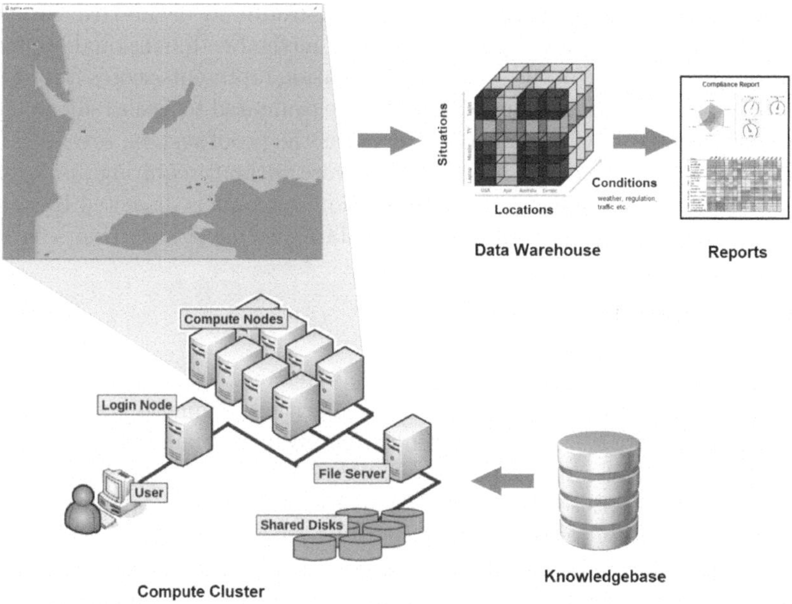

Fig. 5. A massive set of simulated scenarios are processed in several stages to generate a performance report capturing autonomous software behavior.

Simulation Scale-Up & Reporting: The containerized design of a *simulule* ensures that scaling up the simulation is fairly trivial using a HPC-cluster. Figure 5 is a reference architecture for a simulation infrastructure. The simulation workflow runs through the several stages according a choreographed sequence of steps:

Scenario Generation: A simulation definition program, selecting the set of scenarios to evaluate, generates permutations of *simulule* profiles storing it on the file system. The program also generates a task file for the cluster workload manager (e.g.:SLURM) to run simulations in parallel.

Cluster Runner: A runner script loads the task file submitted to the workload manager to spawn individual *simulules* as individual tasks across nodes on the HPC cluster. The *simulule* may interact with backend database (knowledgebase) and micro services during its run to access historical data, causality maps and other forms of domain knowledge required to orchestrate the simulation.

Data Aggregator: Upon completion of all simulations, an aggregator script ingests simulation score results stored in local cache database on each node to export it into a central OLAP database. Data stored in the OLAP database maps simulation performance along aspects of matitime scenarios, covering: situations, locations and conditions (e.g.: weather, traffic, jurisdiction etc.).

Report Generation: Finally, a customizable reporting tool interacts with the OLAP database to help visualize the data. A front-end dashboard with heat maps present aggregate simulation scores along navigable dimensional intersects.

The output database of the scaled-up simulation represents scores from a multiverse of hypothetical situations where AVs are evaluated to assure safe behavior in a composite system. This multiverse serves as the proof system, revealing both delinquencies and traits of the tested AV software without requiring disclosure of its internal workings. Analysis of the simulation outcome is dissected by analyzing the collated scored results stored in the database using reporting solutions.

5 Illustration

This section presents an illustrative case study demonstrating the application of our platform to assure AV compliance with maritime regulations (COLREGs). Whereas a vessels are typically expected to comply with a family of international (e.g.:COLREG, MASS) and coastal regulatory protocols, our case study focuses exclusively on COLREG safety verification. However, the tools and techniques used in this case study is directly transferable to any analogous family of vessel safety protocols. In the interest of brevity, the reader is advised that this section only provides glimpses into the key features of the system. A thorough treatment of the practice is intended for a future sibling publication focusing exclusively on *Legata*.

5.1 Assurance Solution for COLREG Compliance

The COLREG are a set of rules established by the International Maritime Organization (IMO) to ensure safe navigation and prevent collisions between vessels; they are essentially the driving rules for vessels at open sea. The COLREGs encompass a wide range of scenarios, encompassing various circumstance that arise at sea: the conduct of vessels in various visibility conditions, the responsibilities of vessels in terms of right of way, and the actions to be taken to avoid collisions. The ambiguity of COLREGs exemplifies the challenges in ensuring autonomous machines comply with current regulated environments; thus serving as the ideal test bed demonstrating the applicability of our methodology to similar cases.

Conventional COLREG verification systems (COLREG-VS) are buttressed by a conceptual framework and a knowledge base. Whereas the knowledge base captures domain characteristics (e.g., properties of the environment) and behaviors (e.g., actions possible within the environment), the conceptual framework typically interprets knowledge for testing purposes to dynamically synthesizing test scenarios in real-time based on observed environmental situations. Verification systems typically embed both capabilities into monolithic individual test cases, a problematic issue because it scales poorly to situational diversity. Breaking convention, the verification system on the COS platform externalizes environmental, situational, and practical knowledge into external artifacts (files, databases, etc.). This expands the scope of verification, while also enabling a gradual system enrichment, by incorporating rich modeling paradigms, data sources, and algorithmic techniques through external artifacts. The COLREG-VS employs specialized *faculties* to a) synthesize real-time test scenarios to verify concepts, b) respond to simulation events and state information from the test environment to ensure realism and c) evaluate situations and generate test scores. This 'gang of faculties' collectively ensures broader assurances on safety coverage and reliability by exposing the tested algorithms to a wider range of operating conditions. Within the COLREG-VS we distinguish two types of rules that govern the behavior of a simulation: *physical rules* - immutable physical laws that govern the natural world expressed as mathematical equations in the simulation, and *regulations* - regulatory constructs that 'police' the simulation to prevent or minimize circumstances of contention or accidents; maritime regulations fall in this category.

Encoding Regulations: Since regulations like COLREG are notoriously imprecise, abstract, vague, and conceptual, cross-referential, dispositional, and deferential to exceptions, our approach to systematize and interpret it involves two phases:

- *Pipelining:* Process events in the simulation through a decision flow that progressively elevates observations to higher levels of abstraction. In our COLREG model, situations transform physical observations (e.g., movement of vessels) into logical occurrences. Regulatory clauses can then be used to interpret these occurrences, transforming them into regulatory occurrences and scoring them based on a verification scheme. (Figure 4)
- *Conceptualizing:* Regulatory clauses require situations to provide context, necessitating an abstract, conceptual language and algebra of concepts for encoding. *Legata* transcriptions of COLREGs, fills this gap by providing a language to capture legal abstractions.

Encoding Physical Rules: Modeling physics into the simulation is straightforward [21]. The example below shows how standard vessel dynamics equations [5] and weather behavior are typically incorporated into realistic simulations of a vessels at sea. Several such models including weather patterns, radio & sonic transmission models and optical visibility models are easily incorporated using physics programs implemented as faculties to orchestrate various elements of the simulation.

Example: To simulate ship dynamics, a simplified 3-degrees-of-freedom (DoF) ship maneuvering model [7] is used as presented in Eq. 1.

$$\dot{\boldsymbol{\eta}} = \mathbf{R}(\psi)\boldsymbol{\nu} \tag{1a}$$

$$\mathbf{M}\dot{\boldsymbol{\nu}} + \mathbf{C}(\boldsymbol{\nu})\boldsymbol{\nu} + \mathbf{D}(\boldsymbol{\nu})\boldsymbol{\nu} = \boldsymbol{\tau} \tag{1b}$$

$$\mathbf{R}(\psi) = \begin{bmatrix} \cos(\psi) & -\sin(\psi) & 0 \\ \sin(\psi) & \cos(\psi) & 0 \\ 0 & 0 & 1 \end{bmatrix} \tag{1c}$$

Ship states consist of $\boldsymbol{\eta} = [x, y, \psi]^{\mathrm{T}}$, i.e., position and heading angle in the Earth-fixed Cartesian coordinate frame, and $\boldsymbol{\nu} = [u, v, r]^{\mathrm{T}}$, i.e., surge, sway velocities and yaw rate in the body-fixed coordinate frame. $\mathbf{M}$, $\mathbf{C}(\cdot)$, $\mathbf{D}(\cdot)$ are Inertia, Coriolis-centripetal, and Damping matrices respectively, and a rotation matrix $\mathbf{R}(\cdot)$ is used to transform body-fixed frame to earth-fixed frame. $\boldsymbol{\tau}$ represents forces and moments in the surge, sway directions, and yaw axis, that result from the steering and propulsion systems. Note that for simulating surface vessels it is customary to employ a simplified 3-degrees-of-freedom (DoF), whereas more sophisticated schemes of physics models with 6-degrees-of-freedom (DoF) is generally applied to simulate aerial drones at sea and underwater vessels moving in 3-dimensions.

6 Discussion

Our approach to implementing the COLREG assurance platform delivers significantly more scenario coverage than conventional tools. It thus ensures improved safety of AI algorithms used in ASVs. However, the experience building our platform left us with several important lessons, learned along the way:

- *Multi-faceted approaches are required to tackle AI verification and compliance:* Our case study revealed how an alchemy of paradigms, platform, modeling and tools (e.g.:compilers) are required to broadly address the challenge.
- *One-size does not fit all:* The case study demonstrates that optimal coverage requires getting closer to specifics of the domain and developing tools that specialized for the domain. Although platforms are general usable, tools have to be developed with specificity and locality in mind.
- *Precise assurances require rich datasets:* Historical (e.g.: traffic and weather) and factual data (e.g.: maps, vessel models) are critical to assuring the simulations imitate reality as closely as possible. This ensures the accuracy of the results generated by the proof system.

- *Regulations are nuanced, assurance systems have to be too:* Assurance platforms ought to have the flexibility to test a wide range of situations, in particular rules are nuanced by interpretations, whether attributed to linguistic or jurisdictional interpretations does not matter, but they will all need to be assured.
- *Multi-disciplinary skills are required for modeling:* Modular platforms, flexible enough to adapt to several domains make modeling for AI compliance possible is crucial. However, creating the models also requires a team with multi-disciplinary skills to imbue the simulations with rich realistic models that mimic the physical world.

Several limitations also became evident to us along the way:

- *What you model is what you assure:* There is no silver bullet to assurances on total AI safety. But it is pragmatically possible to assure adequate safety for all practical purposes. The catch however is that the scope of assurances must be bound by the scope of what the assurance model can test [41].
- *Massive demands for data and compute limits model accuracy:* The implicit requirement for a HPC infrastructure, and the dependency on massive (e.g.: weather, traffic, accidents) or regulated (e.g.: risk models or data based on proprietary/legal documents) datasets can restrict access to the methodology to but the largest organizations [28].

7 Conclusion

In this paper we address the critical challenge of modeling platforms to ensure the safety and reliability of AVs. We present a systematic approach to compliance verification leveraging large-scale, representationally accurate simulations and a novel domain specific computer language for COLREGs that demonstrates how compliance coverage can be significantly enhanced than is conventionally possible. Our research create a solution that complementary conventional practices by maximizing test coverage in a virtual test environment thus reducing the current excessively high cost and burden of conducting comprehensive physical tests [18]. The applicability of our approach reveals principles we believe applies to broader applications of safety and compliance assurance across AI regulated sectors - healthcare, transportation and hospitality - where autonomous systems are rapidly gaining traction.

Future work will focus not just on expanding the coverage of maritime regulations but also harnessing recent advances in AI including small language models and graph neural networks to augment the generative testing capabilities of our platform. Also on the roadmap is fusion of aerial, underwater and surface vessels into a universal simulation platform, expanded support for sensors & instrumentation and advancement of a public knowledgebase of simulation data.

Acknowledgments. This work and the related research project is part of SFI AutoShip and funded by the Research Council of Norway under project number 309230.

Disclosure of Interests. The authors declared no potential conflicts of interest with respect to the research, authorship, and/or publication of this article.

References

1. Baldauf, M., Benedict, K., Fischer, S., Motz, F., Schröder-Hinrichs, J.U.: Collision avoidance systems in air and maritime traffic. Proc. Inst. Mech. Eng. Part O: J. Risk Reliab. **225**(3), 233–245 (2011)
2. Burmeister, H.C., Constapel, M.: Autonomous collision avoidance at sea: a survey. Front. Robot. AI **297**, 739013 (2021)
3. Corso, A., Moss, R., Koren, M., Lee, R., Kochenderfer, M.: A survey of algorithms for black-box safety validation of cyber-physical systems. J. Artif. Intell. Res. **72** (2021). https://doi.org/10.1613/jair.1.12716
4. DNV GL, Kongsberg, SINTEF Ocean, NTNU, 2018. Open Simulation Platform, September 2018. www.opensimulationplatform.com
5. Fossen, T.I.: Handbook of Marine Craft Hydrodynamics and Motion Control. Wiley, Hoboken, 2nd edn (2021)
6. Foster, S., Gleirscher, M., Calinescu, R.: Towards deductive verification of control algorithms for autonomous marine vehicles 2020 25th International Conference on Engineering of Complex Computer Systems (ICECCS), pp. 113–118. IEEE (2020)
7. Fremont, D.J., et al.: Mehta formal scenario-based testing of autonomous vehicles: from simulation to the real world. In: IEEE 23rd International Conference on Intelligent Transportation Systems (ITSC), pp. 1–8 (2020)
8. Hagen, I.B., Vassbotn, O., Skogvold, M., Johansen, T.A., Brekke, E.F.: Safety and COLREGs evaluation for marine collision avoidance algorithms. Ocean Eng. **288**, 115991 (2022)
9. Hagen, I.B., Kufoalor, M.K., Brekke, E.F., Johansen,T.A.: Scenario-based model predictive control with several steps for COLREGs compliant ship collision avoidance. In: 14th IFAC Conference on Control Applications in Marine Systems, Robotics and Vehicles (CAMS) (2022)
10. Hawkins, J., Lewis, M., Klukas, M., Purdy, S., Ahmad, S.: A framework for intelligence and cortical function based on grid cells in the neocortex. Front. Neural Circ. **12** (2019). https://doi.org/10.3389/fncir.2018.00121
11. Hawkins, J., Ahmad, S., Cui, Y.: Why does the neocortex have columns, a theory of learning the structure of the world (2017) https://doi.org/10.1101/162263
12. Hawkins, J., Ahmad, S., Cui, Y.: A theory of how columns in the neocortex enable learning the structure of the world. Front. Neural Circ. **11** (2017). https://doi.org/10.3389/fncir.2017.00081
13. Hawkins, J., Blakeslee, S.: On Intelligence. Times Books, Manhattan, NY, USA (2004)
14. He, Y., Li, Z., Mou, J., Hu, W., Li, L., Wang, B.: Collision-avoidance path planning for multi-ship encounters considering ship manoeuvrability and COLREGs. Transp. Saf. Environ. (2021). https://doi.org/10.1093/tse/tdab004
15. Huang, Y., Chen, L., Chen, P., Negenborn, R.R., Van Gelder, P.H.A.J.M.: Ship collision avoidance methods: state-of-the-art. Saf. Sci. **121**, 451–473 (2020)
16. Lindvall, M., Porter, A., Magnusson, G., Schulze, C.: Metamorphic model-based testing of autonomous systems. In: 2017 IEEE/ACM 2nd International Workshop on Metamorphic Testing (MET), pp. 35–41. IEEE (2017)

17. Khastgir, S., Brewerton, S., Thomas, J., Jennings, P.: Systems approach to creating test scenarios for automated driving systems. Reliab. Eng. Syst. Saf. **215**, 107610 (2021)
18. Liu, J., Yang, F., Li, S., Lv, Y., Hu, X.: Testing and evaluation for intelligent navigation of ships: current status, possible solutions, and challenges. Ocean Eng. **295**, 116969 (2024). https://doi.org/10.1016/j.oceaneng.2024.116969
19. Öztürk, Ü., Akdag, M., Ayabakan, T.: A review of path planning algorithms in maritime autonomous surface ships: navigation safety perspective. Ocean Eng. **251**, 111010 (2022)
20. Mahler, T.: Regulating artificial general intelligence (AGI). In: Custers, B., Fosch-Villaronga, E. (eds.) Law and Artificial Intelligence. Information Technology and Law Series, vol. 35. T.M.C. Asser Press, The Hague (2022)
21. Menges, D., Rasheed, A.: An environmental disturbance observer framework for autonomous ships (2022). https://doi.org/10.48550/arXiv.2211.08360
22. Minne, P.K.E.: Automatic testing of maritime collision avoidance algorithms. In: NTNU (2017)
23. Minsky, M.L.: A framework for representing knowledge. In: Winston, P.H. (ed.). The Psychology of Computer Vision, McGraw-Hill (1977). [aLWB]
24. Minsky, M.L.: The society of mind. Simon & Schuster (1985)
25. Park, J., Kim, J.: autonomous docking of an unmanned surface vehicle based on reachability analysis. In: 2020 20th International Conference on Control Automation and Systems (ICCAS), pp. 962–966 (2020)
26. Navarro, A., Sanchis, J., Maté, A., Trujillo, J.: An approach aligned with model driven development to evaluate the quality of explainable artificial intelligence. In: International Conference on Conceptual Modeling, pp. 284–293 (2023). https://doi.org/10.1007/978-3-031-47112-4-27
27. Pedersen, T., Glomsrud, J.A., Haugen, O.I.: Towards simulation-based verification of autonomous navigation systems. In: Proceedings of the International Seminar on Safety and Security of AVs (ISSAV) and European STAMP Workshop and Conference (ESWC) (2019). https://doi.org/10.2478/9788395669606-00
28. Pedersen, T., Vasanthan, C., Karolius, K., Engelhardtsen, Ø., Houweling, K., Jørgensen, A.: Generating structured set of encounters for verifying automated collision and grounding avoidance systems (2023). https://doi.org/10.1088/1742-6596/2618/1/012013
29. Pedersen, T., et al.: Evolution of safety in marine systems: from system-theoretic process analysis to automated test scenario generation. J. Phys: Conf. Ser. **2311**, 012016 (2022). https://doi.org/10.1088/1742-6596/2311/1/012016
30. Peled, D., Vardi, M.Y., Yannakakis, M.: Black box checking. In: Wu, J., Chanson, S.T., Gao, Q. (eds.) Formal Methods for Protocol Engineering and Distributed Systems. IAICT, vol. 28, pp. 225–240. Springer, Boston, MA (1999). https://doi.org/10.1007/978-0-387-35578-8_13
31. Riedmaier, S., Schneider, J., Danquah, B., Schick, B., Diermeyer, F.: Non-deterministic model validation methodology for simulation-based safety assessment of automated vehicles. Simulat. Model. Pract. Theor. **109**, 102274 (2021)
32. Rokseth, B., Haugen, O.I., Utne, I.B.: Safety verification for autonomous ships. In: MATEC Web of Conferences EDP Sciences (2019)
33. Rumelhart, D. E., McClelland, J.L.: The PDP Research Group: Parallel distributed processing: Explorations in the microstructure of cognition:, vol. 1. MIT Press, Foundations (1986)
34. Russell, S.J.: Artificial IntelligenceâĂŕ: A Modern Approach. Upper Saddle River, N.J., Prentice Hall (2010)

35. Shokri-Manninen, F., Vain, J., Waldén, M.: Formal verification of COLREG-based navigation of maritime autonomous systems. In: de Boer, F., Cerone, A. (eds.) SEFM 2020. LNCS, vol. 12310, pp. 41–59. Springer, Cham (2020). https://doi.org/10.1007/978-3-030-58768-0_3
36. Sormunen, O. V., Goerlandt, F., Kujala, P.: A risk-informed ship collision avoidance system: framework and model development. Risk Anal. **38**(5), 1049–1067 (2018). Exploration of the Human-Machine Interface in Autonomous Systems
37. Stankiewicz, P.G., Mullins, G.E.: Improving evaluation methodology for autonomous surface vessel COLREGs compliance. In: OCEANS 2019-Marseille, pp. 1-7. IEEE (2019)
38. Torben, T.R., Glomsrud, J.A., Pedersen, T.A., Utne, I.B., Sørensen A.J.: Automatic simulation-based testing of autonomous ships using Gaussian processes and temporal logic. In: Proceedings of the Institution of Mechanical Engineers, Part O: Journal of Risk and Reliability, vol. 237, p. 1748006X2110692 (2022). https://doi.org/10.1177/1748006X211069277
39. Vagale, A., Bye, R.T., Oucheikh, R., Osen, O.L., Fossen, T.I.: Path planning and collision avoidance for autonomous surface vehicles II: a comparative study of algorithms. J. Mar. Sci. Technol. **26**(4), 1307–1323 (2021)
40. Woerner, K.L.: COLREGS-compliant Autonomous Collision Avoidance Using Multi-Objective Optimization with Interval Programming. MIT, Cambridge (2014)
41. Woerner, K.L., Benjamin, M.R., Novitzky, M., Leonard, J.J.: Collision avoidance road test for COLREG-constrained autonomous vehicles. In: OCEANS, vol. 2016 MTS/IEEE Monterey, pp. 1–6 (2016). [148]
42. Wooldridge, M.: An Introduction to MultiAgent Systems. 2nd Edition. Wiley, Hoboken (2009)

LLM4Modeling

2nd Workshop on Modeling in the Age of Large Language Models (LLM4Modeling)

Hans-Georg Fill[1], Peter Fettke[3], and Julius Köpke[2]

[1] University of Fribourg, Switzerland
hans-georg.fill@unifr.ch
[2] Saarland University and German Research Center for Artificial Intelligence (DFKI), Germany
julius.koepke@aau.at
[3] University of Klagenfurt, Austria
peter.fettke@dfki.de

Large language models (LLMs) have recently received enormous attention in practice and science. It is evident that LLMs have the potential to develop some rudimentary aspects of a domain model quickly. However, it is unclear which precision and quality can be achieved. The question is how modeling will deal with LLMs in the future. Which influence will LLMs have on modeling? How will the tasks of modeling change? Will modeling lose its importance?

The workshop aimed at illuminating the potential and challenges of LLMs in modeling. We report here on the second iteration of the Workshop on Modeling in the Age of Large Language Models (LLM4Modeling) at ER'2024 after the first LLM4Modeling Workshop at the Modellierung 2024 conference in Potsdam.

We received in total seven submissions. Three papers were carefully selected based on rigorous reviews for presentation and inclusion in the proceedings. Each paper received at least three reviews in a double-blind review process.

The paper "An LLM Assistant for Characterizing Conceptual Modeling Research Contributions" reports on creating a fine-tuned ChatGPT model (assistant) for analyzing the content of research articles in the domain of Conceptual Modeling.

In "AI-Assisted Analytics – An Automated Approach to Data Visualization", the authors propose an LLM-based approach for AI-assisted analytics focusing on visualizations. A central component is a conceptualization of analytical tasks as a taxonomy to assist an LLM in identifying tasks.

The paper "Combining Natural Language Generation and Graph Algorithms to Explain Causal Maps through Meaningful Paragraphs" presents an LLM-based method for automatically translating causal maps into natural language. To tackle large graphs, the approach automatically generates sub-graphs for LLM processing. Therefore, a considerable number of graph algorithms and LLMs are evaluated.

Acknowledgements. We would like to express our gratitude to everyone involved in making the second LLM4Modeling Workshop a success: the authors of all papers, the Program Committee members and additional reviewers for reviewing each paper, and the speakers who shared their valuable work. We also thank the ER 2024 chairs and organizers for their support in preparing the Workshop.

LLM4Modeling Organization

Program Chairs

Hans-Georg Fill	University of Fribourg, Switzerland
Peter Fettke	German Research Center for Artificial Intelligence (DFKI), Germany
Julius Köpke	University of Klagenfurt, Austria

Program Committee

Dominik Bork	Vienna University of Technology, Austria
Robert Andrei Buchmann	Babeş-Bolyai University of Cluj Napoca, Romania
Patrick Delfmann	University of Koblenz-Landau, Germany
Chiara Di Francescomarino	University of Trento, Italy
Felix Härer	University of Fribourg, Switzerland
Manfred Jeusfeld	University of Skövde, Sweden
Florian Johannsen	University of Bremen, Germany
Agnes Koschmider	University of Bayreuth, Germany
Henrik Leopold	Kühne Logistics University, Germany
Oscar Pastor	Universidad Politécnica de Valencia, Spain
Dimitris Plexousakis	FORTH Institute of Computer Science, Greece
Henderik A. Proper	Vienna University of Technology, Austria
Bernhard Rumpe	RWTH Aachen University, Germany
Kurt Sandkuhl	The University of Rostock, Germany
Maribel Yasmina Santos	University of Minho, Portugal
Reinhard Schütte	University of Duisburg-Essen, Germany
Cogan Shimizu	Wright State University, USA
Pnina Soffer	University of Haifa, Israel
Wilfrid Utz	OMILAB gGmbH, Germany
Maxim Vidgof	Vienna University of Economics and Business, Austria
Sandra Zilker	Technische Hochschule Nürnberg Georg Simon Ohm, Germany

Additional Reviewers

Syed Juned Ali
Katerina Papantoniou
Yorck Zisgen
Alexander Lüpges
Fabian Muff

An LLM Assistant for Characterizing Conceptual Modeling Research Contributions

Stephen W. Liddle[1(✉)], Heinrich C. Mayr[2], Oscar Pastor[3], Veda C. Storey[4], and Bernhard Thalheim[5]

[1] Brigham Young University, Provo, UT, USA
liddle@byu.edu
[2] Alpen-Adria-Universität, Klagenfurt, Austria
[3] Universitat Politècnica de València, Valencia, Spain
[4] Georgia State University, Atlanta, GA, USA
[5] Christian-Albrechts-Universität, Kiel, Germany

Abstract. Research in conceptual modeling has led to such a vast and diverse body of publications that it is difficult for any one research group to digest it all. Approaches such as the Characterizing Conceptual Modeling Research framework have been proposed to help organize these contributions, but it is unrealistic to expect human experts to manually characterize all of this research. LLM-based generative AI tools like ChatGPT offer the promise of helping with this tedious manual work. In this paper, we show how to create and tune a customized version of ChatGPT to help with this task. Using this approach, it is feasible to create a truly usable knowledge survey for the evolving body of conceptual modeling research contributions.

Keywords: LLM-based content characterization · Characterizing Conceptual Modeling Research framework (CCMR) · AI assistant for ER research evaluation

1 Introduction

The field of conceptual modeling (CM) has evolved over decades of research and practice. Given the large number of publications in the field of CM and the variety of subfields covering, for example, methods, languages, and models [17], concentrated characterizations of CM research contributions could be very helpful for different user groups. Consider, for example, conference participants who want a quick overview of the individual paper contributions to put together their individual plan of presentations to attend; or a practitioner or scientist who wants to compile relevant CM material for a planned project. Publicly available brief characterizations of research contributions could make these tasks more manageable and efficient.

M. Saeki et al. (Eds.): ER 2024 Workshops, LNCS 14932, pp. 325–342, 2025.
https://doi.org/10.1007/978-3-031-75599-6_23

We use the CCMR (Characterizing Conceptual Modeling Research) framework as a starting point [9] for characterizing CM research contributions. This framework comprises a set of dimensions that are relevant for CM research initiatives and is supported by a tool allowing for recording characterizations in a database. However, the number of relevant publications in the field of CM is so large that it is unrealistic to expect experts to create and record such characterizations manually for all relevant publications.

Inspired by recent advances in the field of artificial intelligence (AI), we pose the **research question**, *"To what extent and quality level can an AI-based tool be created and applied in a useful way for analyzing the content of CM research articles and the characterization of their contributions?"* Generative AI tools like OpenAI's ChatGPT, Google's Gemini, and Anthropic's Claude.ai are useful in a wide variety of contexts. We seek to understand whether such technology could be effectively applied in to characterize CM research contributions effectively.

Although there is much debate about the philosophical underpinnings of LLMs, capacities and weaknesses need to be assessed. We, therefore, report our analysis in a concrete, practical case, namely on our experience in creating and using CCMR Assistant, which is a version of ChatGPT specifically customized for the analysis of entity-relationship (ER) and CM research articles. The results from its application indicate that this assistant delivers very good characterization results in most cases, although some revision might be required, which the CCMR Assistant itself can do when prompted appropriately. We conclude that a large base of knowledge could be accumulated in a reasonable amount of time, making the huge body of knowledge in ER and CM research more transparent and more accessible for both researchers and practitioners.

We describe the creation of the custom GPT tool, showing how the prompts we employed increasingly improved its understanding of CCMR and the characterization task. We carefully report a sequence of actions:

1. We asked ChatGPT to create an expert assistant (so-called CCMR Assistant, the tool to be used in our practical experiment) intended to have the skills and personality of a research scientist in the field of CM. We instructed ChatGPT to do this based on the CCMR description from a reference paper. We also supplied additional CM knowledge to fine-tune the custom GPT.
2. After creating the CCMR Assistant and choosing a name and a logo for it, we started training the CCMR Assistant in the analysis and conceptual characterization of CM research papers. The main answers to be provided included: (1) a summary of the central contribution of the selected paper, (2) the classification of the primary contribution of the research according to the CCMR taxonomy and (3) an explanation of the relevance of the paper to the CM field.
3. The subsequent sequence of prompts was intended to instruct ChatGPT to improve its answers. This process provided us with a set of interesting insights into how relevant the prompting style was for obtaining correct answers. The "prompt engineering" dimension of this problem will also be discussed at the end of this paper.

The remainder of this paper is organized as follows: Sect. 2 provides an overview of the main objectives and structure of the CCMR framework. In Sect. 3 we discuss the development of our CCMR Assistant and its use. Section 4 presents some results of the application of the CCMR Assistant to selected research articles and discusses the quality of the characterizations provided by the assistant. Section 5 provides an overview of related work. Section 6 summarizes and concludes the paper with suggestions for future work.

2 The Characterizing Conceptual Modeling Research Framework

Characterizing Conceptual Modeling Research (CCMR), upon which we base the training of our AI tool for characterizing CM research contributions, is described in detail in [9]. We therefore only provide a brief overview of the main structural elements of the framework here.

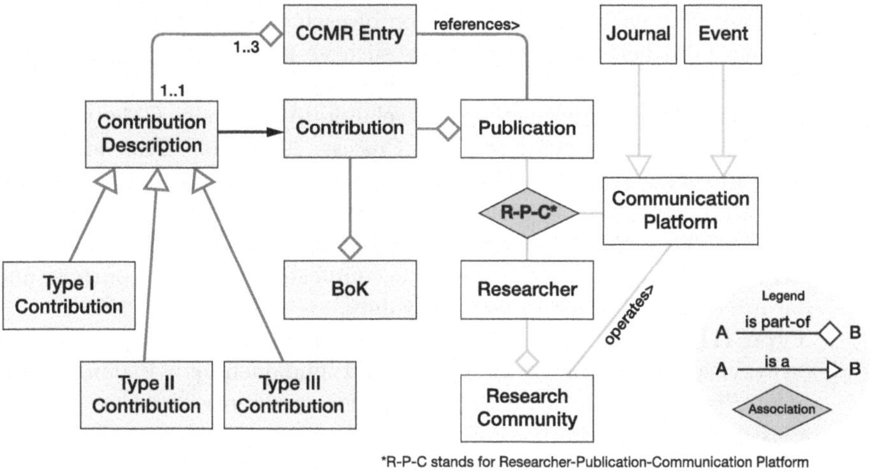

Fig. 1. Conceptual model for CCMR's universe of discourse [9]

Figure 1 shows a conceptualization of the aspects that are relevant in the context of CCMR and this investigation, with the following three main parts:

1. **Who contributes where** (yellow, on the right side of the figure): *Researchers* author *Publications* in *Communication Platforms* (association *R-P-C*) operated by *Research Communities* where *Communication Platforms* include *Journals* and *Events* (e.g. conferences where papers are published in the proceedings). *Researchers* are part of (belong to) *Research Communities.*
2. **The contribution and its area** (blue, lower two concepts in the middle): Through their publications, researchers make *Contributions* to the *Body of Knowledge* (*BoK*) of a research field; here, the field of conceptual modeling.

3. **Description of the contribution** (green, top concept in middle, plus entire left side): A *CCMR Entry* can describe up to three types of contributions, labeled as follows (see Table 1 for an example).
   - **Type I:** A concrete CM-based artifact as a created, valuable object (a kind of "what the CM is" aspect): *Model, Metamodel, Language, Notation, etc.* A Type I contribution includes a description of the specific accomplishment with its purpose and nature. Such contributions can be further explained using the paradigm of the Triptych of Conceptual Modeling [16] which features three dimensions with its three wings: *language*, *model*, and *meaning*. Even if we take a very general concept of language as a basis, we can assume that languages used to represent models have a defined notation and certain grammatical composition rules. The model dimension defines the structure of the models in different levels of an abstraction hierarchy. One example is the Object Management Group's MetaObject Facility (MOF) where a metamodel defines the intended modeling concepts. The meaning dimension provides the grounding of the concepts introduced in the model dimension at all levels, e.g., through an ontological or encyclopedic definition of each concept or through a thesaurus, data dictionary, or glossary such as a "company manual" that defines all of the terms used in a given company [27].
   - **Type II:** The procedural strategy to elaborate or manage CMs (the "how the CM is built" aspect): *Method, Process, Algorithm, Tool, etc.* This type is for characterizing work that contributes a method, a process, an algorithm, a tool, a methodology, or something similar. The focus is on the process followed to elaborate or manage models. A Type II contribution includes a description of the specific accomplishment with its purpose and nature, each with a list of possible values.
   - **Type III:** The principles that guide and support the CM process (the "why, visionary" aspect that explains CM fundamentals): *Vision, Philosophy, Principles, Review, etc.* This type focuses on research that presents a vision for the field, a discussion of philosophy or principles, a broad survey paper, an approach to pedagogy or education in conceptual modeling, or an application of conceptual modeling to an interesting domain.

Based on this framework, a schema for the detailed description of contributions along with a prototype web-based tool to capture CCMR characterizations (see https://ccmr.byu.edu/) has been developed. Figure 2 shows a screenshot of the tool's overview page with its four main sections:

1. bibliographic information,
2. the significant contribution of a work,
3. a detailed characterization of the contribution within 3 main contribution types
4. any additional information a user wishes to record.

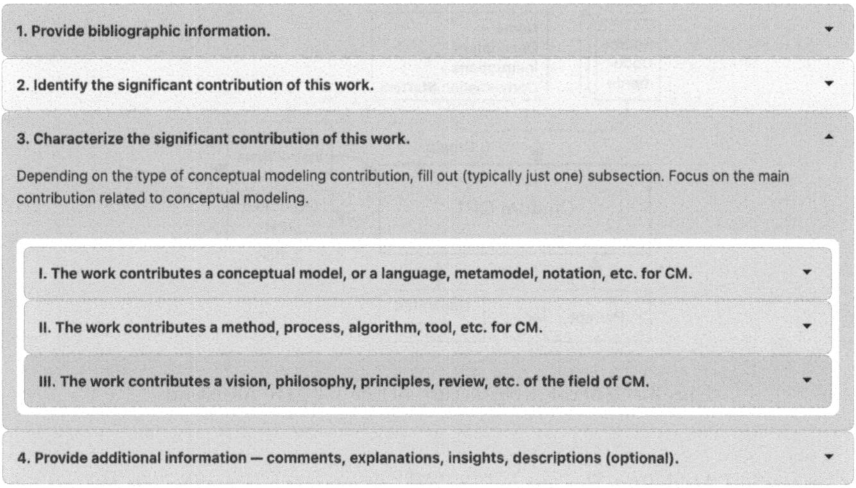

Fig. 2. Overview page of the CCMR tool [9]

3 The CCMR Assistant

To test whether LLM-based AI can provide meaningful assistance in filling out CCMR forms, we used OpenAI's ChatGPT [2] to create a custom GPT (Generative Pre-trained Transformer) that we called "CCMR Assistant" using the latest GPT-4o model. Any ChatGPT Plus subscriber with the link can access the CCMR Assistant custom GPT (see [1]).

Figure 3 shows the general architecture of the CCMR Assistant. It is a custom GPT configured (step 1) by supplying an initial set of source documents (in PDF format) along with identifying fields and textual instructions. After the initial configuration of the custom GPT, the developer can give additional instructions to refine its behavior through textual prompts. Steps 2 (editing) and 3 (usage) can be performed repeatedly and in any order. Only the custom GPT developer can perform steps 1 and 2 (this is the *training* of the tool). Anyone with access to the custom GPT can perform step 3 (tool usage). The prompts detailed in this section are all parts of steps 1 and 2, not step 3 end-user prompts. In this section, when we state that we submitted a paper to the custom GPT for evaluation, it was done in a separate step 3 conversation. The step 3 prompt was always something similar to "*Characterize this paper using CCMR.*"

To train the CCMR Assistant, we first designed a creation prompt consisting of the following text:

- *Create an expert assistant called CCMR Assistant that has the skills and personality of a research scientist in the field of conceptual modeling, which is a sub-discipline of computer science, information systems, informatics, and knowledge management. The assistant will analyze research papers to summarize their contributions to conceptual modeling (CM). Use the Characterizing*

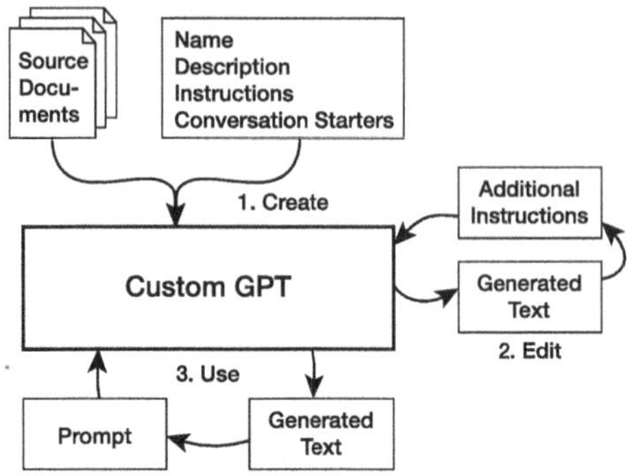

Fig. 3. General architecture of the CCMR Assistant.

Conceptual Modeling Research (CCMR) framework described in the attached manuscript (A Structured Perspective on Conceptual Modeling Research) as a guide for how to characterize CM research papers. Favor concise answers. Do not be verbose.

- *When a user uploads a PDF of a research paper, use the CCMR framework to summarize the paper. There are four parts to CCMR: bibliographic information, identify the significant contribution, characterize the significant contribution, and provide additional information. Ignore the bibliographic information section and instead start by answering the questions under "identify the significant contribution". Especially indicate what are the key questions addressed in the work, what is the central contribution of the work, and how is the work relevant to CM. Be brief when answering the relevance question. The question on CM users targeted/assumed/mentioned in the work probably won't apply for many CM papers. It's okay to say N/A in such cases. Be concise if you answer this question, or say "N/A". Likewise, the question on "application of CM" should only be answered (and briefly) if the application of CM is a significant part of the paper's contribution. It's okay to say "N/A" when appropriate.*
- *Do not guess. Make statements based on verifiable facts. When a field is optional, do not comment on it unless it applies. Use a professional, concise way of speaking. Do not get pedantic or overly formal. When special terminology is required, that's okay, but prefer clear, concise, professional language. Use language in a way that an international audience will understand clearly. Use the uploaded documents I have given you to inform your knowledge of the field of conceptual modeling.*
- *In addition to giving an initial characterization as described above, also characterize the central contribution by classifying a research paper according to Type I (the "what" of CM, focused on a conceptual model as an artifact), Type II (the "how" of CM, focused on processes of conceptual modeling), or Type III (other aspects of CM, such as vision, philosophy, application, education, and so forth). Analyze the CCMR framework to understand these three types.*

- *When asked for more detail, provide a full CCMR characterization of the paper and its primary contribution. In some cases there may be more than one primary contribution, and those contributions could be of different types.*
- *When the user uploads a paper, start by telling the user about that paper's key questions, central contribution, and relevance to conceptual modeling. Also indicate the type of the central contribution.*

Along with this creation prompt, we also uploaded PDF files to give the CCMR Assistant direct access to additional CM knowledge. Because the CCMR framework is core to this custom GPT, we provided the full text of the 2024 submitted manuscript explaining CCMR in detail [9]. Likewise, since the Triptych of Conceptual Modeling mentioned in Sect. 2 is a vital component of the CCMR framework, we provided the full text of that work [16]. We also provided the full text of several books on conceptual modeling, including the 2000 book by Thalheim [28], the 2001 book by Pastor et al. [23], and the 2007 book by Olivé [20]. To give some historical context we provided the full text of surveys from the 1980's on semantic data models [14,24]. The paper by Mylopoulos [18] is often cited for its definition of "conceptual modeling." Wand and Weber's 2002 research commentary on information systems and conceptual modeling is influential in the IS community [29], and Guizzardi's 2005 PhD thesis gives broad and detailed background for the conceptual modeling ontology community [11].

We had initially attempted to upload many more helpful CM resources, only to discover that custom GPTs are constrained to a maximum of 10 files.[1] We could in the future bundle a number of helpful papers into a single PDF, but in this exploratory phase we simply deleted the other files.

The next step was to use the CCMR Assistant custom GPT to characterize various papers that we had already manually characterized. We found the majority of its answers to be fairly good, but it clearly deviated from human expert judgment in many cases and often did not follow the full detailed instructions it was given.

We initially created the CCMR Assistant using these materials and then realized that it was not fully exploiting the details of the CCMR framework. This was because much of the CCMR framework is presented in the 2024 manuscript as screenshots. We, therefore, applied an OCR tool to the PDF and re-uploaded it. Then we verified that the CCMR Assistant could repeat back the various sections of the CCMR framework accurately by asking the creation tool detailed questions about CCMR's various parts. We instructed the custom GPT to use the CCMR framework as it had repeated it back to us. The accuracy of answers and fidelity to the CCMR framework improved after this corrective step. Indeed, the CCMR Assistant was able essentially to quote the CCMR manuscript [9], which uses CCMR to describe itself.

After testing the custom GPT on conceptual modeling papers, we observed that, in spite of repeated instructions to be concise, the tool was still giving fairly verbose answers, and especially so when answering the CCMR question

[1] OpenAI has since increased the limit to 20 files with a maximum of 2,000,000 tokens each, checked August 21, 2024.

You
Be more concise when answering the question about relevance to CM, giving at most a couple of sentences.

GPT Builder
Understood! I will now provide more concise answers regarding relevance to the field of conceptual modeling (CM) whenever requested. Here's the updated behavior description:

Name: CCMR Assistant

Description: Expert in conceptual modeling research analysis, now more concise on CM relevance.

Context: The CCMR Assistant serves as a specialized resource in conceptual modeling, focusing on the analysis and summarization of research contributions using the Characterizing Conceptual Modeling Research (CCMR) framework. It targets academic and professional users, providing concise summaries of key questions, central contributions, and relevance to conceptual modeling. The assistant evaluates research papers, identifying their significant contributions and classifying them into one of three types: Type I (artifact-oriented), Type II (process-oriented), and Type III (encompassing broader aspects like vision, philosophy, or application). When discussing the relevance to the field of conceptual modeling, the assistant now gives succinct, focused responses.

Abilities: dalle, browser, python

Does this update meet your requirements? If yes, I'll confirm the change!

You
Yes

GPT Builder
Updating GPT...

Fig. 4. Sample dialog for tweaking custom GPT parameters.

about how the work is relevant to the field of conceptual modeling. Therefore, we issued the instruction, "*Be more concise when answering the question about relevance to CM, giving at most a couple of sentences*" and approved the change as Fig. 4 illustrates. This resulted in some improvement.

As we asked the CCMR Assistant to characterize additional papers, we discovered that further instructions were often necessary. For example, the custom GPT tool would still tend to be verbose, and sometimes it would go outside of the structure of the CCMR framework in describing a paper. So we tried the prompt, "*Be sure to use the form of the CCMR framework. Address the questions in the order shown in the CCMR framework. Give me the 'identify the significant contribution' section along with a contribution type characterization.*" This improved the quality of the output, but after submitting several more papers for characterization we still saw a fair amount of undesirable variety in structure generated by the tool. For example, in one case the tool returned an answer with the uploaded paper's title, authors, type of contribution, summary, key contributions, and relevance to conceptual modeling (which was still a lengthy paragraph). So we gave the prompt, "*I thought the CCMR had the fields of 'key questions', 'central contribution', 'relevance to CM', 'intended CM users', and 'application domain'.*" This led to an answer structured the way we wanted, but still too lengthy, so we introduced the following prompt:

- *Your answers vary in format too much. When you characterize or summarize a research paper using CCMR, be sure to give answers in the 'Identifying the Significant Contribution' section. Start by listing the key questions addressed in the paper, then describe its central contribution (including a determination of the type of the central contribution—Type I, II, or III). Then very briefly describe its relevance to CM. One sentence is probably enough on the relevance question. If applicable, answer the questions on intended CM users and application domain. Remember that for most papers those last two fields won't be needed and you can just answer 'N/A' for them. If the user asks for more details, give detailed answers according to the 'Characterizing the Significant Contribution' section of the CCMR form.*

At this point the CCMR Assistant gave responses that were more consistent in format and better aligned with CCMR when asked to characterize various research papers, as we show in Table 2. Indeed, the characterization obtained with the CCMR Assistant mimicked characterizations done by a human expert, as the one shown in Table 1.

4 Application of the CCMR Assistant

In this section we discuss how humans use tools in general and then more specifically explore our application of the CCMR Assistant tool.

4.1 The Pattern of Tool Usage

When humans use tools, and in today's context, especially when we use AI tools, it is possible to achieve an initial result productively and quite quickly. But, at the same time, it is important to emphasize the preparation and follow-up, depending on the quality we need from the initial tool output. Generative AI is prone to "hallucinate" [30], so careful human supervision is required even (or especially) with powerful generative AI technology. This general pattern of well-thought-out and professional use of tools is common practice in both craftsmanship and engineering. A practitioner knows:

- which tools should be prepared or be available, and at which level of quality,
- which framework of action and the order to follow,
- what would be a good result from using the given tools; and
- how to achieve a completely satisfactory result by using these tools.

Tool selection, work preparation and post-processing follow a guiding activity model and are determined by specific concerns. This model is described as a three-step mechanism:

Table 1. Characterization of [19] by a Human Expert

About this Work	
Title:	An Ontology for Context Modeling in Smart Spaces
Authors:	Leonardo Vianna do Nascimento and José Palazzo M. de Oliveira
Other info:	ER 2023, LNCS 14320, pp. 354–371, 2023.
Communities:	Developers of intelligent user-centered systems – including user-context adaptation – especially for smart systems
Identifying the Significant Contribution	
Key questions:	RQ1: How can context information about the user be captured for smart environments in a coherent, economical and sufficiently complete form? RQ2: Can a small but sophisticated ontology be developed as a standard vocabulary for the exchange of user context information for intelligent environments? RQ3: Which of the existing ontologies can be used in whole or in part as a starting point, or should a new and independent ontology be developed for smart spaces?
Central contribution:	Proposes an ontology-based model for user and usage context in smart (intelligence enhanced) environments. The novel SpaceCOn ontology was tested and trialed for data collection from wearables. The complete development and testing of ontologies was presented as a generalizable teaching example for analog data collection.
Relevance to CM:	Development of a usage/user context-tracking model capturing usage, users, and quality parameters
Intended CM users:	Developers of smart devices in similar applications; ontology researchers with a teaching example; modelers and programmers of services with an explicit integration of service quality.
Application domain:	Development of personalization means for smart devices and application to wearables
Characterizing the Significant Contribution	
I. Contributes a conceptual model, or a language, metamodel, notation, etc. for CM.	
Specific accomplishment:	Introduction of an ontology of contextual elements, with which the context quality can also be recorded according to assignments to various categories
Purpose:	Development and testing of an ontology for standardized exchange form of user context
Nature:	☑ **Definition** ☑ **Evaluation through a case study** ☑ **Formalization**
Modeling artifacts:	Categorized and prioritized contextual elements as containers with additional data on quality of context, time, and context category
Additional Information	
Special application case for design and development of web information systems with actors as context of a system.	

Table 2. Characterization of [19] by the CCMR Assistant Custom GPT Tool

About this Work	
Title:	An Ontology for Context Modeling in Smart Spaces
Authors:	Leonardo Vianna do Nascimento, José Palazzo Moreira de Oliveira
Other info:	ER 2023, LNCS 14320, pp. 354–371, 2023.
Communities:	*No answer provided*
Identifying the Significant Contribution	
Key questions:	1. How can context data in smart environments be semantically represented? 2. What are the essential requirements for an ontology that supports context modeling in smart spaces? 3. How can the developed ontology integrate context data from different sources in large smart environments like smart universities and cities?
Central contribution:	The central contribution of this paper is the development and presentation of an ontology called SpaceCOn (Smart Spaces Context Ontology). This ontology is designed to semantically represent context information in smart environments, addressing the need for a standardized approach to integrate context data from various sources.
Relevance to CM:	The work is relevant to the field of conceptual modeling as it provides a structured and semantically rich ontology for representing context data in smart environments. This contribution is significant because it enhances the ability to model, integrate, and utilize context information in ubiquitous computing applications, which is a growing area within conceptual modeling and information systems.
Intended CM users:	The primary users targeted by this research include developers and researchers working on ubiquitous computing applications, particularly those involved in designing and implementing smart environments such as smart cities and smart universities.
Application domain:	The application domain for this research is smart environments, specifically focusing on smart spaces like smart universities and cities. The ontology aims to facilitate the integration and utilization of context data to improve the functionality and user experience within these environments.
Characterizing the Significant Contribution	
I. Contributes a conceptual model, or a language, metamodel, notation, etc. for CM.	
Specific accomplishment:	Development of the SpaceCOn ontology for context modeling in smart spaces.
Purpose:	The ontology is developed to provide a standard way to semantically represent context information, facilitating data integration and interoperability in smart environments.
Nature:	*No answer provided*
Semantic Grounding:	Ensures that the context data represented by the ontology is unambiguous and interpretable across different systems and applications.
Modeling Artifacts:	The ontology itself is a modeling artifact that defines various context-related concepts and their relationships.
Linguistic Development:	Defines a common vocabulary and structure for context data, enabling consistent communication and integration.
Additional Information	
This paper makes a significant artifact-oriented contribution to the field of conceptual modeling by providing a robust ontology that addresses a critical need in the domain of smart environments. By doing so, it enhances the ability to model and integrate context data, which is essential for the development of sophisticated, context-aware applications in ubiquitous computing.	

1. First, an organizational framework and a scheme of action is adopted based on the concern.
2. Then the tools can be used according to their professional use.
3. Finally, the result obtained is processed in order to fully achieve the objective.

One application of an AI tool could be a booklet for a conference that can be adapted to specific needs. This could help resolve the information deficit of participants for conferences that only inform their participants about the proceedings at the on-site registration or shortly before the first session. Participants are thus relegated to a quick, quasi-random selection if they have not actively informed themselves in advance of the program. Sometimes the presentations lack time for discussion or only random questions are asked in a session.

A possible solution is a CCMR booklet, which could be further developed by respective participants and specialists through subsequent discussions and adaptation to their interests. Following the tool analogy, we can envision three steps:

1. A framework for describing conference contributions using CCMR is provided and used as a configuration for an AI tool.
2. With this configuration, an initial booklet can be created with the AI tool, which also supports a quick understanding of the contributions.
3. The booklet can then be enriched and potentially corrected, and printed as a nice accordion folding (or *leporello*) with further descriptions for the respective contributions. In this way, a scientific classification of the contributions is also carried out immediately.

Such an extended booklet could also form the basis for an overview presentation, for example, by a student reporting to a working group after a conference (especially useful when parallel sessions do not allow attendance at all presentations).

4.2 Evaluating the CCMR Assistant Tool

During the building phases of the CCMR Assistant training, we asked the assistant to evaluate all 11 of the papers characterized in the CCMR manuscript [9] one or more times. Since that manuscript provides human expert-created characterizations, it is possible that the custom GPT could have repeated back the characterizations given in that manuscript. However, that only occurred for one paper, which was for the CCMR manuscript itself. To assess whether the results were more generally applicable, during training we also submitted other papers for characterization. Across all of these documents ($n = 11$) the performance was roughly the same.

To test the capabilities of the CCMR Assistant more carefully, we compared the characterization we had written manually for an ER2023 paper [19] (as Table 1 shows) with a tool-generated characterization (as Table 2 shows). For space reasons we have formatted the AI output as a CCMR table rather than providing a screenshot; all non-boldface text in Table 2 is machine generated.

The AI-generated responses for the various CCMR fields tend to be more verbose than those written by a human expert, in spite of repeated instructions to be concise, direct, and brief. This is somewhat understandable, since generative AI tools exist expressly to generate text. Further prompts by the CCMR Assistant user could lead to more concise output. The AI tool also did not initially provide answers for the research communities represented in this work and the nature of the significant Type I contribution. When instructed, "*What CM-related research communities is this work mainly associated with? (Give a list, not a paragraph describing them.)*" the tool generated a list of 8 communities. In response to "*Give me just the top three.*" the tool truncated the list after three, apparently interpreting "top" as "first". In response to "*I don't mean the 'first' three, but the most relevant three.*" the tool listed "ubiquitous computing," "context-aware systems," and "ontology engineering." This is a reasonable answer. When prompted with "*From the CCMR list of possible choices for nature of the significant contribution, which choices apply to this paper?*" the tool generated five selections, including two of the triptych dimensions (which is nonsensical) along with "definition," "extension," and "discussion of philosophical basis." Arguments can be made in favor of all of these choices. The human expert likewise chose "definition," but also "evaluation through a case study" and "formalization."

Comparing the AI and human-generated answers for central contribution, we conclude that both gave valid summaries of the primary contribution. Comparing the relevance, intended users, and application domain responses, the AI tool is still more verbose than we would prefer. Prompted with "*Reduce the relevance, intended users, and application domain responses each to a single sentence or phrase.*" the tool generated what we consider to be better answers. These included (respectively):

- *Enhances modeling and integration of context data in ubiquitous computing applications.*
- *Developers and researchers in ubiquitous computing and smart environments.*
- *Smart environments, specifically smart cities and smart universities.*

On the triptych-related dimensions, the AI tool gave responses for all three dimensions, where the human expert saw the contribution mainly in light of the modeling artifacts. The tool's answer for the modeling artifacts dimension is reasonable. Overall, for this paper the CCMR Assistant did an acceptable job of characterizing the contribution. The tool was verbose and could improve in nuance, but it performed arguably better than graduate students in a separate human-centric test of the CCMR framework [22].

To further test the capabilities of the CCMR Assistant, we uploaded all 22 papers from ER2023 [8], one at a time, prompting with, "*Characterize this paper using CCMR.*" For two of the papers, answers returned by the CCMR Assistant were not in the structure expected, but trying again (with refined step 3 end-user prompts), the results were improved. 43 pages of screenshots of the tool-generated characterizations for all of these papers are at the following URL

(note also that this document could form the basis for a conference booklet as described in Sect. 4.1):
https://ccmr.byu.edu/ER2023PapersCharacterizedByAI.pdf.
Matching our expectations, it appears that a human expert could likely add important nuances to the AI-generated characterizations. But exceeding our initial expectations, the tool's responses are generally reasonable across all the papers—a promising result. Notably, AI hallucination was not a frequent problem in our experiments with the CCMR Assistant.

To simplify further evaluation of the AI tool, we conducted one additional experiment. Human experts had evaluated five ER'79 papers and five ER2022 papers to determine their central contributions and the CCMR contribution types [9]. For the five ER'79 papers, we prompted the CCMR Assistant with "*For these papers, list the primary contribution (just very briefly) and give the CCMR type for each contribution.*" We did the same for the ER2022 papers. For the ER'79 papers, all the tool's summaries of primary contributions were compatible with what the human experts wrote. Three of the five CCMR type characterizations were consistent with the human experts, whereas, in two cases, the tool chose Type I when the human experts had chosen Type II. For the ER2022 papers, the contribution summaries were likewise compatible with those of the human experts. Four of the five CCMR type characterizations were compatible with the choices of the human experts. It is, thus, likely that the AI tool would benefit from further training in how to determine what fits each of the CCMR contribution type categories and how to better use some of the other parts of the CCMR form. However, caution is warranted in interpreting this variation. In seven of ten cases, the AI tool matched human experts, but this does not mean the failure rate was 30%. We expect diversity even among human experts as they evaluate papers, and it is usually the case that multiple complementary perspectives can all be "correct". We have found that this diversity of evaluation leads to discussion and improved understanding, and so some variation is desirable and expected [9].

5 Related Work

In conceptual modeling, initial work has already been conducted on how and at what level of quality conceptual models can be created using ChatGPT. Fill et al. [12] report on initial experiments. Härer [13] describes an LLM-based "Conceptual Model Interpreter". To the best of our knowledge, our work is the first attempt to use LLM-based generative AI to create characterizations of CM-related research contributions systematically, though we report on an earlier ad hoc attempt to use the SciSpace Copilot tool [25] for this purpose in [9].

More broadly, there are several notable tools that relate to our goals with the CCMR Assistant. SciSpace [25] offers tools to assist with literature review, answer questions based on a PDF, extract data from multiple files, and paraphrase small amounts of text. Consensus [4] is an academic search engine that uses AI to answer yes/no questions from analyzing over 200 million papers. It also has tools to synthesize the results of several papers and to generate content in response to prompts. Elicit [5] provides tools for obtaining one-sentence summaries of abstracts, finding other papers similar to a given set, extracting details from multiple papers into an organized table, and identifying common concepts across multiple papers. Scite [7] answers questions by searching the literature, summarizing findings, and exporting cited works in a preferred format. It can also classify papers based on whether they support or contradict a finding, and can screen the literature to help authors ensure they are citing high-quality references. ChatPDF [3] lets one upload PDF files and then pose questions about those specific files. Research Rabbit [6] includes a discovery tool specifically designed to assist with literature search, review, and mapping tasks. It identifies other papers similar to a given set, curate collections of papers, and visualize connections between papers. These tools can be helpful for conceptual modeling, but the unique aspect of our project is using the CCMR framework to specifically identify nuanced conceptual modeling aspects of relevant papers.

There is another important concept connected to our work in this paper. Generative AI tools operate according to the prompting approach: a user supplies a textual prompt and the tool responds to the prompt by generating what it predicts is the best answer (see [15] for a formal discussion of prompts in NLP). The prompt cycle can iterate as many times as the user wishes, building on previous prompts and previously generated responses. Variations in prompts lead to variations in the quality of the responses, resulting in the need for "prompt engineering", where users actively seek to improve the response quality by adjusting aspects of the prompts [15].

A considerable amount of energy is being invested in the complex area of prompt engineering. Sahoo et al. [26], for example, provide a taxonomy of prompt engineering approaches that catalogs 29 specific approaches in 12 application areas. The 2024 Web Conference hosted a workshop on prompt engineering [10]. A practitioner-oriented overview of prompt engineering [21] is available from OpenAI. The website also provides extensive links to libraries, tools, guides, video courses, and research papers.

Although we have used several prompt engineering techniques, this is an actively evolving area. No doubt, it will be possible to enhance the prompt engineering of our CCMR Assistant, thereby improving its performance.

6 Conclusion

In this paper, we illustrated how an LLM-based tool, named CCMR Assistant, can produce reasonably good CCMR characterizations quickly, although human supervision and editing is still required. We have presented and discussed our results, showing that it is a feasible approach for automating the characterization of the large amount of research that has been conducted on conceptual modeling.

Much future work could be carried out. The CCMR Assistant could be integrated into CCMR using ChatGPT's API access. Then a user could simply upload a PDF of a paper and use suggestions from the CCMR Assistant in the style of auto-complete. If the LLM-based creation process becomes good enough, we could automate more of the characterization process. Additional sophisticated prompt engineering strategies could be developed to address various parts of the CCMR framework. In our use, we had to ask multiple times to obtain research communities. Perhaps more chain-of-thought prompts could enable the model to first focus on one question, and then lead it to others, in a divide-and-conquer type of strategy. After improving the prompt engineering approach, we could initiate a "gatekeeper" user to submit a large body of conceptual modeling papers and capture the results in our database (https://ccmr.byu.edu). AI-generated results would be labeled as such, and then the community of experts could review and curate the work, making revisions to AI-generated material as appropriate. Perhaps the tool could even be trained to answer the question, "Is this a conceptual modeling paper?" to screen papers.

We intend to improve the CCMR framework's controlled vocabularies by identifying the variety proposed by the LLM across the vast body of CM papers, and curating that list; for example for different research communities. It should be possible to generate a finite list of selections to choose from. We could use such a list to re-train the LLM, with re-application to each paper to yield better, automatic results.

As much research demonstrates, LLM-based generative AI tools are sufficiently mature to help human experts with certain tedious or voluminous tasks. In our research, we have explored this possibility for characterizing the large body of research in conceptual modeling. It is likely feasible to apply such a tool to other areas of research as well. One first needs to develop a canonical framework for the description of contributions in a given discipline and then use it to configure custom GPT as we have done here for conceptual modeling.

We note that automatic AI-based text summarization and research characterization could be the first step towards a credible and sustainable body of knowledge for conceptual modeling. Many works shed light on multiple aspects and problem domains, and therefore need to be seen in different contexts. Therefore, we propose to our community to open up the legacy of conceptual modeling in discussion groups for particularly valuable works. There are hundreds of such works that could otherwise fall into oblivion or somehow be reinvented. We can use regular world-wide virtual discussion groups to preserve this scientific heritage and keep it available through exchange.

References

1. CCMR assistant custom GPT created using the ChatGPT platform (2024). https://chatgpt.com/g/g-FFUJeSht2-ccmr-assistant. Accessed 27 May 2024
2. ChatGPT.com home page (2024). https://chatgpt.com. Accessed 28 May 2024
3. ChatPDF home page (2024). https://www.chatpdf.com/. Accessed 28 May 2024
4. Consensus home page (2024). https://consensus.app/. Accessed 28 May 2024
5. Elicit home page (2024). https://elicit.com/. Accessed 28 May 2024
6. Research rabbit home page (2024). https://www.researchrabbit.ai/. Accessed 28 May 2024

7. scite home page (2024). https://scite.ai/. Accessed 28 May 2024
8. Almeida, J.P.A., Borbinha, J., Guizzardi, G., Link, S., Zdravkovic, J. (eds.): Conceptual Modeling - 42nd International Conference, ER 2023, Lisbon, Portugal, 6–9 November 2023, Proceedings. LNCS, vol. 14320. Springer (2023). https://doi.org/10.1007/978-3-031-47262-6
9. Delcambre, L.M., Liddle, S.W., Pastor, O., Storey, V.C., Mayr, H.C., Thalheim, B.: A structured perspective on conceptual modeling research (2024). Submitted
10. Graux, D., Montella, S., Jabeen, H., Gardent, C., Pan, J.Z.: [PromptEng] First international workshop on prompt engineering for pre-trained language models. In: Companion Proceedings of the ACM on Web Conference 2024, WWW 2024, Singapore, Singapore, 13–17 May 2024, pp. 1311–1312. ACM (2024). https://doi.org/10.1145/3589335.3641292
11. Guizzardi, G.: Ontological foundations for structural conceptual models. Ph.D. thesis, University of Twente (2005)
12. Fill, H.-G., Fettke, P.: Conceptual modeling and large language models: impressions from first experiments with ChatGPT. Enterp. Model. Inf. Syst. Archit. (EMISAJ) - Int. J. Conceptual Model. **18**(3) (2023). https://doi.org/10.18417/emisa.18.3
13. Härer, F.: Conceptual model interpreter for large language models. In: ER Forum Proceedings. CEUR Workshop Proceedings, vol. 3618. CEUR-WS.org (2023). https://ceur-ws.org/Vol-3618/forum_paper_11.pdf
14. Hull, R., King, R.: Semantic database modeling: survey, applications, and research issues. ACM Comput. Surv. **19**(3), 201–260 (1987). https://doi.org/10.1145/45072.45073
15. Liu, P., Yuan, W., Fu, J., Jiang, Z., Hayashi, H., Neubig, G.: Pre-train, prompt, and predict: a systematic survey of prompting methods in natural language processing. ACM Comput. Surv. **55**(9), 195:1–195:35 (2023). https://doi.org/10.1145/3560815
16. Mayr, H.C., Thalheim, B.: The triptych of conceptual modeling - a framework for a better understanding of conceptual modeling. Softw. Syst. Model. **20**(1), 7–24 (2021). https://doi.org/10.1007/S10270-020-00836-Z
17. Michael, J., Bork, D., Wimmer, M., Mayr, H.C.: Quo vadis modeling? Findings of a community survey, an ad-hoc bibliometric analysis, and expert interviews on data, process, and software modeling. Softw. Syst. Model. **23**(1), 7–28 (2024). https://doi.org/10.1007/S10270-023-01128-Y
18. Mylopoulos, J.: Conceptual modeling and Telos. In: Conceptual Modelling. Databases and CASE: An Integrated View of Information Systems Development, pp. 49–68. Wiley, New York (1992)
19. do Nascimento, L.V., de Oliveira, J.P.M.: An ontology for context modeling in smart spaces. In: Almeida, J.P.A., Borbinha, J., Guizzardi, G., Link, S., Zdravkovic, J. (eds.) ER 2023. LNCS, vol. 14320, pp. 354–371. Springer, Cham (2023). https://doi.org/10.1007/978-3-031-47262-6_19
20. Olivé, A.: Conceptual Modeling of Information Systems. Springer, Berlin (2007). https://doi.org/10.1007/978-3-540-39390-0
21. OpenAI: Prompt engineering (2024). https://platform.openai.com/docs/guides/prompt-engineering. Accessed 28 May 2024
22. Panach, J.I., et al.: Evaluating a framework of conceptual modelling research through a family of experiments (2024). Working paper
23. Pastor, O., Gómez, J., Insfrán, E., Pelechano, V.: The OO-method approach for information systems modeling: from object-oriented conceptual modeling to automated programming. Inf. Syst. **26**(7), 507–534 (2001)
24. Peckham, J., Maryanski, F.J.: Semantic data models. ACM Comput. Surv. **20**(3), 153–189 (1988). https://doi.org/10.1145/62061.62062

25. Roy, T., et al.: SciSpace Copilot: empowering researchers through intelligent reading assistance. In: Proceedings of the AAAI Conference on Artificial Intelligence, vol. 38, pp. 23826–23828 (2024). https://doi.org/10.1609/AAAI.V38I21.30578
26. Sahoo, P., Singh, A.K., Saha, S., Jain, V., Mondal, S., Chadha, A.: A systematic survey of prompt engineering in large language models: techniques and applications. CoRR abs/2402.07927 (2024). https://doi.org/10.48550/ARXIV.2402.07927
27. Storey, V.C., Thalheim, B.: Conceptual modeling: enhancement through semiotics. In: Mayr, H.C., Guizzardi, G., Ma, H., Pastor, O. (eds.) ER 2017. LNCS, vol. 10650, pp. 182–190. Springer, Cham (2017). https://doi.org/10.1007/978-3-319-69904-2_15
28. Thalheim, B.: Entity-Relationship Modeling: Foundations of Database Technology. Springer, Heidelberg (2000). https://doi.org/10.1007/978-3-662-04058-4
29. Wand, Y., Weber, R.: Research commentary: information systems and conceptual modeling - a research agenda. Inf. Syst. Res. **13**(4), 363–376 (2002). https://doi.org/10.1287/isre.13.4.363.69
30. Zuccon, G., Koopman, B., Shaik, R.: ChatGPT hallucinates when attributing answers. In: Ai, Q., Liu, Y., Moffat, A., Huang, X., Sakai, T., Zobel, J. (eds.) Annual International ACM SIGIR Conference on Research and Development in Information Retrieval in the Asia Pacific Region, SIGIR-AP 2023, Beijing, China, 26–28 November 2023, pp. 46–51. ACM (2023). https://doi.org/10.1145/3624918.3625329

AI-Assisted Analytics – An Automated Approach to Data Visualization

Alberto Alves[1(✉)], João Moura Pires[1], Maribel Yasmina Santos[2], Andreia Almeida[2], and Ana León[3]

[1] School of Science and Technology, NOVA University of Lisbon, Lisbon, Portugal
alberto.pires.alves@gmail.com, jmp@fct.unl.pt

[2] ALGORITMI Research Center, University of Minho, Guimarães, Portugal
maribel@dsi.uminho.pt, a89250@alunos.uminho.pt

[3] Research Center on Software Production Methods (PROS), Universitat Politècnica de València, València, Spain
aleon@vrain.upv.es

Abstract. In all areas of human activity, the generation and storage of data are universal and growing. The extraction of knowledge from this data is a generally complex and very demanding task in terms of human resources, both for domain experts and data analysts. The need to automate and simplify the process, in particular for the domain specialist, is increasingly imperative for the effective use of data in decision-making processes. In this work, based on an extensive survey of literature regarding analytical tasks, we propose a taxonomy of analytical tasks (independent of the domain), and evaluate the performance of several state-of-the-art Large Language Models (LLMs) in the decomposition of questions of the domain into a set of analytical tasks, for 5 different domains. Only after this decomposition we perform the necessary tasks on the domain data and propose a ranking of visualizations that best respond to the question of the domain, using a Visualization Recommendation System (VRS). The two-step separation: (i) decomposition into analytical tasks; (ii) execution of tasks, including the generation of views, distinguishes our approach from most proposals that use LLMs for analytical activities. Another aspect that distinguishes this work is the presentation of an ordered set of views in a declarative way utilizing Vega-Lite as the rendering environment.

Keywords: Visual Analytics · Analytical Tasks · Visualization Recommendation System · Generative AI · Data Visualization

1 Introduction

Data Analytics builds upon the assertion that if processed and correctly analyzed unstructured data can provide valuable insights [7]. Data Analytics is relevant in different areas, from businesses to academia. The process of data analytics typically begins with a domain question and then the need to establish the set of

M. Saeki et al. (Eds.): ER 2024 Workshops, LNCS 14932, pp. 343–358, 2025.
https://doi.org/10.1007/978-3-031-75599-6_24

analytical tasks that allows us to answer the initial question, often culminating in the presentation of results through visualizations. Importantly, this process is iterative, as initial domain questions may undergo some refinement, or new questions may emerge during the analysis [23]. A key aspect of this iterative process is the interaction between the domain user and the data engineer, enabling the latter to gain a deeper understanding of domain concepts and data. However, from the perspective of the domain user, this process can be both demanding and susceptible to issues of interpretation. The primary challenges include the process's resource-intensive nature [26], and the inherent complexity of domains and their data [13].

Several approaches have been drawn in order to tackle these challenges, which are central to the discussion of this paper. For example, Münzner [23] justifies the need to formulate actionable abstractions that allow for domain questions to be decomposed into analytical tasks. This reasoning stems from the fact that different domain questions can be represented by a finite set of domain-independent analytical tasks, which can be systematically processed to generate suitable answers. The author illustrates two examples of different domains, an epidemiologist presenting the domain question "How does the prognosis of patients who were intubated in the ICU contrast?", and a biologist investigating immune system responses asking "Do results for the tissue samples treat with LL-37 match up with the ones without the peptide?". In both examples, the underlying analytical task is the same (**Compare**) even if the terminologies "match up" and "contrast" are different. Thus, translating and decomposing domain questions into analytical tasks is crucial in lessening the complexity and resource intensity by precisely describing the user's objectives.

Another hurdle ties in with the difficulty of selecting appropriate and efficient visualizations to answer a domain question. This involves not only the expressiveness of specific visual elements [23], such as position and color, but the effectiveness of certain types of visualizations concerning specific analytical tasks [29], and the inherent preferences of individual users [5]. Given the iterative nature of the analytical process, there is an opportunity to streamline the workflow from the domain user's perspective, by making it faster and more efficient. Consequently, our objective is to automate and enhance this process in a way that minimizes the interaction between domain users and data engineers.

Taking inspiration from Munzner's premise, the work presented in this paper proposes an approach to automate data analytics with an AI-driven methodology, leveraging both Large Language Models (LLMs) and Visualization Recommendation Systems (VRSs). LLMs will be employed in the translation and decomposition of domain questions into analytical tasks, due to their multidisciplinary capabilities being a key factor in their selection. Concurrently, the VRS's objective is to guide users by suggesting visualizations based on data characteristics, analytical tasks, domain knowledge, visual ease, or user preferences [32]. Within our approach, the VRS will process the analytical tasks and generate and rank visualizations that align with these tasks. These technologies will utilize our proposed taxonomy of analytical tasks, which was developed to ensure that these tasks would be actionable and could be systematically processed to create visualizations, simultaneously serving as context for LLMs to accurately decompose domain questions into terms present in the taxonomy.

By implementing this approach, we expect a significant reduction in the human resource intensity demands, both in terms of time and expertise. This contrasts with traditional methods, which typically require a human-in-the-loop, i.e. data engineer, to study the domain and manually design the visualizations.

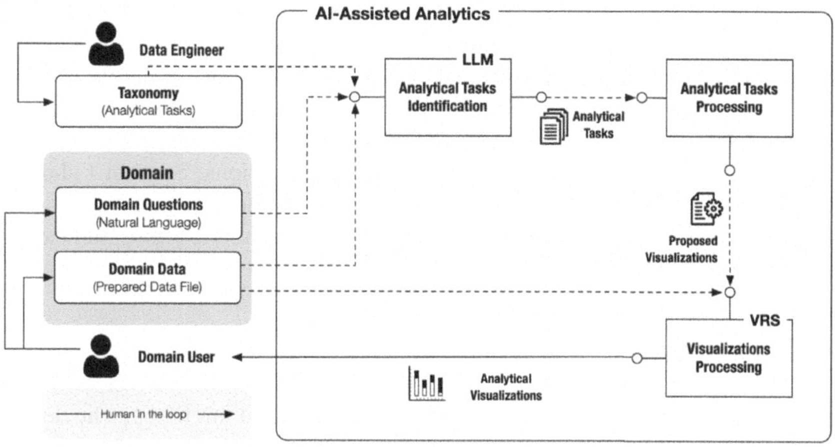

Fig. 1. Proposed AI-assisted analytics foundational methodology.

This work's approach overview, shown in Fig. 1, focus on four main components:

- **Taxonomy of Analytical Tasks**. A taxonomy of Analytical Tasks is proposed (see Sect. 3.1) as a response to the wide range of existing analytical tasks, within the literature. This happens as a consequence of underlying differences between works since tasks can diverge significantly depending on their ultimate goals [24]. The taxonomy is built under the premise of being utilized and easily assimilated by LLMs, allowing these models to contextually identify analytical tasks from domain questions.
- **Analytical Tasks Identification**. The identification of Analytical Tasks (see Sect. 3.2) within our approach relies upon the LLM's ability to translate and decompose domain questions. A focal point of our approach and one of the motivations behind the creation of the taxonomy was to experiment and evaluate these model's translation and decomposition abilities.
- **Analytical Tasks Processing**. Processing sequences of analytical tasks, aimed to manipulate data, allows for the determination of Visualizations deemed more effective [28]. In our approach, visualizations are influenced by specific design choices that are tied to the individual analytical tasks capable of generating visualizations. Therefore, rendering the system to process

the analytical tasks and directly choose, based on our rules and constraints, what visualizations should be created. This decision supports both the will to further increase automation and efficiency (see Sect. 3.3).
- **Visualization Processing**. Analytical visualizations are the final tangible results of our approach, hence why we need to design and display them. This component will be responsible for generating visualizations, by analyzing the set of analytical tasks that compose the domain question's answer. Besides this processing, it will also rank and display the most appropriate visualizations (see Sect. 3.3).

This paper is organized as follows. Section 2 summarizes the related work, with the contextualization and needed comparison between available literature and the work here proposed. Section 3 presents the proposed taxonomy and the use of LLMs to support the identification and processing of the analytical tasks, as well as the processing of analytical visualizations. Section 4 shows an illustrative case study following the proposed methodology and the obtained results. Section 5 highlights the presented work and its contributions and explores possible future work.

2 Related Work

In this work, guided by the proposed approach found in Fig. 1, the focus is on conducting an in-depth survey related to organizing and detailing a set of **Analytical Tasks** where the suitability to the **LLMs** environment was a key motivating factor. These models play an important role in the process of translating and decomposing domain-specific questions into sets of analytical tasks, which can thereafter be processed into adequate **Analytical Visualizations**.

Analytical Tasks - As mentioned in the previous section, our study/survey concerning analytical tasks was conducted following two principles: firstly, the lack of a generalized consensus means that the choice of any already existing set of tasks suffers from inherent limitations. Secondly, the need to feed our analytical tasks to an LLM would mean that the tasks need to be easily digestible by these models.

According to Nickerson [25], our taxonomy mirrored a fundamentally *ad hoc* proposal. This intuitive approach bases itself around the researcher's understanding of the domain based on their perceptions of what is necessary to achieve its goals. Instead of defining the characteristics and meta-characteristics, we surveyed existing literature works that helped us determine a taxonomy within our established goals. As mentioned in the previous section, our survey concerning analytical tasks was conducted following three principles: firstly, solve the question regarding the inexistence of a literature standard, tailoring a set of analytical tasks to solve our expected goals, and finally the need to have a set of tasks that could be easily contextualized to an LLM.

Conducted research on analytical tasks' literature had a basis in Münzner's work [23], which had already inspired our adoption of analytical tasks. We then directed our attention to other publications found in ACM, dblp, IEEE, and Springer libraries, as well as author-published books, that concluded our survey. These were found primarily through their keywords, with concepts such as analytical task, visual task, taxonomy, visualization, data visualization, and visual encoding. The remaining collection of works was incorporated due to being conceptually similar [3,19,31,33], showing an effort toward organizing/categorizing analytical tasks [2,12,21,37], or comprising surveys of existing literature [6,27]. Table 1 shows all studied publications ordered chronologically, and existing analytical tasks that perform the same task.

Table 1. Summary table of agreeing analytical tasks and taxonomies.

Similar Tasks / Literature Works	Wehrend et al. 1990 [28]	Amar et al. 2005 [3]	Valiati et al. 2006 [27]	Abela 2008 [2]	Yau 2011 [32]	Few 2012 [10]	Münzner 2014 [21]	Laha et al. 2015 [17]	Börner 2019 [5]	Quadri et al. 2021 [21]	Li et al. 2023 [18]
Comparison / Compare / Nominal Comparison / Differences	X	-	X	X	X	X	X	-	X	X	X
Relationship / Correlate / Relationships / Correlation / Correlations	X	X	-	X	X	X	-	-	X	X	X
Distribution / Characterize Distribution / Distributions / Determine	X	X	X	X	-	X	-	-	X	X	-
Composition/ Part-to-whole / Proportions / Compositions	-	-	-	X	X	X	-	-	X	-	X
Identify / Retrieve Value	-	X	X	-	-	-	X	-	-	X	-
Rank / Order / Sort / Ranking	X	X	-	-	-	X	-	-	X	-	-
Search / Locate	X	-	X	-	-	-	X	X	-	-	-
Cluster	X	X		-	-	-	-	-	-	X	-
Derive / Compute Derived Value	-	X	-	-	-	-	X	-	-	X	-
Determine Range	-	X	-	-	-	-	-	-	-	X	-
Find Anomalies		X		-	-	-	-	-	-	X	-
Find Extremum	-	X	-	-	-	-	-	-	-	X	-
Identify / Explore	X	-	-	-	-	-	X	-	-	-	-
Infer / Discover	-	-	X	-	-	-	X	-	-	-	-
Spatial Understanding / Distribution	-	-	-	-	-	-	-	X	-	-	X

Table 1 is ordered from top to bottom, from the most to the least common tasks. A significant difference is tangible between the number of occurrences of common tasks such as ***Compare*** or ***Correlate*** when compared with ***Discover*** and ***Spatial Understanding*** – other tasks existed but as a single instance within all works, and therefore did not feature in this table. Existence of tasks with similar names that perform different analytical actions and of tasks with different names that perform very similarly are noticeable in Table 1. These inconsistencies stood out to our team as a direct alignment with our statement regarding the lack of consensus in the literature. In Sect. 3 we will discuss further our analytical task taxonomy proposal.

Large Language Models in Data Analytics - Generative AI's data visualization literature is steadily growing and its impact is branching out toward automatic visualization generation frameworks and visualization generation through LLM interaction.

The automatic visualization generation approach is typically restricted to only data. These systems evaluate the data properties and try to display rudimentary visualizations that might be helpful to the user [10,16,34,38]. Regrettably, the best outcome these approaches can do is to try to make an educated prediction of how the data properties can relate to one another, in order to create simple visualizations. Since there is no input from the user, besides the raw data, i.e. no domain concepts or questions, the framework has to propose visualizations without any domain knowledge.

The other branch where LLMs are being utilized, has a wider range of available works. Some are comprised of language models being used for dataset exploration and data knowledge-gathering, where the user interacts mostly with the data at hand [8]. These interfaces, as some authors call them, are very useful in tackling ambiguity and developing domain knowledge [14]. Others, directly achieve visualizations through the usage of LLMs to analyze and summarize data, and generate code to display visualizations [9]. These approaches share an underlying limitation, the lack of support for domain questions and leveraging user requirements.

However, within our specialized utilization of LLMs, domain questions are part of the analysis and are a foundational pillar of the approach. We only found a single work [11] where there was an effort, very similar to ours, to consider the user's questions as part of the approach and abstract them into tasks that influence the resulting visualizations.

Analytical Visualization Generation and Design - Regarding the approach, generating visualizations through the processing of analytical tasks is an obligatory step in delivering an answer to the domain user. Our objective of providing a higher degree of automation, in relation to the traditional data analytics approach, mixes with the aim of designing meaningful visualizations, with well-versed design choices.

Through the usage of visualization recommendation systems, there is a path that allows us to go from analytical information to visualizations. For this reason, tools are typically utilized to guide users by suggesting visualizations akin to their data characteristics, user requirements, and user-specific preferences [17]. Literature typically categorizes these systems into: Data-driven models, where data is used to predict relationships through similarity which is calculated by machine learning models [1,10,16,35,38]. Knowledge-based models utilize information/knowledge, usually in the form of metrics, guidelines, or constraints, to make predictions about possible correlations between data objects [20,36]. Lastly, hybrid models are essentially a system that blends data-driven and knowledge-based principles to attain design choices and render visualizations [22].

Since the visualizations are being created through the execution of analytical tasks, then the tasks must be related to some sort of visual expressiveness. Conceptually, it is a hard-to-achieve premise since domain questions tend to not have a one-size-fits-all solution, for example, domain questions with the same sequence of analytical tasks can immensely benefit from different types of visualizations. Literature suggests that the results from typical/common data analysis methods (e.g. Compare [18,28], Correlate [27]) can be easier to perceive when paired with a suitable visualization [15,39]. If this is the case, then analytical tasks also have suitable visualization and therefore adequate design options. In Sect. 3 we will explore this topic further and leverage it with our taxonomy's analytical tasks.

Considering the features and methodology we are proposing, finding an approach that offers similar properties is difficult. Our hindsight suggests that this approach, along with its testing and validation, demonstrates a state-of-the-art case study in this branch of literature, with positive end results.

3 Analytical Tasks Identification and Processing

Identification and processing are connected through the usage of different analytical tasks. This happens since there is a fundamental need to leverage the user's questions to a less domain-specific layer, in order to become adequately answerable. Within the scope of our approach, we define a **Domain Question** as a question about a specific domain in which the user imposes the concern of gathering a response, and an **Analytical Task** as an abstraction of the actions that must be enforced to reach a full, or partial, response – e.g. within a supermarket domain, a user has the following question: "What's the difference between prices of product A and B, in each existing store?". The domain question initially must be translated and then decomposed into the necessary analytical tasks, available in Fig. 2. In this context, the word "difference" has an underlying meaning of "comparing" the product's prices. Therefore, an adequate task to answer this domain question would be ***Compare***. This example demonstrates how analytical tasks can bestow a helping hand, not only to data engineers but equally to the GenAI, more specifically LLMs, which are an essential part of our approach.

The potential drawbacks and limitations involved with adopting an independent study about analytical tasks were considerable. Hence why the reason we considered taking another path by proposing a **Taxonomy** of analytical tasks.

3.1 Proposed Taxonomy

An analytical taxonomy works in a fairly identical way to a common taxonomy, it classifies concepts that share similar foundations. Our proposal is encompassed by a hierarchical taxonomy, comprised of primary tasks and their respective sub-tasks. **Identify**, **Compare**, **Determine Distribution**, **Organize**, and **Derive**, as seen in Fig. 2, are the main tasks.

The task **Identify** uses the available data to find and gather information. It is a common analytical task because its primary objective is directly related to acquiring knowledge regarding the domain's data. We sub-divided **Identify**, creating a small hierarchy, into five sub-tasks that were considered to be worthwhile when evaluating our approach's vision. These sub-tasks were characterized as the following:

- **Relate**: Identifies how data interacts within itself (relationships), the main objective is to obtain useful insights.

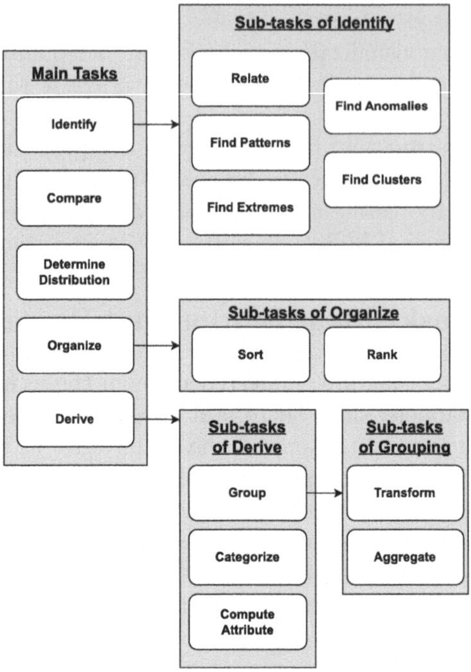

Fig. 2. Proposed taxonomy's hierarchical diagram.

- **Find Patterns**: Patterns can be found through regular/irregular periods of data fluctuations (trends) in the dataset.
- **Find Extremes**: Extremes are found due to being interpolated as the higher or lower values, within a certain range.
- **Find Anomalies**: Similar to finding extremes, but in this case the objective is to find possible outliers in the data. This can be done both locally or globally, concerning the dataset.
- **Find Clusters**: Finding clusters of data uses categories or labels, since clusters are typically groups of data that share the same attributes or similar values of a specific attribute, in a non-deterministic way.

Compare is a widely used task in data analysis due to the intrinsic need to compare and evaluate specific data values/characteristics. It is utilized to assess differences between data, some of the other analytical tasks present in our proposal use implicit comparative methods.

Another important task, in the spectrum of data analysis, is the capacity of **Determining Distributions**. They are primarily tied with showing the true distribution of data, within a certain dataset, of specific values or attributes. This task is deeply connected to statistical analysis.

Organize originates from the need to reorganize existing data by using common sorting concepts (e.g. alphabetically or ascending/descending) and by allowing the ranking of data with user-created heuristics. In contrast with the formerly seen tasks, this one does not provide the possibility of creating a visualization.

Finally, **Derive** is not concerned with creating visualizations, but with manipulating data. These transforming functions occupy a particular and paramount role in data analysis. Data might be incapable of answering domain questions without deriving new attributes, values, or datasets. **Derive** shows itself as a focal task that operates only on data and always precedes the visualization processing step. It is composed of the following set of sub-tasks:

- **Group**: Creates groups of data entries that must be generated deterministically by a user's criteria. This sub-task has two additional grouping tasks relative to a specific operation.
  - **Transform** - Responsible for executing mathematical/transformation operations to every data entry of a formed group.
  - **Aggregate** - A function that allows for the usage of statistical operations in a specified group.
- **Categorize**: Classifies and labels data into user-created categories that are not present in the original dataset. It can be seen as a refined task of grouping/clustering, with additional input from the user.
- **Compute Attribute**: Provides the possibility of generating new data attributes based on data from the dataset. New attributes are designed to be recorded into a new version of the dataset.

Although we conducted an extensive study relative to analytical taxonomies, present in the literature work, the main focus was to achieve a proposal with a degree of stability and appropriate integration. We did not seek to make our proposal relate one-to-one to Table 1. However, the overall knowledge acquired by conducting this survey is mirrored in our taxonomy. It is important to state that our proposal is arranged in a way that is open to the merging of new analytical tasks if necessary.

3.2 Task Identification and Processing with LLMs

In a non-automated setting, as the example shown at the beginning of Sect. 3, the generation of visualizations through the identification and processing of analytical tasks originating from domain questions should behave in a three-step order: translation, decomposition, and processing. Domain questions are translated and decomposed into analytical tasks, and the processing of such tasks will result in visualizations.

This methodology centers on users' questions and domain concept assimilation to achieve adequate answers. While reliable, it requires significant resources to address a single question. Our goal was to explore automation technologies to streamline this process, focusing on the use of LLMs.

Through iterative testing, we evaluated the LLMs' proficiency in translating and decomposing domain questions into analytical tasks using our taxonomy. Preliminary insights revealed that the models could achieve satisfactory results, especially if evaluating common domains. However, hallucinations and problems with out-of-context answers were still present.

The iterative process of testing and evaluation was conducted a total of three times. Initial tests with GPT-3.5[1], using a generic business domain, exhibited promising results in the automation of translation and decomposition of analytical tasks but highlighted issues relative to the LLMs, i.e. hallucinations and out-of-context answers. These preliminary results served as a foundation to refine our taxonomy by enhancing the context specificity and adding new tasks.

A second iteration of tests was executed as a further assessment of LLM's capabilities. The model that underwent testing was again GPT-3.5, but the total number of questions increased and the number of domains was extended to five (business, temporal, spatial, socio-economical, and human genome). These tests had the objective of understanding the model's behavior and performance when dealing with various domains of contrasting difficulties. The model answers were then compared to our team's and judged on a scale from one to five, where one represents a model answer completely divergent from ours and five reflects a complete match between answers (1–2 are inadequate answers, and 3–5 are adequate answers). Table 2 exemplifies a translation and decomposition of a domain question, from the second testing iteration. Once again, results came with a positive average on common domains, but a lower performance on more difficult domains, i.e. human genome and spatial. Even though the results were compatible with the ones obtained in the first tests. The wider range of domains, the low number of questions, and the different levels of difficulty between domains, paired with the testing environment being limited to a single model, could influence our results.

Table 2. Example of an LLM translation of a domain question, respective answer, and the evaluation compared to our team's answer.

Domain Question	Model Answer	Experts Answer	Evaluation
"How many cities are represented from each country?"	1. **Derive**: *Group*: Group the cities in your dataset by their respective countries. 2. **Derive**: *Aggregate*: Aggregate data within each country group to count the number of cities in each country. 3. **Determine Distribution**: Determine the distribution of the number of cities per country.	1. **Derive**: *Aggregate*: Count the number of cities per country. 2. **Determine Distribution**: Check the distribution of cities per country.	4

The last series of tests were done with a new structure and methodology, which we believed could yield better results. Firstly, we applied a few-shot learning strategy that generally provides better outcomes, when it comes to results related to LLMs [4]. Besides this addition, we created new domain questions

[1] https://openai.com/chatgpt/.

and dichotomized them into **direct** and **interpretative** categories, this way the chance of having high fluctuations of difficulty in domain questions would be less likely. Finally, the evaluation was also revised and now is comprised of three separate categories:

- **Domain Knowledge** - Determines the model's ability to demonstrate its in-depth knowledge of the domain at hand. Evaluated on a scale from one to five, similar to the one utilized in the second phase of testing, where one represents a bad interpretation of the domain's contexts while five is an excellent interpretation.
- **Question Understanding** - Classifies the judgment the model exhibits regarding a domain question. Uses a range from one, a bad perception of the domain question, to five, which presents a great cognizance of the question.
- **Task Selection** - Rates the degree of adequateness of the answer given by the model. Carries the same evaluation seen in the second phase of testing for model's answers.

Testing setting was expanded to uphold five different models, i.e. GPT-3.5, GPT-4, GPT-4 (Bing)[2], Gemini 1.0[3], and Mixtral 8x7B[4]. However, it was assumed that the default parameters and baselines were on equal conditions despite the inherent differences between the models and their environments.

A blunt overview of the results from this final phase of testing, presented in Fig. 3, provides interesting insight that some of the models are capable of, on average, giving slightly above-average (three) results.

The positive answers supported our belief in the possibility of automating the process of going from domain questions to analytical tasks, using natural language. Since there is still some theoretical potential to obtain better results, if we were to create a future fine-tuned model, our team holds the thought that these results could still improve substantially. More information regarding the testing conditions and results can be examined in the GitHub repository[5].

3.3 Visualization Processing with Support of VRSs

The evaluation of our approach relies on delivering visual answers to the users. As a means to generate resulting analytical visualizations, it was necessary to have a tool that would be capable of creating these resources. After performing a survey on eight VSRs [1,10,16,20,22,35,36,38] and examining the results, based on the models' characteristics, we had to decide which one we would include in the approach. The visualization recommendation system chosen was Draco because its knowledge-based approach and constraint learning tasks made it possible to implement our taxonomy within the system. Another positive aspect

[2] https://copilot.microsoft.com/.
[3] https://gemini.google.com/.
[4] https://huggingface.co/chat/.
[5] https://github.com/AMPAlves/Repositorio-Final-Tese.

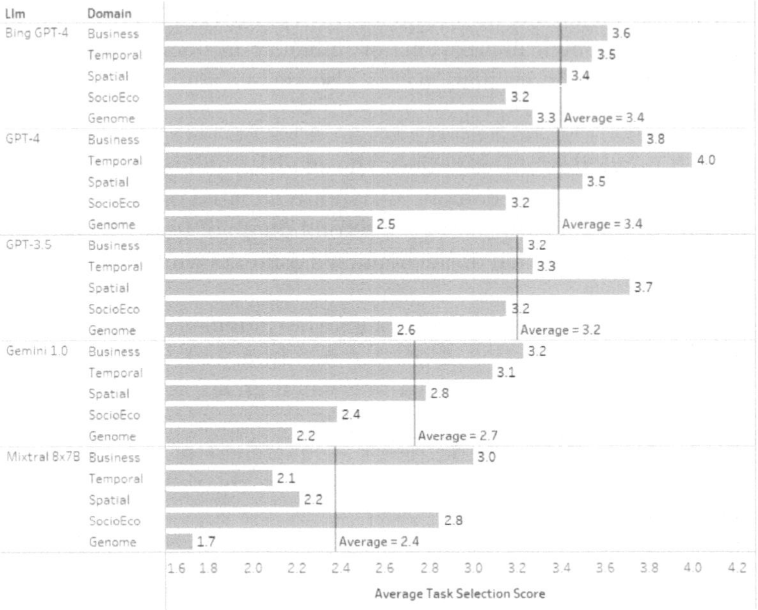

Fig. 3. Distribution of models' average **Task Selection** score, for individual domains, from the best to the worst-performing model.

was the possibility of creating rules associated with analytical tasks. This meant that we could customize the design choices of each task.

The system's inner workings require the input of a specific file, with information related to the data and tasks under execution. This knowledge is analyzed by the answer set programming system and translated to Vega-Lite [30], where the mapping of data and visual encodings happen. Because the system could treat tasks as actionable functions, it is possible for the system to both process analytical tasks and render visualizations.

4 Illustrative Case Study

In this section, a comprehensive example will be executed through the lens of our proposed approach. In the first instance, it is necessary to establish what domain will be studied and analyzed. Considering this, the example will explore a generic domain related to **Business & Sales**.

For the sake of this example, we will only take into consideration the classes **Order** and **Item**, where an order is comprised of multiple items, and the relevant data fields are *Profit*, a continuous data type, and *Sub-Category*, a nominal data type.

After mapping the domain data to the respective domain concepts, which is out of this paper's scope, we can proceed to the domain question analysis and analytical task identification. To serve this example, the chosen domain question was **"What is the total profit for each sub-category of items?"**. Following the approach's rationale, the question must be translated and broken down into analytical tasks, which will be done through the usage of **LLMs** – specifically, in this example, GPT-4 since it was the best-performing model in the aforementioned testing environment in Sect. 3.2. The model's answer suggested that this question should be answered by employing the task ***Aggregate*** – by applying a **Sum** function on the *Profit* field, grouped by *Sub-Category* – and ***Compare*** which is utilized to enable the comparison of the *Sub-Category* profits and generate a visualization. This happens due to the fact that **Aggregate** is not able to produce visualizations. Currently, our example utilizes the ***Compare*** task as a means to establish a visualization. However, this results in three visualizations that excel performance-wise in providing comparisons, i.e. bar chart, line chart, and radial chart. These visualizations were the top three chosen by the VRS, which ranked them internally by applying our sets of constraints. Although the graphics in Fig. 4 are adequate to answer the domain question, they lack a depth of precision because the y-axis can only provide an estimate of the total profit instead of the exact number.

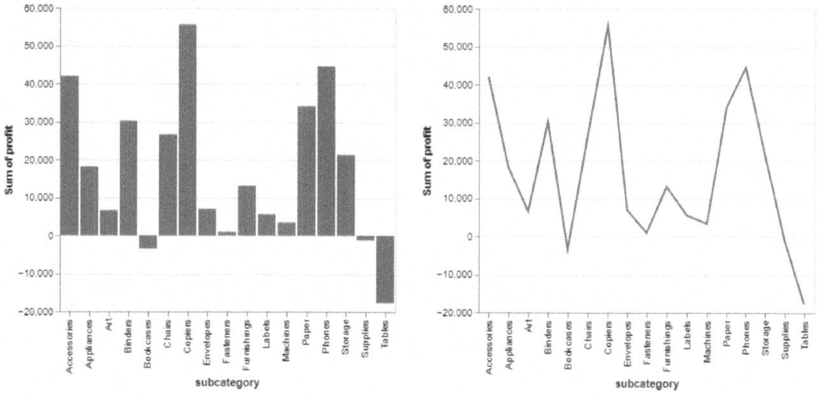

Fig. 4. Best-ranked visualizations according to the VRS. Ranked 1st and 2nd from left to right. Obtained by the VRS when answering the domain question **"What is the total profit for each sub-category of items?"**, with the analytical task ***Compare***.

This example was noteworthy by virtue of demonstrating our approach working and yielding favorable results. Nevertheless, it is also valuable since it exhibits some of the limitations and hurdles intrinsic to our work and research. Such hindrances will be categorized as feasible components of our future work.

5 Conclusion

In summary, our objective was to present an approach capable of providing automated support to data visualization through the usage of LLM while acknowledging domain concepts and users' domain questions. Our approach tries to minimize issues concerning LLMs such as hallucinations and the black-box effect by providing a clear division of the necessary analytical steps. Overall, the core analysis ensures that the implementation of our approach can be seen as sound since it achieves our objectives and is simultaneously coherent with the works that serve as our foundations. The use case studies, show the potential and effectiveness of our approach by utilizing existing domain questions and correctly assessing them with the projected top-ranked visualizations from the recommendation system.

Currently, our approach presents some limitations. For example, the taxonomy does not include any aspect of interaction on data visualizations which should be considered since it is very relevant in Visual Analytics. Additionally, the recommendation visualization system, although useful, draws multiple limitations regarding visualization design options, expressiveness, and available dataset training.

These limitations provide a guide to the possible future work concerning our approach. Taxonomy enhancements might be needed since currently it lacks the option of interactability between the visualizations and the end-user. Broaden the current evaluation and create an empirical evaluation of visualizations with users. Enhancing the current visualization recommendation system, or adopting another option, will offer a higher depth of design expressiveness, versatility, and adequate visualizations. Successfully fine-tuning an LLM to translate and decompose domain questions into analytical tasks would prove to be vital work capable of bettering the existing results regarding translation while minimizing the rate of ineffective responses.

Acknowledgements. This work has been supported by *FCT – Fundação para a Ciência e Tecnologia* within the R&D Units Project Scope UIDB/00319/2020 (ALGORITMI) and UIDB/04516/2020 (NOVA LINCS), and by the Spanish Ministry of Universities and the Universitat Politècnica de València under the Margarita Salas Next Generation EU grant. This paper uses icons made available by www.flaticon.com.

References

1. Parameswaran, A., Karahalios, K.: Zenvisage (2019). https://zenvisage.github.io/. Accessed 2 Feb 2024
2. Abela, A.: Advanced Presentations by Design: Creating Communication that Drives Action. Pfeiffer Essential Resources for Training and HR Professionals. Wiley (2008). https://books.google.pt/books?id=z2S0Fz_gD2wC
3. Amar, R., Eagan, J., et al.: Low-level components of analytic activity in information visualization. In: Proceedings of the 2005 IEEE Symposium on Information Visualization, INFOVIS 2005, USA, p. 15. IEEE Computer Society (2005). https://doi.org/10.1109/INFOVIS.2005.24
4. Brown, T.B., Mann, B., Ryder, N., et al.: Language models are few-shot learners (2020). https://doi.org/10.48550/arXiv.2005.14165
5. Brusilovsky, P.: Methods and techniques of adaptive hypermedia. User Model. User-Adap. Interact. **6**, 87–129 (1996). https://api.semanticscholar.org/CorpusID:16808655

6. Börner, K., Bueckle, A., et al.: Data visualization literacy: definitions, conceptual frameworks, exercises, and assessments. In: Proceedings of the National Academy of Sciences of the United States of America (2019). https://doi.org/10.1073/pnas.1807180116
7. Cao, L.: Data science: a comprehensive overview. ACM Comput. Surv. (CSUR) **50**(3), 1–42 (2017)
8. Dhamdhere, K., McCurley, K.S., et al.: Analyza: exploring data with conversation. In: Proceedings of the 22nd International Conference on Intelligent User Interfaces, IUI 2017, pp. 493–504. Association for Computing Machinery, New York (2017). https://doi.org/10.1145/3025171.3025227
9. Dibia, V.: LIDA: a tool for automatic generation of grammar-agnostic visualizations and infographics using large language models (2023). https://arxiv.org/abs/2303.02927
10. Dibia, V., Demiralp, Ç.: Data2Vis: automatic generation of data visualizations using sequence to sequence recurrent neural networks (2018)
11. Eliseeva, U., Heiß, S., et al.: Query-to-vis: conceptualization of a broad-coverage automated visualization pipeline (2024). Presented at IV 2024 Conference, Coimbra
12. Few, S.: Show Me the Numbers: Designing Tables and Graphs to Enlighten. Analytics Press (2012). https://books.google.pt/books?id=1xiHLgEACAAJ
13. Gandomi, A., Haider, M.: Beyond the hype: big data concepts, methods, and analytics. Int. J. Inf. Manag. **35**(2), 137–144 (2015). https://doi.org/10.1016/j.ijinfomgt.2014.10.007
14. Gao, T., Dontcheva, M., et al.: DataTone: managing ambiguity in natural language interfaces for data visualization. In: Proceedings of the 28th Annual ACM Symposium on User Interface Software & Technology (2015). https://api.semanticscholar.org/CorpusID:2110110
15. Harrison, L., Yang, F., Franconeri, S., et al.: Ranking visualizations of correlation using weber's law. IEEE Trans. Vis. Comput. Graph. **20**, 1943–1952 (2014). https://doi.org/10.1109/TVCG.2014.2346979
16. Hu, K.Z., Bakker, M.A., et al.: VizML: a machine learning approach to visualization recommendation. In: Proceedings of the 2019 CHI Conference on Human Factors in Computing Systems (2018)
17. Kaur, P., Owonibi, M.: A review on visualization recommendation strategies (2017). https://doi.org/10.5220/0006175002660273
18. Kay, M., Heer, J.: Beyond weber's law: a second look at ranking visualizations of correlation. IEEE Trans. Vis. Comput. Graph. **22**(1), 469–478 (2016). https://doi.org/10.1109/TVCG.2015.2467671
19. Laha, B., Bowman, D.A., et al.: A classification of user tasks in visual analysis of volume data. In: 2015 IEEE Scientific Visualization Conference (SciVis), pp. 1–8 (2015). https://doi.org/10.1109/SciVis.2015.7429485
20. Li, H., Wang, Y., et al.: KG4Vis: a knowledge graph-based approach for visualization recommendation. IEEE Trans. Vis. Comput. Graph. **28**(1), 195–205 (2022). https://doi.org/10.1109/tvcg.2021.3114863
21. Li, T., Wei, X., Wang, Y.: A requirements-driven framework for automatic data visualization. In: van der Aa, H., Bork, D., Proper, H.A., Schmidt, R. (eds.) BPMDS EMMSAD 2023. LNBIP, vol. 479, pp. 297–311. Springer, Cham (2023). https://doi.org/10.1007/978-3-031-34241-7_21
22. Luo, Y., Qin, X., et al.: DeepEye: towards automatic data visualization, pp. 101–112 (2018). https://doi.org/10.1109/ICDE.2018.00019

23. Munzner, T.: Visualization Analysis and Design. A K Peters/CRC Press (2014). https://doi.org/10.1201/b17511
24. Mylavarapu, P., Yalcin, A., et al.: Ranked-list visualization: a graphical perception study. In: Proceedings of the 2019 CHI Conference on Human Factors in Computing Systems, CHI 2019, pp. 1–12. Association for Computing Machinery, New York (2019). https://doi.org/10.1145/3290605.3300422
25. Nickerson, R.C., Varshney, U., Muntermann, J.: A method for taxonomy development and its application in information systems. Eur. J. Inf. Syst. **22**, 336–359 (2013)
26. Pope, C., Ziebland, S., Mays, N.: Qualitative research in health care: analysing qualitative data. BMJ: Br. Med. J. **320**(7227), 114 (2000)
27. Quadri, G.J., Rosen, P.: A survey of perception-based visualization studies by task. CoRR abs/2107.07477 (2021). https://arxiv.org/abs/2107.07477
28. Saket, B., Endert, A., Demiralp, Ç.: Task-based effectiveness of basic visualizations. IEEE Trans. Vis. Comput. Graph. **25**(7), 2505–2512 (2019). https://doi.org/10.1109/TVCG.2018.2829750
29. Sarikaya, A., Gleicher, M.: Scatterplots: tasks, data, and designs. IEEE Trans. Vis. Comput. Graph. **24**(1), 402–412 (2018). https://doi.org/10.1109/TVCG.2017.2744184
30. Satyanarayan, A., Moritz, D., et al.: Vega-lite: a grammar of interactive graphics. IEEE Trans. Vis. Comput. Graph. **23**(1), 341–350 (2017). (Proc. InfoVis). http://idl.cs.washington.edu/papers/vega-lite
31. Valiati, E.R.A., Pimenta, M.S., et al.: A taxonomy of tasks for guiding the evaluation of multidimensional visualizations. In: Proceedings of the 2006 AVI Workshop on BEyond Time and Errors: Novel Evaluation Methods for Information Visualization, BELIV 2006, pp. 1–6. Association for Computing Machinery, New York (2006). https://doi.org/10.1145/1168149.1168169
32. Vartak, M., Huang, S., et al.: Towards visualization recommendation systems. SIGMOD Rec. **45**(4), 34–39 (2017). https://doi.org/10.1145/3092931.3092937
33. Wehrend, S., Lewis, C.H.: A problem-oriented classification of visualization techniques. In: Proceedings of the First IEEE Conference on Visualization: Visualization 1990, pp. 139–143 (1990)
34. Wills, G.J., Wilkinson, L.: AutoVis: automatic visualization. Inf. Vis. **9**, 47–69 (2010). https://api.semanticscholar.org/CorpusID:1372993
35. Wongsuphasawat, K., Moritz, D., et al.: Voyager: exploratory analysis via faceted browsing of visualization recommendations. IEEE Trans. Vis. Comput. Graph. **22**(1), 649–658 (2016). https://doi.org/10.1109/TVCG.2015.2467191
36. Yang, J., Gyarmati, P.F., Zeng, Z., Moritz, D.: Draco 2: an extensible platform to model visualization design (2023)
37. Yau, N.: Visualize This: The FlowingData Guide to Design, Visualization, and Statistics. Wiley Pub. (2011). https://books.google.pt/books?id=otpRtAEACAAJ
38. Zhou, M., Li, Q., et al.: Table2Charts: recommending charts by learning shared table representations. In: Proceedings of the 27th ACM SIGKDD Conference on Knowledge Discovery & Data Mining, KDD 2021. ACM (2021). https://doi.org/10.1145/3447548.3467279
39. Zhou, M.X., Feiner, S.K.: Visual task characterization for automated visual discourse synthesis. In: Proceedings of the SIGCHI Conference on Human Factors in Computing Systems, CHI 1998, pp. 392–399. ACM Press/Addison-Wesley Publishing Co. (1998). https://doi.org/10.1145/274644.274698

Combining Natural Language Generation and Graph Algorithms to Explain Causal Maps Through Meaningful Paragraphs

Tyler J. Gandee[1] and Philippe J. Giabbanelli[2(✉)]

[1] Miami University, Oxford, OH, USA
gandeetj@miamioh.edu
[2] Virginia Modeling, Analysis, and Simulation Center (VMASC), Old Dominion University, Norfolk, VA, USA
pgiabban@odu.edu

Abstract. Causal maps, consisting of labeled nodes and directed edges, capture individual mental models, which can be aggregated to form complex group-level maps. While aggregate maps leverage distributed expertise, they often lose transparency, creating barriers for community members. Software solutions have attempted to address this issue, but diagrammatic representations can still hinder accessibility. Large Language Models (LLMs) have been proposed to automatically explain conceptual models as text, but they lost information and often focused on sentence generation whereas we need reports formed of paragraphs. In this paper, we design, implement, and evaluate a method that automatically translates causal maps into coherent narratives without model loss. Our evaluation compares 24 community detection algorithms to decompose maps into topical communities and utilizing 3 LLMs to generate coherent paragraphs. The optimal combination produces text with readability levels comparable to human-written paragraphs. Our method is open-source, allowing modeling groups to adapt it for their stakeholders.

Keywords: Automatic Explanations · Conceptual Model · GPT · Gemini · Llama · Network Science

1 Introduction

Conceptual models of complex socio-environmental systems are often built by groups of individuals (or 'participants'). This allows to distribute expertise, as various participants can contribute to mapping different facets of a system thanks to their lived experiences and/or professional background. The practice of *participatory modeling* has devised several methods to arrive at a shared model [48], based on considerations such as the expected characteristics of the system (e.g., whether it includes loops), the required level of details for a project (e.g., should relations be expressed over time, weighted, or typed?), or the ability to engage a broad spectrum of participants through a flexible format. A wealth of

M. Saeki et al. (Eds.): ER 2024 Workshops, LNCS 14932, pp. 359–376, 2025.
https://doi.org/10.1007/978-3-031-75599-6_25

studies has documented the benefits of creating shared artifacts in the forms of maps as they externalize individual perspectives (or 'mental models') about a system of interest, thus allowing analysts to find leverage points and perform trade-off analyses [14], compare viewpoints among participants or with respect to prevailing frameworks, or extent a map into a simulation model.

Transparency is essential in building conceptual models in a participatory modeling setting, since participants are both data providers and consumers of the ensuing analysis. Without transparency, we lose some of the expected benefits of collaborative conceptual modeling such as learning among participants, fostering engagement, or buy-in from key actors [40]. Transparency is necessarily a trade-off: "for modeling to be able to offer genuine analytical support for participatory management, it must be simple and transparent for local stakeholders and at the same time it must of be of sufficient rigor" [35]. Techniques such as cognitive mapping can transparently elicit maps from individuals by asking a set of questions (e.g., in a semi-structured interview), thus gradually teasing out relevant nodes and relationships. Studies demonstrated that participants can navigate their own causal maps [14], interpret the labels of the nodes (e.g., 'drought', 'crop yield') and their associated edges (e.g., "drought $\xrightarrow{+}$ crop yield" means that an increase in drought will lower the yield).

A *group-level map* is obtained by combining the individual maps, thus it has many more nodes and edges, which can engender several structures that are important for the dynamics of a problem (e.g., feedback loops) yet difficult to comprehend. There have been recurrent criticisms of the lack of transparency in group-level maps. A case in point is the Foresight Obesity Map, which is now portrayed as looking like a "spilled plate of spaghetti" [22] rather than examined for its intrinsic scientific value [44]. The lack of transparency of aggregate maps is an important challenge for participatory modeling and group-based conceptual modeling in general, because it creates a barrier to learning (individuals can navigate their own small maps but not the work of the collective) and potentially decreases buy-in from participants. While there are numerous software to support participatory modeling in fields such as educational technology (to solve open-ended complex problems) or environmental management, the focus is usually on supporting participants to analyze the quality of their maps using quantitative metrics [12] or to test the implications of their knowledge base on a set of scenarios [21]. There are fewer specialized software to support interacting with the large systems maps originating from participatory modeling studies. In addition, usability studies have shown that participants struggled with these soft-ware solutions, since navigating large interactive node-link diagrams was much less familiar than reading reports [10].

Several studies recently explored using Large Language Models (LLMs) to enable transformations between conceptual models (e.g., cognitive maps, causal loop diagrams, UML) and text [9,20,46]. While results on generating textual explanations about small models are encouraging, experiments suggest that even recent LLMs such as GPT-4 struggle with processing large models [37]. Prototypes thus decomposed large models into smaller parts (Fig. 1), but these

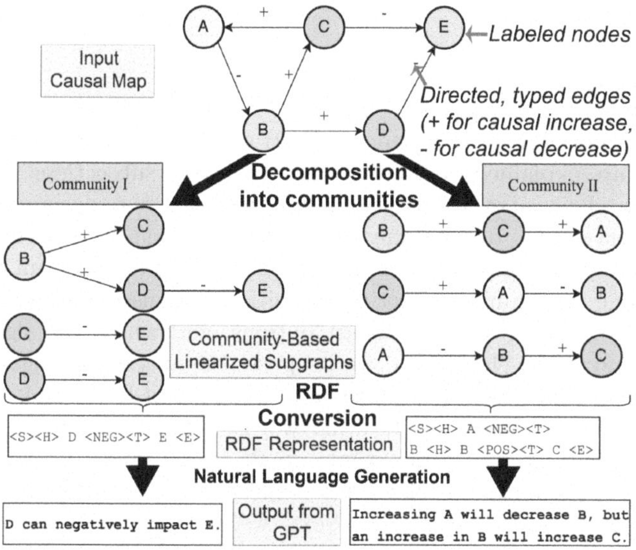

Fig. 1. Steps involved in prior works [46].

decomposition algorithms lost some content [46]. In addition, prior experiments on small models emphasized sentence-level generation (within a single paragraph), whereas *larger models must be arranged into paragraphs* with meaningful topics and an appropriate flow. Consequently, this paper pursues the following research question: can we combine graph algorithms and improved uses of LLMs to convey causal maps as paragraphs without information loss? This question translates to the main contribution of our paper, as we design, implement, and evaluate an LLM-based system that seeks to improve transparency in participatory modeling by transforming conceptual maps into paragraphs that are sufficiently readable for our target audience consisting of model-users (e.g., community members, decision-makers) rather than modelers. We focus on *causal maps* as they are widely employed used in participatory modeling [48]. Our work specifically addresses the limitations of recent studies as we (i) decompose a causal map into components that *preserve* its entire content, and we (ii) turn these components into *topical paragraphs* that are sufficiently readable.

The remainder of this paper is organized as follows. Our methods are detailed in Sect. 2, including our optimization via 24 graph algorithms to navigate and decompose a system without information loss, and our use of LLMs to produce paragraphs. Results are evaluated across multiple versions of GPT (3, 3.5, 4) along with Gemini 1.0 (Gemini-1.0-pro) and Llama-2 (Llama-2-7b-chat-hf) in Sect. 3 and contextualized in Sect. 4 with respect to advancing the application of LLMs in conceptual modeling.

2 Methods

2.1 Overview

The complete workflow of this paper (Fig. 2) can be articulated into four main steps, which are explained in the following dedicated subsections. We start by optimizing the choice of overlapping community detection to decompose a model, with set criteria seeking to avoid any information loss and balance the partitions' sizes (to promote paragraphs of similar lengths). This differs from prior works where only one community detection algorithm was used instead of optimizing its selection among state-of-the-art options, and where the algorithm lost both nodes and edges [46]. Then, we propose a new series of algorithms that traverse the communities and produce an ordered list of RDF triplets (shown in Fig. 1 and detailed in Sect. 2.3). In other words, a large conceptual model that may contain cycles is broken down into small acyclic parts, ordered in a way that ultimately promotes the flow of sentences, and represented using a tagging system that LLMs can handle. Next, we fine-tune GPT (to create individual sentences) by expanding an open dataset related to suicide, which consists of a large causal map developed in a participatory modeling setting along with manually crafted pairs of potential inputs (subgraphs) and desired outputs (sentences) [4]. Finally, we perform experiments on the suicide case study to demonstrate the feasibility of our approach in generating paragraphs, together with the identification of optimal configurations in terms of temperature settings (the 'creativity' variable of LLMs), number of sentences to assemble per paragraph (denoted as 'bundle size'), and LLM. For a comprehensive evaluation, we include five models: three versions of OpenAI's GPT (GPT-3.5-Turbo, GPT-4, and GPT-4-Turbo-Preview), Google's Gemini (gemini-1.0), and Meta's Llama-2 (Llama-2-7b-chat-hf). Our evaluation uses well-established automatic metrics from the literature on assessing LLMs. Specifically, we evaluate the quality of the output at the paragraph-level (Flesch Reading Ease score for readability) and at the sentence-level (BLEU, ROUGE, BERTScore) by comparison with an authoritative document on the same topic. An ablation study allows to specifically evaluate the effects of packing sentences into several paragraphs instead of accumulating them in a single (massive) paragraph. To support replicability and reuse, our code (as Jupyter Notebooks) and its use on the case study is openly accessible on an anonymized third-party repository at https://doi.org/10.5281/zenodo.12636643.

2.2 Decomposition Algorithms

We seek to decompose a given causal map into communities with a small amount of *shared content* (i.e., overlapping communities), since paragraphs need to be connected through shared elements rather than jumping abruptly be-tween topics. Consequently, we focus on community detection algorithms in static networks and evaluate them with respect to two requirements. First, we seek to *preserve* the graph, as the union of all communities should be as close as possible to the original graph. This criterion ensures that the paragraphs cover the content of the causal map. This criterion is measured as *coverage*, which counts the fraction of nodes from the given causal map that are included in at least one community; the target is a coverage of 1. Second, we value communities with similar number of nodes (i.e., *balanced* communities) as paragraphs should not differ noticeably in length. This is also a common problem in community detection, as some algorithms lead to the "creation of monster communities" [42], typically with the first community being at least one order of magnitude larger than the rest. We measure balance as the *entropy* of the distribution of the number of nodes across communities. A high entropy is desired, as it means that communities' sizes are more similar. While optimizing these two criteria is essential, other features can be desirable. We thus also track the Girvan-Newman *Modularity*, which measures community structure (higher numbers can lead to more topical paragraphs), and the *overlap ratio*, which measures how many nodes exist in more than one community (higher numbers can facilitate transitions between paragraphs at the expense of redundancy). We report our two required metrics and two additional features on 24 overlapping community detection algorithms, 19 of which are optimized as they have hyperparameters (Table 2).

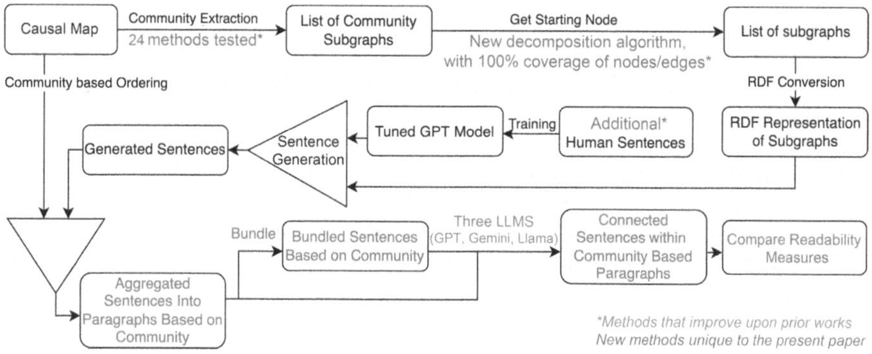

Fig. 2. Our detailed flowchart identifies improvements upon Shrestha *et al.*'s [46]. While we use the same methods to generate paragraphs, we emphasize choosing the right community detection algorithm (to avoid information loss), utilizing graph traversal algorithms for each community, and optimizing the bundle size. Note that 'human sentences' are a set of ground-truth sentences that are manually written by a combination of graduate and undergraduate students; we gave them RDF subgraphs and tasked them with writing natural sentences in varied styles so that we could fine-tune the RDF-to-text GPT model.

After selecting the best overlapping community detection algorithm given our criteria, we break each community into a set of components as illustrated in Fig. 3. In short, there are two levels of subdivisions: the communities, and

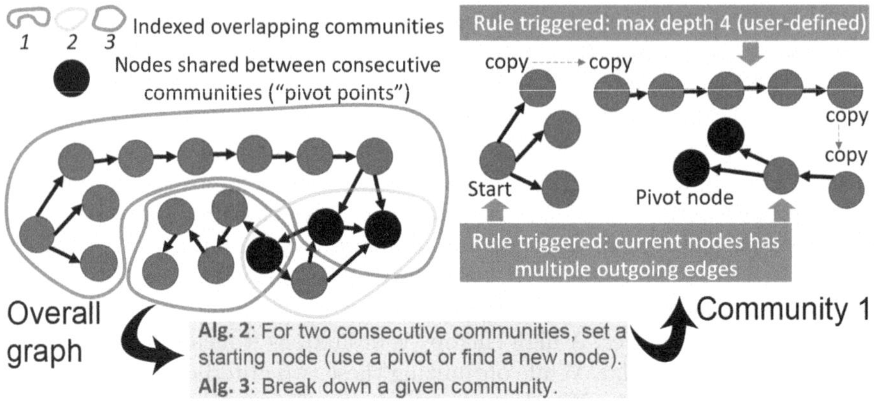

Fig. 3. Algorithm 1 dispatches pairs of consecutive communities to Algorithm 2 to find a starting node for each community, either using a pivot with the prior community (when avail-able) or by finding the furthest node from the pivot with the next community. Algorithm 3 then repeatedly uses a Breadth-First Search modified with two rules to subdivide each community without loss.

Algorithm 1. Initialize and dispatch

Input: List of n communities
Output: List of graph components

function INIT(graph with communities)
  Remove self-loops in the graph
  for every node v **do**
    `/* A node is in a list of (at least one) communities */`
    for i from 1 to $n-1$ **do**
      if v is both in community i and $i+1$ **then**
        then flag v as pivot
  Call Alg. 2 on community 1 to get start node
  Pass start node to Alg. 3 to break 1st community
  for i from 2 to n **do**
    if communities i and $i-1$ share a pivot **then**
      set it as start node
    else
      find start node in i via Alg. 2
    Run Alg. 3 on i from the starting node
  return component list accumulated from Alg. 3

their smaller components. Algorithm 1 navigates through communities, identifying shared concepts or 'pivot nodes' (when they exist) that will be used to flow from the end of one paragraph to the beginning of the next one. Algorithm 2 sets the starting node for the paragraph. When a paragraph flows from a prior one (i.e., they shared nodes), one of these pivot nodes is used as the start. For the first paragraph or for disjoint paragraphs, the starting node is identified as the furthest from the end of its paragraph. Algorithm 3 repeatedly divides the current community into components. We prevent components from being exceedingly large by (i) capping long chains of causes and consequences $X_i \rightarrow \ldots \rightarrow X_k$ at a user-defined limit, and (ii) stopping when a node fans out to many consequences $X_i \rightarrow \{X_j, \ldots, X_k\}$. Algorithm 3 ensures that no node or edge gets lost in the decomposition process.

Algorithm 2. Select the starting node

Input: First two communities
Output: Starting node

function GETSTARTNODE(comm. j, comm. $j+1$)
  if there are pivots between j and $j+1$ **then**
    use the first pivot as target node
  else
    use source of 1st edge as target node
  Reverse direction of the graph
  Perform depth-first search from the target node to find the farthest node
  `/* If there are many nodes with the same farthest distance, use 1st encountered */`
  return the farthest node

2.3 RDF Conversion and Fine-Tuning

Each of the components created through the process outlined in the previous subsection is transformed into an RDF representation. In short, each pair of nodes $\mathbb{A}$ and $\mathbb{B}$ connected by an edge of type $\mathbb{T}$ will be turned into $< S >< H > \mathbb{A} < \mathbb{T} >< T > \mathbb{B} < E >$. S and E mark the start and end of a block, respectively; H and T represent the head and target node, respectively. For example, in our case study on suicide and Adverse Childhood Experiences (ACEs), one component of 9 edges can be turned into the following (where POS and NEG indicate positive and negative causations respectively):

$< S >< H >$ Stigma of the ACE $< POS >< T >$ Cumulative trauma $< E >< S >< H >$ Fighting in the house $< POS >< T >$ Family risk factors $< E >< S >< H >$ Interpersonal problems $< POS >< T >$ ACEs $< E >$ $< S >< H >$ ACEs of siblings $< POS >< T >$ ACEs $< E >< S >< H >$ Cultural norms that ACEs aren't problems $< POS >< T >$ ACEs $< E >$ $< S >< H >$ Chronic exposure to unsafe messaging $< POS >< T >$ Feeling unsafe $< E >< S >< H >$ Healthy mentoring $< NEG >< T >$ ACEs $< E >< S >< H >$ Peer victimization $< POS >< T >$ ACEs $< E >< S >< H >$ Positive childhood experiences $< NEG >< T >$ ACEs $< E >$

Algorithm 3. Traverse and break community

Input: community i, start node, max depth
Output: list of components from community i

```
function TraverseBreak(i, head, max depth)
    Queue of nodes Q ← {head}
    List of components L ← ∅
    while edges exist in community i do
        current component C ← ∅
        while Q is not empty do
            current depth d ← 1
            current component c ← ∅
            /* Starts a constrained breadth-first search */
            repeat
                current node v ← next in Q
                add to C all outgoing edges/nodes of v
                add to Q all outgoing nodes of v
                remove from i all outgoing edges of v
                increment depth d
            until outdegree(v) > d or d ≥ maxdepth
            add component C to L
    return components L
```

We manually created a dataset for fine-tuning, consisting of the desired text output for 697 edges. GPT was fine-tuned with 85% of our manually labeled data for training, 7.5% for validation, and 7.5% for testing. These proportions are similar to other studies that fine-tune LLMs by devoting from 80% to 90% of the data to training [13,28,47] and using the rest either equally for validation and testing [13] or with a minimum of 5% devoted to testing [47]. For fine-tuning, we used gpt-3.5-turbo-1106 with 3 epochs, a batch size of 1, an LR multiplier of 2, and different trained tokens depending on the case study (233,865 for suicide and 196,230 for obesity).

All sentences were generated, one by one, through fine-tuned GPT models. We emphasized that this fine-tuned model only served to generate *individual* sentences, while all LLMs were compared in their ability to *combine* sentences into paragraphs.

2.4 Paragraph Generation and Evaluation

To obtain a *baseline*, we output individual sentences in the paragraph exactly as they were generated in the previous subsection. Since a fine-tuned LLM is only aware of one sentence at a time, it cannot smooth out a transition with the sentences immediately before or after. We contrast this baseline with our proposed *bundling approach*, which takes in a user-defined number of sentences (the 'bundle size') and assembles them in a paragraph. We used the prompt "You are a helpful assistant that combines a list of sentence into one paragraph in

Table 1. Studies evaluating Flesch Reading Ease scores across different applications using various versions of ChatGPT and GPT-3 technologies.

Study	Application	Technology	Average Flesch Reading Ease score (± standard deviation, when provided)
[31]	radiology	ChatGPT 3.5*	83.5 ± 5.6
[36]	ophthalmology	ChatGPT 4.0	From 28.1 ± 7.5 for epiretinal membrane to 34.4 ± 7.7 for macular hole
[52]	dermatology	ChatGPT 4.0	42.67 (range 26.55–62.98)
[24]	drug-drug interactions	ChatGPT 3.5*	27.64 ± 10.85 on asking whether 2 drugs can be taken together; 14.85 ± 1.97 on why they shouldn't
[38]	4th grade history class	ChatGPT 3.5*	In English, 50 by default and averages 65 to 75 in child-friendly mode
[30]	college engineering class	GPT-3	43

*The specific version not stated by the authors and was inferred by publication dates

a way that a 15th grader could understand." For role-based models like GPT, this prompt is inserted as the system prompt for every paragraph. We thus have three parameters: LLM, bundle size, temperature. We optimized each LLM via a grid search by considering bundle sizes of {5, 10, 15, 20} and four values for temperature. LLMs have various ranges for temperature. GPT models are on a scale of 0 to 2, however temperatures higher than 1.0 tend to yield poor results in information and text generation. For consistency, we use the values {0.25, 0.5, 0.75, 1.0} for all models.

At the paragraph-level, we measure readability via the Flesch Reading Ease score, which scales from 0 to 100. Scores below 50 are difficult or "academic" (30–50), and scores below 30 are very difficult to read (0–30). This score has been used in several recent studies that generated text via GPT. These reports have primarily been in medical fields, and secondarily from fields such as education. These scores can range widely (Table 1), as they are the result of both variations in the use of technology as well as considerable differences in the inherent difficulty of texts originating from a given context. For example, we may expect a 4th grade explanation to have a higher readability level than surgical reports. It is thus important to contextualize these scores by also estimating the readability of *human* written texts for the same application.

At the sentence-level, we compared our generated text with the CDC's Suicide Prevention Resource [4], which was independently written by subject-matter experts on the same topic. We performed an n-gram comparison using the standard BLEU and ROUGE metrics. We also utilize BERTScore, which accounts for semantic similarity instead of being limited to matching n-grams.

3 Results

The input consists of a large causal map on Adverse Childhood Experiences (ACEs) and suicide in youth. This map was developed through a participatory modeling process detailed in [11], where fifteen subject matter experts provided individual maps that were combined into an aggregate with 361 nodes and 946 edges. This map illustrates the problem addressed by our method: each expert provides a small map that is viewable and understandable by them, but participants cannot learn from each other given the complexity of the aggregated map. Our results focus on choosing the best overlapping community detection algorithm for this causal map and performing a quantitative analysis of our generated text. We stress that our method can be replicated to other causal maps via the code that we openly released on an anonymized third-party repository at https://doi.org/10.5281/zenodo.12636643.

3.1 Overlapping Community Detection

Table 2 shows our parameter search along with the best set of parameters based on Girvan-Newman Modularity. We utilize all ideal parameters alongside 5 more algorithms that do not require calibration, and evaluate based on Girvan-Newman modularity, entropy, coverage, and overlap (Table 3). We achieved the highest Girvan-Newman modularity score of 0.49 using an ensemble approach through EnDNTM [23]. However, given the set of parameters, all communities were disjoint. The second-best score with 100% coverage and some overlap is Link Partitioning Around Medoids (LPAM) [43] with a modularity score of 0.32. Core expansion [6], Cluster-Overlap Newman Girvan Optimized (CONGO) [16], and Label Propagation Algorithm with Neighbor Node Influence (LPANNI) [34] achieved similar scores, all within 0.05 of the second-highest modularity score. However, Core Expansion and LPANNI are disjoint. CONGO and LPAM also have an equal overlap ratio, however CONGO has a significantly higher level of entropy. Given the significant jump in entropy, we sacrifice the slight decrease in modularity and utilize CONGO for processing our network traversal algorithms.

3.2 Evaluation of Paragraphs

To set expectations about the desired readability level, we tasked a team of human participants with writing paragraphs in relation to the causal map. They manually wrote 27 paragraphs, achieving a Flesch Reading Ease score of 53.92. For our automated system, we divided the causal map into overlapping communities using the CONGO overlapping community detection algorithm, calibrated for the highest modularity score.

Figure 4 displays Flesch Reading Ease heatmaps for all GPT models with varying temperatures and bundle sizes. Here we can see we achieve the best *readability* scores with GPT-3.5-Turbo with a temperature of 0.5 and bundle

Table 2. We performed a grid search to optimize the Girvan-Newman modularity (score) across 19 algorithms with different number of parameters ('param').

Algorithm	Parameter	Range	Score	Param
Angel [45]	Threshold	0, 0.01, ..., 1.0	0.028	0.73
	Min. community size	0, 1, ..., 49		3
CoAch [50]	Density threshold	0, 0.0833, ..., 1	0.173	0
	Affinity threshold	0, 0.0833, ..., 1		0.1667
	Closeness	0, 0.0833, ..., 1.0		0.0833
CONGA [16]	communities	10, 20, ..., 50	0.342	10
CONGO [16]	communities	10, 20, ..., 50	0.271	50
	Height	1, 2, 3		2
Core [6]	Tolerance	0.0001, 0.0011, ..., 1.0	0.305	0.0191
DEMON [8]	Epsilon	0.1, 0.2, ..., 1.0	0.220	0.5
	Min. community size	0, 1, ..., 49		10
Ego Networks	Level	0, 1, ..., 99	0.178	2
EnDNTM [23][a]	Epsilon	0.000, 0.001, ..., 100.0	0.490	0.0
IPCA [32]	t_{in}	0, 0.1, ..., 1.0	0.163	1.0
K-clique [41]	k	2, 3, ..., 9999	0.230	2
Lemon [33][2]	Min. community size	10, 20, 30	0.000	20
	Max. community size	40, 50, ..., 100		40
	Expand, subst., walk	1, 2, ..., 5 (three params)		1
	Biased?	True, False		True
LFM [29]	Alpha	0.0000, 0.0042, ..., 0.8375	0.216	0.8249
LPAM [43]	k	25, 50	0.317	25
	Threshold	0.00010, 0.50005, 1.0		0.0001
LPANNI [34]	Threshold	0.0001, 0.0344, ..., 1.0000	0.275	0.0001
MULTICOM [19]	Seed node	0, 1, ..., 9	0.012	1
OSSE [49][b]	n_{inf}?	True, False	0.037	True
	Expansion	ppr', vppr'		'ppr'
	Alpha	0.00, 0.01, ..., 1.0		0.04
	Delta	0.0, 0.1, ..., 1.0		0
SLPA [51]	t	10, 11, ..., 50	0.362	29
	r	0.0, 0.1, 1.0		0.2
Walkscan [18]	#steps, min. sample	1, 2, ..., 10 (2 params)	0.117	6
	EPS	0.00, 0.01, ..., 1.0		0.0101

[a] EnDNTM is an ensembling approach, and we used the default disjoint algorithms used by CDLib: Louvain [3], Label Propagation [7], and Walkscan [18]. [b] These algorithms utilized seed nodes, which we defaulted to "ACEs", "Suicide ideation", and "Suicide attempt"

size of 5, and a worst score using GPT-4-Turbo-Preview with a temperature of 1.0 and bundle size of 20.

Our average Flesch reading ease score was 36.371 ± 6.754. Llama-2 holds the top 6 scores with the best score of 46.88 using a temperature of 0.25 and bundle size of 15. Of those 6 results, none used a bundle size of 20. After the top Llama-2 scores, Gemini-1.0-Pro achieved a Flesch score of 45.86 with a temperature of 0.25 and bundle size of 10. The bottom 10 Flesch reading ease scores are GPT-4 and GPT-4-Turbo-Preview, with the worst score being 21.13 with a temperature of 1.0 and bundle size of 20. Our original fine-tuned sentences spliced together (i.e., baseline without paragraph bundling) achieved a score of 31.17.

Our BLEU scores are significantly low (maximum is 0.006), which is to be expected given that BLEU is designed for local text similarities rather than large documents [17]. GPT-4 and GPT-4-Turbo-Preview achieve ROUGE-1 scores over 0.3, with the highest score of 0.313. More precisely, the top 8 ROUGE-1 scores are all GPT-4 and GPT-4-Turbo-Preview models with a bundle size of 5. The next 6 scores are GPT-4 and GPT-4-Turbo-Preview models with a bundle size of 10, with the closest competitor being Gemini at 0.256 with temperature 1.0 and bundle size of 5. We see similar trends with ROUGE-2 and ROUGE-L, but our scores are significantly lower. Again, this is expected when we increase the n-gram length. BERTScore achieves significantly better results, with an average precision of 0.780 ± 0.009, recall of 0.728 ± 0.005, and F1-score of 0.753 ± 0.006.

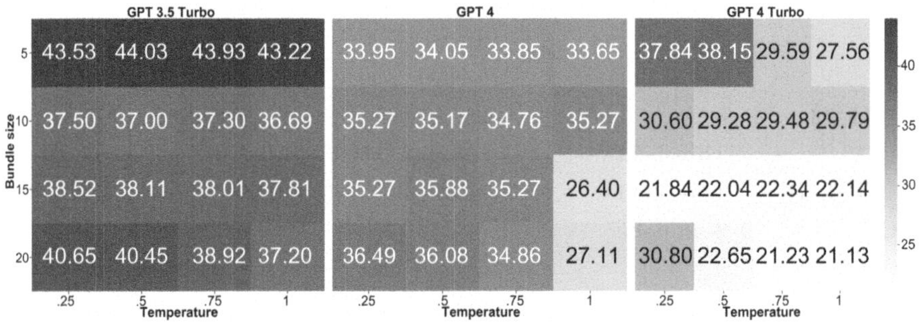

Fig. 4. Flesch Reading Ease Grid search on GPT models with varying temperature and bundle size. *This high resolution figure can be zoomed in.*

Table 3. Evaluation of calibrated algorithms, with the best scores displayed in bold. A negative NG modularity score is believed to be an implementation error, as scores less than 0 should not exist [39].

Algorithm	NGModularity	Coverage	Entropy	Overlap
Angel [45]	0.01	0.47	3.70	0.03
ASLPAw [51]	0.04	0.99	0.69	0.00
CoAch [50]	0.18	0.86	5.31	0.16
CONGA [15]	0.21	**1.00**	0.94	0.02
CONGO* [16]	0.27	**1.00**	5.21	0.02
Core Expansion [6]	0.30	**1.00**	4.14	0.00
Demon [8]	0.23	**1.00**	4.41	0.04
EBGC [27]	0.05	**1.00**	7.79	0.00
Ego-networks	0.18	**1.00**	**8.00**	0.14
EnDNTM [23]	**0.49**	**1.00**	3.27	0.00
Graph Entropy [26]	0.08	**1.00**	7.72	0.00
IPCA [32]	0.16	0.88	6.69	0.07
k-clique [41]	0.00	**1.00**	0.00	0.00
LAIS2 [2]	−0.02	0.29	4.91	**0.48**
Lemon [33]	−0.05	0.09	0.00	0.00
LPAM* [43]	0.32	**1.00**	3.57	0.02
LPANNI [34]	0.27	**1.00**	2.10	0.00
LFM* [29]	0.22	**1.00**	1.75	0.02
MULTICOM [19]	−0.01	0.46	2.15	0.15
OSSE [49]	0.03	0.41	1.54	0.20
PercoMVC [25]	−0.02	0.17	1.89	0.05
SLPA [51]	0.08	**1.00**	0.91	0.01
UMSTMO [1]	0.04	**1.00**	7.29	0.00
Walkscan [18]	0.05	**1.00**	0.27	0.01

*Algorithm scores are the average of 200 runs

4 Discussion

In this paper, we have proposed, implemented, and evaluated a new process to automatically turn a large conceptual model in the form of a causal map (currently difficult to use for lay participants) into textual narratives (as a more accessible format). For our case study of suicide in youth, we have identified a suitable overlapping community detection algorithm (CONGO), explained and applied our network traversal algorithms, generated ordered sentences using the output from network traversal and a fine-tuned GPT model, and performed a grid search on combining those sentences into paragraphs using various LLMs. The readability of the paragraphs was at the college-level (categorized as the

30 to 50 range). Our result show that Llama-2 had a higher score (46.88) than Gemini, which in turn outperformed GPT. While these rankings can change as new LLMs are proposed, our results emphasize that the choice of LLM can impact the readability of the text describing a conceptual model.

Our qualitative inspection of the generated paragraphs found that they had coherent topics and an appropriate flow from one paragraph to the next. For quantitative evaluation, it is necessary to have human-written text as a reference point. While there is an abundance of large causal maps, none of them has so far been entirely explained through a *companion text document*. In this paper, we utilized the CDC's Suicide Prevention Resource [4]. While the report and our causal map both seek to *address the same topic* comprehensively, we cannot expect them to contain the same information, thus we should obtain lower evaluation scores than on a narrative built from the causal map. To perform a complementary evaluation, we thus employed a set of human evaluators to create paragraphs. We note that hand-crafting paragraphs is a highly time consuming activity, which prevents an evaluation across a large set of case studies. As our solution is open source, we encourage other groups to report performances on their own case studies. Should performances differ, an investigation of the *characteristics* of the case studies and their impact on performances would be a valuable goal for future work.

There are several limitations to this study, apart from the number of case studies as mentioned above. There exist many community detection algorithms, thus it is possible that another option could yield more balanced communities. As LLMs continue to improve, their sophistication may eventually suffice to orchestrate a large map into meaningful paragraphs without needing algorithms that 'spoon-feed' a map into the LLM by decomposing it into small parts. Finally, the quality of our summaries should ultimately be assessed by our target audience, but this audience is not homogeneous (e.g., community members, decision-makers) thus dedicated human studies would be needed.

Our method requires *overlapping* communities, because paragraphs must have some shared elements in order to create the pivots that would be expected in fluent writing. However, this requirement does not necessarily limit us to using overlapping community detection algorithms. Indeed, our process could be revised to take in *disjoint* communities and expanding them to create overlaps, such as looking for edges whose endpoints reside in different communities. Several solutions can already infer overlapping communities based on multiple disjoint community structures [5], such as the recent Expansion with Contraction method for Overlapping Community Detection (ECOCD) [53]. This could allow us to expand our search space and use algorithms for disjoint communities, which may enhance our results in regards to modularity and entropy. However, it adds one component to our process, as we would have to optimize the disjoint community algorithm *and* the algorithm that creates overlaps.

Disclosure of Interests. The authors have no competing interests to declare that are relevant to the content of this article.

References

1. Asmi, K., Lotfi, D., El Marraki, M.: Overlapping community detection based on the union of all maximum spanning trees. Libr. Hi Tech **38**(2), 276–292 (2020)
2. Baumes, J., Goldberg, M., Magdon-Ismail, M.: Efficient identification of overlapping communities. In: Kantor, P., et al. (eds.) ISI 2005. LNCS, vol. 3495, pp. 27–36. Springer, Heidelberg (2005). https://doi.org/10.1007/11427995_3
3. Blondel, V.D., Guillaume, J.L., Lambiotte, R., Lefebvre, E.: Fast unfolding of communities in large networks. J. Stat. Mech: Theory Exp. **2008**(10), P10008 (2008)
4. Centers for Disease Control and Prevention (CDC): Suicide prevention resource for action: a compilation of the best available evidence. National Center for Injury Prevention and Control, CDC, Atlanta (2022). Accessed 6 Mar 2024
5. Chakraborty, T., Ghosh, S., Park, N.: Ensemble-based overlapping community detection using disjoint community structures. Knowl.-Based Syst. **163**, 241–251 (2019)
6. Choumane, A., Awada, A., Harkous, A.: Core expansion: a new community detection algorithm based on neighborhood overlap. Soc. Netw. Anal. Min. **10**, 1–11 (2020)
7. Cordasco, G., Gargano, L.: Community detection via semi-synchronous label propagation algorithms. In: 2010 IEEE International Workshop on: Business Applications of Social Network Analysis (BASNA), pp. 1–8. IEEE (2010)
8. Coscia, M., Rossetti, G., Giannotti, F., Pedreschi, D.: DEMON: a local-first discovery method for overlapping communities. In: Proceedings of the 18th ACM SIGKDD International Conference on Knowledge Discovery and Data Mining, pp. 615–623 (2012)
9. Fill, H.G., Fettke, P., Köpke, J.: Conceptual modeling and large language models: impressions from first experiments with ChatGPT. Enterp. Model. Inf. Syst. Archit. (EMISAJ) **18**, 1–15 (2023)
10. Giabbanelli, P.J., Baniukiewicz, M.: Navigating complex systems for policymaking using simple software tools. In: Giabbanelli, P.J., Mago, V.K., Papageorgiou, E.I. (eds.) Advanced Data Analytics in Health. SIST, vol. 93, pp. 21–40. Springer, Cham (2018). https://doi.org/10.1007/978-3-319-77911-9_2
11. Giabbanelli, P.J., et al.: Pathways to suicide or collections of vicious cycles? Understanding the complexity of suicide through causal mapping. Soc. Netw. Anal. Min. **12**(1), 60 (2022)
12. Giabbanelli, P.J., Tawfik, A.A., Wang, B.: Designing the next generation of map assessment systems: open questions and opportunities to automatically assess a student's knowledge as a map. J. Res. Technol. Educ. **55**(1), 79–93 (2023)
13. Gira, M., Zhang, R., Lee, K.: Debiasing pre-trained language models via efficient fine-tuning. In: Proceedings of the Second Workshop on Language Technology for Equality, Diversity and Inclusion, pp. 59–69 (2022)
14. Gray, S., et al.: Assessing (social-ecological) systems thinking by evaluating cognitive maps. Sustainability **11**(20), 5753 (2019)
15. Gregory, S.: An algorithm to find overlapping community structure in networks. In: Kok, J.N., Koronacki, J., Lopez de Mantaras, R., Matwin, S., Mladenič, D., Skowron, A. (eds.) PKDD 2007. LNCS (LNAI), vol. 4702, pp. 91–102. Springer, Heidelberg (2007). https://doi.org/10.1007/978-3-540-74976-9_12

16. Gregory, S.: A fast algorithm to find overlapping communities in networks. In: Daelemans, W., Goethals, B., Morik, K. (eds.) ECML PKDD 2008. LNCS (LNAI), vol. 5211, pp. 408–423. Springer, Heidelberg (2008). https://doi.org/10.1007/978-3-540-87479-9_45
17. Guo, J., Lu, S., Cai, H., Zhang, W., Yu, Y., Wang, J.: Long text generation via adversarial training with leaked information. In: Proceedings of the AAAI Conference on Artificial Intelligence, vol. 32 (2018)
18. Hollocou, A., Bonald, T., Lelarge, M.: Improving PageRank for local community detection. arXiv preprint arXiv:1610.08722 (2016)
19. Hollocou, A., Bonald, T., Lelarge, M.: Multiple local community detection. ACM SIGMETRICS Perform. Eval. Rev. **45**(3), 76–83 (2018)
20. Hosseinichimeh, N., Majumdar, A., Williams, R., Ghaffarzadegan, N.: From text to map: a system dynamics bot for constructing causal loop diagrams. arXiv preprint arXiv:2402.11400 (2024)
21. Hudson-Doyle, E.E., Harrison, S.E., Hill, S.R., Williams, M., Paton, D., Bostrom, A.: Eliciting mental models of science and risk for disaster communication: a scoping review of methodologies. Int. J. Disaster Risk Reduct. **77**, 103084 (2022)
22. Jack, A.: Foresight report on obesity-author's reply. The Lancet **370**(9601), 1755 (2007)
23. Jaiswal, R., Ramanna, S.: Detecting overlapping communities using ensemble-based distributed neighbourhood threshold method in social networks. Intell. Decis. Technol. **15**(2), 251–267 (2021)
24. Juhi, A., et al.: The capability of ChatGPT in predicting and explaining common drug-drug interactions. Cureus **15**(3), e36272 (2023)
25. Kasoro, N., Kasereka, S., Mayogha, E., Vinh, H.T., Kinganga, J.: PercoMCV: a hybrid approach of community detection in social networks. Procedia Comput. Sci. **151**, 45–52 (2019)
26. Kenley, E.C., Cho, Y.R.: Detecting protein complexes and functional modules from protein interaction networks: a graph entropy approach. Proteomics **11**(19), 3835–3844 (2011)
27. Kenley, E.C., Cho, Y.R.: Entropy-based graph clustering: application to biological and social networks. In: 2011 IEEE 11th International Conference on Data Mining, pp. 1116–1121. IEEE (2011)
28. Lajkó, M., Csuvik, V., Vidács, L.: Towards JavaScript program repair with generative pre-trained transformer (GPT-2). In: Proceedings of the Third International Workshop on Automated Program Repair, pp. 61–68 (2022)
29. Lancichinetti, A., Fortunato, S., Kertész, J.: Detecting the overlapping and hierarchical community structure in complex networks. New J. Phys. **11**(3), 033015 (2009)
30. Lesage, J., et al.: Exploring natural language processing in mechanical engineering education: implications for academic integrity. Int. J. Mech. Eng. Educ. **52**(1), 88–105 (2023)
31. Li, H., et al.: Decoding radiology reports: potential application of OpenAI ChatGPT to enhance patient understanding of diagnostic reports. Clin. Imaging **101**, 137–141 (2023)
32. Li, M., Chen, J., Wang, J., Hu, B., Chen, G.: Modifying the DPClus algorithm for identifying protein complexes based on new topological structures. BMC Bioinform. **9**, 1–16 (2008)
33. Li, Y., He, K., Bindel, D., Hopcroft, J.E.: Uncovering the small community structure in large networks: a local spectral approach. In: Proceedings of the 24th International Conference on World Wide Web, pp. 658–668 (2015)

34. Lu, M., Zhang, Z., Qu, Z., Kang, Y.: LPANNI: overlapping community detection using label propagation in large-scale complex networks. IEEE Trans. Knowl. Data Eng. **31**(9), 1736–1749 (2018)
35. Mendoza, G.A., Prabhu, R.: Participatory modeling and analysis for sustainable forest management: overview of soft system dynamics models and applications. Forest Policy Econ. **9**(2), 179–196 (2006)
36. Momenaei, B., et al.: Appropriateness and readability of ChatGPT-4 generated responses for surgical treatment of retinal diseases. Ophthalmol. Retina **7**(10), 862–868 (2023)
37. Muff, F., Fill, H.G.: Limitations of ChatGPT in conceptual modeling: insights from experiments in metamodeling. In: Modellierung 2024 Satellite Events, p. 10–18420. Gesellschaft für Informatik eV (2024)
38. Murgia, E., et al.: ChatGPT in the classroom: a preliminary exploration on the feasibility of adapting ChatGPT to support children's information discovery. In: Adjunct Proceedings of the 31st ACM Conference on User Modeling, Adaptation and Personalization, pp. 22–27 (2023)
39. Newman, M.E., Girvan, M.: Finding and evaluating community structure in networks. Phys. Rev. E **69**(2), 026113 (2004)
40. Nguyen, L.K.N., Kumar, C., Jiang, B., et al.: Implementation of systems thinking in public policy: a systematic review. Systems **11**(2), 64 (2023)
41. Palla, G., Derényi, I., Farkas, I., Vicsek, T.: Uncovering the overlapping community structure of complex networks in nature and society. Nature **435**(7043), 814–818 (2005)
42. Parés, F., et al.: Fluid communities: a competitive, scalable and diverse community detection algorithm. In: Cherifi, C., Cherifi, H., Karsai, M., Musolesi, M. (eds.) COMPLEX NETWORKS 2017 2017. SCI, vol. 689, pp. 229–240. Springer, Cham (2018). https://doi.org/10.1007/978-3-319-72150-7_19
43. Ponomarenko, A., Pitsoulis, L., Shamshetdinov, M.: Overlapping community detection in networks based on link partitioning and partitioning around medoids. PLoS ONE **16**(8), e0255717 (2021)
44. Rigby, B.P., Dodd-Reynolds, C.J., Oliver, E.J.: The understanding, application and influence of complexity in national physical activity policymaking. Health Res. Policy Syst. **20**(1), 59 (2022)
45. Rossetti, G.: ANGEL: efficient, and effective, node-centric community discovery in static and dynamic networks. Appl. Netw. Sci. **5**(1), 26 (2020)
46. Shrestha, A., Mielke, K., Nguyen, T.A., Giabbanelli, P.J.: Automatically explaining a model: using deep neural networks to generate text from causal maps. In: 2022 Winter Simulation Conference (WSC), pp. 2629–2640. IEEE (2022)
47. Värtinen, S., Hämäläinen, P., Guckelsberger, C.: Generating role-playing game quests with GPT language models. IEEE Trans. Games **16**(1), 127–139 (2022)
48. Voinov, A., et al.: Tools and methods in participatory modeling: selecting the right tool for the job. Environ. Model. Softw. **109**, 232–255 (2018)
49. Whang, J.J., Gleich, D.F., Dhillon, I.S.: Overlapping community detection using seed set expansion. In: Proceedings of the 22nd ACM International Conference on Information & Knowledge Management, pp. 2099–2108 (2013)
50. Wu, M., Li, X., Kwoh, C.K., Ng, S.K.: A core-attachment based method to detect protein complexes in PPI networks. BMC Bioinform. **10**, 1–16 (2009)

51. Xie, J., Szymanski, B.K., Liu, X.: SLPA: uncovering overlapping communities in social networks via a speaker-listener interaction dynamic process. In: 11th International Conference on Data Mining Workshops, pp. 344–349. IEEE (2011)
52. Young, J.N., et al.: The utility of ChatGPT in generating patient-facing and clinical responses for melanoma. J. Am. Acad. Dermatol. **89**(3), 602–604 (2023)
53. Zhuo, Z., Chen, B., Yu, S., Cao, L.: Overlapping community detection using expansion with contraction. Neurocomputing **565**, 126989 (2023)

Author Index

M. Saeki et al. (Eds.): ER 2024 Workshops, LNCS 14932, pp. 377–378, 2025.
https://doi.org/10.1007/978-3-031-75599-6

SPRINGER NATURE

GPSR Compliance

The European Union's (EU) General Product Safety Regulation (GPSR) is a set of rules that requires consumer products to be safe and our obligations to ensure this.

If you have any concerns about our products, you can contact us on ProductSafety@springernature.com

In case Publisher is established outside the EU, the EU authorized representative is:

Springer Nature Customer Service Center GmbH
Europaplatz 3
69115 Heidelberg, Germany

The manufacturer's authorised representative in the EU is Springer Nature Customer Service Centre GmbH, Europaplatz 3, 69115 Heidelberg, Germany. If you have any concerns regarding our products, please contact ProductSafety@springernature.com

Printed and bound by CPI Group (UK) Ltd, Croydon, CR0 4YY
01/10/2026
02225834-0012